The West

Encounters & Transformations

Volume 2: Since 1550

Third Edition

Brian Levack

University of Texas at Austin

Edward Muir

Northwestern University

Meredith Veldman

Louisiana State University

Longman

Boston   Columbus   Indianapolis   New York   San Francisco   Upper Saddle River
Amsterdam   Cape Town   Dubai   London   Madrid   Milan   Munich   Paris   Montréal   Toronto
Delhi   Mexico City   São Paulo   Sydney   Hong Kong   Seoul   Singapore   Taipei   Tokyo

Editorial Director: Craig Campanella
Executive Editor: Jeff Lasser
Editorial Assistant: Amanda Dykstra
Senior Development Editor: Gerald Lombardi
Editor-in-Chief of Development: Rochelle Diogenes
Director of Marketing: Brandy Dawson
Senior Marketing Manager: Maureen E. Prado Roberts
Marketing Assistant: Marissa O'Brien
Senior Managing Editor: Ann Marie McCarthy
Project Managers: Lynn Savino; Debra Wechsler
Senior Manufacturing and Operations Manager for Arts and Sciences: Nick Sklitsis
Operations Specialists: Christina Amato; Sherry Lewis
Senior Art Director: Maria Lange
AV Project Manager: Mirella Signoretto
Manager, Visual Research: Beth Brenzel

Photo Researcher: Francelle Carapetyan
Manager, Rights and Permissions: Zina Arabia
Image Permission Coordinator: Michelina Viscusi
Manager, Cover Visual Research & Permissions: Karen Sanatar
Cover Art: "Marco Polo (1254–1324)." Galleria Nazionale d'Arte Moderna, Rome, Italy/The Bridgeman Art Library
Director of Media: Brian Hyland
Media Editor: Sarah Kinney
Supplements Editor: Emsal Hassan
Full-Service Project Management: Elm Street Publishing Services
Composition: Integra Software Services Pvt. Ltd.
Printer/Binder: Courier/Kendallville
Cover Printer: Coral Graphics Services, Inc.
Text Font: 10/12 Sabon

Credits and acknowledgments borrowed from other sources and reproduced, with permission, in this textbook appear on appropriate page within text (or on page C-1).

Library of Congress Cataloging-in-Publication Data
Levack, Brian P.
  The West : encounters & transformations/Brian Levack, Edward Muir, Meredith Veldman.—3rd ed.
      p. cm.
  "Combined volume."
  Includes bibliographical references and index.
  ISBN-13: 978-0-13-213284-8 (combined vol. : alk. paper)
  ISBN-10: 0-13-213284-2 (combined vol. : alk. paper)
  1. Civilization, Western—History—Textbooks. I. Muir, Edward. II. Veldman, Meredith. III. Title.
CB245.W455 2011
909'.09821—dc22

                                                                                2009053898

10 9 8 7 6 5 4 3 2 1

Longman
is an imprint of

PEARSON
www.pearsonhighered.com

ISBN 10:   0-13-213286-9
ISBN 13: 978-0-13-213286-2

à la carte edition
ISBN 10:   0-205-79779-2
ISBN 13: 978-0-205-79779-0

CONTENTS

Preface   ix
About the Authors   xviii

What is the West?   2
THE SHIFTING BORDERS OF THE WEST   2
CHANGING IDENTITIES WITHIN THE WEST   4
WESTERN VALUES   5
ASKING THE RIGHT QUESTIONS   6
    The "What" Question   6
    The "When" Question   6
    The "Where" Question   8
    The "Who" Question   8
    The "How"Question   8
    The "Why" Question   9

CHAPTER 15
The Age of Confessional Division   456
THE PEOPLES OF EARLY MODERN EUROPE   458
    The Population Recovery   458
    The Thriving Cities   460
    The Price Revolution   461
DISCIPLINING THE PEOPLE   463
    Establishing Confessional Identities   463
    Regulating the Family   464
    JUSTICE IN HISTORY: The *Auto-da-Fé*: The Power of Penance   466
    ENCOUNTERS AND TRANSFORMATIONS: The Introduction of the Table Fork: The New Sign of Western Civilization   468
HUNTING WITCHES   469
    DIFFERENT VOICES: Were There Really Witches?   472
THE CONFESSIONAL STATES   472
    The French Wars of Religion   474
    Philip II, His Most Catholic Majesty   477
    The Dutch Revolt   478
    Literature in the Age of Confessional Division   480
STATES AND CONFESSIONS IN EASTERN EUROPE   483
    The Dream World of Emperor Rudolf   483
    The Renaissance of Poland-Lithuania   485
    The Troubled Legacy of Ivan the Terrible   488
CONCLUSION: THE DIVISIONS OF THE WEST   490

CHAPTER 16
Absolutism and State Building in Europe, 1618–1715   492
THE NATURE OF ABSOLUTISM   493
    The Theory of Absolutism   493
    The Practice of Absolutism   494
    Warfare and the Absolutist State   494
THE ABSOLUTIST STATE IN FRANCE AND SPAIN   495
    The Foundations of French Absolutism   496
    Absolutism in the Reign of Louis XIV   497
    Louis XIV and the Culture of Absolutism   499
    The Wars of Louis XIV, 1667–1714   500
    Absolutism and State Building in Spain   501
ABSOLUTISM AND STATE BUILDING IN CENTRAL AND EASTERN EUROPE   506
    Germany and the Thirty Years' War, 1618–1648   506
    The Growth of the Prussian State   507
    The Austrian Habsburg Monarchy   510
    The Ottoman Empire: Between East and West   511
    DIFFERENT VOICES: Western Writers Evaluate the Ottoman Turks   512
    Russia and the West   513
    ENCOUNTERS AND TRANSFORMATIONS: St. Petersburg and the West   515
RESISTANCE TO ABSOLUTISM IN ENGLAND AND THE DUTCH REPUBLIC   516
    The English Monarchy   517
    The English Civil Wars and Revolution   517
    JUSTICE IN HISTORY: The Trial of Charles I   519
    Later Stuart Absolutism and Glorious Revolution   521
    The Dutch Republic   523
CONCLUSION: THE WESTERN STATE IN THE AGE OF ABSOLUTISM   526

CHAPTER 17
The Scientific Revolution   528
THE DISCOVERIES AND ACHIEVEMENTS OF THE SCIENTIFIC REVOLUTION   529
    Astronomy: A New Model of the Universe   530
    Physics: The Laws of Motion and Gravitation   532

Chemistry: Discovering the Elements of Nature 534
Biology: The Circulation of the Blood 534
THE SEARCH FOR SCIENTIFIC KNOWLEDGE 535
Observation and Experimentation 535
Deductive Reasoning 536
Mathematics and Nature 536
The Mechanical Philosophy 536
THE CAUSES OF THE SCIENTIFIC REVOLUTION 537
Developments Within Science 537
Developments Outside Science 539
DIFFERENT VOICES: Copernicus and the Papacy 540
THE INTELLECTUAL CONSEQUENCES
OF THE SCIENTIFIC REVOLUTION 543
Education 543
Skepticism and Independent Reasoning 543
Science and Religion 544
JUSTICE IN HISTORY: The Trial of Galileo 546
HUMANS AND THE NATURAL WORLD 548
The Place of Human Beings in
the Universe 548
The Control of Nature 548
Women, Men, and Nature 549
CONCLUSION: SCIENCE AND WESTERN CULTURE 550

CHAPTER 18
The West and the World: Empire, Trade, and War, 1650–1815 552

EUROPEAN EMPIRES IN THE AMERICAS
AND ASIA 554
The Rise of the British Empire 554
The Scattered French Empire 556
The Commercial Dutch Empire 557
JUSTICE IN HISTORY: The Trial of the
Mutineers on the Bounty 558
The Vast Spanish Empire 560
The Declining Portuguese Empire 560
The Russian Empire in the Pacific 561
WARFARE IN EUROPE, NORTH AMERICA,
AND ASIA 561
Mercantile Warfare 562
Anglo-French Military Rivalry 563
THE ATLANTIC WORLD 565
The Atlantic Economy 567
ENCOUNTERS AND TRANSFORMATIONS:
Chocolate in the New World and the Old 568
The Atlantic Slave Trade 570

DIFFERENT VOICES: The Abolition of the
Slave Trade 572
Ethnic Diversity in the Atlantic World 573
ENCOUNTERS BETWEEN EUROPEANS
AND ASIANS 575
Political Control of India 575
Changing European Attitudes Toward Asian
Cultures 576
THE CRISIS OF EMPIRE AND THE ATLANTIC
REVOLUTIONS 579
The American Revolution,
1775–1783 579
The Haitian Revolution,
1789–1804 581
The Irish Rebellion, 1798–1799 582
National Revolutions in Spanish America,
1810–1824 583
CONCLUSION: THE RISE AND RESHAPING
OF THE WEST 584

CHAPTER 19
Eighteenth-Century Society and Culture 586

THE ARISTOCRACY 587
The Wealth of the Aristocracy 588
The Political Power of the Aristocracy 590
The Cultural World of the Aristocracy 591
CHALLENGES TO ARISTOCRATIC
DOMINANCE 592
Encounters with the Rural Peasantry 593
The Social Position of the Bourgeoisie 594
The Bourgeois Critique of the Aristocracy 595
THE ENLIGHTENMENT 596
Themes of Enlightenment Thought 596
ENCOUNTERS AND TRANSFORMATIONS:
The Enlightenment, Pacific Islanders, and
the Noble Savage 598
DIFFERENT VOICES: The Enlightenment
Debate over Progress 602
Voltaire and the Spirit of Enlightenment 602
JUSTICE IN HISTORY: A Case of Infanticide
in the Age of the Enlightenment 604
Enlightenment Political Theory 606
Women and the Enlightenment 609
The Enlightenment and Sexuality 610
THE IMPACT OF THE ENLIGHTENMENT 610
The Spread of Enlightened Ideas 610

The Limits of the Enlightenment 612

The Political Legacy of the
Enlightenment 613

Enlightened Absolutism 613

The Enlightenment and Revolution 615

CONCLUSION: THE ENLIGHTENMENT
AND WESTERN IDENTITY 616

CHAPTER 20
The Age of the French
Revolution, 1789–1815 618

THE FIRST FRENCH REVOLUTION
1789–1791 620

The Beginning of the Revolution 620

The Creation of a New Political Society 622

THE FRENCH REPUBLIC, 1792–1799 623

The Establishment of the Republic, 1792 623

DIFFERENT VOICES: The Rights of Man
and Woman 624

The Jacobins and the Revolution 627

The Reign of Terror, 1793–1794 628

JUSTICE IN HISTORY: The Trial of Louis XVI 630

The Directory, 1795–1799 632

CULTURAL CHANGE IN FRANCE DURING
THE REVOLUTION 634

The Transformation of the Cultural
Institutions 634

The Creation of a New Political Culture 635

THE NAPOLEONIC ERA, 1799–1815 638

Napoleon's Rise to Power 638

Napoleon and the Revolution 640

Napoleon and the French State 640

Napoleon, the Empire, and Europe 642

The Downfall of Napoleon 644

ENCOUNTERS AND TRANSFORMATIONS:
The French Encounter the Egyptians, 1798–1801 646

THE LEGACY OF THE FRENCH REVOLUTION 650

CONCLUSION: THE FRENCH REVOLUTION
AND WESTERN CIVILIZATION 652

CHAPTER 21
The Industrial Revolution 654

THE NATURE OF THE INDUSTRIAL
REVOLUTION 655

New Industrial Technology 655

Mineral Sources of Energy 658

The Growth of Factories 659

New Methods of Transportation 660

CONDITIONS FAVORING INDUSTRIAL
GROWTH 662

Population Growth 662

Agricultural Productivity 663

Capital Formation and Accumuluation 663

Demand from Consumers and Producers 664

THE SPREAD OF INDUSTRIALIZATION 665

Great Britain and the Continent 666

Features of Continental Industrialization 667

Industrialization in the United States 669

Industrial Regionalism 669

THE EFFECTS OF INDUSTRIALIZATION 670

Population and Economic Growth 670

Standards of Living 671

Women, Children, and Industry 672

Class and Class Consciousness 673

DIFFERENT VOICES: The Social and Cultural
Effects of Industrialization 674

JUSTICE IN HISTORY: The Sadler
Committee on Child Labor 676

The Industrial Landscape 679

INDUSTRY, TRADE AND EMPIRE 680

East Asia: The Opium War, 1839–1842 680

India: Annexation and Trade 681

Latin America: An Empire of Trade 681

Ireland: The Internal Colony 682

CONCLUSION: INDUSTRIALIZATION AND
THE WEST 682

CHAPTER 22
Ideological Conflict and National
Unification, 1815–1871 684

NEW IDEOLOGIES IN THE EARLY
NINETEENTH CENTURY 685

Liberalism: The Protection of Individual
Freedom 686

Conservatism: Preserving the Established
Order 686

Socialism: The Demand for Equality 687

DIFFERENT VOICES: Liberals and Socialists
View the Middle Class 688

Nationalism: The Unity of the People 690

Culture and Ideology 692

IDEOLOGICAL ENCOUNTERS IN EUROPE,
1815–1848 695

Liberal and Nationalist Revolts,
1820–1825   695

Liberal and Nationalist Revolts, 1830   697

Liberal Reform in Britain, 1815–1848   699

The Revolutions of 1848   702

JUSTICE IN HISTORY: Prostitution, Corporal
Punishment, and Liberalism in Germany   706

NATIONAL UNIFICATION IN EUROPE AND
AMERICA, 1848–1871   708

Italian Unification: Building a Fragile
Nation-State   709

German Unification: Conservative
Nation-Building   711

Unification in the United States: Creating
a Nation of Nations   712

Nationalism in Eastern Europe: Preserving
Multinational Empires   714

INTERNATIONAL CONFLICT AND DOMESTIC
POLITICS, 1853–1871   716

Russian and the Crimean War, 1853–1856   716

France and the Franco-Prussian War,
1870–1871   717

CONCLUSION: THE IDEOLOGICAL
TRANSFORMATION IN THE WEST   718

CHAPTER 23
The Coming of Mass Politics: Industrialization, Emancipation, and Instability, 1870–1914   720

ECONOMIC TRANSFORMATION   721

Economic Depression   721

Industrial Expansion and Development   722

On the Move: Emigration and
Urbanization   724

Growing Social Unrest   724

DEFINING THE POLITICAL NATION   725

Nation-Making   726

Nation-Making: The Examples of France,
Russia, and Ireland   728

JUSTICE IN HISTORY: The Dreyfus Affair:
Defining National Identity in France   731

BROADENING THE POLITICAL NATION   735

The Politics of the Working Class   735

The Politics of Race and Nation   738

OUTSIDE THE POLITICAL NATION? THE
EXPERIENCE OF WOMEN   741

Changes in the Position of Middle-Class
Women   742

Women and the Law   742

Finding a Place: Employment and Education   744

No More Angels   744

The Fight for Women's Suffrage   745

DIFFERENT VOICES: The Debate over
Women's Suffrage   746

CONCLUSION: THE WEST IN AN AGE
OF MASS POLITICS   748

CHAPTER 24
The West and the World: Cultural Crisis and the New Imperialism, 1870–1914   750

SCIENTIFIC TRANSFORMATIONS   750

Medicine and Microbes   751

The Triumph of Evolutionary Science   753

Social Darwinism and Racial Hierarchies   755

The Revolution in Physics   755

Social Thought: The Revolt against
Positivism   756

CULTURAL CRISIS: THE *FIN-DE-SIÈCLE*
AND THE BIRTH OF MODERNISM   757

The *Fin-de-Siècle*   757

Tightening Gender Boundaries   758

JUSTICE IN HISTORY: The Trial of Oscar Wilde   760

The Birth of Modernism   762

Popular Religion and Secularization   764

THE NEW IMPERIALISM   765

Understanding the New Imperialism   766

ENCOUNTERS AND TRANSFORMATIONS:
Picasso Goes to the Museum   768

DIFFERENT VOICES: Advocates of New
Imperialism   770

The Scramble for Africa   773

Asian Encounters   775

A Glimpse of Things to Come: The Boer War   781

CONCLUSION: RESHAPING THE WEST:
EXPANSION AND FRAGMENTATION   782

CHAPTER 25
The First World War   784

THE ORIGINS OF THE FIRST WORLD WAR   784

Nationalism in Eastern Europe: Austria-
Hungary and the Problem of Serbia   785

International Competition and Rival
Alliance Systems   787

Mobilization Plans and the Industrialized
Military 788
The Will to War 790
THE EXPERIENCE OF TOTAL WAR 792
The Western Front: Stalemate in the
Trenches 792
DIFFERENT VOICES: The Cultural Impact
of the Western Front 794
The War in Eastern Europe 795
The World at War 798
THE HOME FRONTS 802
Industrial War 802
The World Turned Upside Down 804
Identifying the Enemy: From Propaganda
to Genocide 805
WAR AND REVOLUTION 807
The Russian Revolutions 807
JUSTICE IN HISTORY: Revolutionary
Justice: The Nontrial of Nicholas
and Alexandra 810
The Failure of Wilson's Revolution 813
The Making of the Modern Middle East 816
CONCLUSION: THE WAR AND THE WEST 818

CHAPTER 26

Reconstruction, Reaction, and Continuing Revolution: The 1920s and 1930s

820

CULTURAL DESPAIR AND DESIRE 821
The Waste Land 821
Building Something Better 822
Scientific Possibilities 823
OUT OF THE TRENCHES: RECONSTRUCTING
NATIONALISM AND GENDER POLITICS IN
THE 1920s 824
The Reconstruction of Imperial Russia:
The Soviet Union 824
The Reconstruction of National Politics in
Eastern and Central Europe 825
The Reconstruction of Gender 828
JUSTICE IN HISTORY: The Trial of Adolf
Hitler 829
THE RISE OF THE RADICAL RIGHT 833
The Fascist Alternative 833
The Nazi Revolution 835
Women and the Radical Right 838

THE POLARIZATION OF POLITICS IN
THE 1930s 839
The Soviet Union: Revolution Reconstructed,
Terror Extended 840
The Response of the Democracies 843
DIFFERENT VOICES: The Cult of the Leader 844
THE WEST AND THE WORLD: IMPERIALISM
IN THE INTERWAR ERA 847
The Irish Revolution 847
Changing Power Equations: Ideology and
Economics 848
Postwar Nationalism, Westernization,
and the Islamic Challenge 849
Moral Revolution in India 851
The Power of the Primitive 851
ENCOUNTERS AND TRANSFORMATIONS:
From Mohandas to Mahatma: Gandhi's
Transformation 852
CONCLUSION: THE KINGDOM
OF CORPSES 853

CHAPTER 27

World War II

856

THE COMING OF WAR 857
An Uneasy Peace 858
The Expansion of Nazi Germany 858
Evaluating Appeasement 860
EUROPE AT WAR, 1939–1941 861
A New Kind of Warfare 861
DIFFERENT VOICES: Appeasement and the
Munich Agreement 862
The Invasion of the Soviet Union 864
THE WORLD AT WAR, 1941–1945 869
The Globalization of the War 869
THE TURNING POINT: MIDWAY, EL ALAMEIN,
AND STALINGRAD 869
THE ALLIED VICTORY IN EUROPE 871
The Air War, the Atom Bomb, and the
Fall of Japan 874
THE WAR AGAINST THE JEWS 877
From Emigration to Extermination: The
Evolution of Genocide 878
Genocide by Assembly Line 879
The Allies' Response 880
JUSTICE IN HISTORY: The Trial of Adolf
Eichmann 881

THE HOME FRONT: THE OTHER WARS   883
    The Limits of Resistance   883
    Civil War in Yugoslavia   884
    Under Occupation   885
    The Women's War   886
    What Are We Fighting For?   887
CONCLUSION: THE NEW WEST: AFTER AUSCHWITZ AND THE ATOM BOMB   888

CHAPTER 28
Redefining the West After World War II   890

A DUBIOUS PEACE, 1945–1949   891
    Devastation, Death, and Continuing War   892
    From Hot to Cold War   892
    JUSTICE IN HISTORY: Show Time: The Trial of Rudolf Slánský   898
THE WEST AND THE WORLD: DECOLONIZATION AND THE COLD WAR   900
    The End to the Age of European Empires   900
    The Globalization of the Cold War   904
    DIFFERENT VOICES: Torture and Terrorism in the French-Algerian War   906
THE SOVIET UNION AND EASTERN EUROPE IN THE 1950s AND 1960s   911
    De-Stalinization under Khruschev   912
    Re-Stalinization and Stagnation: The Brezhnev Era   913
    Diversity and Dissent in Eastern Europe   914
THE WEST: CONSENSUS, CONSUMPTION, AND CULTURE   915
    The Triumph of Democracy   916
    Prosperity in the West   917
    Western Culture and Thought in the Age of Consumption   918
    Social Encounters in the Age of Affluence   923
CONCLUSION: NEW DEFINITIONS, NEW DIVISIONS   927

CHAPTER 29
The West in the Contemporary Era: New Encounters and Transformations   928

ECONOMIC STAGNATION AND POLITICAL CHANGE: THE 1970s AND 1980s   929
    The 1970s: A More Uncertain Era   930
    The 1980s: The End of Political Consensus in the West   931
REVOLUTION IN THE EAST   934
    The Crisis of Legitimacy in the East   934
    Gorbachev and Radical Reform   937
    ENCOUNTERS AND TRANSFORMATIONS: Rock and the Velvet Revolution   938
    Revolution in Eastern Europe   940
    The Disintegration of the Soviet Union   942
IN THE WAKE OF REVOLUTION   943
    Russia after the Revolution   943
    Central and Eastern Europe: Toward Democracy?   945
    The Breakup of Yugoslavia   946
RETHINKING THE WEST   949
    The European Union   949
    Islam, Terrorism, and European Identity   951
    JUSTICE IN HISTORY: The Sentencing of Salman Rushdie   953
    Into the Postmodern Era   957
    DIFFERENT VOICES: History in a Postmodern World   960
    The West in the 21st Century   964
CONCLUSION: WHERE IS THE WEST NOW?   964

Glossary   G-1
Suggestions for Further Reading   R-1
Notes   N-1
Photo Credits   C-1
Index   I-1

We wrote this textbook to answer questions about the identity of the civilization in which we live. Journalists, politicians, and scholars often refer to our civilization, its political ideologies, its economic systems, and its cultures as "Western" without fully considering what that label means and why it might be appropriate. The classification of our civilization as Western has become particularly problematic in the age of globalization. The creation of international markets, the rapid dissemination of ideas on a global scale, and the transmission of popular culture from one country to another often make it difficult to distinguish what is Western from what is not. *The West: Encounters & Transformations* offers students a history of Western civilization in which these issues of Western identity are given prominence. Our goal is neither to idealize nor to indict that civilization, but to describe its main characteristics in different historical periods.

The West: Encounters & Transformations gives careful consideration to two basic questions. The first is, how did the definition of the West change over time? In what ways did its boundaries shift and how did the distinguishing characteristics of its cultures change? The second question is, by what means did the West—and the idea of the West—develop? We argue that the West is the product of a series of cultural encounters that occurred both outside and within its geographical boundaries. We explore these encounters and the transformations they produced by detailing the political, social, religious, and cultural history of the regions that have been, at one time or another, a part of the West.

DEFINING THE WEST

What is the West? How did it come into being? How has it developed throughout history? Many textbooks take for granted which regions or peoples of the globe constitute the West. They treat the history of the West as a somewhat expanded version of European history. While not disputing the centrality of Europe to any definition of the West, we contend that the West is not only a geographical realm with ever-shifting boundaries, but also a cultural realm, an area of cultural influence extending beyond the geographical and political boundaries of Europe. We so strongly believe in this notion that we have written the introductory essay "What Is the West?" to encourage students to think about their understanding of Western civilization and to guide their understanding of each chapter. Many of the features of what we call Western civilization originated in regions that are not geographically part of Europe (such as North Africa and the Middle East), while ever since the fifteenth century various social, ethnic, and political groups from non-European regions (such as North and South America, eastern Russia, Australia, New Zealand, and South Africa) have identified themselves, in one way or another, with the West. Throughout the text, we devote considerable attention to the boundaries of the West and show how borderlines between cultures have been created, especially in eastern and southeastern Europe.

Considered as a geographical and cultural realm, *the West* is a term of recent origin, and the civilization to which it refers did not become clearly defined until the eleventh century, especially during the Crusades, when western European Christians developed a distinct cultural identity. Before that time we can only talk about the powerful forces that created the West, especially the dynamic interaction of the civilizations of western Europe, the Byzantine Empire, and the Muslim world.

Over the centuries Western civilization has acquired many salient characteristics. These include two of the world's great legal systems (civil law and common law), three of the world's monotheistic religions (Judaism, Christianity, and Islam), certain political and social philosophies, forms of political organization (such as the modern bureaucratic state and democracy), methods of scientific inquiry, systems of economic organization (such as industrial capitalism), and distinctive styles of art, architecture, and music. At times one or more of these characteristics has served as a primary source of Western identity: Christianity in the Middle Ages, science and rationalism during the Enlightenment, industrialization in the nineteenth and twentieth centuries, and a defense of individual liberty and democracy in the late twentieth century. These sources of Western identity, however, have always been challenged and contested, both when they were coming into prominence and when they appeared to be most triumphant. Western culture has never been monolithic; even today references to the West imply a wide range of meanings.

CULTURAL ENCOUNTERS

The definition of the West is closely related to the central theme of our book, which is the process of cultural encounters. Throughout *The West: Encounters & Transformations,* we examine the West as a product of a series of cultural encounters both outside the West and within it. We show that the West originated and developed through a continuous process of inclusion and exclusion resulting from a series of encounters among and within different groups. These encounters can be described in a general sense as external, internal, or ideological.

External Encounters

External encounters took place between peoples of different civilizations. Before the emergence of the West as a clearly defined entity, external encounters occurred between such diverse peoples as Greeks and Phoenicians, Macedonians and Egyptians, and Romans and Celts. After the eleventh century, external encounters between Western and non-Western peoples occurred mainly during periods of European exploration, expansion, and imperialism. In the sixteenth and seventeenth centuries, for example, a series of external encounters took place between Europeans on the one hand and Africans, Asians, and the indigenous people of the Americas on the other. Two chapters of *The West: Encounters & Transformations* (Chapters 13 and 18) and a large section of a third (Chapter 24) explore these external encounters in depth and discuss how they affected Western and non-Western civilizations alike.

Internal Encounters

Our discussion of encounters also includes similar interactions between different social groups *within* Western countries. These internal encounters often took place between dominant and subordinate groups, such as between lords and peasants, rulers and subjects, men and women, factory owners and workers, masters and slaves. Encounters between those who were educated and those who were illiterate, which recurred frequently throughout Western history, also fall into this category. Encounters just as often took place between different religious and political groups, such as between Christians and Jews, Catholics and Protestants, and royal absolutists and republicans.

Ideological Encounters

Ideological encounters involve interaction between comprehensive systems of thought, most notably religious doctrines, political philosophies, and scientific theories about the nature of the world. These ideological conflicts usually arose out of internal encounters, when various groups within Western societies subscribed to different theories of government or rival religious faiths. The encounters between Christianity and polytheism in the early Middle Ages, between liberalism and conservatism in the nineteenth century, and between fascism and communism in the twentieth century were ideological encounters. Some ideological encounters had an external dimension, such as when the forces of Islam and Christianity came into conflict during the Crusades and when the Cold War developed between Soviet communism and Western democracy in the second half of the twentieth century.

* * *

The West: Encounters & Transformations illuminates the variety of these encounters and clarifies their effects. By their very nature encounters are interactive, but they have taken different forms: They have been violent or peaceful, coercive or Cooperative. Some have resulted in the imposition of Western ideas on areas outside the geographical boundaries of the West or the perpetuation of the dominant culture within Western societies. More often than not, however, encounters have resulted in a more reciprocal process of exchange in which both Western and non-Western cultures, or the values of both dominant and subordinate groups, have undergone significant transformation. Our book not only identifies these encounters, but also discusses their significance by returning periodically to the issue of Western identity.

COVERAGE

The West: Encounters & Transformations offers both comprehensive coverage of political, social, and culture history and a broader coverage of the West and the world.

Comprehensive Coverage

Our goal throughout the text has been to provide comprehensive coverage of political, social, and cultural history and to include significant coverage of religious and military history as well. Political history defines the basic structure of the book, and some chapters, such as those on Hellenistic civilization, the age of confessional divisions, absolutism and state building, the French Revolution, and the coming of mass politics, include sustained political narratives. Because we understand the West to be a cultural as well as a geographical realm, we give a prominent position to cultural history. Thus, we include rich sections on Hellenistic philosophy and literature, the cultural environment of the Italian Renaissance, the creation of a new political culture at the time of the French Revolution, and the atmosphere of cultural despair and desire that prevailed in Europe after World War I. We also devote special attention to religious history, including the history of Islam as well as that of Christianity and Judaism. Unlike many other textbooks, our coverage of religion continues into the modern period.

The West: Encounters & Transformations also provides extensive coverage of the history of women and gender. Wherever possible the history of women is integrated into the broader social, cultural, and political history of the period. But there are also separate sections on women in our chapters on classical Greece, the Renaissance, the Reformation, the Enlightenment, the Industrial Revolution, World War I, World War II, and the postwar era.

The West and the World

Our book provides broad geographical coverage. Because the West is the product of a series of encounters, the external areas with which the West interacted are of major importance. Three chapters deal specifically with the West and the world.

- Chapter 13, "The West and the World: The Significance of Global Encounters, 1450–1650"
- Chapter 18, "The West and the World: Empire, Trade, and War, 1650–1815"
- Chapter 24, "The West and the World: Cultural Crisis and the New Imperialism, 1870–1914"

These chapters present substantial material on sub-Saharan Africa, Latin America, the Middle East, India, and East Asia. Our text is also distinctive in its coverage of eastern Europe and the Muslim world, areas that have often been considered outside the boundaries of the West. These regions were arenas within which significant cultural encounters took place. Finally, we include material on the United States and Australia, both of which have become part of the West. We recognize that most American college and university students have the opportunity to study American history as a separate subject, but treatment of the United States as a Western nation provides a different perspective from that usually given in courses on American history. For example, this book treats America's revolution as one of four Atlantic revolutions, its national unification in the nineteenth century as part of a broader western European development, its pattern of industrialization as related to that of Britain, and its central role in the Cold War as part of an ideological encounter that was global in scope.

What's New to This Edition?

- In preparing this edition we have thoroughly revised every chapter to ensure that we include the most recent research in the field and to make it even more accessible to students. Most significantly, we have reduced the length of each chapter by approximately 20 to 25 percent.
- We have written separate chapters on Hellenistic civilization and the Roman Republic. In the second edition we had included both subjects in the same chapter because Rome was a part of the Hellenistic world and absorbed large doses of Greek culture. Separate chapters, however, allow us not only to devote more space to each topic, but also to clarify the ways in which republican Rome developed a distinctive brand of Hellenism.
- The discussion of ancient Egypt, which was divided between Chapters 1 and 2 in the second edition, has been consolidated into Chapter 1 for ease of teaching. Discussion of the ancient Hebrews, now in Chapter 2, has been expanded.
- Instead of including three separate primary source documents in each chapter we have

included two documents that present different and often contradictory positions on the same person, event, or development. These documents, which are followed by questions for discussion, appear in the "Different Voices" feature in each chapter.
- We have written new "Encounters and Transformations" features in Chapters 2, 5, 6, 11, and 12, and new "Justice in History" features for Chapters 2, 4, 13, and 14.

FEATURES AND PEDAGOGICAL AIDS

In writing this textbook we have endeavored to keep both the student reader and the classroom instructor in mind at all times. The text includes the following features and pedagogical aids, all of which are intended to support the themes of the book.

"What Is the West?"

The West: Encounters & Transformations begins with an essay to engage students in the task of defining the West and to introduce them to the notion of cultural encounters. "What Is the West?" guides students through the text by providing a framework for understanding how the West was shaped. Structured around the six questions of What? When? Where? Who? How? and Why?, this framework encourages students to think about their understanding of Western civilization. The essay serves as a blueprint for using this textbook.

"Encounters and Transformations"

These features, which appear in about half the chapters, illustrate the main theme of the book by identifying specific encounters and showing how they led to significant transformations in the cultures of the West.

ENCOUNTERS AND TRANSFORMATIONS

**The Introduction of the Table Fork:
The New Sign of Western Civilization**

Sometime in the sixteenth century, western Europeans encountered a new tool that initiated a profound and lasting transformation in Western society: the table fork. Before the table fork, people dined in a way that, to our modern sensibilities, seems disgusting. Members of the upper classes indulged themselves by devouring meat in enormous quantities. Whole rabbits, lambs, and pigs roasted on a spit were placed before diners. A quarter of veal or venison or even an entire roast beef, complete with its head, might

be heaved onto the table. Diners used knives to cut off a piece of meat that they then ate with their hands, allowing the juices to drip down their arms. They used the long sleeves of their shirts to wipe meat juices, sweat, and spittle from their mouths and faces. These banquets celebrated the direct physical contact between the body of the dead animal and the bodies of the diners themselves who touched, handled, chewed, and swallowed it.

During the sixteenth century, puritanical reformers who were trying to abolish the cruder aspects of popular culture also promoted new table manners.

THE INTRODUCTION OF THE TABLE FORK
During the late sixteenth century the refinement of manners among the upper classes focused on dining. No innovation was more revolutionary than the spread of the use of the table fork. Pictured here is the travel cutlery, including two table forks, of Queen Elizabeth I.

These features show, for example, how camels enabled encounters among nomadic tribes of Arabia, which led to the rapid spread of Islam; how the Mayans' interpretation of Christian symbols transformed European Christianity into a hybrid religion; how the importation of chocolate from the New World to Europe changed Western consumption patterns and the rhythms of the Atlantic economy; and how Picasso's encounter with African art contributed to the transformation of modernism. Each of these essays concludes with questions for discussion.

"Justice in History"

Found in every chapter, this feature presents a historically significant trial or episode in which different notions of justice (or injustice) were debated and resolved. The "Justice in History" features illustrate cultural encounters within communities as they try to determine the fate of individuals from all walks of life.

Many famous trials dealt with conflicts over basic religious, philosophical, or political values, such as those of Socrates, Jesus, Joan of Arc, Martin Luther, Charles I, Galileo, and Adolf Eichmann. Other "Justice in History" features show how judicial institutions, such as the ordeal, the Inquisition, and revolutionary tribunals, handled adversarial situations in different societies. These essays, therefore, illustrate the way in which the basic values of the West have evolved through attempts to resolve disputes and conflict.

Each "Justice in History" feature includes two pedagogical aids. "For Discussion" helps students explore the historical significance of the episode just examined. These questions can be used in classroom discussion or as student essay topics. "Taking It Further" provides the student with a few references that can be consulted in connection with a research project.

JUSTICE IN HISTORY

The *Auto-da-Fé*: The Power of Penance

Performed in Spain and Portugal from the sixteenth to eighteenth centuries, the *auto-da-fé* merged the judicial processes of the state with the sacramental rituals of the Catholic Church. An *auto* took place at the end of a judicial investigation conducted by the inquisitors of the Church after the defendants had been found guilty of a sin or crime. The term **auto-da-fé** means "act of faith," and the goal was to persuade or force a person who had been judged guilty to repent and confess. Organized through the cooperation of ecclesiastical and secular authorities, autos-da-fé brought together an assortment of sinners, criminals, and heretics for a vast public rite that dramatized the essential elements of the sacrament of penance: *contrition*, by which the sinner recognized and felt sorry for the sin; *confession*, which required the sinner to admit the sin to a priest; and *satisfaction* or *punishment*, by which the priest absolved the sinner and enacted some kind of penalty. The auto-da-fé transformed penance, especially confession and satisfaction, into a spectacular affirmation of the faith and a manifestation of divine justice.

The *auto* symbolically anticipated the Last Judgment. By suffering bodily pain in this life the soul

miters or hat:
their sin, four
devils, and th
their necks tc
tives. The sin
sent their lacl
escaped arres
sion by effigi
who had died
carried in the
appeared bef
zens stripped
dressed only
Among them
mous *sanben*
yellow strip d
painted with
the unrepent

The proces
platform on w
lic penances a
their knees, p
and to plead f
church. For th
announced th
from the pain:
auto. The sent
tial procession

"Different Voices"

Each chapter contains a new feature consisting of two primary source documents that present different and often opposing views regarding a particular person, event, or development. An introduction to the documents provides the necessary historical context, identifies the authors of the documents and suggests the different perspectives they take. A set of questions for discussion follows the two documents.

DIFFERENT VOICES WERE THERE REALLY WITCHES?

Even during the height of the witch-hunt the existence of witches was controversial. Most authorities assumed that the devil worked evil on earth and that hunting witches, therefore, was an effective means of defending Christians. These authorities used the church and secular courts to interrogate alleged witches, sometimes supplemented by torture, to obtain confessions and the identities of other confederate witches. These authorities considered the hunting of witches part of their duty to protect the public from harm. Others accepted the reality of witchcraft but doubted the capacity of judges to determine who was a witch. A few doubted the reality of witchcraft altogether.

Johann Weyer (1515?–1588) was a physician who argued that most witches were deluded old women who suffered from depression and need medical help rather than legal punishment. The devil deceived them into thinking they had magical powers, but because Weyer had a strong belief that only God had power over nature, he did not credit the devil or witches with any special powers. No one else during the sixteenth century disputed the reality of the powers of witches as systematically as he. Jean

permission and
and storms, he
them to use th
when the troub
witches are cor
have caused it.
make hail and
deluded and bl
whom they hav
they think that
storms. Not on
godless lives sh
severely....

Our witches
phantasy by th
they have done
pen or caused
did not take pl
cially under to
causing many t
them and for a
them when the
themselves to t

Chapter Review and Questions for Discussion

This edition of *The West* offers three different sets of questions in each chapter.

- Each of the major sections of the chapter begins with the main question that the section addresses. These questions are printed in blue. These section questions appear once again at the end of the chapter under the heading "Chapter Questions."
- At the end of each chapter a set of questions under the heading "Taking It

Further" ask the student to think about some of the more specific issues discussed in the chapter.
- Each Justice in History and Different Voices feature is followed by a set of questions under the heading "For Discussion."

Maps and Illustrations

Artwork is a key component of our book. We recognize that many students often lack a strong familiarity with geography, and so we have taken great care to develop maps that help sharpen their geographic skills. Complementing the book's standard map program, we include maps focusing on areas outside the borders of Western civilization. More than 300 images of fine art and photos tell the story of Western civilization and help students visualize the past: the way people lived, the events that shaped their lives, and how they viewed the world around them.

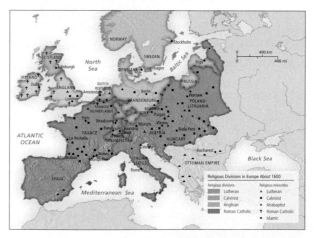

Chronologies

Each chapter includes a varying number of chronologies that list in tabular form the events relating to a particular topic discussed in the text. Chronologies present the sequence of events and can be helpful for purposes of review.

CHRONOLOGY: SPAIN AND THE NETHERLANDS, 1568–1648

1568	Edict against Morisco culture
1580	King Philip II inherits Portugal and the Portuguese Empire
1584	Assassination of William the Silent
1588	Defeat of the Spanish Armada, failed Spanish invasion of England; the seven northern provinces of the Netherlands becomes a republic
1609	Expulsion of the Moriscos from Spain
1648	Treaty of Westphalia recognizes independence of the Netherlands

Key Terms and Glossary

We have sought to create a work that is accessible to students with little prior knowledge of the basic facts of Western history or geography. Throughout the book we have explained difficult concepts at length. For example, we present in-depth explanations of the concepts of Zoroastrianism, Neoplatonism, Renaissance humanism, the various Protestant denominations of the sixteenth century, capitalism, seventeenth-century absolutism, nineteenth-century liberalism and nationalism, fascism, and modernism. We have identified these concepts as key terms by printing them in bold in the text. Key terms for each chapter are listed at the end of each chapter, and all key terms are listed in alphabetical order, together with their definitions, in the Glossary at the end of the book.

Suggested Readings

An annotated list of suggested readings for all the chapters appears at the end of the book. The items listed there are not scholarly works for the benefit of the instructor, but suggestions for students who wish to explore a topic in greater depth or to write a research paper. References to books or articles relevant to the subject of the "Justice in History" feature appear in each chapter under the heading "Taking it Further."

A Note About Dates and Transliterations

In keeping with current academic practice, *The West: Encounters & Transformations* uses B.C.E. (before the common era) and C.E. (common era) to designate dates. We also follow the most current and widely accepted English transliterations of Arabic. *Qur'an*, for example, is used for *Koran; Muslim* is used for *Moslem*. Chinese words appearing in the text for the first time are written in pinyin, followed by the older Wade-Giles system in parentheses.

ANCILLARY MATERIALS

The ancillary materials that accompany *The West: Encounters and Transformations*, Third Edition, are designed to reinforce and enliven the richness of the past and inspire students with the excitement of studying the history of Western Civilization.

For Instructors

THE INSTRUCTOR'S RESOURCE CENTER (www. pearsonhighered.com) Text-specific materials, such as the instructor's manual, and the test item file, are available for downloading by adopters.

INSTRUCTOR'S RESOURCE MANUAL/TEST ITEM FILE The Instructor's Manual contains chapter outlines, summaries, key points and vital concepts, and information on audio-visual resources that can be used in developing and preparing lecture presentations. The Test Item File includes 1,200 multiple-choice and essay test questions. **Available on the Instructor's Resource Center: www.pearsonhighered.com/irc/**

MYTEST MyTest is an online test management program. The program allows instructors to select items from the Test Item File in order to create tests. It also allows for online testing. **Available on the Instructor's Resource Center: www.pearsonhighered.com/irc/**

DIGITAL TRANSPARENCY MASTERS AND POWER-POINTS The Digital Transparency Masters are full-color PDFs containing high-resolution images of all the maps and line art that appear in the text. These files are suitable for both printing to acetate or electronic display. The PowerPoints contain chapter outlines and full-color images of maps and line art. Both are text specific and available for download from the Instructor's Resource Center. **Available on the Instructor's Resource Center: www.pearsonhighered.com/irc/**

For Instructors and Students

MYHISTORYLAB (www.myhistorylab.com) **SAVE TIME. IMPROVE RESULTS.** MyHistoryLab is a

dynamic website that provides a wealth of resources geared to meet the diverse teaching and learning needs of today's instructors and students. MyHistoryLab's many accessible tools will encourage students to read their text and help them improve their grade in their course.

Here are some of the features that will help you and your students save time and improve results:

■ Pearson eText—Just like the printed text, students can highlight and add their own notes. Students save time and improve results by having access to their book online.
■ Gradebook—Students can follow their own progress and instructors can monitor the work of the entire class. Automated grading

of quizzes and assignments helps both instructors and students save time and monitor their results throughout the course.
■ History Bookshelf—Students may read, download, or print 100 of the most commonly assigned history works like Homer's *The Iliad* or Machiavelli's *The Prince.*
■ MySearchLab—This website provides students access to a number of reliable sources for online research, as well as clear guidance on the research and writing process.

COURSESMART TEXTBOOKS ONLINE www.coursesmart.com. provides students an inexpensive alternative to purchasing the print textbook by subscribing to the same text online. Features include search, online note-taking, a print option and bookmarking.

For Students

Please contact your Pearson Arts and Sciences representative for ordering information.

LIVES AND LEGACIES: BIOGRAPHIES IN WESTERN CIVILIZATION, SECOND EDITION Extensively revised, *Lives and Legacies* includes brief, focused biographies of 60 individuals whose lives provide insight into the key developments of Western civilization. Each biography includes an introduction, pre-reading questions, and suggestions for additional reading.

Volume One: ISBN-10: 0205649157 | ISBN-13: 9780205649150
Volume Two: ISBN-10: 0205649149 | ISBN-13: 9780205649143

A variety of Penguin-Putnam texts are available at a discounted prices when bundled with *The West: Encounters & Transformations*, Third Edition. The complete list of titles is available at www.pearsonhighered.com/penguin

 THE PRENTICE HALL ATLAS OF WESTERN CIVILIZATION, SECOND EDITION Produced in collaboration with Dorling Kindersley, the leader in cartographic publishing, the updated second edition of *The Prentice Hall Atlas of Western Civilization* applies the most innovative cartographic techniques to present western civilization in all of its complexity and diversity. Copies of the atlas can be bundled with *The West: Encounters & Transformations*, Third Edition, for a nominal charge. Contact your Pearson Arts and Sciences sales representative for details. ISBN-10: 0136042465 | ISBN-13: 9780136042464

A GUIDE TO YOUR HISTORY COURSE: WHAT EVERY STUDENT NEEDS TO KNOW Written by Vincent A. Clark, this concise, spiral-bound guidebook orients students to the issues and problems they will face in the history classroom. Available at a discount when bundled with *The West: Encounters & Transformations*, Third Edition. ISBN-10: 0131850873 | ISBN-13: 9780131850873

A SHORT GUIDE TO WRITING ABOUT HISTORY, SEVENTH EDITION Written by Richard Marius, late of Harvard University, and Melvin E. Page, Eastern Tennessee State University, this engaging and practical text helps students get beyond merely compiling dates and facts. Covering both brief essays and the documented resource paper, the text explores the writing and researching processes, identifies different modes of historical writing, including argument, and concludes with guidelines for improving style. ISBN-10: 0205673708 | ISBN-13: 9780205673704

ACKNOWLEDGMENTS

We wish to thank Michael Maas, whose contributions to the second edition have been incorporated into Chapters 1–8 of this edition. We are also grateful to Priscilla McGeehon, for her support during the production of all three editions of the book; Janet Lanphier, for helping us plan the third edition; Gerald Lombardi, for his editorial comments on the first eight chapters; and Charles Cavaliere, who guided us through the long process of preparing the third edition.

We would also like to thank the following friends and colleagues for their valuable advice and suggestions: Gabor Agoston, Catherine Clinton, Catherine Evtuhov, Wojciech Falkowski, Andrzej Kaminski, Adam Kozuchowski, Christopher Lazarski, David Lindenfeld, John McNeill, Suzanne Marchand, John Merriman, James Miller, Daria Nalecz, Karl Roider, and Mark Steinberg. Finally, we wish to thank Graham Nichols for telecommunications assistance and expertise.

ABOUT THE AUTHORS

 **Brian Levack** grew up in a family of teachers in the New York metropolitan area. From his father, a professor of French history, he acquired a love for studying the past, and he knew from an early age that he too would become a historian. He received his B.A. from Fordham University in 1965 and his Ph.D. from Yale in 1970. In graduate school he became fascinated by the history of the law and the interaction between law and politics, interests that he has maintained throughout his career. In 1969 he joined the history department of the University of Texas at Austin, where he is now the John Green Regents Professor in History. The winner of several teaching awards, Levack teaches a wide variety of courses on British and European history, legal history, and the history of witchcraft. For eight years he served as the chair of his department, a rewarding but challenging assignment that made it difficult for him to devote as much time as he wished to his teaching and scholarship. His books include *The Civil Lawyers in England, 1603–1641: A Political Study* (1973), *The Formation of the British State: England, Scotland and the Union, 1603–1707* (1987), *The Witch-Hunt in Early Modern Europe* (3rd edition, 2006), and *Witch-Hunting in Scotland: Law, Politics, and Religion* (2008).

His study of the development of beliefs about witchcraft in Europe over the course of many centuries gave him the idea of writing a textbook on Western civilization that would illustrate a broader set of encounters between different cultures, societies, and ideologies. While writing the book, Levack and his two sons built a house on property that he and his wife, Nancy, own in the Texas hill country. He found that the two projects presented similar challenges: It was easy to draw up the design, but far more difficult to execute it. When not teaching, writing, or doing carpentry work, Levack runs along the jogging trails of Austin and has recently discovered the pleasures of scuba diving.

 **Edward Muir** grew up in the foothills of the Wasatch Mountains in Utah, close to the Emigration Trail along which wagon trains of Mormon pioneers and California-bound settlers made their way westward. As a child he loved to explore the broken-down wagons and abandoned household goods left at the side of the trail and from that acquired a fascination with the past. Besides the material remains of the past, he grew up with stories of his Mormon pioneer ancestors and an appreciation for how the past continued to influence the present. During the turbulent 1960s, he became interested in Renaissance Italy as a period and place that had been formative for Western civilization. His biggest challenge is finding the time to explore yet another new corner of Italy and its restaurants.

Muir received his Ph.D. from Rutgers University, where he specialized in the Italian Renaissance and did archival research in Venice and Florence, Italy. He is now the Clarence L. Ver Steeg Professor in the Arts and Sciences at Northwestern University and former chair of the history department. At Northwestern he has won several teaching awards. His books include *Civic Ritual in Renaissance Venice* (1981), *Mad Blood Stirring: Vendetta in Renaissance Italy* (1993 and 1998), *Ritual in Early Modern Europe* (1997 and 2005), and *The Culture Wars of the Late Renaissance: Skeptics, Libertines, and Opera* (2007). His books have also been published in Italian.

Some years ago Muir began to experiment with the use of historical trials in teaching and discovered that students loved them. From that experience he decided to write this textbook, which employs trials as a central feature. He lives beside Lake Michigan in Evanston, Illinois. His twin passions are skiing in the Rocky Mountains and rooting for the Chicago Cubs, who manage every summer to demonstrate that winning isn't everything.

 **Meredith Veldman** grew up in the western suburbs of Chicago, where she learned to love winter and the Cubs—which might explain her preference for all things improbable and impractical. Certainly that preference is what attracted her to the study of history, filled as it is with impractical people doing the most improbable things. Veldman majored in history at Calvin College in Grand Rapids, Michigan, and then earned a Ph.D. in modern European history, with a concentration in nineteenth-and twentieth-century Britain, from Northwestern University in 1988.

As an associate professor of history at Louisiana State University, Veldman teaches courses in nineteenth- and twentieth-century British history and twentieth-century Europe, as well as the second half of "Western Civ." In her many semesters in the Western Civ. classroom, Veldman tried a number of different textbooks but found herself increasingly dissatisfied. She wanted a text that would convey to beginning students at least some of the complexities and ambiguities of historical interpretation, introduce them to the exciting work being done in cultural history, and, most important, tell a good story. The search for this textbook led her to accept the offer made by Levack and Muir to join them in writing *The West: Encounters & Transformations*.

An award-winning teacher, Veldman is also the author of *Fantasy, the Bomb, and the Greening of Britain: Romantic Protest, 1945–1980* (1994). She and her family ride out the hurricanes in Baton Rouge, Louisiana. She remains a Cubs fan and she misses snow.

What Is the West?

Many of the people who influence public opinion—politicians, teachers, clergy, journalists, and television commentators—refer to "Western values," "the West," and "Western civilization." They often use these terms as if they do not require explanation. But what *do* these terms mean? The West has always been an arena within which different cultures, religions, values, and philosophies have interacted; any definition of the West will inevitably arouse controversy.

The definition of the West has always been disputed. Note the difference in the following two poems, the first by Rudyard Kipling (1865–1936), an ardent promoter of European imperialism who wrote "The Ballad of East and West" at the height of the British Empire:

> OH, East is East, and West is West, and never the twain shall meet,
> Till Earth and Sky stand presently at God's great Judgment Seat....

The second, "East/West Poem," is by a Chinese-American living in Hawaii, Wing Tek Lum (1946–), who expresses the confusion caused by terms that designate both cultural traits and directions around the globe:

> O
> East is East
> and
> West is West.
> but
> I never did
> understand
> why
> in Geography class
> the East was west
> and
> the West was east
> and that no

> one ever
> cared
> about the difference.

This textbook cares about the difference. It also shows that East and West have, in contrast to Kipling's view, often "met." These encounters created the idea of the East and the West and helped identify the ever shifting borders between the two.

THE SHIFTING BORDERS OF THE WEST

The most basic definition of the West is of a place. Western civilization is now typically thought to comprise the regions of Europe, the Americas, Australia, and New Zealand. However, this is a contemporary definition of the West. The inclusion of these places in the West is the result of a long history of European expansion through colonization and conquest.

This textbook begins about 10,000 years ago in what is now Iraq; the final chapter returns to discuss the Iraq War, but in the meantime the Mesopotamian region is only occasionally a concern for Western history. The history of the West begins with the domestication of animals, the cultivation of the first crops, and the establishment of long-distance trading networks in the Tigris, Euphrates, and Nile River valleys. Cities, kingdoms, and empires in those valleys gave birth to the first civilizations in the West. By about 500 B.C.E., the civilizations that were the cultural ancestors of the modern West had spread from southwestern Asia and north Africa to include the entire Mediterranean basin—areas influenced by Egyptian, Hebrew, Greek, and Roman thought, art, law, and religion. The resulting Greco-Roman

THE TEMPLE OF HERA AT PAESTUM, ITALY:

Greek colonists in Italy built this temple in the sixth century B.C.E. Greek ideas and artistic styles spread throughout the ancient world, both from Greek colonists, such as those at Paestum, and from other peoples who imitated the Greeks.

culture created the most enduring foundation of the West. By the first century C.E. the Roman Empire drew the map of what historians consider the heartland of the West: most of western and southern Europe, the coastlands of the Mediterranean Sea, and the Middle East.

For many centuries, these ancient foundations defined the borders of the West. During the last century, however, the West came to be less about geography than about culture, identity, and technology. When Japan, an Asian country, accepted human rights and democracy after World War II, did it become part of the West? Most Japanese might not think they have adopted "Western" values, but the thriving capitalism and stable democracy of this traditional Asian country

that was never colonized by a European power complicates the idea of what is the West. Or consider the Republic of South Africa, which the white minority—people descended from European immigrants—ruled until 1994. The oppressive white regime violated human rights, rejected full legal equality for all citizens, and jailed or murdered those who questioned the government. Only when democratic elections open to blacks replaced that government did South Africa fully embrace what the rest of the West would consider Western values. To what degree was South Africa part of the West before and after these developments?

Or how about Russia? Russia long saw itself as a Christian country with cultural, economic,

WHERE IS THE WEST?
The shifting borders of the West have moved many times throughout history, but they have always included the areas shown in this satellite photo. These include Europe, north Africa, and the Middle East.

CHANGING IDENTITIES WITHIN THE WEST

In addition to being a place, the West is the birthplace of Western civilization, a civilization that encompasses a cultural history—a tradition stretching back thousands of years to the ancient world. Over this long period the civilization we now identify as Western gradually took shape. The many characteristics that identify it emerged over this time: forms of governments, economic systems, and methods of scientific inquiry, as well as religions, languages, literature, and art.

Throughout the development of Western civilization, the ways in which people identified themselves changed as well. People in the ancient world had no such idea of the common identity of the West, only of being members of a tribe, citizens of a town, or subjects of an empire. But with the spread of Christianity and Islam between the first and seventh centuries, the notion of a distinct civilization in these "Western" lands subtly changed. People came to identify themselves less as subjects of a particular empire and more as members of a community of faith—whether that community comprised followers of Judaism, Christianity, or Islam. These communities of faith drew lines of inclusion and exclusion that still exist today. Starting about 1,600 years ago, Christian monarchs and clergy began to obliterate polytheism (the worship of many gods) and marginalize Jews. From 1,000 to 500 years ago, Christian authorities fought to expel Muslims from Europe. Europeans developed definitions of the West that did not include Islamic communities, even though Muslims continued to live in Europe, and Europeans traded and interacted with the Muslim world. The Islamic countries themselves erected their own barriers, seeing themselves in opposition to the Christian West, even as they continued to look back to the common cultural origins in the ancient world that they shared with Jews and Christians.

During the Renaissance in the fifteenth century, these ancient cultural origins became an alternative to religious affiliation for thinking

and political ties with the rest of Europe. The Russians have intermittently identified with their Western neighbors, especially during the reign of Peter the Great (1682–1725), but their neighbors were not always sure about the Russians. After the Mongol invasions of the thirteenth and fourteenth centuries much of Russia was isolated from the rest of the West, and during the Cold War from 1949 to 1989 Western democracies considered communist Russia an enemy. When was Russia "Western" and when not?

Thus, when we talk about where the West is, we are almost always talking about the Mediterranean basin and much of Europe (and later, the Americas). But we will also show that countries that border "the West," and even countries far from it, might be considered Western in many aspects as well.

about the identity of the West. From this Renaissance historical perspective Jews, Christians, and Muslims descended from the cultures of the ancient Egyptians, Hebrews, Greeks, and Romans. Despite their differences, the followers of these religions shared a history. In fact, in the late Renaissance a number of Jewish and Christian thinkers imagined the possibility of rediscovering the single universal religion that they thought must have once been practiced in the ancient world. If they could just recapture that religion, they could restore the unity they imagined had once prevailed in the West.

The definition of the West has also changed as a result of European colonialism, which began about 500 years ago. When European powers assembled large overseas empires, they introduced Western languages, religions, technologies, and cultures to many distant places in the world, making Western identity a transportable concept. In some of these colonized areas—such as North America, Argentina, Australia, and New Zealand—the European newcomers so outnumbered the indigenous people that these regions became as much a part of the West as Britain, France, and Spain. In other European colonies, especially on the Asian continent, Western cultures failed to exercise similar levels of influence.

As a result of colonialism Western culture sometimes merged with other cultures, and in the process, both were changed. Brazil, a South American country inhabited by large numbers of indigenous peoples, the descendants of African slaves, and European settlers, epitomizes the complexity of what defines the West. In Brazil, almost everyone speaks a Western language (Portuguese), practices a Western religion (Christianity), and participates in Western political and economic institutions (democracy and capitalism). Yet in Brazil all of these features of Western civilization have become part of a distinctive culture in which indigenous, African, and European elements have been blended. During Carnival, for example, Brazilians dressed in indigenous costumes dance in African rhythms to the accompaniment of music played on European instruments.

MARINER'S COMPASS

The mariner's compass was a navigational device intended for use primarily at sea. The compass originated in China; once adopted by Europeans, it enabled them to embark on long ocean voyages around the world.

WESTERN VALUES

For many people today, the most important definition of the West involves adherence to "Western" values. The values typically identified as Western include democracy, individualism, universal human rights, toleration of religious diversity, ownership of private property, equality before the law, and freedom of inquiry and expression. These values, however, have not always been part of Western civilization. In fact, they describe ideals rather than actual realities; these values are by no means universally accepted throughout the West. Thus, there is nothing inevitable about these values; Western history at various stages exhibited quite different ones. Western societies seldom prized legal or political equality until quite recently. In ancient Rome and throughout most of medieval Europe, the wealthy and the powerful enjoyed more protection under the law than did slaves or the poor. Most medieval Christians were completely convinced of the virtue of making war against Muslims and heretics and curtailing the actions of Jews. Before the end of the eighteenth century, few Westerners questioned the practice of slavery, a social hierarchy of birth that remained powerful in the West through the nineteenth century; in addition, most women were excluded from equal economic and educational opportunities until well into the twentieth century. In many places women still do not have equal opportunities. In the twentieth century, millions of Westerners followed leaders who stifled free inquiry, denied basic human rights to many of their citizens, made terror an instrument of the state, and censored authors, artists, and journalists.

The values that define the West have not only changed over time, they also remain fiercely contested. One of the most divisive political issues today, for example, is that of "gay marriage." Both sides in this debate frame their arguments in terms of "Western values." Supporters of the legalization of same-sex marriages highlight equality and human rights: They demand that all citizens have equal access to the basic legal protections afforded by marriage. Opponents emphasize the centrality of the tradition of monogamous heterosexual marriage to Western legal, moral, and religious codes. What this current debate shows us is that no single understanding of "Western values," or of the West itself, exists. These values have always been contended, disputed, and fought over. In other words, they have a history. This text highlights and examines that history.

ASKING THE RIGHT QUESTIONS

So how can we make sense of the West as a place and an identity, the shifting borders and definitions of the West, and Western civilization in general? In short, what has Western civilization been over the course of its long history—and what is it today?

Answering these questions is the challenge this book addresses. There are no simple answers to any of these questions, but there is a method for finding answers. The method is straightforward. Always ask the *what, when, where, who, how,* and *why* questions of the text.

The "What" Question

What is Western civilization? The answer to this question will vary according to time and place. In fact, for much of the early history covered in this book, "Western civilization" did not exist. Rather, a number of distinctive civilizations emerged in the Middle East, northern Africa, and Europe, each of which contributed to what later became Western civilization. As these cultures developed and intermingled, the idea of Western civilization slowly began to form. Thus, the understanding of Western civilization will change from chapter to chapter. The most extensive change in the place of the West was through the colonial expansion of the European nations between the fifteenth and twentieth centuries. Perhaps the most significant cultural change came with acceptance of the values of scientific inquiry for solving human and philosophical problems, an approach that did not exist before the seventeenth century but became one of the distinguishing characteristics of Western civilization. During the late eighteenth and nineteenth centuries, industrialization became the engine that drove economic development in the West. During the twentieth century, industrialization in both its capitalist and communist forms dramatically gave the West a level of economic prosperity unmatched in the nonindustrialized parts of the world.

The "When" Question

When did the defining characteristics of Western civilization first emerge, and for how long did they prevail? Dates frame and organize the content of each chapter, and numerous short chronologies are offered. These resources make it possible to keep track of what happened when. Dates have no meaning by themselves, but the connections *between* them can be very revealing. For example, dates show that the agricultural revolution that permitted the birth of the first civilizations unfolded over a long span of about 10,000 years—which is more time than was taken by all the other events and developments covered in this textbook. Wars of religion plagued Europe for nearly 200 years before Enlightenment thinkers articulated the ideals of religious toleration. The American Civil War—the war to preserve the union, as President Abraham Lincoln termed it—took place at exactly the same time as wars were being fought for national unity in Germany and Italy. In other words, by paying attention to other contemporaneous wars for national unity, the American experience seems less peculiarly an American event.

By learning *when* things happened, one can identify the major causes and consequences of events and thus see the transformations of Western civilization. For instance, the production of a surplus of food through agriculture and the domestication of animals were prerequisites for the emergence of civilizations. The violent collapse of religious unity after the Protestant Reformation in the sixteenth century led some Europeans to propose the separation of church and state two centuries later. And during the nineteenth century many Western countries—in response to the enormous diversity among their own

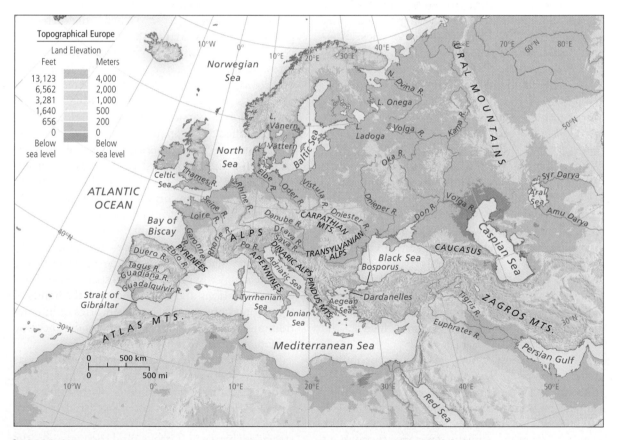

MAP 1

Core Lands of the West

These are the principal geographical features that will appear recurrently throughout this book.

peoples—became preoccupied with maintaining or establishing national unity.

The "Where" Question

Where has Western civilization been located? Geography, of course, does not change very rapidly, but the idea of where the West is does change. By tracing the shifting relationships between the West and other, more distant civilizations with which it interacted, the chapters highlight the changing "where" of the West. The key to understanding the shifting borders of the West is to study how the peoples within the West thought of themselves and how they identified others as "not Western." During the Cold War, for example, many within the West viewed Russia as an enemy rather than as part of the West. In the previous centuries, Australia and North America came to be part of the West because the European conquerors of these regions identified themselves with European cultures and traditions and against non-European values.

The "Who" Question

Who were the people responsible for making Western civilization? Some were anonymous, such as the unknown geniuses who invented the mathematical systems of ancient Mesopotamia. Others are well-known—saints such as Joan of Arc, creative thinkers such as Galileo Galilei, or generals such as Napoleon. Most were ordinary. Humble people, such as the many millions who migrated from Europe to North America or the unfortunate millions who suffered and died in the trenches of World War I, also influenced the course of events.

Perhaps most often this book encounters people who were less the shapers of their own destinies than the subjects of forces that conditioned the kinds of choices they could make, often with unanticipated results. During the eleventh century when farmers throughout Europe began to employ a new kind of plow to till their fields, they were merely trying to do their work more efficiently. They certainly did not recognize that the increase in food they produced would stimulate the enormous population growth that made possible the medieval civilization of thriving cities and magnificent cathedrals. Answering the *who* question requires an evaluation of how much individuals and groups of people were in control of events and how much events controlled them.

The "How" Question

How did Western civilization develop? This is a question about processes—about how things change or stay the same over time. This book identifies and explores these processes in several ways.

First, woven throughout the story is *the theme of encounters and transformations*. What is meant by encounters? When the Spanish *conquistadores* arrived in the Americas some 500 years ago, they came into contact with the cultures of the Caribs, the Aztecs, the Incas, and other peoples who had lived in the Americas for thousands of years. As the Spanish fought, traded with, and intermarried with the natives, each culture changed. The Spanish, for their part, borrowed from the Americas new plants for cultivation and responded to what they considered serious threats to their worldview. Many native Americans, in turn, adopted European religious practices and learned to speak European languages. At the same time, Amerindians were decimated by European diseases, illnesses to which they had never been exposed. The native Americans also witnessed the destruction of their own civilizations and governments at the hands of the colonial powers. Through centuries of interaction and mutual influence, both sides became something other than what they had been.

The European encounter with the Americas is an obvious example of what was, in fact, a continuous process of encounters with other cultures. These encounters often occurred between peoples from different civilizations, such as the struggles between Greeks and Persians in the ancient world or between Europeans and Chinese in the nineteenth century. Other encounters took place among people living in the same civilization. These include interactions between lords and peasants, men and women, Christians and Jews, Catholics and Protestants, factory owners and workers, and capitalists and communists. Western civilization developed and changed, and still does, through a series of external and internal encounters.

Second, *features in the chapters* formulate answers to the question of how Western civilization developed. For example, each chapter contains an essay titled "Justice in History." These essays discuss a trial or some other episode involving questions of justice. Some "Justice in History" essays illustrate how Western civilization was forged in struggles over conflicting values, such as the discussion of the trial of Galileo, which examines the conflict between religious and scientific concepts of truth. Other essays show how efforts to resolve internal cultural, political, and religious tensions helped shape Western ideas about justice, such as the essay on the *auto da fé*, which illustrates how authorities attempted to enforce religious conformity.

Some chapters include another feature as well. The "Encounters and Transformations" features show how encounters between different groups of people, technologies, and ideas were not abstract historical processes, but events that brought people together in a way that transformed history. For example, when the Arabs encountered the camel as an instrument of war, they adopted it for their own purposes. As a result, they were able to conquer their neighbors very quickly and spread Islam far beyond its original home in Arabia.

The "Different Voices" feature in each chapter includes documents from the period that represent contrasting views about a particular issue important at the time. These conflicting voices demonstrate how people debated what mattered to them and in the process formulated what have become Western values. During the Franco-Algerian War of the 1950s and early 1960s, for example, French military officers debated the appropriateness of torture when interrogating Algerian prisoners alleged to be insurgents. The debate about the use of torture against terrorist suspects continues today, revealing one of the unresolved conflicts over the appropriate values of the West.

The "Why" Question

Why did things happen in the way they did in history? This is the hardest question of all, one that engenders the most debate among historians. To take one persistent example, why did Hitler initiate a plan to exterminate the Jews of Europe? Can it be explained by something that happened to him in his childhood? Was he full of self-loathing that he projected onto the Jews? Was it a way of creating an enemy so that he could better unify Germany? Did he really believe that the Jews were the cause of all of Germany's problems? Did he merely act on the deeply seated anti-Semitic tendencies of the German people? Historians still debate the answers to these questions.

Such questions raise issues about human motivation and the role of human agency in historical events. Can historians ever really know what motivated a particular individual in the past, especially when it is so notoriously difficult to understand what motivates other people in the present? Can any individual determine the course of history? The *what, when, where, who,* and *how* questions are much easier to answer; but the *why* question, of course, is the most interesting one, the one that cries out for an answer.

This book does not—and cannot—always offer definitive answers to the *why* question, but it attempts to lay out the most likely possibilities. For example, historians do not really know what disease caused the Black Death in the fourteenth century that killed about one-third of the population in a matter of months. But they can answer many questions about the consequences of that great catastrophe. Why were there so many new universities in the fourteenth and fifteenth centuries? It was because so many priests had died in the Black Death, creating a huge demand for replacements. The answers to the *why* questions are not always obvious, but they are always intriguing; finding the answers is the joy of studying history.

15

The Age of Confessional Division

■ The Peoples of Early Modern Europe   ■ Disciplining the People   ■ Hunting Witches
■ The Confessional States   ■ States and Confessions in Eastern Europe

ON JULY 10, 1584, CATHOLIC EXTREMIST FRANÇOIS GUION, WITH A brace of pistols hidden under his cloak, surprised William the Silent, the Prince of Orange, as he was leaving the dining hall of his palace and shot him at point-blank range. William led the Protestant nobility in the Netherlands, which was in revolt against the Catholic king of Spain. Guion masqueraded as a Protestant for seven years in order to ingratiate himself with William's party, and before the assassination he consulted three Catholic priests who confirmed the religious merit of his plan. Spain's representative in the Netherlands, the Duke of Parma, had offered a reward of 25,000 crowns to anyone who killed William; at the moment of the assassination four other potential assassins were in Delft trying to gain access to the Prince of Orange.

The murder of William the Silent exemplified an ominous figure in Western civilization—the religiously motivated assassin. There had been many assassinations before the late sixteenth century, but those assassins tended to be motivated by the desire to gain political power or to avenge a personal or family injury. Religion hardly ever supplied a motive. In the wake of the Reformation, killing a political leader of the opposing faith to serve God's plan became all too common. The assassination of William illustrated patterns of violence that have since become the *modus operandi* of the political

assassin—the use of deception to gain access to the victim, the vulnerability of leaders who wish to mingle with the public, the lethal potential of easily concealed pistols (a new weapon at that time), the corruption of politics through vast sums of money, and the obsessive hostility of zealots against their perceived enemies. The widespread acrimony among the varieties of Christian faith created a climate of religious extremism during the late sixteenth and early seventeenth centuries.

Religious extremism was just one manifestation of an anxiety that pervaded European society at the time—a fear of hidden forces controlling human events. In an attempt to curb that anxiety, the European monarchs formulated their politics based on the **confessions** of faith, or statements of religious doctrine, peculiar to Catholics or the various forms of Protestantism. During this age of confessional division, European countries polarized along confessional lines, and governments persecuted followers of minority religions, whom they saw as threats to public security. Anxious believers everywhere were consumed with pleasing an angry God, but when they tried to find God within themselves, many Christians seemed only to find the Devil in others.

The religious controversies of the age of confessional division redefined the West. During the Middle Ages, the West came to be identified with

PROCESSION OF THE CATHOLIC LEAGUE

During the last half of the sixteenth century, Catholics and Protestants in France formed armed militias or leagues. Bloody confrontations between these militias led to prolonged civil wars. In this 1590 procession of the French Catholic League, armed monks joined soldiers and common citizens in a demonstration of force.

the practice of Roman Catholic Christianity. The Renaissance added to that identity an appreciation of pre-Christian history going back to Greek and Roman Antiquity. The Reformation of the early sixteenth century eroded the unity of Christian Europe by dividing the West into Catholic and Protestant camps. This division was especially pronounced in western Europe, but less so in eastern Europe because it did not create confessional states. During the late sixteenth and seventeenth centuries, governments reinforced religious divisions and attempted to unify their peoples around a common set of beliefs. How did the encounter between the confessions and the state transform Europe into religiously driven camps?

THE PEOPLES OF EARLY MODERN EUROPE

■ How did the expanding population and price revolution exacerbate religious and political tensions?

During the tenth century if a Rus had wanted to see the sights of Paris—assuming he had even heard of Paris—he could have left Kiev and walked under the shade of trees all the way to France, so extensive were the forests and so sparse the human settlements of northern Europe. By the end of the thirteenth century, the wanderer from Kiev would have needed a hat to protect him on the shadeless journey. Instead of human settlements forming little islands in a sea of forests, the forests were by then islands in a sea of villages and farms, and from almost any church tower the sharp-eyed traveler could have seen other church towers, each marking a nearby village or town. At the end of the thirteenth century, the European continent had become completely settled by a dynamic, growing population, which had cleared the forests for farms.

During the fourteenth century all of that changed. A series of crises—periodic famines, the catastrophic Black Death, and a general economic collapse—left the villages and towns of Europe intact, but a third or more of the population was gone. In that period of desolation, many villages looked like abandoned movie sets, and the cities did not have enough people to fill in the empty spaces between the central market square and the city walls. Fields that had once been put to the plow to feed the hungry children of the thirteenth century were neglected and overrun with bristles and brambles. During the fifteenth century a general European depression and recurrent epidemics kept the population stagnant.

In the sixteenth century the population began to rebound as European agriculture shifted from subsistence to commercial farming.

The sudden swell in human numbers brought dramatic and destabilizing consequences that contributed to pervasive anxiety.

The Population Recovery

During a period historical demographers call the "long sixteenth century" (ca. 1480–1640), the population of Europe began to grow consistently again for the first time since the late thirteenth century. As shown in Figure 15.1, *European Population,* in 1340 on the brink of the Black Death, Europe had about 74 million inhabitants, or 17 percent of the world's total. By 1400 the population of all of Europe had dropped to 52 million or 14 percent of the world's total. Over the course of the long sixteenth century, Europe's population grew to 77.9 million, just barely surpassing the pre–Black Death level.

Figure 15.2, *European Population, 1500–1600,* depicts some representative population figures for the larger European countries during the sixteenth century. Two important facts emerge from these data. The first is the much greater rate of growth in northern Europe compared with southern Europe. England grew by 83 percent, Poland grew by 76 percent, and even the tiny, war-torn Netherlands gained 58 percent. During the same period Italy grew

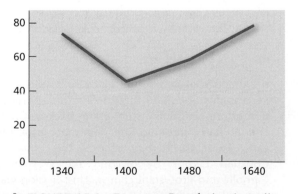

I **FIGURE 15.1** European Population in Millions

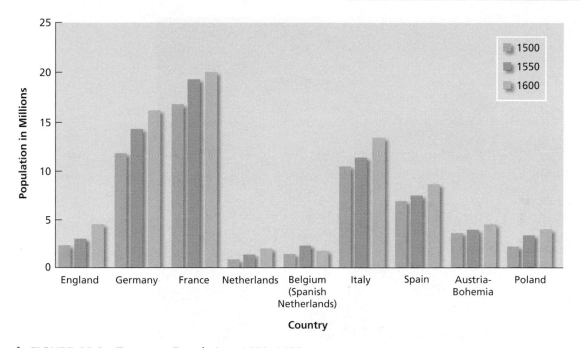

FIGURE 15.2 European Population, 1500–1600

Source: Jan de Vries, "Population," In *Handbook of European History 1400–1600: Late Middle Ages, Renaissance and Reformation,* Vol. 1: *Structures and Assertions,* (eds.) Thomas A. Brady, Jr., Heiko A. Oberman, and James D. Tracy (1994), Table 1, 13. Copyright © 1994 by Brill Academic Publishers. Reproduced with permission of Brill Academic Publishers via Copyright Clearance Center.

by only 25 percent and Spain by 19 percent. These trends signal a massive, permanent shift of demographic and economic power from the Mediterranean countries of Italy and Spain to northern, especially northwestern, Europe. The second fact to note from these data is the overwhelming size of France, which was home to about a quarter of Europe's population. Once France recovered from its long wars of religion, its demographic superiority overwhelmed competing countries and made it the dominant power in Europe, permanently eclipsing its chief rival, Spain.

What explains the growth in the population? To a large extent, the transformation from subsistence to commercial agriculture in certain regions of Europe made it possible. Peasants who practiced subsistence farming consumed about 80 percent of everything they raised, and what little was left over went almost entirely to the landlord as feudal dues and to the church as tithing—the obligation to give to God one-tenth of everything earned or produced. Peasant families lived on the edge of existence. During the sixteenth century, subsistence agriculture gave way to commercial crops, especially wheat, which was sold in town markets and the great cities such as London, Antwerp, Amsterdam, Paris, Milan, Venice, and Barcelona. As commercial agriculture spread, the population grew because the rural population was better fed and more prosperous.

The amount of land available, however, could not provide enough work for the growing farm population. As a result, the landless were forced to take to the road to find their fortunes. These vagabonds, as they were called, exemplified the social problems that emerged from the uneven distribution of

THE RISE OF COMMERCIAL AGRICULTURE
During the sixteenth century commercial agriculture began to produce significant surpluses for the expanding population of the cities. This scene depicts a
windmill for grinding grain and a train of wagons hauling produce from the
country to be marketed in a city.

wealth created by the new commerce. Because large-scale migrations to the Americas had not yet begun, except from Spain, the landless had few options other than to seek opportunities in a city.

The Thriving Cities

By the 1480s cities began to grow, but the growth was uneven with the most dramatic growth occurring in the cities of the North, especially London, Antwerp, and Amsterdam. The surpluses of the countryside, both human and agricultural, flowed into the cities during the sixteenth century. Compared with even the prosperous rural villages, the cities seemed incomparably rich. Half-starved vagabonds marveled at shops piled high with food (white bread, fancy pies, fruit, casks of wine, roasting meats); they wistfully passed taverns full of drunken,

laughing citizens; and they begged for alms in front of magnificent, marble-faced churches.

Every aspect of the cities exhibited dramatic contrasts between the rich and poor, who lived on the same streets and often in different parts of the same houses. Around 1580 Christian missionaries brought a Native American chief to the French city of Rouen. Through an interpreter he was asked what impressed him the most about European cities, so unlike the villages of North America. He replied that he was astonished that the rag-clad, emaciated men and women who crowded the streets did not grab the plump, well-dressed rich people by the throat.

City officials recognized the social problems caused by the disparities in wealth. Every city maintained storehouses of grain and regulated the price of bread and the size of a loaf so that the poor could be fed. The impulse to feed the poor was less the result of humanitarian motives than fear of a hungry mob. Cities guarded carefully against revolts and crime. Even for petty crime, punishment was swift, sure, and gruesome. The beggar who stole a loaf of bread from a baker's cart had his hand amputated on a chopping block in the market square. A shabbily dressed girl who grabbed a lady's glittering trinket had her nose cut off so that she could never attract a man. A burglar was tortured, drawn, and quartered, with his severed head impaled on an iron spike at the town gate as a warning to others.

However talented or enterprising, new arrivals to the city had very limited opportunities. They could hardly start up their own business because all production was strictly controlled by the guilds, which were associations of merchants or artisans organized to protect their interests. Guilds rigidly regulated their membership and required an apprenticeship of many years. Guilds also prohibited technological innovations, guaranteed certain standards of workmanship, and did not allow branching out into new lines. Given the limited opportunities for new arrivals, immigrant men and women begged on the streets or took charity from the public dole. The men picked up any heavy-labor jobs they could find. Both men and women became servants, a job that paid poorly but at least guaranteed regular meals.

Among the important social achievements of both Protestant and Catholic Reformations were efforts to address the problems of the destitute urban poor, who constituted at least a quarter of the population, even in the best of times. In Catholic countries such as Italy, Spain, southern Germany, and France, there was an enormous expansion of credit banks, which were financed by charitable contributions in order to provide small loans to the poor. Catholic cities established convents for poor young women who were at risk of falling into prostitution and for women who had retired from the sex trade. Catholic and Protestant cities established orphanages, hospitals for the sick, hospices for the dying, and public housing. Both Catholic and Protestant cities attempted to distinguish between the "honest" poor—those who were disabled and truly deserving—and the "dishonest" poor who were thought to be malingerers. Protestant cities established poorhouses, which segregated the poor, subjected them to prisonlike discipline, and forced the able-bodied to work.

The more comfortable classes of the cities enjoyed large palaces and luxurious lifestyles. They hired extensive staffs of servants, feasted on meat and fine wines, and purchased exotic imports such as silk cloth, spices from the East, and, in the Mediterranean cities, slaves from eastern Europe, the Middle East, or Africa. Rich merchants maintained their status by marrying within their own class, monopolizing municipal offices, and educating their children in the newly fashionable humanist schools. The wealthy of the cities were the bastions of social stability. They possessed the financial resources and economic skills to protect themselves from the worst consequences of economic instability, especially the corrosive wave of price inflation that struck the West after about 1540.

The Price Revolution

Price inflation became so pervasive during the last half of the sixteenth century that it contributed to the widespread fear that hidden forces controlled events. After a long period of falling or stable prices that stretched back to the fourteenth century, Europe experienced sustained price increases, beginning around 1540, in what historians called the **Price Revolution**. The inflation lasted a century, forcing major economic and social changes that permanently altered the face of Western society. During this period overall prices across Europe multiplied five- or sixfold.

What caused the inflation? The basic principle is simple. The price paid for goods and services is fundamentally the result of the relationship between *supply* and *demand*. If the number of children who need to be fed grows faster than the supply of grain, the price of bread goes up. This happens simply because mothers who can afford it will be willing to pay a higher price to save their children from hunger. If good harvests allow the supply of grain to increase at a greater rate than the demand for bread, then prices go down. Two other factors influence price. One is the *amount of money in circulation.* If the amount of gold or silver available to make coins increases, there is more money in circulation. When more money is circulating, people can buy more things, which creates the same effect as an increase in demand—prices go up. The other factor is called the *velocity of money in circulation,* which refers to the number of times money changes hands to buy things. When people buy commodities with greater frequency, it has the same effect as increasing the amount of money in circulation or of increasing demand—again, prices go up.

The precise combination of these factors in causing the great Price Revolution of the sixteenth century has long been a matter of considerable debate. Most historians would now agree that the primary cause of inflation was population growth, which increased demand for all kinds of basic commodities, such as bread and woolen cloth for clothing. As Europe's population finally began to recover, it meant that more people needed and desired to buy more things. This explanation is most obvious for commodities that people need to survive, such as grain to make bread. These commodities have what economists call *inelastic demand,* that is, consumers do not have a great deal of discretion in purchasing them. Everybody has to eat. The commodities that people could survive without if the price is too high are said to have *elastic demand,* such as dancing shoes and lace collars. In England between 1540 and 1640 overall prices rose by 490 percent. More telling, however, is that the price of grain (inelastic demand) rose by a stunning 670 percent, whereas the price of luxury goods (elastic demand) rose much less, by 204

percent. Thus, inflation hurt the poor, who needed to feed their children, more than the rich, whose desires were more elastic.

Monetary factors also contributed to inflation. The Portuguese brought in significant amounts of gold from Africa, and newly opened mines in central Europe increased the amount of silver by fivefold as early as the 1520s. The discovery in 1545 of the fabulous silver mine of Potosí (in present-day Bolivia) brought to Europe a flood of silver, which Spain used to finance its costly wars. As inflation began to eat away at royal incomes, financially strapped monarchs all across western Europe debased their currency because they believed, mistakenly, that producing more coins containing less silver would buy more. In fact, the minting of more coins meant each coin was worth less and would buy less. In England, for example, debasement was a major source of inflation during the 1540s and 1550s.

The Price Revolution severely weakened governments. Most monarchs derived their incomes from their own private lands and taxes on property. As inflation took hold, property taxes proved dangerously inadequate to cover royal expenses. Even frugal monarchs such as England's Elizabeth I (r. 1558–1603) were forced to take extraordinary measures, in her case to sell off royal lands. Spendthrift monarchs faced disaster. Spain was involved in the costly enterprise of nearly continuous war during the sixteenth century. To pay for the wars, Charles V resorted to a form of deficit financing in which he borrowed money by issuing *juros,* which provided lenders an annuity yielding between three and seven percent on the amount of the principal. By the 1550s, however, the annuity payments of the *juros* consumed half of the royal revenues. Charles's son, Philip II, inherited such an alarming situation that in 1557, the year after he assumed the throne, he was forced to declare bankruptcy. Philip continued to fight expensive wars and borrow wildly, and thus failed to get his financial house in order. He declared bankruptcy again in 1575 and 1596. Philip squandered

Spain's wealth, impoverishing his own subjects through burdensome taxes and contributing to inflation by borrowing at high rates of interest and debasing the coinage. Although the greatest military power of the sixteenth century, Spain sowed the seeds of its own decline by fighting on borrowed money.

Probably the most serious consequence of the Price Revolution was that the hidden force of inflation caused widespread human suffering. During the late sixteenth and early seventeenth centuries, people felt their lives threatened, but they did not know the source and so they imagined all kinds of secret powers at work, especially supernatural ones. The suspicion of religious differences created by the Reformation provided handy, if utterly false, explanations for what had gone wrong. Catholics suspected Protestants, Protestants suspected Catholics, both suspected Jews, and they all worried about witches. Authorities sought to relieve this widespread anxiety by looking in all the wrong places—disciplining the populace, hunting for witches, and battling against enemies from the opposite side of the confessional divide.

DISCIPLINING THE PEOPLE

■ How did religious and political authorities attempt to discipline the people?

The first generation of the Protestant and Catholic Reformations had been devoted to doctrinal disputes and to either rejecting or defending papal authority. Subsequent generations of reformers faced the formidable task of building the institutions that would firmly establish a Protestant or Catholic religious culture. Leaders of all religious confessions, whether Lutheran, Calvinist, Catholic, or Anglican, attempted to revitalize the Christian community by disciplining nonconformists, enforcing moral rigor, and attacking popular culture. Discipline required cooperation between church and secular authorities, but it was not entirely imposed from above. Many people wholeheartedly cooperated with moral correction and even encouraged reformers to go further. Others actively or resentfully resisted it.

Establishing Confessional Identities

Between 1560 and 1650 religious confessions reshaped European culture. A confession consisted of the adherents to a particular statement of religious doctrine—the Confession of Augsburg for Lutherans, the Helvetic Confessions for Calvinists, the Thirty-Nine Articles for Anglicans, and the decrees of the Council of Trent for Catholics.

The process of establishing confessional identities did not happen overnight. During the second half of the sixteenth century, Lutherans turned from the struggle to survive within the hostile Holy Roman Empire to building Lutheranism wherever it was the chosen religion of the local prince. They had to recruit clergy and provide each clergyman with a university education, which was made possible by scholarship endowments from the Lutheran princes of the empire. Once established, the Lutheran clergy became a branch of the civil bureaucracy, received a government stipend, and enforced the will of the prince. Calvinist states followed a similar process, but where they were in a minority, as in France, Calvinists had to go it alone, and the state often discriminated against them. In those places confessional identities were established in opposition to the state and the dominant confession. Catholics responded with their own aggressive plan of training new clergymen, educating the laity, and reinforcing the bond between church and state. Just as with the Lutheran princes, Catholic princes in the Holy Roman Empire associated conformity to Catholicism with loyalty to themselves, making religion a pillar of the state.

Everywhere in western Europe (except for Ireland, the Netherlands, a few places in the Holy Roman Empire, and for a time France) the only openly practiced religion was the religion of the state. The eastern European states of Poland, Bohemia, Hungary, and Transylvania offered greater religious freedom.

Regulating the Family

One matter on which Calvinists, Lutherans, and Catholics agreed was that the foundation of society should be the authority fathers had over their families. This principle of patriarchy, as discussed in Chapter 12, was a traditional *ideal*. The *reality* of high mortality from disease, however, destabilized family life during the fifteenth and sixteenth centuries. Unstable families often lacked fathers and senior males, making it difficult if not impossible to sustain patriarchy in daily life. The confessions that emerged from the Reformation attempted to combat this trend by reinforcing patriarchy. According to an anonymous treatise published in 1586 in Calvinist Nassau, the three pillars of Christian society were the church, the state, and the household. This proposition made the father's authority parallel to the authority of the clergy and king. To enforce patriarchy, ecclesiastical and secular authorities regulated sexuality and the behavior of children. The authorities' goal seems to have been to encourage self-discipline as well as respect for elders. Self-discipline reached into all aspects of life from sexual behavior to table manners. (See *Encounters and Transformations* in this chapter.)

Despite the near universal acceptance of the theory of patriarchy, the reality of the father's and husband's authority varied a great deal. Since the early Middle Ages in northwestern Europe—in Britain, Scandinavia, the Netherlands, northern France, and western Germany—couples tended to wait to marry until their mid- or late twenties, well beyond the age of sexual maturity. The couple had to be economically independent before they married, which meant both had to accumulate savings or the husband needed to inherit from his deceased father before he could marry. When

they did finally marry, they established their own household separate from either of their parents. Husbands were usually only two or three years older than their wives, and that proximity of age tended to make those relationships more cooperative and less authoritarian than the theory of patriarchy might suggest. By contrast, in southern Europe, men in their late twenties or thirties married teenaged women over whom they exercised authority by virtue of the age difference. In eastern Europe, both spouses married in their teens and resided in one of the parental households for many years, which placed both spouses for extended periods under the authority of one of their fathers.

The marriage pattern in northwestern Europe required prolonged sexual restraint by young men and women until they were economically self-sufficient. In addition to individual self-control, sexual restraint required social control by church and secular authorities. Their efforts seem to have been generally successful. For example, in sixteenth-century Geneva, where the elders were especially wary about sexual sins, the rates of illegitimate births were extremely low. The elders were particularly concerned to discipline women and keep them subservient. In 1584 in another Swiss town, Calvinist elders excommunicated Charlotte Arbaleste and her entire household because she wore her hair in curls, which the elders thought were too alluring.

Northwestern European families also tended to be smaller, as married couples began to space their children through birth control and family planning. These self-restrained couples practiced withdrawal, the rhythm method, or abstinence. When mothers no longer relied on wet nurses and nursed their own infants, often for long periods, they also reduced their chances of becoming pregnant. Thus, limiting family size became the social norm in northwestern Europe, especially among the educated and urban middle classes. Protestant families tended to have fewer children than Catholic families, but Catholics in this region also practiced some form of birth control, even though Church law prohibited all forms except abstinence.

The moral status of marriage also demonstrated regional variations during the early modern period. Protestants no longer considered husbands and wives morally inferior to celibate monks and nuns, and the wives of preachers in Protestant communities certainly had a respected social role never granted to the concubines of priests. But the favorable Protestant attitude toward marriage did not necessarily translate into a positive attitude toward women. In Germany the numerous books of advice, called the Father of the House literature, encouraged families to subordinate the individual interests of servants, children, and the mother to the dictates of the father, who was advised to be fair but who always had to be obeyed. Even if a wife was brutally treated by her husband, she could neither find help from authorities nor expect a divorce.

Discipline also played a large role in raising children. The *Disquisition on the Spiritual Condition of Infants* (1618) pointed out that because of original sin, babies were naturally evil. The godly responsibility of the father was to break the will of his evil offspring, taming them so that they could be turned away from sin toward virtue. The very title of a 1591 Calvinist treatise revealed the strength of the evil-child argument: *On Disciplining Children: How the Disobedient, Evil, and Corrupted Youth of These Anxious Last Days Can Be Bettered.* The treatise advised that the mother's role should be limited to her biological function of giving birth. In order to break the will of their infants, mothers were encouraged to wean them early and turn them over for a strict upbringing by their fathers. It directed fathers to be vigilant so that their wives did not corrupt the children, because women "love to accept strange, false beliefs, and go about with benedictions and witches' handiwork."[1]

THE DOMESTIC IDEAL

During the late sixteenth and seventeenth centuries, idealized depictions of harmonious family life became very popular, especially in the Netherlands. This painting by Pieter De Hooch is a prime example of the simple pleasures of domesticity. A young child opens the door to a bedroom while her mother is making a bed.

Source: Pieter de Hooch (Dutch 1629–1684), "The Bedroom" ca. 1658/1660. Oil on canvas. 20" × 23 1/2" (51.0 × 60.0 cm). Widener Collection. 1942.9.33. Photograph © Board of Trustees, National Gallery of Art, Washington, D.C.

JUSTICE IN HISTORY

The *Auto-da-Fé:* The Power of Penance

Performed in Spain and Portugal from the sixteenth to eighteenth centuries, the *auto-da-fé* merged the judicial processes of the state with the sacramental rituals of the Catholic Church. An *auto* took place at the end of a judicial investigation conducted by the inquisitors of the Church after the defendants had been found guilty of a sin or crime. The term **auto-da-fé** means "act of faith," and the goal was to persuade or force a person who had been judged guilty to repent and confess. Organized through the cooperation of ecclesiastical and secular authorities, autos-da-fé brought together an assortment of sinners, criminals, and heretics for a vast public rite that dramatized the essential elements of the sacrament of penance: *contrition,* by which the sinner recognized and felt sorry for the sin; *confession,* which required the sinner to admit the sin to a priest; and *satisfaction* or *punishment,* by which the priest absolved the sinner and enacted some kind of penalty. The auto-da-fé transformed penance, especially confession and satisfaction, into a spectacular affirmation of the faith and a manifestation of divine justice.

The *auto* symbolically anticipated the Last Judgment. By suffering bodily pain in this life the soul might be relieved from worse punishments in the next. Officers of the Inquisition forced the sinners, convicts, and heretics, now considered penitents, to march in a procession that went through the streets of the city from the cathedral to the town hall or place of punishment. These processions would typically include some 30 or 40 penitents, but in moments of crisis they could be far larger. In Toledo in 1486 there were three *autos*—one parading 750 penitents and two displaying some 900 each.

A 1655 *auto* in Córdoba illustrates the symbolic character of the rites. Soldiers carried torches to light the pyre for those to be burnt. Following them in a procession came three bigamists who wore on their heads conical

miters or hats painted with representations of their sin, four witches whose miters depicted devils, and three criminals with harnesses around their necks to demonstrate their status as captives. The sinners carried unlit candles to represent their lack of faith. Criminals who had escaped arrest were represented in the procession by effigies made in their likeness; for those who had died before punishment, effigies were carried in their coffins. The marching sinners appeared before their neighbors and fellow citizens stripped of the normal indicators of status, dressed only in the emblems of their sins. Among them walked a few who wore the infamous *sanbenitos,* a kind of tunic or vest with a yellow strip down the back, and a conical hat painted with flames. These were the *relajados,* the unrepentant or relapsed sinners.

The procession ended in the town square at a platform on which the sinners performed their public penances as on the stage of a theater. Forced to their knees, priests asked the penitents to confess and to plead for readmission into the bosom of the church. For those who did confess, a herald announced the sentence that would rescue them from the pains of Purgatory and the flames of the *auto.* The sentence required them to join a penitential procession for a certain number of Fridays, perform self-flagellation in public, or wear a badge of shame for a prescribed period of time. Those who failed to confess faced a more immediate sentence.

The most horrendous scenes of suffering awaited the *relajados.* If holdouts confessed prior to the reading of the sentence, then the *auto* was a success, a triumph of the Christian faith over its enemies. Therefore, priests attempted everything that they could to elicit confessions, including haranguing, humiliating, and torturing the accused until their stubborn will broke. If the accused finally confessed after the herald read the sentence, then the executioner would strangle them before burning, but if they held out to the very end, the executioner lit the flames while

❙ *AUTO-DA-FÉ* IN LISBON

they were still living. From the ecclesiastics' point of view, the refusal to confess was a disaster for the entire Church because the flames of the pyre opened a window into Hell. They would certainly prefer to see the Church's authority acknowledged through confession than to see the power of Satan manifest in such a public fashion.

Eyewitnesses reported that crowds watched the violence of the autos-da-fé with silent attention in a mood of deep dread, not so much of the inquisitors, it seems, as for the inevitability of the final day of divine judgment that would arrive for them all. The core assumption of the auto-da-fé was that bodily pain could save a soul from damnation. As one contemporary witness put it, the inquisitors removed "through external ritual [the sinners'] internal crimes." Church authorities assumed that the public ritual framework for the sacrament of penance would have a salutary effect on those who witnessed the *auto* by encouraging them to repent before they too faced divine judgment.

For Discussion

1. How did the auto-da-fé contribute to the formation of an individual and collective sense of being a Catholic?

2. In the auto-da-fé, inflicting physical pain was more than punishment. How was pain understood to have been socially and religiously useful?

Taking It Further

Flynn, Maureen. "Mimesis of the Last Judgment: The Spanish *Auto da fé*," *Sixteenth Century Journal* 22 (1991): 281–297. The best analysis of the religious significance of the auto-da-fé.

Flynn, Maureen. "The Spectacle of Suffering in Spanish Streets," In Barbara A. Hanawalt and Kathryn L. Reyerson (eds.), *City and Spectacle in Medieval Europe* (1994). In this fascinating article Flynn analyzes the spiritual value of physical pain.

ENCOUNTERS AND TRANSFORMATIONS

The Introduction of the Table Fork: The New Sign of Western Civilization

Sometime in the sixteenth century, western Europeans encountered a new tool that initiated a profound and lasting transformation in Western society: the table fork. Before the table fork, people dined in a way that, to our modern sensibilities, seems disgusting. Members of the upper classes indulged themselves by devouring meat in enormous quantities. Whole rabbits, lambs, and pigs roasted on a spit were placed before diners. A quarter of veal or venison or even an entire roast beef, complete with its head, might be heaved onto the table. Diners used knives to cut off a piece of meat that they then ate with their hands, allowing the juices to drip down their arms. They used the long sleeves of their shirts to wipe meat juices, sweat, and spittle from their mouths and faces. These banquets celebrated the direct physical contact between the body of the dead animal and the bodies of the diners themselves who touched, handled, chewed, and swallowed it.

During the sixteenth century, puritanical reformers who were trying to abolish the cruder aspects of popular culture also promoted new table manners.

THE INTRODUCTION OF THE TABLE FORK

During the late sixteenth century the refinement of manners among the upper classes focused on dining. No innovation was more revolutionary than the spread of the use of the table fork. Pictured here is the travel cutlery, including two table forks, of Queen Elizabeth I.

New implements made certain that diners did not come into direct physical contact with their food before they placed it in their mouths. In addition to napkins—which came into widespread use to replace shirt sleeves for wiping the mouth—table forks appeared on upper-class tables. It became impolite to transfer food directly from the common serving plate to the mouth. Food first had to go onto each individual's plate and then be cut into small portions and raised to the mouth. A French treatise of 1672 warned that "meat must never be touched…by hand, not even while eating."[2]

This prohibition had nothing to do with cleanliness because bacteria were not discovered until the end of the nineteenth century. The use of the table fork had more to do with civility than hygiene. Certain foods, such as bread or many fruits such as cherries, were and still are always eaten with the hands. In determining when to use a fork it was not cleanliness that mattered, but the kind of food consumed. Forks enabled sixteenth-century diners to avoid their growing sense of discomfort with the textures and juices of meats that reminded them of an animal's flesh and blood.

Forks, then, enabled cultured people to distance themselves from the dead animal that they were eating. More generally, the spreading use of the fork was part of a set of changes linked to growing revulsion with the more physical aspects of human nature, such as reproduction—or the killing and consumption of animals. Just as sixteenth-century church authorities sought to regulate sexuality, so table manners regulated meat eating.

Paradoxically, the civility that resulted from the use of the table fork both created and eroded social divisions. Eating meat with a fork became one more way for those in the upper social ranks to distinguish themselves from the "uncivilized" masses below. Yet everyone—regardless of their social origins—could learn how to use a fork. A clerk or governess could disguise a humble background simply by learning how to eat properly. Gradually—very gradually—behavior replaced birth as a marker of "good breeding." In the end, the transformations that occurred in Western society because of its encounter with the table fork—the blurring of class distinctions and creation of a universal code of manners—were so gradual and subtle that few of us who use a table fork daily are even aware of its profound significance.

For Discussion

How do manners, both good and bad, communicate messages to other people? Why is it important to have good manners?

HUNTING WITCHES

■ Why did people in the sixteenth century think witches were a threat?

The most catastrophic manifestation of the widespread anxiety of the late sixteenth and seventeenth centuries was the great **witch-hunt.** The judicial prosecution of alleged witches in either church or secular courts dramatically increased about the middle of the sixteenth century and lasted until the late seventeenth, when the number of witchcraft trials rapidly diminished and stopped entirely in most of Europe.

Throughout this period, people accepted the reality of two kinds of **magic.** The first kind was natural magic, such as the practice of alchemy or astrology, which involved the manipulation of occult forces believed to exist in nature. The fundamental assumption of natural magic was that everything in nature is alive. The trained magician could coerce the occult forces in nature to do his bidding. During the Renaissance many humanists and scientific thinkers were drawn to natural magic because of its promise of power over nature. Natural magic, in fact, had some practical uses. Alchemists, for example, devoted themselves to discovering what they called the "philosopher's stone," the secret of transmuting base metals into gold. In practice this meant that they learned how to imitate the appearance of gold, a very useful skill for counterfeiting coins or reducing the content of precious metals in legal coins. Natural magic did not imply any kind of contact with devils. Most practitioners of natural magic desired to achieve good, and many considered it the highest form of curative medicine.

Many people of the sixteenth and seventeenth centuries also believed in a second kind of magic—demonic magic. The practitioner of this kind of magic—usually but not always a female witch—called upon evil spirits to gain access to power. Demonic magic was generally understood as a way to work harm by ritual means. Belief in the reality of harmful magic can be found in the Bible and had been widespread for centuries, but only in the fifteenth century did ecclesiastical and secular authorities, convinced that large groups of people were engaging in such heretical practices, prosecute them in large numbers. By the sixteenth century the Protestants' literal readings of the Bible and the disorienting conflicts of the Reformation contributed to fears about witches.

People in many different places—from shepherds in the mountains of Switzerland to Calvinist ministers in the lowlands of Scotland—thought they perceived the work of witches in human and natural events. The alleged practice of witchcraft took two forms: *maleficia* (doing harm by magical means) and *diabolism* (worshiping the devil). There were many kinds of *maleficia*, including coercing an unwilling lover by sprinkling dried menstrual blood in his food, sickening a pig by cursing it, burning a barn after marking it with a hex sign, bringing wasting diarrhea to a child by reciting a spell, and killing an enemy by stabbing a wax statue of him.

Midwives and women who specialized in healing were especially vulnerable to accusations of witchcraft. The intention behind a particular action they might have performed was often obscure, making it difficult to distinguish between magic designed to bring beneficial results, such as the cure of a child, and *maleficia* designed to bring harmful ones. With the high infant mortality rates of the sixteenth and seventeenth centuries, performing magical rituals for a sick baby could be very risky. The logic of witchcraft beliefs implied that a bad ending must have been caused by bad intentions.

While some people certainly attempted to practice *maleficia,* the second and far more serious kind of ritual practice associated with demonic magic, diabolism, certainly never took place. The theory behind diabolism was that the alleged witch made a pact with the Devil, by which she received her magical power, and worshiped him as her god.

The most influential witchcraft treatise, *The Hammer of Witches* (1486), had an extensive discussion of the ceremony of the pact. After the prospective witch had declared her intention to enter his service, Satan appeared to her, often in the alluring form of a handsome young man who offered her rewards, including a demonic lover, called an *incubus.* To obtain these inducements, the witch was obligated to renounce her allegiance to Christ, usually signified by stomping on the cross. The Devil then rebaptized the witch, guaranteeing that her soul belonged to him. To signify that she was one of his own, the Devil marked her body in a hidden place, creating a sign, which could easily be confused with a birthmark or blemish. To an inquisitor or judge, a mark on the skin that did not bleed and was insensitive to pain when pierced with a long pin often confirmed the suspicion that she was a witch.

After making the pact witches allegedly gathered in large numbers to worship the devil at nocturnal assemblies known as sabbaths. The devil was believed to have given them the power to fly to these gatherings. At these assemblies, so it was claimed, witches killed and ate babies, danced naked, and had promiscuous sexual relations with other witches and demons. The belief that witches attended sabbaths, which judicial authorities confirmed by forcing them to confess under severe torture, explains why witch-hunting took a high toll in human life. Between 1450 and 1750, approximately 100,000 people in Europe

BURNING OF A WITCH

Authorities burned a young woman accused of witchcraft, Anne Hendricks, in Amsterdam in 1571.

were tried for witchcraft, and about 50,000 were executed. Approximately half of the trials took place in the German-speaking lands of the Holy Roman Empire, where the central judicial authorities exercised little control over the determination of local judges to secure convictions. Prosecutions were also extensive in Switzerland, France, Scotland, Poland, Hungary, and Transylvania. Relatively few witches were executed in Spain, Portugal, Italy, Scandinavia, the Netherlands, England, and Ireland.

The determination of both Catholics and Protestants to discipline deviants of all sorts and to wage war against the Devil intensified the hunt for witches. The great majority of trials occurred between 1560 and 1650, when religious tensions were strong and economic conditions severe. The trials rarely occurred in a steady flow, as one would find for other crimes. In many cases the torture of a single witch would lead to her naming many alleged accomplices, who would then also be tried. This would lead to a witch panic in which scores and sometimes hundreds of witches would be tried and executed. Eighty percent of accused witches were women, especially those who were unmarried or widowed, but men and even young children could be accused of witchcraft as well. The hunts came to an end when judicial authorities recognized that no one was safe, especially during witch panics, and when they realized that legal evidence against witches was insufficient for conviction. The Dutch Republic was the first to ban witch trials in 1608. (See *Different Voices* in this chapter.)

DIFFERENT VOICES WERE THERE REALLY WITCHES?

Even during the height of the witch-hunt the existence of witches was controversial. Most authorities assumed that the devil worked evil on earth and that hunting witches, therefore, was an effective means of defending Christians. These authorities used the church and secular courts to interrogate alleged witches, sometimes supplemented by torture, to obtain confessions and the identities of other confederate witches. These authorities considered the hunting of witches part of their duty to protect the public from harm. Others accepted the reality of witchcraft but doubted the capacity of judges to determine who was a witch. A few doubted the reality of witchcraft altogether.

Johann Weyer (1515?–1588) was a physician who argued that most witches were deluded old women who suffered from depression and need medical help rather than legal punishment. The devil deceived them into thinking they had magical powers, but because Weyer had a strong belief that only God had power over nature, he did not credit the devil or witches with any special powers. No one else during the sixteenth century disputed the reality of the powers of witches as systematically as he. Jean Bodin (1529?–1596) was one of the greatest legal philosophers of the sixteenth century. Although he was once skeptical of the reality of witchcraft, he changed his mind after witnessing several cases in which women voluntarily confessed to performing evil acts under the guidance of Satan. He considered witchcraft a threat to society and condemned Weyer's soft-hearted view.

Johan Weyer's letter to Johann Brenz (1565)

Witches have no power to make hail, storms, and other evil things, but they are deceived by the devil. For when the devil, with the permission and decree of God, can make hail and storms, he goes to his witches and urges them to use their magic and charms, so that when the trouble and punishment come, the witches are convinced that they and the devil have caused it. Thus, the witches cannot make hail and other things, but they are deluded and blinded by the devil himself to whom they have given themselves. In this way they think that they have made hail and storms. Not on that account but for their godless lives should they be punished severely....

Our witches have been corrupted in their phantasy by the devil and imagine often that they have done evil things that didn't even happen or caused natural occurrences that actually did not take place. In their confessions, especially under torture, they admit to doing and causing many things which are impossible for them and for anyone. One should not believe them when they confess that they have bound themselves to the devil, given themselves to his will, promised to follow his evil goals, just as we do not believe their confession that they make hail and storms, disturb and poison the air, and other impossible deeds....

Even if an old woman, in deep depression, gives herself to the devil, one should not immediately condemn her to the fire but instead have regard for her confused, burdened, and depressed spirits and use all possible energy to convert her that she may avoid evil, and give herself to Christ. In this way we may bring her to her senses again, win her soul, and save her from death....

THE CONFESSIONAL STATES

■ How did religious differences provoke violence and start wars?

The Religious Peace of Augsburg of 1555 provided the model for a solution to the religious divisions produced by the Reformation. According to the principle of *cuius regio, eius religio* (he who rules determines the religion of the land), each prince in the Holy Roman Empire determined the religion to be followed by his subjects; those who disagreed were obliged to convert or emigrate. Certainly, forced exile was economically

Jean Bodin, On the Demonic Madness of Witches (1580)

The judgment which was passed against a witch in a case to which I was called on the last day of April, 1578, gave me occasion to take up my pen in order to clarify the subject of witches—persons who seem strange and wondrous to everyone and incredible to many. The witch whom I refer to was named Jeanne Harvillier, a native of Verbery near Compiegne. She was accused of having murdered many men and beasts, as she herself confessed without questioning or torture, although she at first stubbornly denied the charges and changed her story often. She also confessed that her mother presented her at the age of twelve years to the devil, disguised as a tall black man, larger than most men and clothed in black. The mother told him that as soon as her daughter was born she had promised her to him, whom she called the devil. He in turn promised to treat her well and to make her happy. And from then on she had renounced God and promised to serve the devil. And at that instant she had had carnal copulation with the devil, which she had continued to the age of 50, or thereabouts, when she was captured. She said also that [the] devil presented himself to her when she wished, always dressed as he had been the first time, booted and spurred, with a sword at his side and his horse at the door. And no one saw him but her. He even fornicated with her often without her husband noticing although he lay at her side....

Now we have shown that ordinarily women are possessed by demons more often than men and that witches are often transported bodily but also often ravished in an ecstasy, the soul having separated itself from the body, by diabolical means, leaving the body insensible and stupid. Thus, it is completely ridiculous to say that the illness of the witches originates in melancholy, especially because the diseases coming from melancholy are always dangerous.... Thus, Weyer must admit that there is a remarkable incongruity for one who is a doctor, and a gross example of ignorance (but it is not ignorance) to attribute to women melancholy diseases which are as little appropriate for them as are the praiseworthy effects of a tempered melancholy humor. This humor makes a man wise, sober, and contemplative (as all of the ancient philosophers and physicians remark), which are qualities as incompatible with women as fire with water. And even Solomon, who as a man of the world knew well the humor of women, said that he had seen a wise man for every 1,000 men, but that he had never seen a wise woman. Let us therefore abandon the fanatic error of those who make women into melancholics.

Source: Robert M. Kingdon (ed.), *Transition and Revolution: Problems and Issues of European Renaissance and Reformation History* (Minneapolis: Burgess Publishing Company, 1974), 221–232. Reprinted by permission.

For Discussion

1. How can the uncoerced confessions of women to witchcraft be explained?

2. Why would an otherwise intelligent observer such as Jean Bodin be so willing to believe in the reality of the power of witches?

and personally traumatic for those who emigrated, but it preserved what was almost universally believed to be the fundamental principle of successful rulership—one king, one faith, one law. In other words, each state should have only one church. Except in the states of eastern Europe and a few small troubled principalities in the Holy Roman Empire, few thought it desirable to allow more than one confession in the same state.

The problem with this political theory of religious unity was the reality of religious divisions created by the Reformation. In some places there were as many as three active confessions— Catholic, Lutheran, and Calvinist—in addition to the minority sects, such as the Anabaptists and the Jewish communities. The alternative to religious unity would have been religious toleration, but hardly anyone in a position of authority was willing to advocate that. John Calvin expelled advocates of religious toleration, and Martin Luther was aggressively hostile to those who disagreed with him on seemingly minor theological points. After 1542 with the establishment of the Universal Inquisition, the Catholic Church was committed to exposing and punishing anyone who professed a different faith, with the exception of Jews in Italy, who were under papal protection. Geneva and Rome became competing missionary centers, each flooding the world with polemical tracts and specially trained missionaries willing to risk their lives by going behind the enemy lines to console their co-religionists and evangelize for converts.

Religious passions ran so high that during the late sixteenth century a new word appeared to describe a personality type that may not have been entirely new but was certainly much more common—the **fanatic**. Originally referring to someone possessed by a demon, *fanatic* came to mean a person who expressed immoderate enthusiasm in religious matters, a person who pursued a supposedly divine mission, often to violent ends. Fanatics from all sides of the religious divide initiated waves of political assassinations and massacred their opponents. François Guion, the assassin of William the Silent, whose story began this chapter, was in many ways typical of fanatics in his steadfast pursuit of his victim and his willingness to masquerade for years under a false identity. During the sixteenth and seventeenth centuries, no religious community had a monopoly on fanatics. They served the pope as well as the Protestant churches.

Wherever there were significant religious minorities within a state, the best that could be hoped for was a condition of anxious tension, omnipresent suspicion, and periodic hysteria (see **Map 15.1**). The worst possibility was civil war in which religious affiliations and political rivalries intertwined in such complicated ways that finding peaceful solutions was especially difficult. Between

1560 and 1648 several religious civil wars broke out, including the French Wars of Religion, the Dutch revolt against Spain, the Thirty Years' War in Germany, and the English Civil War. (The latter two will be discussed in Chapter 16.)

The French Wars of Religion

When King Henry II (r. 1547–1559) of France died unexpectedly from a jousting accident, he left behind his widow, the formidable Catherine de' Medici (1519–1589), and a brood of young children—including his heir, Francis II (r. 1559–1560), who was only 15. Henry II had been a peacemaker. In contrast, Catherine and her children, including three sons who successively ascended to the throne, utterly failed to keep the peace, and for some 40 years France was torn apart by a series of desperate civil wars.

THE HUGUENOTS: THE FRENCH CALVINIST COMMUNITY By 1560 Calvinism had made significant inroads into predominantly Catholic France. Pastors sent from Geneva had been especially successful in the larger provincial towns, where their evangelical message appealed to enterprising merchants, professionals, and skilled artisans. One in ten of the French had become Calvinists, or **Huguenots** as French Protestants were called. The political strength of the Huguenots was greater than their numbers might indicate, because between one-third and one-half of the lower nobility professed Calvinism. Calvinism was popular among the French nobility for two reasons. One involved the imitation of social superiors. The financial well-being of any noble depended on his patron, an aristocrat of higher rank who had access to the king and who could distribute jobs and lands to his clients. When a high aristocrat converted to Protestantism, he tended to bring into the new faith his noble clientele, who converted through loyalty to their patron or through the patron's ability to persuade those who were financially dependent on him. As a result of a few aristocratic conversions in southwest France, Calvinism spread through "a veritable religious spider's web,"[3] as one contemporary put it.

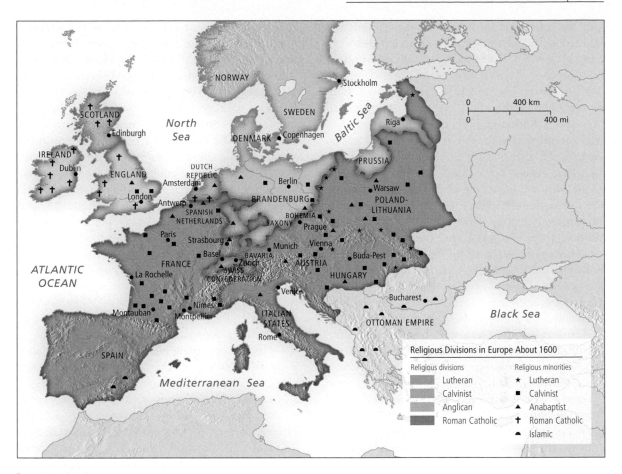

MAP 15.1

Religious Divisions in Europe About 1600

After 1555 the religious borders of Europe became relatively fixed, with only minor changes in confessional affiliations to this day.

A second reason for the spread of Calvinism was the influence of aristocratic women. The sister of King Francis I of France (r. 1515–1547), Marguerite of Angoulême (1492–1549), married the King of Navarre (an independent kingdom situated between France and Spain) and created a haven in Navarre for Huguenot preachers and theologians. Her example drew other aristocratic ladies to the Huguenot cause, and many of the Huguenot leaders during the French Wars of Religion were the sons and grandsons of these early female converts. Marguerite's daughter, Jeanne d'Albret, sponsored Calvinist preachers

for several years before she publicly announced her own conversion in 1560. Her son, Henry Bourbon (Henry of Navarre), became the principal leader of the Huguenot cause during the **French Wars of Religion** and the person responsible for eventually bringing the wars to an end.

THE ORIGINS OF THE RELIGIOUS WARS Like all civil wars, the French Wars of Religion exhibited a bewildering pattern of intrigue, betrayal, and treachery. Three distinct groups constituted the principal players. The first group was the royal family, consisting of Queen Catherine de' Medici and her four sons by Henry II—King Francis II (r. 1559–1560), King Charles IX (r. 1560–1574), King Henry III (r. 1574–1589), and Duke Francis of Alençon (1554–1584)—and her daughter, Marguerite Valois (1553–1615). The royal family remained Catholic but on occasion reconciled themselves with the Huguenot opposition, and Marguerite married into it. The second group was the Huguenot faction of nobles led by the Bourbon family who ruled Navarre. The third group was the hard-line Catholic faction led by the Guise family. These three groups vied for supremacy during the successive reigns of Catherine de' Medici's three sons.

During the reign of the sickly and immature Francis II, the Catholic Guise family dominated the government and raised the persecution of the Huguenots to a new level. In response to that persecution, a group of Huguenot nobles plotted in 1560 to kill the Guises. The Guises got wind of the conspiracy and surprised the plotters as they arrived in small groups at the royal chateau of Amboise. Some were ambushed, some drowned in the Loire River, and some hanged from the balconies of the chateau's courtyard. A tense two years later in 1562, the Duke of Guise was passing through the village of Vassy just as a large Huguenot congregation was holding services in a barn. The duke's men attacked the worshipers, killing some 740 of them and wounding hundreds of others.

Following the massacre at Vassy, civil war broke out in earnest. For nearly 40 years religious wars sapped the strength of France. Most of the battles were indecisive, which meant neither side sustained military superiority for long. Both sides relied for support on their regional bases: The Huguenots' strength was in the southwest; the Catholics', in Paris and the north. Besides military engagements, the French Wars of Religion spawned political assassinations and massacres.

MASSACRE OF ST. BARTHOLOMEW'S DAY   After a decade of bloody yet inconclusive combat, the royal family tried to resolve the conflict by making peace with the Protestants, a shift of policy signified by the announcement of the engagement of Marguerite Valois, daughter of Henry II and Catherine de' Medici, to Henry Bourbon, the son of the Huguenot King of Navarre. At age 19, Marguerite—or Queen Margot, as she was known—was already renowned for her brilliant intelligence—and for her wanton morals. To complicate the situation further, on the eve of the wedding Marguerite was having an affair with another Henry, the young Duke of Guise who was the leader of the intransigent Catholic faction. The marriage between Marguerite and Henry of Navarre was to take place in Paris in August 1572, an event that brought all the Huguenot leaders to the heavily armed Catholic capital for the first time in many years. The gathering of all their enemies in one place presented too great a temptation for the Guises, who hatched a plot to assassinate the Huguenot leaders. Perhaps because she had become jealous of the Huguenots' growing influence on her son, King Charles IX, Catherine suddenly switched sides and became implicated in the plot.

Catherine somehow convinced the weak-willed king to order the massacre of the Huguenot nobles gathered in Paris. On August 14, 1572, St. Bartholomew's Day, the people of Paris began a slaughter. Between 3,000 and 4,000 Huguenots were butchered in Paris and more than 20,000 were put to death throughout the rest of France. Henry of Navarre saved his life by pretending to convert to Catholicism, while most of his companions were murdered.

Catherine's attempted solution for the Huguenot problem failed to solve anything. Henry of Navarre escaped his virtual imprisonment in the royal household, set Marguerite up in an isolated castle, returned to Navarre and his faith, and reinvigorated Huguenot resistance.

The wars of religion continued until the assassination of King Henry III, brother of the late Charles IX. Both Charles IX and Henry III had been childless, a situation that made Henry Bourbon of Navarre the rightful heir to the throne, even though he was a Huguenot. Henry Bourbon became King Henry IV (r. 1589–1610). He recognized that predominantly Catholic

ST. BARTHOLOMEW'S DAY MASSACRE

A Protestant painter, François Dubois, depicted the merciless slaughter of Protestant men, women, and children in the streets of Paris in 1572. The massacre was the most bloody and infamous in the French Wars of Religion and created a lasting memory of atrocity.

France would never accept a Huguenot king, and so in 1593 with his famous quip, "Paris is worth a mass," Henry converted to Catholicism. Most Catholic opposition to him collapsed. Once Henry became a Catholic he managed to have the pope annul his childless marriage to Marguerite so that he could marry Marie de' Medici

and obtain her huge dowry. Affable, witty, generous, and exceedingly tolerant, "Henry the Great" became the most popular king in French history, reuniting the war-torn country by ruling with a very firm hand. With the **Edict of Nantes** of 1598, he allowed the Huguenots to build a quasi-state within the state, giving them the right to have their own troops, church organization, and political autonomy within their walled towns, but banning them from the royal court and the city of Paris.

Despite his enormous popularity, Henry too fell victim to fanaticism. After surviving 18 attempts on his life, in 1610 the king was fatally stabbed by a Catholic fanatic, who took advantage of the opportunity presented when the royal coach unexpectedly stopped behind a cart loading hay. Catholics and Protestants alike mourned Henry's death and considered the assassin mad. Henry's brilliant conciliatory nature and the horrors of the religious wars had tempered public opinion.

Philip II, His Most Catholic Majesty

France's greatest rivals were the Habsburgs, who possessed vast territories in the Holy Roman Empire, controlled the elections for emperor, and had dynastic rights to the throne of Spain. During the late sixteenth century, Habsburg Spain took advantage of French weakness to establish itself as the dominant power in Europe. When Emperor Charles V (who had been both Holy Roman Emperor and king of Spain) abdicated his thrones in 1556, the Habsburg possessions in the Holy Roman Empire and the emperorship went to his brother, Ferdinand I, and the balance of his vast domain to his son, Philip II (r. 1556–1598). Philip's inheritance included Spain,

CHRONOLOGY: THE FRENCH WARS OF RELIGION, 1560–1598

1560	Huguenot conspiracy of Amboise against Catholic Guise family
1572	Massacre of St. Bartholomew's Day, Catholics murder Huguenots
1598	Edict of Nantes granting Huguenots religious toleration

Milan, Naples, Sicily, the Netherlands, scattered outposts on the north coast of Africa, colonies in the Caribbean, Central America, Mexico, Peru, and the Philippines. In 1580 Philip also inherited Portugal and its far-flung overseas empire, which included a line of trading posts from West Africa to the Spice Islands and the vast colony of unexplored Brazil.

This grave, distrustful, rigid man saw himself as the great protector of the Catholic cause and committed Spain to perpetual hostility toward Muslims and Protestants. On the Muslim front he first bullied the Moriscos, the descendants of the Spanish Muslims. The Moriscos had received Christian baptism but were suspected of secretly practicing Islam. In 1568 Philip issued an edict that banned all manifestations of Muslim culture and ordered the Moriscos to turn over their children to Christian priests to educate. The remaining Moriscos were eventually expelled from the country in 1609.

Philip once said he would rather lose all his possessions and die a hundred times than be the king of heretics. (See *Justice in History* in this chapter.) His attitude toward Protestants showed that he meant what he said. Through his marriage to Queen Mary I of England (r. 1553–1558), Philip encouraged her persecutions of Protestants, but they got their revenge. After Mary's death her half-sister, Queen Elizabeth I, refused Philip's marriage proposal and in 1577 signed a treaty to assist the Protestant provinces of the Netherlands, which were in rebellion against Spain. To add insult to injury, the English privateer Sir Francis Drake (ca. 1540–1596) conducted a personal war against Catholic Spain by raiding the Spanish convoys bringing silver from the New World. In 1587 Drake's embarrassing successes culminated with a daring raid on the great Spanish port city of Cadiz, where, "singeing the king of Spain's beard," he destroyed the anchored Spanish fleet and many thousands of tons of vital supplies.

Philip retaliated by building a huge fleet of 132 ships armed with 3,165 cannons, which in 1588 sailed from Portugal to rendezvous with the Spanish army stationed in the Netherlands and launch an invasion of England. As the Invincible Armada, as it was called, passed through the English Channel, it was met by a much smaller English fleet, assembled out of merchant ships refit for battle. Unable to maneuver as effectively as the English in the fluky winds of the channel and mauled by the rapid-firing English guns, the **Spanish Armada** suffered heavy losses and was forced to retreat to the north, where it sustained further losses in storms off the coast of Scotland and Ireland. Barely more than half of the fleet finally straggled home. The defeat severely shook Philip's sense of invincibility.

The reign of Philip II illustrated better than any other the contradictions and tensions of the era. No monarch had at his grasp as many resources and territories as Philip, and yet defending them proved extremely costly. The creaky governmental machinery of Spain put a tremendous burden on a conscientious king such as Philip, but even his unflagging energy and dedication to his duties could not prevent military defeat and financial disaster. Historians remember Philip's reign for its series of state bankruptcies and for the loss of the Dutch provinces in the Netherlands, the most precious jewel in the crown of Spain.

The Dutch Revolt

The Netherlands boasted some of Europe's richest cities, situated amid a vast network of lakes, rivers, channels, estuaries, and tidal basins that periodically replenished the exceptionally productive soil through flooding. The Netherlands consisted of 17 provinces, each with its own distinctive identity, traditions, and even language. The southern provinces were primarily French-speaking; those in the north spoke a bewildering variety of Flemish and Dutch dialects. When Philip II became king of Spain he also inherited all of the Netherlands. With his characteristic bureaucratic mentality, Philip treated Dutch affairs as a management problem rather than a political sore spot, an attitude that subordinated the Netherlands to Spanish interests. Foreign rule irritated the Dutch, who had long enjoyed ancient privileges including the right to raise their own taxes and muster their own troops.

Philip's harsh attitude toward Protestants upset the Netherlands' delicate balance among Catholic, Lutheran, Calvinist, and Anabaptist communities, as did the arrival of Huguenot refugees from the French Wars of Religion. In 1566 Calvinist fanatics occupied many Catholic churches and destroyed paintings and statues.

In response Philip issued edicts against the heretics and strengthened the Spanish Inquisition. The Inquisition in Spain was an arm of the monarchy charged with ensuring religious conformity, but when introduced in the Netherlands, it became an investigating agency devoted to finding, interrogating, and, if necessary, punishing Protestants.

Philip also dispatched 20,000 Spanish troops under the command of the Duke of Alba (1508–1582), a veteran of the Turkish campaigns in North Africa and victories over the Lutheran princes in the Holy Roman Empire. Alba directly attacked the Protestants. He personally presided over the military court, the Council of Troubles, which became so notoriously tyrannical that the people called it the Council of Blood. As an example to others, he systematically razed several small villages where there had been incidents of desecrating Catholic images and slaughtered every inhabitant. Alba himself boasted that during the campaign against the rebels, he had 18,000 people executed, in addition to those who died in battle or were massacred by soldiers. Sixty thousand refugees, about two percent of the population, went into exile.

The Prince of Orange, William the Silent (1533–1584), organized the **Dutch Revolt** to resist to Alba. Within a few short years, William the Silent seized permanent control of the provinces of Holland and Zealand, which were then flooded by Calvinist refugees from the southern provinces.

His policies a failure, Alba was recalled to Spain in 1573. After Alba's departure, no one kept control of the unpaid Spanish soldiers, who in mutinous rage turned against cities loyal to Spain, including Brussels, Ghent, and most savagely Antwerp, the rich center of trade. Antwerp lost 7,000 citizens and one-third of its houses to the "Spanish fury," which permanently destroyed its prosperity.

Alba's replacement, the shrewd statesman and general the Duke of Parma (r. 1578–1592), ultimately subdued the southern provinces, which remained a Spanish colony. The seven northern provinces, however, united in 1579, declared independence from Spain in 1581, and formally organized as a republic in 1588 (see **Map 15.2**). William the Silent became the *stadholder* (governor) of the new United Provinces, and after his assassination in 1584 his 17-year-old son, Maurice of Nassau, inherited the same title.

The Netherlands' struggle for independence transformed the population of the United

MAP 15.2

The Netherlands During the Dutch Revolt, ca. 1580

During the late sixteenth century the northern United Provinces separated from the Spanish Netherlands. The independence of the United Provinces was not recognized by the other European powers until 1648.

CHRONOLOGY: SPAIN AND THE NETHERLANDS, 1568–1648

1568	Edict against Morisco culture
1580	King Philip II inherits Portugal and the Portuguese Empire
1584	Assassination of William the Silent
1588	Defeat of the Spanish Armada, failed Spanish invasion of England; the seven northern provinces of the Netherlands becomes a republic
1609	Expulsion of the Moriscos from Spain
1648	Treaty of Westphalia recognizes independence of the Netherlands

Provinces from mixed religions to staunch Calvinism. The alliance with England, which provided much-needed financial and moral support, reinforced the Protestant identity of the Dutch, and the failure of the Spanish Armada to land Parma's men in England guaranteed the survival of an independent Netherlands. The Dutch carried on a sporadic and inconclusive war against Spain until the end of the Thirty Years' War in 1648, when the international community recognized the independent United Provinces of the Netherlands, known as the Dutch Republic.

Literature in the Age of Confessional Division

Churches and monarchs everywhere demanded religious conformity in word and deed, a situation that would seem to stifle creativity, and yet the late sixteenth and early seventeenth centuries were one of the most remarkable periods in the history of creative literature. Some literary figures did find their works banned and some had political or personal troubles with their monarch. But the controversies of the day seemed to have stimulated rather than inhibited great writers. Political and religious turmoil led them to rise above the petty religious squabbles that preoccupied so many of their contemporaries and to ask penetrating questions about the meaning of life. And importantly, they did so in their native languages. During this period the native or **vernacular languages** of western Europe became literary languages, replacing Latin as the dominant form of expression, even for the educated elite.

FRENCH LITERATURE DURING THE RELIGIOUS TURMOIL In France royal decrees in 1520 and 1539 substituted French for Latin in official legal and government documents. A century later, with the founding of the Académie Française, it became government policy to promote, protect, and refine the French language. The greatest masters of French prose during this crucial period were François Rabelais (ca. 1483–1553) and Michel de Montaigne (1533–1592).

Trained as a lawyer, Rabelais became a friar and priest but left the Church under a cloud of heresy to become a physician. Rabelais's satirical masterpiece, a series of novels recounting the fantastic and grotesque adventures of the giants Gargantua and Pantagruel, combined an encyclopedic command of humanist thought with stunning verbal invention that has had a lasting influence on humorous writers to this day. Rabelais's optimistic vision of human nature represented a startling contrast to the growing anxiety provoked by the religious controversies of his time. Rabelais's controversial work was banned, and he was briefly forced into exile.

It is ironic that Montaigne became a master of French prose. His mother was a Catholic of Spanish-Jewish origin, and the young Michel spoke only Latin for the first six years of his life because his German tutor knew no French. After a modestly successful legal career, Montaigne retired to the family chateau to discover himself by writing essays, a literary form well suited to reflective introspection. In his essays, Montaigne struggled with his lasting grief over the premature death from dysentery of a close friend, reflected on his own experience of the intense physical pain of illness, and diagnosed the absurd causes of the French Wars of Religion. Montaigne's essays were a profound series of meditations on the meaning of life and death, presented in a calm voice of reason to an age of violent fanaticism. In one essay, for example, he exposed the presumption of human beings: "The most vulnerable and frail of all creatures is man, and at the same time the most arrogant." Montaigne thought it presumptuous that human beings picked themselves out as God's favorite creatures. How did they know they were superior to other animals? "When I play with my cat, who knows if I am not a pastime to her more than she is to me?"[4] His own skepticism about religion insulated him from the sometimes violent passions of his era. His essay "On Cannibals" pointed to the hypocrisy of Christians who condemned the alleged cannibalism of the native Americans but justified the torture and murder of other Christians over some minor theological dispute. Montaigne argued that the capacity to understand and tolerate cultural and religious differences, not rigid adherence to biblical laws, defined a truly ethical, truly Christian person.

STIRRINGS OF THE GOLDEN AGE IN IBERIA The literary tradition in the Iberian peninsula thrived in several languages: Basque, Galician, Portuguese, Castilian, and Catalan. The greatest lyric poet of the peninsula, Luís Vaz de Camões (1524–1580), lost an eye in battle and was sent to the Portuguese East Indies after he killed a royal official in a street brawl. When he returned years later, he completed his epic poem *The Lusiads* (1572), a celebration of Vasco da Gama's discovery of the sea route to India, which became the national poem of Portugal. Camoes modeled this work on the ancient epics, especially the *Aeneid*, the greatest Latin epic of ancient Rome, and even included the gods of Olympus as commentators on the human events of Camões's time. By connecting Portugal directly to the glories of the ancient empires, Camões elevated the adventures of his fellow Portuguese in Asia to an important moment in the history of the world.

The period when Spain was the dominant power in Europe coincided with the Golden Age of Spanish literature. Because Spain was unified around the crown of Castile, the Castilian language became the language we now call Spanish. The greatest literary figure was Miguel de Cervantes Saavedra (1547–1616), an impoverished son of an unsuccessful doctor with little formal education. Like Camões, Cervantes survived many adventures. He lost the use of his left hand at the naval Battle of Lepanto and spent five years languishing in a Turkish prison after his capture by Algerian pirates. The disabled veteran wrote plays for the Madrid theater and worked as a tax collector, but was still imprisoned several times for debts. Desperate to make money, Cervantes published a serial novel in installments between 1605 and 1615. It became the greatest masterpiece in Spanish literature, *Don Quixote*.

The prototype of the modern novel form, *Don Quixote* satirizes chivalric romances. Cervantes presented reality on two levels, the "poetic truth" of the master and dreamer Don Quixote and the "historic truth" of his squire and realist Sancho Panza. Don Quixote's imagination persistently ran away with him as he tilted at windmills, believing they were fierce dragons. It remained to Sancho Panza to point out the unheroic truth. Cervantes pursued the interaction between these two incongruous views of truth as a philosophical commentary on existence. For Cervantes there was no single, objective truth, only psychological truths revealed through the interaction of the characters, an idea that contrasted with the notion of dogmatic religious truth that dominated the time.

THE ELIZABETHAN RENAISSANCE During the reign of Elizabeth I (r. 1558–1603), the Renaissance arrived in England. The daughter of Henry VIII and Anne Boleyn, Elizabeth faced terrible insecurity as a girl. Her father had her mother beheaded, she was declared illegitimate, and her half-sister Mary imprisoned her in the Tower of London for treason. After she ascended to the throne in 1558, however, she proved to be a brilliant leader. Elizabeth prevented the kind of religious civil wars that broke out in France by establishing a moderate form of Protestantism as the official religion. She presided over the beginnings of England's rise as a major European power. Perhaps most remarkably, she became a patron and inspiration for England's greatest age of literature.

The principal figure of the Elizabethan Renaissance was a professional dramatist, William Shakespeare (1564–1616). In a series of theaters, including the famous Globe on the south side of the Thames in London, Shakespeare wrote, produced, and acted in comedies, tragedies, and history plays. Shakespeare's enormous output of plays, some of which made veiled allusions to the politics of Elizabeth's court, established him not only as the most popular dramatist of his time, but the greatest literary figure in the English language. The power of his plays derives from the subtle understanding of human psychology found in his characters and the stunning force of his language. For Shakespeare, as for Montaigne, the source of true knowledge was self-knowledge, which most people lacked. Pride and human authority prevented people from knowing themselves:

But man, proud man,
Drest [dressed] in a little brief authority,

QUEEN ELIZABETH I OF ENGLAND
Carried by her courtiers Elizabeth presided over the greatest age of English literature.

Most ignorant of what he's most assured,
His glassy [dull] essence, like an angry ape,
Plays such fantastic tricks before high
    heaven
As make the angels weep.
(*Measure for Measure* II, ii, 117)

Unlike most contemporary authors, Shakespeare wrote for a broad audience of paying theater goers that included common workers as well as highly educated members of Elizabeth's court. This need to appeal to a large audience who gave instant feedback helped him hone his skills as a dramatist.

STATES AND CONFESSIONS IN EASTERN EUROPE

■ How did the countries of eastern Europe during the late sixteenth century become enmeshed in the religious controversies that began in western Europe during the early part of the century?

The religious diversity of eastern Europe contrasted with the religious conformity of western Europe's confessional states. Whereas in western Europe the religious controversies stimulated writers to investigate deeply the human condition but made them cautious about expressing nonconforming religious opinions, writers and creative people in eastern Europe during this period were able to explore a wide range of ideas in a relatively tolerant atmosphere. Bohemia and Poland, in particular, allowed levels of religious diversity unheard of elsewhere. During the last decades of the sixteenth century and early decades of the seventeenth, however, dynastic troubles compromised the relative openness of the eastern states, enmeshing them in conflicts among themselves that had an increasingly strong religious dimension. In the Holy Roman Empire, the weakness of the mad Emperor Rudolf permitted religious conflicts to fester, setting the

stage for the disastrous Thirty Years' War (1618–1648) that pitted Catholic and Protestant princes against one another.

Around the Baltic Sea, rivalries among Lutheran Sweden, Catholic Poland-Lithuania, and Orthodox Russia created a state of almost permanent war in a tense standoff among three very different political and religious states. The enormous confederation of Poland-Lithuania sustained the most decentralized, religiously diverse state anywhere in Europe. By the end of the century, it remained politically decentralized but had become an active theater of the Catholic Reformation where dynastic policy firmly supported the Roman Church. Russia began to strengthen itself under the authoritarian rule of the tsars, who began to transform it into a major European power.

The Dream World of Emperor Rudolf

In Goethe's *Faust,* set in sixteenth-century Germany, drinkers in a tavern sing:

The dear old Holy Roman Empire,
How does it hang together?

Good question. How did this peculiarly decentralized state—neither holy, nor Roman, nor an empire, as Voltaire would later put it—hang together? In the late sixteenth century the empire consisted of one emperor; seven electors; 50 bishops and archbishops, 21 dukes, margraves, and landgraves; 88 independent abbots and assorted prelates of the Church; 178 counts and other sovereign lords; about 80 free imperial cities; and hundreds of free imperial knights. The emperor presided over all, and the Imperial Diet served as a parliament, but the Holy Roman Empire was, in fact, a very loose confederation of semi-independent, mostly German-speaking states, many of which ignored imperial decrees that did not suit them. During the first half of the sixteenth century the empire faced a number of challenges—the turmoil within the empire created by Lutheranism, endless French enmity on the western borders, and the tenacious Ottoman threat on the eastern frontier. Only the universal vision and firm hand of Emperor Charles V kept the empire together. The universal vision and firm hand disappeared in the succeeding generations of emperors to be replaced by petty dynastic squabbles and infirm minds.

The crippling weakness of the imperial system became most evident during the reign of Rudolf II (r. 1576–1612). The Habsburg line had a strain of insanity going back to Joanna "The Mad," the mother of Emperors Charles V (r. 1519–1558) and Ferdinand I (r. 1558–1564), who happened to be Rudolf's two grandfathers, giving him a double dose of Habsburg genes. Soon after his election to the imperial throne, Rudolf moved his court from bustling Vienna to the lovely quiet of Prague in Bohemia. Fearful of noisy crowds and impatient courtiers, stand-offish toward foreign ambassadors who presented him with difficult decisions, paranoid about scheming relatives, and prone to wild emotional gyrations from deep depression to manic grandiosity, Rudolf was hardly suited for the imperial throne. In fact, many contemporaries, who had their own reasons to underrate him, described him as hopelessly insane. Rudolf certainly suffered from moments of profound melancholy and irrational fears that may have had genetic or organic causes, but he was probably unhinged by the conundrum of being the emperor, a position that trapped him between the glorious universal imperial ideal and the ignoble reality of unscrupulous relatives and petty rivalries.

Incapable of governing, Rudolf transmuted the imperial ideal of universality into a strange dream world. In Prague he gathered around him a brilliant court of humanists, musicians, painters, physicians, astronomers, astrologers, alchemists, and magicians. These included an eclectic assortment of significant thinkers—the great astronomers Tycho Brahe and Johannes Kepler, the notorious occult philosopher Giordano Bruno, the theoretical mathematician and astrologer John Dee, and the remarkable inventor of surrealist painting

Giuseppe Arcimboldo. Many of these figures became central figures in the Scientific Revolution, but Rudolf also fell prey to fast-talking charlatans. These included Cornelius Drebber who claimed to have invented a perpetual-motion machine. This weird court, however, was less the strange fruit of the emperor's hopeless dementia than the manifestation of a striving for universal empire. Rudolf sought to preserve the cultural and political unity of the empire, to eradicate religious divisions, and to achieve peace at home. Rudolf's court in Prague was perhaps the only place left during the late sixteenth century where Protestants, Catholics, Jews, and even radical heretics such

EMPEROR RUDOLF II

Among the many creative people in the Emperor Rudolf's court was the Italian surrealist painter Giuseppe Arcimboldo, who specialized in creating images out of fruits, vegetables, flowers, and animals. This is a portrait of the Emperor Rudolf.

as Bruno could gather together in a common intellectual enterprise. The goal of such gatherings was to discover the universal principles that governed nature, principles that would provide the foundations for a single unifying religion and a cure for all human maladies. It was a noble, if utterly improbable, dream.

While Rudolf and his favorite courtiers isolated themselves in their dream world, the religious conflicts within the empire reached a boiling point. Without a strong emperor, confessional squabbles paralyzed the Imperial Diets. In 1607, the Catholic Duke of Bavaria annexed Donauworth—a city with a Lutheran majority—to his own territories. Despite the illegality of the duke's action, Rudolf passively acquiesced, causing fear among German Protestants that the principles of the Religious Peace of Augsburg of 1555 might be ignored. The Religious Peace had allowed princes and imperial free cities, such as Donauworth, to determine their own religion. The Duke of Bavaria's violation of Donauworth's status as a free city jeopardized not only civic liberty but religious liberty. In the following decade, more than 200 religious revolts or riots took place. In 1609 the insane Duke John William of Jülich-Cleves died without a direct heir, and the most suitable claimants to the Catholic duchy were two Lutheran princes. The succession of a Lutheran prince to this Catholic dukedom would have seriously disrupted the balance between Catholics and Protestants in Germany. Religious tensions boiled over. As Chapter 16 will describe, in less than a decade the empire began to dissolve in what became the Thirty Years' War.

The Renaissance of Poland-Lithuania

As the major power in eastern Europe, Poland-Lithuania engaged in a tug-of-war with Sweden over control of the eastern Baltic and almost constant warfare against the expansionist ambitions of Russia (see **Map 15.3**). Nevertheless, during the late sixteenth and early seventeenth centuries, Poland-Lithuania experienced a remarkable cultural and political renaissance inspired by influences from Renaissance Italy linked to strong commercial and diplomatic ties to the Republic of Venice and intellectual connections with the University of Padua. But perhaps the most remarkable achievement of Poland-Lithuania during this contentious time was its unparalleled level of religious toleration and parliamentary rule.

Very loosely joined since 1385, the Kingdom of Poland and the Grand Duchy of Lithuania formally united as the Polish-Lithuanian Commonwealth in 1569. The republican thought from Renaissance Italy directly influenced the political structure and values of the Commonwealth. Polish jurists studied law at the universities of Padua and Bologna where they learned to apply the civic values of Italy to the Polish context. Under these influences, the Polish constitution guaranteed that there would be no changes of the law, no new taxes, and no limitations on freedoms without the consent of the parliament, known as the Sejm. The novel feature of the Commonwealth was how the nobles (*szlachta*) reserved power for themselves through their control of regional assemblies, which in turn dominated the Sejm. The *szlachta* consisted of between 6.6 and 8 percent of the population and nearly 25 percent of ethnic Poles. Elsewhere in Europe, except for Spain, the nobility accounted for no more than 1 to 3 percent of the population. Thus, a much higher percentage of the population of Poland-Lithuania enjoyed political rights than in any other country in Europe. In 1573 the Sejm introduced a highly limited monarchy for Poland. The Sejm elected the king and treated him, at best, as a hired manager. While the rest of Europe moved toward ever more authoritarian monarchies, Poland moved in the opposite direction toward broader political participation.

The Warsaw Confederation of 1573 prohibited religious persecution, making the Commonwealth the safest and most tolerant place in Europe. Poland-Lithuania contained an incomparable religious mixture of Roman

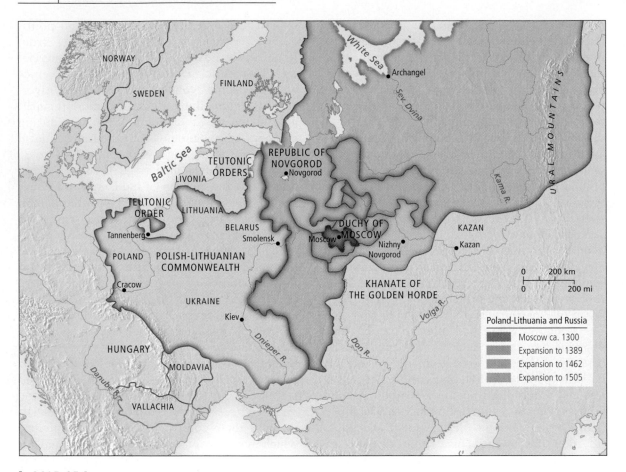

MAP 15.3

Poland-Lithuania and Russia

These countries were the largest in Europe in the size of their territories but were relatively under populated compared to the western European states.

Catholics, Lutherans, Calvinists, Russian Orthodox, Anabaptists, Unitarians, Armenians, and Jews. These communities, however, were strongly divided along geographic and social lines. Lutheranism was a phenomenon of the German-speaking towns, the peasants of Poland remained Catholic, those in Lithuania were Orthodox, and many of the nobles were attracted to Calvinism.

During the late sixteenth century, however, many Protestants in Poland returned or converted to the Roman Catholic faith. The key to the transformation was the changing attitude of the Polish *szlachta,* who had promoted religious diversity because they believed that religious liberty was the cornerstone of political liberty. The revival of Catholicism owed a great deal to Stanislas Hosius (1504–1579), who had studied in Italy before he returned to Poland to become successively a diplomat, bishop, and cardinal. Imbued with the zeal of the Italian Catholic Reformation, Hosius invited the Society of Jesus (Jesuits) into Poland

and worked closely with the papal *nuncios* (the diplomatic representatives of the pope), who organized a campaign to combat all forms of Protestantism. Between 1565 and 1586, 44 Polish nobles studied at the Jesuit college in Rome. When they returned, they took up the most influential church and government offices in Poland. Jesuit colleges sprouted up in many Polish towns, attracting the brightest sons of the nobility and urban bourgeoisie. A close alliance between the kings of Poland and the Jesuits enhanced the social prestige of Catholicism.

The cultural appeal of all things Italian also helped lure many members of the Polish nobility back to Catholicism. Through the spread of elite education, Catholicism returned to Poland largely through persuasion rather than coercion. But the transformation did not occur without violent repercussions. Lutheran, Calvinist, and Bohemian Brethren churches were burned. In Cracow armed confrontations between Protestant and Catholic militants led to casualties. In 1596 the Polish king and Catholic fanatics imposed Catholicism on the Orthodox in the eastern parts of the Commonwealth. Although allowed to retain their rites, Orthodox believers had to accept the authority of the pope. Despite the growing religious hostility, Poland did not degenerate into civil war, as did France or the Netherlands over much the same issues.

Not all Poles and Lithuanians interpreted the Italian influence as affirming the Catholic Reformation. In 1580 Count Jan Zamoyski (1542–1605) founded the city of Zamość, designed as an ideal Renaissance city on the Italian model. Zamoyski had studied at Padua and returned to Poland determined to build his own Padua. He invited Armenians and Jews to inhabit the new town as citizens. A forceful advocate of civic freedom against royal authority and religious toleration, he built a Roman Catholic Church, a Calvinist chapel, an Armenian Orthodox church, and two synagogues. In Zamoyski's planned town the religions of the West encountered one another on a daily basis

ZAMOŚĆ

One of the finest examples of a Renaissance planned-town, Zamość in eastern Poland imitated the arcaded streets of Padua, Italy.

and exemplified one of the most attractive features of the Polish Renaissance.

Perhaps most remarkable was the position of Jews in Poland. During the early modern period Poland-Lithuania became the center of European Jewish culture. Jews described Vilnius as the "new Jerusalem." Jews had their own parliament and sent nonvoting representatives to the Sejm, a form of unequal citizenship but a guarantee of certain rights without parallel elsewhere in Europe. Unlike other parts of Europe, in Poland-Lithuania Jews were not forced to assimilate or hide and were allowed to develop their own distinctive communities.

The Troubled Legacy of Ivan the Terrible

While Poland experimented with a decentralized confederation dominated by nobles that severely restricted the king's initiative, Russia did the opposite. During the late fifteenth and sixteenth centuries, the grand dukes of Moscow who became the tsars of Russia gradually expanded their power over the **boyars** (the upper-level nobles who dominated Russian society) and challenged Moscow's neighbors—Poland-Lithuania and the Republic of Novgorod.

Although well integrated into the European diplomatic community and engaged in trade with its western neighbors, Russia for more than 300 years had been under the "Tartar Yoke," a term describing the Mongolian tribes that overran the country, pillaging and depopulating it. Ivan III, "The Great" (1462–1505), succeeded in gradually throwing off the Tartar Yoke by refusing to continue to pay tribute to the Mongols.

Ivan's marriage to Zoë, the niece of the last Greek emperor of Constantinople, gave him the basis for claiming that the Russian rulers were the heirs of Byzantium and the exclusive protectors of Orthodox Christianity, the state religion of Russia. Following the Byzantine tradition of imperial pomp, Ivan practiced Byzantine court ceremonies, and his advisers developed the theory of the Three Romes. According to this theory, the authority of the

THE MOSCOW KREMLIN

The Kremlin in Moscow was the seat of government for the Russian tsars until 1712. Originally built in 1156, the present enclosure of the Kremlin dates from the sixteenth century and reflects the influence of Italian architects brought to Moscow as well as traditional Byzantine styles. This view shows the Cathedral of St. Michael the Archangel and Bell Tower of Ivan the Great.

ancient Roman Empire had passed first to the Byzantine Empire, which God had punished with the Turkish conquest, and then to Moscow as the third and last "Rome." Ivan celebrated this theory by assuming the title of tsar (or "Caesar"). With his wife's assistance, he hired Italian architects to rebuild the grand ducal palace, the Kremlin.

With his capture of the vast northern territories of the Republic of Novgorod, Ivan expanded the Russian state north to the White Sea and east to the Urals. In 1478 Ivan sent his army to Novgorod, massacred the population, abolished the parliament, and burned the archive, ending the rich republican tradition of northern Russia. Ivan's invasion of parts of Lithuania embroiled Russia in a protracted conflict with Poland that lasted more than a century. Like his fellow monarchs in western Europe, Ivan began to bring the aristocrats under control by incorporating them into the bureaucracy of the state.

Ivan III's grandson, Ivan IV, "The Terrible" (1533–1584), succeeded his father at age three and became the object of innumerable plots, attempted coups, and power struggles among his mother, uncles, and the boyars. The trauma of his childhood years and a painful disease of the spine made him inordinately suspicious and prone to acts of impulsive violence. When at age 17 Ivan was crowned, he reduced the power of the dukes and the boyars. He obliged them to give up their hereditary estates. In return he redistributed lands to them with the legal obligation to serve the tsar in war. In weakening the boyars, Ivan gained considerable

support among the common people and was even remembered in popular songs as the people's tsar. At first, he was a great reformer who introduced a code of laws and a church council. By setting aside half of the realm as his personal domain, he created a strong financial base for the army, which led to military successes in the prolonged wars against Poland-Lithuania and Sweden.

Nevertheless, Ivan distrusted everyone, and his struggle with the boyars led him to subvert his own reforms. He often arrested people on charges of treason, just for taking trips abroad. In a cruel revenge to his enemies among the boyars, he began a reign of terror in which he personally committed horrendous atrocities. His massacre in 1570 of the surviving inhabitants of Novgorod, whom he suspected of harboring Polish sympathies, contributed to his reputation as a bloody tyrant. During his reign, the Polish threat and boyar opposition to his rule revealed signs of the fragility of Russian unity.

Then, during the **"Time of Troubles"** (1604–1613), Russia fell into chaos. Boyar families struggled among themselves for supremacy, the Cossacks from the south led a popular revolt, and Poles and Swedes openly interfered in Russian affairs. Finally, the Time of Troubles ended when in 1613 the national assembly elected Tsar Michael Romanov, whose descendants ruled Russia until 1917. During the seventeenth century the Romanovs gradually restored order to Russia, eroded the independence of local governments, and introduced serfdom to keep the peasants on the land. By the

CHRONOLOGY: STATES AND CONFESSIONS IN EASTERN EUROPE

1480	Grand Duke and later Tsar Ivan III, "The Great," of Russia refuses to pay tribute to Tartars
1569	Constitutional Union established Polish-Lithuanian Commonwealth
1604–1613	Time of Troubles in Russia
1613	Michael Romanov elected Tsar of Russia

end of the seventeenth century Russia was strong enough to reenter European affairs as a major power.

CONCLUSION

The Divisions of the West

During the late sixteenth and early seventeenth centuries, hidden demographic and economic pressures eroded the confidence and security of many Europeans, creating a widespread sense of unease. Most people retreated like confused soldiers behind the barricades of a rigid confessional faith, which provided reassurance that was unavailable elsewhere. To compensate for the absence of predictability in daily life, societies everywhere imposed strict discipline—discipline of women, children, the poor, criminals, and alleged witches. The frenzy for social discipline displaced the fear of those things that could not be controlled (such as price inflation) onto the most easily controllable people, especially the weak, the subordinate, and those perceived to be different in some way.

The union between religion and political authority in the confessional states bolstered official religious faith with the threat of legal or military coercion. Where different religious confessions persisted within one state—most notably France and the Netherlands—the result was riots, assassinations, and civil war. The West had become divided along religious lines in two ways. The first kind of division was within countries with religiously mixed populations, where distinctive religious communities competed for political power and influence. In these countries religion became the cornerstone to justify patriotism or rebellion, loyalty or disloyalty to the monarch. The second kind of division was international. The confessional states formed alliances, crafted foreign policies, and went to war, with religion determining friend and foe. Over the subsequent centuries, religious differences mutated into ideological differences, but the sense that alliances among states should be linked together by a common set of beliefs has persisted to this day as a legacy from the sixteenth century.

During the period of the middle seventeenth to eighteenth centuries, confessional identity and the fear of religious turmoil led monarchs throughout Europe to build absolutist regimes, which attempted to enforce stability through a strengthened, centralized state. The principles of religious toleration and the separation of church and state were still far in the future. They were made possible only as a consequence of the hard lessons learned from the historical turmoil of the late sixteenth and seventeenth centuries.

KEY TERMS

confessions	French Wars of Religion
Price Revolution	Edict of Nantes
auto-da-fé	Spanish Armada
witch-hunt	Dutch Revolt
magic	vernacular languages
fanatic	boyars
Huguenots	Time of Troubles

CHAPTER QUESTIONS

1. How did the expanding population and price revolution exacerbate religious and political tensions? (page 458)
2. How did religious and political authorities attempt to discipline the people? (page 463)
3. Why did people in the sixteenth century think witches were a threat? (page 469)

4. How did religious differences provoke violence and start wars? (page 472)
5. How did the countries of eastern Europe during the late sixteenth century become enmeshed in the religious controversies that began in western Europe during the early part of the century? (page 483)

TAKING IT FURTHER

1. Why was it so difficult to establish religious toleration in the sixteenth century?

2. A common emotion during the age of confessional division was fear. How do you explain the spread of collective fears?
3. How did religious fanatics perceive the world during this period?

✓●─[**Practice** on **MyHistoryLab**]

16

Absolutism and State Building, 1618–1715

- The Nature of Absolutism ■ The Absolutist State in France and Spain
- Absolutism and State Building in Central and Eastern Europe
- Resistance to Absolutism in England and the Dutch Republic

IN 1651 THOMAS HOBBES, AN ENGLISH PHILOSOPHER LIVING IN EXILE IN France, was convinced that the West had descended into chaos. As he looked around him, Hobbes saw nothing but political instability, rebellion, and civil war. The turmoil had begun in the late sixteenth century, when the Reformation sparked the religious warfare described in the last chapter. In 1618 the situation deteriorated when another cycle of political strife and warfare erupted. The Thirty Years' War (1618–1648) began as a religious and political dispute in the Holy Roman Empire but soon became an international conflict involving the armies of Spain, France, Sweden, England, and many German states. The war wreaked economic and social havoc in Germany, decimated its population, and forced governments throughout Europe to raise large armies and tax their subjects to pay for them. The entire European economy suffered as a result.

During the 1640s, partly as a result of that devastating conflict, the political order of Europe collapsed. In England a series of bloody civil wars led to the destruction of the monarchy and the establishment of a republic. In France a civil war over constitutional issues drove the royal family from Paris. In Spain the king faced rebellions in four of his territories, while in Ukraine Cossacks staged a military uprising against the Polish-Lithuanian Commonwealth, killing more than one million people.

Hobbes proposed a solution to this multifaceted crisis. In *Leviathan* (1651), a theoretical treatise on the origin of political power, he argued that in the absence of a strong government society would degenerate into a constant state of war. In this dangerous world life would soon become, in Hobbes's famous words, "solitary, poor, nasty, brutish, and short."[1] The only way for people to find political stability would be to agree with their neighbors to form a political society by surrendering their independent power to a ruler who would make laws, administer justice, and maintain order. In this society the ruler would not share power with others. His subjects, having agreed to endow him with such extensive power, could not resist or depose him. The term used to designate the type of government Hobbes was recommending is **absolutism.** In the most general terms, absolutism means a political arrangement in which one ruler possesses unrivaled power.

During the seventeenth and early eighteenth centuries many European monarchs tried to introduce absolutism and increase the wealth and power of the states they ruled. These efforts always met with resistance. In most cases the rulers and their ministers prevailed, and Europe entered the "age of absolutism," which did not end until the outbreak of the French Revolution in 1789. This chapter addresses this question: Why did some European rulers achieve greater success than others in realizing these political objectives?

THE FRONTISPIECE OF THOMAS HOBBES'S TREATISE _LEVIATHAN_, PUBLISHED IN LONDON IN 1651

The ruler is depicted as incorporating the bodies of all his subjects, as they collectively authorized him to govern.

THE NATURE OF ABSOLUTISM

■ What did absolutism mean, both as a political theory and as a practical program, and how was absolutism related to the growth of the power of the state?

Seventeenth-century absolutism had both a theoretical and a practical dimension. Theoretical absolutists included writers such as Hobbes who described the nature of power in the state and explained the conditions for its acquisition and continuation. Practical absolutists were the rulers who took concrete political steps to gain control over all other political authorities within the state.

The Theory of Absolutism

When seventeenth-century political writers referred to the monarch's absolute power, they usually meant that he did not share the power to make law with representative assemblies. Hobbes, for example, referred to the absolute ruler as "sole legislator," while the French magistrate Jean Bodin (1530–1596), one of the earliest proponents of absolutist theory, argued in _Six_

Books of a Commonwealth (1576) that the most important power of an absolute ruler was the right to make law by himself.

Absolute rulers also claimed that they were above the law. This meant that when monarchs acted for reason of state, that is, for the benefit of the entire kingdom, they did not have to obey the law of their kingdoms. Nor could they be held legally accountable for their actions because they had no legal superior to judge them. Being above the law, however, did not mean monarchs could act arbitrarily, illegally, or despotically, even though some of them did so from time to time. Absolutist theorists claimed monarchs were obliged to respect the property rights of their subjects whenever they were not acting for reason of state. Under all circumstances monarchs were expected to follow the law of God.

Some absolutist theorists, although not Hobbes, claimed that rulers received their power directly from God. This theory of **divine right** supported royal absolutism, so the theorists claimed, because God would only invest the ruler he appointed with powers that resembled his own. The theory of divine right also supported the absolutist argument that subjects could not resist their monarch under any circumstances.

The Practice of Absolutism

In their quest for absolute power European monarchs employed three strategies. First, they sought to eliminate or weaken national legislative assemblies. In France, which historians consider the most absolutist state in seventeenth-century Europe, the monarchy stopped summoning its national legislature, the **Estates General,** in 1614. In Spain monarchs sought to reduce the powers of the legislative assemblies, the **Cortes,** of their various kingdoms, while in Germany many princes stopped consulting the **diets** of their territorial states.

The second strategy of absolutist rulers was to subordinate the nobility to the king and make them dependent on his favor. Monarchs who aspired to a position of unrivaled power in their kingdoms took steps to keep the nobility in line by suppressing aristocratic challenges to their authority and by appointing men from different social groups as their chief ministers. Yet the king could not afford to alienate these wealthy and high-ranking men, upon whom he still relied for running his government and maintaining order in the localities. Absolute monarchs, therefore, offered nobles special privileges, such as exemption from taxation, positions in the king's government, and freedom to exploit their peasants in exchange for their recognition of the king's absolute authority. In this way, nobles became junior partners in the management of the absolutist state.

The third strategy of absolute monarchs was to control the administrative machinery of the state and use it to enforce royal policy throughout their kingdoms. Absolute monarchs were by nature state builders. They established centralized bureaucracies that extended the reach of their governments down into the smallest towns and villages and out into the most remote regions of their kingdoms. The business conducted by these centrally controlled bureaucracies included the collection of taxes, the recruitment of soldiers, and the operation of the judicial system. Some absolute monarchs used the power of the state to impose and maintain religious conformity. As the seventeenth century advanced, they also used the same power to regulate the price of grain, stimulate the growth of industry, and relieve the plight of the poor. In these ways, absolutist policies had an impact on the lives of all royal subjects, not just noblemen and royal councilors.

Warfare and the Absolutist State

The growth of European states in the seventeenth century was closely related to the conduct of war. During the period from 1600 to 1721, European powers were almost constantly at war. To meet the demands of war, rulers began keeping men under arms at all times. By the middle of the seventeenth century, after the Thirty Years' War had come to an end, most European states had acquired such **standing armies.** These military forces not only served their rulers in foreign wars, but also helped to maintain order and enforce royal policy at home. Standing armies became one of the main props of royal absolutism.

European armies also became larger, in many cases tripling in size. In the 1590s Philip II of Spain had mastered Europe with an army of 40,000 men. By contrast, in the late seventeenth century Louis XIV of France needed an army of 400,000 men to become the dominant power on the continent. The increasing size of these forces partly stemmed from the introduction and extensive use of gunpowder in the fifteenth and sixteenth centuries. Gunpowder led to the widespread use of the musket, a heavy shoulder firearm carried by a foot soldier. The use of the musket demanded the recruitment and equipment of large armies of infantry, who marched in square columns with men holding long pikes (long wooden shafts with pointed metal heads) to protect the musketeers from enemy attacks. As the size of these armies of foot soldiers grew, the role of mounted soldiers, who had dominated medieval warfare, shrank.

Changes in military technology and tactics also necessitated more intensive military training. In the Middle Ages mounted knights had acquired great individual skill, but they did not need to work in precise unison with other men under arms (see "The Military Revolution" in Chapter 11). Seventeenth-century foot soldiers, however, had to learn to march in formation, to coordinate their maneuvers, and to fire without harming their comrades in arms. Therefore, they needed to be drilled. Drilling took place in peacetime as well as during war. The wearing of uniforms, which began when the state assumed the function of clothing its thousands of soldiers, gave further unity and cohesion to the trained fighting force.

The cost of recruiting, training, and equipping these mammoth armies was staggering. In the Middle Ages individual lords often had sufficient financial resources to assemble their own private armies. By the beginning of the seventeenth century the only institution capable of putting the new armies in the field was the state itself. The same was true for navies, which now consisted of heavily armed sailing ships, each of which carried as many as 400 sailors. To build these large armies and navies, as well as to pay the increasing cost of waging war itself (which rose 500 percent between 1530 and 1630), governments had to identify new methods of raising and collecting taxes. In times of war as much as 80 percent of state revenue went for military purposes.

The equipment and training of military forces and the collection and allocation of the revenue necessary to subsidize these efforts stimulated the expansion and refinement of the state bureaucracy. Governments employed thousands of new officials to supervise the collection of new taxes. To make the system of tax collection more efficient governments often introduced entirely new administrative systems. Some states completely reorganized their bureaucracies to meet the demands of war. They created new departments to supervise the recruitment of soldiers, the manufacture of equipment and uniforms, the building of fleets, and the provisioning of troops in time of war.

THE ABSOLUTIST STATE IN FRANCE AND SPAIN

■ How did France and Spain implement absolutism in the seventeenth century and how powerful did those states become?

The first two European monarchies to become absolutist states were France and Spain. The political development of these two countries, however, followed very different courses. The kingdom of France became a model of state building and gradually emerged as the most powerful country in Europe. The Spanish monarchy, on the other hand, struggled to introduce absolutism at a time when the overall economic condition of the country was deteriorating and its military forces were suffering a series of defeats.

The Foundations of French Absolutism

The first serious efforts to establish absolutism in France took place during the reign of Louis XIII (r. 1610–1643). When Louis was only eight years old, a Catholic assassin killed his father, Henry IV (1589–1610). Louis's mother, Marie de' Medici, assumed the leadership of the government during his youth. This period of **regency,** in which aristocratic factions vied for supremacy at court, exposed the main weakness of the monarchy, which was the rival power of the great noble families of the realm. The statesman who addressed this problem most directly was Louis's main councilor, Cardinal Armand Jean du Plessis de Richelieu (1585–1642), who became the king's chief minister in 1628. Richelieu directed all his energies toward centralizing the power of the French state in the person of the king.

Richelieu's most immediate concern was to bring the independent nobility to heel and subordinate their local power to that of the state. He suppressed several conspiracies and rebellions led by noblemen and restricted the independent power of the provincial assemblies and the eight regional **parlements,** which were the highest courts in the country. Richelieu's great administrative achievement was the strengthening of the system of the **intendants.** These paid crown officials, who were recruited from the professional classes and the lower ranks of the nobility, became the main agents of French local administration. Responsible only to the royal council, they collected taxes, supervised local administration, and recruited soldiers for the army.

Richelieu's most challenging task was increasing the government's yield from taxation, a task

CARDINAL RICHELIEU
Triple portrait of Cardinal Richelieu, who laid the foundations of French absolutism.

that became more demanding during times of war. Levying taxes on the French population was always a delicate process; the needs of the state conflicted with the privileges of various social groups, such as the nobles, who were exempt from taxation, and the estates of individual provinces, such as Brittany, that claimed the right to tax the people themselves. Using a variety of tactics, Richelieu managed to increase the yield from the *taille,* the direct tax on land, as much as threefold during the period from 1635 to 1648. He supplemented the taille with taxes on office-holding. Even then, the revenue was insufficient to meet the extraordinary demands of war.

Richelieu's protégé and successor, Jules Mazarin (1602–1661), continued his policies but was unable to prevent civil war from breaking out in 1648. This challenge to the French state, known as the *Fronde* (a pejorative reference to a Parisian game in which children flung mud at passing carriages), had two phases. The first, the Fronde of the Parlement (1648–1649), began when the members of the Parlement of Paris, the most important of all the provincial parlements, refused to register a royal edict that required them to surrender four years' salary. This act of resistance led to demands that the king sign a document limiting royal authority. The rebels put up barricades in the streets of Paris and forced the royal family to flee the city. The second and more violent phase was the Fronde of the Princes (1650–1653), during which the Prince de Condé and his noble allies waged war on the government and even formed an alliance with France's enemy, Spain. Only after Condé's military defeat did the entire rebellion collapse.

The Fronde stands as the great crisis of the seventeenth-century French state. It revealed the strength of the local, aristocratic, and legal forces with which the king and his ministers had to contend. In the long run, however, these forces could not destroy the achievement of Richelieu and Mazarin. By the late 1650s the damage had been repaired and the state had resumed its growth.

Absolutism in the Reign of Louis XIV

The man who presided over the development of the French state for the next 50 years was the king himself, Louis XIV (r. 1643–1715), who assumed direct control of his government after the death of Mazarin in 1661. In an age of absolute monarchs, Louis towered over his contemporaries. His reputation as the most powerful ruler of the seventeenth century derives as much from the image he conveyed as from the policies he pursued. Artists, architects, dramatists, and members of his immediate entourage helped the king project an image of incomparable majesty and authority. Paintings and sculptures of the king depicted him in sartorial splendor, holding the symbols of power and displaying expressions of regal superiority that bordered on arrogance. At Versailles, about ten miles from Paris, Louis

CHRONOLOGY: FRANCE IN THE AGE OF ABSOLUTISM

1598	The Edict of Nantes grants toleration to French Calvinists, known as Huguenots
1610	Assassination of Henry IV of France, who was succeeded by Louis XIII (r. 1610–1643)
1628	Cardinal Richelieu becomes chief minister of Louis XIII of France
1643	Death of Louis XIII of France and accession of Louis XIV; Louis's mother, Anne of Austria, becomes queen regent with Cardinal Mazarin as his minister
1648–1653	The Fronde
1661	Death of Cardinal Mazarin; Louis XIV assumes personal rule
1685	Revocation of the Edict of Nantes
1715	Death of Louis XIV of France; succeeded by his grandson, Louis XV

constructed a lavishly furnished palace that became his main residence and the center of his court. The palace was built in the **baroque** style, which emphasized the size and grandeur of the structure while also conveying a sense of unity and balance among its diverse parts. The sweeping façades of baroque buildings gave them a dynamic quality that evoked an emotional response from the viewer. The baroque style, criticized by contemporaries for its exuberance and pomposity, appealed to absolute monarchs who wished to emphasize their unrivaled position within society and their determination to impose order and stability on their kingdoms.

Court life at Versailles revolved entirely around the king. Court dramas depicted Louis, who styled himself "the sun king," as Apollo, the god of light. The paintings in the grand Hall of Mirrors at Versailles, which recorded the king's

military victories, served as reminders of his unrivaled accomplishments. Louis's formal routine in receiving visitors created appropriate distance between him and his courtiers while keeping his subjects in a state of subservient anticipation of royal favor.

Louis's greatest political achievement was securing the complete loyalty and dependence of the old nobility. This he achieved first by requiring the members of these ancient families to come to Versailles for a portion of every year, where they stayed in apartments within the royal palace itself. At Versailles Louis involved them in the elaborate cultural activities of court life and in ceremonial rituals that emphasized their subservience to the king. He also excluded these nobles from holding important offices in the government of the realm, a strategy designed to prevent them from building an independent power

VERSAILLES PALACE, CENTER OF THE COURT OF LOUIS XIV AFTER 1682
The palace was constructed between 1669 and 1686. Its massiveness and grandeur and the order it imposed on the landscape made it a symbol of royal absolutism.

base within the bureaucracy. Instead he recruited men from the mercantile and professional classes to run his government. This policy of taming the nobility and depriving them of central administrative power could work only if they received something in return. Like all the absolute monarchs of western Europe, Louis used the patronage at his disposal to grant members of the nobility wealth and privileges in exchange for their loyalty to the crown. In this way the monarchy and the nobility served each other's interests.

In running the actual machinery of government Louis built upon and perfected the centralizing policies of Richelieu and Mazarin. After the death of Mazarin in 1661, the king, then 23 years old, became his own chief minister, presiding over a council of state that supervised the work of government. An elaborate set of councils at the highest levels of government set policy that department ministers then implemented. The provincial intendants became even more important than they had been under Richelieu and Mazarin, especially in providing food, arms, and equipment for royal troops. The intendants secured the cooperation of local judges, city councils, and parish priests as well as the compliance of the local population. If necessary they could call upon royal troops to enforce the king's policies, but for the most part they preferred to rely on the more effective tactics of negotiation and compromise with local officials. The system, when it worked properly, allowed the king to make decisions that directly affected the lives and beliefs of his 20 million subjects.

In the late seventeenth century the French state also became involved in the economic and financial life of the country. The minister most responsible for this increase in state power was Jean Baptiste Colbert (1619–1683), a protégé of Mazarin who in 1661 became controller general of the realm. Born into a family of merchants, and despised by the old nobility, Colbert epitomized the type of government official Louis recruited into his service. Entrusted with the supervision of the entire system of royal taxation, Colbert increased royal revenues by reducing the cut taken by tax collectors.

Even more important, Colbert exploited the country's economic resources for the benefit of the state. The theory underlying this set of policies was **mercantilism,** which held that the wealth of the state depended on its ability to import fewer commodities than it exported. Its goal was to secure the largest possible share of the world's monetary supply. Colbert increased the size of France's merchant fleet, founded overseas trading companies, and levied high tariffs on France's commercial rivals. To make France economically self-sufficient, he encouraged the growth of the French textile industry, improved the condition of the roads, built canals throughout the kingdom, and reduced some of the burdensome tolls that impeded internal trade.

The most intrusive exercise of the power of the state during Louis XIV's reign was his decision to enforce religious uniformity. In 1598 the Edict of Nantes had given French Calvinists, known as Huguenots, the freedom to practice their religion. Louis considered the existence of this large Huguenot minority within his kingdom an affront to his sense of order. In 1685 therefore Louis revoked the Edict, thereby denying freedom of religious worship to about one million of his subjects. The army enforced public conversions to Catholicism and closed Protestant churches. Large numbers of Huguenots emigrated to the Netherlands, England, Germany, and North America. Few exercises of absolute power in the seventeenth century caused more disruption in the lives of ordinary people than this attempt to realize Louis's ideal of "one king, one law, one faith."

Louis XIV and the Culture of Absolutism

A further manifestation of the power of the French absolutist state was Louis's success in influencing and transforming French culture. Kings had often served as patrons of the arts by providing income for artists, writers, and musicians and endowing cultural and educational institutions. Louis took this type of royal patronage to a new level, making it possible for him to control the dissemination of ideas and the very production of culture itself. During Louis's reign royal patronage, emanating from the court, extended the king's influence over the entire cultural landscape. The architects of the palace at Versailles, the painters of historical scenes that hung in its hallways and galleries, the composers of the plays and operas performed in its theaters, the sculptors who created busts of the king to decorate its chambers, and the historians and pamphlet writers who celebrated the king's achievements in print all benefited from Louis's direct financial support.

Much of Louis's patronage went to cultural institutions. He took over the Academy of Fine Arts in 1661, founded the Academy of Music in 1669, and chartered a theater company, the *Comédie Française,* in 1680. Two great French dramatists of the late seventeenth century, Jean Baptiste Molière (1622–1673), the creator of French high comedy, and Jean Racine (1639–1699), who wrote tragedies in the classical style, benefited from the king's patronage. Louis even subsidized the publication of a new journal, the *Journal des savants,* in which writers advanced their ideas. In 1666 Louis extended his patronage to the sciences with the founding of the *Académie des Sciences,* which had the twofold objective of advancing scientific knowledge and glorifying the king. It also benefited the state by devising improvements in ship design and navigation.

Of all the cultural institutions that benefited from Louis XIV's patronage, the *Académie Française* had the most enduring impact on French culture. This society of literary scholars founded in 1635, sought to standardize the French language and preserve its integrity. In 1694, 22 years after Louis became the academy's patron, the first official French dictionary appeared in print. This achievement of linguistic uniformity, in which words received authorized spellings and definitions, reflected the pervasiveness of Louis's cultural influence as well as the search for order that became the defining characteristic of his reign.

The Wars of Louis XIV, 1667–1714

Colbert's financial and economic policies, coupled with the military reforms of the Marquis de Louvois, laid the foundation for the creation of a formidable military machine. In 1667 Louis XIV began unleashing its full potential. With an army 20 times larger than the French force that had invaded Italy in 1494, Louis fought four separate wars against an array of European powers between 1667 and 1714. His goal in all these wars was territorial acquisition (see **Map 16.1**). In this case Louis set his sights mainly on the German and Spanish territories in the Rhineland along the eastern borders of his kingdom. Contemporaries

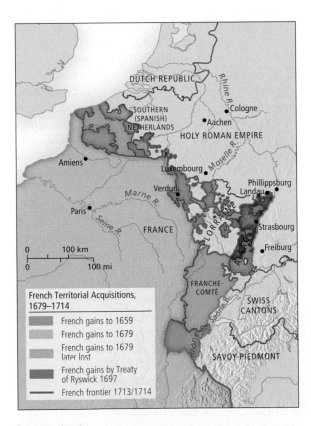

MAP 16.1

French Territorial Acquisitions, 1679–1714

Louis XIV thought of the Rhine River as France's natural eastern boundary, and territories acquired in 1659 and 1697 allowed it to reach that limit.

suggested, however, that he was thinking in grander terms than traditional French dynastic ambition. Propagandists for the king in the late 1660s claimed that Louis harbored visions of establishing a "universal monarchy" or an "absolute empire," reminiscent of the empires of ancient Rome, Charlemagne in the ninth century, and Charles V in the sixteenth century.

Louis never attained the empire of his dreams. After he launched an offensive against German towns along the Rhine River in 1688, Great Britain, the Dutch Republic, Spain, and Austria formed a coalition against him. Finally matched by the combined military strength of these allies, forced to wage war on many different fronts (including North America), and unable to collect enough taxes to pay for the war, France felt compelled to conclude peace in 1697. The Treaty of Ryswick marked the turning point in the expansion of the French state and laid the groundwork for the establishment of a **balance of power** in the next century, an arrangement whereby various countries form alliances to prevent any one state from dominating the others.

The Treaty of Ryswick, however, did not mark the end of French territorial ambition. In 1701 Louis went to war once again, this time as part of an effort to place a French Bourbon candidate, his grandson Duke Philip of Anjou, on the Spanish throne. The impending death of the mentally weak, sexually impotent, and chronically ill King Charles II of Spain (r. 1665–1700) without heirs had created a succession crisis. In 1698 the major European powers had agreed to a treaty that would divide Spanish lands between Louis and the Holy Roman Emperor, both of whom were Charles's brothers-in-law. By his will, however, Charles left the Spanish crown and all its overseas possessions to Philip. This bequest offered France more than it would have received on the basis of the treaty. If the will had been upheld, the Pyrenees Mountains would have disappeared as a political barrier between France and Spain, and France, as the stronger of the two kingdoms, would have controlled unprecedented expanses of European and American territory.

Dreaming once again of universal monarchy, Louis rejected the treaty in favor of King Charles's will. The British, Dutch, and Austrians responded by forming a Grand Alliance against France and Spain. After a long and costly conflict, known as the War of the Spanish Succession (1701–1713), the members of this coalition were able to dictate the terms of the Treaty of Utrecht (1713). Philip, who suffered from fits of manic depression and went days without dressing or leaving his room, remained on the Spanish throne as Philip V (r. 1700–1746), but only on the condition that the French and Spanish crowns would never be united. Spain ceded its territories in the Netherlands and in Italy to the Austrian Habsburg Monarchy and its strategic port of Gibraltar at the entrance to the Mediterranean to the British. Britain also acquired large parts of French Canada, including Newfoundland and Nova Scotia, The treaty thus dashed Louis's hopes of universal monarchy and confirmed the new balance of power in Europe.

The loss of French territory in North America, the strains placed on the taxation system by the financial demands of war, and the weakening of France's commercial power as a result of this conflict made France a less potent state at the time of Louis's death in 1715 than it had been in the 1680s. Nevertheless, the main effects of a century of French state building remained, including a large, well-integrated bureaucratic edifice that allowed the government to exercise unprecedented control over the population and a military establishment that remained the largest and best equipped in Europe.

Absolutism and State Building in Spain

The history of Spain in the seventeenth century is almost always written in terms of failure, as the country endured a long period of economic decline that began in the late sixteenth century. With a precipitate drop in the size of the population, the monarchy became progressively weaker under a series of ineffective kings, To make matters worse,

LOUIS XIV

Portrait of Louis XIV in military armor, with his plumed helmet and his crown on the table to the right. The portrait was painted during the period of French warfare. In the background is a French ship.

the country suffered a series of military defeats, most of them at the hands of the French. As a result, Spain lost its position as the major European power (see **Map 16.2**). By the early eighteenth century Spain was a shadow of its former self, and its culture reflected uncertainty, pessimism, and nostalgia for its former imperial greatness. None of this failure, however, should obscure the fact that

Spain, like France, underwent a period of state building during the seventeenth century, and that its government, like that of France, gravitated toward absolutism.

The Spanish monarchy in 1600 ruled more territory than did France, but its many principalities and small kingdoms possessed far more independence than even the most remote and peripheral French provinces. The center of the monarchy was the kingdom of Castile, with its capital at Madrid. This kingdom, the largest and wealthiest territory within the Iberian Peninsula, had been united with the kingdom of Aragon in 1479 when King Ferdinand II of Aragon (r. 1479–1516), the husband of Queen Isabella of Castile (r. 1474–1504), ascended the throne. These two kingdoms, however, continued to exist as separate states after the union, each having its own representative institutions and administrative systems. Each of them, moreover, contained smaller, semiautonomous kingdoms and provinces that retained their own distinctive political institutions. Outside the Iberian Peninsula the Spanish monarchy ruled territories in the Netherlands, Italy, and the New World.

The only institution besides the monarchy itself that provided any kind of administrative unity to all these Spanish territories in the seventeenth century was the Spanish Inquisition, a centralized ecclesiastical court with a supreme council in Madrid and 21 regional tribunals in different parts of Spain, Italy, and America.

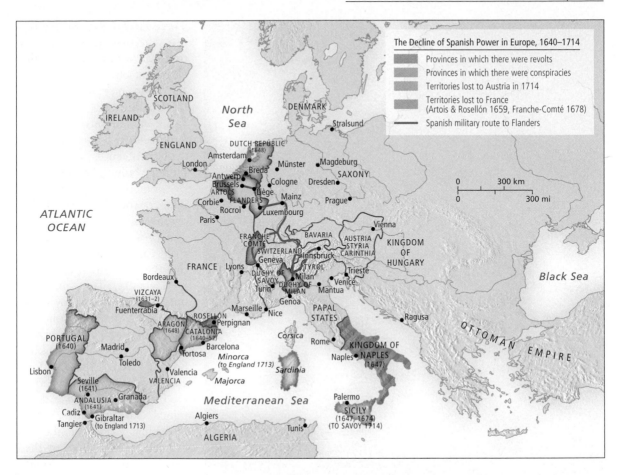

MAP 16.2

The Decline of Spanish Power in Europe, 1640–1714

Revolts in the United Provinces of the Netherlands and Portugal account for two of the most significant losses of Spanish territory. Military defeat at the hands of the French in 1659 and Austria in 1714 account for the loss of most of the other territories.

The great challenge for the Spanish monarchy in the seventeenth century was to integrate the various kingdoms and principalities of Spain into a more highly centralized state and make the machinery of that state more efficient and profitable. The statesman who made the most sustained efforts at realizing these goals was the energetic and authoritarian Count-Duke of Olivares (1587–1645), the contemporary of Richelieu during the reign of the Spanish king Philip IV (1621–1665). Olivares faced a daunting task. As a result of decades of warfare, the Spanish

monarchy in the 1620s was penniless, the kingdom of Castile had gone bankrupt, and the entire country had entered a period of protracted economic decline.

To deal with these deep structural problems Olivares proposed a reform of the entire financial system, the establishment of national banks, and the replacement of the tax on consumption, the *millones*, with proportional contributions from towns and villages in Castile. He also tried to make all the Spanish kingdoms and principalities contribute to the national

DIEGO DE VELÁZQUEZ, PORTRAIT OF THE PRINCE BALTASAR CARLOS, HEIR TO THE SPANISH THRONE

The depiction of the six-year-old prince on a rearing horse was intended to suggest military and political power at a time when the monarchy was losing both. The prince died in 1646, before he could succeed to the throne.

Three factors explain his failure. The first was the opposition he confronted within Castile itself, especially from the cities represented in the Cortes, over the question of taxation. The second, a problem facing Spain throughout the seventeenth century, was military failure. Spanish losses to France during the final phase of the Thirty Years' War aggravated the financial crisis and prevented the monarchy from capitalizing on the prestige that usually attends military victory. The third and most serious impediment was opposition to the policy of subordinating the outlying Spanish regions to the kingdom of Castile. The kingdoms and provinces on the periphery of the country were determined to maintain their individual laws and liberties, especially the powers of their own Cortes. The problem became more serious when Olivares, in the wake of military defeat by the French and Dutch, put more pressure on these outlying kingdoms and provinces to contribute to the war effort. During the tenure of Olivares, Spain faced separatist revolts in Portugal, Catalonia, Sicily, and Naples. With the exception of Portugal, which recovered its sovereignty in 1640, the monarchy managed to retain its provincial and Italian territories, but it failed to bring these areas under central government control.

The relative weakness of the Spanish monarchy became most apparent in the late seventeenth century, the age of Louis XIV. In two important respects the Spanish government failed to match

defense on a proportionate basis. His goal was to unify the entire peninsula in a cohesive Spanish national state, similar to that of France. This policy involved suppression of the historic privileges of the various kingdoms and principalities and the direct subordination of each area to the king. It was, in other words, a policy based on the principles of royal absolutism.

Olivares was unable to match the state-building achievement of Richelieu in France.

CHRONOLOGY: INTERNATIONAL CONFLICT IN THE SEVENTEENTH CENTURY

1609	Truce between the seven Dutch provinces and Spain
1618	Bohemian revolt against Habsburg rule; beginning of the Thirty Years' War
1620	Imperial forces defeat Bohemians at Battle of White Mountain
1648	Treaty of Westphalia, ending the Thirty Years' War; Treaty of Münster, ending the Dutch War of Independence
1667	Beginning of the wars of Louis XIV
1672	William III of Orange-Nassau becomes captain-general of Dutch; beginning of the war against France (1672–1678)
1688–1697	War of the League of Augsburg (Nine Years' War); England and Scotland join forces with Prussia, Austria, the Dutch Republic, and many German states against France
1697	Treaty of Ryswick
1700–1721	Great Northern War in which Russia eventually defeated Sweden; emergence of Russia as a major power
1701–1713	War of the Spanish Succession
1713	Treaty of Utrecht

the achievement of the French. First, Spain could never escape the grip that the old noble families had on the central administration. The unwillingness of the nobility to recruit ministers and officials from the mercantile and professional groups in society (which were small to begin with in Spain) worked against the achievement of bureaucratic efficiency and made innovation almost impossible. Second, unlike the French government during Colbert's ministry, the Spanish government failed to encourage economic growth. The hostility of the aristocratic ruling class to mercantile affairs, coupled with a traditional Spanish unwillingness to follow the example of foreigners (especially when they were Protestants) prevented the country from stemming its own economic decline and the government from solving the formidable financial problems facing it. To make matters worse, the Spanish government failed to make its system of tax collection more efficient.

The mood that prevailed within the upper levels of Castilian society in the seventeenth century reflected the failure of the government and the entire nation. The contrast between the glorious achievements of the monarchy during the

reign of Philip II (r. 1555–1598) and the somber realities of the late seventeenth century led most members of the ruling class to retreat into the past, a nostalgia that only encouraged further economic and political stagnation. The work of Miguel de Cervantes (1547–1616), the greatest Spanish writer of the seventeenth century, reflected this change in the Spanish national mood. In 1605 and 1615 Cervantes published (in two parts) *Don Quixote,* the story of an idealistic wandering nobleman who pursued dreams of an elusive military glory. This work, which as we have seen in Chapter 15, explored the relationship between illusion and reality, served as a commentary on a nobility that had lost confidence in itself.

Paradoxically Spanish painting entered its Golden Age at the time the country began to lose its economic, political, and military vitality. Little in the paintings of the great Spanish artist Diego de Velázquez (1599–1660) would suggest the malaise that was affecting Spain and its nobility at the time. Velázquez painted in the baroque style that was in favor in European courts. He depicted his subjects in heroic poses and imbued them with a sense of royal or aristocratic dignity. One of his historical paintings, *The Surrender of Breda* (1634), commemorated a rare Spanish military victory over the Dutch in 1625 and the magnanimity of the Spanish victors toward their captives. All this was intended to reinforce the prestige of the monarchy, the royal family, and Spain itself at a time when the imperial grandeur of the past had faded. Velázquez's painting reflected the ideals of absolutism but ignored the realities of Spanish political and military life.

ABSOLUTISM AND STATE BUILDING IN CENTRAL AND EASTERN EUROPE

■ What was the nature of royal absolutism in central and eastern Europe, and how did the policies of the Ottoman Empire and Russia help to establish the boundaries of the West during this period?

The forces that led to the establishment of absolutism and state building in France and Spain also made an impact on central and eastern Europe. In Germany the Thirty Years' War led to the establishment of two absolutist states, Prussia and the Austrian Habsburg Monarchy. Farther to the east, the Ottoman and Russian Empires developed political systems that shared many of the same characteristics as states in western and central Europe. These policies challenged the traditional European perception that both empires belonged entirely to an Eastern, Asian world.

Germany and the Thirty Years' War, 1618–1648

Before 1648 the main political power within the geographical area known as Germany was the Holy Roman Empire. This large political formation was a loose confederation of kingdoms, principalities, duchies, ecclesiastical territories, and cities, each of which had its own laws and political institutions. The emperor, who was elected by a body of German princes, exercised immediate jurisdiction only in his own dynastic possessions and in the imperial cities. He also convened a legislative assembly known as the *Reichstag*, over which he exercised limited influence. The emperor did not have a large administrative or judicial bureaucracy through which he could enforce imperial law in the localities. The empire was not in any sense a sovereign state, even though it had long been a major force in European diplomacy. It had acquired and maintained that international position by relying on the military and financial contributions of its imperial cities and the lands controlled directly by the Habsburg emperors.

The Thirty Years' War permanently altered the nature of this intricate political structure. That war began as a conflict between Protestant German princes and the Catholic emperor over religious and constitutional issues. The incident that triggered it in 1618 was the so-called Defenestration of Prague, when members of the predominantly Protestant Bohemian legislature, known as the Diet, threw two imperial officials out a castle window as a protest against the religious policies of their recently elected king, the future emperor Ferdinand II. The Diet proceeded to depose Ferdinand, a Catholic, and elect a Protestant prince, Frederick V of the Palatinate, to replace him. The war soon broadened into a European-wide struggle over the control of German and Spanish territory, as the Danes, Swedes, and French successively entered the conflict against the emperor and his Spanish Habsburg relatives. For a brief period in the late 1620s England also entered the conflict against Spain. The war, which was fought mainly on German soil, had a devastating effect on the country. More than one million soldiers marched across German lands, sacking towns and exploiting the resources of local communities. Germany lost up to one-third of its population, while the destruction of property retarded the economic development of the country for more than 50 years.

DEFENESTRATION OF PRAGUE, MAY 23, 1618
The Thirty Years' War was touched off when Protestant nobles in the Bohemian legislature threw two Catholic imperial governors out the window of a castle in Prague.

The political effects of the war were no less traumatic. By virtue of the Treaty of Westphalia, which ended the war in 1648, the empire was permanently weakened, although it continued to function until 1806 (see **Map 16.3**). The individual German territories within the empire developed more institutional autonomy than they had before the war. They became sovereign states, with their own armies, foreign policies, and central bureaucracies. Two of these German states became major European powers and developed their own forms of absolutism. The first was Brandenburg-Prussia, a collection of various territories in northern Germany that was transformed into the kingdom of Prussia at the beginning of the eighteenth century. The second state was the Austrian Habsburg Monarchy, which in the eighteenth century was usually identified simply as Austria. The Habsburgs had long dominated the Holy Roman Empire and continued to secure election as emperors after the Treaty of Westphalia. In the late seventeenth century, however, the Austrian Habsburg Monarchy acquired its own institutional identity, distinct from that of the Holy Roman Empire. It consisted of the lands that the Habsburgs controlled directly in the southeastern part of the empire and other territories, including the kingdom of Hungary, which lay outside the territorial boundaries of the empire.

The Growth of the Prussian State

In 1648, at the end of the Thirty Years' War, Prussia could barely claim the status of an independent state, much less an absolute monarchy. The core of the Prussian state was Brandenburg,

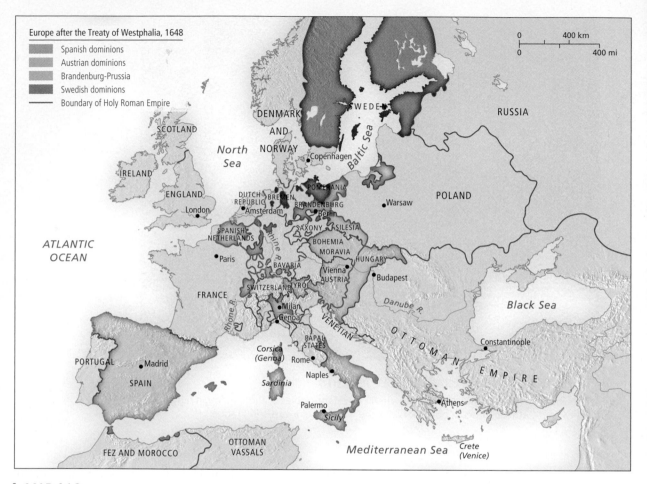

Europe after the Treaty of Westphalia, 1648

■ Spanish dominions
■ Austrian dominions
■ Brandenburg-Prussia
■ Swedish dominions
— Boundary of Holy Roman Empire

MAP 16.3

Europe after the Treaty of Westphalia, 1648

The Holy Roman Empire no longer included the Dutch Republic, which was now independent of Spain. Some of the lands of the Austrian Habsburg Monarchy and Brandenburg-Prussia lay outside the boundaries of the Holy Roman Empire. Italy was divided into a number of small states in the north, while Spain ruled Naples, Sicily, and Sardinia.

which was an electorate because its ruler cast one of the ballots to elect the Holy Roman Emperor. The Hohenzollern family, which controlled the electorate, held lands that lay scattered throughout northern Germany and stretched into eastern Europe. The largest was Prussia, a Baltic territory lying outside the boundaries of the Holy Roman Empire. As ruler of these disparate and noncontiguous lands, the Elector of Brandenburg had virtually no state

bureaucracy, collected few taxes, and commanded only a small army. Most of his territories, moreover, lay in ruins in 1648, having been devastated by Swedish and imperial troops at various times during the war.

The Great Elector Frederick William (r. 1640–1688) began the long process of turning this ramshackle structure into a powerful and cohesive German state (see **Map 16.4**). His son and grandson, King Frederick I (r. 1688–1713)

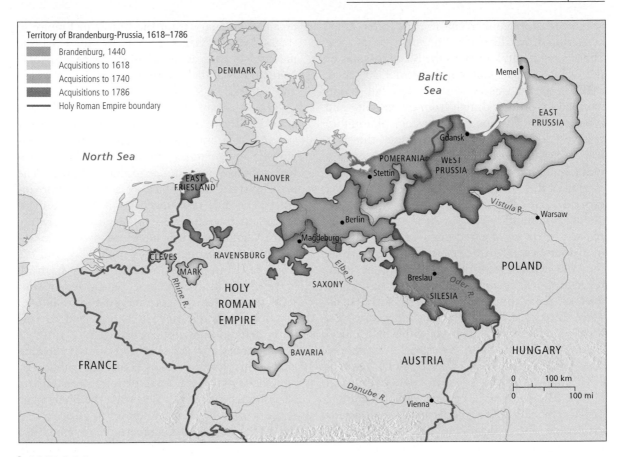

MAP 16.4

The Growth of Brandenburg-Prussia, 1618–1786

By acquiring lands throughout northern Germany, Prussia became a major European power. The process began during the early seventeenth century, but it continued well into the eighteenth century. The Prussian army, which was the best trained fighting force in Europe in the eighteenth century, greatly facilitated Prussia's growth.

and Frederick William I (r. 1713–1740), completed the transformation. The key to their success, as it was for all aspiring absolute monarchs in eastern Europe, was to secure the compliance of the traditional nobility, who in Prussia were known as **Junkers.** The Great Elector Frederick William achieved this end by granting the Junkers a variety of privileges, including exemption from import duties and the excise tax. The most valuable concession was the legal confirmation of their rights over their serfs. During the previous 150 years Prussian peasants had lost their freedom, becoming permanently bound to

the estates of their lords and completely subject to the Junkers' arbitrary brand of local justice. The Junkers had a deeply vested interest in perpetuating this oppressive system of serfdom, and the lawgiver Frederick was able to provide them with the legal guarantees they required.

With the loyalty of the Junkers secure, Frederick William began building a powerful Prussian state with a standing army and a large bureaucracy that superintended military and financial affairs. The army grew rapidly, rising to 30,000 men in 1690 and 80,000 by 1740. It consisted of a combination of carefully recruited volunteers, foreign mercenaries, and, after 1713, conscripts from the general population. Its most famous regiment, known as the Blue Prussians or the Giants of Potsdam, consisted of 1,200 men, each of whom was at least six feet tall. Commanded by officers drawn from the nobility and reinforced by Europe's first system of military reserves, this army quickly became the best trained fighting force in Europe. Prussia became a model military state, symbolized by the transformation of the royal gardens into an army training ground during the reign of Frederick William I.

As this military state grew in size and complexity, its rulers acquired many of the attributes of absolute rule. Most significantly, they became the sole legislators within the state. The main representative assembly in the electorate, the Diet of Brandenburg, met for the last time in 1652. Frederick William and his successors, however, continued to consult with smaller local assemblies, especially in the matter of taxation. The naming of Frederick I as king of Prussia in 1701 marked a further consolidation of royal power. His son's style of rule, which included physical punishment of judges whose decisions displeased him, suggested that the Prussian monarchy not only had attained absolute power, but could occasionally abuse it.

The Austrian Habsburg Monarchy

The Austrian Habsburgs were much less successful than the Hohenzollerns in building a centralized, consolidated state along absolutist lines. The various territories that made up the Austrian Habsburg Monarchy in the late seventeenth century were larger and more diverse than those that belonged to Prussia. **Map 16.3** shows that in addition to the cluster of duchies that form present day Austria, the Austrian Habsburg monarchy embraced two subordinate kingdoms. The kingdom of Bohemia, lying to the north, had struggled against Habsburg control for nearly a century and included the provinces of Moravia and Silesia. The kingdom of Hungary, lying to the southeast, included the large semiautonomous principality of Transylvania. The Habsburgs

regained Hungary from the Ottoman Empire in stages between 1664 and 1718. In 1713 the monarchy also acquired the former Spanish Netherlands and the Italian territories of Milan and Naples.

The Austrian Habsburg monarchs of the seventeenth and early eighteenth centuries never succeeded in integrating these ethnically, religiously, and politically diverse lands into a unified, cohesive state similar to that of France. The main obstacle was a lack of a unified bureaucracy. The only centralized administrative institutions in this amalgam of kingdoms were the Court Chamber, which superintended the collection of taxes throughout the monarchy, and the Austrian army, which included troops from all Habsburg lands. Even these centralized institutions had difficulty operating smoothly. For all practical purposes, the Habsburgs had to rule their various kingdoms separately.

In governing its Austrian and Bohemian lands, this decentralized Habsburg monarchy nonetheless acquired some of the characteristics of absolutist rule. After defeating the Bohemians at the Battle of White Mountain in 1620 during the Thirty Years' War, Emperor Ferdinand II (r. 1618–1637) strengthened his authority not only in Bohemia, but over all the territories under his direct control. After punishing the rebels and exiling many of the Protestant nobility, he undertook a deliberate expansion of his legislative and judicial powers, and he secured direct control over all his administrative officials.

A policy of severe religious repression accompanied this increase in the emperor's authority. Ferdinand assumed that Protestantism served as a justification for rebellion, and he therefore decided that its practice could not be tolerated. He required that Protestants in all the emperor's territories take a Catholic loyalty oath, and he banned Protestant education.

Habsburgs were not so successful in trying to impose absolutism on Hungary in the late seventeenth and eighteenth centuries. Hungarians had a long tradition of limited, constitutional rule in which the national Diet exercised powers of legislation and taxation, just as Parliament did in England. Habsburg emperors made some limited inroads on these traditions but they were never able to break them. They also were unable to achieve the same degree of religious uniformity that they had imposed on their other territories. In Hungary the Habsburgs encountered the limits of royal absolutism.

The Ottoman Empire: Between East and West

In the seventeenth and early eighteenth centuries the southeastern border of the Habsburg monarchy separated the kingdom of Hungary from the Ottoman Empire. This militarized frontier marked not only the political boundary between two empires, but a deeper cultural boundary between East and West.

As we have seen in previous chapters, the West is not just a geographical area. It is also a cultural area; the people who inhabit this territory share many of the same religious, political, legal, and philosophical traditions. In the eyes of most Europeans, the Ottoman Turks, who posed a recurrent military threat to the Habsburg monarchy, did not belong to this Western world. Because the Ottoman Turks were Muslims, Europeans considered them enemies of Christianity, infidels who were bent on the destruction of Christendom. Ottoman emperors, known as sultans, were reputedly despots who ruled over their subjects as slaves. Western literature also depicted the sultans as cruel and brutal tyrants, the opposite of the ideal Christian prince. One French play of 1612 showed the mother of the sultan Mehmed the Conquerer (r. 1451–1481) drinking the blood of a victim.

These stereotypes of the Turks gave Europeans a sense of their own Western identity. Turks became a negative reference group with whom Europeans could compare themselves. The realities of Ottoman politics and culture, however, were quite different from their representations in European literature. Turkish despotism, the name Europeans gave to the Ottoman system of government, existed only in theory. Ever since the fourteenth century Ottoman writers had claimed for

the sultan extraordinary powers, including the right to seize the landed property of his subjects at will. In practice, however, the sultan never exercised unlimited power. The spirit of Muslim law limited his prerogatives, and he shared power with the grand vizier, his chief executive officer. By the 1660s, when most European states had entered the age of absolutism, the sultan's power had become largely titular. Moreover, the Ottoman practice of tolerating non-Muslim religions within the empire made the sultans less absolutist than most of their seventeenth-century European counterparts. (See *Different Voices* in this chapter.)

Even the Ottoman Empire's high degree of administrative centralization did not extend to all the territories it ruled. Many of its provinces, especially those in the Balkans, enjoyed a considerable measure of autonomy, especially in the seventeenth century. The Balkans, which were geographically part of Europe, never experienced the full force of direct Turkish rule. As in most monarchies of western and central Europe, a complex pattern of negotiation between the central imperial administration and local officials characterized Ottoman rule. In Europe the Ottoman Empire bore the closest resemblance to the Spanish monarchy, which also ruled many far-flung territories. Like Spain, the Ottoman Empire declined in power during the seventeenth century and lost effective control of some of its outlying provinces.

Ottoman Turks and Europeans frequently went to war against each other, but their interactions with the West were not always hostile. The Turks had been involved in European warfare since the fifteenth century, and they had formed diplomatic alliances with the French against the Austrian Habsburgs on a number of occasions. Europeans and Ottomans often acquired military technology and administrative techniques from each other. Trade between European countries and the Ottoman Empire remained brisk throughout this period. Europe supplied hardware and textiles to the Turks while they in turn shipped coffee, tobacco, and tulips to European ports. Communities of Turks and other Muslims lived in European cities, while

DIFFERENT VOICES WESTERN WRITERS EVALUATE THE OTTOMAN TURKS

Western commentators displayed ambivalent feelings toward the Ottoman Turks in the seventeenth century. On the one hand, Westerners were impressed with the power of the Sultan, the size of the Ottoman Empire, the discipline of their soldiers, and the political obedience of their subjects to their sovereign. On the other hand, Westerners considered the Turks barbarous. Richard Knolles (1550–1610) reflected this ambivalence in the preface to his history of the Turks with an analysis of their greatness. He then condemned the ways in which this barbarous people violated international and natural law. Thomas Smith, a clergyman at Oxford University, agreed with Knolles that the Turks were a barbarous nation, but he attributed this trait to their lack of interest in education and their intolerance of other religions.

An English Writer Criticizes the Turks for Violating the Law

But to come nearer unto the causes of the Turks greatness, ... first in them is to be noted an ardent and infinite desire of sovereignty, wherewith they have long since promised unto themselves the monarchy of the whole world, a quick motive unto their so haughty designs. Then, such a rare unity and agreement amongst them, as well in the manner of their religion (if it be so to be called) as in matters concerning their state (especially in all their enterprises to be taken in hand for the augmenting of their Empire) as that thereof they call themselves *Islami*, that is to say, men of one mind, or at peace among themselves; so as it is not to be marveled, if thereby they grow strong themselves, and dreadful to others. Join unto this their courage, conceived by the wonderful success of their perpetual fortune, their notable vigilance in taking the advantage of

every occasion for the enlarging of their monarchy, their frugality and temperateness in their diet and other manner of living, their straight observing of their ancient military discipline, their cheerful and almost incredible obedience unto their princes and Sultans; such, as in that point no nation in the world was to be worthily compared unto them—all great causes why their empire hath so mightily increased and so long continued....

And yet these great ones not contented by such commendable and lawful means still to extend or establish their far spreading empire, if that point once come in question, they stick not in their devilish policy to break and infringe the laws both of nations and nature. Their leagues grounded upon the law of nations, be they with never so strong capitulations concluded, or solemnity of oath confirmed, have with them no longer force than stands with their own profit, serving indeed but as snares to entangle other princes in, until they have singled out him whom they purpose to devour; the rest fast bound still looking on as if their own turn should never come, yet with no more assurance of their safety by their leagues than had the other whom they see perish before their faces. As for the kind law of nature, what can be thereunto more contrary than for the father most unnaturally to embrue his hands in the blood of his own children and the brother to become the bloody executioner of his own brethren, a common matter among the Ottoman emperors? All which most execrable and inhumane murders they cover with the pretended safety of their state, as thereby freed from the fear of all aspiring competitors (the greatest torment of the mighty) and by the preservation of the integrity of their Empire, which they thereby keep whole and entire unto themselves, and so

numerous European merchants resided in territories under Ottoman control.

These encounters between Turks and Europeans suggest that the militarized boundary

between the Habsburgs and the Ottoman Empire was more porous than its fortifications suggested. Military conflict and Western contempt for Turks disguised a complex process of political and

deliver it as it were by hand from one to another, in no part dismembered or impaired. By these and such like means is this barbarous empire (of almost nothing) grown to that height of majesty and power, as that it hath in contempt all the rest, being it self not inferior in greatness and strength unto the greatest monarchies that ever yet were upon the face of the earth, the Roman Empire only excepted.

Source: Richard Knolles, *The General History of the Turks from the First Beginnings of That Nation to the Rising of the Ottoman Family*, 1603.

An English Clergyman Comments on the Learning and Religious Intolerance of the Turks

The Turks are justly branded with the character of a barbarous nation, which censure does not relate either to the cruelty and severity of their punishments...or to want of discipline...or to want of civil behavior among themselves...but to the intolerable pride and scorn wherewith they treat all the world besides.

Their temper and genius, the constitution of their government, and the principles of their education incline them to war, where valor and merit are sure to be encouraged, and have their due reward. They have neither leisure nor inclination to entertain the studies of learning or the civil arts, which take off the roughness and wildness of nature, and render men more agreeable in their conversation. And though they are forced to commend and admire the ingenuity of the Western Christians, when they see any mathematical instrument, curious pictures, map, or sea-charts, or open the leaves of any printed book, or the like; yet they look upon all this as a curiosity, that not only may be spared, but what ought to be

carefully avoided, and kept out of their empire, as tending to soften men's minds, and render them less fit for arms, which they look upon as the best and truest end of life, to enlarge their greatness and their conquests.

But it is not so much their want of true and ingenuous learning which makes them thus intractable and rude to strangers as a rooted and inveterate prejudice against and hatred of all others who are of a different religion. It is not to be expected that where this principle prevails, and is looked upon as a piece of religion and duty, they who embrace it should be guilty of any act of kindness and humanity; except when they are bribed to it with hope of reward and gain, or forced to it by the necessities of state, or wrought upon more powerfully, as it were against their wills by the resentments of some favors and kindnesses received, which may happen now and then in some of better natures and more generous tempers.

Source: Thomas Smith, *Remarks upon the Manners, Religion and Government of the Turks*, 1678.

For Discussion

1. Which characteristics of the Turks given in the two documents did the authors view as positive and which did they view as negative?

2. To what extent do these two descriptions of the Turks support the Western view that the Ottoman Empire was an "oriental despotism"?

3. These two writers based their assessments of the Turks upon reports from travelers. What value do such reports have as historical evidence?

cultural interaction between the two civilizations. Europeans tended to think of the Ottoman Empire as "oriental," but it is more accurate to view it as a region lying between the East and the West.

Russia and the West

The other power that marked the boundary between East and West was the vast Russian Empire, which stretched from its boundary with

Poland-Lithuania in the west to the Pacific Ocean in the east. Until the end of the seventeenth century, the kingdom of Muscovy and the lands attached to it seemed, at least to Europeans, part of the Asiatic world. Dominated by an Eastern Orthodox branch of Christianity, Russia drew very little upon the cultural traditions associated with western Europe. Unlike its Slavic neighbor Poland, Russia had not absorbed large doses of German culture. It also appeared to Europeans to be another example of "oriental despotism," a state in which the ruler, known as the tsar (the Russian word for Caesar), could rule his subjects at will, "not bound up by any law or custom."

During the reign of Tsar Peter I, known as Peter the Great (r. 1682–1725), Russia underwent a process of Westernization, bringing it more into line with the culture of European countries and becoming a major European power. This policy began after Peter visited England, the Dutch Republic, northern Germany, and Austria in 1697 and 1698. Upon his return he directed his officials and members of the upper levels of Russian society to adopt Western styles of dress and appearance, including the removal of men's beards. (Scissors were kept in the customs house for this purpose alone.) Beards symbolized the backward, Eastern Orthodox culture from whose grip Peter hoped to extricate his country. Young Russian boys were sent abroad for their education. Women began to participate openly in the social and cultural life of the cities, in violation of Orthodox custom. Smoking was permitted despite the Church's insistence that Scripture condemned it. The calendar was reformed and books were printed in modern Russian type. Peter's importation of Western art and the imitation of Western architecture complemented this policy of enforced cultural change.

Westernization also involved military and political reforms that changed the character of the Russian state. During the first 25 years of his reign Peter had found himself unable to achieve sustained military success against his two great enemies, the Ottoman Turks to the south and the Swedes to the west. During the Great Northern War with Sweden (1700–1721), Peter introduced

a number of military reforms that eventually turned the tide against his enemy. Having learned about naval technology from the British and Dutch, he built a large navy. He introduced a policy of conscription, giving him a standing army of more than 200,000 men. A central council, established in 1711, not only directed financial administration but also levied and supplied troops.

This new military state also acquired many of the centralizing and absolutist features of western European monarchies. Efforts to introduce absolutism in Russia had begun during the reigns of Alexis (r. 1645–1676) and Fedor (r. 1676–1682), who had strengthened the central administration and brutally suppressed peasant rebellions. Peter built upon his predecessors' achievement. He created a new structure for managing the empire, appointing twelve governors to superintend Russia's 43 separate provinces. He brought the Church under state control. By establishing a finely graded hierarchy of official ranks in the armed forces, the civil administration, and the court, Peter not only improved administrative efficiency, but he also made it possible for men of nonaristocratic birth to attain the same privileged status as the old landowning nobility. He won the support of all landowners by introducing **primogeniture** (inheritance of the entire estate by the eldest son), which prevented the subdivision of their estates, and supporting the enserfment of the peasants. In dealing with his subjects Peter claimed more power than any other absolute monarch in Europe. Muscovites often told foreign visitors that the tsar treated them like slaves, punishing them at will and executing them without due process.[2] During the trial of his own son, Alexis, for treason in 1718, Peter told the clergy that "we have a sufficient and absolute power to judge our son for his crimes according to our own pleasure."[3]

The most visible sign of Peter's policy of westernization was the construction of the port city of St. Petersburg on the Gulf of Finland, which became the new capital of the Russian Empire. One of the main objectives of Russian foreign policy during Peter's reign was to secure access to the Baltic Sea, allowing Russia to open

ENCOUNTERS AND TRANSFORMATIONS

St. Petersburg and the West

The building of a new capital city, St. Petersburg, symbolized the encounter between Russia and the West during the reign of Peter the Great. Peter had seized the land on which the city was located, the marshy delta of the Neva River, from Sweden during the Northern War. The construction of the city, which first served as a fortress and then a naval base, occurred at a tremendous cost in treasure and human life. Using the royal powers he had significantly augmented earlier in his reign, Peter ordered more than 10,000 workers (and possibly twice that number) from throughout his kingdom to realize this ambitious and risky project. The harsh weather conditions, the ravages of malaria and other diseases, and the chronic shortages of provisions in a distant location resulted in the death of thousands of workers. Beginning in 1710 Peter ordered the transfer of central governmental, commercial, and military functions to the new city. The city became the site for Peter's Winter Palace, the residences of Russia's foreign ambassadors, and the headquarters of the Russian Orthodox Church. The Academy of Fine Arts and the Academy of Sciences were built shortly thereafter. During the 1730s Russia's first bourse, or exchange, fulfilled the prophecy of a British observer in 1710 that the city, with its network of canals, "might one day prove a second Amsterdam or Venice." Thus, St. Petersburg came to embody all the modernizing and westernizing achievements of Peter the Great.

The location of the new city and its architecture reflected Russia's encounter with the West. With access to the Baltic Sea, the new city, often described as "a window on the West," looked toward the European ports with which Russia increased its commerce and the European powers that Russia engaged in battle and diplomacy. The architects, stonemasons, and interior decorators that Peter commissioned came from France, Italy, Germany, and the Dutch Republic, and they constructed the buildings in contemporary European styles. The general plan of the city, drawn up by a French architect, featured straight, paved streets with stone paths that are now called sidewalks. St. Petersburg thus became a port through which Western influences entered Russia. The contrast with the old capital, Moscow, which was situated in the center of the country and embodied the spirit of the old Russia that Peter strove to modernize, could not have been clearer.

The construction of St. Petersburg played a central role in transforming Russia from a medieval kingdom on the fringes of Europe into a modern, Western power. It did not, however, eliminate the conflict in Russia between those who held the West up as the cultural standard that Russia should emulate and those who celebrated Russia's cultural superiority over the West. This conflict, which began in the eighteenth century, has continued to the present day. During the period of communism in the twentieth century, when St. Petersburg was renamed Leningrad and Moscow once again became the political capital of the country, the tradition that emphasized Russia's Eastern orientation tended to prevail. It was no coincidence that the collapse of communism and the disintegration of the Union of Soviet Socialist Republics in 1989 led to a renewed emphasis on Russia's ties with the West. The restoration of St. Petersburg's original name in 1991 and the celebration of its 300th anniversary in 2003 were further attempts to integrate Russia more fully into the West.

For Discussion

1. How did the founding of St. Petersburg contribute to the growth of the Russian state?

2. How did Peter the Great's absolute power facilitate the growth of the city?

PICTURE OF ST. PETERSBURG (1815)
This view of St. Petersburg from the quay in front of the Winter Palace reveals the city's Western character. The buildings lying across the Neva River, including the bourse, were designed by European architects. The gondolas, seen in the foreground docking at the quay, enhanced St. Petersburg's reputation as "Venice of the North."

Taking It Further

Russell Bova (ed.), *Russia and Western Civilization: Cultural and Historical Encounters.* (2003).

Lindsey Hughes, *Russia in the Age of Peter the Great.* (1998).

maritime trade with Europe and become a Western naval power. By draining a swamp on the estuary of the Neva River, Peter laid the foundations of a city that became the new capital of his empire. Construction began in 1703, and within 20 years St. Petersburg had a population of 40,000 people. With his new capital city now looking westward, and an army and central administration reformed on the basis of Prussian and French example, Peter could enter the world of European diplomacy and warfare as both a Western and an absolute monarch. (See *Encounters and Transformations* in this chapter.)

RESISTANCE TO ABSOLUTISM IN ENGLAND AND THE DUTCH REPUBLIC

■ Why did absolutism fail to take root in England and the Dutch Republic during the seventeenth century?

Royal absolutism did not succeed in all European states. In Poland-Lithuania and Hungary, for example, where the nobility exercised considerable political power, legislative assemblies continued to meet throughout the seventeenth and eighteenth centuries. Both countries had long traditions of constitutional government, and the Poles elected their kings. In western Europe the kingdom of England and the northern provinces of the Netherlands also resisted efforts to implement royal absolutism. In England this resistance to absolutism resulted in the temporary destruction of the monarchy in the middle of the seventeenth century and the permanent limitation of royal power after 1688. In the northern Netherlands, an even more resounding rejection of absolutism occurred. After winning their independence from absolutist Spain, the Dutch established a republic with a decentralized form of government that lasted the entire seventeenth and eighteenth centuries.

The English Monarchy

At different times in the seventeenth century English monarchs tried to introduce royal absolutism, but the political traditions of the country stood as major obstacles to their designs. The most important of these traditions was that the king could not make law or tax his subjects without the consent of Parliament, which consisted of the House of Lords (the nobility and the bishops) and the House of Commons, an elected assembly that included the lesser aristocracy, lawyers, and townsmen.

In the early seventeenth century some members of the House of Commons feared that this tradition of parliamentary government might come to an end. The first Stuart king, James I (r. 1603–1625), aroused some of these fears as early as 1604 when he called his first parliament. James thought of himself as an absolute monarch, and in a number of speeches and published works he emphasized the height of his independent royal power, which was known in England as the **prerogative.** James's son, Charles I (r. 1625–1649), gave substance to these fears of absolutism by forcing his subjects to lend money to the government during a war with Spain (1625–1629), imprisoning men who refused to make these loans, and collecting duties on exports without parliamentary approval. When

members of the House of Commons protested against these policies, Charles dismissed Parliament in 1629 and decided to rule without summoning it again.

This period of nonparliamentary government, known as the **personal rule,** lasted until 1640. During these years Charles, unable to collect taxes by the authority of Parliament, used his prerogative to bring in new revenues, especially by asking all subjects to pay "ship-money" to support the outfitting of ships to defend the country against attack. During the personal rule the king's religious policy fell under the control of William Laud, who was named archbishop of Canterbury in 1633. Laud's determination to restore many of the rituals associated with Roman Catholicism alienated large numbers of the more zealous Protestants, known as Puritans, and led to a growing perception that members of the king's government were engaged in a conspiracy to destroy both England's ancient constitution and the Protestant religion.

The personal rule might have continued indefinitely if Charles had not once again faced the financial demands of war. In 1636 the king tried to introduce a new religious liturgy in his northern kingdom of Scotland. The liturgy included a number of rituals that the firmly Calvinist Scottish population considered Roman Catholic. The new liturgy so angered a group of women in Edinburgh that they threw their chairs at the bishop when he introduced it. In response to this affront to their religion, the infuriated Scots signed a National Covenant (1638) pledging to defend the integrity of their Church, abolished episcopacy (government of the church by bishops) in favor of a Presbyterian system of church government, and mobilized a large army. To secure the funds to fight the Scots, Charles was forced to summon his English Parliament, thereby ending the period of personal rule.

The English Civil Wars and Revolution

Tensions between the reconvened English Parliament and Charles led to the first revolution of modern times. The Long Parliament, which met in November 1640, impeached many of the king's ministers and judges and dismantled the judicial apparatus of the eleven years of personal rule, including the courts that had been active in the prosecution of Puritans. Parliament declared the king's nonparliamentary taxes illegal and enacted a law limiting the time between the meetings of Parliament to three years.

This legislation did not satisfy the king's critics in Parliament. Their suspicion that the king was conspiring against them and their demand to approve all royal appointments created a poisoned political atmosphere in which neither side trusted the other. In August 1642 civil war began between the Parliamentarians, known as Roundheads because many of the artisans who supported them had close-cropped hair styles, and the Royalists or Cavaliers, who often wore their hair in long flowing locks. Parliament, with the military support of the Scots and a well-trained, efficient fighting force, the New Model Army, won this war in 1646 and took Charles prisoner. The king's subsequent negotiations with the Scots and the English Presbyterians, who had originally fought against him, led to a second civil war in 1648. In this war, which lasted only a few months, the New Model Army once again defeated Royalist forces.

This defeat of the king's forces led to a revolution. Following the wishes of the army, Parliament set up a court that tried and executed the king in January 1649. (See *Justice in History* in this chapter.) Shortly thereafter the House of Commons abolished the monarchy itself, thus making England a republic. This revolutionary change in the form of English government, however, did not lead to the establishment of a democratic regime. Democracy, in which a large percentage of the adult male population could vote, was the goal of the Levellers, a political party that originated in the New Model Army and attracted considerable support in London. The Levellers called for annual parliaments, the separation of powers between the executive and legislative branches of government, and the introduction of universal suffrage for men. The army officers, however, resisted these demands, and after an unsuccessful mutiny in the army, the Leveller party collapsed. The defeat of the Levellers guaranteed that political power in the new English republic would remain in the hands of men who occupied the upper levels of English society, especially those who owned property in land.

The republican government established in 1649 did not last. Tensions between the army and Parliament, fueled by the belief that the

CHRONOLOGY: A CENTURY OF REVOLUTION IN ENGLAND AND SCOTLAND

1603	James VI of Scotland (r. 1567–1625) becomes James I of England (r. 1603–1625)
1625	Death of James I and accession of Charles I (r. 1625–1649)
1629–1640	Personal rule of Charles I
1640	Opening of the Long Parliament
1642–1646	Civil War in England, ending with the capture of King Charles I
1648	Second Civil War
1649	Execution of Charles I of England and the beginning of the Republic
1653	End of the Long Parliament; Oliver Cromwell becomes Protector of England, Scotland, and Ireland
1660	Restoration of the monarchy in the person of Charles II
1685	Death of Charles II and accession of his brother, James II (r. 1685–1688)
1688–1689	Glorious Revolution in England and Scotland
1707	England and Scotland politically joined to form the United Kingdom of Great Britain

JUSTICE IN HISTORY

The Trial of Charles I

In January 1649, after the New Model Army had defeated Royalist forces in England's second civil war and purged Parliament of its Presbyterian members, the few remaining members of the House of Commons voted by a narrow margin to erect a High Court of Justice to try King Charles I. This trial, which resulted in Charles's execution, marked the only time in European history that a monarch was tried and executed while still holding the office of king.

The decision to try the king formed part of a deliberate political strategy. The men who arranged the proceeding knew that they were embarking upon a revolutionary course by declaring that the House of Commons, as the elected representative of the people, was the highest power in the realm. They also knew that the republican regime they were establishing did not command a large body of popular support. By trying the king publicly in a court of law and by ensuring that the trial was reported in daily newspapers (the first such trial in history), they hoped to prove the legitimacy of their cause and win support for the new regime.

The decision to bring the king to justice created two legal problems. The first was to identify a crime upon which the trial would be based. For many years members of Parliament had insisted that the king had violated the ancient laws of the kingdom. The charge read that he had "wickedly designed to erect an unlimited and tyrannical power" and had waged war against his people in two civil wars. His prosecutors claimed that those activities amounted to the crime of treason. The problem was that treason in England was a crime a subject committed against the king, not the king against his subjects. In order to try the king for this crime, his accusers had to construct a new theory of treason, according to which he had attacked his own political body, which they identified with the kingdom or the state.

The second problem was to make the court itself a legitimate tribunal. According to English constitutional law, the king possessed the highest legal authority in the land. He appointed his judges, and the courts represented his authority. Parliament could vote to erect a special court, but the bill authorizing it would become law only if the king agreed to it. In this case the House of Commons had set up the court by its own authority, and it had named 135 men, most of whom were army officers, to serve as its judges. The revolutionary nature of this tribunal was difficult to disguise, and Charles made its illegality the basis of his defense. When asked how he would plead, he refused, demanding to be told by what authority he had been brought into court.

The arguments presented by King Charles and John Bradshawe, the president of the court, regarding the legitimacy of the court reflected the main constitutional conflict in seventeenth-century England. On the one hand was the doctrine of divine-right absolutism, according to which the king received his authority from God. He was therefore responsible to God alone, not the people. His subjects could neither try him in a court of law nor fight him on the battlefield. "A king," said Charles, "cannot be tried by any superior jurisdiction on earth." On the other hand was the doctrine of popular sovereignty, which held that political power came from the people. As Bradshawe said in response to Charles's objection, "Sir, as the law is your superior, so truly Sir, there is something that is superior to the law, and that is indeed the parent or author of law, and that is the people of England." This trial, therefore, involved not only a confrontation between Charles and his revolutionary judges but an encounter between two incompatible political ideologies.

In 1649 the advocates of popular sovereignty triumphed over those of divine right. Charles was convicted as a "tyrant, traitor, murderer, and public enemy of the good people of this nation." The verdict was never in doubt, although only 67 of

TRIAL OF CHARLES I AT WESTMINSTER HALL, JANUARY 1649

The king is sitting in the prisoner's box in the foreground, facing the commissioners of the High Court of Justice. His refusal to plead meant that a full trial could not take place.

the 135 men originally appointed as judges voted to convict the king, and a mere 59 signed the death warrant. The trial succeeded only to the extent that it facilitated the establishment of the new regime. With Charles gone, the revolutionaries move ahead with the abolition of the monarchy and the establishment of a republic. But in dramatic terms the trial was a complete failure. Charles, a small shy man with a nervous stammer, was expected to make a poor impression, but he spoke eloquently when he refused to plead, and he won support from spectators in the gallery. In the greatest show trial of the seventeenth century, the royal defendant stole the show.

When Charles's son, Charles II, was restored to the throne in 1660, Royalists finally had their revenge against the judges of this court. Those who could be found alive were hanged, disemboweled, and quartered. For those who were already dead, there was to be another type of justice. In 1661 Royalists exhumed the badly decomposed corpses of Bradshawe, Henry Ireton, and Oliver Cromwell, the three men who bore the largest responsibility for the execution of the king. The three cadavers were hanged and their skulls were placed on pikes on top of Westminster Hall. This macabre ritual served as the Royalists' way of vilifying the memory of the judges of this illegal and revolutionary trial, and their unpardonable sin of executing an anointed king.

For Discussion

1. The men who brought King Charles to trial often spoke about bringing him to "justice." How is justice best understood in this context?

2. How does this trial reveal the limitations of divine-right absolutism in England?

Taking It Further

Peacey, Jason (ed). *The Regicides and the Execution of Charles I.* 2001. A collection of essays on various aspects of this episode and the men who signed the death warrant.

Wedgewood, C. V. *The Trial of Charles I.* 1964. Presents a full account and analysis of the trial.

---

government was not creating a godly society, resulted in the army's dissolution of the Long Parliament in 1653 and the selection of a small legislative assembly consisting of zealous Puritans who were nominated by the army. When this "Parliament of the Saints" broke down later that year, Oliver Cromwell (1599–1658), the commander in chief of the army and the most prominent member of the republican government after 1649, assumed the title of Lord Protector. The protectorate, in which Cromwell shared legislative power with Parliament, represented an effort to return to a more traditional form of government. Cromwell however, relied primarily on the army to maintain power, thereby alienating many of the members of the landed class. After Cromwell's death in 1658, renewed tension between the army and Parliament led to a period of political chaos. In 1660 the army and Parliament decided to restore the monarchy by inviting Charles, the son of Charles I, to return from exile. When he returned, not only the monarchy but also the House of Lords and the Church of England were restored. The revolution had officially come to an end.

Later Stuart Absolutism and the Glorious Revolution

Charles II (r. 1660–1685) and his brother James II (r. 1685–1688) were both absolutists who admired the political achievement of their cousin, Louis XIV of France. They realized, however that they could never return to the policies of their father, much less adopt those of Louis. Neither of them attempted to rule indefinitely without Parliament, as Charles I had. Instead they sought to destroy the independence of Parliament by packing it with their own supporters and using the prerogative to weaken the force of the parliamentary statutes to which they objected.

The main political crisis of Charles II's reign was the attempt by a group of members of Parliament, headed by the Earl of Shaftesbury (1621–1683) and known by their opponents as Whigs, to exclude the king's brother, James, from the throne on the grounds that he was a Catholic. Charles opposed this strategy because it violated the theory of hereditary divine right, according to which God sanctioned the right of the king's closest heir to succeed him. Those members of Parliament who supported Charles on this issue, called Tories, thwarted the designs of the Whigs in three successive parliaments between 1679 and 1681.

An even more serious political crisis occurred after James II succeeded to the throne in 1685. James began to exempt his fellow Catholics from the penal laws, which prevented them from worshiping freely, and from the Test Act of 1673, which denied them the right to hold political office. James began appointing Catholics to positions in the army, the central administration, and local government. These efforts to grant toleration and political power to Catholics revived the traditional English fears of absolutism and "popery." Not only the Whigs but also the predominantly Anglican Tories became alarmed at the king's policies. The birth of a Catholic son to James by his second wife, the Italian princess Mary of Modena, in June 1688 created the fear that the king's religious policy might continue indefinitely. A group of seven Whigs and Tories, including the Bishop of London, invited William III of Orange, the captain-general of the military forces of the Dutch Republic and James's nephew, to come to England to defend their Protestant religion and their constitution. William was married to James's eldest daughter, the Protestant Princess Mary, and as the king's nephew he also had a claim to the throne himself.

Invading with an international force of 12,000 men, William gathered substantial support from the English population. When James's army defected, the king was forced to flee to France without engaging William's forces in battle. The Convention, a special parliament convened by William in 1689, offered the crown to William and Mary while at the same time securing their assent to the Declaration of Rights, a document that later became the parliamentary statute known as the Bill of Rights. This bill, which the English consider the cornerstone of their constitution, corrected many of the abuses of royal power at the hands of James and

Charles, especially the practice of exempting individuals from the penalties of the laws made by Parliament. By proclaiming William king and by excluding Catholics from the throne, the Bill of Rights also destroyed the theory of hereditary divine right.

The events of 1688–1689 were decisive in defeating once and for all the absolutist designs of the Stuart kings and in guaranteeing that Parliament would form a permanent and regular place in English government. The Glorious Revolution also prompted the publication of a political manifesto, John Locke's *Two Treatises of Government* (1690). Locke, a radical Whig, had written the *Treatises* in the early 1680s as a protest against the absolutist policies of Charles II, but only after the abdication and flight of James II could he safely publish his manuscript. Like Hobbes, Locke argued that people left the state of nature and agreed to form a political society mainly to protect their property Unlike Hobbes, however, Locke asserted that the people never relinquished their sovereignty and could replace a government that had violated the trust placed in it. Locke's treatises constituted an uncompromising attack on the system of royal absolutism, which he equated with slavery.

We have seen that the success of absolutism in continental European countries led to the expansion of state power. Paradoxically, the defeat of absolutism in England fostered the growth of the English state. As long as Parliament had remained suspicious of the Stuart kings, it had been reluctant to facilitate the growth of the state, which until 1688 was under direct royal control. Once the Glorious Revolution permanently restricted king's power, and Parliament emerged as the highest power within the country, Members of Parliament (MPs) had less to fear from the executive branch of government. The inauguration of a long period of warfare against France in 1689 required the development of a large army and navy, the expansion of the bureaucracy, government borrowing on an unprecedented scale, and an increase in taxes. By

1720 the kingdom of Great Britain, which had been created by the parliamentary union of England and Scotland in 1707, could rival the French state in military power, wealth, and diplomatic prestige.

The Dutch Republic

In many respects the United Provinces of the Netherlands, known as the Dutch Republic, forms the most striking exception to the pattern of state building in seventeenth-century Europe. Formally established in 1588 during its revolt against Spanish rule, the Dutch Republic was the only major European power to maintain a republican form of government throughout the seventeenth century. As a state it also failed to conform to the pattern of centralization and consolidation that became evident in virtually all European monarchies. Having successfully resisted the centralizing policies of a large multinational Spanish monarchy, the Dutch Republic never acquired much of a centralized bureaucracy of its own. The provinces formed little more than a loose confederation of sovereign republican states. Each of the provinces sent deputies to the States General, where unanimity was required on all important issues, such as the levying of taxes, the declaration of war, and the ratification of treaties.

Political power in the Dutch Republic lay mainly with the wealthy merchants and bankers who served as regents in the councils of the towns. The members of this bourgeois elite did not tend to seek admission to landed society in the way that successful English merchants often did. Nor were they lured into becoming part of an ostentatious court in the manner of the French nobility. Immersed in the world of commerce, they remained part of mercantile society and used their political power to guarantee that the Dutch state would serve the interests of trade.

The political prominence of Dutch merchants reflected the commercial character of the Dutch economy. Shortly after its truce with Spain in 1609, the Dutch cities, especially the port city of Amsterdam in Holland, began to dominate European and world trade. The Dutch served as middlemen and shippers for all the other powers of Europe, transporting grain from the Baltic, textiles from England, timber from Scandinavia, wine from Germany, sugar from Brazil and Ceylon, silk from Persia and China, and porcelain from Japan to markets throughout the world. The Dutch even served as middlemen for their archenemy Spain, providing food and manufactured goods to the Spanish colonies in the New World in exchange for silver from the mines of Peru and Mexico. As part of this process Dutch trading companies, such as the Dutch East India Company, began to establish permanent outposts in India, Indonesia, North America, the Caribbean, South America, and South Africa. Thus, a relatively small country with one-tenth the population of France became a colonial power.

To support their dynamic mercantile economy, Dutch cities developed financial institutions and techniques favorable to trade. An Exchange Bank in Amsterdam, which had a monopoly on the exchange of foreign currencies, eased international transactions. A stock market, also situated in Amsterdam, facilitated the buying and selling of shares in commercial ventures. Dutch merchants developed rational and efficient methods of bookkeeping. Even lawyers contributed to the success of Dutch commerce. In *The Freedom of the Sea* (1609), the great legal and political philosopher Hugo Grotius (1583–1645) defended the freedom of merchants to use the open seas for trade and fishing, thereby challenging the claims of European monarchs who wished to exclude foreigners from the waters surrounding their countries. Grotius, who also wrote *The Law of War and Peace* (1625), gained a reputation as the founder of modern international law.

One of the most striking contrasts between the Dutch Republic and the kingdom of France

THE AMSTERDAM STOCK EXCHANGE IN 1668
Known as the Bourse, this multipurpose building served as a gathering point for merchants trading in different parts of the world. The main activity was the buying and selling of shares of stock in trading companies during trading sessions that lasted for two hours each day.

in the seventeenth century lay in the area of religious policy. Whereas in France the revocation of the Edict of Nantes represented the culmination of a policy enforcing religious uniformity and the suppression of Protestant dissent, the predominantly Calvinist Dutch Republic gained a reputation for religious toleration. The Dutch Reformed Church did not always deserve this reputation, but secular authorities, especially in the cities, proved remarkably tolerant of different religious groups. Amsterdam, which attracted a diverse immigrant population during its period of rapid growth, contained a large community of Jews, including the philosopher Baruch Spinoza (1632–1677). The country became the center for religious exiles and political dissidents,

accommodating French Huguenots who fled their country after the repeal of the Edict of Nantes in 1685 as well as English Whigs (including the Earl of Shaftesbury and John Locke) who were being pursued by the Tory government in the 1680s.

This tolerant bourgeois republic also made a distinct contribution to European culture during the seventeenth century, known as its Golden Age. The Dutch cultural achievement was greatest in the area of the visual arts, where Rembrandt van Rijn (1606–1669), Franz Hals (ca. 1580–1666), and Jan Steen (1626–1679) belonged to an astonishing concentration of artistic genius in the cities of Amsterdam, Haarlem, and Leiden. Dutch painting reflected the

REMBRANDT, *SYNDICS OF THE CLOTHMAKERS OF AMSTERDAM* (1662)
Rembrandt's realistic portrait depicted wealthy Dutch bourgeoisie, who had great political as well as economic power in the Dutch Republic.

religious, social, and political climate of this era. The Protestant Reformation had ended the tradition of devotional religious painting that had flourished during the Middle Ages, and the absence of a baroque court culture reduced the demand for royal and aristocratic portraiture and for paintings of heroic classical, mythological, and historical scenes. Instead the Dutch artists of the Golden Age produced intensely realistic portraits of merchants and financiers, such as Rembrandt's famous *Syndics of the Clothmakers of Amsterdam* (1662). Realism became one of the defining features of Dutch painting, evident in the numerous street scenes, still lifes, and landscapes that Dutch artists painted and sold to a largely bourgeois clientele.

In the early eighteenth century the Dutch Republic lost its position of economic superiority to Great Britain and France, which developed even larger mercantile empires of their own and began to dominate world commerce. The long period of war against France, which ended in 1713, took its toll on Dutch manpower and wealth, and the relatively small size of the country and its decentralized institutions made it more difficult for it to recover its position in European diplomacy and warfare. As a state it could no longer fight above its weight, and it became vulnerable to attacks by the French in the nineteenth century and the Germans in the twentieth. But in the seventeenth century this highly urbanized and commercial country showed that a small, decentralized republic could hold its own with the absolutist states of France and Spain as well as with the parliamentary monarchy of England.

CONCLUSION

The Western State in the Age of Absolutism

Between 1600 and 1715 three fundamental political changes helped redefine the West. The first was the dramatic and unprecedented growth of the state. During these years all Western states grew in size and strength. They became more cohesive as they brought the outlying provinces of kingdoms more firmly under central governmental control. The administrative machinery of the state became more complex and efficient. The armies of the state could be called upon at any time to take action against internal rebels and foreign enemies. The income of the state increased as royal officials collected higher taxes, and governments became involved in the promotion of trade and industry and in the regulation of the economy. By the beginning of the eighteenth century one of the most distinctive features of Western civilization was the prevalence of these large, powerful, bureaucratic states. There was nothing like them in the non-Western world.

The second change was the introduction of absolutism into these Western states. With the notable exception of Poland and Hungary, rulers aspired to complete and unrivaled power. These efforts achieved varying degrees of success, and in two states, England and the Dutch Republic, they ended in failure. Nevertheless, during the seventeenth and eighteenth centuries the absolutist state became the main form of government in the West. For this reason historians refer to the period of Western history beginning in the seventeenth century as the age of absolutism.

The third change was the conduct of a new style of warfare by Western absolutist states. The West became the arena where large armies, funded, equipped, and trained by the state, engaged in long, costly, and bloody military campaigns. The conduct of war on this scale threatened to drain the state of its financial resources, destroy its economy, and decimate its civilian and military population. Western powers were not unaware of the dangers of this type of warfare. The development of international law and the attempt to achieve a balance of power among European powers represented efforts to place restrictions on seventeenth-century warfare. These efforts, however, were not completely successful, and in the eighteenth and nineteenth centuries warfare in the West entered a new and even more dangerous phase, aided by the technological innovations that the Scientific and Industrial Revolutions made possible. To the first of those great transformations, the revolution in science, we now turn.

KEY TERMS

absolutism	baroque
divine right	balance of power
Estates General	mercantilism
Cortes	Junkers
diets	balance of power
standing armies	primogeniture
regency	prerogative
parlements	personal rule
intendants	

CHAPTER QUESTIONS

1. What did absolutism mean, both as a political theory and as a practical program, and how was absolutism related to the growth of the power of the state? (page 493)
2. How did France and Spain implement absolutism in the seventeenth century and how powerful did those states become? (page 495)
3. What was the nature of royal absolutism in central and eastern Europe, and how did the policies of the Ottoman Empire and Russia help to establish the boundaries of the West during this period? (page 506)

4. Why did absolutism fail to take root in England and the Dutch Republic during the seventeenth century? (page 516)

TAKING IT FURTHER

1. Absolutist rulers sought unrivalled power, but they frequently encountered resistance. Why were they often unable to achieve the power they desired?
2. The Thirty years' War was a major turning point in German and European history. What impact did it have on the development of absolutist theory and the development of modern states?
3. Many American notions of liberty originated in seventeenth-century England. How did developments in the two English Revolutions of the seventeenth century contribute to the ideology of religious liberty?
4. How would you define the political and cultural boundaries of the West by the beginning of the eighteenth century.

✓•─ **Practice** on **MyHistoryLab**

17

The Scientific Revolution

- The Discoveries and Achievements of the Scientific Revolution
- The Search for Scientific Knowledge ■ The Causes of the Scientific Revolution
- The Intellectual Consequences of the Scientific Revolution
- Humans and the Natural World

IN 1609 GALILEO GALILEI, AN ITALIAN MATHEMATICIAN AT THE UNIVERSITY OF Padua, directed a new scientific instrument, the telescope, toward the heavens. Having heard that a Dutch artisan had put together two lenses in a way that magnified distant objects, Galileo built his own such device. Anyone who has looked through a telescope can appreciate his excitement. Objects that appeared one way to the naked eye looked entirely different when magnified by his new "spyglass," as he called it. The surface of the moon, long believed to be smooth, uniform, and perfectly spherical, now appeared full of mountains and craters. Galileo's spyglass showed that the sun, too, was imperfect, marred by spots that appeared to move across its surface. Such sights challenged traditional science, which assumed that "the heavens," the throne of God, were perfect and thus never changed. Traditional science was shaken even further, when Galileo showed that Venus, viewed over many months, appeared to change its shape, much as the moon did in its phases. This discovery provided evidence for the relatively new theory that the planets, including Earth, revolved around the sun rather than the sun and the planets around the Earth.

Galileo shared the discoveries he made not only with fellow scientists, but also with other educated members of society. He also staged a number of public demonstrations of his new astronomical instrument, the first of which took place on top of one of the city gates of Rome in 1611. To convince those who doubted the reality of the images they saw, Galileo turned the telescope toward familiar landmarks in the city. Interest in the new scientific instrument ran so high that a number of amateur astronomers acquired telescopes of their own.

Galileo's discoveries were part of what historians call the Scientific Revolution. This development changed the way Europeans viewed the natural world, the supernatural realm, and themselves. It led to controversies in religion, philosophy, and politics and changes in military technology, navigation, and business. It also set the West apart from the civilizations of the Middle East, Asia, and Africa and provided a basis for claims of Western superiority over the people in those lands.

The scientific culture that emerged in the West by the end of the seventeenth century was the product of a series of cultural encounters. It resulted from a complex interaction among scholars proposing different ideas of how nature operated. Some of these ideas originated in Greek philosophy. Others came from Christian sources. Still other ideas came from a tradition of late medieval science that had been influenced by the scholarship of the Islamic Middle East.

The main question this chapter seeks to answer is this: How did European scientists in the sixteenth and seventeenth centuries change the way in which people in the West viewed the natural world?

THE TELESCOPE

The telescope was the most important of the new scientific instruments that facilitated discovery. This engraving depicts an astronomer using the telescope in 1647.

THE DISCOVERIES AND ACHIEVEMENTS OF THE SCIENTIFIC REVOLUTION

■ What were the achievements and discoveries of the Scientific Revolution?

Unlike political revolutions, such as the English Revolution of the 1640s discussed in the last chapter, the Scientific Revolution developed gradually over a long period of time. It began in the mid-sixteenth century and continued into the eighteenth century. Even though it took a relatively long time to unfold, it was revolutionary in the sense that it transformed human thought, just as political revolutions have fundamentally changed systems of government. The most important changes in seventeenth-century science took place in astronomy, physics, chemistry, and biology.

Astronomy: A New Model of the Universe

The most significant change in astronomy was the acceptance of the view that the sun, not the Earth, was the center of the universe. Until the mid-sixteenth century, most natural philosophers—as scientists were known at the time—accepted the views of the ancient Greek astronomer Claudius Ptolemy (100–170 C.E.). Ptolemy's observations and calculations supported the cosmology of the Greek philosopher Aristotle (384–322 B.C.E.). According to Ptolemy and Aristotle, the center of the universe was a stationary Earth, around which the moon, the sun, and the other planets revolved in circular orbits. Beyond the planets a large sphere carried the stars, which stood in a fixed relationship to each other, around the Earth from east to west once every 24 hours, thus accounting for the rising and setting of the stars. Each of the four known elements—earth, water, air, and fire—had a natural place within this universe, with the heavy elements, earth and water, being pulled down toward the center of the Earth and the light ones, air and fire, hovering above it. All heavenly

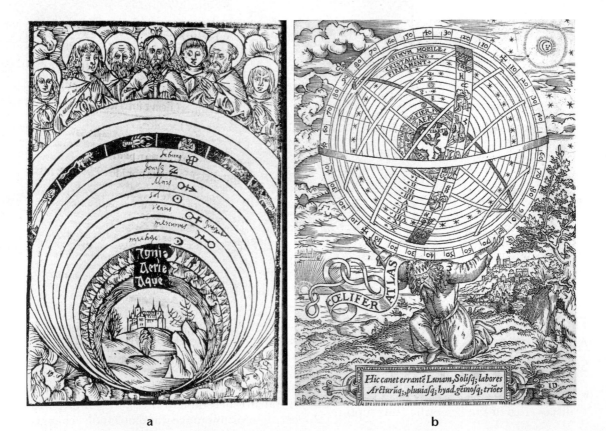

a   b

TWO VIEWS OF THE PTOLEMAIC OR PRE-COPERNICAN UNIVERSE

(a) In this sixteenth-century engraving the Earth lies at the center of the universe and the elements of water, air, and fire are arranged in ascending order above the Earth. The orbit that is shaded in black is the firmament or stellar sphere. The presence of Christ and the saints at the top reflects the view that Heaven lay beyond the stellar sphere. (b) A medieval king representing Atlas holds a Ptolemaic cosmos. The Ptolemaic universe is often referred to as a two-sphere universe: The inner sphere of the Earth lies at the center and the outer sphere encompassing the entire universe rotates around the Earth.

bodies, including the sun and the planets, were composed of a fifth element, called ether, which unlike matter on Earth was thought to be eternal and could not be altered, corrupted, or destroyed.

This traditional view of the cosmos had much to recommend it, and some educated people continued to accept it well into the eighteenth century. The Bible, which in a few passages referred to the motion of the sun, reinforced the authority of Aristotle. And human observation seemed to confirm the motion of the sun. We do, after all, see the sun "rise" and "set" every day, so the idea that the Earth rotates at high speed and revolves around the sun contradicts the experience of our senses. Nevertheless, the Earth-centered model of the universe failed to explain many patterns that astronomers observed in the sky, most notably the paths followed by planets. Whenever ancient or medieval astronomers confronted a new problem as a result of their observations, they tried to accommodate the results to the Ptolemaic model. By the sixteenth century this model had been

modified or adjusted so many times that it had gradually become a confused collection of planets and stars following different motions.

Faced with this situation, a Polish cleric, Nicolaus Copernicus (1473–1543), looked for a simpler and more plausible model of the universe. In *The Revolutions of the Heavenly Spheres*, which was published shortly after his death, Copernicus proposed that the center of the universe was not the Earth but the sun. The book was widely circulated, but it did not win much support for the sun-centered theory of the universe. Only the most learned astronomers could understand Copernicus' mathematical arguments, and even they were not prepared to adopt his central thesis. In the late sixteenth century the great Danish astronomer Tycho Brahe (1546–1601) accepted the argument of Copernicus that the planets revolved around the sun but still insisted that the sun revolved around the Earth.

Significant support for the Copernican model of the universe among scientists began to

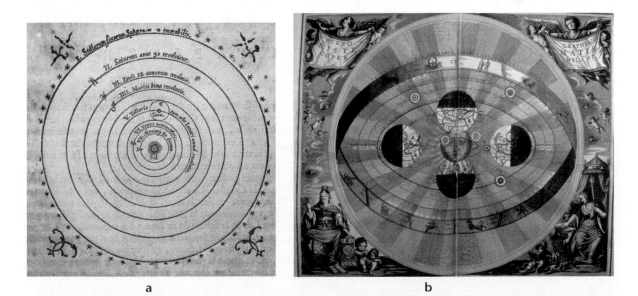

a

b

TWO EARLY MODERN VIEWS OF THE SUN-CENTERED UNIVERSE

(a) The depiction by Copernicus. Note that all the orbits are circular, rather than elliptical, as Kepler was to show they were. The outermost sphere is that of the fixed stars. (b) A late-seventeenth-century depiction of the cosmos by Andreas Cellarius in which the planets follow elliptical orbits. It illustrates four different positions of the Earth as it orbits the sun.

materialize only in the seventeenth century. In 1609 a German astronomer, Johannes Kepler (1571–1630), using data that Brahe had collected, confirmed the central position of the sun in the universe. In *New Astronomy* (1609) Kepler also demonstrated that the planets, including the Earth, followed elliptical rather than circular orbits and that physical laws governed their movements. Not many people read Kepler's book, however, and his achievement was not fully appreciated until many decades later.

Galileo Galilei (1564–1642) was far more successful in gaining support for the sun-centered model of the universe. Galileo had the literary skill, which Kepler lacked, of being able to write for a broad audience. Using the evidence gained from his observations with the telescope, and presenting his views in the form of a dialogue between the advocates of the two competing worldviews, Galileo demonstrated the plausibility and superiority of Copernicus's theory.

The publication of Galileo's *Dialogue Concerning the Two Chief World Systems—Ptolemaic and Copernican* in 1632 won many converts to the sun-centered theory of the universe, but it lost him the support of Pope Urban VIII, who had been one of his patrons. The character in *Dialogue* who defends the Ptolemaic system is named Simplicio (that is, a simple—or stupid—person). Urban wrongly concluded that Galileo was mocking him. In 1633 Galileo was tried before the Roman Inquisition, an ecclesiastical court whose purpose was to maintain theological orthodoxy. The charge against him was that he had challenged the authority of Scripture and was therefore guilty of heresy, the denial of the theological truths of the Roman Catholic Church. (See *Justice in History* in this chapter.)

As a result of this trial, Galileo was forced to abandon his support for the Copernican model of the universe, and *Dialogue* was placed on the Index of Prohibited Books, a list compiled by the papacy of all printed works containing heretical ideas. Despite this setback, by 1700 Copernicanism commanded widespread support among scientists and the educated public. *Dialogue,* however, was not removed from the Index until 1822.

Physics: The Laws of Motion and Gravitation

Galileo made his most significant contributions to the Scientific Revolution in physics. In the seventeenth century the main branches of physics were mechanics (the study of motion and its causes) and optics (the study of light). Galileo formulated a set of laws governing the motion of material objects that challenged the accepted theories of Aristotle regarding motion and laid the foundation of modern physics.

According to Aristotle, whose views dominated science in the late Middle Ages, the motion of every object—except the natural motion of falling toward the center of the Earth—required another object to move it. If the mover stopped, the object fell to the ground or simply stopped moving. But this theory could not explain why a projectile, such as a discus or a spear, continued to move after a person threw it. Galileo's answer to that question was a theory of inertia, which became the basis of a new theory of motion. According to Galileo, an object continues to move or lie at rest until something external to it intervenes to change its motion. Thus, motion is neither a quality inherent in an object nor a force that it acquires from another object. It is simply a state in which the object finds itself.

Galileo also discovered that the motion of an object occurs only in relation to things that do not move. A ship moves through the water, for example, but the goods that the ship carries do not move in relationship to the moving ship. This insight explained to the critics of Copernicus how the Earth can move even though we do not experience its motion. Galileo's most significant contribution to mechanics was his formulation of a mathematical law of motion that explained how the speed and acceleration of a falling object are determined by the distance it travels during equal intervals of time.

The greatest achievements of the Scientific Revolution in physics belong to English scientist Sir Isaac Newton (1642–1727). His research changed the way future generations viewed the world. As a boy Newton felt out of place in his small village, where he worked on his mother's farm and attended school. Fascinated by mechanical devices, he spent much of his time building wooden models of windmills and other machines. When playing with his friends he always found ways to exercise his mind, calculating, for example, how he could use the wind to win jumping contests. It became obvious to all who knew him that Newton belonged at a university. In 1661 he entered Cambridge University, where, at age 27, he became a chaired professor of mathematics.

Newton formulated a set of mathematical laws to explain the operation of the entire physical world. In 1687 he published his theories in *Mathematical Principles of Natural Philosophy*. The centerpiece of this monumental work was the **universal law of gravitation,** which demonstrated that the same force holding an object to the Earth also holds the planets in their orbits. This law represented a synthesis of the work of other scientists, including Kepler on planetary motion and Galileo on inertia. Newton paid tribute to the work of these men when he said, "If I have seen farther, it is by standing on the shoulders of giants." But Newton went further than any of them by establishing the existence of a single gravitational force and by giving it precise mathematical expression. His book revealed the unity and order of the entire physical world and thus offered a scientific model to replace that of Aristotle.

SIR ISAAC NEWTON

This portrait was painted by Sir Godfrey Kneller in 1689, two years after the publication of *Mathematical Principles of Natural Philosophy*.

CHRONOLOGY: DISCOVERIES OF THE SCIENTIFIC REVOLUTION

1543	Copernicus publishes *The Revolutions of the Heavenly Spheres*
1609	Johannes Kepler publishes *New Astronomy*
1628	William Harvey publishes *On the Motion of the Heart and Blood in Animals*
1632	Galileo publishes *Dialogue Concerning the Two Chief World Systems*
1638	Galileo publishes *Discourses on the Two New Sciences of Motion and Mechanics*
1659	Robert Boyle invents the air pump and conducts experiments on the elasticity and compressibility of air
1687	Newton publishes *Mathematical Principles of Natural Philosophy*

Chemistry: Discovering the Elements of Nature

At the beginning of the seventeenth century, the science today called chemistry was considered part of either medicine or **alchemy,** the magical art of attempting to turn base metals into gold or silver. The most famous chemist of the sixteenth century was the Swiss physician Paracelsus (1493–1541), who rejected the theory advanced by the ancient Greek physician Galen (129–200 C.E.) that an imbalance of the four "humors" or fluids in the body—blood, phlegm, black bile, and yellow bile—caused diseases. The medical practice of drawing blood from sick patients to cure them by correcting this alleged imbalance was based on Galen's theory. Instead, to cure certain diseases, Paracelsus began to treat his patients with chemicals, such as mercury and sulfur. Paracelsus is often dismissed for his belief in alchemy, but his prescription of chemicals helped give chemistry a respectable place within medical science.

During the seventeenth century chemistry became a legitimate field of scientific research, largely as the result of the work of Robert Boyle (1627–1691). Boyle destroyed the prevailing idea that all basic constituents of matter share the same structure. He contended that the arrangement of their components, which he identified as corpuscles or atoms, determined their characteristics. He also conducted experiments on the volume, pressure, and density of gas and the elasticity of air. Boyle's most famous experiments, undertaken with an air pump, proved the existence of a vacuum. Largely as a result of Boyle's discoveries, chemists won acceptance as legitimate members of the company of scientists.

Biology: The Circulation of the Blood

The English physician William Harvey (1578–1657) made one of the great medical discoveries of the seventeenth century by demonstrating in 1628 that blood circulates throughout the human body. Traditional science had maintained that blood originated in the liver and then flowed outward through the veins. A certain amount of blood

Gulielm Faithorne ad viv delin: et sculp:

ROBERTUS BOYLE ᴴᴿˢ:

PORTRAIT OF ROBERT BOYLE WITH HIS AIR PUMP IN THE BACKGROUND (1664)
Boyle's pump became the center of a series of experiments carried on at the Royal Society in London.

flowed from the liver into the heart, where it passed from one ventricle to the other and then traveled through the arteries to different parts of the body. During its journey this arterial blood was enriched by a special *pneuma* or "vital spirit" that was necessary to sustain life. When this enriched blood reached the brain, it became the body's "psychic spirits," which influenced human behavior.

Through experiments on human cadavers and live animals in which he weighed the blood that the heart pumped every hour, Harvey demonstrated that rather than sucking in blood, the heart pumped it through the arteries by means of contraction and constriction. The only gap in his theory was the question of how blood went from the ends of the arteries to the ends of the veins. This question was answered in 1661, when scientists, using a new instrument known as a microscope, could see the capillaries connecting the veins and arteries. Harvey, however, had set the standard for future biological research.

THE SEARCH FOR SCIENTIFIC KNOWLEDGE

- ■ What methods did scientists use during this period to investigate nature, and how did they think nature operated?

The natural philosophers who made these scientific discoveries worked in different disciplines, and each followed his own procedures for discovering scientific truth. In the sixteenth and seventeenth centuries there was no "scientific method." Many natural philosophers, however, shared similar views about how nature operated and the means by which humans could acquire knowledge of it. In searching for scientific knowledge, these scientists observed and experimented, used deductive reasoning, expressed their theories in mathematical terms, and argued that nature operated like a machine. These features of scientific research ultimately defined a distinctly Western approach to solving scientific problems.

Observation and Experimentation

The most prominent feature of scientific research in sixteenth- and seventeenth-century Europe was the observation of nature, combined with the testing of hypotheses by rigorous experimentation. This was primarily a process of **induction,** in which theories emerged only after the accumulation and analysis of data. It assumed a willingness to abandon preconceived ideas and base scientific conclusions on experience and observation. This approach is also described as empirical: **empiricism** demands that all scientific theories be tested by experiments based on observation of the natural world.

In *New Organon* (1620), the English philosopher Francis Bacon (1561–1626) promoted this

DISSECTION

The English surgeon William Cheselden giving an anatomical demonstration to spectators in London around 1735. As medical science developed in the sixteenth and seventeenth centuries, the dissection of human corpses became a standard practice in European universities and medical schools. Knowledge of the structure and composition of the human body, which was central to the advancement of physiology, could best be acquired by cutting open a corpse to reveal the organs, muscles, and bones of human beings. The practice reflected the emphasis scientists placed on observation and experimentation in conducting scientific research.

empirical approach to scientific research. Bacon complained that all previous scientific endeavors, especially those of ancient Greek philosophers, relied too little on experimentation. In contrast, his approach involved the thorough and systematic investigation of nature, a process that Bacon, who was a lawyer and judge, compared to the interrogation of a person suspected of committing a crime. For Bacon, scientific experimentation was "putting nature to the question," a phrase that referred to questioning a prisoner under torture to determine the facts of a case.

Deductive Reasoning

The second feature of sixteenth- and seventeenth-century scientific research was the use of **deductive reasoning** to establish basic scientific truths or principles. From these principles other ideas or laws could be deduced logically. Just as induction is linked to empiricism, so deduction is connected to **rationalism.** Unlike empiricism—the idea that we know truth through what the senses can experience—rationalism insists that the mind contains rational categories independent of sensory observation.

Unlike the inductive experimental approach, which found its most enthusiastic practitioners in England, the deductive approach had its most zealous advocates on the European continent. The French philosopher and mathematician René Descartes (1596–1650) became the foremost champion of this methodology. In his *Discourse on the Method* (1637), Descartes recommended that to solve any intellectual problem, a person should first establish fundamental principles or truths and then proceed from those ideas to specific conclusions.

Mathematics, in which one also moves logically from certain premises to conclusions by means of equations, provided the model for deductive reasoning. Although rational deduction proved to be an essential feature of scientific methodology, the limitations of an exclusively deductive approach became apparent when Descartes and his followers deduced a theory of gravitation from the principle that objects could influence each other only if they actually touched. This theory, as well as the principle upon which it was based, lacked an empirical foundation and eventually had to be abandoned.

Mathematics and Nature

The third feature of scientific research in the sixteenth and seventeenth centuries was the application of mathematics to the study of the physical world. Scientists working in both the inductive and the deductive traditions used mathematics. Descartes shared with Galileo the conviction that nature had a geometrical structure and could therefore be understood in mathematical terms. The physical dimensions of matter, which Descartes claimed were its only properties, could of course be expressed mathematically. Galileo claimed that mathematics was the language in which philosophy was written in "the book of the universe."

Isaac Newton's work provided the best illustration of the application of mathematics to scientific problems. Newton used observation and experimentation to confirm his theory of universal gravitation, but he wrote his *Mathematical Principles of Natural Philosophy* in the language of mathematics. His approach to scientific problems, which became a model for future research, used examples derived from experiments and deductive, mathematical reasoning to discover the laws of nature.

The Mechanical Philosophy

Much of seventeenth-century scientific experimentation and deduction assumed that the natural world operated as if it were a machine made by a human being. This **mechanical philosophy** of nature appeared most clearly in the work of Descartes. Medieval philosophers had argued that natural bodies had an innate tendency to change, whereas artificial objects, that is, those constructed by humans, did not. Descartes, as well as Kepler, Galileo, and Bacon, denied that assumption. Mechanists argued that nature operated in a mechanical way, just like a piece of machinery. The only difference was that the operating structures of natural mechanisms could not be observed as readily as the structures of a machine.

Mechanists perceived the human body itself as a machine. Harvey, for example, described the heart as "a piece of machinery in which, though one wheel gives motion to another, yet all the wheels seem to move simultaneously." The only difference between the body and other machines was that the mind could move the body, although how it did so was controversial. According to Descartes, the mind was completely different from the body and the rest of the material world. Unlike the body, the mind was an immaterial substance that could be not be extended in space, divided, or measured mathematically, the way one could record the dimensions of the body. Because Descartes made this sharp distinction between the mind and the body, we describe his philosophy as **dualistic.**

Descartes and other mechanists argued that matter was completely inert or dead. It did not possess a soul or any innate purpose. Its only property was "extension," or the physical dimensions of length, width, and depth. Without a spirit or any other internal force directing its action, matter simply responded to the power of the other bodies with which it came in contact. According to Descartes, all physical phenomena could be explained by reference to the dimensions and the movement of particles of matter. He once claimed, "Give me extension and motion and I will construct the universe."[1]

The view of nature as a machine implied that it operated in a regular, predictable way in accordance with unchanging laws of nature. Scientists could use reason to discover what those laws were and thus learn how nature performed under any circumstances. The scientific investigations of Galileo and Kepler were based on those assumptions, and Descartes made them explicit. The immutability of the laws of nature implied that the entire universe was uniform in structure, an assumption that underlay Newton's formulation of the laws of motion and universal gravitation.

THE CAUSES OF THE SCIENTIFIC REVOLUTION

■ Why did the Scientific Revolution take place in western Europe at this time?

Why did the Scientific Revolution take place at this particular time, and why did it originate in western European countries? There is no simple answer to this question. We can, however, identify developments that inspired these scientific discoveries. Some of these developments arose out of earlier investigations conducted by natural philosophers in the late Middle Ages, the Renaissance, and the sixteenth century. Others emerged from the religious, political, social, and economic life of early modern Europe.

Developments Within Science

The three internal causes of the Scientific Revolution were the research into motion conducted by natural philosophers in the fourteenth century, the scientific investigations conducted by Renaissance humanists, and the collapse of the dominant conceptual frameworks, or paradigms, that had governed scientific inquiry and research for centuries.

LATE MEDIEVAL SCIENCE Modern science can trace some of its origins to the fourteenth century, when the first significant modifications of Aristotle's scientific theories began to emerge. The most significant of these refinements was the theory of impetus. Aristotle had argued that an object would stop as soon as it lost contact with the object that moved it. Late medieval scientists claimed that objects in motion acquire a force that stays with them after they lose contact with the mover. This theory of impetus questioned Aristotle's authority, and it influenced some of Galileo's early thought on motion.

Natural philosophers of the fourteenth century also began to recommend direct, empirical observation in place of the traditional tendency to accept preconceived notions regarding the operation of nature. This approach to answering scientific questions did not result in the type of rigorous experimentation that Bacon demanded three centuries later, but it did encourage scientists to base their theories on the facts that emerged from an empirical study of nature.

The contribution of late medieval science to the Scientific Revolution should not be exaggerated. Philosophers of the fourteenth century continued to accept Ptolemy's cosmology and Galen's anatomical theories. The unchallenged position of theology as the dominant subject in late medieval universities also guaranteed that new scientific ideas would receive little favor if they challenged Christian doctrine.

RENAISSANCE SCIENCE   Natural philosophers during the Renaissance contributed more than their late medieval predecessors to the rise of modern science. Many of the scientific discoveries of the late sixteenth and seventeenth centuries drew their inspiration from Greek scientific works that had been rediscovered during the Renaissance. Copernicus, for example, found the idea of his sun-centered universe in the writings of Aristarchus of Samos, a Greek astronomer of the third century B.C.E. whose work had been unknown during the Middle Ages. Similarly, the works of the ancient Greek philosopher Democritus in the late fifth century B.C.E. introduced the idea, developed by Boyle and others in the seventeenth century, that matter was divisible into small particles known as atoms. The works of Archimedes (287–212 B.C.E.), which had been virtually unknown in the Middle Ages, stimulated interest in the science of mechanics. The recovery and translation of previously unknown texts also made scientists aware that Greek scientists did not always agree with each other and thus provided a stimulus to independent observation and experimentation as a means of resolving their differences.

Renaissance revival of the philosophy of **Neoplatonism** (see Chapter 7) made an even more direct contribution to the birth of modern science. While most medieval natural philosophers relied on the ideas of Aristotle, Neoplatonists drew on the work of Plotinus (205–270 C.E.), the last great philosopher of antiquity who synthesized the work of Plato, other ancient Greek philosophers, and Persian religious traditions. Neoplatonists stressed the unity of the natural and spiritual worlds. Matter is alive, linked to the divine soul that governs the entire universe. To unlock the mysteries of this living world, Neoplatonists turned to mathematics, because they believed the divine expressed itself in geometrical harmony, and to alchemy, because they sought to uncover the shared essence that linked all creation. They also believed that the sun, as a symbol of the divine soul, logically stood at the center of the universe.

Neoplatonic ideas influenced seventeenth-century scientists. Copernicus, for example, took from Neoplatonism his idea of the sun sitting at the center of the universe, as "on a royal throne ruling his children, the planets which circle around him." From his reading in Neoplatonic sources Kepler acquired his belief that the universe was constructed according to geometric principles. Newton was fascinated by the subject of alchemy, and the original inspiration of his theory of gravitation probably came from his Neoplatonist professor at Cambridge, who insisted on the presence of spiritual forces in the physical world. Modern science resulted from an encounter between the mechanical philosophy, which held that matter was inert, and Neoplatonism, which claimed that the natural world was alive.

THE COLLAPSE OF PARADIGMS   The third internal cause of the Scientific Revolution was the collapse of the intellectual frameworks that had governed scientific research since antiquity. In all historical periods scientists prefer to work within an established conceptual framework, or what the scholar Thomas Kuhn has referred to as a **paradigm,** rather than introduce new theories. Every so often, however, the paradigm that has governed scientific research for an extended period of time can no longer account for many different observable phenomena. A scientific revolution occurs when the old paradigm collapses and a new paradigm replaces it.[2]

The revolutionary developments we have discussed in astronomy and biology were partly the result of the collapse of old paradigms. In astronomy the paradigm that had governed scientific inquiry in antiquity and the Middle Ages was the Ptolemaic model, in which the sun and the planets revolved around the Earth. By the sixteenth century, however, new observations had so confused and complicated this model that, to men like Copernicus, it no longer provided a satisfactory explanation for the material universe. Copernicus looked for a simpler and more plausible model of the universe. His sun-centered theory became the new paradigm within which Kepler, Galileo, and Newton all worked.

In biology a parallel development occurred when the old paradigm constructed by Galen, in which the blood originated in the liver and traveled from the heart through the arteries, also collapsed because it could not explain the findings of medical scholars. Harvey introduced a new paradigm, in which the blood circulated through the body. As in astronomy, Harvey's new paradigm served as a framework for subsequent biological research and helped shape the Scientific Revolution.

Developments Outside Science

Nonscientific developments also encouraged the development and acceptance of new scientific ideas. These developments include the spread of Protestantism, the patronage of scientific research, the invention of the printing press, and military and economic change.

PROTESTANTISM Protestantism played a limited role in causing the Scientific Revolution. In the early years of the Reformation, Protestants were just as hostile as Catholics to the new science. Reflecting the Protestant belief in the literal truth of the Bible, Luther referred to Copernicus as "a fool who went against Holy Writ." Throughout the sixteenth and seventeenth centuries, moreover, Catholics as well as Protestants engaged in scientific research. Indeed, some of the most prominent European natural philosophers, including Galileo and Descartes, were devout Catholics. Nonetheless, Protestantism encouraged the emergence of modern science in three ways.

First, as the scientific revolution gained steam in the seventeenth century, Protestant governments were more willing than Catholic authorities to allow the publication and dissemination of new scientific ideas. Protestant governments, for example, did not prohibit the publication of books that promoted novel scientific ideas on the grounds

that they were heretical, as the papacy did in compiling the Index of Prohibited Books. The greater willingness of Protestant governments, especially those of England and the Dutch Republic, to tolerate the expression of new scientific ideas helps to explain why the main geographical arena of scientific investigation shifted from the Catholic Mediterranean to the Protestant North Atlantic in the second half of the seventeenth century. (See *Different Voices* in this chapter.)

Second, seventeenth-century Protestant writers emphasized the idea that God revealed his intentions not only in the Bible, but also in nature itself. They claimed that individuals therefore had a duty to study nature, just as it was their duty to read Scripture to gain knowledge of God's will. Kepler's claim that the astronomer was "as a priest of God to the book of nature" reflected this Protestant outlook.

Third, many seventeenth-century Protestant scientists believed that the millennium, a period of one thousand years when Christ would come again and rule the world, was about to begin. Millenarians believed that during this period knowledge would increase, society would improve, and humans would gain control over nature. Protestant scientists, including Boyle and Newton, conducted their research and experiments believing that their work would contribute to this improvement of human life after the Second Coming of Christ.

PATRONAGE Scientists could not have succeeded without financial and institutional support. Only an organizational structure could give science a permanent status, let it develop as a discipline, and give its members a professional identity. The universities, which today support scientific research, were not the main source of that support in the seventeenth century. They remained predominantly clerical institutions with a vested interest in defending the medieval fusion of Christian theology and Aristotelian science. Instead of the universities, scientists depended on the patronage of wealthy and influential individuals, especially the kings, princes, and great nobles who ruled European states.

DIFFERENT VOICES COPERNICUS AND THE PAPACY

In dedicating his book, On the Revolution of the Heavenly Spheres *(1543), to Pope Paul II (r. 1464–1471), Copernicus explained that he drew inspiration from ancient philosophers who had imagined that the Earth moved. Anticipating condemnation from those who based their astronomical theories on the Bible, he appealed to the pope for protection while showing contempt for the theories of his opponents. Paul II neither endorsed nor condemned Copernicus's work, but in 1616, the papacy suspended the book's publication because it contradicted Scripture.*

Copernicus on Heliocentrism and the Bible

...I began to chafe that philosophers could by no means agree on any one certain theory of the mechanism of the Universe, wrought for us by a supremely good and orderly Creator...I therefore took pains to read again the works of all the philosophers on whom I could lay my hand to seek out whether any of them had ever supposed that the motions of the spheres were other than those demanded by the mathematical schools. I found first in Cicero that Hicetas had realized that the Earth moved. Afterwards I found in Plutarch that certain others had held the like opinion....

Taking advantage of this I too began to think of the mobility of the Earth; and though the opinion seemed absurd, yet knowing now that others before me had been granted freedom to imagine such circles as they chose to explain the phenomena of the stars, I considered that I also might easily be allowed to try whether, by assuming some motion of the Earth, sounder explanations than theirs for the revolution of the celestial spheres might so be discovered.

Thus assuming motions, which in my work I ascribe to the Earth, by long and frequent observations I have at last discovered that, if the motions of the rest of the planets be brought into relation with the circulation of the Earth and be reckoned in proportion to the circles of each planet...the orders and magnitudes of all stars and spheres, nay the heavens themselves, become so bound together that nothing in any part thereof could be moved from its place without producing confusion of all the other parts and of the Universe as a whole....

It may fall out, too, that idle babblers, ignorant of mathematics, may claim a right to pronounce a judgment on my work, by reason of a certain passage of Scripture basely twisted to serve their purpose. Should any such venture to criticize and carp at my project, I make no account of them; I consider their judgment rash, and utterly despise it.

This group included Pope Urban VIII, ruler of the Papal States.

Patronage, however, could easily be withdrawn. Scientists had to conduct themselves and their research to maintain the favor of their patrons. Galileo referred to the new moons of Jupiter that he observed through his telescope as the Medicean stars to flatter the Medici family that ruled

CHRONOLOGY: THE FORMATION OF SCIENTIFIC SOCIETIES

1603	Prince Cesi founds the Academy of the Lynx-Eyed in Rome
1657	Cosimo II de' Medici founds the Academy of Experiment in Florence
1662	Founding of the Royal Society of London under the auspices of Charles II
1666	Founding of the Academy of Sciences in Paris

Source: From Nicolaus Copernicus, *De Revolutionibus Orbium Coelestium* (1543), trans. by John F. Dobson and Selig Brodetsky in *Occasional Notes of the Royal Astronomical Society,* 2(10), 1947. Reprinted by permission of Blackwell Publishing.

Papal Decree against Heliocentrism, 1616

Decree of the Holy Congregation of his Most Illustrious Lord Cardinals especially charged by His Holiness Pope Paul V and by the Holy Apostolic See with the index of books and their licensing, prohibition, correction and printing in all of Christendom....

This Holy Congregation has also learned about the spreading and acceptance by many of the false Pythagorean doctrine, altogether contrary to the Holy Scripture, that the earth moves and the sun is motionless, which is also taught by Nicholaus Copernicus's *On the Revolutions of the Heavenly Spheres* and by Diego de Zuñiga's *On Job*. This may be seen from a certain letter published by a certain Carmelite Father, whose title is *Letter of the Reverend Father Paolo Antonio Foscarini on the Pythagorean and Copernican Opinion of the Earth's Motion and Sun's Rest and on the New Pythagorean World System*...in which the said Father tries to show that the above mentioned doctrine of the sun's rest at the center of the world and the earth's motion is consonant with the truth and does not contradict Holy Scripture. Therefore, in order that this opinion may not creep any further to the prejudice of Catholic truth, the Congregation has decided that the books by Nicholaus Copernicus (*On the Revolution of Spheres*) and Diego de Zuniga (*On Job*) be suspended until corrected; but that the book of the Carmelite Father Paolo Antonini Foscarini be completely prohibited and condemned; and that all other books which teach the same be likewise prohibited, according to whether with the present decree it prohibits condemns and suspends them respectively. In witness thereof this decree has been signed by the hand and stamped with the seal of the Most Illustrious and reverend Lord cardinal of St. Cecilia. Bishop of Albano, on March 5, 1616.

Source: From *The Galileo Affair: A Documentary History,* ed. and trans. by Maurice A. Finocchairo, copyright © 1989 by The Regents of the University of California, is reprinted by permission of the University of Calfornia Press.

For Discussion

1. Why did the papal authorities prohibit and condemn the work by Antonini Foscarini but only suspend those of Copernicus and Diego de Zuñia?
2. How did Copernicus and the papal authorities differ about classical antiquity and the truth of Holy Scripture?

Florence. His publications were inspired as much by his obligation to glorify Grand Duke Cosimo II as by his belief in the sun-centered theory.

Academies in which groups of scientists could share ideas and work served as a second important source of patronage. One of the earliest of these institutions was the Academy of the Lynx-Eyed in Rome, named after the animal whose sharp vision symbolized the power of observation required by the new science. Founded in 1603 by Prince Cesi, the Academy published many of Galileo's works. In 1657 Cosimo II founded a similar institution in Florence, the Academy of Experiment. These academies offered a more regular source of patronage than scientists could acquire from individual positions at court, but they still served the function of glorifying their founders, and they depended on patrons for their continued existence. The royal academies established in the 1660s, however, especially the Royal Academy of Sciences in France and the Royal Society in England (1662), became in effect public institutions that operated with a minimum of royal intervention and made possible a continuous program of work.

THE FOUNDING OF THE FRENCH ACADÈMIE DES SCIENCES

Like the Royal Society in England, the French Academy of Sciences was dependent upon royal patronage. Louis XIV, seen sitting in the middle of the painting, used the occasion to glorify himself as a patron of the sciences as well as the arts. The painting also commemorates the building of the Royal Observatory in Paris, which is shown in the background.

the authors supplied. Illustrations, diagrams, tables, and other schematic drawings that helped to convey the author's findings could also be printed. The entire body of scientific knowledge thus became cumulative. Printing also made members of the nonscientific community aware of the latest advances in physics and astronomy and so helped to make science an integral part of the culture of educated Europeans.

The mission of the Royal Society in England was the promotion of scientific knowledge through experimentation. It also placed the results of scientific research at the service of the state. Members of the Royal Society, for example, did research on ship construction and military technology. These attempts to use scientific technology to strengthen the power of the state show how the growth of the modern state and the emergence of modern science were related.

THE PRINTING PRESS   Printing made it much easier for scientists to share their discoveries with others. During the Middle Ages, books were handwritten. Errors could creep into the text as it was being copied, and the number of copies that could be made of a manuscript limited the spread of scientific knowledge. The spread of printing ensured that scientific achievements could be preserved more accurately and presented to a broader audience. The availability of printed copies also made it much easier for other scientists to correct or supplement the data that

MILITARY AND ECONOMIC CHANGE   The Scientific Revolution occurred at roughly the same time that both the conduct of warfare and the European economy were undergoing dramatic changes. As territorial states increased the size of their armies and arsenals, they demanded more accurate weapons with longer range. Some of the work that physicists did during the seventeenth century was deliberately meant to improve weaponry. Members of the Royal Society in England, for example, conducted extensive scientific research on the trajectory and velocity of missiles, and so followed Francis Bacon's recommendation that scientists place their research at the service of the state.

The needs of the emerging capitalist economy also influenced scientific research. The study of mechanics, for example, led to new techniques to ventilate mines and raise coal or ore from them, thus making mining more profitable. Some of the questions discussed at the meetings of the Royal Society suggest that its members undertook research to make capitalist ventures more productive and profitable. The research did not always produce immediate results, but ultimately it increased economic profitability and contributed to the English economy in the eighteenth century.

THE INTELLECTUAL CONSEQUENCES OF THE SCIENTIFIC REVOLUTION

■ How did the Scientific Revolution influence philosophical and religious thought in the seventeenth and early eighteenth centuries?

The Scientific Revolution profoundly affected the intellectual life of educated Europeans. The discoveries of Copernicus, Kepler, Galileo, and Newton, as well as the assumptions on which their work was based, influenced what educated people in the West studied, how they approached intellectual problems, and what they thought about the supernatural realm.

Education

During the seventeenth and early eighteenth centuries, especially between 1680 and 1720, science and the new philosophy that was associated with it became an important part of university education. Outside academia, learned societies, public lectures, discussions in coffeehouses, and popular scientific publications spread the knowledge of science among the educated members of society. In this way science secured a permanent foothold in Western culture.

The spread of science did not go unchallenged. It encountered academic rivals committed not only to traditional Aristotelianism but also to Renaissance humanism. In the late seventeenth century, a conflict arose between "the ancients," who revered the wisdom of classical authors, and "the moderns," who emphasized the superiority of the new scientific culture. The most concrete expression of this conflict was the Battle of the Books, an intellectual debate that raged over the question of which group of thinkers had contributed more to human knowledge. No clear winner in this battle emerged, and the conflict between the ancients and the moderns was never completely resolved. The humanities and the sciences, while included within the same curriculum at many universities, are still often regarded as representing separate cultural traditions.

Skepticism and Independent Reasoning

The Scientific Revolution encouraged the habit of **skepticism,** the tendency to doubt what we have been taught and are expected to believe. This skepticism formed part of the method that seventeenth-century scientists adopted to solve philosophical problems. As we have seen, Descartes, Bacon, Galileo, and Kepler all refused to acknowledge the authority of classical or medieval texts. They preferred to rely upon the knowledge they acquired from observing nature and using their own rational faculties.

In *Discourse on the Method,* Descartes showed the extremes to which this skepticism could be taken. Descartes doubted the reality of his own sense perceptions and even his own existence until he realized that the very act of doubting proved his existence as a thinking being. As he wrote in words that have become famous, "I think, therefore I am."[3] Upon this foundation Descartes went on to prove the existence of God and the material world, thereby conquering the skepticism with which he began his inquiry. In the

CHRONOLOGY: THE IMPACT OF THE SCIENTIFIC REVOLUTION

1620	Francis Bacon argues for the necessity of rigorous experimentation
1633	Galileo tried by the Roman Inquisition
1637	René Descartes publishes *Discourse on the Method*
1670	Baruch Spinoza publishes *Treatise on Religion and Political Philosophy,* challenging the distinction between spirit and matter
1686	Bernard de Fontenelle publishes *Treatises on the Plurality of Worlds*

process, however, he developed an approach to solving intellectual problems that asked people to question authority and think clearly and systematically for themselves. The effects of this method became apparent in the late seventeenth century, when skeptics invoked Descartes' methodology to challenge both orthodox Judaism and Christianity. Some of the most radical of those opinions came from Baruch Spinoza (1632–1677), who grew up in Amsterdam in a community of Spanish and Portuguese Jews who had fled the Inquisition. Although educated as an Orthodox Jew, Spinoza also studied Latin and read Descartes and other Christian writers. From Descartes, Spinoza learned "that nothing ought to be admitted as true but what has been proved by good and solid

BARUCH SPINOZA
Spinoza was one of the most radical thinkers of the seventeenth century. His identification of God with nature made him vulnerable to charges of atheism. His followers in the Dutch Republic, who were known as freethinkers, laid the foundations for the Enlightenment in the eighteenth century.

reason." This skepticism and independence of thought led to his excommunication from the Jewish community at age 24.

Spinoza used Descartes' skepticism to challenge Descartes himself. He rejected Descartes' separation of the mind and the body and his radical distinction between the spiritual and the material. For Spinoza there was only one substance in the universe, which he identified with both God and nature. The claim that God and nature were two names for the same reality challenged not only the ideas of Descartes, but also the fundamental tenets of Christianity, including the belief in a personal God who had created the natural world by design and continued to govern it. In *A Treatise on Religion and Political Philosophy* (1670), Spinoza described "a universe ruled only by the cause and effect of natural laws, without purpose or design."

Spinoza's skeptical approach to solving philosophical and scientific problems revealed the radical intellectual potential of the new science. The freedom of thought that Spinoza advocated, as well as the belief that nature followed unchangeable laws and could be understood in mathematical terms, served as important links between the Scientific Revolution and the Enlightenment of the eighteenth century. We will discuss those connections more fully in Chapter 19.

Science and Religion

The new science presented two challenges to traditional Christian belief. The first involved the apparent contradiction between the sun-centered theory of the universe and biblical references to the sun's mobility. Because the Bible was considered the inspired word of God, the Church took everything it said, including any passages regarding the operation of the physical world, as literally true. The Bible's reference to the sun moving across the sky served as the basis of the papal condemnation of sun-centered theories in 1616 and the prosecution of Galileo in 1633.

The second challenge to traditional Christian belief was the implication that if the universe functioned as a machine, on the basis of unchanging natural laws, then God played little part in its operation. God was akin to an engineer, who had designed the perfect machine, and therefore had no need to interfere with its workings. This position, which thinkers known as **deists** adopted in the late seventeenth and eighteenth centuries, denied the Christian belief that God was constantly active in the operation of the world. More directly, it rejected the possibility of miracles. None of the great scientists of the seventeenth century were themselves deists, but their acceptance of the mechanical philosophy made them vulnerable to the charge that they denied Christian doctrine.

Although the new science and seventeenth-century Christianity appeared to be on a collision course, some scientists and theologians insisted that there was no conflict between them. They argued that religion and science had different concerns. Religion dealt with the relationship between humanity and God. Science explained how nature operated. As Galileo wrote in 1615, "The intention of the Holy Ghost is to teach us how one goes to heaven, not how heaven goes."[4] Scripture was not intended to explain natural phenomena, but to convey religious truths that human reason could not grasp.

Another argument for the compatibility of science and religion was the claim that the mechanical philosophy, rather than relegating God to the role of a retired engineer, actually manifested God's unlimited power. In a mechanistic universe God was still the creator of the physical world and the maker of the laws by which nature operated. He was still all-powerful and present everywhere. According to Boyle and Newton, moreover, God played a supremely active role in governing the universe. Not only had he created the universe, but as Boyle argued, he also continued to keep all matter constantly in motion. This theory served the purpose of redefining God's power without diminishing it in any way. Newton arrived at a similar position in his search for an immaterial agent who would cause gravity to operate. He proposed that God himself, who he believed "endures always and is present everywhere," made bodies move according to gravitational laws. Throughout the early eighteenth century this feature of Newtonian natural philosophy served as a powerful argument for the active involvement of God in the universe.

As the new science became more widely accepted, many theologians, especially Protestants, accommodated scientific knowledge to their religious beliefs. Some Protestants welcomed the discoveries of science as an opportunity to purify the Christian religion by combating the superstition, magic, and ignorance that they claimed the Catholic Church had been promoting. Clergymen argued that because God worked through the processes of nature, scientific inquiry could lead to knowledge of God. Religion and science could illuminate each other.

Theologians and philosophers also began to expand the role that reason played in religion. The English philosopher John Locke (1632–1704) argued that reason should be the final judge of the existence of the supernatural and the true meaning of the Bible. This new emphasis on the role of reason in religion coincided with a rejection of the religious zeal that had prevailed during the Reformation and the wars of religion. Increasingly, political and ecclesiastical authorities condemned religious enthusiasm as dangerous and irrational.

The new emphasis on the reasonableness of religion and the decline of religious enthusiasm are often viewed as evidence of a trend toward the **secularization** of European life, a process in which religion gave way to more worldly concerns. In one sense this secular trend was undeniable. By 1700, theology had lost its dominant position at the universities and religion had lost much of its influence on politics, diplomacy, and economic activity.

Religion, however, had not lost its relevance. It remained a vital force in the lives of most Europeans. Many of those who accepted the new science continued to believe in a providential God and the divinity of Christ. Moreover, a small but influential group of educated people, following the lead of the French scientist and philosopher Blaise Pascal (1623–1662), argued that religious faith occupied a higher sphere of knowledge that reason and science could not penetrate. Pascal, the inventor of a calculating machine and the promoter of a system of public coach service in Paris, was an

JUSTICE IN HISTORY

The Trial of Galileo

The events leading to the trial of Galileo for heresy in 1633 began in 1616, when a committee of theologians reported to the Roman Inquisition that the sun-centered theory of Copernicus was heretical. Those who accepted this theory were declared to be heretics not only because they questioned the Bible itself, but because they denied the exclusive authority of the Catholic Church to interpret the Bible. The day after this report was submitted, Pope Paul V (r. 1605–1621) instructed Cardinal Robert Bellarmine (1542–16210, a theologian who was on good terms with Galileo, to warn him to abandon his Copernican views. Galileo had written extensively in support of the sun-centered thesis, especially in his *Letters on Sunspots* (1613) and his *Letter to the Grand Duchess Christina* (1615), although he had never admitted that the theory was proved conclusively. Then he was told not to hold, teach, or defend in any way the opinion that the sun was stable or the Earth moved. If he ignored that warning, he would be prosecuted as a heretic.

During the next 16 years Galileo published two books. The first, *The Assayer* (1623), attacked the views of an Italian philosopher regarding comets. The book won Galileo support, especially from the new pope, Urban VIII (r. 1623–1644), who was eager to be associated with the most fashionable intellectual trends. Urban took Galileo under his wing and made him the intellectual star of his court. Urban even declared that support for Copernicanism was rash but not heretical.

The pope's patronage may have emboldened Galileo to exercise less caution in writing his second book of this period, *Dialogue Concerning the Two Chief World Systems* (1632). Ostensibly an impartial presentation of the rival Ptolemaic and Copernican cosmologies, this book promoted Copernicanism in its own quiet way. Galileo sought proper authorization from ecclesiastical authorities to put the book in print, but he allowed it to be published in Florence before it received official approval from Rome.

The publication of *Dialogue* precipitated Galileo's fall from the pope's favor. Urban, accused of leniency with heretics, ordered the book taken out of circulation in the summer of 1632 and appointed a commission to investigate Galileo's activities. After receiving their report, he turned the matter over to the Roman Inquisition, which charged Galileo with heresy.

The Roman Inquisition had been established in 1542 to preserve the Catholic faith and prosecute heresy. Like the Spanish Inquisition, this Roman ecclesiastical court has acquired a reputation for being harsh and arbitrary, for administering torture, for proceeding in secrecy, and for denying the accused the right to know the charges before the trial. There is some validity to these criticisms, although the Inquisition did not torture Galileo or deny him the opportunity to defend himself. The most unfair aspect of the proceeding, and of inquisitorial justice in general, was that the same judges who had brought the charges against the accused and conducted the interrogation also decided the case. This meant that in a politically motivated trial such as Galileo's, the verdict was a foregone conclusion. To accept Galileo's defense would have been a sign of weakness and a repudiation of the pope.

Although the underlying issue in the trial was whether Galileo was guilty of heresy for denying the sun's motion and the Earth's immobility, the more technical question was whether by publishing *Dialogue* he had violated the prohibition of 1616. In his defense Galileo claimed he had only written *Dialogue* to present "the physical and astronomical reasons that can be advanced for one side or the other." He denied holding Copernicus's opinion to be true.

In the end the court determined that by publishing *Dialogue*, Galileo had violated the injunction of 1616. He had disseminated "the false opinion of

THE TRIAL OF GALILEO, 1633

Galileo is shown here presenting one of his four defenses to the Inquisition. He claimed that his book *Dialogue Concerning the Two Chief World Systems* did not endorse the Copernican model of the universe.

Source: Gérard Blot/Art Resource/ Reunion des Musees Nationaux

the Earth's motion and the sun's stability," and he had "defended the said opinion already condemned." Even Galileo's efforts "to give the impression of leaving it undecided and labeled as probable" was still a serious error, because there was no way that "an opinion declared and defined contrary to divine Scripture may be probable." The court also declared that Galileo had obtained permission to publish the book in Florence without telling the authorities there that he was under the injunction of 1616.

Throughout the trial every effort was made to distance the pope from his former protégé. The papal court feared that because the pope had been Galileo's patron and had allowed him to develop his ideas, he himself would be implicated in Galileo's heresy. Information regarding the pope's earlier support for Galileo would not be allowed to surface during the trial. The court made sure, for example, that no one from the court of the Grand Duke of Tuscany in Florence, who had secured Galileo's appointment at the University of Padua and had defended him throughout this crisis, would testify for him. The trial tells us as much about Urban VIII's efforts to save face as about the Catholic Church's hostility to the new science.

The Inquisition required Galileo to renounce his views and avoid further defense of Copernicanism.

After making this humiliating submission to the court, he was sent to Siena and later that year was allowed to return to his villa near Florence, where he remained under house arrest until his death in 1642.

For Discussion

1. Galileo was silenced because of what he had printed. Why had he published these works, and why did the Church consider his publications a threat?

2. Should disputes between science and religion be resolved in a court of law? Why or why not?

Taking It Further

Finocchiaro, Maurice (ed). *The Galileo Affair: A Documentary History.* 1989. A collection of original documents regarding the controversy between Galileo and the Roman Catholic Church.

Sharratt, Michael. *Galileo: Decisive Innovator.* 1994. A study of Galileo's place in the history of science that provides full coverage of his trial and papal reconsiderations of it in the late twentieth century.

advocate of the new science. He endorsed the Copernican model of the universe and opposed the condemnation of Galileo. He introduced a new scientific theory regarding fluids that later became known as Pascal's law of pressure. But by claiming that knowledge of God comes from the heart rather than the mind, Pascal challenged the contention of Locke and Spinoza that reason was the ultimate arbiter of religious truth.

HUMANS AND THE NATURAL WORLD

■ How did the Scientific Revolution change the way in which seventeenth- and eighteenth-century Europeans thought of the place of human beings in nature?

The spread of scientific knowledge not only redefined the views of educated people regarding the supernatural, but also led them to reconsider their relationship to nature. This process involved three separate but related inquiries: to determine the place of human beings in a sun-centered universe, to investigate how science and technology had given human beings greater control over nature, and to reconsider the relationship between men and women in light of new scientific knowledge about the human mind and body.

The Place of Human Beings in the Universe

The astronomical discoveries of Copernicus, Kepler, and Galileo offered a new outlook about the position of human beings in the universe. The Earth-centered Ptolemaic cosmos that dominated scientific thought during the Middle Ages was also human-centered. Human beings inhabited the planet at the very center of the universe, and on that planet they enjoyed a privileged position. They were, after all, created in the image of God, according to Christian belief.

The acceptance of a sun-centered model of the universe began to change these views of humankind. Once it became apparent that the Earth was not the center of the universe, human beings began to lose their privileged position in nature. The Copernican universe was neither Earth-centered nor human-centered. Scientists such as Descartes continued to claim that human beings were the greatest of nature's creatures, but their habitation of a tiny planet circling the sun inevitably reduced the sense of their own importance. Moreover, as astronomers began to recognize the incomprehensible size of the cosmos, the possibility emerged that there were other habitable worlds in the universe, calling into further question the unique status of humankind.

In the late sixteenth and seventeenth centuries a number of literary works explored the possibility of other inhabited worlds and forms of life. Kepler's *Somnium,* or *Lunar Astronomy* (1634), a book that combined science and fiction, described various species of moon dwellers, some of whom were rational and superior to humans. The most ambitious of these books on extraterrestrial life was Bernard de Fontenelle's *Conversations on the Plurality of Worlds* (1686). This fictional work by a dramatist and poet who was also well versed in scientific knowledge became immensely popular throughout Europe and was more responsible than any purely scientific achievement for leading the general reading public to call into question the centrality of human beings in Creation.

The Control of Nature

The Scientific Revolution strengthened the confidence human beings had in their ability to control nature. By disclosing the laws governing the operation of the universe, the new science gave humans the tools they needed to make nature serve them more effectively than it had in the past. Francis Bacon, for example, believed that knowledge of the laws of nature could restore the dominion over nature that humans had lost in the biblical Garden of Eden. Bacon thought that nature existed for human beings to control and exploit for their own benefit. His famous saying, "knowledge is power," conveyed his confidence that science would give human beings this type of control. This optimism regarding human control of nature found support in the belief that God permitted such mastery, first by creating a regular and uniform universe and then by giving humans the rational faculties by which they could understand nature's laws.

Many seventeenth-century scientists emphasized the practical applications of their research, just as scientists often do today. Descartes, who used his knowledge of optics to improve the grinding of lenses, considered how scientific knowledge could drain marshes, increase the velocity of bullets, and use bells to make clouds give rain. In his celebration of the French Academy of Sciences in 1699, Fontenelle wrote that "the application of science to nature will constantly grow in scope and intensity and we shall go on from one marvel to the next; the day will come when man will be able to fly by fitting on wings to keep him in the air...till one day we shall be able to fly to the moon."[5]

The hopes of seventeenth-century scientists for the improvement of human life by means of technology remained in large part unfulfilled until the eighteenth century. Only then did the technological promise of the Scientific Revolution begin to be realized, most notably with the innovations that preceded or accompanied the Industrial Revolution (see Chapter 21). By the middle of the eighteenth century, the belief that science would improve human life became an integral part of Western culture. Faith in human progress also became one of the main themes of the Enlightenment, which will be discussed in Chapter 19.

Women, Men, and Nature

The new scientific and philosophical ideas challenged ancient and medieval notions about women's physical and mental inferiority to men but not other traditional ideas about gender roles.

Until the seventeenth century, a woman's sexual organs were thought to be imperfect versions of a man's, an idea that made woman an inferior version of man and, in some respects, a freak of nature. During the sixteenth and seventeenth centuries, scientific literature advanced the new idea that women's sexual organs were perfect in their own right and served distinct functions in reproduction. Aristotle's view that men made a more important contribution to reproduction than women also came under attack. Semen was long believed to contain the form of both the body and the soul, while a woman only contributed the formless matter on which the semen acted. By 1700, however, most scholars agreed that both sexes contributed equally to the process of reproduction.

Some seventeenth-century natural philosophers also questioned ancient and medieval ideas about women's mental inferiority to men. In making a radical separation between the mind and the human body, Descartes, for example, found no difference between the minds of men and women. As one of his followers wrote in 1673, "The mind has no sex."[6] A few upper-class women provided evidence to support this revolutionary claim of female intellectual equality. Princess Elisabeth of Bohemia, for example, carried on a long correspondence with Descartes during the 1640s and challenged many of his ideas on the relationship between the body and the soul. The English noblewoman Margaret Cavendish (1623–1673) wrote scientific and philosophical works and conversed with leading philosophers. In early eighteenth-century France, small groups of women and men gathered in the salons or private sitting rooms of the nobility to discuss philosophical and scientific ideas. In Germany women helped their husbands run astronomical observatories.

Although seventeenth-century science laid the foundations for a theory of sexual equality, it did not challenge other traditional ideas that compared women unfavorably with men. Most educated people continued to ground female behavior in the humors, claiming that because women were cold and wet, as opposed to hot and dry, they were naturally more deceptive, unstable, and melancholic than men. They also continued to identify women with nature itself, which had always been depicted as female.

ASTRONOMERS IN SEVENTEENTH-CENTURY GERMANY

Elisabetha and Johannes Hevelius working together with a sextant in a German astronomical observatory. More than 14 percent of all German astronomers were female. Most of them cooperated with their husbands in their work.

Bacon's use of masculine metaphors to describe science and his references to "man's mastery over nature" therefore seemed to reinforce traditional ideas of male dominance over women. His language also reinforced traditional notions of men's superior rationality.[7] In 1664 the secretary of the Royal Society, which excluded women from membership, proclaimed that the mission of that institution was to develop a "masculine philosophy."[8]

The new science thus strengthened the theoretical foundations for the male control of women at a time when many men expressed concern over women's "disorderly" and "irrational" conduct. In a world populated with witches, rebels, and other women who refused to adhere to conventional standards of proper feminine behavior, the adoption of a masculine philosophy was associated with the reassertion of patriarchy.

CONCLUSION

Science and Western Culture

Unlike many of the cultural developments in the history of the West, the Scientific Revolution owes very little to Eastern influences. During the Middle Ages the Islamic civilizations of the Middle East produced a rich body of scientific knowledge that influenced the development of medieval science in Europe, but by the time of the Scientific Revolution, Middle Eastern science no longer occupied the frontlines of scientific research. Middle Eastern natural philosophers had little to offer their European counterparts as they made their contributions to the Scientific Revolution.

China and India had also accumulated a large body of scientific knowledge in ancient and medieval times. When Jesuit missionaries began teaching Western science and mathematics to the Chinese in the sixteenth and seventeenth centuries, they learned about earlier Chinese technological advances, including the invention of the compass, gunpowder, and printing. They also learned that ancient Chinese astronomers had been the first to observe solar eclipses and comets. By the time the Jesuits arrived, however, Chinese science had entered a period of decline. When those missionaries returned home, they introduced Europeans to many aspects of Chinese culture but very few scientific ideas that Europeans natural philosophers found useful.

None of these Eastern civilizations had a scientific revolution comparable to the one that occurred in the West in the late sixteenth and seventeenth centuries. For China the explanation probably lies in the absence of military and political incentives to promote scientific research at a time when the vast Chinese empire was relatively stable. In the Middle East the explanation is more likely that Islam during these years failed to give priority to the study of the natural world. In Islam nature was either entirely secular (that is, not religious) and hence not worthy of study on its own terms or so heavily infused with spiritual value that it could not be subjected to rational analysis. In Europe, however, religious and cultural traditions allowed scientists to view nature as both a product of supernatural forces and something that was separate from the supernatural. Nature could therefore be studied objectively without losing its religious significance. Only when nature was viewed as both the creation of God and at the same time as independent of God, could it be subjected to mathematical analysis and brought under human control.

Scientific and technological knowledge became a significant component of Western culture, and in the eighteenth century Western science gave many educated Europeans a new source of identity. These people believed that their knowledge of science, in conjunction with their Christian religion, their classical culture, and their political institutions made them different from, if not superior to, people living in the East.

The rise of Western science and technology played a role in the growth of European dominance over Africa, Asia, and the Americas. Science gave Western states the military and navigational technology that helped them gain control of foreign lands. Knowledge of botany and agriculture allowed Western powers to develop the resources of the areas they colonized and use these resources to improve their own societies. Some Europeans even appealed to science to justify their dominance of the people in the lands they settled and ruled. To this process of Western imperial expansion we now turn.

KEY TERMS

universal law of gravitation	mechanical philosophy
alchemy	dualistic
induction	Neoplatonism
empiricism	paradigm
deductive reasoning	skepticism
rationalism	deists
	secularization

CHAPTER QUESTIONS

1. What were the achievements and discoveries of the Scientific Revolution? (page 529)
2. What methods did scientists use during this period to investigate nature, and how did they think nature operated? (page 535)
3. Why did the Scientific Revolution occur in Western Europe at this particular time? (page 537)
4. How did the Scientific Revolution influence philosophical and religious thought in the seventeenth and early eighteenth centuries? (page 543)
5. How did the Scientific Revolution change how Europeans thought about the place of human beings in nature? (page 548)

TAKING IT FURTHER

1. Were the changes in astronomy, physics, chemistry, and biology in the sixteenth and seventeenth centuries revolutionary? In which field were the changes most significant?
2. Scientists today often refer to the scientific method. Was there a scientific method in the seventeenth century or did scientists employ various methods?
3. Why did the scientific revolution occur at this time? Did it owe its development more to internal or external developments? Scientists today often refer to the scientific method. Was there a scientific method in the seventeenth century or did scientists employ various methods?
4. What does the conflict between the supporter of a sun-centered theory and the Catholic Church suggest about the compatibility of science and religion in the seventeenth century?

✓•⟦Practice⟧ on MyHistoryLab

18

The West and the World: Empire, Trade, and War, 1650–1815

■ European Empires in the Americas and Asia ■ Warfare in Europe, North America, and Asia ■ The Atlantic World ■ Encounters Between Europeans and Asians ■ The Crisis of Empire and the Atlantic Revolutions

IN 1789 OLAUDAH EQUIANO, A FREED SLAVE LIVING IN GREAT BRITAIN, wrote an account of his experiences in captivity. Equiano's narrative recounted his seizure in the Gambia region of Africa and his transportation on a slave ship to the British Caribbean colony of Barbados. He described the unmerciful floggings to which the Africans on his ship were subjected, the unrelieved hunger they experienced, and the insufferable heat and smells they endured in the hold of the ship. He witnessed the suicide of those who threw themselves into the sea to avoid further misery. He was terrified that his white captors would eat him, and he wished for a merciful death.

Once the ship had reached its destination the Africans were herded into pens where white plantation owners examined, purchased, and branded them. The most moving part of Equiano's narrative is his account of the cries he heard as family members were sold to different masters. "O you nominal Christians," wrote Equiano, "might not an African ask you, learned you this from your God? Is it not enough that we are torn from our country and friends to toil for your luxury and lust of gain? Must every tender feeling be sacrificed to your avarice?"[1]

Between 1650 and 1815 millions of African men and women took journeys similar to Equiano's. The forced emigration of black Africans from their homelands, their sale to white landlords, and their subjection to inhumane treatment number among the abiding horrors of Western civilization. To understand how these horrors could have occurred, especially at the hands of men who proclaimed a commitment to human freedom, we must study the growth of European empires during these centuries.

As European states grew in size, wealth, and military power in the sixteenth and seventeenth centuries, the most powerful of them acquired large overseas empires. By the end of the seventeenth century the British, French, and Dutch had joined the Portuguese and the Spanish as overseas imperial powers. As we discussed in Chapter 13, the first stage of empire-building, which lasted from 1500 until about 1650, had many different motives. The search for gold and silver, the mission to Christianize the indigenous populations, the desire of some colonists to escape religious persecution, the urge to plunder, the efforts of monarchs to expand the size of their dominions, and the desire to profit from international trade all

JEAN-BAPTISTE DEBRET, *PUNISHMENT OF A SLAVE*

This image of the flogging of a slave in Brazil conveys the brutality of Atlantic slavery. The French painter Jean Baptiste Debret included this engraving in his three-volume study, *A Pictureque and Historic Voyage to Brazil* (1834–1839).

Source: Biblioteca Nacional, Rio de Janiero Brazil/The Bridgeman Art Library

figured in the process. In 1625 the English government recognized many of these motives when it declared the purpose of the colony of Virginia to be "the propagation of the Christian religion, the increase of trade, and the enlarging of the royal empire."[2]

During the second stage of empire-building, which lasted from about 1650 to 1815, the economic motive for acquiring overseas possessions became dominant. More than anything else, the desire for profit within a world economy shaped imperial policy. In the eyes of western European governments, all colonies were economic enterprises. They supplied the parent country, often referred to as the **metropolis,** with agricultural products, raw materials, and minerals. Overseas colonies also provided the metropolis with markets for its manufactured goods.

The growth of these empires expanded the geographical boundaries of the West. It also resulted in the spread of Western ideas, political institutions, and economic systems to Asia and the Americas. At the same time, encounters between Europeans and non-Western peoples, especially those of Asia, changed the cultures of the West.

EUROPEAN EMPIRES IN THE AMERICAS AND ASIA

■ How did the composition and organization of European empires change during the seventeenth and eighteenth centuries?

The main political units in Europe during this long period of history are usually referred to as **states.** A state is a consolidated territorial area that has its own political institutions and recognizes no higher authority. Thus, we refer to France, England (which became Great Britain after its union with Scotland in 1707), Prussia, the Dutch Republic, and Portugal as states. As we have discussed in Chapter 16, most of these states acquired larger armies and administrative bureaucracies during the sixteenth and seventeenth centuries, mainly to meet the demands of war. Consequently, they became more highly integrated and cohesive political structures.

Many European states formed the center or core of much larger political formations known as **empires.** The main characteristic of empires in the seventeenth and eighteenth centuries was that they contained many different kingdoms or territorial possessions. The metropolis controlled these imperial territories, but did not fully integrate them into its administrative structure. Some of the territories that formed a part of these empires were located in Europe. The Austrian Habsburg monarchy, for example, had jurisdiction over a host of separate kingdoms and principalities in central and eastern Europe, including Hungary and Bohemia. The Spanish monarchy controlled many different kingdoms and provinces in the Iberian Peninsula as well as territories in southern Italy and the Netherlands. On the eastern and southeastern periphery of Europe lay two other empires: the Russian and the Ottoman, which controlled vast expanses of land not only in eastern Europe, but also in Asia. As in previous centuries, the Russian and Ottoman empires marked the ever-shifting boundaries between East and West.

Beginning in the fifteenth century, as the result of transoceanic voyages of exploration and the establishment of overseas colonies, western European states acquired, settled, or controlled territories in the Americas, Africa, and Asia. Mastery of these lands came much more quickly in the New World than in Asia. The peoples of North and South America whom Europeans encountered when they arrived were able fighters, but diseases introduced by the Europeans drastically reduced their numbers. European settlers, who had the added advantage of superior military technology, were able to gain the upper hand in battle, seize or purchase their lands, and force those who survived to retreat to less inhabited areas.

When Europeans started to develop extensive trading routes in Asia, however, that continent was already highly developed politically and militarily. Three Muslim empires—the Ottoman, the Safavid (Persia), and the Mughal (India)—and the neighboring Chinese Empire in East Asia occupied the mass of land from the Balkans to the Pacific Ocean. Only when these Asian empires began to fall apart, giving greater autonomy to the smaller, subordinate states within their boundaries, were Europeans able to exploit the situation, secure favorable trading arrangements with provincial rulers in Asia, and ultimately gain control over some Asian territories.

The Rise of the British Empire

The fastest-growing of the new European overseas empires during this period was that of Great Britain. England had begun its overseas empire in the late twelfth century, when it conquered the neighboring island of Ireland, but only in the seventeenth century did it begin to acquire lands in the New World and Asia. By 1700 the English empire in the Americas included colonies on the eastern North American seaboard, a vast territory in the northern part of Canada, and a cluster of islands in the Caribbean, most notably Barbados, Jamaica, and the Bahamas.

These Caribbean or West Indian colonies developed an economy that used slave labor, and therefore black slaves brought there from Africa soon outnumbered Europeans by a significant margin. In the colonies on the mainland of North America, however, most of the colonists were white, even in the southern colonies, where black slaves accounted for less than half the population.

Many English settlers, especially in the northern colonies, emigrated so that they might practice their religion without legal restraint. During the 1630s communities of English Protestants known as Puritans settled in New England. They objected to the control of the English Church by bishops, especially during the period from 1633 to 1641, when William Laud served as archbishop of Canterbury. Their main complaint was that the church services authorized by Laud too closely resembled those of Roman Catholicism. During the same years small groups of English Catholics, who were denied the right to practice their religion, took refuge in Maryland. In the late seventeenth century a dissenting Protestant sect known as Quakers (so called because their founder, George Fox, told them to quake at the word of the Lord), smarting under legislation that denied them religious freedom and political power, emigrated to Pennsylvania.

During the seventeenth century the English also established trading posts, known as factories, along the coast of India. They settled at Surat in 1612, Madras in 1640, Bombay in 1661, and Calcutta in 1690. These mercantile depots differed markedly from the colonies in the Caribbean and on the North American mainland. The number of British settlers in India, who were mostly members of the East India Company (which had a monopoly of British trade with India), remained small, and they did not establish large plantations. Consequently, they did not introduce slave labor.

SAMUEL SCOTT, *A THAMES WHARF* (1750s)
British merchants conducted a brisk trade with Asia and the Americas in the eighteenth century.

As **Map 18.1** shows, the British also acquired influence and ultimately political control of the area from Southeast Asia stretching down into the South Pacific. In the late seventeenth century the British began to challenge the Dutch and the Portuguese for control of the trade with Indonesia, and in the second half of the eighteenth century British merchants established a thriving trade with the countries on the Malay Peninsula. In the late eighteenth century the British also began to explore the South Pacific, which remained the last part of the inhabited world that Europeans had not yet visited. (See *Justice in History* in this chapter.) In 1770 the British naval officer and explorer Captain James Cook (1728–1779) claimed the entire eastern coast of Australia for Britain, and in 1788 the British established a penal colony in the southeastern corner of the Australian continent at Botany Bay.

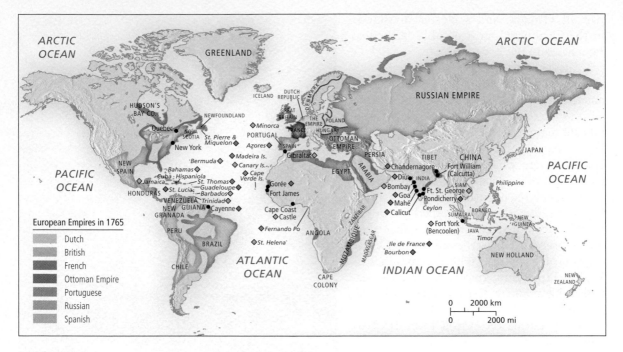

MAP 18.1

European Empires in 1763

This map shows the overseas possessions of Britain, France, the Dutch Republic, Spain, and Portugal. Russian overseas expansion into North America had not yet begun.

The Scattered French Empire

French colonization of North America and India paralleled that of Great Britain, but it never achieved the same degree of success. As the British were establishing footholds in the West Indies and the mainland of North America, the French acquired their own islands in the Caribbean and laid claim to large sections of Canada and the Ohio and Mississippi River valleys in the present-day United States. In the West Indies the French first drew their labor supply from servants indentured for periods of three years, but in the eighteenth century they began to follow the British and Spanish pattern of importing slaves to provide labor for the sugar plantations. In North America French settlers did not require a large labor supply, as their main economic undertakings were the fur trade and fishing, and so they did not introduce slaves to those areas.

The parallel between French and British overseas expansion extended to India, where in the early eighteenth century the French East India Company established factories at Pondicherry, Chandenagar, and other locations. Rivalry with the British also led the French to make alliances with native governors of Indian provinces, to assist them in a series of military conflicts with the British between 1744 and 1815. The British ultimately prevailed in this struggle, reducing the French presence in India to a few isolated factories by the early nineteenth century.

The waning of French influence in India coincided with a series of territorial losses in the New World. Defeats suffered at the hands of the British during the Seven Years' War (1756–1763) resulted in the transfer of French Canada and the territory east of the Mississippi River to Great Britain. During that conflict France also ceded the vast region of Louisiana between the Mississippi River and the Rocky Mountains to Spain. France regained Louisiana in 1801 but then promptly sold the entire territory to the United States in 1803. The following year the French Caribbean colony of Saint Domingue became independent, although France retained possession of its other West Indian colonies.

The Commercial Dutch Empire

The tiny Dutch Republic acquired almost all of its overseas possessions in the first half of the seventeenth century, at about the same time that the British and French were establishing their first colonies in Asia and the New World. The formation of the Dutch empire went hand in hand with the explosive growth of the Dutch economy in the seventeenth century. At that time the Dutch Republic became the center of a global economy, and its overseas colonies in the New World, Asia, and Africa helped the Dutch Republic maintain its commercial supremacy. Dutch overseas settlements, just like Dutch port cities in the metropolis, were dedicated almost exclusively to serving the interests of trade.

The Dutch were more eager than other European powers to use military and naval power to acquire and fortify trading depots. They seized two trading posts from the Portuguese on the West African coast in 1637, and in 1641 they also acquired from Portugal the African islands of São Tomé and Principe. In 1654 they seized two small West Indian islands and plantation colonies on the Guiana coast of South America, mainly in present-day Surinam. From these settlements in Africa and the Caribbean the Dutch carried on trade with the Spanish, Portuguese, French, and British colonies. Through these ports the Dutch brought more than 500,000 slaves to Brazil, the Spanish colonies, and the French and British West Indies.

In addition to their African and Caribbean possessions, the Dutch established a presence in three other parts of the world. In the early seventeenth century they settled a colony in the Hudson River valley on the North American mainland. They named the colony New Netherland and its main port, at the mouth of the river, New Amsterdam. In 1664 the Dutch lost the colony to the English, who renamed the colony and the port New York. The second area was in Asia, where the Dutch East India Company established a fort at Batavia (now Jakarta in Indonesia) and factories in India, China, and Japan. These possessions allowed the Dutch to engage in trade throughout Asia. In the eighteenth century, however, the British began to take control of Dutch trading routes.

THE DUTCH FACTORY OF BATAVIA IN INDONESIA, CA. 1665

The Dutch Republic dominated the Asian trade in the seventeenth century. Batavia (now Jakarta) was the most important of their settlements in Southeast Asia. The efforts of the Dutch to transplant their culture is evident in this building's Dutch style of architecture.

JUSTICE IN HISTORY

The Trial of the Mutineers on the *Bounty*

In December 1787 a British ship named the *Bounty,* under the captainship of William Bligh, left Portsmouth, England, on a momentous journey to Tahiti, an island in the South Pacific that Captain James Cook had first visited in 1769. The goal of the voyage of the *Bounty* was neither exploration nor colonial expansion, but to bring home breadfruit trees that Cook had discovered on his second trip to the island in 1773. The trees, so it was hoped, would be introduced to the West Indies as a source of food for the slaves and hence the survival of the plantation economy. The voyage of the *Bounty* was therefore part of the operation of the new global economy that European expansion had made possible. The total size of the crew, all of whom had volunteered for service, was 46. The master's first mate, who became the main leader of a mutiny against Bligh, was Fletcher Christian.

The mutiny did not take place until after the ship had remained at Tahiti for a number of months, loaded its cargo of more than one thousand breadfruit plants, and begun its return voyage. The main reason for the mutiny was Captain Bligh's abusive and humiliating language. Unlike many other officers who faced the task of maintaining order on their ships and commanding the obedience of their crews, Bligh did not flog his men. In that regard Bligh's behavior was mild. Instead he went into tantrums and verbally abused them, belittling them and calling them scoundrels. Just before the mutiny Bligh called Fletcher

Christian a cowardly rascal and falsely accused him of stealing from him. On the morning of April 28, 1788, Christian arrested Bligh at bayonet point, tied his hands behind his back, and threatened him with instant death if he should speak a word. Claiming that "Captain Bligh had brought all this on himself," Christian and his associates put Bligh and 18 other members of the crew into one of the ship's small launch boats and set them adrift, leaving them to reach a nearby island by their own power.

The mutineers sailed on to the island of Tubuai, where after a brief stay they split into two groups. Nine of them, headed by Christian and accompanied by six Tahitian men and twelve women, established a settlement on Pitcairn Island, where their descendents still reside today. The remaining 16 mutineers returned to Tahiti. All but two of these men

THE MUTINEERS CASTING BLIGH ADRIFT IN THE LAUNCH, ENGRAVING BY ROBERT DODD (1790)

This was the central act in the mutiny led by Fletcher Christian. Captain Bligh is standing in the launch in his nightclothes. Some of the breadfruit trees loaded on the ship at Tahiti can be seen on the top deck.

were apprehended in 1791 by Captain Edwards of the H.M.S. *Pandora,* which had sailed to Tahiti to arrest and return them to England for trial. At the beginning of its return voyage the *Pandora* was shipwrecked, and four of the prisoners drowned. The rest reached England aboard another ship in 1792. They were promptly charged before a navy court-martial with taking the *Bounty* away from its captain and with desertion, both of which were capital offenses under the Naval Discipline Act of 1766.

The trial took place aboard a British ship, H.M.S. *Duke,* in Portsmouth harbor in September 1792. The proceeding had all the markings of a state trial, a proceeding initiated by the government for offenses against the Crown. Mutiny and desertion represented challenges to the state itself. During the second period of imperial expansion navies became major instruments of state power. Even when ships were used for purposes of exploration rather than naval combat, they served the interests of the state. The captain of the ship represented the power of the sovereign at sea. Because of the difficulty of maintaining order in such circum-stances, the captain was given absolute authority. He could use whatever means necessary, including the infliction of corporal punishment, to preserve order. To disobey or challenge the captain was interpreted as an act of rebellion.

The trial was based on the assumption that the mutiny was illegal and seditious. The only ques-tion was the extent of individual involvement in the act itself. The degree of involvement was measured by evidence of one's co-operation with Christian or his loyalty to Bligh. The mere fact that some men had remained with Christian on the *Bounty* did not prove that they had supported the mutiny. Four of those men gave little evidence of having voluntarily cooperated with Christian, and those four men were eventually acquitted. The testimony of Captain Bligh, who declared that those four crew members had been reluctant to put him in the launch boat, was decisive in securing their not-guilty verdicts.

The remaining six men were convicted and sentenced to die by hanging. Three of those men were eventually spared their lives. Peter Heywood and James Morrison were well connected to influential people in the navy and the government and received royal pardons. William Muspratt, one of only three mutineers to hire a lawyer, entered a protest against the procedures of the court. In a court-martial, unlike a criminal trial at the common law, a prisoner could not call witnesses in his own defense. At the time of his conviction Muspratt protested that he had been "debarred calling witnesses whose evidence I have reason to believe would have tended to prove my innocence." The difference between the two systems of criminal justice, he claimed, "is dreadful to the subject and fatal to me." On this ground Muspratt was reprieved.

The three men who were executed died as model prisoners, proclaiming the illegality of their rebellion. By securing their conviction and dramatizing it with a widely publicized hanging, the government had upheld its authority and thus reinforced the power of the Crown.

For Discussion

1. How would you characterize the different ideals of justice adhered to by the mutineers on the *Bounty* and the British admiralty court that tried them?

2. What does the journey of the *Bounty* tell us about the role of the British navy in the process of imperial expansion? What prob-lems were inherent in using British ships for these purposes?

Taking it Further
Rutter, Owen (ed.) *The Court-Martial of the "Bounty" Mutineers.* 1931. Contains a full transcript of the trial.

The third area was the southern tip of Africa, where in 1652 the Dutch settled a colony at the Cape of Good Hope, mainly to provide support for ships engaged in commerce with the East Indies. In this colony some 1,700 Dutch settlers, most of them farmers known as **boers,** developed an agricultural economy on plantations that employed slave labor. The loss of this colony to the British at the end of the eighteenth century reflected a more general decline of Dutch military and imperial strength.

The Vast Spanish Empire

Of the five western European overseas empires, the Spanish monarchy controlled the most land. At the height of its power in 1650, the Spanish Empire covered the western part of North America from California to Mexico and from Mexico down through Central America. It also included Florida and the Caribbean islands of Cuba, San Domingo, and Puerto Rico. It embraced almost all of South America except Brazil, which was under Portuguese control. In Asia the main Spanish possessions were the Philippine Islands, which served as the main base from which the Spanish engaged in trade with other Asian countries.

Spanish overseas possessions formed part of a much more authoritarian imperial system than those of the British. Like all mercantilist enterprises, the Spanish colonial empire served the purposes of trade. Until the eighteenth century a council known as the House of Trade, situated in Seville, exercised a monopoly over all colonial commerce. It funneled trade with the colonies from the southwestern Spanish port of Cadiz to selected ports on the eastern coasts of Spanish America, from which it was then redirected to other ports. The ships returned to Spain carrying the gold and silver from Mexican and Peruvian mines.

The Bourbon kings of Spain, who came to power in 1700, introduced political reforms that were intended to increase the volume of the colonial trade and prevent the smuggling that threatened to undermine it. On the one hand, they opened up the colonial trade to more Spanish and American ports and also permitted more trade within the colonies. On the other hand, the Bourbons, especially Charles III (r. 1759–1788), brought their overseas territories under more direct control of Spanish royal officials and increased the efficiency of the tax collection system. These **Bourbon reforms** made the empire more manageable and profitable, but they also created tension between the Spanish-born bureaucrats and the **creoles,** the people of Spanish descent who had been born in the colonies. These tensions eventually led in the early nineteenth century to a series of wars of independence from Spain that we shall discuss in a later section.

The Declining Portuguese Empire

The Portuguese had been the first European nation to engage in overseas exploration and colonization. During the late fifteenth and sixteenth centuries, they had established colonies in Asia, South America, and Africa (see Chapter 13). By the beginning of the eighteenth century, however, the Portuguese Empire had declined in size and wealth in relation to its rivals. The Portuguese continued to hold a few ports in India, most notably the small island of Goa. They also retained a factory at Macao off the southeastern coast of China. In the New World the major Portuguese plantation colony was Brazil, which occupied almost half the land mass of South America and supplied Europe with sugar, cacao (from which chocolate is made), and other agricultural commodities. Closely linked to Brazil were the Portuguese colonies along and off the West African coast. These possessions were all deeply involved in the transatlantic trade, especially in slaves. The Portuguese also had a series of trading stations and small settlements on the southeastern coast of Africa, including Mozambique.

A relatively weak European power, Portugal did not fare well in the fierce military conflicts that ensued in South America and Asia over control of the colonial trade. Portugal's main military and economic competition came from the Dutch, who seized many of its Asian, African, and South American colonies, thereby acquiring many Portuguese trading routes. Most of those losses took place in Asia between 1600 and 1670. The Portuguese Empire suffered further attrition when the crown relinquished Bombay and the northern African port of Tangier to the English as part of the dowry for the Portuguese princess Catherine of Braganza when she married King Charles II of Great Britain in 1661.

Brazil remained by far the most important of the Portuguese possessions during the late seventeenth and eighteenth centuries. The colony suffered from an unfavorable balance of trade with Portugal, but it expanded in population and wealth during this period, especially after the discovery of gold and diamonds led to large-scale mining in the interior. The slave trade increased in volume to provide additional labor in the mines and on the sugar plantations. In the first quarter of the nineteenth century, as the British slave trade declined and came to an end, Portuguese ships carried 871,600 slaves to Brazil. Between 1826 and 1850 the number increased to an astonishing 1,247,700. As a result of this massive influx of Africans, slaves accounted for approximately 40 percent of the entire Brazilian population in the nineteenth century.

Like most other European countries, Portugal tightened the control of its imperial possessions during the second half of the eighteenth century. During the ministry of the dictatorial Marquis of Pombal from 1755 to 1777, the Portuguese government increased its control over all aspects of colonial life. Like the Bourbon reforms in Spanish America, this legislation created considerable resentment among the creoles. As in Spanish America, these tensions led to demands for Brazil's autonomy in the nineteenth century.

The Russian Empire in the Pacific

The only eastern European state that established an overseas empire during the eighteenth century was Russia. Between the fifteenth and the early eighteenth centuries Russia had gradually acquired a massive overland empire stretching from St. Petersburg in the west across the frigid expanse of Siberia to the Pacific Ocean. The main impulse of Russian expansion had been the search for exotic furs that were in high demand in the colder climes of Russia and northern Europe. During the reign of the empress Catherine the Great (r. 1762–1796), Russia entered a period of further territorial expansion. On its western frontier it took part in the successive partitions of Poland between 1772 and 1795, while to the south it held the Crimean region within the Ottoman Empire between 1783 and 1792.

In the late eighteenth and early nineteenth centuries Russia extended its empire overseas. Russian traders and explorers undertook numerous expeditions to Hawaii and other islands in the Pacific Ocean, sailing as far south as Mexico. They did not, however, establish colonies in these locations. Further expeditions brought Russia across the northern Pacific, where they encroached upon the hunting grounds of the native Aleuts in Alaska. The Russian-American Company, established in 1789, built trading posts along the Pacific seaboard from Alaska down to Fort Ross in northern California. These claims led to a protracted territorial dispute with Spain, which had established a string of missions and settlements on the California coast as far north as San Francisco. In this way the two great European empires of Russia and Spain, advancing from opposite directions, confronted each other on the western coast of North America. Russian expansion into Alaska and California also led to territorial disputes with the United States, which was engaged in its own process of territorial expansion westward toward the Pacific during the nineteenth century.

WARFARE IN EUROPE, NORTH AMERICA, AND ASIA

■ In what ways did the wars waged by European powers during this period involve competition for overseas possessions and trading routes?

Until the middle of the seventeenth century, European states engaged each other in battle almost exclusively within their own continent.

The farthest their armies ever traveled was to the Near East to fight the Turks or to Ireland to conquer the native Celts. The acquisition of overseas empires and the disputes that erupted between European powers over the control of global trade brought those European conflicts to new and distant military theaters. Wars that began over territory in Europe were readily extended to America in one direction and to Asia in the other. The military forces that fought in these imperial battles consisted not only of metropolitan government troops but also colonists. These colonial forces were often supplemented by the troops drawn from the local population, such as when the French recruited Native Americans to fight with them against the British in North America. This pattern of recruiting soldiers from the indigenous population, which began in the eighteenth century, became the norm during the third and final phase of empire-building in the nineteenth and early twentieth centuries.

Wars fought overseas placed a premium on naval strength. Ground troops remained important, both in Europe and overseas, but naval power increasingly proved to be the crucial factor. All of the Western imperial powers either possessed or acquired large navies. Great Britain and the Dutch Republic rose to the status of world powers on the basis of sea power, while the French strengthened their navy considerably during the reign of Louis XIV. The Dutch used their naval power mainly against the Portuguese and the British, while the British directed theirs against the French and the Spanish and also the Dutch. The overwhelming success that the British realized in these conflicts resulted in the establishment of British maritime and imperial supremacy.

Mercantile Warfare

An increasingly important motive for engaging in warfare in the late seventeenth and eighteenth centuries was the protection and expansion of trade. The theory that underlay and inspired these imperial wars was mercantilism. As discussed in Chapter 16, mercantilists believed that the wealth of a state depended on its ability to import fewer commodities than it exported and thus acquire the largest possible share of the world's monetary supply. Mercantilists encouraged domestic industry and placed heavy customs duties or tariffs on imported goods. Mercantilism was therefore a policy of **protectionism,** the shielding of domestic industries from foreign competition. Mercantilists also sought to increase the size of the country's commercial fleet, establish colonies to promote trade, and import raw materials from the colonies to benefit domestic industry. The imperial wars of the seventeenth and eighteenth centuries, which were fought over the control of colonies and trading routes, thus formed part of a mercantilist policy.

The earliest of these mercantile wars took place between the emerging commercial powers of England and the Dutch Republic in the third quarter of the seventeenth century (1652–1654, 1664–1667, 1672–1675). The Dutch resented the passage of English laws, known as the Navigation Acts, which excluded them from trade with English colonies. The Dutch also claimed the right, denied to them by the English, to fish in British waters. Not surprisingly, many of the engagements in these Anglo-Dutch wars took place at sea and in the colonies. The most significant result of these conflicts was the Dutch loss of the port city of New Amsterdam, now renamed New York, to the English.

Shortly after the first Anglo-Dutch conflict, England went to war against Spain (1655–1657). Although this war pitted Protestants against a Catholic power, the two countries fought mainly over economic issues. The war resulted in the British acquisition of Jamaica, one of its most important Caribbean colonies, in 1655. When Britain tried to smuggle more goods than it was allowed by the Treaty of Utrecht (1713) into the Spanish trading post of Portobelo on the Isthmus of Panama, the Spanish retaliated by cutting off the ear of Robert Jenkins, an English captain. This incident led to the War of Jenkins' Ear in 1739. In 1762, during another war against Spain (as well as France), armed forces from Britain and the North American colonies seized the Cuban port of Havana, which Britain returned to Spain in exchange for Florida. Acquisition of Florida gave the British control of the entire North American eastern seaboard.

Anglo-French Military Rivalry

Anglo-Spanish conflict paled in comparison with the bitter commercial rivalry between Great Britain and France during the eighteenth century. Anglo-French conflict was one of the few consistent patterns of eighteenth-century European warfare. It lasted so long and had so many different phases that it became known as the second Hundred Years' War, a recurrence of the bitter period of warfare between England and France from the middle of the fourteenth century to the middle of the fifteenth century.

THE WARS OF THE SPANISH AND AUSTRIAN SUCCESSIONS, 1701–1748 This eighteenth-century Anglo-French rivalry had its roots in the War of the Spanish Succession (1701–1713). The war began as an effort to prevent France from putting Louis XIV's grandson, Philip, on the Spanish throne (see Chapter 16). By uniting French and Spanish territory the proposed succession would have created a massive French-Spanish empire not only in Europe, but in the Western Hemisphere as well. This combination of French and Spanish territory and military power threatened to eclipse the British colonies along the North American coast and deprive British merchants of much of their valuable trade.

The ensuing struggle in North America, known in the British colonies as Queen Anne's War, was settled in Britain's favor by the Treaty of Utrecht in 1713. Philip V (r. 1700–1746) was allowed to remain on the Spanish throne, but French and Spanish territories in Europe and America were kept separate. Even more important, the French ceded their Canadian territories of Newfoundland and Nova Scotia to the British. The treaty, which also gave Britain the contract to ship slaves to the Spanish colonies for 30 years, marked the emergence of Britain as Europe's dominant colonial and maritime power.

The next phase of Anglo-French warfare, the War of the Austrian Succession (1740–1748), formed part of a European conflict that engaged the forces of Austria, Prussia, and Spain in addition to those of Britain and France. In this conflict European dynastic struggles once again intersected with competition for colonial advantage overseas. The ostensible cause of this war was the impetuous decision by the new king of Prussia, the absolutist Frederick II, to seize the large German-speaking province of Silesia from Austria upon the succession of Maria Theresa (r. 1740–1780) as the ruler of the hereditary Habsburg lands (see **Map 18.2**). Frederick struck with devastating effectiveness, and by the terms of the treaty that ended the war he acquired most of the province.

CHRONOLOGY: A CENTURY OF ANGLO-FRENCH WARFARE

1701–1713	War of the Spanish Succession (Queen Anne's War in North America): Spain is allied with France
1740–1748	War of the Austrian Succession (Europe): France is allied with Spain and Prussia; Britain is allied with Austria and the Dutch Republic
1744–1748	King George's War (North America)
1754–1763	French and Indian War (North America): French and British are allied with different Indian tribes
1756–1763	Seven Years' War (Europe): France is allied with Austria; Britain is allied with Prussia
1775–1783	American War of Independence: France is allied with United States against Britain in 1778
1781–1783	Warfare in India
1792–1815	French Revolutionary and Napoleonic Wars: Britain is allied at various times with Austria, Prussia, Spain, and the Dutch Republic; warfare at times in the West Indies and India

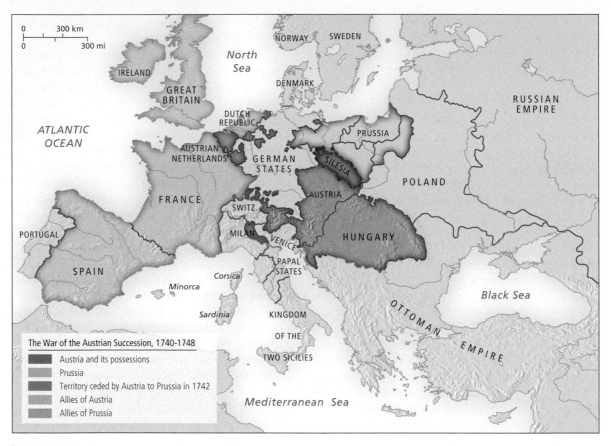

MAP 18.2

The War of the Austrian Succession, 1740–1748

Austria lost Silesia to Prussia during the War of the Austrian Succession in 1742. Maria Theresa's efforts to regain the province in the Seven Years' War were unsuccessful.

Frederick's aggression enticed other European powers to join the conflict. Eager to acquire Habsburg territories in different parts of Europe, France and Spain both declared war on Austria. Britain then entered the war against France, mainly to keep France from acquiring Austria's possessions in the Netherlands.

The colonial phase of this war, known in British North America as King George's War, opened in 1744, when the French supported the Spanish in a war that Spain had been waging against Britain since 1739 over the Caribbean trade. Clashes between French and British trading companies in India also began in the same year. The main military engagement of this war was the seizure of the French port and fortress of Louisbourg on Cape Breton Island in Canada by 4,000 New England colonial troops and a large British fleet. At the end of the war, however, the British returned Louisbourg to the French in exchange for the factory of Madras in India, which the French had taken during the war.

THE SEVEN YEARS' WAR, 1756–1763 European and colonial rivalries became even more entangled in the next round of Anglo-French warfare, known as the Seven Years' War (1756–1763) in Europe and the French and Indian War (1754–1763) in

North America. In Europe the conflict arose as a result of Maria Theresa's eventually unsuccessful attempt to regain Silesia. In this encounter, however, she joined forces with her former enemies, France and Russia, after Great Britain signed a defensive alliance with Prussia. This "diplomatic revolution" of 1756 shifted all the traditional alliances among European powers, but it did not affect Anglo-French rivalry in the colonies, which continued unabated.

The fighting in North America was particularly brutal and inflicted extensive casualties. In their struggle to gain control of eastern port cities and interior lands, the British and the French secured alliances with different Indian tribes. Among the many victims were some of France's Indian allies who contracted smallpox when British-American colonists sold them blankets deliberately contaminated with the disease—the first known use of germ warfare in the West.

This colonial war also had an Asian theater, in which French and British forces, most of them drawn from the trading companies of their respective countries, vied for mercantile influence and the possession of factories along the coast of the Indian Ocean. This conflict led directly to the British acquisition of the Indian province of Bengal in 1765.

The Treaty of Paris of 1763 ended this round of European and colonial warfare. In Europe Prussia managed to hold on to Silesia, although its army incurred heavy casualties and its economy suffered from the war. In North America all of French Canada east of the Mississippi, including the entire province of Quebec, with its predominantly French population and French system of civil law, passed into British control (see **Map 18.3**). Even more important, the treaty secured British naval and mercantile superiority in the Atlantic, Caribbean, and Indian oceans. By virtue of its victories over France, Britain gained control of the lion's share of world commerce. This commercial superiority had profound implications for the economic development of Britain. Partly because of its ability to acquire raw materials from its colonies and to market its products throughout the world, Britain became the first country to experience the Industrial Revolution.

THE AMERICAN AND FRENCH REVOLUTIONARY WARS, 1775–1815 Despite the British victory over the French in 1763, the long conflict between the two countries continued into the early nineteenth century. During the American War of Independence (1775–1783), the North American colonists secured French military aid, a British fleet attacked the French colony of Martinique, and the French dispatched an expedition against the British at Savannah that included hundreds of Africans and **mulattos,** or people of mixed race, drawn from the population of the West Indies. In India further conflicts between the French and British occurred, mainly between 1781 and 1783. These simultaneous military engagements in various parts of the world turned this phase of Anglo-French conflict into the first truly global war.

Anglo-French rivalry entered yet another phase between 1792 and 1815, during the era of the French Revolution (see Chapter 20). The British were able to maintain their military and naval superiority, although once again it required an alliance with many European powers and the creation of a new balance of power against France. Even during this later phase of this French-British rivalry the British pursued imperial objectives. They expanded their empire in India and consolidated their territory there under the governorship of Richard Wellesley (1760–1842). In 1795, in the midst of the war against France, the British also acquired the Dutch colony at the Cape of Good Hope, giving them a base for their claims to much larger African territories in the nineteenth century.

THE ATLANTIC WORLD

■ How did European empires create an Atlantic economy in which the traffic in slaves was a major feature?

By the beginning of the eighteenth century, the territorial acquisitions of the five European

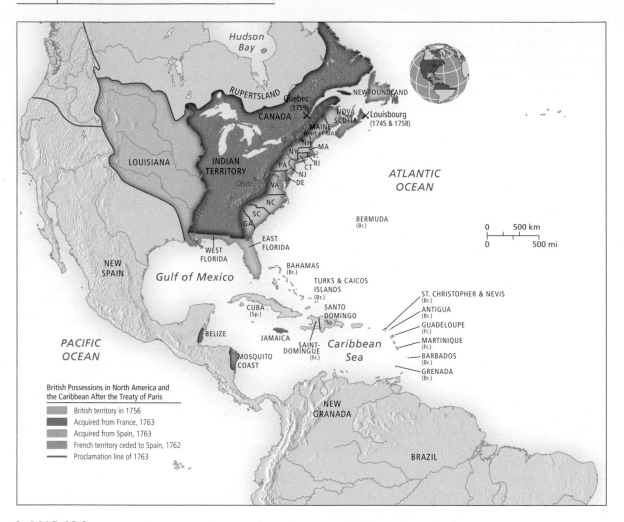

MAP 18.3
British Possessions in North America and the Caribbean After the Treaty of Paris, 1763

The British acquisition of French territory marked a decisive moment in the expansion of the British Empire.

maritime powers had moved the geographical center of the West from the European continent to the Atlantic Ocean itself. The Atlantic, rather than separating large geographical land masses, gave them a new unity. The boundaries of this new Western world were the four continents that bordered the Atlantic: Europe, Africa, North America, and South America. The main thoroughfares that linked them were maritime routes across the Atlantic and up and down its coasts. The main points of commer-cial and cultural contact between the four continents, until the end of the eighteenth century, were the coastal areas and ports that bordered on the ocean. Within this Atlantic world arose new patterns of trade and economic activity, new interactions between ethnic and racial groups, and new political institutions. The Atlantic world also became the arena in which political and religious ideas were transmitted across the ocean and transformed within new environments.

The Atlantic Economy

The exchange of commercial goods and slaves between the western coasts of Europe, the African coasts, and the ports of North and South America created a major economic enterprise (see **Map 18.4**). The ships that brought the slaves from Africa to the Americas used the profits gained from their transactions to acquire precious metals

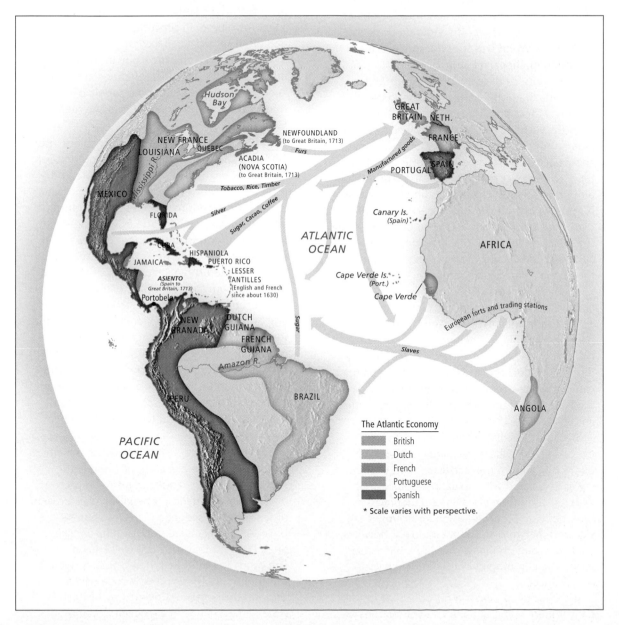

MAP 18.4

The Atlantic Economy in the Mid-Eighteenth Century

Commodities and African slaves were exchanged between the four continents of North America, South America, Europe, and Africa.

ENCOUNTERS AND TRANSFORMATIONS

Chocolate in the New World and the Old

One product of the encounters that took place between Spaniards and the indigenous people of the New World was the widespread consumption of chocolate among western Europeans in the seventeenth century. Long before the Spanish Conquest of the sixteenth century, Aztecs and Mayans produced chocolate from the seeds of the cacao tree, which was indigenous to South America. They consumed chocolate mainly as a beverage and used it, like tobacco (another native American plant), in religious and political ceremonies and for medicinal purposes. Spanish colonists received gifts of chocolate from Indians and soon began to enjoy the pleasurable physiological effects of this commodity, which contains chemical agents that act like amphetamines.

By the beginning of the seventeenth century, chocolate made its way from colonial America across the Atlantic to Spain. Shortly thereafter it became available in other western European countries. Its widespread use prepared the way for the introduction of two other stimulants that came originally from the Middle East and Asia in the latter half of the seventeenth century: coffee and tea.

Because chocolate was grown in non-Christian lands where Spaniards believed that demons inhabited the landscape, and because it was associated with sexual pleasure, it met with harsh disapproval. Clerics denounced it— together with tobacco—as an inducement to vice and the work of Satan. Gradually, however, chocolate came to be viewed in purely secular terms as a commodity, without any religious significance.

The European demand for chocolate contributed to three major transformations of Western life. The first was the growth of the Atlantic trade and a global economy. Among the products that were shipped from the Americas to Europe in exchange for slaves and manufactured goods, cacao was second only to sugar in volume. In preconquest America cacao had often served as an exchange currency. Now it was assigned a specific value in the world marketplace. As the price of chocolate escalated, Spain established a monopoly over the trade, and thus integrated it into the mercantilist system.

Second, the introduction of chocolate into Europe transformed Western drinking patterns. There had been nothing like chocolate in the diets of Europeans before its arrival, and when it was introduced, new rituals of consumption developed. Cups with handles were designed specifically for drinking the hot beverage, the same cups later used for coffee and tea. Europeans adopted the Aztec custom of scooping the foam from the top of a chocolate drink. The European desire to sweeten chocolate, and also coffee and tea, increased the demand for sugar, which in turn encouraged the growth of slavery on the sugar plantations in the West Indies. Sweetened chocolate eventually began to be served as a candy, and by the nineteenth century chocolate candy became the main form in which the commodity was consumed.

Finally, chocolate became a part of the emerging bourgeois sexual culture of eighteenth-century France and England. Just as in preconquest Spanish America, it began to play a role in rituals of sexual seduction. It is no accident that boxes of chocolate are popular gifts on Valentine's Day and that the most well-known chocolate candy in the United States, Godiva, features the English noblewoman who rode naked through the streets of Coventry in 1140. The sustained exchange of a delectable commodity between the New World and the Old World thus contributed to a transformation of Western culture.

THE CHOCOLATE HOUSE (1787)

Men and women drinking chocolate, tea, and coffee at the White Conduit House, Islington, London.

Source: Thomas Rowlandson (1756–1827), "The Chocolate House," 1787. HIP/Art Resource, NY

For Discussion

1. To what extent did the tastes of European consumers determine the nature of the Atlantic economy in the seventeenth and eighteenth centuries?

2. Why did political leaders and clerics differ in their views regarding the value of chocolate in the seventeenth and eighteenth centuries?

Taking it Further

Louis Grivetti and Howard-Yana Shapiro (eds.), *Chocolate: History, Culture, and Heritage*, 2009. A massive scholarly collection of 57 articles on all aspects of the subject.

and agricultural products for the European market. They then returned to western European Atlantic ports, where the goods were sold.

The Atlantic economy was fueled by the demand of a growing European population for agricultural products that were unavailable in Europe and were more costly to transport from Asia. Sugar was the most important of these commodities, but tobacco, cotton, rice, cacao, and coffee also became staples of the transatlantic trade. (See *Encounters and Transformations* in this chapter.) For their part, North and South American colonists created a steady demand for manufactured goods, especially cutlery and metal tools produced in Europe.

Two of the commodities imported from the colonies, tobacco and coffee, were criticized for their harmful effects. "Tobacco, that outlandish weed," read one popular rhyme, "It spends the brain and spoils the seed." Critics also claimed that it had a hallucinatory effect. Coffee, a stimulant that originally came from the Middle East but later from Haiti and Brazil, was believed to encourage political radicalism, probably because the coffeehouses served as gathering places for political dissidents. Contemporaries also identified coffee's capacity to produce irritability and depression.

The Atlantic economy had its own rhythms but was also part of a global economy. As Europeans had expanded the volume of their imports from America, those markets were fully integrated into this world system. The system was capitalist in the sense that private individuals produced and distributed commodities for profit in a systematic way. European governments had an interest in this capitalist economy because as mercantilists they wanted their countries to acquire the largest possible share of world trade, but they did not control the actual operations of the marketplace. Their role was mainly to authorize individuals or trading companies to conduct trade in a particular geographical area.

The Atlantic Slave Trade

The slave trade became the linchpin of the Atlantic economy, and all five western European imperial powers—Britain, France, the Dutch Republic, Spain, and Portugal—participated in it. The trade arose to meet the demand of plantation owners in the New World for agricultural labor. In the seventeenth century this demand became urgent when disease ravaged the indigenous Indian population and when indentured whites who had emigrated from Europe in search of a more secure future gained their freedom. Slave labor possessed considerable advantages over free labor. Plantation masters could discipline slaves more easily and force them to work longer hours. Slaves became a vital part of a plantation economy in which one authority, the plantation master, directed the growing, harvesting, and processing of sugar and agricultural commodities. The use of slave labor also allowed the economies of European countries, especially

A SATIRE AGAINST COFFEE AND TOBACCO
A seventeenth-century satirical depiction of two European women smoking tobacco and drinking coffee. Turkey, represented by the figure to the right, was the main source of coffee in the seventeenth century. An African servant, to the left, pours the coffee. Tobacco came from the Americas.

Britain, to develop. Those who had invested in the colonial trade received attractive returns on their investment, while agricultural profits acquired from crops produced by slaves encouraged the growth of domestic manufacturing.

The slave trade formed the crucial link in the triangular pattern of commercial routes that began when European vessels traveled to ports along the western coast of Africa. There they exchanged European goods, including guns, for slaves that African merchants had captured in the interior and had marched to the sea. At these ports European slave traders branded the slaves with initials indicating to which nation they belonged. Traders then packed them into ships that transported them across the Atlantic to the coast of South America, to the Caribbean, or as far north as Maryland. This was the notorious **Middle Passage,** the second leg of the triangular journey, which was completed when the ships returned to their points of origin loaded with the plantation products of America. Once they had arrived in the Americas, the slaves were sold to the owners of plantations in the tropical areas of the Caribbean and the south Atlantic and in the more moderate climates of the North American mainland.

The African slave trade conducted by Europeans differed from other forms of slavery in world history in three respects. The first was its size: it was the largest involuntary, transoceanic transportation of human beings in world history. Between 1519 and 1867 more than eleven million slaves were shipped from Africa to the New World. Deaths at sea reduced the number of slaves who actually arrived in the Americas to about 9.5 million. Nine out of every ten of these slaves were sent to Brazil or the Caribbean region, including the northern coast of South America.

The second distinctive feature of African slavery in the Americas was its racial character. In this respect it differed from the forms of slavery that had existed in ancient Greece, Rome, and medieval Europe, where people of different races and ethnicities had been enslaved. It also differed from Muslim slavery, which involved the captivity of white European Christians as well as black Africans. As the slave trade brought millions of black Africans into the Americas, slavery came to be equated with being black, and Europeans referred to the color of the slaves' skin as evidence that they were inferior to white people.

The third distinctive feature of the Atlantic slave trade was its commercial character. Its sole function was to provide slave traders with a profit and slave owners with a supply of cheap labor. Europeans defended the right of slave masters to own their slaves as they would other pieces of property. The Atlantic slave trade turned African slaves into commercial commodities and treated them in a manner that deprived them of all human dignity. To justify such treatment their owners insisted that they "were beasts and had no more souls than beasts."[3]

One harrowing incident on the British slave ship *Zong* reveals the way in which financial calculations determined the fate of slaves. The *Zong* set sail in 1781 from Africa with 442 African slaves on board. When the slaves began to fall ill and die from malnutrition and disease, the captain of the ship, Luke Collingwood, feared that the owners of the ship would suffer a financial loss. If, however, the slaves were to be thrown overboard on the pretext that the safety of the crew was in jeopardy, those who had insured the voyage would absorb the loss. Accordingly Collingwood tied 132 slaves together, two by two, and flung them into the sea. When the ship owners went to court to collect the insurance, they argued that slaves were no different from horses and that they had a perfect right to throw the slaves overboard to preserve the safety of the ship.

The slave trade itself became the object of intense competition, as each country tried to establish a monopoly over certain routes. During the seventeenth century the British managed to make inroads into the French slave trade, and eventually the British surpassed the Portuguese and the Dutch as well. By 1700 British ships were transporting more than 50 percent of all slaves to the Americas. The dominance that Britain established in the slave trade reinforced its growing maritime and commercial strength. With an enormous merchant marine and a navy that could support it, the British came to dominate the slave trade in the same way they came to dominate the entire world economy. Both revealed how far mercantile capitalism had triumphed in Britain and its overseas possessions.

In the late eighteenth century, however, a movement arose in all European countries to end both the slave trade and the institution of slavery itself. (See *Different Voices* in this chapter.) The movement drew much of its inspiration from religious zeal, especially among evangelical Protestants in Britain and Jesuits in Spain and Portugal. The movement gradually acquired widespread support. In Britain more than 300,000 people

DIFFERENT VOICES THE ABOLITION OF THE SLAVE TRADE

In 1787 Quobna Ottobah Cugoano (1757–1791), a former slave, published a treatise calling for the abolition of the African slave trade. Like the narrative written by Olaudah Equiano quoted at the beginning of this chapter, Cugoano's book described the horrors of the African slave trade that he himself had experienced. In this passage Cugoano deplored the effect that the slave trade had on his native Africa. In Great Britain the politician and philanthropist William Wilberforce (1759–1833) spearheaded the campaign to abolish the slave trade in the late eighteenth and early nineteenth centuries. His was a lonely voice when he gave his first speech to parliament on this subject in 1789, 18 years before Britain ended the slave trade. Wilberforce also discussed the deleterious effects of the slave trade on Africa.

A former slave exposes the effects of the slave trade on Africa

That base traffic of kid-napping and stealing men was begun by the Portuguese on the coast of Africa, and as they found the benefit of it for their own wicked purposes, they soon went on to commit further depredations. The Spaniards followed their infamous example, and the African slave trade was thought most advantageous for them, to enable themselves to live in ease and affluence by the cruel subjection and slavery of others. The French and English, and some other nations in Europe, as they founded settlements or colonies in the West Indies or in America, went on in the same manner, and joined hand in hand with the Portuguese and Spaniards to rob and pillage Africa and desolate the inhabitants of the western continent. But the European depredators and pirates have not only robbed and pillaged the people of Africa themselves; but, by their instigation, they have infested the inhabitants with some of the vilest combinations of fraudulent and treacherous villains, even among their own people, and have set up their forts and factories as a reservoir of public and abandoned thieves and as a den of desperadoes, where they may ensnare, entrap and catch men. So that Africa has been robbed of its inhabitants, its freeborn sons and daughters have been stolen, and kid-napped and violently taken away and carried into captivity and cruel bondage. And it may be said in respect to that diabolical traffic which is still carried on by the European depredators, that Africa has suffered as much and more than any other quarters of the globe.

Source: Quobna Ottobah Cugoano, *Thoughts and Sentiments on the Evil and Wicked Traffic of the Slavery and Commerce of the Human Species* (London, 1787).

An English politician launches a campaign to end the slave trade Slave Trade in 1789

What should we suppose must naturally be the consequence of our carrying on a slave trade with Africa? With a country vast in its extent, not utterly barbarous, but civilized in a very small degree? Does one suppose a slave trade would

supported the cause of abolition by refusing to buy sugar—the largest consumer boycott the world had ever known. British capitalists also came to the conclusion that slavery was no longer economically advantageous. Goods produced by free labor, especially by machine, made slavery appear less cost-effective than in the past.

By the first decade of the nineteenth century opposition to slavery began to achieve limited success. In 1807 the British parliament legislated an end to the trade within the British Empire, and in the following year the United States refused to allow any of its ports to accept slave ships. The Dutch ended their slave trade in 1814, the French in 1815, and the Spanish in 1838. The Portuguese continued to import slaves to Brazil until 1850.

Liberation of the slaves generally came later. The British dismantled the system within

help their civilization? Is it not plain that she must suffer from it?...that her barbarous manners must be made more barbarous; and that the happiness of her millions of inhabitants must be prejudiced with her intercourse with Britain? Does not everyone see that a slave trade, carried on around her coasts, must carry violence and desolation to her very center? That in a Continent just emerging from barbarism, if a trade in men is established, if her men are all converted into goods, and become commodities that can be bartered, it follows, they must be subject to ravage just as goods are; and this, too, at a period of civilization, when there is no protecting legislature to defend this their only sort of property, in the same manner as the rights of property are maintained by the legislature of every civilized country....In Africa it is the personal avarice and sensuality of their kings...[T]hese two vices we stimulate in all these African princes, and we depend upon these vices for the very maintenance of the slave trade....

I must speak of the transit of the slaves in the West Indies. This I confess, in my opinion, is the most wretched part of the whole subject. So much misery condensed in so little room is more than the human imagination had ever before conceived....Let anyone imagine to himself 6 or 700 of these wretches chained two and two, surrounded with every object that is nauseous and disgusting, diseased, and struggling under every kind of wretchedness! How can we bear to think of such a scene as this? One would think it had been

determined to heap upon them all the varieties of bodily pain, for the purposes of blunting the feelings of the mind....Exclusive of those who perish before they set sail, not less than $12\frac{1}{2}$ per cent perish in the passage. Besides these the Jamaica report tells you that not less than $4\frac{1}{2}$ per cent die on the shore before the day of sale, which is only a week or two from the time of landing. One third more die in the seasoning, and this in a country exactly like their own, where they are healthy and happy as some of the evidences would pretend....Upon the whole, however, there is a mortality of about 50 per cent, and this amongst negroes who are not bought unless healthy at first, and unless (as the phrase is with cattle) they are sound in wind and limb.

Source: From *Cobbett's Parliamentary History* 28, pp. 41–43

For Discussion

1. How did Cugoano and Wilberforce differ in their views of Africa?

2. The slave trade in Britain was not abolished until 1807, 20 years after the publication of Cugoana's treatise and 18 years after Wilberforce began his parliamentary campaign. Why might other legislators in Britain have resisted their efforts?

3. Why was the mortality rate of slaves transported to the West Indies higher than those shipped to other destinations?

their empire between 1834 and 1838. Slavery persisted until 1848 in the French Caribbean, 1863 in the southern United States, 1886 in Cuba, and 1888 in Brazil.

Ethnic Diversity in the Atlantic World

European countries had always possessed some ethnic diversity, but the emigration of people from many different parts of Europe and Africa to America, followed by their intermarriage, created societies of much greater complexity. Even white European communities in the colonies were more ethnically diverse than in the metropolis. The British colonies, for example, attracted not only English, Scottish, and Irish settlers, but also Germans, French, and Swiss.

***THE SLAVE SHIP* BY J. M. W. TURNER (1840)**

The English painter J. M. W. Turner captured the horror of the incident that took place aboard the slave ship *Zong,* when the crew threw 132 slaves overboard in 1781.

Source: Joseph Mallord William Turner (English 1775–1851), "Slave Ship (Slavers Throwing Overboard the Dead and Dying. Typhoon Coming On)." 1840. Oil on canvas. 90.8 × 122.6 (35 3/4 × 48 1/4 in). Henry Lillie Pierce Fund. 99.22. Courtesy, Museum of Fine Arts, Boston. Reproduced with permission. © 2006 Museum of Fine Arts, Boston. All Rights Reserved.

CHRONOLOGY: VOLUME OF THE TRANSATLANTIC SLAVE TRADE FROM AFRICA, 1519–1867

1519–1600	266,100
1601–1650	503,500
1651–1675	239,800
1676–1700	510,000
1701–1725	958,600
1725–1750	1,311,300
1751–1775	1,905,200
1776–1800	1,921,100
1801–1825	1,645,100
1826–1850	1,621,000
1851–1867	180,800
Total	11,062,500

Source: David Eltis, "The Volume and Structure of the Transatlantic Slave Trade: A Reassessment," *William and Mary Quarterly,* 3rd series, 58 (2001), Table II.6

The ethnicity of colonial populations was more varied in Latin America than in North America. The higher proportion of African slaves, more frequent intermarriage among different groups, and the free status achieved by many blacks and mulattos created highly stratified societies. In these colonies divisions arose not only between the recently arrived Europeans and the creoles, but also among the various groups that Europeans considered socially inferior.

The most complex social structure in the New World developed in Brazil. Portuguese bureaucrats stood at the top of the Brazilian social hierarchy, holding a social position just above a large and wealthy group of planter creoles. These two elite groups dominated a lower-class social hierarchy of **mestizos** (people of mixed white and Indian ancestry), indigenous people, mulattos, freed blacks, and slaves.

ENCOUNTERS BETWEEN EUROPEANS AND ASIANS

■ How did cultural encounters between European and Asian peoples during this period of empire-building, change Western attitudes toward outsiders?

In Asia, European powers initially did not try to acquire and govern large territories and subjugate their populations, as they did in America. Europeans first came to Asia to trade, not to conquer or establish large colonies. Europeans did not engage in fixed battles with Asians, take steps to reduce the size of their populations, or force them to migrate, as they did in the New World. Nevertheless, during the period from 1650 to 1815 European powers established or greatly expanded their empires in Asia.

When Europeans used military force in Asia, it was almost always against rival European powers, not the indigenous population. When European countries did eventually use force against Asians, they discovered that victory was much more difficult than it had been in the New World. Indeed, Asian peoples already possessed or were acquiring sufficient military strength to respond to European military might. In China and Japan the possession of this military power prevented Europeans from even contemplating conquest or exploitation until the nineteenth century. Establishment of European hegemony in Asia, therefore, took longer and was achieved more gradually than in the Americas.

Political Control of India

Despite their original intentions, Europeans eventually began to acquire political control over large geographical areas in Asia and subject Asians to European rule. The first decisive steps in this process took place in India during the second half of the eighteenth century. Until that time the British in India, most of whom were members of the British East India Company, remained confined to the factories that were established along the Indian coast. We saw earlier that the main purpose of these factories was to engage in trade not only with Europe, but also with other parts of Asia. In conducting this trade the British had to deal with local Indian merchants and compete with the French, the Portuguese, and the Dutch, who had established factories of their own. They also found it advantageous to make alliances with the provincial governors, known as **nawabs,** who controlled the interior of the country. It became customary for each European power to have its own candidate for nawab, with the expectation that he would provide favors for his European patrons once he took office.

MILITARY CONFLICT AND TERRITORIAL ACQUISITIONS, **1756–1856** In 1756 this pattern of trading and negotiating resulted in armed military conflict in the city of Calcutta in the northeastern province of Bengal. The British had established a factory at Calcutta in 1690, and they continued to carry on an extensive trade there with Indian merchants, many of whom were Hindus. Bengal's nawab, the Muslim Siraj-ud-Daulah, had contempt for all Europeans, especially the British, and he was determined that he would not be beholden to any of them. In June 1756 he sent an army of 50,000 Muslims against Calcutta, burning and plundering the city and besieging the East India Company's Fort William, which was manned by 515 troops in the service of the company. The entire British population of the city, together with more than 2,000 Hindus, had taken refuge in the fort. After a long struggle, which resulted in the death of hundreds of Indians, the fort fell to the nawab's forces, and some of the British officers and magistrates, including the governor of Calcutta, fled by sea.

During this siege the shooting death of a Bengali guard led to an incident that became permanently emblazoned on the emerging imperial consciousness of the British people. In response to the shooting, officers in the nawab's army crammed the entire remaining British contingent, a total of 146 men and women, into the fort's lockup or prison, known as the Black Hole of Calcutta. Measuring 18' × 14', it was meant to hold only three or four prisoners overnight.

WARREN HASTINGS

Warren Hastings (1732–1818), who was appointed the first governor-general of India in 1773, represented the ambiguities of early British rule in that country. An officer in the British East India Company, he was sympathetic to Indian culture. He was, however, accused of gross misconduct in the management of Indian affairs. His impeachment by the British Parliament in 1786 for corruption in his administration and cruelty toward some of the native people in Bengal lasted 145 days but resulted in an acquittal in 1787.

Source: Thomas Gainsborough (1727–88), "Lord Hastings (1732–1818), Governor of India," 1780s, oil on canvas. Museu de Arte, Sao Paulo, Brazil/Giraudon/The Bridgeman Art Library

The deaths of these British men and women in the Black Hole of Calcutta led the British to seek swift and brutal retribution against the nawab. In 1757, under the direction of the British military officer Robert Clive, a force of 800 British troops and 2,000 native Indian soldiers known as **sepoys** retook Calcutta and routed Siraj-ud-Daulah's army at the Battle of Plassey. The British executed Siraj-ud-Daulah and replaced him with a nawab more amenable to their interests. A few years later the British East India Company secured the right to collect taxes and thus exercise political control over the entire province of Bengal. The enormous revenue from these taxes enabled the company to acquire a large army, composed mainly of sepoys. This force grew to 115,000 men by 1782. The British then used this army, equipped with Western military technology, to gain control of other provinces in India and defeat their French rivals in subsequent engagements during the early nineteenth century.

These further acquisitions of Indian territory led eventually to the establishment of British dominance throughout the South Asian subcontinent (see **Map 18.5**). New territories were brought under British control in the early years of the nineteenth century, and during the tenure of Lord Dalhousie as governor-general of India from 1848 to 1856 the British annexed eight Indian states, including the great Muslim state of Oudh in 1856. The expansion of British control went hand in hand with the introduction of Western technology and literature, the English language, and British criminal procedure. After suppressing a mutiny of sepoys against British rule in 1857, the British government abolished the East India Company and assumed direct control of the entire South Asian continent.

Changing European Attitudes Toward Asian Cultures

European imperialism in Asia played a crucial role in the formation of Western identity. Until the seventeenth century Europeans thought of "the East" mainly as the Near East, an area that was largely subsumed within the Ottoman Empire. The Far East, comprising South Asia (India), East Asia

The stench was so bad that many prisoners vomited on the people squeezed next to them. The insufferable heat and lack of water and air were stifling. Only 22 men and one woman survived until the next morning, when the nawab released them. The remainder either had been trampled to death or had asphyxiated.

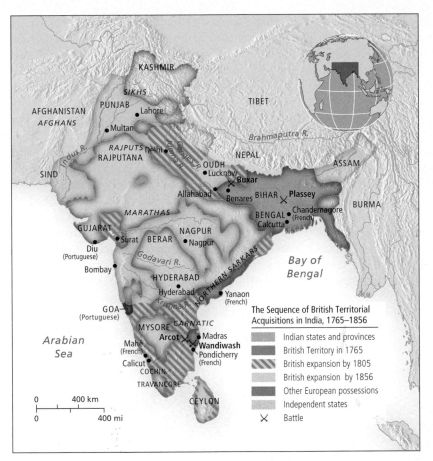

MAP 18.5

The Sequence of British Territorial Acquisitions in India, 1765–1856

British political control of large territories on the South Asian subcontinent began more than a century after the establishment of the first factories along the coast.

(China, Japan), and Southeast Asia (Burma, Siam, Indonesia), generally did not enter into European perceptions of "the Orient." Europeans had little contact with this part of the world, and much of what they knew about it was shrouded in mystery. During this period Europeans viewed the Far East mainly as an exotic land, rich in spices, silk, and other luxury commodities.

As Western missionaries and merchants made more frequent contacts with Asian society, Europeans developed more informed impressions of these distant lands and peoples. Some

of those impressions were negative, especially when they dealt with the political power of Asian rulers, but many other characterizations of the East were positive. Interest in and admiration for Indian and Chinese culture were most widespread during the middle years of the eighteenth century. More and more European scholars committed themselves to the systematic study of Asian languages, especially Chinese and Sanskrit. European writers and thinkers used Asian comparisons to reinforce their criticisms of the West. The French writer Voltaire (1694–1778), for example, regarded Asian cultures as superior to those of Europe in many respects. Voltaire also found the East unaffected by the superstition and the fanaticism that characterized Western Christianity, which he loathed. To him, the main philosophical tradition of China, Confucianism, which embodied a strict moral code, was a more attractive alternative. Eastern religion, especially Hinduism, also won admiration for its ethical content and its underlying belief in a single deity.

This mid-eighteenth-century admiration of Asian culture even extended to Chinese and Indian political institutions. Voltaire transformed the despotic Chinese Empire into an enlightened monarchy, while the French Jesuit priest Guillaume Thomas Raynal (1713–1796) idealized the "purity and equity" of the ancient Indian political system. Comparison of contemporary Indian politics with the corruption of governments in Europe made native Asian political systems look good by comparison. In Britain there was more disrespect for the members of the East India Company, known as **nabobs,** than there was for native Indian officials.

This intellectual respect for Asian philosophy and politics coincided with a period of widespread Asian influences on Western art, architecture, and design. Eastern themes began to influence British buildings, such as in the Brighton Pavilion, designed by John Nash. Small cottages, known as bungalows, owed their inspiration to Indian models. French architects built pagodas (towers with the roof of each story turning upward) for their clients. Chinese gardens, which unlike classical European gardens were not arranged geometrically, became popular in England and France.

A new form of decorative art that combined Chinese and European motifs, known in French as **chinoiserie,** became highly fashionable. Wealthy French people furnished their homes with Chinese wallpaper and hand-painted folding screens. The demand for Chinese porcelain, known in English simply as china, was insatiable. Vast quantities of this porcelain, technically and aesthetically superior to the stoneware produced in Germany and England, left China for the ports of western Europe.

Asian styles also influenced styles of dress and types of recreation. Indian and Chinese silks were in high demand, and Europeans preferred Indian cotton over that produced in the New World. A style of Indian nightwear known as pajamas became popular in England. A new sport, polo, which had originated to India, made its entry into the upper levels of European society at this time.

During the late eighteenth and early nineteenth centuries the high regard in which many Europeans held Asian culture began to wane. As the European presence in Asia increased, as the British began to exercise more control in India,

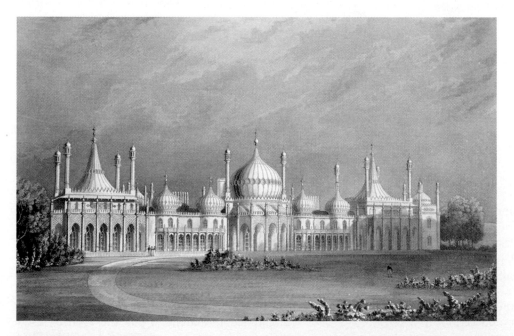

BRIGHTON PAVILION

This building, designed by John Nash, reflected the incorporation of Eastern styles into English architecture, and was inspired by the description of Kubla Khan's palace in Samuel Taylor Coleridge's poem "Kubla Khan" (1816).

and as merchants began to monopolize the Asian trade, Western images of the East became more negative. Europeans now tended to view Chinese philosophy not as a repository of ancient ethical wisdom, but rather irrational when compared with that of the West. Confucianism fell out of favor, and Eastern religion in general came to be regarded as being inferior to Christianity. European thinkers ranked Asian political systems below those of the more "advanced" countries of Europe. English writers claimed that the Chinese did not deserve their reputation for industry, ingenuity, and technological innovation.

Western ideas of racial difference reinforced Europeans' belief in their superiority over Asians. European argued that differences in skin color and facial features reflected their superiority over the Chinese, dark-skinned South Asians, and Polynesians. Intellectual theories of race, which emerged in Europe during the late eighteenth century and were applied mainly to black Africans, provided a supposedly empirical and scientific foundation for these assumptions. Westerners used the color of South Asians' complexion, which had determined position of a person in the Hindu caste system, to identify them as "coloreds." Chinese people, previously described in the West as white, were now referred to as being nonwhite or yellow.

THE CRISIS OF EMPIRE AND THE ATLANTIC REVOLUTIONS

- Why did European powers begin to lose control of some of their colonies, especially those in the Americas, between 1775 and 1825?

During the period from 1780 to 1825, European empires experienced a crisis that marked the end of the second stage of European overseas expansion. As a result of this crisis, British, French, and Spanish governments lost large segments of their empires in the Americas. New states were carved out of the older sprawling empires.

The crisis was to some extent administrative. Having acquired large expanses of territory overseas, European states faced the challenging problem of governing them from a distance. They not only had to rule large areas inhabited by non-European peoples (Indians and African slaves), but they also faced the difficulty of maintaining the loyalty of people of European descent who were born in the colonies. These creoles became the main protagonists in the struggles that led to the independence of the North American colonies from Britain in 1776 and the South American colonies from Spain a generation later.

In the French colony of Saint Domingue and in Britain's European colony of Ireland, different stories unfolded. In Saint Domingue, the location of the only successful revolution in the Caribbean region, the revolution was led not by white creoles but by people of color, including the slaves who worked on the plantations. In Britain's European colony of Ireland, where an unsuccessful revolution against British rule took place in 1798, the urge for independence came both from settlers of British descent and the native Irish population.

The American Revolution, 1775–1783

The first Atlantic revolution began with the revolt of the 13 North American colonies in 1775 and resulted in the establishment of their independence from British rule in 1783. During the second half of the eighteenth century, tension arose between the British government and its transatlantic colonies. These overseas British colonies had developed traditions of self-government, but various governmental bodies responsible to the British Parliament continued to exercise control over their activities. The colonies had their own militias, but they also received protection from British troops when conflicts developed with the French.

The crisis that led to the American Revolution had its roots in the situation that emerged at the end of the French and Indian War. To maintain the peace of 1763, the British government stationed troops on the frontiers of the colonies.

It argued that because the troops were protecting the colonists, they should contribute financially to their own defense. To this end the government began imposing new taxes on the colonists. In 1765 the British Parliament passed the Stamp Act, which forced colonists to purchase stamps for almost anything that was printed. This piece of legislation raised the central constitutional issue of whether Parliament had the power to legislate for British subjects in lands that did not elect members of that Parliament. "Taxation without representation is tyranny" became the main rallying cry of the colonists. Opposition to the Stamp Act was so strong that Parliament repealed the act the following year, but it later passed a statute declaring that it had the authority to tax the colonists as it pleased. When the government imposed new taxes on the tea imported from Britain in 1773, colonists dressed as Indians threw the tea into Boston Harbor.

The government responded to this "Boston Tea Party" by passing a series of statutes, known in the colonies as the Intolerable Acts, in 1774. One of these acts specified that the port of Boston be closed until the colonists had repaid the cost of the tea. The Intolerable Acts led to organized resistance to British rule, and in the following year military conflict broke out at Lexington and Concord in Massachusetts. On July 4, 1776, 13 of the colonies on the North American mainland, stretching from New Hampshire to Georgia, approved a Declaration of Independence from Great Britain. A long revolutionary war, in which the colonists received assistance from France in 1778, ended with the defeat of British troops at Yorktown in 1781 and the recognition of the republic of the United States of America in the Treaty of Paris in 1783.

The case that the American colonists made for independence from Britain drew upon four distinct sources. First, the political theories of John Locke, who justified resistance against the Stuart monarchy at the time of the Glorious

THE BOSTONIANS' PAYING THE EXCISE MAN OR TARRING & FEATHERING

THE BOSTONIANS' PAYING THE EXCISE MAN OR TARRING AND FEATHERING (1774)

This satirical engraving reflects the hatred of colonial Americans at the collection of taxes levied on them without their consent. The Boston Tea Party is depicted in the background. The colonists are forcing the tax collector to drink the tea on which he is trying to collect taxes.

Revolution and who placed limits on legislative as well as executive power, became the main inspiration of the Declaration of Independence. Second, the Revolution found support in the customs and traditions embodied in the English common law, especially the principle that governments could not encroach upon property rights. Third, republican ideas, drawn both from ancient Greece and Rome and revived at the time of the Renaissance, offered colonists a model of a community of virtuous men joined in a commitment to the body politic. Finally, the belief that all men had a natural right to life, liberty, and the pursuit of happiness, provided a philosophical inspiration to the colonists' cause (see Chapter 19).

The Haitian Revolution, 1789–1804

The second successful revolution in the Atlantic world took place in the French Caribbean colony of Saint Domingue, known later as Haiti, which occupied the western portion of the island of Hispaniola. This revolution resulted in the establishment of the colony's independence, but the revolt was directed not so much against French rule as against the island's white planters. Just like their counterparts in Spanish and British Caribbean colonies, these planters, known in Haiti as *colons*, had little desire for national independence. They wished to remain within the protective custody of the French state. Because they formed a distinct minority of the total population, they did not think of themselves as constituting a separate national community. Successful resistance to imperial rule, moreover, would have required them to arm their slaves, which would have threatened their control of the black population.

The Haitian revolution began in 1789 when the people defined legally as free coloreds, most of whom were mulattos, rose up in protest against the refusal of the white planters, who were creoles, to give them representation in the revolutionary French National Assembly as well as in local assemblies in Saint Domingue. This rebellion led directly to a massive slave revolt in 1791. At that time slaves constituted about 90 percent of the population. Their uprising took place after the French National Assembly voted to abolish slavery in France, but not in the French colonies. In this revolt 12,000 African slaves, armed with machetes and reacting to their brutal treatment by their masters, destroyed a thousand plantations and killed hundreds of whites. Their tactics, which included cutting white planters in half, raping their wives and daughters, and decapitating their children, were matched by those of the planters, who retaliated by torturing blacks and hanging them in the streets.

Spanish and British armies, frightened that this slave rebellion would spread to their colonies, occupied Saint Domingue and massacred thousands of slaves, many of them after they surrendered. In 1795, however, the Spanish withdrew from Saint Domingue and ceded their portion of the island of Hispaniola to France. The British were likewise forced to leave the colony in 1798, having lost as many as 40,000 soldiers, most of them from disease. The man who had assumed the leadership of the slave revolt, the freed slave Toussaint L'Ouverture, then proceeded to conquer the entire island in 1801, abolish slavery, and proclaim himself the governor-general of an autonomous province.

In 1801 a French army of 20,000 men occupied Saint Domingue. The purpose was to make the colony the centerpiece of a restored French Empire, which was to include Florida, Louisiana, French Guiana, and the French West Indies. The French secured the surrender of L'Ouverture, but when it was learned that the French were planning to reintroduce slavery, two black generals, Jean-Jacques Dessalines and Henri Christophe, whom the French had enlisted to suppress the revolt, united freed blacks and slaves against the French forces. In 1803 these united forces drove the French out of the colony, and in 1804 they established the independent state of Haiti.

This new state of Haiti was far different from the United States, in that it was governed entirely by people of color and it banned slavery. It proclaimed racial equality by defining all Haitians as black. Haiti's new government destroyed the plantation system, redistributed the land among free blacks, and forbade foreigners to hold property. Deciding upon the form of government took time, however, because the new rulers of the country were divided between those who wished to establish a monarchy and those who favored a republic. Those divisions led to a prolonged civil war from 1807 until 1822, when the warring northern and southern provinces were integrated into a single republic.

The Haitian revolution was the most radical and egalitarian of the Atlantic revolutions of the late eighteenth and early nineteenth centuries. Its unqualified declaration of human equality and its abolition of slavery served as an inspiration to abolitionist movements in other countries, including the United States, throughout the nineteenth century. The destruction of the plantation system, however, transformed the country's economy. As a French possession Saint Domingue was quite possibly the richest colony in the world, producing about two-fifths of the world's sugar and half of its coffee. After the revolution, with its economy severed from that of France, the country could no longer compete successfully in the Atlantic economy.

The Irish Rebellion, 1798–1799

The success of the American Revolution directly inspired a revolution in the kingdom of Ireland. Unlike the residents of the 13 colonies in North America, the Gaelic people of Ireland had long thought of themselves as a distinct nation. The English, however, had begun a conquest of this Irish nation in the twelfth century, and during the next 500 years had struggled to rule it effectively. One of their methods was to settle English landlords on Irish lands. They had done this in the Middle Ages by giving large estates to English feudal lords, but those old Anglo-Irish families had gradually begun to think of themselves as Irish, and after the Reformation they had remained Catholic, while most English people had become Protestant.

In the sixteenth century the English government began to settle colonies of English Protestants on plantations in various parts of Ireland. The purpose of this policy was to gain tighter control over the country and to promote the loyalty of Irish landowners to the English government. In the early seventeenth century James VI of Scotland (who had also become James I of England in 1603) had settled both Scottish Presbyterians, later known as the Scots Irish, and English Anglicans in the northern Irish province of Ulster. These Protestants of Scottish and English descent had become the core of the ruling establishment throughout Ireland, especially after

the failure of Catholic rebellions in 1641–1649 and again in 1689–1690.

In the eighteenth century these Irish Protestants began to resent their subservient relationship to the British government. Just like the American colonists, they recognized the way in which the Irish economy was serving British rather than Irish interests, and they resented the control that Britain had over the Irish parliament. A reform association known as the Society of United Irishmen, led by the Protestant Ulsterman Wolfe Tone, succeeded in building common ground between Protestants and Catholics. The United Irishmen demanded the repeal of the laws that denied Catholics the right to hold office and sit in the Irish parliament.

The ideals of the United Irishmen drew on many different sources. A long tradition of Presbyterian republican radicalism found reinforcement in the ideals of the American Revolution. The Irish objected to paying tithes to the established Church of England, and like the American colonists in the 1760s, they resented paying taxes to support the British war against the French during the 1790s.

In 1798 the United Irishmen aligned themselves with lower-class Catholic peasants known as **Defenders,** and these Irish groups staged a rebellion against British rule with the intention of establishing an Irish republic. Like the American colonists, the Irish revolutionaries sought French aid, but it came too little and too late, and the rebellion failed. The revolt, which featured atrocities on both sides, left 30,000 people dead.

The British government recognized that its arrangement for ruling Ireland, in which the nationalist republican movement had originated, could no longer work. It decided therefore to bring about a complete union between Great Britain and Ireland. By the terms of this arrangement, which took effect in 1801, Ireland's parliament ceased to meet. Instead, the Irish elected a limited number of representatives to sit in the British parliament. Ireland thus became a part of the United Kingdom, which had been formed when England and Scotland were united in 1707. The proximity of Ireland to Britain, which made the prospect of Irish independence much more dangerous, was a major factor in making the British determined to hold on to this "internal colony." The forces of Irish nationalism could not be contained, however, and during the nineteenth century new movements for Irish independence arose.

National Revolutions in Spanish America, 1810–1824

The final set of revolutions against European imperial powers occurred between 1810 and 1824 in six Spanish American colonies. These struggles, like the American Revolution, turned colonies into new states and led to the building of new nations. The first of these revolutions began in Mexico in 1810, and others soon arose in Venezuela, Argentina, Colombia, Chile, and Peru. In these revolutions creoles played a leading role, just as they had in the American War of Independence. The main sources of creole discontent were the Bourbon reforms, which ironically had sought to make the Spanish Empire more efficient and thus preserve it. The reforms had achieved this goal, however, by favoring commercial interests at the expense of the traditional aristocracy, thereby reversing or threatening the position of many creole elites. The creoles also faced increasingly heavy taxation, as the Spanish government sought to make them support the expenses of colonial administration.

CHRONOLOGY: THE ATLANTIC REVOLUTIONS, 1775–1824

1775–1783	United States of America
1789–1804	Haiti
1798–1799	Ireland
1810–1821	Mexico
1810–1819	Colombia
1810–1821	Venezuela
1810–1816	Argentina
1810–1818	Chile
1821–1824	Peru

During the late eighteenth century Spanish creole discontent had crystallized into demands for greater political autonomy, similar to the objectives of British American colonists. South American creoles began to think of themselves as Spanish Americans and sometimes simply as Americans. Like British American colonists, they also read and found inspiration in the works of French political philosophers. Nevertheless, the Spanish creole struggle against imperial rule did not commence until some 30 years after the North American colonies had won their independence. One reason for this slow development of revolutionary action was that Spanish American creoles still looked to the Spanish government to provide them with military support against the threat of lower-class rebellion. Faced with this threat, which continued to plague them even after independence, creoles were reluctant to abandon the military and police support provided by the metropolis.

The event that eventually precipitated these wars for national independence was the collapse of the Spanish monarchy after the French army invaded Spain in 1808 (see Chapter 20). This development left the Spanish Empire, which had always been more centralized than the British Empire, in a weakened position. In an effort to reconstitute the political order in their colonies, creoles sought to establish greater autonomy. Once the monarchy was restored, this demand for autonomy led quickly to armed resistance. This resistance began in Mexico, but it soon spread throughout Spanish America and quickly acquired popular support.

The man who took the lead in these early revolts against Spanish rule was the fiery Venezuelan aristocrat Símon Bolívar (1783–1830). Bolívar led uprisings in his homeland in 1811 and 1814 and eventually defeated the Spanish there in 1819. Unlike most creoles, Bolívar was not afraid to recruit free coloreds and blacks into his armies. His hatred of European colonial governors knew few boundaries. At one point he reportedly commanded his soldiers to shoot and kill any European on sight. He vowed never to rest until all of Spanish America was free. Bolívar carried the struggle for liberation to Peru, which became independent in 1824, and created the state of Bolivia in 1825. He was more responsible than any one individual for the liberation of Spanish America from Spanish rule. Independent states were established in Argentina in 1816, Chile in 1818, Colombia in 1819, and Mexico in 1821. By then the Spanish, who in the sixteenth century had the largest empire in the world, retained control of only two colonies in the Western Hemisphere: Puerto Rico and Cuba.

CONCLUSION

The Rise and Reshaping of the West

During the second period of European empire-building, the West not only expanded geographically, but also acquired a large share of the world's resources. By dominating the world's carrying trade, and by exploiting the agricultural and mineral resources of the Americas, Western states gained control of the world economy. The slave trade, with all its horrors, formed an important part of this economy and served as one of the main sources of Western wealth.

Western economic power laid the foundations for Western political control. In Asia European states assumed political control over territories slowly and reluctantly, as Britain's gradual and piecemeal acquisition of territory in India revealed. In the Americas, European powers acquired territory with relative ease, and European possessions in the New World soon became part of the West. By 1700, as we have seen, the geographical center of the West had become the Atlantic Ocean.

The American territories that were brought under European political control also became, at least to some extent, culturally part of the West. The European colonists who settled in the Americas preserved the languages, the religions, and many of the cultural traditions of the European countries from which they came. When some of

the British and Spanish colonies in the Americas rebelled against European regimes in the late eighteenth and early nineteenth centuries, the identity of the colonists who led the resistance remained essentially Western. Even the political ideas that inspired national resistance to European regimes had their origins in Europe.

The assertion of Western political and economic power in the world cultivated a sense of Western superiority. The belief that Europeans, regardless of their nationality, were superior to those from other parts of the world originated in the encounters that took place between Europeans and both African slaves and the indigenous peoples in the Americas. In the late eighteenth century a conviction also developed, although much more slowly, that the West was culturally superior to the civilizations of Asia. This belief in Western superiority became even more pronounced when the economies of Western nations began to experience more rapid growth than those of Asia. The main source of this new Western economic strength was the Industrial Revolution, which will be the subject of Chapter 21.

KEY TERMS

metropolis	Middle Passage
states	mestizos
empires	nawabs
boers	sepoys
Bourbon reforms	nabobs
creoles	chinoiserie
protectionism	Defenders
mulattos	

CHAPTER QUESTIONS

1. How did the composition and organization of European empires change during the seventeenth and eighteenth centuries? (page 554)
2. In what ways did the wars waged by European powers during this period involve competition for overseas possessions and trading routes? (page 561)

3. How did European empires create an Atlantic economy in which the traffic in slaves was a major feature? (page 565)

4. How did cultural encounters between European and Asian peoples during this period of empire-building change Western attitudes toward outsiders? (page 575)

5. Why did European powers begin to lose control of some of their colonies, especially those in the Americas, between 1775 and 1825? (page 579)

TAKING IT FURTHER

1. Why did Britain become the major European imperial power by the beginning of the nineteenth century?

2. Why did wars between European powers in the eighteenth century spread to the Americas and Asia?

3. How could Europeans who professed to believe in the dignity of human beings justify placing Africans in slavery?

4. Which of the Atlantic Revolutions was the most radical and why?

5. How did the growth of European empires contribute to a redefinition of the West?

✓•─Practice on MyHistoryLab

19

Eighteenth-Century Society and Culture

■ The Aristocracy ■ Challenges to Aristocratic Dominance
■ The Enlightenment ■ The Impact of the Enlightenment

IN 1745 THOMAS BROWN AND ELEVEN OTHER MEN LIVING ON THE ESTATE OF the Earl of Uxbridge, an English nobleman, were jailed for up to one year for shooting deer and rabbits on the earl's land. All twelve defendants were poor. Brown eked out a living as a coal miner in the earl's mines and rented a cottage and five acres of land from him. Like many of his fellow villagers, Brown supplemented his family's diet by shooting game from time to time, usually as he was walking to work through the earl's vast estate. This poaching violated a set of English parliamentary statutes known as the game laws, which restricted the shooting or trapping of wild animals to wealthy landowners.

The earl and other noblemen defended the game laws on the grounds that they were necessary to protect their property. The laws, however, served an even more important purpose of maintaining social distinctions between landowners and the common people. Members of the landed class believed that only they should have the right to hunt game and to serve deer, pheasants, and hares at lavish dinners attended by their social equals. For a poor person like Thomas Brown, who was described in a court document as "a rude disorderly man and a most notorious poacher," to enjoy such delicacies was a challenge to the social order.

This mid-eighteenth-century encounter between the Earl of Uxbridge and his tenants reflected the tensions that simmered beneath the calm surface of eighteenth-century European society. These tensions arose between the aristocracy, a small but wealthy governing elite, and the masses of tenants and laborers who formed the overwhelming majority of the population. The aristocracy occupied a dominant position in eighteenth-century society and politics. They controlled an enormous portion of their countries' wealth, much of it in land. They staffed the state bureaucracies, the legislative assemblies, the military officer corps, and the judiciaries of almost all European states.

By 1800 the social and political dominance of the aristocracy had begun to wane. Their legitimacy as a privileged elite was increasingly called into question. In a few countries political power began to pass from them to other social groups. This change began during a period of political stability between 1750 and the outbreak of the French Revolution in 1789.

The decline of the aristocracy was the result of a series of cultural encounters. In the first, aristocratic landowners confronted peasants and agricultural laborers who resented the repressive features of upper-class rule. In the second increasingly literate, politically active people who

FIRST LECTURE IN THE SALON OF MADAME GEOFFRIN, 1755

The speaker is lecturing on Voltaire's *The Orphan of China* before a predominantly aristocratic audience of men and women.

Source: Lemonnier, Anicet Charles Gabriel (1743–1824), "Reading of Voltaire's tragedy 'L'orphelin de la Chine' at the salon of Madame Geoffrin". 1755. Oil on canvas, 129 × 196 cm. D. Arnaudet. Chateaux de Malmaison et Bois-Preau, Rueil-Malmaison, France. RMN Reunion des Musees Nationaux/Art Resource, NY

occupied the middle ranks of society, such as merchants and skilled artisans criticized the aristocracy and demanded political reform. The third set of encounters was the cultural and intellectual movement known as the Enlightenment. Even though many of the Enlightenment's most prominent thinkers came from the ranks of the aristocracy, they advanced a set of political, social, economic, and legal ideas that inspired the creation of a more egalitarian society. This chapter will explore the following question: How did these social and cultural encounters change the political and intellectual cultures of the West?

THE ARISTOCRACY

■ **What social groups belonged to the aristocracy and how did they exercise their power and influence during the eighteenth century?**

During the eighteenth century a relatively small, wealthy group of men dominated European society and politics. This social and ruling elite is often referred to as the **aristocracy,** a term derived from a Greek word meaning the men best fit to rule. In the eighteenth and nineteenth centuries the term *aristocracy* also referred to the

587

wealthiest members of society, especially those who owned land.

Within the aristocracy those who received official recognition of their hereditary status, including their titles of honor and special legal privileges, were known as the **nobility.** In the Middle Ages the nobility consisted mainly of warriors who prided themselves on their courage and military skill. Over the course of many centuries these military functions became less important, although many noblemen, especially in central and eastern Europe, continued to serve as military officers in the armies of the state.

The aristocracy for the most part lived on their estates in the countryside, but they also spent time in the cities and towns, where many of them owned townhouses or even palaces. In cities that were centers of national government, such as Madrid and Berlin, aristocrats were prominent members of the royal court, and many of them served as royal judges. The aristocracy, therefore, maintained a visible and powerful presence in urban society.

By the eighteenth century most European aristocracies included a relatively small group of titled noblemen (such as dukes and counts) who possessed great wealth and political influence and a much larger group of lesser aristocrats, occasionally referred to as gentry, who did not necessarily have hereditary titles. In Spain a vast gulf separated a few hundred titled noblemen, the *titulos*, and thousands of sometimes poverty-stricken *hidalgos*. In Britain a few hundred titled noblemen, known as peers, took precedence over some 50,000 families that belonged to the gentry. In Poland the nobility, known as the *szlachta*, was divided between a tiny, powerful group of magnates and some 700,000 noblemen of more modest means who constituted more than ten percent of the entire population.

The aristocracy was not completely closed to outsiders. Commoners could gain entrance to it, especially its lower ranks, on the basis of acquired wealth or government service. Lawyers, wealthy merchants, or accomplished state servants might accumulate wealth during their careers, use that wealth to purchase land, and then acquire a title

of nobility. Many of the Russians who received titles of nobility in the early eighteenth century were commoners. In France many of the royal officials who belonged to the **nobility of the robe** in the eighteenth century could not trace their noble status back further than two generations.

Women of non-noble birth occasionally gained entry into aristocratic society by marriage. This usually occurred when a nobleman who was greatly in debt arranged to marry his son to the daughter of a wealthy merchant to secure the dowry from the father of the bride. The dowry became the price of the daughter's admission to the nobility.

In the sixteenth and seventeenth centuries the size of the aristocracy had grown faster than the general population as a result of economic prosperity and the expansion of the state bureaucracy. In the eighteenth century the size of the aristocracy stabilized and in many countries declined, as nobles took steps to restrict the number of newcomers from the lower orders. It was never a very large social group. The number of titled nobles was almost always less than one percent of the total population, and even when lesser nobles or gentry are taken into account, their total numbers usually amounted to no more than four percent. Only in Poland and Hungary did the percentages climb to more than ten percent.

Because of the small size of this social group, many members of the aristocracy knew each other, especially those who had seats in the same political assembly or served together at court. The aristocracy was, in fact, the only real **class** in European society before the early nineteenth century, in the sense that they formed a cohesive social group with similar economic and political interests, which they were determined to protect.

The Wealth of the Aristocracy

The aristocracy was the wealthiest social group in all European countries, and during the eighteenth century many of its members became even wealthier. The most prosperous aristocratic families lived in stupendous luxury. They built magnificent homes on their country estates and surrounded them with finely manicured gardens. In the cities, where service at court demanded more of their time, they built spacious palaces, entertained guests on a lavish scale, and purchased everything from expensive clothes to artistic treasures. This ostentatious display of wealth confirmed their social importance and status.

Most of the income that supported the lifestyle of the aristocracy came directly or indirectly from land. In all European countries the aristocracy owned at least one-third of all the land, and in some countries, such as England and Denmark, they owned more than four-fifths of it.

Even in the Italian states, where many of the nobility had come from families of merchants, they controlled large estates. Land provided the aristocracy with either feudal dues or rents from the peasants or laborers who lived and worked on their estates. Because noblemen did not engage in manual labor themselves, some social critics later condemned them as unproductive parasites living off the labor of others.

During the first half of the eighteenth century the collective wealth of the European aristocracy reached new heights. In eastern Europe that new wealth came mainly from the dramatic

MARRIAGE INTO THE NOBILITY

This painting by William Hogarth, in a series titled *Marriage à la Mode,* depicts the negotiation of a marriage contract between an English earl and a wealthy London merchant. The earl, seated to the left and pointing to his family tree, is negotiating with the merchant sitting across the table. The marriage will take place between the earl's vain son, sitting to the far right, and the distracted daughter of the merchant, sitting next to him. The two individuals who are about to be married have no interest in each other. The earl has incurred large debts from building the large mansion depicted in the rear, and he intends to use the dowry to recover financially. By virtue of this transaction the daughter will enter aristocratic society.

Source: © National Gallery, London/Art Resource, NY

increase in the size of the population. With more serfs under their control, the landed nobility could increase the wealth they gained from these poor people's labor and feudal dues. In western Europe, most notably Britain and France, the members of the aristocracy increasingly participated in other forms of economic activity. They operated rural industries such as mining and forestry. They entered the financial world by lending money to the government. They became involved in urban building projects and in the economic development of overseas colonies. Some members of old noble families considered such commercial pursuits to be beneath their status, but by investing at a distance, nobles could give the impression that they were not actually engaged in the sordid transactions of the marketplace.

Although some historians have argued that the members of the eighteenth-century aristocracy were social and economic conservatives who were unable or unwilling to act in an entrepreneurial manner, aristocratic involvement in financial and commercial projects suggests a different conclusion. Even on their agricultural estates, many members of the aristocracy, both titled and untitled, adopted capitalist techniques to make their lands more productive. In

England a nobleman, Charles Townshend, became widely known as "Turnip Townshend" when he introduced a crop rotation that included the lowly turnip. This type of agricultural entrepreneurship accounts for the accumulation of many aristocratic fortunes.

The Political Power of the Aristocracy

The mid-eighteenth century also marked the apex of political power for the aristocracy in Europe. Having recovered from the economic and political turmoil of the mid-seventeenth century, when they experienced a temporary eclipse of their power, aristocrats pursued various strategies to increase or preserve their share of local and national political power. In England, where the Glorious Revolution had restricted royal power, the aristocracy gained political dominance. A small group of noblemen sat in the House of Lords, while the gentry formed the large majority of members of the House of Commons. After 1689 the English king could not rule without the cooperation of these two Houses of Parliament. The monarchy tried to control the proceedings of that assembly by creating parties of royal supporters within both houses. Because those parties were controlled by

SIZE OF THE ARISTOCRACY IN EUROPEAN STATES IN THE EIGHTEENTH CENTURY			
Country	Date	Number of Nobles	Percent of the Population
Austria	1800	90,000	1.15%
France	1775	400,000	1.60
Great Britain and Ireland	1783	50,000	3.25
Hungary	1800	400,000	11.25
Poland	1800	700,000	11.66
Russia	1800	600,000	1.66
Spain	1797	402,000	3.80
Sweden	1757	10,000	0.50
Venice	1797	1,090	0.80

Sources: A. Corvisier, *Armies and Society in Europe, 1494–1789* (1976), 113, 115; J. Meyer, *Noblesses et pouvoirs dans l'Europe d'Ancien Régime* (1973); M. Reinard and A. Armenguard, *Histoire Générale de la Population Modiale* (1961); J. Dewald, *The European Nobility* (1996), 22–27.

the king's ministers, who were themselves members of the nobility, the system allowed the aristocracy to dominate.

In absolute monarchies members of the aristocracy exercised political power by dominating the institutions through which the monarchy exercised its power. As we saw in Chapter 16, absolute monarchs appeased the aristocracy by giving them control over provincial government and recruiting them to occupy positions in the central bureaucracy of the state. In France, for example, noblemen of the robe, a privileged group of approximately 2,000 officials, dominated the state bureaucracy. In Russia tsars granted the nobility privileges to secure their assistance in running local government.

The aristocracy also exercised political power through the judiciary. Members of the aristocracy often served as judges of the law courts of their kingdoms. In England noblemen and gentry served as the judges of almost all the common law courts, hearing cases both at the center of government at Westminster and in the provinces. In France noblemen staffed the nine regional *parlements* that registered royal edicts and acted as a court of appeal in criminal cases. The nobility controlled the central tribunals of the German kingdoms and principalities. At the local level the aristocracy exercised either a personal jurisdiction over the peasants who lived on their lands or an official jurisdiction as magistrates, such as the justices of the peace in each English county.

The Cultural World of the Aristocracy

During the eighteenth century aristocracies in western European countries adopted a lifestyle that emphasized their learning, refinement, and appreciation of the fine arts. It had not always been that way. As late as the fifteenth century the aristocracy had a reputation for their indifference or even hostility to learning, and their conduct was often uncouth if not boorish. In eastern Europe a tradition of aristocratic illiteracy persisted into the eighteenth century. In western and central Europe, however, the pattern began to change in the sixteenth century, when members of the aristocracy started providing for the education of their children either at universities or in private academies. Even more important, aristocratic families began to acquire the manners and social graces that would be acceptable at court. By the eighteenth century the aristocracy, especially its upper ranks, became the backbone of what was then called "polite society."

The aristocracy also developed a sophisticated appreciation of high culture. Their homes housed large private collections of artwork that occasionally rivaled those of contemporary European monarchs. They were the main participants in the cultural life of European cities, especially Paris, London, Rome, Vienna, and Berlin. They formed the audiences of musical recitals, attended plays and operas in large numbers, and frequented the art galleries that were established in all the capitals of Europe. They also became the patrons of musicians, writers, and artists.

The homes of the eighteenth-century aristocracy reflected their preference for **classicism,** a style in art, architecture, music, and literature that emphasized proportion, adherence to traditional forms, and a rejection of emotion and enthusiasm. The classicism of the eighteenth century marked a step away from the more dynamic, imposing baroque style, which had flourished in the seventeenth century. Classicism celebrated the culture of ancient Greece and Rome. The revival of that culture in the eighteenth century in art and architecture is often referred to as **neoclassicism.** The residences of the eighteenth-century aristocracy built in the classical style were perfectly proportioned and elegant without being overly decorated. Their Greek columns and formal gardens, lined with statues of classical figures, served as symbols of their cultural heritage. The classical architecture of the eighteenth century reflected the quiet confidence of the aristocracy that they, like their Greek and Roman forebears, occupied a dominant position in society.

CHISWICK HOUSE

This house was built by Lord Burlington as a library and reception hall on his estate near London about 1725. Symmetrical, balanced, and restrained, the building embodies many of the features of classicism. Chiswick House was modeled on the architecture of the Italian Andrea Palladio (1518–1580), who in turn drew his inspiration from the buildings of ancient Rome.

Eighteenth-century music, which is likewise referred to as classical, reflected a concern for formal design, proportion, and concise melodic expression. The two greatest composers of the eighteenth century, Franz Joseph Haydn (1732–1809) and Wolfgang Amadeus Mozart (1756–1791), whose music was played before predominantly aristocratic audiences, became the most famous composers in this tradition. Classical music appealed less to the emotions than either the baroque music of the seventeenth century or the romantic music of the nineteenth century. The dominance of classicism in music and architecture during the eighteenth century reflected broader cultural currents in European intellectual life, when science and philosophy placed the highest value on the rationality and order of all material and human life.

CHALLENGES TO ARISTOCRATIC DOMINANCE

■ How did subordinate social groups, most notably the rural peasantry and those who lived in the towns, challenge the aristocracy during the late eighteenth century?

Starting around the middle of the eighteenth century, the aristocracy endured increasingly acrimonious challenges to their power and criticisms of their values and lifestyles. They gradually lost the respect that they commanded from the lower ranks of society. By the end of the century many European aristocracies had suffered a loss of political power and an erosion of their privileges. A claim of nobility began to be viewed more as a sign of vanity than as a natural right to rule. The revolution that took place in France in the last decade of the eighteenth century, followed by the reform movements that developed in its wake throughout Europe in the early nineteenth century, brought the age of aristocracy to an end. Members of the aristocracy managed to regain some of what they had lost in the French Revolution, and they also showed their resourcefulness by accommodating themselves to the new order, but they never recovered the dominant position they had held in the eighteenth century.

Encounters with the Rural Peasantry

One set of challenges to the aristocracy came from the peasants and serfs who lived and worked on agricultural estates. This was the social group over whom the aristocracy exercised the most direct control. In central and eastern Europe, where the institution of serfdom persisted, aristocratic control over the rural masses was most oppressive. Landlords not only determined where serfs lived and when they married, but they also collected burdensome financial duties from the serfs. Royal edicts that eliminated some of the duties of serfdom in the late eighteenth century only partially relieved the plight of the rural masses.

In western Europe, where serfdom had for the most part given way to tenant ownership and leasehold tenure, the condition of the rural population was only marginally better than in Prussia, Austria, and Russia. After 1720, famines in western Europe became less common than in the late seventeenth century, making it possible for peasants to eke out an existence, but other economic pressures, including the elimination of common pasture rights and an increase in taxation, continued to weigh heavily on them. Over the course of the eighteenth century the number of peasants owning small plots of land declined. Many of those who leased land were forced to sell it as landowners consolidated their holdings. Consequently, the number of landless laborers who worked for wages increased. By 1789 almost half the peasants in France had no land at all.

Under these circumstances the relationship between peasants and aristocratic landowners continued to deteriorate. The realities of the marketplace gradually eroded the paternalistic concern that the nobility had traditionally shown for the welfare of their serfs or tenants. As the relationship between landlord and peasant became predominantly economic, visual and personal contact between lord and peasant became less frequent. Landlords built their mansions away from the local village, and by surrounding their homes with acres of parkland and gardens, they shielded themselves from the sight of the peasants working in the fields. The most direct contact a landlord made with the members of the lower classes was with the servants who worked in their homes.

As economic pressures on peasants mounted, conflicts between them and their landlords increased. In some countries, most notably France, peasants brought their grievances before village assemblies. These democratic institutions frequently succeeded in upholding peasants' demands, especially when royal officials in the provinces, who wished to collect their own taxes from the peasants, sided with them against the aristocracy.

Another option for the peasants was to file lawsuits against the lords, often with the assistance of the royal government. In Burgundy numerous peasant communities hired lawyers to take their **seigneurs** or lords to court to prevent the imposition of new financial dues or the confiscation of communal village land. In these lawsuits, which became common in the second half of the eighteenth century, peasants challenged not only the imposition of seigneurial dues but the very institution of aristocratic lordship. In 1765 one lawyer representing a peasant community argued that the rights claimed by landowners "derive from the violence of seigneurs" and had always been "odious." The language used in these cases inspired much of the rhetoric employed in the abolition of feudal privilege at the time of the French Revolution (see Chapter 20).

Peasants occasionally took more direct action against their landlords. In eastern France the number of incidents of rural violence against the property of seigneurs who tried to collect new financial exactions increased toward the end of the eighteenth century. In Ireland a group known as the Whiteboys maimed cattle and tore down fences when landowners denied tenants their common grazing rights. Other forms of peasant action included poaching on the lands of landowners who claimed the exclusive right to hunt or trap game on their estates. The hunting activities of the tenants of the Earl of Uxbridge discussed at the beginning of this chapter were just one example of this type of lower-class resistance to aristocratic privilege.

In eastern Europe the deteriorating economic condition of the peasantry led to large-scale rebellion. Bohemia, Hungary, and Croatia, all of which lay within the boundaries of the Austrian Habsburg monarchy, witnessed large peasant revolts in the 1780s. The bloodiest of these rebellions occurred in the province of Transylvania in 1784, when 30,000 peasants butchered hundreds of noblemen and their families after those landowners had raised the dues owed to them as much as 1,000 percent.

The largest eastern European rural rebellion took place in Russia between 1773 and 1774. Pretending to be the murdered Tsar Peter III (d. 1762), the Cossack Emelian Pugachev (1726–1775) set out to destroy the Russian government of Catherine the Great and the nobility that served it. Pugachev assembled an army of 8,000 men, which staged lightning raids against government centers in the southern Urals. The most serious phase of this uprising took place when these troops marched into the agricultural regions of the country and inspired as many as three million serfs to revolt. Pugachev promised to abolish serfdom, end taxation, and eliminate the lesser aristocracy. The rebellion took a heavy toll, as the serfs and soldiers murdered some 3,000 nobles and officials. The Russian upper class feared that the rebellion would spread and destroy the entire social order, but government troops prevented that from happening by brutally suppressing the rising. They locked Pugachev in an iron cage and carried him to Moscow, where he was hanged, quartered, and burned.

Neither Pugachev nor the serfs who joined his rebellion envisioned the creation of a new social order. They still spoke in conservative terms of regaining ancient freedoms that had been lost. But this massive revolt, like others that resembled it, reflected the depth of the tension that prevailed between landlord and peasant, between nobleman and serf, in the apparently stable world of the eighteenth century. That tension served as one of the most striking and ominous themes of eighteenth-century social history.

The Social Position of the Bourgeoisie

In the cities and towns the most serious challenges to the aristocracy came not from the urban masses, who posed an occasional threat to all urban authorities, but from the **bourgeoisie**. This social group was more heterogeneous than the aristocracy. It consisted of untitled people of property who lived in the cities and towns. Prosperous merchants and financiers formed the upper ranks of the bourgeoisie, while members of the legal and medical professions, second-tier government officials, and emerging industrialists occupied a social niche just below them. The bourgeoisie also included some skilled artisans and shopkeepers who were far more prosperous than the large mass of urban laborers. The size of the bourgeoisie grew as the urban population of Europe expanded during the eighteenth century, even before the advent of industrialization. This social group was far more numerous in the North Atlantic countries of France, the Dutch Republic, and Britain than in the states of central and eastern Europe. In England the bourgeoisie accounted for about 15 percent of the total population in 1800, whereas in Russia they constituted no more than three percent.

Because it was possible for some members of the bourgeoisie to achieve upward social mobility and join the ranks of the aristocracy, the social and economic boundaries separating wealthy townsmen from the lower aristocratic ranks were often blurred. In French towns it was often difficult to distinguish between wealthy financiers and noble bureaucrats. Although the two groups received their income from different sources, they both belonged to a wealthy, propertied elite. The middle and lower ranks of the bourgeoisie, however, gradually emerged as a social group that acquired its own social, political, and cultural identity, distinct from that of the aristocracy.

Bourgeois identity originated in the towns, which had their own political institutions and their own social hierarchies. The bourgeoisie also possessed the means of effectively communicating with each other and thus were capable of forming common political goals. Their high rates of literacy made them the core of the new political force of public opinion that emerged in the eighteenth century. The bourgeoisie were the main audience of the thousands of newspapers, pamphlets, and books that rolled off the presses. A "public sphere" of activity, in which politically conscious townsmen participated, became a peculiar feature of bourgeois society. During the eighteenth and early nineteenth centuries the bourgeoisie became the leaders of movements seeking political change. They organized and became the main participants in protests, demonstrations, petitioning drives, and efforts to overthrow established regimes.

The Bourgeois Critique of the Aristocracy

At the core of bourgeois identity lay a set of values that contrasted with those attributed to the aristocracy, especially the noblemen and noblewomen who gathered at court. Not all members of the bourgeoisie shared these values, nor did all members of the nobility embody those attributed to them. Nonetheless, the bourgeois critique of aristocratic society, which flourished mainly among the lower or middle bourgeoisie rather than the great merchants and financiers, contributed to the formation of bourgeois identity and helped to erode respect for the traditional aristocracy.

The bourgeois critique of the aristocracy consisted of three related claims. First, the bourgeoisie alleged that the aristocracy lived a life of luxury, hedonism, and idleness that contrasted with the values of the thrifty, sober, hardworking bourgeoisie. Unlike the aristocracy, the bourgeoisie did not display their wealth. Second, the bourgeoisie accused court nobles of sexual promiscuity and immorality and depicted their wives as vain flirts. There was some foundation to this charge, especially because the predominance of arranged marriages within the nobility had induced many noble husbands and wives to seek sexual partners outside marriage. By contrast, the bourgeoisie tended to enter into marriages in which both partners remained faithful to each

JOSHUA REYNOLDS, *MARY, DUCHESS OF RICHMOND* (CA. 1765)

At a time when most European noblewomen were attracting criticism for their luxury and vanity, this prominent English duchess was depicted as being engaged in the simple domestic task of needlepoint. Some members of the aristocracy were able to deflect criticism of their lifestyle by adopting the habits of the bourgeoisie.

Source: Sir Joshua Reynolds (1723–92), "Mary, Duchess of Richmond (1740–96)," 1746–67, oil on canvas. Private Collection/The Bridgeman Art Library

other. Third, the bourgeoisie considered the members of the aristocracy participants in a decadent international culture that often ignored or degraded their own wholesome, patriotic values.

This bourgeois critique of the aristocracy had profound political implications. It contributed to bourgeois demands for the right to participate fully in the political process. These demands came not from wealthy financiers, merchants, and capitalists who had the opportunity to ascend into the ranks of the nobility, but from men of more modest means: holders of minor political offices, shopkeepers, and even skilled artisans. Criticism of aristocratic values and the demands for an expansion of the franchise received support from intellectuals who are usually identified with the movement known as the **Enlightenment.** Not all of these thinkers and writers came from the middle ranks of society. Many of them were, in fact, members of the aristocracy or the beneficiaries of aristocratic patronage. Nevertheless, their goal was to bring about the reform of society, and that inevitably led to a critique of aristocratic values and behavior.

THE ENLIGHTENMENT

■ What were the main features of Enlightenment thought and how did it present a threat to the old order?

The Enlightenment was the defining intellectual and cultural movement of the eighteenth century. Contemporaries used the word *enlightenment* to describe their own intellectual outlook and achievements. For Immanuel Kant (1724–1804), the renowned German philosopher and author of *Critique of Pure Reason* (1781), enlightenment was the expression of intellectual maturity, the attainment of understanding solely by using one's reason without being influenced by dogma, superstition, or another person's opinion. For Kant, enlightenment was both the process of thinking for oneself and the knowledge of human society and human nature that one achieved as a result. His

famous exhortation, "Have the courage to know!" could serve as a slogan for the entire Enlightenment.

The Enlightenment is often referred to as a French movement, and it is true that the most famous of the European writers and thinkers of the Enlightenment, known as **philosophes,** were French. But French philosophes found inspiration in seventeenth-century English sources, especially the writings of Isaac Newton (1647–1727) and John Locke (1632–1704), while German, Scottish, Dutch, Swiss, and Italian writers made their own distinctive contributions to Enlightenment thought. The ideas of the Enlightenment also spread to the Americas, where they inspired movements for political reform and national independence. The men and women of the Enlightenment thought of themselves not so much as French, British, or Dutch, but as members of an international **Republic of Letters,** not unlike the international community of scholars that had arisen within the ancient Roman Empire and again at the time of the Renaissance. This cosmopolitan literary republic knew no geographical boundaries, and it was open to ideas from all lands (see **Map 19.1**). Its literary achievements, however, bore a distinctly Western stamp, and the ideas its members promoted became essential components of Western civilization.

Themes of Enlightenment Thought

Because the Enlightenment spanned the entire European continent and lasted for more than a century, it is difficult to establish characteristics that all its participants shared. The Enlightenment was more a frame of mind, an approach to obtaining knowledge, as Kant claimed, than a set of clearly defined beliefs. Enlightenment writers, however, emphasized several intellectual themes that gave the entire movement a certain degree of unity and coherence.

REASON AND THE LAWS OF NATURE   The first theme that Enlightenment thinkers emphasized was the elevation of human reason to a position of paramount philosophical importance. Philosophes

MAP 19.1

The European Enlightenment

The map shows the birthplaces and birthdates of thinkers and writers of the Enlightenment. The greatest number came from France and Britain, but all European countries were represented. The map does not draw sharp distinctions between the territorial boundaries of European states because the men and women of the Enlightenment thought of themselves as belonging to an international "Republic of Letters" that knew no political boundaries.

placed almost unlimited confidence in the ability of human beings to understand how the world operated. In previous ages philosophers had always found a place for human reason, but they also placed limits on it, especially when it came into conflict with religious faith. In the eighteenth century, however, philosophes placed greater emphasis on reason alone, which they believed to be superior to religious faith and the final arbiter of all philosophical and theological disputes.

Confidence in human reason underlay the effort of Enlightenment thinkers to discover

ENCOUNTERS AND TRANSFORMATIONS

The Enlightenment, Pacific Islanders, and the Noble Savage

When European explorers visited the Pacific islands for the first time in the late eighteenth century, they encountered peoples who had had no previous contact with the West. Enlightenment thinkers, who delighted in studying cultures that were different from their own, seized upon the descriptions of these people, especially the natives of Tahiti, as evidence of the real nature of human beings, before the advent of civilization. From this commentary emerged a picture of the noble savage, who was viewed as being closer to nature than contemporary Europeans. The most positive assessment of the primitive culture of the Pacific islanders appeared in Denis Diderot's *Supplement to the Voyages of Bougainville*, written in 1772 and published in 1796. Regarding the Tahitians, Diderot wrote:

> The life of savages is so simple, and our societies are such complicated machines! The Tahitian is close to the origin of the world, while the European is closer to its old age...they understand nothing about our manners or our laws, and they are bound to see in them nothing but shackles disguised in a hundred different ways. These shackles could only provoke the indignation and scorn of creatures in whom the most profound feeling is a love of liberty.

Diderot (1713–1784) admired these islanders' natural religion, their lack of sexual inhibitions, and their superior sense of morality and justice. His depiction of Tahitian society provided support for the argument of Jean-Jacques Rousseau in *Discourse on Inequality* (1754) that civilization itself had a profoundly negative effect on human society.

Western encounters with the noble savages in the "New World" of the Pacific presented an unprecedented challenge to the dominant Western view of the natural state of human beings. Neither Thomas More, who contrasted the evils of European society with the virtues of a fictional island society in *Utopia* (1516), nor Bartolome las Casas, the Spanish priest who condemned conquistadors for their brutal treatment of Native Americans, idealized human beings in a natural, uncivilized state. The Christian belief that all people are born in a state of original sin prevented them from taking this position. Even John Locke, who described a peaceful state of nature in *Two Treatises of Government* (1690), referred to "the viciousness of man" in that state and contended that the inconveniences of the state of nature necessitated the formation of government. Only when Enlightenment thinkers, with their emphasis on natural

DENIS DIDEROT

Diderot's *Encyclopedia*, which he co-authored with D'Alembery, stands as a classic statement of the range and themes of Enlightenment thought. In *Supplement to the Voyages of Bougainville*, Diderot presented his radical ideas regarding religion and sexuality morality.

law and their hostility to traditional Christianity, encountered Pacific peoples who were untouched by Western civilization did the image of the noble savage fully emerge. Interest in these uncivilized people was so great that Tahitian natives were transported to Paris and London where they became the darlings of literate society.

The idealization of primitive Pacific Islanders by Enlightenment thinkers gave Westerners a standard by which they could gain a clearer sense of their own identity. As we saw in Chapter 16, the boundaries of the West became blurred in the early eighteenth century, as both the Ottoman Empire and Russia became more closely tied to Europe. Eighteenth-century descriptions of "uncivilized" Pacific islanders who had radically different customs from those of the West made it possible for Westerners to determine who they were by observing who they were not. For those philosophes who believed that these islanders were noble savages, this self-evaluation was not very favorable. It transformed earlier appeals for reform, such as those urged by More and Las Casas, into demands for a fundamental restructuring of society.

For Discussion

1. In what ways did Diderot's idealization of the culture of Pacific islanders challenge traditional Christianity?

2. How might a person who did not subscribe to the ideas of the Enlightenment have criticized Diderot's argument regarding the noble savage?

Taking it Further

Denis Diderot, *Rameau's Nephew and D'Alembert's Dream*, 1976. These two works by Diderot, unpublished during his lifetime, provide further insights into Diderot's criticism of conventional morality, society, and religion.

---

scientific laws that governed not only the operation of the natural world, but also the functioning of human society. The belief that scientific laws governed human behavior was the most novel feature of Enlightenment thought. For example, the Scottish philosopher David Hume (1711–1776) proposed a science of the human mind in his *Treatise of Human Nature* (1739–1740) and a science of politics in *Political Discourses* (1752). The Scottish economist Adam Smith (1723–1790), who described the operation of economic life in *The Wealth of Nations* (1776), believed that the economy followed inviolable laws, just like those that governed the movement of the heavens. The Enlightenment thus gave birth to modern social science. Economics, political science, sociology, anthropology, and psychology all trace their origins as intellectual disciplines to this time. They are all based on the premise that reason can discover the laws or principles of human nature.

The search for natural laws governing all human life provides an explanation for the unprecedented interest of eighteenth-century writers in non-European cultures. During the Enlightenment, European writers subjected the peoples of the world to detailed description, classification, and analysis. The first thorough, scholarly studies of Indian, Chinese, and Arab cultures appeared in print during the middle and late eighteenth century. Egypt, which had been isolated from the West since the sixteenth century, became the subject of an extensive literature, especially after the French occupied the country in 1798. Books on societies that Europeans were encountering for the first time, including the indigenous peoples of northwestern Canada, Australia, and Tahiti, also became readily available in the bookshops of Paris and London.

RELIGION AND MORALITY The spread of scientific knowledge in the eighteenth century gave the thinkers of the Enlightenment a new understanding of God and his relationship to humankind. The Christian God of the Middle Ages and the Reformation period was an all-knowing, personal God who often intervened in the life of human beings. He could be stern and severe or gentle and merciful, but he was always involved in the affairs of humankind, which he governed through Providence. The gradual recognition that the universe was of unfathomable size and that it operated in accordance with natural laws made God appear more remote. Most philosophes believed that God was still the creator of the universe and the author of the natural laws that governed it, but they did not believe that he was still actively involved in its operation. God was the playwright of the universe, but not its director. This belief that God had created the universe, given it laws, and then allowed it to operate in a mechanistic fashion is known as **deism.** In deism there was no place for the traditional Christian belief that God became human to redeem humankind from original sin.

Enlightenment thinkers, especially those who were deists, believed that human beings could use reason to discover the natural laws God had laid down at the time of creation. This inquiry included the discovery of the principles of morality, which no longer were to be grounded in the Bible. To observe the laws of God now meant not so much keeping his commandments, but discovering what was natural and acting accordingly. In a certain sense God was being remade in a human image and was being identified with the natural instincts of human beings. Religion had become equated with the pursuit of human happiness.

Because Enlightenment thinkers believed that God established natural laws for all humanity, doctrinal differences between religions became less important. In the Enlightenment view, all religions were valid to the extent that they led to an understanding of natural law. This denial of the existence of one true religion led to a demand for toleration of all religions, including those of non-Western peoples.

Enlightenment thinkers were highly critical of the superstitious and dogmatic character of contemporary Christianity, especially Roman Catholicism. French philosophes in particular had little use for priests, whom they castigated relentlessly in their letters and pamphlets. They minimized the importance of religious belief in the conduct of human life and substituted rational for religious values. They had little respect for the academic discipline of theology. The German-born Parisian writer Barond'-Holbach (1723–1789), one of the few philosophes who could be considered an atheist (one who denied the existence of God), dismissed theology as a "pretended science." He claimed that its principles were "only hazardous suppositions, imagined by ignorance, propagated by enthusiasm or knavery, adopted by timid credulity, preserved by custom which never reasons, and revered solely because not understood."[1]

In *An Enquiry Concerning Human Understanding* (1748), David Hume epitomized the new religious outlook of the Enlightenment. Hume challenged the claim of the seventeenth-century rationalist philosopher René Descartes that God implants clear and distinct ideas in our minds, from which we are able to deduce other truths. Hume argued instead that our understanding derives from sense perceptions, not innate ideas. Even more important, he denied that there was any certain knowledge, thereby calling into question the authority of revealed truth and religious doctrine.

Hume's writing on religion reflected his skepticism. Raised a Presbyterian, he nevertheless rejected the revealed truths of Christianity on the ground that they had no rational foundation. The concept of Providence was completely alien to his philosophical position. An avowed agnostic, he expressed contempt for organized religion, especially Catholicism in France and Anglicanism in England. Organized religion, according to Hume, "renders men tame and submissive, is acceptable to the magistrate, and seems inoffensive to the people; till at last the priest, having firmly established his

WILLIAM HOGARTH, *CREDULITY, SUPERSTITION, AND FANATICISM* (1762)

Hogarth was a moralist who embodied the rationalism and humanitarianism of the Enlightenment. In this engraving he exposes the effects of fanatical religion, witchcraft, and superstition. The sermon has whipped the entire congregation into a highly emotional state. The woman in the foreground is Mary Tofts, who was believed to have given birth to rabbits. The boy next to her, allegedly possessed by the Devil, vomits pins. The Protestant preacher's wig falls off, exposing the shaven head of a Roman Catholic monk. An unemotional Turk observes this scene from outside the window.

Source: William Hogarth (1697–1764), "Credulity, Superstition and Fanaticism," 1762, engraving. The Israel Museum, Jerusalem, Israel/Vera & Arturo Schwarz Collection of Dada and Surrealist Art/The Bridgeman Art Library

authority, becomes the tyrant and disturber of human society."[2]

PROGRESS AND REFORM Theories regarding the stages of human development, coupled with the commitment of philosophes to the improvement and ultimate transformation of society, contributed to the Enlightenment belief in the progress of civilization. (See *Different Voices* in this chapter.) Until

the eighteenth century the very notion of progress was alien to even the most highly educated Europeans. Programs of reform were almost always associated with the restoration of a superior golden age rather than the realization of something new and different. If movement took place, it was cyclical rather than progressive. In the eighteenth century, however, the possibility of improvement began to dominate philosophical and political discussion. The Enlightenment was largely responsible for making this belief in progress, especially toward the attainment of social justice, a prominent feature of modern Western culture.

Another source of the Enlightenment's belief in progress was the conviction that corrupt institutions could be reformed. State bureaucracies, established churches, and the institution of monarchy itself all became the targets of Enlightenment reformers. The judicial institutions of government were particularly susceptible to this type of reforming zeal. Campaigns arose to eliminate the administration of judicial torture and capital punishment. Philosophes hoped that these reforms would lead to the creation of a more humane, civilized society.

The Italian jurist Cesare Beccaria (1738–1794) provided the intellectual inspiration of the movement for legal reform. In his *Essay on Crimes and Punishments* (1764), Beccaria argued that punishment should be used not to exact retribution for crimes, but to rehabilitate the criminal and to serve the interests of society. "In order that every punishment may not be an act of violence committed by one or by many against a private member of society," wrote Beccaria, "it should be above all things public, immediate, and necessary, the least possible in the case given, proportioned to the crime, and determined by the laws."[3] Beccaria called for the abolition of capital punishment and the imprisonment of convicted felons. The prison, which prior to the eighteenth century had been little more than a jail or holding facility, now became a symbol of the improvement of society.

DIFFERENT VOICES THE ENLIGHTENMENT DEBATE OVER PROGRESS

The Enlightenment produced two radically different views of the course of human development. The more optimistic of these, expressed most clearly by the French mathematician and political reformer the Marquis de Condorcet (1743–1794), envisioned human beings gradually progressing toward perfection. The more pessimistic view, exemplified by the Swiss born philosopher and political theorist Jean-Jacques Rousseau, saw civilization as inherently corrupting and degenerative. Rousseau developed this pessimistic view in his historical analysis of the causes of social and economic inequality. His description of the state of nature offered a philosophical foundation for the Enlightenment's ideal of the noble savage. (See Encounters and Transformations in this chapter.)

The Marquis of Condorcet Celebrates the Progress of the Human Mind

All these causes of the improvement of the human species, all these means that assure it, will by their nature act continuously and acquire a constantly growing momentum.... [W]e could therefore already conclude that the perfectibility of man is unlimited, even though, up to now, we have only supposed him endowed with the same natural faculties and organization. What then would be the certainty and extent of our hopes if we could believe that these natural faculties themselves and this organization are also susceptible of improvement? This is the last question remaining for us to examine.

The organic perfectibility or degeneration of races in plants and animals may be regarded as one of the general laws of nature. This law extends to the human species; and certainly no one will doubt that progress in medical conservation [of life], in the use of healthier food and housing, a way of living that would develop strength through exercise without impairing it by excess, and finally the destruction of the two most active causes of degradation—misery and too great wealth—will prolong the extent of life and assure people more constant health and a more robust constitution. We feel that the progress of preventive medicine as a preservative, made more effective by the progress of reason and social order, will eventually banish communicable or contagious illnesses and those diseases in general that originate in climate, food, and the nature of work. It would not be difficult to prove that this hope should extend to almost all other diseases, whose more remote causes will eventually be recognized. Would it be absurd now to suppose that the improvement of the human race should be regarded as capable of unlimited progress? That a time will come when death would result only from extraordinary accidents or the more and more gradual wearing out of vitality, and that, finally, the duration of the average interval between birth and wearing out has itself no specific limit whatsoever? No doubt man will not become immortal, but cannot the span constantly increase between the moment he begins to live and the time when naturally, without illness or accident, he finds life a burden?

Voltaire and the Spirit of the Enlightenment

The philosophe who captured all the main themes and the spirit of the Enlightenment was the writer and philosopher François Marie Arouet (1694–1778), known universally by his pen name, Voltaire. Born into a French bourgeois family, Voltaire became one of the most prominent and prolific writers of the eigh-teenth century. Although he wrote for a fairly broad, predominantly bourgeois audience, and although he decried the injustices of aristocratic society, he was comfortable in the homes of the nobility and at the courts of European monarchs. Voltaire's main career was as an author. He wrote plays, novels, poems, letters, essays, and history. These writings revealed commitment to scientific rationality, contempt

Source: Marie Jean Antoine Nicolas Caritat, Marquis de Condorcet, *Esquisse d'un tableau historique des progrès de l'esprit humain* (Paris: Masson et Fils, 1822), pp. 279–285, 293–294, 303–305.

Rousseau on the Degeneration of Humankind (1754)

Many writers have hastily concluded that man is naturally cruel and requires civil institutions to make him more mild; whereas nothing is more gentle than man in his primitive state, as he is placed by nature at an equal distance from the stupidity of brutes and the fatal ingenuity of civilized man. Equally confined by instinct and reason to the sole care of guarding himself against the mischiefs which threaten him, he is restrained by natural compassion from doing any injury to others, and is not led to do such a thing even in return for injuries received.... The example of savages, most of whom have been found in this state, seems to prove that men were meant to remain in it, that it is the real youth of the world, and that all subsequent advances have been apparently so many steps towards the perfection of the individual, but in reality towards the decrepitude of the species.

Before the invention of signs to represent riches, wealth could hardly consist in anything but lands and cattle, the only real possessions men can have. But, when inheritances so increased in number and extent as to occupy the whole of the land, and to border on one another, one man could aggrandize himself only at the expense of another.... Thus, as

the most powerful or the most miserable considered their might or misery as a kind of right to the possessions of others, equivalent, in their opinion, to that of property, the destruction of equality was attended by the most terrible disorders. Usurpations by the rich, robbery by the poor, and the unbridled passions of both, suppressed the cries of natural compassion and the still feeble voice of justice, and filled men with avarice, ambition and vice. Between the title of the strongest and that of the first occupier, there arose perpetual conflicts, which never ended but in battles and bloodshed. The new-born state of society thus gave rise to a horrible state of war; men thus harassed and depraved were no longer capable of retracing their steps or renouncing the fatal acquisitions they had made, but, laboring by the abuse of the faculties which do them honor, merely to their own confusion, brought themselves to the brink of ruin.

Source: Jean-Jacques Rousseau, *Discourse on Inequality* (1754).

For Discussion

1. What is the basis of Condorcet's optimism that human beings are progressing toward perfection?

2. What is the basis of Rousseau's contention that the human species was degenerating?

3. Do you think modern Western society is progressing or deteriorating?

for established religion, and unflagging pursuit of liberty and justice.

Like many men of the Enlightenment, Voltaire developed a deep interest in science. He acquired much of his scientific knowledge from a learned noblewoman, Madame du Châtelet (1706–1749), a scientist and mathematician who translated the works of Newton into French. Madame du Châtelet became Voltaire's mistress,

and the two lived together with her tolerant husband in their country estate in eastern France. The sexual freedom they experienced was characteristic of many Enlightenment figures, who rejected the Christian condemnation of sexual activity outside marriage and who justified their behavior on the basis of natural law and the pursuit of happiness. From Madame du Châtelet, Voltaire acquired not only an understanding of

JUSTICE IN HISTORY

A Case of Infanticide in the Age of the Enlightenment

A mid-eighteenth-century trial of a young French woman charged with killing her newborn child provides a window into the life of women who occupied the lower rungs of French society, in contrast to those who frequented the court and met in salons. The trial also raises the larger question, debated during the Enlightenment, whether the punishments prescribed for infanticide were proportionate to the crime.

In August 1742 Marie-Jeanne Bartonnet, a 21-year-old unmarried woman from a small French village in Brie, moved to Paris, where she took up residence with Claude le Queux, whom she had known in her youth, and Claude's sister. At that time Bartonnet was seven months pregnant. On October 22 Bartonnet caused a ruckus in the middle of the night when she went to the toilet and began groaning loudly and bleeding profusely. When her neighbors found her, and when she asked for towels for the blood, they suspected that she had had a miscarriage and called for a midwife. By the time the midwife arrived, it was clear that the delivery had already taken place and that the infant had fallen down the toilet to the cesspool five stories below. Suspecting that Bartonnet had killed the baby, the proprietress of the building reported her to the nearest judicial officer. The next day authorities returned to the building and found the dead infant in the cesspool. An autopsy revealed that either a blunt instrument or a fall had dented the child's skull. After a medical examination of Bartonnet revealed the signs of having just delivered a baby, she was arrested and imprisoned for the crime of infanticide.

Bartonnet came very close to being executed, but the strict procedures of French justice saved her from paying the ultimate price for her apparent crime. In the seventeenth and eighteenth centuries French criminal justice had established clear criteria for determining the guilt or innocence of a person accused of a crime. These procedures involved a systematic interrogation of the accused (only rarely under torture), the deposition of witnesses, the evaluation of physical evidence, and the confrontation of the accused with the witnesses who testified against

A WOMAN ACCUSED OF MURDER IN THE EIGHTEENTH CENTURY

With the exception of infanticide—the crime for which Marie-Jeanne Bartonnet was tried and convicted—few women were tried for capital crimes in the eighteenth century. One exception was Sarah Malcolm, a 22-year-old Englishwoman, shown here in a portrait by William Hogarth (1733). Malcolm was executed for slitting the throat of a wealthy lady in London.

her. There also was a mandatory review of the case, which involved a further interrogation of the defendant, before the Parlement of Paris, the highest court in northern France.

The interrogations of Bartonnet did not give her judges much evidence on which they could convict her. When asked the name of the village where she had lived in Brie, she told her interrogators, "It's none of your business." She denied that she had even known she was pregnant, refused to name the man with whom she had had intercourse, and claimed that she had mistaken her labor pains for colic or diarrhea. She denied picking her baby off the floor of the toilet after the delivery and throwing it into the cesspool. When presented with the baby's corpse, she claimed she did not recognize it.

After this interrogation, Bartonnet was given the opportunity to challenge the testimony of the witnesses who had seen her the night of the delivery. The most damning testimony came from Madame Pâris, the wife of the proprietor, who had found Bartonnet on the toilet and thus could verify the circumstances of the clandestine delivery. Bartonnet's inability to challenge the testimony of Madame Pâris led directly to her initial conviction. After reviewing the entire dossier of evidence, the king's attorney recommended conviction for concealing her pregnancy, hiding her delivery, and destroying her child. French criminal procedure entrusted the decision of guilt or innocence to the judges themselves, and on November 27 they voted that Bartonnet should be executed by hanging.

Marie-Jeanne Bartonnet's fate, however, was not yet sealed. When her case was appealed to the Parlement of Paris, Bartonnet repeated her statement that she had gone to the toilet but did not know whether she had given birth. Even though her execution was warranted by terms of a law of 1557 that defined the crime of infanticide, the judges of this court voted to commute her sentence to a public whipping, banishment from the jurisdiction of the Parlement of Paris, and confiscation of her property. The basis of this decision appears to have been the absence of any proof that she had

deliberately killed her baby. Indeed, its injuries could have been caused by its fall down the drain pipe into the cesspool. There was also the persistent refusal of the defendant to make a confession. She may have been lying, but it is equally possible that once she had delivered the baby, which happened very quickly, she convinced herself that it had not happened.

Bartonnet's trial for infanticide stands at the end of a long period of intense prosecution of this crime. Trials of this sort declined as cities built foundling hospitals for abandoned infants and as moral criticism of illegitimacy was redirected from the pregnant mother to the father. The new legal values promoted at the time of the Enlightenment, moreover, made it less likely that any woman or man would be executed for this or any other crime.

For Discussion

1. As in many trials, the facts of this case can be used to support different claims of justice. If you had been the prosecutor in this trial, what position would you have taken to prove the crime of infanticide? If you had been defending Marie-Jeanne Bartonnet, what arguments would you have used in her defense?

2. In his *Essay on Crimes and Punishments* (1764), Beccaria recommended that punishments be determined strictly in accordance with the social damage committed by the crime. What would Beccaria have said about the original sentence of death in this case? What would he have said about the modified sentence handed down by the Parlement of Paris?

Taking It Further

Michael Wolfe (ed.) *Changing Identities in Early Modern France.* 1997. Gives a full account of Marie-Jeanne Bartonnet's trial for infanticide.

Mark Jackson (ed.) *Infanticide: Historical Perspectives on Child Murder and Concealment, 1550–2000.* (Ashgate, 2002). A collection of essays on infanticide in various countries.

Newton's scientific laws, but also a commitment to women's education and equality. Voltaire lived with her until she died in 1749 while giving birth to a child that neither Voltaire nor her husband had fathered.

Voltaire's belief in a Newtonian universe—one governed by the universal law of gravitation—laid the foundation for his deism and his attacks on contemporary Christianity. In his *Philosophical Dictionary* (1764), he lashed out at established religion and the clergy, Protestant as well as Catholic. In a letter to another philosophe attacking religious superstition he pleaded, "Whatever you do, crush the infamous thing." In Voltaire's eyes Christianity was not only unreasonable, but

MADAME DU CHÂTELET

In her *Institutions de physique* (1740) this French noblewoman, the mistress of Voltaire, made an original and impressive attempt to give Newtonian physics a philosophical foundation.

also vulgar and barbaric. He condemned the Catholic Church for the slaughter of millions of indigenous people in the Americas on the grounds that they had not been baptized, as well as the executions of hundreds of thousands of Jews and heretics in Europe. All of these people were the victims of "barbarism and fanaticism."[4]

Voltaire's indictment of the Church for these barbarities was matched by his scathing criticism of the French government for a series of injustices, including his own imprisonment for insulting the regent of France. While living in England for three years, Voltaire became an admirer of English legal institutions, which he considered more humane and just than those of his native country. A tireless advocate of individual liberty, he became a regular defender of victims of injustice. One of the victims he defended was Jean Calas, a Protestant shopkeeper from Toulouse who had been tortured and executed for allegedly murdering his son because he had expressed a desire to convert to Catholicism. The boy had, in fact, committed suicide.

Voltaire showed a commitment to placing his knowledge in the service of humanitarian causes. In his most famous novel, *Candide* (1759), the character by that name challenged the smug confidence of Dr. Pangloss, the tutor who repeatedly claimed that they lived in "the best of all possible worlds." At the end of the novel Candide responded to this refrain by saying that "we must cultivate our garden." Voltaire, instead of being content with the current condition of humankind, was demanding that we work actively to improve society.

Enlightenment Political Theory

Enlightenment thinkers are known most widely for their political theories, especially those that supported the causes of liberty and reform. They did not share a common political ideology or agree on the most desirable type of political society, but they did share a belief that politics was a science that had its own natural laws. They also thought of the state in secular rather than religious terms. There was little place in Enlightenment thought for the divine right of kings. Nor was there a place for the Church in the government of the state. On other issues, however, there was little consensus. Three thinkers in particular illustrate the range of Enlightenment political thought: Montesquieu, Rousseau, and Paine.

BARON DE MONTESQUIEU: THE SEPARATION OF POWERS The most influential political writer of the Enlightenment was the French philosophe Charles-Louis de Secondat, Baron de Montesquieu (1689–1755). The son of a nobleman of the robe from Bordeaux, Montesquieu had a legal education and also developed an interest in science, history, and anthropology. In *Spirit of the Laws* (1748), Montesquieu argued that there were three forms of government: republics, monarchies, and despotisms, each of which had an activating or inspirational force. In republics that force was civic virtue, in monarchies it was honor, and in despotisms it was fear. In each form of government there was a danger that the polity could degenerate: The virtue of republics could be lost, monarchies could become corrupt, and despotisms could lead to repression. The key to maintaining moderation and preventing this degeneration of civil society was the law of each country.

Montesquieu used his knowledge of the British political system, which he had studied firsthand while living in England for two years, to argue that the key to good government was the separation of executive, legislative, and judicial power. He was particularly concerned about the independence of the judiciary. Montesquieu was unaware that legislative and executive powers actually overlapped in eighteenth-century Britain, but his emphasis on the importance of a separation of powers became the most durable of his ideas. It had a profound influence on the drafting of the Constitution of the United States of America in 1787.

CHRONOLOGY: LITERARY WORKS OF THE ENLIGHTENMENT

1687	Isaac Newton, *Mathematical Principles of Natural Philosophy*
1690	John Locke, *An Essay Concerning Human Understanding*
1721	Baron de Montesquieu, *The Persian Letters*
1738	Voltaire, *Elements of the Philosophy of Newton*
1738	David Hume, *Treatise of Human Nature*
1748	Baron de Montesquieu, *Spirit of the Laws*
	David Hume, *An Enquiry Concerning Human Understanding*
1751	First volume of Diderot and d'Alembert's *Encyclopedia*
1755	Jean-Jacques Rousseau, *Discourse on the Origin of Inequality Among Men*
1759	Voltaire, *Candide*
1762	Jean-Jacques Rousseau, *The Social Contract* and *Emile, or On Education*
1763	Voltaire, *Treatise on Toleration*
1764	Cesare Beccaria, *Essay on Crimes and Punishments*
	Voltaire, *Philosophical Dictionary*
1776	Adam Smith, *The Wealth of Nations*
1781	Immanuel Kant, *Critique of Pure Reason*
1791	Thomas Paine, *The Rights of Man*
1792	Mary Wollstonecraft, *A Vindication of the Rights of Woman*
1795	Marquis de Condorcet, *Progress of the Human Mind*

JEAN-JACQUES ROUSSEAU: THE GENERAL WILL   Also influential as a political theorist was the Swiss philosophe Jean-Jacques Rousseau (1712–1778), who as a young man moved from Geneva to Paris and became a member of a prominent intellectual circle. Rousseau did not conform to the model of the typical Enlightenment thinker. His distrust of human reason and his emotionalism separated him from Hume, Voltaire, and Diderot. That distrust laid the foundations for the romantic reaction against the Enlightenment in the early nineteenth century (see Chapter 22). Instead of celebrating the improvement of society as it evolved into higher forms, Rousseau had a negative view of the achievements of civilization. He idealized the uncorrupted condition of human beings in the state of nature, supporting the theory of the "noble savage." Human beings could never return to that original natural state, but Rousseau held out the hope of recreating an idealized golden age when they were not yet alienated from themselves and their environment.

Rousseau's political theories were hardly conventional, but they appealed to some segments of the reading public. In his *Discourse on the Origin of Inequality Among Men* (1755) and *The Social Contract* (1762), he challenged the existing political and social order with an uncompromising attack on aristocracy and monarchy. He linked absolute monarchy, which he referred to as despotism, with the court and especially with the vain, pampered, conceited, and over-decorated aristocratic women who wielded political influence with the king and in the salons. As an alternative to this aristocratic, monarchical, and feminized society, Rousseau proclaimed the sovereignty of the people. Laws were to be determined by the General Will, by which he meant the true and inherent interest of the community, not the vote of the majority.

As a result of his writings, Rousseau became associated with radical republican and democratic ideas that flourished at the time of the French Revolution. One indication of that radicalism was the fact that *The Social Contract* was banned not only in absolutist France, but also in the republics of the Netherlands and Switzerland.

DIFFERENCES AMONG THE PHILOSOPHERS

This satirical print shows Rousseau, to the left, and Voltaire engaged in heated debate. The two men were both major figures in the Enlightenment, but they differed widely in temperament and in their philosophical and political views. Rousseau was very much the rebel; unlike Voltaire, he distrusted reason and articulated highly egalitarian political principles.

Source: Bibliotheque Nationale de France

Rousseau was also criticized for justifying authoritarian rule. His argument that the General Will placed limits on individual civil liberty encouraged autocratic leaders, such as the radical Maximilien Robespierre at the time of the French Revolution, to claim that their dictatorial rule embodied that General Will.

THOMAS PAINE: THE RIGHTS OF MAN   Of all the Enlightenment political theorists, the English publicist and propagandist Thomas Paine (1737–1809) was arguably the most radical. Paine was influenced by Rousseau, Diderot, and Voltaire, but his radicalism developed mainly as a result of his intense involvement in the political world of revolutionary America. In *Common Sense* (1776), Paine presented the case for American independence from Britain. This included a passionate statement of human freedom, equality, and rationality. It also involved a trenchant attack on hereditary monarchy and an eloquent statement for the sovereignty of the law. At the time of the French Revolution, Paine continued to call for the establishment of a republic in France and in his native country. In his most widely circulated work, *The Rights of Man* (1791), he linked the institution of monarchy with the aristocracy, which he referred to as "a seraglio of males, who neither collect the honey nor form the hive but exist only for lazy enjoyment."

The title of *The Rights of Man* established a theme that appeared in much Enlightenment writing. Like Diderot and Rousseau, Paine spoke the language of natural rights. Until the Enlightenment, rights were considered legal privileges acquired by royal charter or by inheritance. One had a right, for example, to a particular piece of land or to elect representatives from one's county or town. Those rights could be surrendered under certain circumstances, such as when a person sold land. The new emphasis on natural law, however, led to the belief that simply by being a human being one acquired natural rights that could never be taken away. The American Declaration of Independence (1776), drafted by Thomas Jefferson, presented an eloquent statement of these God-given inalienable rights, which included "life, liberty and the pursuit of happiness."

Women and the Enlightenment

The emphasis that Enlightenment thinkers placed on natural law led to two very different views regarding the position of women in society. A large number of philosophes, including Diderot and Rousseau, argued that because women are different in nature from men, they should be confined to an exclusively domestic role as wives and mothers. Rousseau also insisted on the separate education of girls. This patriarchal argument supported the emerging theory of **separate spheres,** which held that men and women should conduct their lives in different social and political environments. The identification of women with the private, domestic sphere laid the foundation for the ideology of female domesticity, which became popular in bourgeois society in the nineteenth century. This ideal denied women the freedom that aristocratic women in France had acquired during the eighteenth century, especially those who belonged to polite society. It also continued to deny them civil rights. Eighteenth-century women could not vote and could not initiate lawsuits. They were not full members of civil society.

A small minority of Enlightenment thinkers rejected this theory of the separate spheres, demanding the full equality of men and women. The first of these appeals came from the Marquis de Condorcet, who published *On the Admission of Women to the Rights of Citizenship* in 1789. In this pamphlet Condorcet proposed that all women who owned property be given the right to vote. He later called for universal suffrage for all men and women on the grounds that they shared a common human nature.

Condorcet's English contemporary, Mary Wollstonecraft (1759–1797), also made an eloquent appeal for extending civil and political rights to women. In *A Vindication of the Rights of Woman* (1792), Wollstonecraft argued that girls should receive the same education as boys and learn how to support themselves. Only in this way could women take control of their lives and become the social and political equals of men. Thus, Wollstonecraft challenged the belief of Rousseau and other male Enlightenment thinkers that cultural and social differences between men and women were "natural."

The Enlightenment and Sexuality

One facet of Enlightenment thought that had a profound effect on the position of women in society was the appeal for greater sexual permissiveness. Many philosophes, including Voltaire, Diderot, and Holbach, remained openly critical of the strict standard of sexual morality enforced by Christian churches. The basic argument of the philosophes was that sexual activity should not be restricted because it was pleasurable and a source of happiness. The arbitrary prohibitions imposed by the Church contradicted human nature. Enlightenment thinkers used European encounters with pagan natives of the South Pacific, who were reported to enjoy great sexual permissiveness, to reinforce this argument. Diderot appealed to the sexual code of the Tahitians in his attack on Christian sexual morality.

Many philosophes, including Voltaire, practiced what they preached and lived openly with women out of wedlock. Other members of wealthy society adopted an even more libertine lifestyle. The Venetian adventurer and author Giacomo Casanova (1725–1798), who was expelled from a seminary for his immorality, gained fame for his life of gambling, spying, and seducing hundreds of women. To one young Spanish woman, who resisted his advances to protect her virginity, he said: "You must abandon yourself to my passion without any resistance, and you may rest assured I will respect your innocence." Casanova's name soon became identified with sexual seduction.

The violent excesses to which this type of eighteenth-century sexual permissiveness could lead can be seen in the career of the Marquis de Sade (1740–1814). The author of licentious libertine narratives, including his own memoirs and an erotic novel, *Justine* (1793), de Sade described the use of violence in sexual encounters and thus gave rise to the word *sadism* to describe the pleasurable administration of pain. He spent 27 years in prison for his various sexual offenses.

It makes sense that noblemen like Casanova and de Sade would have adopted the libertine values of the Enlightenment thinkers. Somewhat more remarkable was the growth of public sexual permissiveness among all social groups, including the rather prim and proper bourgeoisie and the working poor. Erotic literature, such as John Cleland's *Memoirs of a Woman of Pleasure* (1749), and pornographic prints achieved considerable popularity in an increasingly commercialized society, while prostitution became more open and widespread. Voltaire and Diderot might not have approved of this literature or these practices, but the libertine, anti-Christian, materialist outlook of these philosophes helped to prepare the ground for their acceptance.

THE IMPACT OF THE ENLIGHTENMENT

■ What impact did the Enlightenment have on Western culture and politics?

The ideas of the Enlightenment spread to every country in Europe and the Americas. They inspired programs of reform and radical political movements. Enlightenment thought, however, did not become the property of the entire population. It appealed mainly to the educated and the relatively prosperous, and it failed to penetrate the lower levels of society.

The Spread of Enlightened Ideas

The ideas of the Enlightenment spread rapidly among the literate members of society, mainly by means of print. During the eighteenth century, print became the main medium of formal communication. The technology of printing allowed for the publication of materials on a scale unknown a century before. Pamphlets, newspapers, and books rolled off presses not only in the major cities, but in provincial towns as well. Literacy rates increased dramatically throughout western Europe. By 1750 more than half the male population of France and England could read basic texts. The foundation of public libraries in all the major cities of western Europe made printed materials more widely available. In many bookshops, rooms were set aside for browsing in the hope that readers would eventually purchase the books they consulted.

One of the most widely circulated publications of the Enlightenment was the *Encyclopedia* compiled by Denis Diderot and the mathematician Jean le Rond d'Alembert. This massive 17-volume work, which was published between 1751 and 1765, contained thousands of articles on science, religion, politics, and the economy. The entries in the *Encyclopedia* were intended not only to promote knowledge, but also to advance the ideas of the Enlightenment. Included, for example, were two entries on natural law, which was described as being "perpetual and unchangeable." Other articles praised the achievements of science and technology and gave special attention to industrial crafts and trades. Underlying the entire enterprise was the belief that knowledge was useful, that it could contribute to the improvement of human life. In these respects, the *Encyclopedia* became the quintessential statement of the worldview of the Enlightenment, and its publication stands as a crowning achievement of the entire movement.

Encyclopedias, pamphlets, newspapers, and novels were not the only means by which the ideas of the Enlightenment spread. Literary societies and book clubs, which proliferated in the major cities of western Europe, encouraged the public reading and discussion of the latest publications. Scientific societies sponsored lectures on developments in physics, chemistry, and natural history. One of the most famous of these lectures demonstrated the power of electricity by charging a young boy, suspended from the ground, with static electricity. This "electrified boy," who was not harmed in the process, attracted objects from a stool placed below him. Lectures like this one attracted large crowds.

Equally important in the spread of the scientific and cultural ideas of the Enlightenment were museums, where an increasingly curious and educated public could view scientific and cultural artifacts, many of them gathered from around the world. The museums often sponsored exhibits and lectures. Paris became home to many of these museums in the 1780s, and they could be found in all the major cities of Europe by the end of the eighteenth century.

Enlightenment ideas also spread, although more informally, in the coffeehouses that sprang up in cities across Europe. These commercial establishments were open to everyone who could pay the fare, and therefore they proved immensely successful in facilitating the spread of ideas within the bourgeoisie. Newspapers were often read aloud at coffeehouses, and political debates often took place there.

Another set of institutions that promoted the ideas of the Enlightenment were the secret societies of men and women known as **freemasons.** Committed to the principles of liberty and equality, freemasons strove to create a society based on reason and virtue. Freemasonry first appeared in England and Scotland in the seventeenth century and then spread to France, the Dutch Republic, Germany, Poland, and Russia during the eighteenth century. Some of the most famous figures of the Enlightenment, including Voltaire, belonged to masonic lodges. In the 1770s there were more than 10,000 freemasons in Paris alone. In the lodges philosophes interacted with merchants, lawyers, and government leaders. The pope condemned the freemasons in 1738, and many civil authorities considered their ideas subversive.

The most famous informal cultural institutions of the Enlightenment were the **salons,** the private sitting rooms or parlors of aristocratic women where discussions of philosophy, science, literature, and politics took place. The salons of Madame Geoffrin and Madame du Deffand in Paris won international fame. The women who hosted these meetings invited the participants, entertained those who attended, and used their conversational skills to direct and facilitate the conversation. They also used their influence to secure aristocratic patronage of the young male writers and scientists whom they cultivated.

Most of the prominent male figures of the French Enlightenment participated in these meetings, at least during the early years of their careers.

The salons became the target of contemporary criticism because they allowed women a place in public life and because they epitomized aristocratic culture. What mattered most in the salons, however, was not gender or social status, but quickness of wit, conversational skill, and intellectual appeal. Thus, the salon contributed to the creation of a society based on merit rather than birth alone.

The Limits of the Enlightenment

The ideas of the Enlightenment spread rapidly across Europe, but their influence was limited. The market for books by philosophes such as Voltaire and Rousseau was quite small. Diderot and d'Alembert's *Encyclopedia* sold a remarkable 25,000 copies by 1789, but that was exceptional, and libraries purchased a large number of them. Paine's *The Rights of Man* also reached a fairly broad audience, mainly because it was written in a simple direct style and its price was deliberately kept low. Most books on social and political theory and scholarly works on science did not sell very well. Rousseau's *Social Contract* was a commercial failure.

Books on other topics had much better sales. Inspirational religious literature continued to be immensely popular, indicating the limits of Enlightenment secularism. Novels, a relatively new genre of fiction that appealed to the bourgeoisie, were almost as successful. Rousseau and Voltaire both used novels to advance their radical social views. In France, books that were banned because of their pornographic content or their satirical attacks on the monarchy, the clergy, or ministers in the government also proved to be best-sellers in the huge underground French book market.

Pseudoscientific popular literature also revealed the limited influence of the Enlightenment. The reading public did not show much interest in genuinely scientific books, but they did purchase thousands of copies of publications on such technological developments as hot-air balloons, which became a new fad in the 1780s, and on the monsters supposedly sighted in distant lands. They also bought books on **mesmerism.** The Viennese physicist and physician Franz Anton Mesmer (1734–1815), who moved to Paris in 1778, claimed that he had discovered a fluid that permeated and surrounded all bodies and was the source of heat, light, electricity, and magnetism. Sickness was caused by the obstruction to the flow of this fluid in the human body. To restore this flow patients were massaged, hypnotized, or "mesmerized" with the intention of producing a convulsion or crisis that restored health. Mesmerism developed into a form of spiritualism in which its patients engaged in séances with spirits, and its practitioners dabbled in the occult. This pseudo-science, which the French Academy of Science rejected as a hoax, became the subject of numerous pamphlets and newspaper articles that fascinated the reading public.

Those who read books about mesmerism had only a tenuous connection with the learned world of the Enlightenment. Among those who were illiterate or barely literate, Enlightenment ideas made even fewer inroads. Throughout the eighteenth century, for example, uneducated villages continued to believe in magic and witchcraft and occasionally lynched neighbors suspected of causing misfortune by such means. Philosophes considered the belief in magic and witchcraft as superstitious and ignorant, but they were unable to change popular mentality.

More physical manifestations of popular culture included cockfighting and baiting bulls, bears, and badgers by tying them down and allowing dogs to attack them. These blood sports, which could attract thousands of spectators at a single event, resulted in the serious injury or death of the animals. Enlightenment thinkers and many others condemned this activity for its cruelty and barbarism and argued that just like the torture and execution of criminals, these pastimes had no place in polite society. Popular sports, however, could not be easily eradicated. They did not begin to disappear until the nineteenth century, often as the result of campaigns conducted by clergymen.

The Political Legacy of the Enlightenment

When we turn to Enlightened political ideas, we confront an even more difficult task of determining the extent of their impact. The main figures of the Enlightenment were intellectuals—men of letters who did not occupy positions of great political importance and who did not devote much thought to the challenging task of putting their theories into practice. Rulers often treated Enlightenment thinkers with suspicion, if only because they criticized established authority. Nevertheless, Enlightenment thought did make its mark on eighteenth-century politics in two strikingly different ways.

Enlightened Absolutism

The first was through the reforms enacted by rulers known as **enlightened despots,** although the term *despot* is misleading because these enlightened rulers were rarely despotic in the sense of exercising power cruelly and arbitrarily. Enlightened absolutists, as these monarchs are more properly called, used royal power to implement reforms that Enlightenment thinkers had proposed. The connection between Enlightenment and royal absolutism is not as unnatural as it might appear. It is true that philosophes tended to be critical of the **Old Regime,** the eighteenth-century political order dominated by an absolute monarch and a privileged nobility and clergy. But many of them, including Voltaire, had little sympathy with democracy, which they identified with irrational mob rule. These philosophes preferred to entrust absolute monarchs with the implementation of the reforms they advocated.

Rulers of central and eastern European countries were particularly receptive to Enlightenment thought. These monarchs had read widely in the literature of the Enlightenment and introduced Western intellectuals to their courts. The most famous of the enlightened absolutists was King Frederick II of Prussia, known as Frederick the Great (r. 1740–1786). A deist who wrote poetry and played the flute, Frederick was enamored of all things French. When the French philosophe d'Alembert visited his court, the king hosted a dinner at which he spoke only French, leaving many of the Prussian guests to sip their soup in stunned silence. Frederick corresponded extensively with Voltaire and invited him to take up residence at his French-style royal palace, "Sans Souci," at Potsdam. The relationship between king and philosopher, however, was often stormy, and when Frederick publicly burned a publication in which Voltaire had lampooned a royal favorite, Voltaire left Potsdam.

The departure of Voltaire did not weaken Frederick's determination to implement policies that reflected the ideals of the Enlightenment. The most noteworthy of these was the introduction of religious toleration throughout his predominantly Lutheran kingdom. Protestants of all denominations and Catholics (but not Jews) received the protection of the law and even benefited from royal patronage. Frederick also introduced legal reforms with the intention of realizing the Enlightenment ideal of making the law both rational and humane. He authorized the codification of Prussian law (an undertaking that was completed after his death in 1794), abolished judicial torture, and eliminated capital punishment. To provide for the training of future servants of the state, he began a system of compulsory education throughout the country. Like most enlightened rulers, Frederick never abandoned his commitment to absolute rule, which he strengthened by winning the support of the nobility. He also remained committed to the militaristic and expansionist policies of his father, Frederick William I. For him there was no contradiction between his style of rule and his commitment to Enlightenment ideals.

In neighboring Austria two Habsburg rulers, Maria Theresa (r. 1740–1780) and her son

Joseph II (r. 1780–1790), pursued reformist policies that gave them the reputation of being enlightened monarchs. Most of Maria Theresa's reforms were of an administrative nature. Stunned by the Prussian invasion and occupation of the Habsburg province of Silesia in 1740, Maria Theresa set out to strengthen the Habsburg monarchy by gaining complete control over taxation and by reorganizing the military and civil bureaucracy. She also took steps to make the serfs more productive, mainly by restricting the work they performed on their lords' lands and by abolishing the feudal dues they paid.

These efforts won the applause of philosophes, but the policies of Maria Theresa that most clearly bore the stamp of the Enlightenment were her legal reforms. Inspired by Beccaria and Montesquieu, she established a commission to reform the entire corpus of Austrian law. She promulgated a new code of criminal law in 1769, and seven years later she issued an edict abolishing judicial torture. Joseph continued this program of legal reform by reorganizing the entire central court system and by eliminating capital punishment. He also revealed the influence of the Enlightenment by granting religious toleration, first to Protestants and eastern Orthodox Christians in 1781, and then to Jews in 1782. With respect to social issues, he completed his mother's work of abolishing serfdom altogether.

The efforts of Catherine II of Russia (r. 1762–1796) to implement the ideas of the Enlightenment followed a different course from those of Maria Theresa and Joseph. The daughter of a German prince, Catherine received an education grounded in a traditional curriculum of history, geography, and Lutheran theology. In 1745 she was married to a distant cousin, Peter, who was in line to inherit the Russian throne from his aunt, the childless Empress Elizabeth (r. 1741–1762). After arriving in St. Petersburg Catherine not only studied Russian language, literature, and religion, but also read widely in western

European sources, including the works of Enlightenment thinkers. She later corresponded with Voltaire and d'Alembert and employed the famous salon hostess Madame Geoffrin at her court. At Catherine's invitation Diderot visited St. Petersburg for six months.

Early in her reign, Catherine embarked on a program of reform similar to those of other enlightened absolutists. In 1767 she appointed a commission to codify Russian law on the basis of western European principles. Her

CATHERINE THE GREAT

Catherine II of Russia on the day she succeeded in taking the throne from her husband, Peter III, at Peterhof in 1762. Catherine, who despised her husband, joined a conspiracy against him right after his accession to the throne. Catherine, like Peter, had several lovers, and her two children, including the future emperor Paul, were reputedly conceived by members of the nobility.

Source: Vigilius Erichsen (1722–82), "Equestrian Portrait of Catherine II (1729–96), the Great of Russia," oil on canvas. Musee des Beaux-Arts, Chartres, France/The Bridgeman Art Library

recommendations to the commission included the abolition of torture and inhumane punishment and the establishment of religious toleration. She was eventually forced to disband the commission, whose members could not agree on a new code, but she later abolished torture and capital punishment on her own authority. Like Maria Theresa, she instituted administrative and educational reforms, including the introduction of primary schooling in the provinces. Catherine, who became known as Catherine the Great, also tried unsuccessfully to provide for the education of girls.

Catherine gained a reputation for being an enlightened European monarch, but she never fully embraced the ideals of the Enlightenment. She admitted that it was easier to subscribe to those ideals than to implement them. On the issue of serfdom, which most Enlightenment thinkers wished to see abolished, she would not yield. Catherine not only preserved that social system to secure the loyalty of the Russian nobility, but also extended it to Ukraine and parts of Poland after Russia incorporated those regions into the empire. Some philosophes called for the dissolution of large imperial structures, but Catherine expanded the Russian Empire by acquiring vast territories in Eastern Europe, East Asia, and Alaska.

Eventually Catherine disavowed the ideals of the Enlightenment altogether. After putting down the Pugachev rebellion in 1774, she began to question the desirability of social reform. The experience of the French Revolution in the 1790s (see Chapter 20) led her to repudiate Enlightenment reformism.

The Enlightenment and Revolution

While Enlightenment thought led to enlightened absolutism, it also led in the opposite direction. The second mark that Enlightenment thought made on eighteenth-century politics was the inspiration it gave to movements for reform and revolution in western Europe and the Americas. The emphasis placed by Enlightenment thinkers on individual liberty, natural rights, and political reform pressured monarchs and the traditional nobility either to make concessions or to relinquish power altogether. Very few philosophes were themselves revolutionaries, but their ideas contributed to the creation of a new political order.

The towering reputation of Voltaire during the French Revolution in 1789, as well as the anger of conservatives who exhumed and burned his bones after the revolution had ended, suggests that this philosophe's passionate criticisms of the Old Regime and his pleas for human freedom played a significant role in the revolutionary developments of the 1790s. The same is true of the radical Rousseau, whose concept of the General Will served as the basis of a revolutionary ideology. Rousseau's democratic and republican ideas were used to justify some of the most important changes that took place during the revolution. Contemporaries either glorified or attacked him, depending on their political philosophy, for having actually caused the revolution. One book published in 1791 was titled *On Jean-Jacques Rousseau Considered as One of the First Authors of the Revolution.*

Yet another application of enlightened ideas to politics took place in the Americas. The advocates of colonial independence from their mother countries, such as Thomas Jefferson in Virginia and Símon Bolívar in Venezuela and Colombia, were all deeply influenced by the Enlightenment concepts of natural law, natural rights, liberty, and popular sovereignty. The Declaration of Independence, which was written by Jefferson, betrayed its debt to the Enlightenment in its reference to the inalienable rights of all men and to the foundation of those rights in "the law of nature and Nature's God." As discussed in Chapter 18, the American Revolution cannot be explained solely in terms of these Enlightenment ideas. The colonists found inspiration in many different sources, including English common law. But the American colonists did wish to create an entirely new world order, just as did many

Enlightenment thinkers. They also adopted some of the most radical political ideas of the Enlightenment, which identified the people as the source of political power.

CONCLUSION

The Enlightenment and Western Identity

The Enlightenment was a distinctly Western phenomenon. It arose in the countries of western Europe and then spread to central and eastern Europe and to the Americas. Many traditions identified today as "Western values" either had their origin or received their most cogent expression in the Enlightenment. In particular, the commitment to individual liberty, civil rights, toleration, and rational decision making all took shape during this period.

It would be misleading to make a simple equation between the ideas of the Enlightenment and the Western intellectual tradition. The ideals of the Enlightenment have never been fully accepted within Western societies. Ever since the original formulation of Enlightenment ideas, conservatives have challenged those ideas on the grounds that they would lead to the destruction of religion and the social order. Those conservative criticisms became most vocal at the time of the French Revolution and during the early years of the nineteenth century.

Even though the values of the Enlightenment have never met with universal approval, they gave many Europeans a clear sense of their own identity with respect to the rest of the world. Educated people who prided themselves on being enlightened knew that their scientific, rational worldview was not shared by Asians, Africans, indigenous Americans, or South Pacific islanders. It did not matter whether Enlightenment thinkers had a positive view of those other cultures, like Voltaire or Rousseau, or a negative one, like Montesquieu. What mattered was that they shared a similar mental outlook and a commitment to individual liberty, justice, and the improvement of civilization. For all of them religious faith was less important, both as an arbiter of morality and as a source of authority, than it was in these other cultures. The men and women of the Enlightenment all looked to the law of their country as a reflection of natural law and as the guardian of civil liberty. Their writings helped their European and colonial audiences think of themselves as even more distinct from non-Western people than they had in the past.

KEY TERMS

aristocracy	Republic of Letters
nobility	deism
nobility of the robe	separate spheres
classicism	freemasons
neoclassicism	salons
seigneurs	mesmerism
bourgeoisie	enlightened despots
Enlightenment	Old Regime
philosophes	

CHAPTER QUESTIONS

1. What social groups belonged to the aristocracy and how did they exercise their power and influence during the eighteenth century? (page 587)
2. How did subordinate social groups, most notably the rural peasantry and those who lived in the towns, challenge the aristocracy during the late eighteenth century? (page 592)
3. What were the main features of Enlightenment thought and how did it present a threat to the old order? (page 596)
4. What impact did the Enlightenment have on Western culture and politics? (page 610)

TAKING IT FURTHER

1. How might a nobleman in the eighteenth century have defended himself from the critiques leveled by members of the bourgeoisie?
2. In what ways did Enlightenment thinkers contribute to the decline of the aristocracy in the late eighteenth century?
3. What were the main issues over which philosophes disagreed? What were the issues that led Rousseau to disagree with Voltaire, Condorcet, and Mary Wollstonecraft?
4. How did the Enlightenment help to define the geographical limits of the West in the late eighteenth century?

✓○─ **Practice** on **MyHistoryLab**

20

The Age of the French Revolution, 1789–1815

■ The First French Revolution, 1789–1791 ■ The French Republic, 1792–1799
■ Cultural Change in France during the Revolution ■ The Napoleonic
Era, 1799–1815 ■ The Legacy of the French Revolution

ON JULY 12, 1789, THE FRENCH JOURNALIST CAMILLE DESMOULINS addressed an anxious crowd of Parisian citizens gathered outside the Palais-Royal, where public debate often took place. Playing upon fears that had been mounting during the past two months, Desmoulins claimed that the government of Louis XVI was preparing a massacre of Parisians. "To arms, to arms," Desmoulins cried out, as he roused the citizens to their own defense. That night Parisians responded to his call by invading arsenals in the city in anticipation of the violence they thought was about to descend upon them. The next day they continued to seize weapons and declared themselves members of the National Guard, a volunteer militia of propertied citizens.

On the morning of July 14, crowds of Parisians moved toward an ancient fortress known as the Bastille, where royal troops were stationed. The Parisians feared that the troops in the Bastille would take violent action against them, and they also wanted to capture the ammunition stored inside the building, which served as an arsenal and a prison. Negotiations with the governor of the Bastille were interrupted when some of the militia, moving into the courtyard of the fortress, demanded the surrender of the troops. Both sides fired shots, and the

exchange led to a full-scale assault upon the Bastille by the National Guard.

After three hours of fighting and the death of 83 people, the governor surrendered. His captors, bearing the arms they had seized, then led him to face charges before the officers of the city government. The crowd, however, crying for vengeance against their oppressors, attacked the soldiers and crushed some of them underfoot. The governor was stabbed hundreds of times, hacked to pieces, and decapitated. The chief magistrate of the city suffered the same fate for his reluctance to issue arms to its citizens. The crowd then placed the heads of the two men on pikes and paraded through the city.

The storming of the Bastille was the first of many violent episodes that occurred during the sequence of events called the French Revolution. That revolution brought about some of the most fundamental changes in European political life since the end of Roman rule. It heralded the destruction of the Old Regime, the eighteenth-century political order that had been dominated by an absolute monarch and a privileged nobility and clergy. It led to the submission of the Catholic Church to state control. A more radical phase of the revolution, beginning in 1792, resulted in the

THE STORMING OF THE BASTILLE, JULY 14, 1789

Parisian citizens attacked the Bastille not because it was a symbol of the Old Regime, but because it contained weapons that they needed to protect themselves from royalist troops.

destruction of the French monarchy and the declaration of a republic. It also led to a period of state-sponsored terrorism in 1793 and 1794, during which one group of revolutionaries engaged in a brutal campaign to eliminate their real and imagined enemies.

The excesses of the revolution led to a conservative reaction, and after a long period of rule by Napoleon Bonaparte between 1799 and 1815,

the French monarchy was restored, marking the end of the revolutionary period. The ideas of the revolution, however, especially its commitment to democratic republicanism and its concept of the nation, continued to dominate politics in the West for the next two hundred years. This chapter will address this question: How did the French Revolution permanently change the political culture of the West?

THE FIRST FRENCH REVOLUTION, 1789–1791

■ Why did the Old Regime in France collapse in 1789, and what revolutionary changes took place in French government and society during the next two years?

The French Revolution consisted of two distinct revolutions. The first, which began in 1789, resulted in a destruction of royal absolutism and the drafting of a constitution. The second and more radical revolution began in 1792 with the abolition of the monarchy and the formation of the French Republic.

The Beginning of the Revolution

The immediate cause of the revolution was a financial crisis that bankrupted the monarchy and deprived it of its authority. The government of Louis XVI (r. 1774–1792) had inherited considerable debts as a result of protracted periods of warfare with Great Britain. The opening of a new phase of this warfare in 1778, when France intervened in the American War of Independence on the side of the United States, pushed the government further into debt and strained the entire French economy. As the crisis deepened the king proposed a direct tax on all landowners. The nobility, however, objected to this plan, which would have perpetuated the absolutist policies of the royal government.

The deterioration of the government's financial condition finally forced the king to yield. When tax returns dried up as the result of an agricultural crisis in the summer months of 1788, the government could no longer pay its creditors. In a desperate effort to save his regime, Louis announced that he would convene the Estates General, a national representative assembly that had not met since 1614.

The meeting of the Estates General was set for May 1789, and during the months leading up to its opening, public debates arose over how the delegates should vote. The Estates General

CHRONOLOGY: THE FIRST FRENCH REVOLUTION, 1789–1791

1788

August 8	Announcement of the meeting of the Estates General

1789

May 5	The Estates General opens at Versailles
June 17	The Third Estate adopts the title of the National Assembly
June 20	Oath of the Tennis Court
July 14	The storming of the Bastille
Late July	The Great Fear in rural areas
August 4	Abolition of feudalism and privileges
August 26	*Declaration of the Rights of Man and Citizen*
October 5	March to Versailles; Louis XVI and National Assembly move to Paris
November 2	Church property is nationalized

1790

July 12	Civil Constitution of the Clergy
November 27	Decree requiring oath of loyalty from the clergy

1791

June 20	Royal family flees to Varennes, is apprehended by the National Guard
October 1	Newly elected Legislative Assembly opens

consisted of representatives of the three orders or social groups, known as **estates**, which made up French society: the clergy, the nobility, and the **Third Estate.** The Third Estate technically contained all the commoners in the kingdom (about 96 percent of the population), ranging from the wealthiest merchant to the poorest peasant. The elected representatives of the Third Estate were propertied non-noble elements of lay society, including many lawyers and military officers.

Before the meeting a dispute arose among the representatives over whether the three groups would vote by estate, in which case the first two estates would dominate the assembly, or by head, in which case the Third Estate would have about the same number of representatives as the other two estates. Each side claimed that it was the best representative of the "nation," a term meaning the entire body of French people.

After the king indicated that he would side with the clergy and the nobility, the Third Estate took the dramatic step of declaring itself a National Assembly and asked members of the other estates to vote with them. When the king locked the Third Estate out of their meeting place without explanation, the outraged members went to a nearby indoor tennis court and took a solemn oath (known as the Oath of the Tennis Court) that they would not disband until the country had been given a constitution. One week later the king ordered the nobility and the clergy to join the National Assembly.

As this political crisis was reaching a climax, a major social crisis, fueled by the high price of bread, caused a breakdown of public order. For many years French agriculture had experienced difficulty meeting the demands of an expanding population. A widespread harvest failure in 1788 reduced the supply even further. As the price of

JACQUES-LOUIS DAVID, *THE OATH OF THE TENNIS COURT*

The oath taken by the members of the Third Estate not to disband until France had a constitution led to the creation of the National Assembly and the legislation that destroyed royal absolutism and feudalism.

bread soared, demand for manufactured goods shrank, thus causing widespread unemployment among artisans. An increasing number of bread riots, peasant revolts, and urban strikes contributed to a sense of panic at the very time that the government's financial crisis deepened. In Paris the situation reached a critical point in June 1789.

At that point the king, a man with little political sense, made the ill-advised decisions to send 17,000 royal troops to Paris to restore order. The arrival of the troops gave the impression that the government was planning to attack the people of the city. In this atmosphere of public paranoia Parisians formed the National Guard and stormed the Bastille.

The fall of the Bastille unnerved the king. When he asked one of his aides, "Is it a revolt?" the aide replied, "No, sire, it is a revolution." The revolution had just begun. It moved into high gear two weeks later when the National Assembly responded to the outbreak of social unrest in the provinces. The scarcity of grain in the countryside gave rise to false rumors that the nobles were engaged in a plot to destroy crops and starve the people into submission. Peasants armed themselves and prepared to fight off the hired agents of the nobility. A widespread panic, known as the "Great Fear," gripped many parts of the country. Townspeople and peasants amassed in large numbers to defend themselves and save the harvest. In response to this panic, which reached its peak in the last two weeks of July, the National Assembly began to pass legislation that destroyed the Old Regime and created a new political order.

The Creation of a New Political Society

Between August 1789 and September 1790 the National Assembly took three revolutionary steps. First, it eliminated noble and clerical privileges. In August the assembly abolished the feudal dues that peasants paid their lords, the private legal jurisdictions of noblemen, the collection of tithes by the clergy, and the exclusive right of noblemen to hunt game on their lands. Ten months later the nobility lost their titles. Instead of a society divided into various corporate groups, each with its own privileges, France would now have only citizens, all of them equal at law. Social distinctions would be based on merit rather than birth.

The second step, taken on August 26, was the promulgation of the *Declaration of the Rights of Man and Citizen*. This document revealed the main influence of the Enlightenment on the revolution. It declared that all men, not just Frenchmen, had a natural right to liberty, property, equality before the law, freedom from oppression, and religious toleration. The statement that the "law is the expression of the general will" reflected the influence of Rousseau's *The Social Contract* (1762), while the statement that every citizen has the right to participate in the formation of that law either personally or through a representative embodied the basic principle of democracy. (See *Different Voices* in this chapter.)

The third step in this revolutionary program was a complete reorganization of the Church. To solve the problem of the national debt, the National Assembly placed land owned by the Church (about ten percent of all French territory) at the service of the nation. The Civil Constitution of the Clergy of July 1790 in effect made the Church a department of the state, with the government paying the clergy directly. To retain their positions, the clergy were required to take an oath of loyalty to the nation.

In 1791 a newly elected Legislative Assembly—replacing the National Assembly—confirmed and extended many of these changes. A constitution, put into effect in October, formalized the end of royal absolutism. The king became a constitutional monarch, retaining only the power to suspend legislation, direct foreign policy, and command the armed forces.

The new constitution formally abolished hereditary legal privileges, thus providing equality of all citizens before the law. Subsequent legislation

TRICOLOR COCKADE
Louis XVI wearing the red liberty bonnet with the tricolor cockade on October 20, 1792. Refusing to be intimidated by a crowd of 20,000 people outside the royal palace, he donned the cap and proclaimed his loyalty to the constitution.

granted Jews and Protestants full civil rights and toleration. A law eliminating primogeniture (inheritance of the entire estate by the eldest son) gave all heirs equal rights to inherited property. The establishment of marriage as a civil contract and the right to end a marriage in divorce supported the idea of the husband and wife as freely contracting individuals.

This body of legislation destroyed the Old Regime and promoted a revolutionary view of French society as a nation composed of equal citizens possessing natural rights. Contemporaries recognized the significance of these changes. The Portuguese ambassador to France, who witnessed the events of 1789 firsthand, reported back to his government, "In all the world's annals there is no mention of a revolution like this."

THE FRENCH REPUBLIC, 1792–1799

■ How did a second, more radical revolution, which began with the establishment of the Republic in 1792, create a regime that used the power of the state to institute the Reign of Terror?

Beginning in 1792 France experienced a second revolution that was much more radical than the first. During this revolution France was transformed from a constitutional monarchy into a republic. The state claimed far greater power than it had acquired in 1789, and it used that power to bring about a radical reform of French society.

The Establishment of the Republic, 1792

During the first two years of the revolution it appeared that the building of a new French nation would take place within the framework of a constitutional monarchy. There was little sentiment among the members of the Legislative Assembly, much less among the general population, in favor of abolishing the institution of monarchy. The only committed republicans—those supporting the establishment of a republic—in the Legislative Assembly belonged to a party known as the **Jacobins,** who found support in political clubs in Paris and in other parts of the country. By the late summer of 1792 this group of radicals, drawing upon the support of militant Parisian citizens known as **sans-culottes** (literally, those without breeches, the pants worn by noblemen), succeeded in bringing about the second, more radical revolution.

King Louis himself was in part responsible for this destruction of the monarchy. The success of constitutional monarchy depended on the king's willingness to play the new role assigned to him. In October 1789 Louis had agreed, under considerable pressure, to move his residence from Versailles to Paris, where the National Assembly

DIFFERENT VOICES THE RIGHTS OF MAN AND WOMAN

The French Revolution gave rise to formal demands for the recognition and enforcement of the rights of man, but it also led to some of the earliest appeals for the equal rights of women. These two documents present the proclamation of the rights of man by the National Assembly and a parallel statement by a female writer who called for fundamental changes in the relations between men and women.

The passage of the Declaration of the Rights of Man and Citizen *by the National Assembly on August 26, 1789, was one of the earliest and most enduring acts of the French Revolution. A document of great simplicity and power, it was hammered out during many weeks of debate. Its concern with natural rights and equality before the law reflected the ideas of the Enlightenment.*

For Olympe de Gouges, the Declaration of the Rights of Man and Citizen *did not guarantee women the same rights as men nor address existing inequalities between the sexes. In a pamphlet titled* Declaration of the Rights of Women and the Female Citizen (1791), *which is a founding document of modern feminism, de Gouges offered a set of principles that paralleled the rights claimed in the National Assembly's demand for universal human rights.*

Declaration of the Rights of Man and Citizen (1789)

1. Men are born free and remain free and equal in rights. Social distinctions may be founded only on the common good.
2. The aim of all political association is the preservation of the natural and imprescriptible rights of man. These rights are liberty, property, security and resistance to oppression.
3. The principle of all authority rests essentially in the nation. No body nor individual may

exercise any authority which does not emanate expressly from the nation.

4. Liberty consists in the freedom to do whatever does not harm another; hence the exercise of the natural rights of each man has no limits except those which assure to the other members of society the enjoyment of the same rights. These limits can only be determined by law....
6. Law is the expression of the general will. Every citizen has the right to participate personally or through his representative in its formation. It must be the same for all, whether it protects or punishes. All citizens, being equal in the eyes of the law, are equally eligible to all dignities and to all public positions and occupations, according to their abilities, and without distinction except that of their virtues and talents.
7. No man may be indicted, arrested, or imprisoned except in cases determined by the law and according to the forms prescribed by law....
10. No one should be disturbed for his opinions, even in religion, provided that their manifestation does not trouble public order as established by law.
11. The free communication of thoughts and opinions is one of the most precious of the rights of man. Every citizen may therefore speak, write, and print freely, but shall be responsible for any abuse of this freedom in the cases set by the law....
17. Property being an inviolable and sacred right, no one may be deprived of it except when public necessity, determined by law, obviously requires it, and then on the

had also relocated. The pressure came mainly from women, who formed the large majority of 10,000 demonstrators who marched from Paris to Versailles demanding a reduction in the price of bread. The king yielded to their demands and

came to Paris. As he entered the city, accompanied by soldiers, monks, and women carrying guns and pikes, he reluctantly agreed to wear the tricolor cockade (a badge) to symbolize his acceptance of the revolution. Louis, however,

condition that the owner shall have been previously and equitably compensated.

Source: From P.-J.-B. Buchez and P.-C. Roux, *Histoire parlementaire de la Révolution française* (Paris, 1834).

Olympe de Gouges, *Declaration of the Rights of Women and the Female Citizen* (1791)

1. Woman is born free and lives equal to man in her rights. Social distinctions can be based only on common utility.

2. The purpose of any political association is the conservation of the natural and imprescriptible rights of woman and man; these rights are liberty, property, security, and especially resistance to oppression.

3. The principle of all sovereignty rests essentially with the nation, which is nothing but the union of woman and man; no body and no individual can exercise any authority which does not come expressly from it [the nation].

4. Liberty and justice consist of restoring all that belongs to others; thus, the only limits on the exercise of the natural rights of woman are perpetual male tyranny; these limits are to be reformed by the laws of nature and reason....

6. The laws must be the expression of the general will; all female and male citizens must contribute either personally or through their representatives to its formation; it must be the same for all: male and female citizens, being equal in the eyes of the law, must be equally admitted to all honors, positions, and public employment according to their capacity and without other distinctions besides those of their virtues and talents.

7. No woman is an exception: she is accused, arrested, and detained in cases determined by law. Women, like men, obey this rigorous law....

10. No one is to be disquieted for his very basic opinions; woman has the right to mount the scaffold; she must equally have the right to mount the rostrum, provided that her demonstrations do not disturb the legally established public order.

11. The free communication of thoughts and opinions is one of the most precious rights of woman, since this liberty assures the recognition of children by their fathers. Any female citizen thus may say freely, I am the mother of your child, without being forced by a barbarous prejudice to hide the truth; as long as she accepts responsibility for any abuse of this liberty [by lying about thee paternity of the child] in cases determined by law....

17. Property belongs to both sexes whether united or separated; for each it is an inviolable and sacred right; no one can be deprived of it, since it is a true patrimony of nature, unless public necessity, determined by law, requires it, and then only with a just compensation, settled in advance.

Source: Olympe de Gouges, *Les Droits de la femme* (Paris, 1791).

For Discussion

1. What is the basis of Olympe de Gouges's demand for equal rights for women?

2. Did the two declarations differ in their views of the nation? Did they differ in their view of the proper function of law?

could not disguise his opposition to the revolution, especially the ecclesiastical legislation of 1789. His opposition led many people to suspect that he was encouraging the powers of Europe to invade France to restore the Old Regime.

Louis XVI had few personal resources upon which he might draw to win the confidence of his subjects. He was not as intelligent as his grandfather, Louis XV, nor did he have the skills necessary to dispel his subjects' growing distrust of him.

SANS-CULOTTES

Male and female dress of the *sans-culottes,* the armed Parisian radicals who supported the Republic. The men did not wear the breeches (*culottes*) that were in style among the members of the French nobility.

Neither Louis nor his Austrian wife, Marie Antoinette, commanded much respect among the people. For many years the royal couple had been the object of relentless, sometimes pornographic satire. Critics lampooned the king for his rumored sexual inadequacies and the queen for a series of alleged infidelities with the king's brother and a succession of female partners. Whatever confidence Parisian citizens might have retained in the royal couple evaporated in June 1791, when the king and queen attempted to flee the country. The National Guard apprehended them at Varennes, close to the eastern French border, and forced them to return to Paris, where they were kept under guard at the palace of the Tuileries.

The development that actually precipitated the downfall of the monarchy and led to the establishment of a republic was the decision by the Legislative Assembly to go to war. After the flight to Varennes and the capture of the royal family, Frederick William II of Prussia and Emperor Leopold II of Austria, the brother of Marie Antoinette, signed an alliance and called upon the other European monarchs "to restore to the king of France complete liberty and to consolidate the bases of monarchical government." In response to this threat a small group of republicans, headed by the eloquent orator Jacques-Pierre Brissot (1754–1793), convinced the assembly that an international conspiracy against the revolution would end in an invasion of their country. Brissot and his supporters also believed that France could be lured into a foreign war, the king and queen would be revealed as traitors, and the monarchy would be destroyed. Exploiting xenophobic and revolutionary sentiment, and claiming that the strength of a citizen army would win a quick and decisive victory, Brissot and his allies won the support of the entire assembly. They also appealed to the international goals of the revolution, claiming that the French army would inspire revolution against "the tyrants of Europe" everywhere they went.

The Legislative Assembly declared war on Austria in April 1792. Instead of a glorious victory, however, the war resulted in a series of disastrous defeats at the hands of the Austrians and their Prussian allies. This military failure contributed to a mood of paranoia in France, especially in Paris. Fears arose that invading armies, in alliance with nobles, would undermine the revolution and destroy the assembly itself. In July the assembly officially proclaimed the nation to be in danger, calling for all citizens to rally against the enemies of liberty at home and abroad. Women petitioned for the right to bear arms. When the Austrians and Prussians threatened to torch the entire city of Paris and slaughter its population if anyone laid a hand on the royal family, Parisian citizens immediately demanded that the king be deposed.

On August 10 a radical republican committee overthrew the Paris commune, the city government that had been installed in 1789, and set up a new, revolutionary commune. A force of about 20,000 men, including volunteer troops from various parts of the kingdom, invaded the Tuileries, which was defended by about 900 Swiss guards. When the members of the royal bodyguard fled, members of the Paris crowds pursued them, stripped them of their red uniforms and hacked 600 of them to death with knives, pikes, and hatchets. The attack on the Tuileries forced the king to take refuge in the nearby Legislative Assembly. The assembly promptly suspended the monarchy and turned the royal family over to the commune, which imprisoned them in the Temple, a medieval fortress in the northeastern part of the city. The Assembly then ordered its own dissolution and called for the election of a new legislative body that would draft a new constitution.

The fall of the monarchy did nothing to allay the siege mentality of the city, especially after further Prussian victories in early September escalated fears of a Prussian invasion. The foreign invasion never materialized. On September 20, 1792 a surprisingly well-disciplined and well-trained army of French citizens, inspired by dedication to France and the revolution, repulsed the Prussian army at Valmy. This victory saved the revolution. Delegates to a new National Convention, elected by **universal male suffrage,** had already arrived in Paris to write a new constitution. On September 22 the Convention declared that the monarchy was formally abolished and that France was a republic. France had now experienced a second revolution, more radical than the first, but dedicated to the principles of liberty, equality, and fraternity, which soon became the motto of the revolution.

The Jacobins and the Revolution

By the time the Republic had been declared, the Jacobins had become the major political party in the Legislative Assembly. Soon, however, factional divisions began to develop within Jacobin ranks. The main split occurred between the followers of Brissot, known as **Girondins,** and the radicals known as Montagnards, or "**the Mountain.**" The latter acquired their name because they occupied the benches on the side of the Convention hall, where the floor sloped upward. The Girondins occupied the lower side of the hall, while the uncommitted deputies, known as "the Plain," occupied the middle.

Both the Mountain and the Girondins claimed to be advancing the goals of the revolution, but they differed widely on which tactics to pursue. The Mountain took the position that as long as internal and external enemies threatened the state, the government needed to centralize authority in the capital. The Mountain thought of themselves as the representatives of the common people, especially the *sans-culottes* in Paris. Many of their leaders, including Georges-Jacques Danton (1759–1794), Jean-Paul Marat (1743–1793), and Maximilien Robespierre (1758–1794), were in fact Parisians. Their mission was to make the revolution even more egalitarian and to establish a republic characterized by civic pride and patriotism, which Robespierre referred to as the **Republic of Virtue.**

The Girondins, known as such because many of their leaders came from the southwestern department of Gironde, took a more conservative position than the Mountain on these issues. Favoring the economic freedom and local control desired by merchants and manufacturers, they were reluctant to support further centralization of state power. They believed that the revolution had advanced far enough and should not become more radical. They were also afraid that the egalitarianism of the revolution, if unchecked, would lead to a leveling of French society and result in social anarchy.

The conflict between the Girondins and the Mountain became apparent in the debate over what to do with the deposed king. Louis had been suspected of conspiring with the enemies of the revolution, and the discovery of his correspondence with the Austrian government led to his trial for treason against the nation. The Girondins had originally expressed reluctance to bring him to trial, preferring to keep him in prison. Once the trial began, they joined the entire National Convention in voting to convict him, but they opposed his execution. This stance led the Mountain to accuse the Girondins of being secret collaborators with the monarchy. By a narrow vote the Convention decided to put the king to death, and on January 21, 1793, Louis was executed at the Place de la Révolution, formerly known as the Place de Louis XV. (See *Justice in History* in this chapter.)

The instrument of death was the guillotine, an efficient and merciful but nonetheless terrifying decapitation machine first pressed into service in April 1792. It took its name from Dr. Joseph-Ignace Guillotin, who had the original idea for such a device, although he did not invent it. The guillotine was inspired by the conviction that all criminals, not just those of noble blood, should be executed in a swift, painless manner. The new device was to be put to extensive use during the next 18 months, and many Girondins fell victim to it.

The split between the Mountain and the Girondins became more pronounced as the republican regime encountered increasing opposition from foreign and domestic enemies. Early in 1793 Great Britain and the Dutch Republic allied with Prussia and Austria to form the First Coalition against France, and within a month Spain and the Italian kingdoms of Sardinia and Naples joined them. The armies of these allied powers defeated French forces in the Austrian Netherlands in March of that year, and once again an invasion seemed imminent. At the same time internal rebellions against the revolutionary regime took place in various outlying provinces, especially in the district of the Vendée in western France. Noblemen and clerics led these uprisings, but they also had popular support, especially from tenant farmers who resented the increased taxation imposed by the new revolutionary government.

In the minds of Robespierre and his colleagues, the Girondins were linked to these provincial rebels, whom they labeled as *federalists* because they opposed the centralization of the French state and thus threatened the unity of the nation. In June 1793, 29 Girondins were expelled from the Convention for supporting local officials accused of hoarding grain. This purge made it apparent that any political opponent of the Mountain, even those with solid republican credentials, could now be identified as an enemy of the revolution.

The Reign of Terror, 1793–1794

To deal with its domestic enemies, the French republican government claimed powers that far exceeded those exercised by the monarchy in the age of absolutism. The Convention passed laws that set up special courts to prosecute enemies of the regime and authorized procedures that deprived those accused of their legal rights. These laws laid the legal foundation for the **Reign of Terror,** a campaign to rid the state of its internal enemies. A Committee of Public Safety, consisting of twelve members entrusted with the executive power of the state, superintended this process. Although technically subordinate to the

CHRONOLOGY: THE FRENCH REPUBLIC AND THE TERROR, 1792–1794

1792

April 20	Declaration of war against Austria
August 10	Attack on the Tuileries; monarchy is suspended
September 20	French victory at the Battle of Valmy
September 21	National Convention meets
September 22	Abolition of the monarchy and establishment of the Republic

1793

January 21	Execution of Louis XVI
February 1	Declaration of war against Great Britain and the Dutch Republic
March 11	Beginning of rebellion in the Vendée
June 2	Purge of Girondins from the Convention
June 24	Ratification of a republican constitution
October 16	Execution of Marie Antoinette

1794

July 28	Tenth of *Thermidor;* execution of Robespierre
November 12	Jacobin clubs closed

Convention, the Committee of Public Safety became, in effect, a revolutionary dictatorship.

The man who emerged as the main figure on the Committee of Public Safety was Maximilien Robespierre. A brilliant student as a youth, Robespierre had taken offense when the royal carriage splashed him with mud as he was waiting to read an address to the king. A man with little sense of humor, he was passionate in his quest for justice. As a lawyer who defended indigent clients, Robespierre was elected to the Third Estate in 1789 and became a favorite of the *sans-culottes,* who called him "The Incorruptible." That he may have been, but he was also susceptible to the temptation to abuse power for partisan political purposes. Like Rousseau, whose work he admired, he was also willing to sacrifice individual liberty in the name of the General Will. He reasoned that because the General Will was indivisible, it could not accommodate dissent. Robespierre was primarily responsible for pushing the revolution to new extremes by establishing the program of state repression that began in the autumn of 1793.

The most intense prosecutions of the Terror took place between October 1793 and June 1794, but they continued until August 1794. By that time the revolutionary courts had executed 17,000 people, while 500,000 had suffered imprisonment. Another 20,000 either died in prison or were killed without any form of trial. Among the victims of the Terror were substantial numbers of clergy and nobility, but the overwhelming majority were artisans and peasants. One Parisian stableboy was guillotined for having said "f . . the Republic," while a baker from Alsace lost his head for predicting that "the Republic will go to hell with all its partisans."[1] Many of the victims came from the outlying regions of the country, especially the northeast, where foreign armies threatened the Republic, and the west, where a brutal civil war between the French army and Catholics and royalists was raging. Special surveillance committees identified these provincial enemies of the regime, and revolutionary tribunals tried them. The guillotine was by no means the only method of execution. In November and December 1793, about 1,800 rebels captured during the uprising in the Vendée were tied to other prisoners, placed in sinking boats, and drowned in the chilly waters of the Loire River.

JUSTICE IN HISTORY

The Trial of Louis XVI

After the abolition of the monarchy and the proclamation of the French Republic in September 1792, the National Convention considered the fate of the deposed king. There was a broad consensus that Louis was guilty of treason against the nation and that he should answer for his crimes, but how he should do so became a subject of heated debate. The Convention was divided between the Girondins and the Mountain. Of the two, the Girondins were more inclined to follow due process, whereas the Mountain considered themselves to be acting as a revolutionary tribunal that had no obligation to adhere to existing French law. The Convention thus became a forum where Louis's accusers expressed competing notions of revolutionary justice.

The most divisive and revealing issue was whether there should be a trial at all. The Mountain originally took the position that because the people had already judged the king on August 10, when the monarchy had fallen and the king was taken prisoner, there was no need for a second judgment. They believed the death sentence should have been carried out immediately. Robespierre argued that a trial would have been counterrevolutionary, for it would have allowed the revolution itself to be brought before the court to be judged. A centrist majority, however, decided that the king had to be charged with specific offenses in a court of law and found guilty by due process before being sentenced.

A second issue, closely related to the first, was the technical legal question of whether Louis could be subject to legal action. Even in a constitutional monarchy, such as had been established in 1789, the legislative branch of the government did not possess authority over the king. The Convention based its decision to try Louis, however, on the revolutionary princi-

ple that he had committed crimes against the nation, which the revolutionaries claimed was a higher authority than the king. Louis, moreover, was no longer king but was now a citizen and, therefore, subject to the law in the same way as anyone else.

The third issue was Louis's culpability for the specific charges in the indictment. These crimes included refusing to call the Estates General, sending an army to march against the citizens of Paris, and conducting secret negotiations with France's enemies. The journalist and deputy Jean-Paul Marat added that "he robbed the citizens of their gold as a subsidy for their foes" and "caused his hirelings to hoard, to create famine, to dry up the sources of abundance that the people might die from misery and hunger." The king, who appeared personally to hear the indictment and then respond to the charges, based his defense on the laws in force at the times he was supposed to have committed his crimes. Thus, he defended his sending of troops to Paris on the grounds that in June and July 1789 he could order troops wherever he wanted. In the same vein, he argued that he had used force solely in response to illegal intimidation. These legalisms, however, only made the members of the Convention more contemptuous of the king. His defense failed to persuade a single convention deputy. He was convicted of treason by a vote of 693–0.

The unanimous conviction of the king did not end the factional debates over the king's fate. Knowing that there was extensive support for the king in various parts of the country, the Girondins asked that the verdict be appealed to the people. They argued that the Convention, dominated by the Mountain and supported by militants in Paris, had usurped the sovereignty of the people. A motion to submit the verdict to the people for ratification lost by a vote of 424–283.

EXECUTION OF LOUIS XVI, JANUARY 21, 1793

Although the king was convicted of treason by a unanimous vote, the vote to execute him carried by a slender majority of only 27 votes.

The last vote, the closest of all, determined the king's sentence. Originally, it appeared that a majority might vote for noncapital punishment. The Marquis de Condorcet, for example, argued that although the king deserved death on the basis of the law of treason, he could not bring himself to vote for capital punishment on principle. The radical response to this argument came from Robespierre, who appealed to the "principles of nature" that justified the death penalty in such cases, "where it is vital to the safety of private citizens or of the public." Robespierre's impassioned oratory carried the day. By a vote of 361–334 the king was sentenced to "death within 24 hours" rather than the alternatives of imprisonment followed by banishment after the war or imprisonment in chains for life. The following day Louis was led to the guillotine.

All public trials, especially those for political crimes, are theatrical events, in that the various parties play specific roles and seek to convey certain messages to their audiences. The men who voted to put Louis XVI on trial wanted to create an educational spectacle in which the already deposed monarch would be stripped of any respect he might still have commanded among the people. Louis was to be tried like any other traitor, and he was to suffer the same fate, execution by the guillotine. The attempt to strip him of all privilege and status continued after his death. His corpse, with his head placed between his knees, was taken to a cemetery, placed in a wooden box, and buried in the common pit. The revolutionaries were determined to guarantee that even in death the king would have the same position as the humblest of his former subjects.

For Discussion

1. How would you describe the standard of justice that the members of the National Convention upheld in voting to execute the king? How did this standard of justice differ from the standard to which King Louis XVI appealed?

2. Evaluate the argument of Robespierre that the death penalty can be justified only in cases of public safety. Compare his argument to that of Enlightenment thinkers such as Cesare Beccaria that capital punishment was an unjust, unnecessary, and uncivilized punishment.

Taking It Further

Jordan, David P. *The King's Trial: The French Revolution vs. Louis XVI*. 1979. The most thorough account of the trial.

Walzer, Michael (ed.) *Regicide and Revolution: Speeches at the Trial of Louis XVI*. 1974. A valuable collection of speeches with an extended commentary.

Some of the most prominent figures of the Enlightenment fell victim to this paranoia. Among them was the Marquis de Condorcet, who believed passionately that all citizens, including women, had equal rights. Having campaigned against capital punishment, he committed suicide in a Parisian prison, just before he was to be executed. Another figure of the Enlightenment, the famous chemist Antoine Lavoisier (1743–1794), who had devoted himself to improving social and economic conditions in France, was executed at the same time. So too was the feminist Olympe de Gouges, who had petitioned for the equal rights of women. Many French revolutionaries, including Robespierre, used the political ideas of the Enlightenment to justify their actions, but the Terror struck down some of the most distinguished figures of that movement. In that sense the Terror marked the end of the Enlightenment in France.

The Committee of Public Safety then went after Danton and other so-called Indulgents who had decided that the Terror had gone too far. Danton's execution made everyone, especially moderate Jacobins, wonder who would be the next victim of a process that had spun completely out of control. In June 1794 the Terror reached a climax as 1,300 people went to their deaths. To stop the process, a group of Jacobins in the Convention organized a plot against Robespierre. Calling him a tyrant, they arrested him and more than 100 of his followers and guillotined them in late July 1794. In the provinces members of the White Terror, so named for the white Bourbon flag they displayed, executed leaders of local revolutionary tribunals. With these reprisals the most violent and radical phase of the French revolution came to an end.

The Reign of Terror had ended, but its memory would never be extinguished. Its horrors served as a constant warning against the dangers inherent in revolutionary movements. The guillotine, the agent of a dysfunctional and indiscriminate state terrorism, became just as closely identified with the French Revolution as its famous slogan of "Liberty, Equality, Fraternity." The contrast between those two symbols, each of them emblematic of a different stage of the revolution, helps to explain how both conservatives and liberals in the nineteenth century would be able to appeal to the experience of the revolution to support their contradictory ideologies.

The Directory, 1795–1799

A desire to end the violence of the Terror allowed moderates in the National Convention to regain control of the state apparatus that Robespierre and his allies had used to such devastating effect. They dismantled the Paris Commune and stripped the Committee of Public Safety of most of its powers. In November 1794 they closed Jacobin clubs throughout the country, which had provided support for the Terror. The moderates who now controlled the government still hoped to preserve the gains of the revolution, while returning the country to more familiar forms of authority. A new constitution of 1795 bestowed executive power on a five-man Directorate, while an assembly consisting of two houses, the Council of Elders and the Council of Five Hundred, proposed and voted on all legislation. The franchise was limited to property holders, allowing only two million men out of an adult male population of seven million to vote. A system of indirect election, in which a person voted for electors who then selected representatives, guaranteed that only the wealthiest members of the country would sit in the legislative councils.

Some of the wealthier and more entrepreneurial citizens of Paris welcomed the new regime, but opposition soon arose, mainly from Jacobins and sans-culottes. When the government relaxed the strict price controls that had been in effect under the Jacobins, the soaring price of bread and other commodities caused widespread social discontent among the populace. The continuation of the interminable war against the foreign powers only aggravated the situation. Wherever French troops went, their constant need of food and other goods resulted in serious shortages of these commodities.

By the end of 1798 conditions had grown even worse. Inflation was running out of control. The collection of taxes was intermittent at best. The paper money known as *assignats*, first issued by the government in 1791 and backed by the value of confiscated church lands, had become almost worthless. Late in 1797 the Directory, as the new regime was called, had to cancel more than half the national debt, a step that further alienated wealthy citizens who had lent money to the government. Military setbacks in 1798 and 1799 brought the situation to a critical point. The formation of a Second Coalition of European powers in 1799, which included Britain, Austria, Russia, Naples, and Turkey, presented a formidable challenge to French power and ensured that the war would not end soon. These military events produced a swing to the political left and raised the specter of another Jacobin coup.

CHRONOLOGY: THE DIRECTORY, 1795–1799

1795

August 22	The National Convention approves a new constitution
October 5	Napoleon suppresses a royalist insurrection in Paris
October 26	End of the Convention; beginning of the Directory

1796

February 19	The issuing of *assignats* halted
April 12	Beginning of a series of victories by Napoleon in Italy

1798

May 13	Napoleon's expedition departs for Egypt
May	Second Coalition (Britain, Austria, Russia, Naples, and Turkey) is formed against Napoleon
July 21	Napoleon wins the Battle of the Pyramids
August 1	Nelson destroys the French fleet at the Battle of the Nile

1799

November 9–10	Napoleon's coup; Consulate established

In the face of this instability, Emmanuel-Joseph Sieyès, who had been elected as one of the directors two years earlier, decided to overthrow the government. Sieyès provided a link between the early years of the revolution, when he had defended the Third Estate, and the government of the Directory. Unlike many other prominent political figures, he had managed to avoid prosecution as the revolution had become more radical. When asked what he had done during the Reign of Terror, Sieyès replied, "I survived." Now he sought to provide the country with strong government, its greatest need in a period of political, economic, and social instability. The person Sieyès selected as his partner in this enterprise, who immediately assumed leadership of the coup, was Napoleon Bonaparte (1769–1821), a 30-year-old general who in 1795 had put down a royalist rebellion in Paris with a "whiff of grapeshot."

Napoleon had already established impressive credentials as a military leader. In 1796 and 1797 he had won major victories in Italy, leading to the Treaty of Campo Formio with Austria in 1797. Those victories and his short-lived success at the Battle of the Pyramids in Egypt had made him enormously popular in Paris, where he was received as a hero when he assumed command of the armed forces in the city in 1799. (See *Encounters and Transformations* in this chapter.) His popularity, his demonstrated military leadership, and his control of a large armed force made this "man on horseback" appear to have the best chance to replace the enfeebled civilian regime of the Directory.

On November 9, 1799, Napoleon addressed the two legislative councils. He reported the discovery of another Jacobin conspiracy and called for a new constitution to give the executive branch of the government more authority. Napoleon encountered resistance from some members of the Council of Five Hundred, who demanded that he be declared an outlaw. At this stage the president of the council, Napoleon's brother Lucien, intervened and called in troops to evict the members who opposed him. The following day France had a new government, known as the Consulate.

Executive power in the new government was to be vested in three consuls. It soon became clear, however, that Napoleon would dominate this trio. In the new constitution of December 1799, which the electorate ratified by **plebiscite** (a vote to accept or reject a proposal), Napoleon was named First Consul. This appointment made him the most powerful man in France and, for all practical purposes, a military dictator. The dictatorship became more apparent in 1802, when Napoleon was named Consul for Life.

CULTURAL CHANGE IN FRANCE DURING THE REVOLUTION

■ **In what ways did the political events of the revolution change French culture?**

The French Revolution was primarily a political revolution, but it also brought about profound changes in French culture. It destroyed the cultural institutions of the Old Regime and created a new revolutionary culture.

The Transformation of Cultural Institutions

Between 1791 and 1794 many of the cultural institutions of the Old Regime were either destroyed or radically transformed, and new institutions under the control of the state took their place.

ACADEMIES   The Parisian scientific and artistic academies established by Louis XIV (see Chapter 16) had a monopoly over the promotion and transmission of knowledge in the sciences and the visual arts. The academies were the epitome of privilege. They controlled their own membership, determined the recipients of their prizes, and monopolized their particular branches of knowledge. They were also heavily aristocratic institutions. As many as three-quarters of their members were nobles or clergy.

During the revolution the academies were abolished as part of a general attack on corporate bodies, and various government committees replaced them. For example, the Commission on Weights and Measures, which had been part of the Academy of Science, became an independent commission. Its task was to provide uniform weights and measures for the entire kingdom. In 1795 it established the meter, calculated as one ten-millionth of the distance from the North Pole to the equator, as the standard measure of distance. Like the decimal system, which was introduced at the same time, the metric system was subsequently adopted as a universal standard in all European countries.

The Popular and Republican Society of the Arts replaced the Royal Academy of Arts. The inspiration for this new republican society, which was open to artists of all social ranks, was Jacques-Louis David (1748–1825), the greatest painter of his generation. Employed at the court of Louis XVI, David became a vocal critic of the academy at the time of the revolution. He painted some of the most memorable scenes of the revolution, including the oath taken at the tennis court by the members of the National Assembly in 1789. During the Republic David depicted heroes of the revolution, such as Jean-Paul Marat (see the illustration on page 638), and he was later appointed First Painter to Napoleon. David presided over a revival of classicism in French painting, employing Greek and Roman motifs and exhibiting a rationalism and lack of sentiment in his work.

LIBRARIES Shortly after the revolution had begun, thousands of books and manuscripts from the libraries of monasteries, royal castles, residences of the nobility, and academies came into the possession of the state. Many of these became part of the Royal Library, which was appropriately renamed the National Library. The government also intended to catalog all the books held in libraries throughout the country. This effort to create the General Bibliography of France was never completed, and while the books were being cataloged, the government decided to get rid of those that dealt with "theology, mysticism, feudalism, and royalism" by sending them to foreign countries. This decision initiated a frenzy of book sales, mainly to private individuals. Altogether about five million books were lost or sold during these years.

MUSEUMS AND MONUMENTS The day after the abolition of the monarchy the Legislative Assembly created a Commission of the Museum, whose charge was "to collect paintings, statues and other precious objects" from royal residences, churches, and houses of émigrés. The museum was to be located in the Louvre, a royal palace that also served as an art gallery. When it opened in August 1793 the Louvre included a majority of paintings with religious themes. These religious works of art remained in the collection even though they appeared to be incompatible with the republican rejection of Christianity. The revolutionaries justified this decision on the grounds that this museum was intended to be entirely historical and have no relevance to contemporary culture.

The revolutionaries did not have the same respect for the bodies of their former kings. On August 10, 1793, the first anniversary of the deposition of Louis XVI, the National Convention ordered the destruction of all the tombs of past French kings. One by one the tombs were opened and the corpses, embalmed in lead, were removed. Metals and valuables were melted down for use in the war effort. The corpses were either left to disintegrate in the atmosphere or dragged unceremoniously to the cemetery, where they were thrown into the common pit. The corpse of Louis XIV landed on top of that of Henry IV. This disrespectful treatment of the remains of France's former kings was intended to erase the memory of monarchy.

The Creation of a New Political Culture

As the state was taking over and adapting the cultural institutions of the Old Regime, revolutionaries engaged in a much bolder and original undertaking: the production of a new, revolutionary political culture. Its sole purpose was to legitimize and glorify the new regime. This culture was almost entirely political; all forms of cultural expression were subordinated to the realization of a pressing political agenda.

The main political doctrine of the revolution was popular sovereignty: the claim that the people were the highest political power in the state. The new political culture was also popular in the sense that the entire populace, not simply the literate elite, adopted it. The people who embraced the new culture most enthusiastically were the *sans-culottes*—the radical shopkeepers, artisans, and laborers of Paris. The dress of these people influenced a change in fashion among the wealthier segments of society. A simple jacket replaced the ruffled coat worn by members of the upper classes, their powdered wigs gave way to natural hair, and long trousers replaced the shorter breeches. They also donned the red liberty cap, to which a tricolor cockade was affixed. The tricolor, which combined the red and blue colors of Paris with the white symbol of the Bourbon monarchy, identified the adherents of the revolution.

Symbols of revolution could be found everywhere. The commercialization of the revolution guaranteed that the tricolor flag, portraits of revolutionary figures, and images of the Bastille appeared on household objects as constant reminders of the public's support for the revolution. An order of the government in 1792 required all men to wear the tricolor cockade. Liberty trees, first planted by peasants as protests against local landlords, became a symbol of the revolution. By May 1792 more than 60,000 trees had been planted throughout the country.

The press, no longer tightly controlled by the government and the printers' guild, became a crucial agent of revolutionary propaganda and a producer of the new culture. Pamphlets, newspapers, brochures, and posters all promoted a distinctive revolutionary language, which became one of the permanent legacies of the revolution. Political leaders used the same rhetoric in their political speeches. *Sans-culottes* sang satirical songs and ballads, many of them to tunes well known in the Old Regime. The most popular of the songs of the revolutionary period was the *Marseillaise,* first sung by soldiers preparing for battle against the Austrians, but soon adopted by the civilian population and sung at political gatherings.

Much of this new political culture stemmed from the conviction that the doctrine of popular sovereignty should be practiced in everyday life. *Sans-culottes* did this by joining the political clubs organized by different factions within the National Assembly, by addressing others as citizens, and by using the more familiar form of the pronoun *you* (*tu* rather than *vous*) in all conversations. They also participated in the revolution by taking public oaths. On the first anniversary of the fall of the Bastille, as many as 350,000 people, many of them members of the "federations" of National Guards throughout the country, gathered on the royal parade ground outside Paris to take an oath "to the Nation, to the Law, to the King." Direct democracy was not possible in a society of 27 million people, but these cultural practices allowed people to believe that they were participating actively in the political process.

The new revolutionary culture was emphatically secular. In its most extreme form, it was blatantly anti-Christian. In September 1793 the radical Jacobin and former priest Joseph Fouché inaugurated a program of **de-Christianization.** Under his leadership, radical Jacobins closed churches and removed religious symbols such as crosses from cemeteries and public venues. In an effort to establish a purely civic religion, they forbade the public practice of religion and renamed churches "temples of reason." In their public pronouncements the architects of de-Christianization avoided reference to the Christian period of French history, which covered the entire national past.

This de-Christianization campaign became the official policy of the Paris Commune and the National Convention. The program, however, did not win widespread support, and even some Jacobins claimed that in rejecting Christianity it had undermined a belief in God and the afterlife. In 1794 Robespierre attempted to modify the excesses of de-Christianization by launching the

OATH TAKING

On July 14, 1790, the first anniversary of the fall of the Bastille, as many as 350,000 people gathered on a field outside Paris to take an oath of loyalty to the new French nation. The event was referred to as the Feast of the Federation, because most of the oath takers were members of the regional federations of National Guards. The oath taking, which had many characteristics of a religious gathering, was led by the king himself, and it marked the most optimistic period of the revolution.

Cult of the Supreme Being. He promoted a series of festivals acknowledging the existence of a deity and the immortality of the soul. This new cult paid lip service to traditional religious beliefs, but it still served secular purposes. The cult was designed to direct the spiritual yearnings of the French people into patriotic undertakings and promote republican virtue.

In an effort to destroy all vestiges of the Old Regime, the government also instituted a new calendar in October 1793. The dates on the calendar began with September 22, 1792, the day the Republic was established. That became the first day of the year I, while the weeks now had ten days instead of seven. The new months were given names to evoke the different seasons, such as *Brumaire* for the first month of wintry weather, *Germinal* for the season of planting, and

Thermidor for the warmest month of the summer. Hostile British contemporaries gave their own humorous renditions of these names, translating them as Freezy, Flowery, Heaty, and so on. The new calendar was intended to make the revolution a part of people's everyday consciousness. It remained in effect until the last day of 1805.

The new revolutionary culture was disseminated widely, but it was always contested. Royalists trampled on the tricolor cockade, refused to adopt the new style of dress, and pulled up the liberty trees. During the Directory many wealthy members of society donned fancy and opulent clothes and revived the high social life of the capital. This resistance from counterrevolutionary forces guaranteed that when the revolution was reversed, much of the new political culture would disappear. Napoleon did little to perpetuate it in

JACQUES-LOUIS DAVID, *THE DEATH OF MARAT* (1793)

The Jacobin journalist Jean-Paul Marat was stabbed to death in his bathtub by a noblewoman, Charlotte Corday, in July 1793. Marat holds the letter from his murderer that gave her entrance to his residence. The painting depicts the slain victim in the manner of the dead Christ in Michelangelo's *Pietà*. The painting thus shows how new secular culture of the revolution incorporated many elements of the Christian culture that had prevailed before the revolution began.

the first decade of the nineteenth century, and the restored monarchy was openly hostile to it. Like the political revolution, however, some elements of revolutionary culture, such as the tricolor and the rhetoric of the revolutionary press, could never be suppressed. Not only did these cultural innovations inspire revolutionaries for the next 100 years, but they also became part of the mainstream of Western civilization.

THE NAPOLEONIC ERA, 1799–1815

■ Did the authoritarian rule of Napoleon Bonaparte from 1799 to 1814 confirm or betray the achievements of the French Revolution, and what impact did his military conquests have on Europe and the world?

The coup d'état on November 9, 1799, or the eighteenth of *Brumaire* on the revolutionary calendar, marked a turning point in the political history of France. The Consulate ushered in a period of authoritarian rule. Liberty was restricted in the interest of order; republicanism gave way to dictatorship. The French Revolution had apparently run its course. But the period between 1799 and 1815 was also a time of considerable innovation, especially in the realm of politics and diplomacy. Those innovations were primarily the work of one man, Napoleon Bonaparte, who controlled the French government for the next 15 years.

Napoleon's Rise to Power

Napoleon Bonaparte was born on the Mediterranean island of Corsica. His father, Charles-Marie de Buonaparte, was an attorney who had supported the cause of winning Corsica's independence from the Italian state of Genoa. His mother, Letizia, came from an old noble family in the northern Italian region of Lombardy. In 1770 the new French government, which had gained control of the island the previous year, accepted the Buonaparte family as nobility. In 1779 the young Napoleon, whose native language was Corsican, received an appointment to a French military school. He survived both the rigors of the course of study and the taunting of his classmates, who mocked him for his accent and his poverty. Displaying a natural gift for military science, he won a position in the artillery section of the national military academy in Paris.

The events of the French Revolution made possible Napoleon's rapid ascent to military prominence and political power. When the revolution broke out, Napoleon returned to Corsica, where he organized the National Guard and petitioned the government to grant full rights of citizenship to his people. After becoming a Jacobin, he was commissioned to attack federalist and royalist positions in the south of France. Unlike many of his fellow Jacobins, he found favor with the Directory. In 1796 Napoleon was given command of the Army of Italy, at which time he abandoned the Italian spelling of his name for Bonaparte. His decisive victories against the

Austrians and his popularity in Paris attracted the attention of Sieyès and others who wished to give the country strong, charismatic leadership.

Napoleon's personality was ideally suited to the acquisition and maintenance of political power. A man of unparalleled ambition, he was driven by an extraordinarily high assessment of his abilities. After one of his military victories he wrote, "I realized I was a superior being and conceived the ambition of performing great things." To the pursuit of his destiny he harnessed a determined and stubborn will and enormous energy. Temporary setbacks never seemed to thwart his single-minded pursuit of glory. He brought enormous energy to his military and political pursuits. He wrote more than 80,000 letters during his life, many of them transmitting orders to his officers and ministers. Authoritarian by nature, he used both intimidation and paternalism to cultivate the loyalty of his subordinates. Like many authoritarian leaders, he had difficulty delegating authority, a trait that weakened his regime. Finally, in an age dominated by high-minded causes, he exhibited an instinctive distrust of ideology and the doctrinaire pronouncements of philosophes such as Rousseau. Napoleon's military training led him to take a pragmatic, disciplined approach to politics, in which he always sought the most effective means to the desired end.

Napoleon's acquisition of power was systematic and shrewd. Playing on the need for a strong leader, and using the army as his main political tool, he maneuvered himself into the position of first consul in 1799. In 1802 he became consul for life, and two years later he crowned himself emperor of the French and his wife Josephine empress. The title of emperor traditionally denoted the height of monarchical power.

EMPEROR NAPOLEON CROWNING HIS WIFE, JOSEPHINE, EMPRESS OF THE FRENCH IN THE CATHEDRAL OF NOTRE DAME, 1804

This painting by Jacques-Louis David depicts secular and religious figures gathered around Napoleon not as members of privileged orders, but as representatives of the nation. Pope Pius VII remains seated as Napoleon places the crown on Josephine's head. Napoleon had already crowned himself emperor of the French.

Source: Jacques Louis David (1748–1825), "Consecration of the Emperor Napoleon I and Coronation of Empress Josephine," 1806–07. Louvre, Paris. Bridgeman-Giraudon/Art Resource, NY

It is ironic that Napoleon, while continuing to hunt down and execute royalists, accepted a title of royalty himself and made his position, just like the French kingship, hereditary. As one royalist declared in 1804, "We have done more than we hoped. We meant to give France a king, and we have given her an emperor." Napoleon's coronation also made a negative impression outside France. The great German composer Ludwig van Beethoven, having dedicated his *Third Symphony* (1803) to Napoleon for overthrowing tyranny in France, scratched the emperor's name from the dedication after he assumed his new title the following year.

Napoleon and the Revolution

What was the relationship between Napoleon's rule and the French Revolution? Did Napoleon consolidate the gains of the revolution or destroy them? Did he simply redirect the revolutionary commitment to liberty, equality, and fraternity into more disciplined channels of expression after 1799? Or did he reverse the political trends that had prevailed from 1789 to 1799, crushing liberty in all its forms and establishing a ruthless, authoritarian dictatorship?

Napoleon always thought of himself as the heir of the revolution rather than its undertaker. He used the radical vocabulary of the revolution to characterize his domestic programs and his military campaigns. He presented himself as the ally of the common man against entrenched aristocratic privilege. He proclaimed a love for the French people and gave his support to the doctrine of popular sovereignty. He often referred to the rulers of other European countries as tyrants and presented himself as the liberator of their subjects.

Yet Napoleon's commitment to liberty was almost entirely rhetorical. Behind the appeals to the slogans of the revolution lurked a domineering will that was stronger than that of any eighteenth-century absolute monarch. Napoleon used the language of liberty and democracy to disguise a thoroughgoing authoritarianism, just as he used the rhetoric of republicanism to legitimize his own dictatorial regime. He orchestrated and controlled elections to make it appear that his rule reflected the will of the people. When the empire was established he told his troops that they had the freedom to vote for or against the new form of government, but that if they voted against it, they would be shot.

We can make a stronger case for Napoleon's egalitarianism. He demonstrated a commitment to providing equality of opportunity in the service of the state, and he supported the equality of all Frenchmen (but not Frenchwomen) before the law. This egalitarianism laid the foundation for the support he received from peasants, soldiers, and workers. He brought equality and political stability to France in exchange for political liberty. He synthesized the egalitarianism of the revolution with the authoritarianism of the Old Regime.

Napoleon was the heir of the revolution in two other ways. First, he continued the centralization and growth of state power and the rational organization of the administration that had begun in 1789. Each of the successive regimes between 1789 and 1815, even the Directory, had contributed to this pattern of state-building, and Napoleon's contribution was monumental. Second, he continued and extended France's military mission to export the revolution to its European neighbors. The two achievements are related to each other because the war effort necessitated the further growth and centralization of state power.

Napoleon and the French State

Once Napoleon had gained effective control of the French state, he sought to make it more efficient, organized, and powerful. In addition to turning the government into a de facto dictatorship, Napoleon settled the long struggle between Church and state, laid down a new law code that imposed legal uniformity on the entire country, and made the civil bureaucracy more centralized and uniform. He did all this with the intention of making the state an effective instrument of social and political control.

CONCORDAT WITH THE PAPACY Napoleon's first contribution to the development of the French state, achieved during the Consulate, was to resolve the bitter struggle between Church and state. A committed secularist, Napoleon was determined to bring the Church under the direct control of the state. This had been the main purpose of the Civil Constitution of the Clergy of 1790. Napoleon also realized, however, that the Civil Constitution had divided the clergy between those who had taken an oath to the nation and those who had refused. Clerical independence had also become a major rallying cry of royalists against the new regime, thereby threatening the stability of the country.

The death of Pope Pius VI (r. 1775–1799), an implacable foe of the revolution, gave Napoleon the opportunity to address this problem. The new pope, Pius VII (r. 1800–1823), who was more sympathetic to liberal causes, was eager to come to terms with the French government. The Concordat, which Napoleon and Pope Pius agreed to in 1801, gave something to both sides, although Napoleon gained more than he conceded. The pope agreed that all the clergy who refused to swear their loyalty to the nation would resign their posts, thus ending the bitter divisions of the past twelve years. The pope would appoint new bishops, but only with Napoleon's prior approval. The state would pay all clerical salaries, and the Church would abandon its claims to the ecclesiastical lands seized by the state at the beginning of the revolution.

These provisions represented formidable concessions to state power, and many French bishops found the terms of the Concordat too unfavorable to the Church. But the pope did manage to secure a statement that Roman Catholicism was the religion of the majority of citizens, and Napoleon agreed to scrap the secular calendar introduced in 1793, thereby restoring Sundays and holy days. Church attendance, having reached historic lows during the period of the Republic, began to rise. The Church regained respect and the freedom to function in French society, and more young recruits joined the clergy. Napoleon did not make many concessions

to the Church, but they were significant enough to alienate a group of liberal philosophers and writers known as the Ideologues, who objected to what they saw as the return of "monkish superstition."

With the pope somewhat appeased, Napoleon took unilateral steps to regulate the administration of the French church. In a set of regulations known as the Organic Articles, which were added to the Concordat in 1802, the French church became a department of state, controlled by a ministry, just like any other bureaucratic department. Pronouncements from the pope required prior government approval, and the clergy were obliged to read government decrees from the pulpit. The state also gained control of Protestant congregations, which were given freedom of worship, and their ministers were also paid by the state. Jews received the protection of the state, but the government did not pay the salaries of rabbis.

THE CIVIL CODE Napoleon's most enduring achievement in the realm of state building was the promulgation of a new legal code, the Civil Code of 1804. A legal code is an authoritative and comprehensive statement of the law of a particular country. The model for modern legal codes in Europe was the *Corpus Juris Civilis* of the Roman Empire, which Justinian decreed at Constantinople between 529 and 534 C.E. That code had replaced the thousands of constitutions, customs, and judicial decisions that had been in effect during the Roman Republic and Empire. In compiling the new French code Napoleon, who had just proclaimed himself emperor of the French, imitated Justinian's legal achievement.

The Civil Code also met a long-standing set of demands to reform the confusing and irregular body of French law. Ever since the Middle Ages, France had been governed by a multiplicity of laws. In the southern provinces of the country, those closest to Italy, the law had been influenced by Roman law. In the north, the law was based on local or provincial customs. France needed a common law for all its people. Efforts to produce an authoritative written law code for all parts of the country had begun during the revolution, but Napoleon completed the project and published the code.

The Civil Code, which consisted of more than 2,000 articles, reflected the values of Napoleonic France. Articles guaranteeing the rights of private property, equality before the law, and freedom of religion enshrined key revolutionary ideas. The values promoted by the Civil Code, however, did not include the equality of the sexes. It granted men control of all family property. Women could not buy or sell property without the consent of their husbands. All male heirs were entitled to inherit equal shares of a family estate, but daughters were excluded from the settlement.

The Civil Code, which dealt only with the rights and relationships of private individuals, was the first and most important of six law codes promulgated by Napoleon. Others dealt with civil procedure (1806), commerce (1807), and criminal law (1811). Renamed the **Napoleonic Code** in 1806, the Civil Code had an impact on the law of several countries outside France. It became the basis for the codification of the laws of Switzerland, northern Italy, Poland, and the Netherlands, and it served as a model for the codes of many German territories controlled by France during the Napoleonic period. The Napoleonic Code also influenced the law of French-speaking North America, including the civil law of the state of Louisiana, which bears signs of its influence even today.

ADMINISTRATIVE CENTRALIZATION   Napoleon laid the foundation of modern French civil administration, which acquired the characteristics of rational organization, uniformity, and centralization. All power emanated from Paris, where Napoleon presided over a Council of State. This body consisted of his main ministers, who handled all matters of finance, domestic affairs, and war and oversaw a vast bureaucracy of salaried, trained officials. The central government also exercised direct control over the provinces. In each of the departments, the administrative

divisions of France organized in 1790, an official known as a *prefect,* appointed by the central government, enforced orders coming from Paris (see **Map 20.1**). Paid the handsome annual salary of 20,000 francs, the prefects were responsible for the maintenance of public order. They enforced conscription, collected taxes, and supervised local public works, such as the construction and improvement of roads.

The men who served in the government of the French Empire belonged to one of two elaborate, hierarchical institutions: the civil bureaucracy and the army officer corps. The two were closely related, because the main purpose of the administrative bureaucracy was to prepare for and sustain the war effort. Both institutions were organized hierarchically, and those who held positions in them were trained and salaried. Appointment and promotion were based primarily on talent rather than birth.

The idea of "a career open to all talents," as Napoleon described it, ran counter to the tradition of noble privilege. This was one of the achievements of the revolution that Napoleon perpetuated during the empire. The new system did not amount to a **meritocracy**, in which advancement depends solely on ability and performance, because Napoleon himself made or influenced many appointments on the basis of friendship or kinship. The system did, however, allow people from the ranks of the bourgeoisie to achieve upward social mobility. To recognize their new status, Napoleon created a new order of nonhereditary noblemen, known as *notables.* Instead of inheriting status, these men acquired their titles by governmental service. Napoleon created more than 3,500 notables during his rule, thereby encouraging service to the state and strengthening loyalty to it.

Napoleon, the Empire, and Europe

Closely related to Napoleon's efforts to build the French state was his creation of a sprawling European empire. This empire was the product of a series of military victories against the armies of Austria, Prussia, Russia, and Spain between

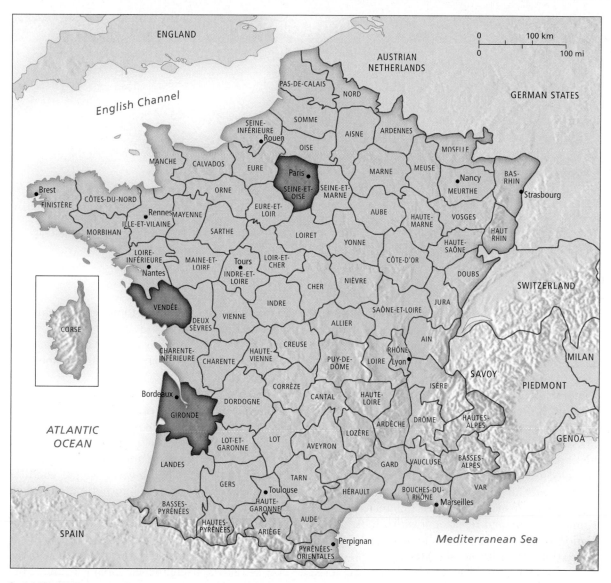

MAP 20.1

French Departments during the Revolution

In 1790 France was divided into the 83 departments, each roughly equal in population. A preoccupation with uniformity, a product of the Enlightenment, became a major feature of French revolutionary culture. Note the departments of Vendée, a major center of counterrevolution in 1793, and Gironde, from which the Girondins, the moderate Jacobin party, took its name.

1797 and 1809. The instrument of these victories was the massive army that Napoleon assembled. With more than one million men under arms, it was the largest military force controlled by one man up to this time in European history.

Napoleon's victories against Austria in 1797 and 1800 resulted in territorial gains in Italy and control over the southern Netherlands, now called Belgium. A temporary peace with Britain in 1802 gave Napoleon free rein to reorganize

CHRONOLOGY: THE CONSULATE AND THE EARLY YEARS OF THE EMPIRE, 1799–1806

1799
December 15   Proclamation of the Constitution of the Consulate
1801
July 15   Concordat with the Papacy
1804
March 21   The Civil Code promulgated
December 2   Napoleon crowned emperor of the French
1805
August   Third Coalition (Britain, Austria, and Russia) formed against France
1806
October 14   French victories at the battles of Jena and Auerstädt
August 6   Formal dissolution of the Holy Roman Empire

the countries that bordered on France's eastern and southeastern boundaries. In Italy he named himself the president of the newly established Cisalpine Republic, and he transformed the cantons of Switzerland into the Helvetic Republic. Victories over Prussian forces at Jena and Auerstädt in 1806 gave him the opportunity to carve a new German kingdom of Westphalia out of Prussian territory in the Rhineland and to install his brother Jerome as its ruler. In the east Napoleon created the duchy of Warsaw out of Polish lands he seized from Prussia and Austria. In 1806 he formally dissolved the ancient Holy Roman Empire and replaced it with a loose association of 16 German states known as the Confederation of the Rhine (see **Map 20.2**).

Napoleon's final step in his effort to achieve mastery of Europe was the invasion and occupation of Spain. This campaign began as an effort to crush Portugal, an ally of Britain. In May 1808, as French armies marched through Spain en route to Lisbon, the Portuguese capital, a popular insurrection against Spanish rule occurred in Madrid. This spontaneous revolt, which led to the abdication of King Charles IV and the succession of his son Ferdinand VII, was the first of many developments that caused the collapse of the Spanish Empire in America. In Europe it led to the absorption of Spain into the French

Empire. Sensing that he could easily add one more territory to his list of conquests, Napoleon forced Ferdinand to abdicate and summoned his own brother, Joseph Bonaparte, to become king of Spain.

Joseph instituted some reforms in Spain, but the abolition of the Spanish Inquisition and the closing of two-thirds of the Spanish convents triggered a visceral reaction from the Spanish clergy and the general populace. Fighting for Church and king, small bands of local guerillas subjected French forces to intermittent and effective sabotage. An invasion by British forces under the command of Arthur Wellesley, later the Duke of Wellington (1769–1852), in what has become known as the Peninsular War (1808–1813), strengthened Spanish and Portuguese resistance.

The Downfall of Napoleon

The turning point in Napoleon's personal fortunes and those of his empire came in 1810. After securing a divorce from Josephine in late 1809 because she had not borne him an heir, he married Marie-Louise, the daughter of the Habsburg emperor. This diplomatic marriage, which produced a son and heir to the throne the following year, should have made the French Empire

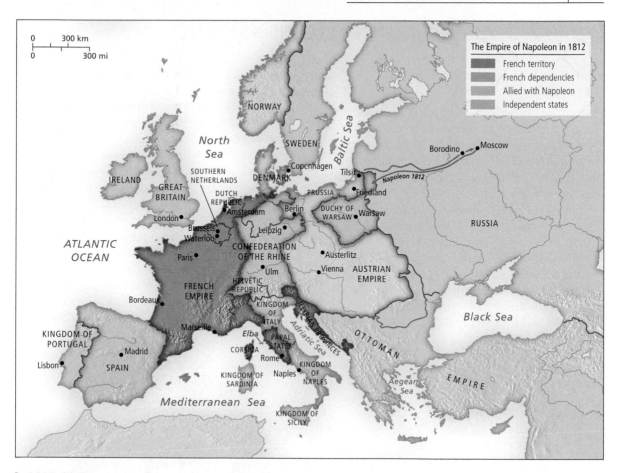

MAP 20.2

The Empire of Napoleon in 1812

At its peak the official French Empire had 44 million inhabitants. The population of dependent states in Spain, Italy, Germany, and Poland brought the population of the "Grand Empire" to 80 million people.

more secure, but it had the opposite effect. For the first time during his rule, Napoleon faced dissent from both the right and the left, provoked in part by his negotiations with the Austrian Habsburgs. Despite the most stringent efforts at censorship, royalist and Jacobin literature poured off the presses. The number of military deserters and those evading conscription increased. Relations with the papacy reached a breaking point when Napoleon annexed the Papal States, at which point Pope Pius VII, who had negotiated the Concordat of 1801, excommunicated him.

Dissent at home had the effect of driving the megalomaniacal emperor to seek more glory and

further conquests. In this frame of mind Napoleon made the ill-advised decision to invade Russia. The motives for engaging in this overly ambitious military campaign were not completely irrational. Victory over Russia promised to give France control of the Black Sea, and that in turn could ultimately have led to the control of Constantinople and the entire Middle East. More immediately, defeating Russia would have been necessary to enforce the French blockade of British goods, which Russia had refused to support.

The problem with a Russian invasion was that it stretched Napoleon's lines of communication

ENCOUNTERS AND TRANSFORMATIONS

The French Encounter the Egyptians, 1798–1801

Napoleon's expedition to Egypt in 1798 marked one of the few times during the revolutionary period that the French came in direct contact with non-Western peoples. The expedition resulted in the military occupation of the country for three years and set the stage for the first extensive encounters between Egyptians and Europeans since the Ottoman conquest of Egypt in the sixteenth century. At that time Egypt had become a semiautonomous province of the Ottoman Empire and had very little contact with the West. Egypt's isolation from the West meant that it had little exposure to the scientific and technological discoveries that had taken place in western Europe during the previous 300 years.

In addition to 38,000 soldiers, Napoleon brought with him 165 scholars who were organized in a Commission of Science and Arts. These men came from virtually every branch of learning: surveyors, cartographers, civil engineers, architects, botanists, physicians, chemists, and mineralogists. The commission also included artists, archaeologists, writers, and musicians. Their purpose was to give Napoleon information on the people and the resources of the country so that he could more easily subject it to French domination. A small group of these scholars set up an Institute of Egypt, whose mission was to propagate the Enlightenment and to undertake

JEAN CHARLES TARDIEU, *THE FRENCH ARMY HALTS AT SYENE, UPPER EGYPT, ON FEBRUARY 2, 1799*

This painting depicts a cultural encounter between French soldiers and Egyptians in the city of Syene (now Aswan) during the Egyptian campaign of 1798–1799. The soldiers are scribbling on the ruins of ancient Egypt, indicating a lack of respect for Egyptian culture.

Source: Jean-Charles Tardieu (1765–1830), "Troops Halted on the Banks of the Nile, 2nd February 1812", oil on canvas. Chateau de Versailles, France/Lauros/Giraudon/The Bridgeman Art Library

research on the history, people, and the economy of the country. This involved the scholarly study of Egyptian antiquities, including the pyramids.

This work of the institute ushered in a long period in which many artifacts of Egyptian antiquity were taken from the country and transported to European museums and palaces. Members of the institute encouraged this cultural plundering, arguing that these Egyptian additions to the collections of the Louvre would embellish the glory of France. This ransacking of native Egyptian antiquities represented a form of cultural imperialism that continued unabated during the nineteenth century.

A description of Egypt, *Travels in Upper and Lower Egypt* (1802), written by a member of the institute, Dominique-Vivant Denon, reflected a different sort of French cultural imperialism. In this two-volume work Vivant Denon described the different "races" of Egyptians whom he had encountered in the port town of Rosetta. He described the Copts, the most ancient Egyptians, as "swarthy Nubians" with flat foreheads, high cheekbones, and short broad noses and tendencies toward "ignorance, drunkenness, cunning, and finesse." He described the physical and personal characteristics of the Arabs and the Turks in more appealing terms, but they too were often reduced to the "degraded state of animals."

Expressions of French cultural superiority permeated other contemporary accounts of Napoleon's expedition. A multivolume work, *The Description of Egypt,* claimed that Napoleon wanted to procure for Egyptians "all the advantages of a perfected civilization." It praised him for bringing modern knowledge to a country that had been "plunged into darkness." These attitudes provided a justification for the subsequent economic exploitation of Egypt, first by the French and later by the British, during the nineteenth century.

For Discussion

In what ways did Vivant Denon's work reflect the values that were cultivated during the Enlightenment?

---

too far and his resources too thin. Even before the invasion it was becoming increasingly difficult to feed, equip, and train the huge army he had assembled. The Grand Army that crossed from Poland into Russia in 1812 was not the efficient military force that Napoleon had commanded in the early years of the empire. Many of his best soldiers were fighting in the guerilla war in Spain. Casualties and desertions had forced Napoleon to call up new recruits who were not properly trained. Half the army, moreover, had been recruited from the population of conquered countries, making their loyalty to Napoleon uncertain.

The tactics of the Russians contributed to the failure of the invasion. Instead of engaging the Grand Army in combat, the Russian army kept retreating, pulling Napoleon further east toward Moscow. On September 7 the two armies clashed at Borodino, suffering a staggering 77,000 casualties in all. The Russian army then continued its retreat eastward. When Napoleon reached Moscow he found it deserted, and fires deliberately set by Muscovites had destroyed more than two-thirds of the city. Napoleon, facing the onset of a dreaded Russian winter and rapidly diminishing supplies, began the long retreat back to France. Skirmishes with the Russians along the way, which cost him 25,000 lives just crossing the Beresina River, conspired with the cold and hunger to destroy his army. During the entire Russian campaign his army lost a total of 380,000 men to death, imprisonment, or desertion. In the midst of this horror Napoleon, oblivious to the suffering of his troops, reported back to Paris, "The health of the emperor has never been better."

Not to be discouraged, Napoleon soon began preparing for further conquests. Once again his enemies formed a coalition against him, pledging to restore the independence of the countries that had become his satellites or dependents. Napoleon scored a few victories in the late summer of 1813, but in October allied forces inflicted a crushing defeat on him in the Battle of the Nations at Leipzig. Austrian troops administered another blow to the French in northern

FRANCISCO GOYA, *THE THIRD OF MAY 1808*
This painting of the suppression of the popular revolt in Madrid in 1808 captures the brutality of the French occupation of Spain. A French unit executes Spanish citizens, including a monk in the foreground. Goya was a figure of the Enlightenment and a Spanish patriot.

Italy, and the British finally drove them out of Spain. Napoleon's army was pushed back into France. A massive allied force advanced into Paris and occupied the city. After extensive political maneuvering, including a vote by the Senate to depose him, Napoleon abdicated on April 6, 1814. The allies promptly exiled him to the Mediterranean island of Elba. As he made the journey to the coast, crowds surrounding his coach shouted "Down with the tyrant!" while some villagers hanged him in effigy.

This course of events led to the restoration of the Bourbon monarchy. By the terms of the first Treaty of Paris of May 1814, the allies restored the brother of Louis XVI, the Count of Provence, to the French throne as Louis XVIII (r. 1814–1824). An implacable foe of the revolution, Louis strove to undermine its achievements. The white Bourbon flag replaced the revolutionary tricolor. Catholicism was once again recognized as the state religion. Exiled royalists returned to their high-ranking positions in the army. Nonetheless, Louis accepted a Constitutional Charter that incorporated many of the changes made between 1789 and 1791. Representative government, with a relatively limited franchise, replaced the absolutism of the Old Regime. The Constitutional Charter reaffirmed equality before the law, freedom of religion, and freedom of expression. Even more important, the powers of the state that the National Assembly and the Directory had extended and Napoleon had enhanced were maintained. The administrative division of France into departments continued, and the Napoleonic Code remained in force.

France had experienced a counterrevolution in 1814, but it did not simply turn the political clock back to 1788. Some of the political achievements of the previous 25 years were preserved.

Despite his disgrace and exile, Napoleon still commanded loyalty from his troops and large segments of the population. While in power he had constructed a legend that drew on strong patriotic sentiment. Supporters throughout France continued to promote his cause in the same way that royalists had maintained that of the Bourbon monarchy since 1792. The strength of the Napoleonic legend became apparent in March 1815, when Napoleon escaped from Elba and landed in southern France. Promising to rid the country of the exiled royalists who had returned and thereby save the revolutionary cause, he won over peasants, workers, and soldiers. Regiment after regiment joined him as he marched toward Paris. By the time he arrived, Louis XVIII had gone into exile once again, and Napoleon found himself back in power.

CHRONOLOGY: THE DOWNFALL OF NAPOLEON, 1810–1815

1810

April 2	Marriage of Napoleon to Marie-Louise

1812

September 7	Battle of Borodino
September 14	Napoleon enters Moscow
October	Retreat from Moscow begins

1813

October 16–19	Battle of the Nations at Leipzig

1814

April 6	Abdication of Napoleon
May 30	First Treaty of Paris
September	Congress of Vienna assembles

1815

March	Napoleon escapes from Elba
June 18	Battle of Waterloo
November 20	Second Treaty of Paris

But not for long. The allied European powers quickly began to assemble yet another coalition. Fearing that the allies would launch a massive invasion of France, Napoleon decided to strike first. He marched an army of 200,000 men into the Austrian Netherlands, where the allies responded by amassing 700,000 troops. Near the small village of Waterloo, south of Brussels, Napoleon met the British forces of the Duke of Wellington, who had turned the tide against him during the Peninsula War. Reinforced by Prussian troops, Wellington inflicted a devastating defeat on the French army, which lost 28,000 men and went into a full-scale retreat. Napoleon abdicated once again and was exiled to the remote South Atlantic island of St. Helena, from which escape was impossible. He died there in 1821.

Even before the Battle of Waterloo, the major powers of Europe had gathered in Vienna to redraw the boundaries of the European states that had been created, dismembered, or transformed during the preceding 52 years (see **Map 20.3**). Under the leadership of the Austrian foreign minister, Prince Klemens von Metternich (1773–1859), this conference, known as the **Congress of Vienna,** worked out a settlement that was intended to preserve the balance of power in Europe and at the same time uphold the principle of dynastic legitimacy. By the terms of a separate Treaty of Paris (the second in two years) the boundaries of France were scaled back to what they had been in 1790, before it had begun its wars of expansion. To create a buffer state on the northern boundary of France, the Congress annexed the Austrian Netherlands to the Dutch Republic, which now became the Kingdom of the Netherlands with William I, a prince of the House of Orange, as its king. The treaty ceded territory along the Rhineland to Prussia, while Austria, now named the Austrian Empire, gained territory in Italy. In place of the defunct Holy Roman Empire, the Congress established a new German Confederation, a loose coalition of 39 separate territories with a weak legislative assembly. The duchy of Warsaw, established in 1807 and renamed the Kingdom of

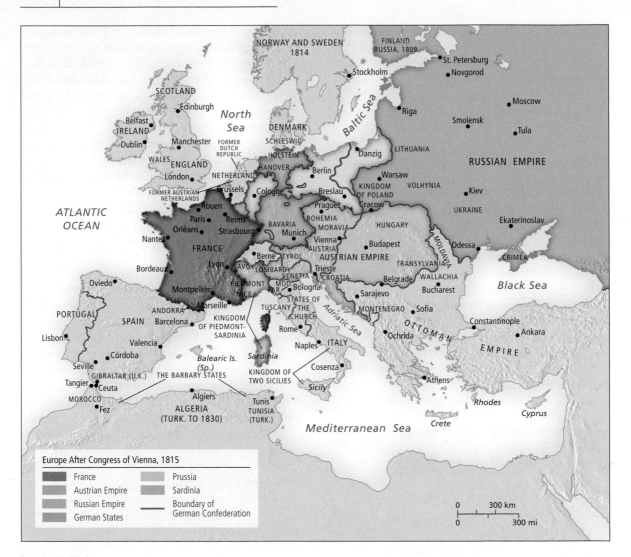

MAP 20.3

Europe After the Congress of Vienna, 1815

The Congress scaled back the boundaries of France to their status in 1790, ceded territory to Austria in western and northeastern Italy; created the kingdom of the Netherlands, a new German Confederation, and a new Kingdom of Poland ruled by Russia. The western part of Poland was ceded to Prussia.

Poland in 1812, was partitioned between Prussia and Russia. The five major powers that had drawn this new map of Europe—Britain, Austria, Prussia, Russia, and France—agreed to meet annually to prevent any one country, especially France but also Russia, from achieving military dominance of the European Continent.

THE LEGACY OF THE FRENCH REVOLUTION

■ What did the French Revolution ultimately achieve and in what ways did it change the course of European and Western history?

With the conclusion of the Congress of Vienna a tumultuous period of European and Western history finally came to an end. Not only had France experienced a revolution, but every country in Europe and America had felt its effects. Governments were toppled in countries as far apart as Poland and Peru. Added to this turbulence was the experience of incessant warfare. France was at war for more than 20 years during the Republic and the Empire, and it had involved almost all European powers in the struggle. With armies constantly in need of provisions and supplies, high taxation, galloping inflation, and food shortages inflicted economic hardship on a large portion of the European population.

The cost of all this instability and warfare in terms of human life was staggering. Within the space of one generation almost two million European soldiers were killed in action, wasted by disease, or starved or frozen to death. In France alone just under 500,000 soldiers died during the revolutionary wars of 1792–1802 and another 916,000 during the wars of the Empire. Internal political disturbances took the lives of hundreds of thousands of civilians from all ranks of society, not only in France, but throughout Europe. Unprecedented fears of internal and external subversion fed the violence at all levels. Government officials, collaborators, counterrevolutionaries, and imagined enemies of the state were all executed. This spate of violence and death—much of it in the name of liberty—occurred almost entirely at the hands of the state or its enemies.

What was achieved at this extraordinary price? How did the France of 1815 differ from the France of 1788? What on balance had changed? Historians once argued that as a result of the revolution the bourgeoisie, composed of merchants, manufacturers, and other commoners of substantial wealth, had replaced the nobility as the dominant social and political class in France. This argument can no longer be sustained. The nobility certainly lost many of their privileges in 1789, and many of them went into exile during the revolutionary period, but the position they had in French society in 1815 did not differ greatly from what it had been under the Old Regime. In both periods

there was considerable blurring of the distinctions between nobility and bourgeoisie. Nor did the revolutionary period witness the emergence of a new class of industrial entrepreneurs. The only group that definitely profited from the revolution in the long run were men of property, regardless of their membership in any social category or "class." Wealthy men emerged triumphant in the Directory, found favor during the Napoleonic period, and became the most important members of political society after the monarchy was restored.

It would be difficult to argue that *women* of any social rank benefited from the revolution. During the early years of the revolution, women participated actively in public life. They were involved in many demonstrations in Paris, including the storming of the Bastille and the march to Versailles. But women never achieved the position of equality with men for which the Marquis de Condorcet and Olympe de Gouges had hoped. The radical Jacobins dealt that goal a major setback when they banned all women's clubs and societies on the grounds that female participation in public life would harm the institution of the family. This action ended the extensive participation of women in political life, which had begun during the eighteenth century, especially in the salons. During the nineteenth century French women exercised influence in the private sphere of the home, but not in the public sphere of politics.

It is even more difficult to identify permanent economic changes as a result of the revolution. The elimination of the remnants of feudalism may have made France marginally more capitalist than it had been before the revolution, but agricultural and mercantile capitalism had long been entrenched in French society. Nor did the Continental System, the blockade of British goods from all European ports initiated in 1806, allow French industry to catch up with that of Great Britain. Whatever economic gains were made under the protective shield of the state were offset by the adverse economic effects of 22 years of nearly continuous warfare. In the long run the revolutionary period delayed the process of industrialization that had entered its preliminary stages in France during the 1780s and retarded the growth of the French economy for the remainder of the nineteenth century.

The permanent legacy of the French Revolution lies in the realm of politics. First, the period from 1789 to 1815 triggered an enormous growth in the competence and power of the state. This trend had begun before the revolution, but the desire of the revolutionaries to transform every aspect of human life in the service of the revolution, coupled with the necessity of utilizing all the country's resources in the war effort, gave the state more control over the everyday life of its citizens than ever before. Fifteen years of Napoleonic rule only accentuated this trend, and after 1815 many of those powers remained with the government.

A second permanent political achievement of the French Revolution was the promotion of the doctrine of popular sovereignty. The belief that the people constituted the highest political authority in the state became so entrenched during the revolution that it could never be completely suppressed, either in France or in the other countries of Europe. Napoleon recognized its power when he asked the people to approve political changes he had already made by his own authority. After the restoration of the monarchy the doctrine of popular sovereignty was promoted mainly by the press, which continued to employ the new revolutionary rhetoric to keep alive the high ideals and aspirations of the revolution. The doctrine also contributed to the formation of two nineteenth-century ideologies, liberalism and nationalism, which will be discussed in Chapter 22.

CONCLUSION

The French Revolution and Western Civilization

The French Revolution was a central event in the history of the West. It began as an internal French affair, reflecting the social and political tensions of the Old Regime, but it soon became a turning point in European and Western history. Proclamations of the natural rights of humanity gave the ideals of the revolution widespread appeal, and a period of protracted warfare succeeded in disseminating those ideals outside the boundaries of France.

Underlying the export of French revolutionary ideology was the belief that France had become the standard-bearer of Western civilization. French people believed they were *la grande nation*, the country that had reached the highest level of political and social organization. They did not believe they had acquired this exalted status by inheritance. Unlike the English revolutionaries of the seventeenth century, the French did not claim that they were the heirs of a medieval constitution. French republicans of the 1790s attributed none of their national preeminence to the monarchy, whose memory they took drastic steps to erase. They considered the secular political culture that emerged during the French Revolution to be entirely new.

The export of French revolutionary political culture during the Republic and the Empire led to widespread changes in the established order. Regimes were toppled, French puppets acquired political power, boundaries of states were redrawn, and traditional authorities were challenged. Liberal reforms were enacted, new constitutions were written, and new law codes were promulgated. The Europe of 1815 could not be mistaken for the Europe of 1789.

The ideas of the French Revolution, like those of the Enlightenment that had helped to inspire them, did not go unchallenged. From the very early years of the revolution they encountered determined opposition, both in France and abroad. As the revolution lost its appeal in France, the forces of conservatism and reaction gathered strength. At the end of the Napoleonic period, the Congress of Vienna took steps to restore the legitimate rulers of European states and to prevent revolution from recurring. It appeared that the revolution would be completely reversed, but that was not the case. The ideas born of the revolution continued to inspire demands for political reform in Europe during the nineteenth century, and those demands, just like those in the 1790s, met with fierce resistance.

KEY TERMS

estates

Third Estate

Jacobins

sans-culottes

universal male suffrage

Girondins

The Mountain

Republic of Virtue

Reign of Terror

plebiscite

de-Christianization

Napoleonic Code

departments

meritocracy

Congress of Vienna

CHAPTER QUESTIONS

1. Why did the Old Regime in France collapse in 1789, and what revolutionary changes took place in French government and society during the next two years? (page 620)

2. How did a second, more radical revolution, which began with the establishment of the Republic in 1792, lead to the creation of a regime that used the power of the state to institute the Reign of Terror? (page 623)

3. In what ways did the political events of the revolution change French culture? (page 634)

4. Did the authoritarian rule of Napoleon Bonaparte from 1799 to 1814 confirm or betray the achievements of the French Revolution, and what impact did his military conquests have on Europe and the world? (page 638)

5. What did the French Revolution ultimately achieve and in what ways did it change the course of European and Western history? (page 650)

TAKING IT FURTHER

1. Did the events of 1789 constitute a revolution in the sense that they brought about a fundamental change in the system of government? In what sense did the establishment of the Republic in 1792 represent a more radical change in French politics?

2. To what extent did the ideas of the Enlightenment inspire the events of the French Revolution?

3. How did the Jacobin commitment to equality lead to the Reign of Terror?

4. Did the French Revolution end in 1799 or did Napoleon perpetuate it in any significant ways?

5. Why did Napoleon fail to realize his diplomatic and military objectives?

✔•⎯Practice on MyHistoryLab

21

The Industrial Revolution

■ The Nature of the Industrial Revolution   ■ Conditions Favoring Industrial
Growth   ■ The Spread of Industrialization   ■ The Effects of Industrialization
■ Industry, Trade, and Empire

IN 1842 A 17-YEAR-OLD GIRL, PATIENCE KERSHAW, TESTIFIED BEFORE A BRITISH parliamentary committee regarding the practice of employing children and women in the nation's mines. When the girl made her appearance, the members of the committee observed that she was "an ignorant, filthy, ragged, and deplorable-looking object, such as one of uncivilized natives of the prairies would be shocked to look upon." Patience, who had never been to school and could not read or write, told the committee that she was one of ten children, all of whom had at one time worked in the coal mines, although three of her sisters now worked in a textile mill. She went to the pit at five in the morning and came out at five at night. Her job in the mines was to hurry coal, that is, to pull carts of coal through the narrow tunnels of the mine. Each cart weighed 300 pounds, and every day she hauled eleven of them one mile. The carts were attached to her head and shoulders by a chain and belt, and the pressure of the cart had worn a bald spot on her head. Patience hurried coal for twelve hours straight, not taking any time for her midday meal, which she ate as she worked. While she was working, the men and boys who dug the coal and put it in the carts would often beat her and take sexual liberties with her. Patience told the committee, "I am the only girl in the pit; there are about 20 boys and 15 men. All the men are naked. I would rather work in a mill than a coal pit."[1]

Patience Kershaw was one of the human casualties of a development that historians refer to as the Industrial Revolution. This process, which fundamentally transformed human life, involved the extensive use of machinery in the production of goods. Much of that machinery was driven by steam engines, which required coal to produce the steam. Coal mining itself became a major industry, and the men who owned and operated the mines tried to hire workers, many of them children, at the lowest possible wage. This desire to maximize profits led to the employment, physical hardship, and abuse of girls like Patience Kershaw.

The Industrial Revolution did more than create harrowing labor conditions. It resulted in a staggering increase in the volume and range of products made available to consumers, from machine-produced clothing to household utensils. It made possible unprecedented and sustained economic growth. The Industrial Revolution facilitated the rapid transportation of passengers as well as goods across large expanses of territory, mainly on the railroads that were constructed in all industrialized countries. It brought about a new awareness of the position of workers in the economic system, and it unleashed powerful political forces intended to improve the lot of these workers.

The Industrial Revolution thus played a crucial role in redefining and reshaping the West. Until the late nineteenth century industrialization took place only in

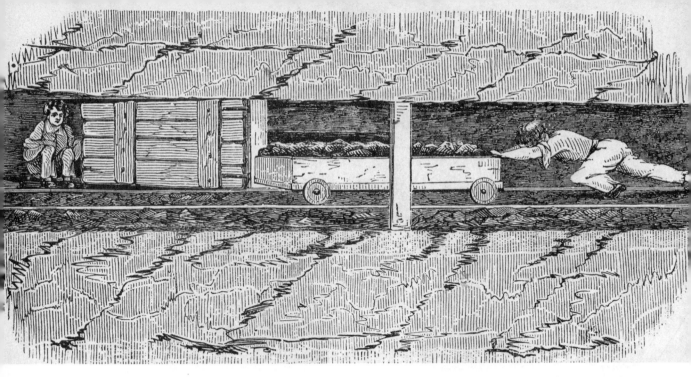

CHILD LABOR IN THE MINES
A child hurrying coal through a tunnel in a mine.

Western nations. During that century "the West" gradually became identified with countries that had industrial economies. When some non-Western countries introduced mechanized industry in the twentieth century, largely by imitating Western example, the geographical boundaries of the West shifted.

This chapter will address the following question: How did the Industrial Revolution transform Western civilization?

THE NATURE OF THE INDUSTRIAL REVOLUTION

■ What do historians mean when they refer to the Industrial Revolution of the late eighteenth and nineteenth centuries?

The Industrial Revolution, which took place in Great Britain during the late eighteenth and early nineteenth centuries and in other European countries and America after 1815, consisted of four closely related developments: the introduction of new industrial technology, the utilization of mineral sources of energy, the concentration of labor in factories, and the development of new methods of transportation.

New Industrial Technology

The Industrial Revolution ushered in the machine age, and to this day machines are the most striking feature of modern industrial economies. In the late eighteenth century industrial machines were novelties, but their numbers increased dramatically in the early nineteenth century. For example, the power loom, a machine used for weaving cloth, was invented in Britain in 1787 but not put into widespread use until the 1820s. By 1836 there were more than 60,000 power looms in just one English county.

Machines became so common in Britain that machine-making itself became a major

EXHIBIT OF MACHINERY AT THE CRYSTAL PALACE EXHIBITION IN LONDON IN 1851

During the Industrial Revolution the manufacture of heavy machinery itself became an industry.

industry, supplying its products to other manufacturers rather than to individual consumers. Machines were introduced in the textile, iron, printing, papermaking, and engineering industries and were used in every stage of manufacture. Machines extracted minerals for use as either raw materials or sources of energy, transported those materials to the factories, saved time and labor in the actual manufacturing of commodities, and carried the finished products to market. Eventually machines were used in agriculture, facilitating both the plowing of fields and the harvesting of crops.

The most significant of the new machines were devices for producing textiles and the steam engine, which were first used in mining and the iron industry. These pieces of machinery became almost synonymous with the Industrial Revolution, and their invention in the 1760s appropriately marks its beginning.

TEXTILE MACHINERY Until the late eighteenth century, Europeans produced textiles entirely by hand. They spun yarn on spinning wheels and wove cloth on handlooms. Wool remained the main textile produced in Europe until the early eighteenth century, when a new material, cotton, became immensely popular, mainly because of its greater comfort. The demand for cotton yarn was greater than the quantities spinners could supply. To meet this demand a British inventor, James Hargreaves, in 1767 constructed a new machine, the spinning jenny, which greatly increased the amount of cotton yarn that could be spun and thus made available for weaving. The original jenny, a hand machine used in the homes of spinners, consisted of only eight spindles, but it later accommodated as many as 120.

The spinning of yarn on the jenny required a stronger warp, the yarn that ran lengthwise on a loom. A power-driven machine, the water frame, introduced by the barber and wigmaker Richard Arkwright in 1769, made the production of this stronger warp possible. In 1779 Samuel Crompton, using tools he had purchased with his earnings as a fiddle player at a local theater,

BROADLIE MILL IN THE 1790s

The earliest textile mills were built in the rural areas, near rivers that supplied water power. This mill was built on the Broadlie farm, near the village of Neilston in southwestern Scotland, about twelve miles from Glasgow. The power to run the mill came from the Levern River. By 1815 there were six cotton mills in the area, supporting a community of about 1,500 workers. Housing for the workers, including some houses for single women, was constructed near the mills.

combined the jenny and the frame in one machine, called the mule. Crompton worked on his machine only at night to keep it secret, and the strange noises coming out of his workshop made his neighbors think his house was haunted. The mule, which could spin as much as 300 times the amount of yarn produced by one spinning wheel, became the main spinning machine of the early Industrial Revolution. Both the water frame and the mule required power, and that requirement led to the centralization of the textile industry in large rural mills located near rivers so that their water wheels could drive the machinery.

The tremendous success of the mule eventually produced more yarn than the weavers could handle on their hand looms. Edmund Cartwright, an Oxford-educated clergyman, supported by

monies from his heiress wife, addressed that need with the invention of the power loom in 1787. In that same year he put his new invention to use in a weaving mill he built near the town of Doncaster. The power loom, like the spinning jenny, the water frame, and the mule, met a specific need within the industry. It also gave the producer a competitive advantage by saving time, reducing the cost of labor, and increasing production. Two power looms run by a 15-year-old boy, for example, could produce more than three times what a skilled hand loom weaver could turn out in the same time using only the old hand device, the flying shuttle. The net effect of all these machines was the production of more than 200 times as much cotton cloth in 1850 as in 1780. By 1800 cotton became Britain's largest industry, producing more than 20 percent of the world's cloth; by 1850 that percentage had risen to more than 50 percent. Indeed, by midcentury, cotton accounted for 70 percent of the value of all British exports.

THE STEAM ENGINE The steam engine was even more important than the new textile machinery because it was used in almost every stage of the productive process, including the operation of textile machinery itself. James Watt, a Scottish engineer, invented the steam engine in 1763. Watt's steam engine improved the engine invented by Thomas Newcomen in 1709, which had been used mainly to drain water from deep mines. The problem with Newcomen's engine was that the steam, which was produced in a cylinder heated by coal, had to be cooled to make the piston return, and the process of heating and cooling had to be repeated for each stroke of the piston. The engine was therefore inefficient and expensive to operate. Watt created a separate chamber where the steam could be condensed without affecting the heat of the cylinder. The result was a more efficient and cost-effective machine that could provide more power than any other source. Watt's pride in his invention was matched only by his pride in his Scottish nationality. Upon receiving a patent for the new device, he boasted, "This was made by a Scot."

After designing the steam engine, Watt teamed up with a Birmingham metal manufacturer, Matthew Boulton, to produce it on a large scale.

CHRONOLOGY: TECHNOLOGICAL INNOVATIONS OF THE INDUSTRIAL REVOLUTION

1763	James Watts's rotative steam engine
1767	James Hargreaves's spinning jenny
1769	Richard Arkwright's water frame
1779	Samuel Crompton's mule
1787	Edmund Cartwright's power loom
1815	George Stephenson's steam locomotive
1846	Elias Howe's sewing machine

Boulton provided the capital necessary to begin this process and to hire the skilled laborers to assemble the machines. He also had ambitious plans for marketing the new invention throughout the world. "It would not be worth my while to make for three countries only," Boulton said, "but I find it well worth my while to make for the whole world."

The steam engine soon became the workhorse of the Industrial Revolution. Not only did it pump water from mines, but it also helped raise minerals such as iron ore from those mines. It provided the intense blast of heat that was necessary to re-smelt pig iron into cast iron, which in turn was used to make industrial machinery, buildings, bridges, locomotives, and ships. Once the engine was equipped with a rotating device, it drove factory machinery in the textile mills, and it eventually powered the railroad locomotives that carried industrial goods to market.

Mineral Sources of Energy

Until the late eighteenth century, either humans or beasts provided the power for most economic activity. Either people tilled the soil themselves, using a spade, or they yoked oxen to pull a plow. Either they carried materials and goods on their backs or they used horses to transport them. In either case the energy for these tasks came ultimately from organic sources, the food that was needed to feed farmers or their animals. If workers needed heat, they had to burn an organic material, wood or charcoal, to produce it. The amount of energy that these sources generated was therefore limited by the capacity of a geographical region to produce sufficient wood, charcoal, or food.

Organic sources of energy were of course renewable, in that new crops could be grown and forests replanted, but the long periods of time that these processes took, coupled with the limited volume of organic material that could be extracted from an acre of land, made it difficult to sustain economic growth. The only viable alternatives to organic sources of energy before the eighteenth century were those that tapped the forces of nature: windmills, which drained fields mainly in the Netherlands, and water wheels, which were driven by water pressure from river currents, waterfalls, or human-made channels that regulated the flow of water. The energy produced by wind and water was difficult to harness, however, and was available only in certain places. Moreover, these natural sources of energy could not produce heat.

The decisive change in harnessing energy for industrial purposes was the successful use of minerals, originally coal but in the twentieth century also oil and uranium, as the main sources of energy in the production and transportation of goods. These minerals were not inexhaustible, but the supplies could last for centuries, and they were much more efficient than any form of energy produced from organic materials, including charcoal and peat. Coal produced the high combustion temperatures necessary to smelt iron, and unlike charcoal it was not limited by the size of a region's forests. Coal therefore became the key to the expansion of the British iron industry in the nineteenth century. It also became the sole source of heat for the new steam engine.

As the Industrial Revolution progressed, it relied increasingly on coal as its main fuel. Largely because of the demands of the mining, textile, and metal industries, coal mining became a major industry itself with an enormous labor force. By 1850 British mines employed about five percent of the entire national workforce. These miners were just as instrumental as textile workers in making Britain an industrial nation.

The Growth of Factories

During the Industrial Revolution, mechanized factories gradually replaced two types of workplaces in which most industrial production took

PHILIPPE JACQUES DE LOUTHERBOURG, *COALBROOKDALE BY NIGHT* (1801)
This painting depicts the intense heat produced by the coal bellows used to smelt iron in Coalbrookdale, an English town in the Severn Valley that was one of the key centers of industrial activity at the beginning of the nineteenth century.

place. These two predecessors of the factory were the rural industrial cottage and the large urban handicraft workshop.

Beginning in the late sixteenth century capitalist entrepreneurs began employing families in the countryside to spin and weave cloth and make nails and cutlery. In this **domestic system** the entrepreneur provided the workers with raw materials and later paid them a fixed rate for each finished product. The workers performed their labor in their cottages, which were situated in agricultural areas. One feature of the domestic system was that all the members of the family, including children, participated in this industrial work, mainly when they were not engaged in planting or harvesting their crops.

In the early nineteenth century rural cottage industry gradually gave way to production in large factories. The great advantage of factory production over that of the rural cottage was mechanization, which became cost-efficient in a central industrial workplace. In factories, moreover, the entrepreneur could reduce the cost of labor and transportation, exercise tighter control over the quality of goods, and increase productivity by concentrating workers in one location. Temporary labor shortages sometimes made the transition from rural industry to factory production imperative.

The second type of industrial workplace that the factory replaced was the large handicraft workshop. Usually located in the towns and cities, rather than in the countryside, these workshops employed relatively small numbers of people with different skills who worked collectively on the manufacture of a variety of items, such as pottery and munitions. The owner of the workshop supplied the raw materials, paid the workers' wages, and gained a profit from selling the finished products.

The large handicraft workshop made possible a **division of labor**—the assignment of one stage of production to each worker or group of workers. The effect of the division of labor on productivity was evident even in the manufacture of simple items such as buttons and pins. In *The Wealth of Nations* (1776), the economist Adam Smith (1723–1790) used a pin factory in London to illustrate how the division of labor could increase per capita productivity from no more than 20 pins a day to the astonishing total of 4,800 pins in the same period of time.

Like the cottages engaged in rural industry, the large handicraft workshop eventually gave way to the mechanized factory. The main difference between the workshop and the factory was that the factory did not require a body of skilled workers. The factory worker's job was simply to tend to the machinery. The only skill factory workers needed was manual dexterity to operate the machinery. Only those workers who made industrial machinery remained craftsmen or skilled workers in the traditional sense of the word.

With the advent of mechanization, factory owners gained much tighter control over the entire production process. Indeed, they began to enforce an unprecedented discipline among their workers, who had to accommodate themselves to the boredom of repetitive work and a timetable set by the machines. Craftsmen who had been accustomed to working at their own pace now had to adjust to an entirely new and more demanding schedule. "While the engine runs," wrote one critical contemporary, "the people must work—men, women, and children yoked together with iron and steam. The animal machine—breakable in the best case, subject to a thousand sources of suffering—is chained fast to the iron machine which knows no suffering and no weariness."[2]

New Methods of Transportation

As industry became more extensive and increased its output, transport facilities, such as roads, bridges, canals, and eventually railroads, grew in number and quality. High industrial productivity required the efficient movement of raw materials to production sites and the transportation of finished products to markets. During the early phase of the Industrial Revolution in Britain, water transportation supplied most of these needs. A vast network of navigable rivers

MULE SPINNING
A large mechanized spinning mill in northern England, about 1835. The workers did not require any great skill to run the machinery.

and human-made canals, eventually more than 4,000 miles in length, transported goods to and from areas that did not have access to the coast. For routes that had no access to water, the most common method of transportation was by horse-drawn carriages on newly built turnpikes or toll roads, many of them made of stone so that they were passable even in wet weather.

The most significant innovation in transport during the nineteenth century was the railroad. Introduced as the Industrial Revolution was gaining momentum, the railroad provided quick, cheap transportation of heavy materials such as coal and iron over long distances. Its introduction in Britain during the 1820s and throughout Europe and America during the following decades illustrated the transition from an economy based on organic sources of energy to one that relied on mineral sources of energy. Driven by coal-burning, steam-powered locomotives, the railroads freed transport from its dependence on animal power, especially the horses that were used to pull coaches along turnpikes, barges

along canals, and carts along parallel tracks in mines. Railroads rapidly became the main economic thoroughfares of the industrial economy. They linked towns and regions that earlier had not been easily accessible to each other. They also changed the travel habits of Europeans by making it possible to cover distances in one-fifth the time it took by coach.

The construction and operation of railroads became a major new industry, employing thousands of skilled and unskilled workers and providing opportunities for investment and profit. The industry created an unprecedented demand for iron and other materials used to build and equip locomotives, tracks, freight cars, passenger cars, and signals, thus giving a tremendous boost to the iron industry and the metalworking and engineering trades. By the 1840s the railroads had become the main stimulus to economic growth throughout western Europe and the United States. Transport in industrialized economies continues to experience frequent innovation. During the twentieth century, for example, new methods of transportation, including automobiles, airplanes, and high-speed rails, sustained economic growth in all industrialized countries and like the railroads, they have become major industries themselves.

CONDITIONS FAVORING INDUSTRIAL GROWTH

■ What social and economic changes made industrial development possible?

The industrial revolution occurred first in Britain because a set of social and economic developments encouraged the mechanization of industry. These conditions were the steady increase in the British population, improved agricultural productivity, the accumulation of large amounts of capital, and sufficient demand for manufactured goods.

Population Growth

Industrialization required a sufficiently large pool of labor to staff the factories and workshops of the new industries. One of the main reasons why the Industrial Revolution occurred first in Britain was that its population during the eighteenth century increased more rapidly than that of any country in continental Europe. Between 1680 and 1820 the population of England more than doubled, while that of France grew at less than one-third that rate, and the population of the Dutch Republic hardly grew at all.

One of the reasons this growth in the British population took place was that famines, which had occurred periodically throughout the early modern period, became less frequent during the eighteenth century. The last great famine in Britain took place in 1740, only a generation before industrialization began. Mortality from epidemic diseases, especially typhus, influenza, and smallpox, also decreased. Plague, which had decimated the European population periodically since the fourteenth century, struck England for the last time in the Great Plague of London of 1665. It made its last European appearance at

INCREASE IN EUROPEAN POPULATION, 1680–1820		
Population Totals (millions)		
	1680	*1820*
France	21.9	30.5
Italy	12.0	18.4
Germany	12.0	18.1
Spain	8.5	14.0
England	4.9	11.5
Netherlands	1.9	2.0
Western Europe	71.9	116.5
Percentage Growth Rates, 1680–1820		
England	133%	
Spain	64	
Italy	53	
Germany	51	
France	39	
Netherlands	8	
Western Europe	73	

Source: E. A. Wrigley, "The Growth of Population in Eighteenth-Century England: A Conundrum Resolved," *Past and Present* 98 (1983): 122, by permission of Oxford University Press.

Marseilles in 1720 but did not spread beyond the southern parts of France.

A second and even more important factor in British population growth was an increase in fertility. More people were marrying, and at a younger age, which increased the birthrate. The spread of rural industry encouraged this early-marriage pattern. Wage-earning textile workers tended to marry a little earlier than agricultural workers, probably because wage earners did not have to postpone marriage to inherit land or to become self-employed, as was the case with farm workers.

This increase in population facilitated industrialization by swelling domestic demand for manufactured goods and by increasing the number of people available to work in the factories and mines. The increase in the British population, however, was not so large that it retarded industrialization. If population growth was too rapid, it could lead to declining incomes, put pressure on agriculture to feed more people than possible, and prevent the accumulation of wealth. Most important, overpopulation could discourage factory owners from introducing costly machinery. If labor was plentiful and cheap, it could cost less for workers to produce the same volume of goods by hand. Industrialization therefore required a significant but not too rapid increase in population—the exact scenario that occurred in Britain during the eighteenth century.

Agricultural Productivity

Like population growth, expanding agricultural output fostered the Industrial Revolution in Britain. Between 1700 and 1800 British agriculture experienced a revolution, resulting in a substantial increase in productivity. A major reason for this increase was the consolidation of all the land farmed by one tenant into compact fields. During the Middle Ages and most of the early modern period, each tenant on a manorial estate leased and farmed strips of land scattered throughout the estate. Decisions regarding the planting and harvesting of crops in these "open fields" were made collectively in the manorial court. Beginning in the sixteenth century, some of the wealthier tenants on these estates agreed to exchange their strips of land with their neighbors to consolidate their holdings into large compact fields, with hedges, bushes, or walls defining their boundaries. This process of **enclosure** allowed individual farmers to exercise complete control over the use of their land. In the eighteenth and nineteenth centuries the number of enclosures increased dramatically when the British Parliament, most of whose members were landowners, passed legislation authorizing them.

With control of their lands, farmers could make them more productive. The most profitable change was to introduce new crop rotations, often involving the alternation of grains such as rye or barley with root crops such as turnips or grasses such as clover. These new crops and grasses restored nutrients to the soil and therefore made it unnecessary to let fields lie

fallow once every three years. Farmers also introduced a variety of new fertilizers and soil additives that made harvests more bountiful. Farmers who raised sheep took advantage of discoveries regarding scientific breeding that improved the quality of their flocks.

More productive farming meant that fewer agricultural workers were required to feed the population. This made it possible for more people to leave the farms to work in the factories and mines. The expanded labor pool of industrial workers, moreover, was large enough that factory owners did not have to pay workers high wages; otherwise the prospect of industrializing would have lost much of its appeal. The hiring of children and women to work in the factories and mines also kept the labor pool large and the costs of labor low.

Capital Formation and Accumulation

A third development that encouraged British industrialization was the accumulation of capital. The term **capital** refers to all the assets used in production. These include both the factories and machines that produce other goods (fixed capital) and the raw materials and finished products that go to market (circulating capital). Other forms of capital are the railroads and barges that transport raw materials to the places of production and finished products to market. Mechanized industry involves the extensive and intensive use of capital to do the work formerly assigned to human beings. An industrial economy therefore requires large amounts of capital, especially fixed capital.

Capital more generally refers to the money that is necessary to purchase these physical assets. This capital can come from individuals, such as wealthy landlords, merchants, or industrialists who invest the profits they have accumulated in industrial machinery or equipment. In many cases the profits derived from industrial production are reinvested in the firm itself. Alternatively, capital can come from financial institutions in the form of loans. Very often a number of individuals make their wealth available to an industrial firm by buying shares of stock in that company's operations. This, of course, is the main way in which most capital is accumulated today. In countries that have only recently begun to industrialize in Latin America and Southeast Asia, capital often comes from public sources, such as governments, or from international institutions, such as the International Monetary Fund.

In Britain the capital needed to achieve industrialization came almost entirely from private sources. Some of it was raised by selling shares of stock to people from the middle and upper levels of society, but an even larger amount came from merchants who engaged in domestic and international trade, landowners who profited from the production of agricultural goods (including those who owned plantations in America), and the industrial entrepreneurs who owned mines, ironworks, and factories. In Britain, where all three groups were more successful than in other parts of Europe, the volume of capital made available from these sources was substantial. These people could invest directly in industrial machinery and mines or, more commonly, make their wealth available to others indirectly in the form of loans from banks where they kept their financial assets.

Banks supplied a considerable amount of the funds necessary for industrialization. In Britain the possibilities for such capital were maximized in the late eighteenth century when financial institutions offered loans at low interest rates and when the development of a national banking system made these funds readily available throughout the country, especially in the new industrial cities, such as Leeds, Sheffield, and Manchester. The number of English banks rose from a mere dozen in 1750 to more than 300 in 1800. Many bankers had close ties with industrialists, thereby facilitating the flow of capital from the financial to the industrial sector of the economy.

Demand from Consumers and Producers

The conditions for industrialization discussed so far all deal with **supply,** that is, the amounts of capital, labor, food, and skill necessary to support the industrial process. The other side of the economic equation is **demand,** which is the desire of consumers to purchase industrial goods and of producers to acquire raw materials and machinery. Much of the extraordinary productivity of the Industrial Revolution arose from the demand for industrial products. Many of the technological innovations that occurred at the beginning of the revolution also originated as responses to the demand for more goods. For example, the demand for more cotton goods spurred the introduction of the spinning jenny, the water frame, and the mule. Likewise, the demand for coal for industrial and domestic use led to the development of an efficient steam engine to drain mines so that those supplies of coal could be extracted.

During the early years of British industrialization the domestic market was the main source of demand for industrial products. Demand was especially strong among the bourgeoisie. A "consumer revolution" had taken place during the eighteenth century, as bourgeois individuals and families strove to acquire goods of all sorts, especially clothing and household products, such as pottery, cutlery, furniture, and curtains. The desire of the bourgeoisie to imitate the spending habits of the aristocracy helped to fuel this consumer revolution, while commercial manipulation, including newspaper advertising, warehouse displays, product demonstrations, and the distribution of samples, helped to facilitate it. An entirely new consumer culture arose, one in which women played a leading role. Advertisements promoting the latest female fashions, housewares, and children's toys became more common than those directed at adult male consumers. One ad in a local British paper in 1777, capitalizing on reports that mice were getting into ladies' hair at night, promoted "night caps made of silver wire so strong that no mouse or even a rat can gnaw through them." Advertisements therefore created a demand for new products and increased the demand for those already on the market.

If this consumer revolution had been restricted to the middle ranks of society, it would have had only a limited effect on the Industrial Revolution. The bourgeoisie constituted at most only 20 percent of the entire population of eighteenth-century Britain, and most of the goods they craved, with the exception of the pottery produced in Josiah Wedgwood's factories (which is still made today), were luxury items rather than the types of products that could be easily mass-produced. A strong demand for manufactured products could develop only if workers were to buy consumer goods such as knitted stockings and caps, cotton shirts, earthenware, coffeepots, nails, candlesticks, watches, lace, and ribbon. The demand for these products came from small cottagers and laborers as well as the middle class. The demand for stockings for both men and women was particularly strong. In 1831 the author of a study of the impact of machinery on British society declared, "Two centuries ago, not one person in a thousand wore stockings; one century ago, not one person in five hundred wore them; now not one person in a thousand is without them."[3]

Demand for manufactured products from the lower classes was obviously limited by the amount of money that wage earners had available for nonessential goods, and real wages did not increase very much, if at all, during the eighteenth century. Nevertheless the income of families in which the wife and children as well as the father worked for wages did increase significantly both during the heyday of rural industry and during the early years of industrialization. In many cases family members worked longer and harder just so they could afford to buy new products coming on the market. As the population increased, so too did this lower-class demand, which helped sustain an economy built around industrial production.

THE SPREAD OF INDUSTRIALIZATION

■ How did industrialization spread from Great Britain to the European continent and America?

The Industrial Revolution did not occur in all European countries at the same time. As we have seen, it began in Britain in the 1760s and for more than four decades was confined exclusively to that country (see **Map 21.1**). It eventually spread to other European and North American countries, where many industrial innovations were modeled on those in Britain. Belgium,

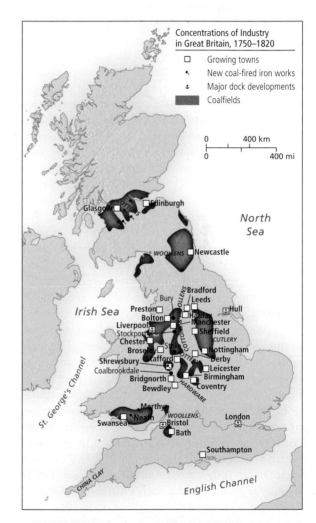

MAP 21.1

The Concentrations of Industry in Great Britain, 1750–1820

The most heavily industrialized regions were in northern England, where the population of cities such as Manchester, Liverpool, and Sheffield grew rapidly.

France, Germany, Switzerland, Austria, Sweden, and the United States all experienced their own Industrial Revolutions by the middle of the nineteenth century. Only in the late nineteenth century did countries outside the traditional boundaries of the West, mainly Russia and Japan, begin to industrialize. By the middle of the twentieth century, industrialization had become a truly global process, transforming the economies of a number of Asian and Latin American countries.

Great Britain and the Continent

Industrialization occurred on the European continent much later than it did in Great Britain. Only after 1815 did Belgium and France begin to industrialize on a large scale, and it was not until 1840 that Germany, Switzerland, and Austria showed significant signs of industrial growth. Other European countries, such as Italy, Spain, and Russia, did not begin serious efforts in this direction until the late nineteenth century. It took continental European states even longer to rival the economic strength of Britain. Germany, which emerged as Britain's main competitor in the late nineteenth century, did not match British industrial output until the twentieth century.

Four factors explain the slower development of industrialization on the Continent. The first relates to the political situations in those countries. Well into the nineteenth century, most continental European states had numerous internal political barriers that impeded the transportation of raw materials and goods from one part of the country to another. In Germany, for example, which was not politically united until 1871, scores of small sovereign territorial units charged tariffs whenever goods crossed their boundaries. Only in 1834 did a customs union, the *Zollverein*, eliminate some of these barriers. In Poland the removal of customs barriers did not take place until 1851. The relatively poor state of continental roads and the inaccessibility of many seaports from production sites aggravated this political situation.

In contrast, Britain achieved economic unity early in the eighteenth century. After 1707, when Scotland was united to England and freedom of internal trade was established between the two countries, the United Kingdom of Great Britain constituted the largest free-trade zone in Europe. Raw materials and finished products could therefore move from one place to another in Britain, up to a distance of more than 800 miles, without payment of any internal customs or duties. The system of inland waterways was complete by 1780, and seaports were accessible from all parts of the country.

A second factor that weakened the industrial potential of many continental European countries was the imposition of protective tariffs on goods imported from other countries. The purpose of this mercantilist policy was to develop national self-sufficiency and maintain a favorable balance of trade, but it also had the negative effect of limiting economic growth. For example, in the Dutch Republic (the Kingdom of the Netherlands after 1815) a long tradition of protecting established industries prevented that country from importing the raw materials and machines needed to develop new industries. Because protectionism invited retaliation from trading partners, it also tended to shrink the size of potential overseas markets. Britain adopted a policy of free trade during the 1840s, and it pressured other European countries to adopt the same policy.

A third obstacle to European industrialization was aristocratic hostility, or at least indifference, to industrial development. British aristocrats were themselves often involved in capitalist enterprise and did not have the same suspicion of industry and trade that their counterparts in France and Spain often harbored. Many members of the British aristocracy, such as the entrepreneur "Turnip Townshend" (see Chapter 19), were agricultural capitalists who improved the productivity of their estates. Others were involved in mining. The Duke of Devonshire encouraged the exploitation of the copper mines on his estate, while the Duke of Bridgewater employed the engineer James Brindley to build a canal from the duke's coal mines in Worsley to the industrial city of Manchester in 1759. One reason for the British aristocracy's support for economic growth was that many of its members, especially the gentry, rose into its ranks from other social and economic groups. These individuals tended to be sympathetic to the values of a commercial and an industrial society. The same attitude toward commerce and industry did not exist among the nobility in France before the revolution, much less among German *Junkers*. These groups had little connection with industrial or commercial society, whose values they held in very low regard. Consequently, they rarely invested in industry.

A final reason for the slow industrialization of continental European countries was that they lacked the abundant raw materials that formed the basis of an industrial economy. Britain's large deposits of coal and iron ore, both of which were indispensable to industrialization, gave it an advantage over other European countries. France and Germany had some coal deposits, but they were more difficult to mine and they were not located near ocean ports. Continental countries also lacked access to other raw materials, especially cotton, which Britain could import from its overseas colonies. With a large empire on four continents and the world's largest merchant marine, Britain could import these raw materials less expensively and in larger quantities than its continental competitors.

Features of Continental Industrialization

During the first half of the nineteenth century, especially after 1830, Belgium, France, Switzerland, Germany, and Austria introduced machinery into the industrial process, used steam power in production, concentrated labor in large factories, and built railroads. This continental European version of the Industrial Revolution was often—but incorrectly—described as an imitative process, one in which entrepreneurs or government officials simply tried to duplicate Britain's economic success by following British example. Although continental European nations did indeed rely to some

extent on British industrial technology, each European nation, responding to its own unique combination of political, economic, and social conditions, followed its own course of industrialization. Three features, however, characterized these diverse industrial paths.

First, once countries such as Belgium and Germany began to industrialize, their governments played a much more active role in encouraging and assisting in the process. In contrast to Britain, whose government allowed private industry to function with few economic controls, continental governments became active partners in the industrial process. They

MAP 21.2

Customs Unions in Continental Europe

One of the reasons for the relatively slow progress of industrialization on the European continent was the existence of internal tariff barriers. This map shows the dates when customs unions, such as the *Zollverein* of 1834 in the German Confederation, were established or the customs barriers were eliminated. By contrast, all internal customs duties within Great Britain had been eliminated more than a century earlier when England and Scotland were united in 1707.

KRUPP STEELWORKS IN ESSEN, GERMANY IN 1875
Smoke rises from the stacks of a steel mill in the Ruhr region, the center of German industry.

supplied capital for many economic ventures, especially building railroads and roads. In Prussia the state owned a number of manufacturing and mining enterprises. Many continental governments also imposed protective tariffs to prevent an influx of cheap British goods from underselling the products of their own fledgling industries. In a few cases, continental European governments even provided financial support for investors in an effort to encourage capital formation.

A second major feature of continental European industrialization was that banks, particularly in Germany and Belgium, played an active role in industrial development. Drawing on the resources of both small and large investors, these corporate banks became in effect industrial banks, building railroads and factories themselves in addition to making capital available for a variety of industrial ventures.

A third distinct feature of continental European industrialization was that the railroads actually contributed to the beginning of industrial development. In Britain the railroads were introduced some 60 years after industrialization had begun and thus helped sustain an ongoing process of economic development. By contrast, the railroads on the Continent provided the basic infrastructure of its new economy and became a major stimulus to the development of other industries. Railroads also gave continental European governments the ability to transport military troops quickly in time of war, which helps to explain why governments supported railroad construction with such enthusiasm. In Belgium, which was the first continental European nation to industrialize, the new government built a national railroad system during the 1830s and 1840s not only to stimulate industry, but also to unify the newly independent nation.

Industrialization in the United States

Industrialization in the United States began during the 1820s, not long after Belgium and France had begun to experience their own industrial revolutions. It occurred first in the textile industry in New England, where factories using water power produced goods for largely rural markets. New England also began producing two domestic hardware products—clocks and guns—for the same market. Between 1850 and 1880 a second region between Pittsburgh and Cleveland became industrialized. This area specialized in heavy industry, especially steelmaking and the manufacture of large machinery, and it relied on coal for fuel.

American industrialization included features of both the British and continental European patterns. As in Britain and France, the development of cottage industry in the United States preceded industrialization. Most of the industrial machinery in the United States during the nineteenth century was modeled on imports from Britain. The most significant American technological innovation before 1900 was the sewing machine, which Elias Howe patented in 1846 and Isaac Singer improved in the 1850s. This new machine was then introduced in Europe, where it was used in the production of ready-to-wear garments.

After 1865, when American industrialization began to spread rapidly across the entire country, American entrepreneurs made a distinctive contribution to the industrial process in the area of business organization, especially the operation of international firms. Toward the beginning of the twentieth century, American manufacturers streamlined the production process by introducing the assembly line, a division of labor in which the product passed from one operation to the next until it was fully assembled. The assembly line required the production of interchangeable parts, another American innovation, first used in the manufacture of rifles for the U.S. government.

Like Britain, the United States possessed vast natural resources, including coal. It also resembled Britain in the absence of governmental involvement in the process of industrialization.

The main difference between the industrializations of the two countries was that during the nineteenth century labor in America was in relatively short supply. This placed workers in a more advantageous situation in dealing with their employers and prevented some of the horrors of early British industrialization from recurring on the other side of the Atlantic. Only with the influx of European immigrants in the late nineteenth century did the condition of American workers deteriorate and begin to resemble the early-nineteenth-century British pattern.

Industrial Regionalism

Although we have discussed the industrialization of entire states, the process usually took place within smaller geographical regions. There had always been regional specialization in agriculture, with some areas raising crops and others livestock. During the Industrial Revolution, however, entire economies acquired a distinctly regional character. Regional economies began to take shape during the days of the domestic system, when merchants employed families in certain geographical areas, such as Lancashire in England, to produce textiles. Related industries, such as those for finishing or dyeing cloth, also sprang up close to areas where spinning and weaving took place.

As industrialization spread outside Britain, this regional pattern became even more pronounced. In France the centers of the textile industry were situated near the northeastern border near Belgium and in the area surrounding Lyons in the east-central part of the country. Both of these areas had attracted rural household industry before the introduction of textile machinery. In Germany the iron industry was centered in the Ruhr region, where most of the country's coal was mined. In the city of Essen on the Ruhr River, the industrialist Alfred Krupp (1812–1887) established an enormous steelmaking complex that produced industrial machinery, railroad equipment, and guns for the Prussian army. Within the Habsburg Empire, most industry was located in parts of Bohemia (now the Czech Republic).

The development of regional economies did not mean that markets were regional. The goods produced in one region almost always served the needs of people outside that particular area. Markets for most industrial goods were national and international, and even people in small agricultural villages created a demand for manufactured goods. The French iron industry, for example, was centered in the eastern part of the country, but it catered to the needs of the wealthier segments of its own and other European populations, as did the iron industry in the Ruhr region in Germany and the textile industry in the north of England.

Regional industrial development helps to explain the striking contrast that persisted well into the twentieth century between the parts of countries that had become heavily industrialized and those that retained at least many of the appearances of a preindustrial life. Some areas in all industrialized countries remained exclusively agricultural, while others continued a tradition of rural industry. This pattern was particularly evident in France, where mechanized industry was concentrated in a limited number of centers in the northeastern half of the country. In 1870 more than two-thirds of the French population still lived in rural areas. As economic growth and industrial development continued, however, agricultural regions eventually began to lose their traditional character. Even if industry itself did not arrive, the larger industrial economy made its mark. Agriculture itself became mechanized, while railroads and other forms of mechanized transport integrated these areas in a national economy.

THE EFFECTS OF INDUSTRIALIZATION

■ What were the economic, social, and cultural effects of the Industrial Revolution?

The Industrial Revolution had a profound impact on virtually every aspect of human life. The changes that it brought about were most evident in Britain, but in time they have occurred in every country that has industrialized, including the United States. Industrialization encouraged the growth of the population and the economy, affected the conditions in which people lived, changed family life, created new divisions within society, and transformed the traditional rural landscape.

Population and Economic Growth

The most significant of these changes was the sustained expansion of both the population and the economy. As we have seen, a significant population increase in the eighteenth century helped to make the Industrial Revolution in Britain possible. That growth had created a plentiful supply of relatively cheap labor, which in turn increased industrial output. As industry grew, population kept pace, and each provided a stimulus to the growth of the other.

Most contemporary observers in the late eighteenth century did not believe that this expansion of both the population and the economy could be sustained. The most pessimistic of these commentators was Thomas Malthus (1766–1834), an English clergyman who wrote *An Essay on the Principle of Population* in 1798. Malthus argued that population had a natural tendency to grow faster than the food supply. Thus, unless couples exercised restraint by marrying late and producing fewer children, the population would eventually outstrip the resources necessary to sustain it, resulting in poor nutrition, famine, and disease. These "positive checks" on population growth, sometimes aggravated by war, would drive population back to sustainable levels. These checks on population growth also ended periods of economic expansion, which generally accompany increases in population. If this demographic and economic pattern had recurred, the significant expansion of the population and the economy that took place in eighteenth-century Britain would have reached its limits, just around the time that Malthus was writing.

This predicted cyclical contraction of both the population and the economy did not take place.

Europe for the first time in its history managed to escape the **Malthusian population trap.** Instead of being sharply reduced after 1800, the population continued to expand at an ever-faster rate, doubling in Britain between 1800 and 1850. At the same time the economy, instead of contracting or collapsing, continued to grow and diversify.

Developments in industry explain why Europe was able to escape the Malthusian population trap. The accumulation of capital over a long period of time was so great that industry could employ large numbers of workers, even during the 1790s and 1800s, when Europe was at war. Because they had income from wages, workers were willing to marry earlier and have larger families. With lower food prices because of higher agricultural productivity, they could also afford to maintain a healthier diet and purchase more manufactured goods. Thus, the Industrial Revolution itself, coupled with the changes in agriculture that accompanied it, proved Malthus wrong.

While the increase of population in all industrialized societies is incontestable, the record of continued economic growth is not so clear. Economic growth in industrialized countries has not always been rapid or continuous. During the first six decades of industrialization in Britain, for example, economic growth was actually fairly slow, mainly because so much capital went into subsidizing the long war against France (1792–1802; 1804–1815). To claim that the Industrial Revolution resulted in sustained economic growth, we have to take a broad view, looking at an overall pattern of economic development and ignoring cyclical recessions and depressions. More important, industrialized nations have not yet experienced the type of economic contraction or collapse that Malthus predicted. For that reason, we can say that the Industrial Revolution has resulted in sustained economic growth in the West.

Standards of Living

Ever since the early years of the Industrial Revolution, a debate has raged over the effect of industrialization on the standard of living and the quality of life of the laboring population. The two main schools of thought on this issue are often referred to as the *optimists* and the *pessimists*. The optimists emphasize the positive effects of both the process of mechanization and the system of industrial capitalism that arose during the revolution. They focus on the success that industrialized nations have achieved in escaping the Malthusian population trap and in experiencing sustained economic growth. The Industrial Revolution, so they argue, has resulted in an unprecedented rise in individual income, which has made it possible for the mass of a country's population to avoid poverty for the first time in human history.

The main yardstick that the optimists use to measure the improvement in living standards is *per capita real income*, that is, income measured in terms of its actual purchasing power. Real income in Britain rose about 50 percent between 1770 and 1850 and more than doubled during the entire nineteenth century. This increase in income allowed workers to improve their diets as well as to purchase more clothing and other basic commodities. These increases, however, were only averages, concealing disparities among workers with different levels of skill. Only in the late nineteenth and twentieth centuries did industrialization raise the real income of all workers to a level that made the benefits of industrialization apparent.

The long-term increase in real income has never been substantial enough to persuade the pessimists that industrialization was on balance a positive good, at least for the working class. Pessimists have always stressed the negative effects of industrial development on the people on the lower levels of society. In their way of thinking, industrialization was an unmitigated disaster. The cause of this disaster in their eyes was not mechanization itself, but the system of **industrial capitalism.** This form of capitalism, which is characterized by the private ownership of factories and the employment of wage labor, involved a systematic effort to reduce costs and maximize profits. In the pursuit of this goal, employers tried to keep wages as low as possible and increase production by introducing labor-saving technology, thus preventing workers from improving their lot.

Pessimists usually claim a moral basis for their position. In this respect they follow in a tradition begun by the poet William Blake (1757–1827), who referred to the new factories as "satanic mills," and the socialist Friedrich Engels (1820–1895), who in *The Condition of the Working Class in England in 1844* (1845) accused the factory owners in England of mass murder and robbery.

Most of the evidence that social critics use to support the pessimist position comes from the early period of industrialization in Britain, when workers' real wages either stagnated or declined and when conditions in factories and towns were most appalling. Working-class housing was makeshift and crowded, and there were few sanitary facilities. A new word, *slum,* was coined to refer to these poverty-stricken working-class neighborhoods. Poor drainage and raw sewage gave rise to a host of new hygienic problems, especially outbreaks of typhus and cholera. Between 1831 and 1866 four epidemics of cholera killed at least 140,000 people in Britain, most of whom lived in poorer districts.

The impact of industrialization and urbanization on the environment was no less harrowing. The burning of coal and the use of industrial chemicals polluted the urban atmosphere. The famous London fogs, which were actually smogs caused by industrial pollutants, presented a serious public health problem throughout the nineteenth century and did not begin to disappear until the introduction of strict regulations on the burning of coal in the 1950s.

While life in the city was bleak and unhealthy, working conditions in the factory were monotonous and demeaning. Forced to submit to a regimen governed by the operation of the machine, workers lost their independence as well as any control whatsoever over the products of their labor. They were required to work long hours, often 14 hours a day, six days a week, with few breaks. Factory masters locked the doors during working hours and assessed fines for infractions such as opening a window when the temperature was unbearable, whistling while working, and having dirty hands while spinning yarn. Work in the mines was a little less monotonous, but it was physically more demanding and far more dangerous. (See *Different Voices* in this chapter.)

Women, Children, and Industry

During the early Industrial Revolution in Britain, the industrial workforce, especially in the textile and mining industries, included large numbers of children and women. In the woolen industry in the western part of England, for example, female and child labor together accounted for 75 percent of the workforce. Children under age 13 made up 13 percent of the cotton factory workforce, and those under age 18 made up 51 percent. This pattern of employment reflected the demands of industrialists, who valued the hand skills and dexterity that children possessed as well as the greater amenability of both children and women to the discipline of factory labor. Some of the machines that were introduced into the textile industry in the late eighteenth century were specifically designed for women and children.

Female and child labor was both plentiful and cheap. Children received only one-sixth to one-third the wages of a grown man, while women generally took home only one-third to one-half of that adult male income. Yet women and children sought these low-paying jobs. In a family dependent on wages, everyone needed to work, even when a large labor pool kept wages depressed.

The participation of women and children in the workforce was *not* new. In an agricultural economy all members of the family contributed to the work, with parents and children, young and old, all being assigned specific roles. Rural industry also involved the labor of all members of the family. When people began working in the factories, however, they were physically separated from the home, making it impossible for workers to combine domestic and occupational labor.

As the workplace became distinct from the household, family life underwent a fundamental change, although it did not occur immediately. During the early years of the Industrial Revolution, members of many families found employment together in the factories and mines. Factory owners also tried to perpetuate many aspects of family life in the new industrial setting, defining the entire factory community as an extended family, in which the factory owner played the paternalistic role. Gradually, however, mothers found it impossible to care for their youngest children on the job, and most of them dropped out of the full-time workforce. The restriction of child labor by the British Factory Act of 1833 reinforced this trend and led to the establishment of a fairly common situation in which the male wage earner worked outside the home while his wife stayed home with the children. As one young girl who worked in the mines testified before a parliamentary commission investigation of child labor in 1842, "Mother takes care of the children." (See *Justice in History* in this chapter.)

The Industrial Revolution did nothing to improve the status of women. Neither the pay these women received nor the jobs they performed gave them financial autonomy or social prestige. Becoming an independent wage earner meant little when women's wages were on average one-third to one-half those of men. The jobs assigned to women within industry, such as operating textile machinery, generally required the least skill. When men and women worked in the same factory, the women were invariably subordinated to the authority of male workers or foremen, thereby perpetuating the patriarchal patterns that prevailed in preindustrial society. Even their exclusion from certain occupations, such as mining by an act of Parliament in 1842, only made the sexual division of labor more rigid than in preindustrial society.

Class and Class Consciousness

As Europe became more industrialized and urbanized, and as the system of industrial capitalism became more entrenched, writers began to use a new terminology to describe the structure of society. Instead of claiming that society consisted of a finely graded hierarchy of ranks to which individuals belonged by virtue of their occupations or their legal status, they divided society into three classes on the basis of the type of property people owned

CAPITAL AND LABOR
This cartoon, drawn by the illustrator Gustave Doré, depicts wealthy industrialists gambling with workers tied together as chips.

DIFFERENT VOICES THE SOCIAL AND CULTURAL EFFECTS OF INDUSTRIALIZATION

Contemporaries and historians have debated whether the condition of the working class improved or deteriorated as a result of the Industrial Revolution. These two descriptions of the working class in England in the first half of the nineteenth century present evidence to support the two sides of the debate. In his history of the cotton industry, which he greatly admired, the English journalist Richard Guest focused on the improved educational opportunities offered to workers, mainly in the Sunday schools. The German social philosopher Friedrich Engels, who collaborated with Karl Marx (1818–1883) in writing The Communist Manifesto (1848), *emphasized the exploitation and brutalization of the lower classes as they were turned into a wage-earning proletariat. In his first book,* The Condition of the Working Class in England in 1844, *which was inspired by his service as a manager in a factory in Manchester, Engels focused on the deplorable living conditions of industrial workers.*

A Journalist Celebrates the Improvement in the Life of Industrial Workers

The progress of the cotton manufacture introduced great change in the manners and habits of the people. The operative workmen being thrown together in great numbers, had their faculties sharpened and improved by constant communication. Conversation wandered over a variety of topics not before essayed; the questions of peace and war, which interested them importantly, inasmuch as they might produce a rise or fall of wages, became highly interesting, and this brought them into the vast field of politics and discussions on the character of their government and the men who composed it. They took a greater interest in the defeats and victories of their country's arms, and from being only a few degrees above their cattle in the scale of intellect, they became political citizens.

To these changes the establishment of Sunday Schools has very much contributed; they have been a great means of forwarding this wonderful alteration. Before their institution the lower orders were extremely illiterate; very few of them could read, and still fewer of them could write, and when one of them learned to read, write and cast accounts, those requirements elevated him to a superior rank. His clerkly skill exempted him from manual labour, and as shopman, book-keeper or town's officer—perchance in the higher dignity of parish clerk or schoolmaster—he rose a step above his original station in life....

The facility with which the weavers changed their masters, the constant effort to find out and obtain the largest remuneration for their labor, the excitement to ingenuity which the higher wages for fine manufacturers and skilful workmanship produced, and a conviction that they depended mainly on their own exertions produced in them that invaluable feeling, a spirit of freedom and independence, and that guarantee for good conduct and improvement of manners, a consciousness of the value of character and of their own weight and importance.

Source: Richard Guest, *A Compendious History of the Cotton Manufacture* (1823).

and the manner in which they acquired it. At the top of this new social hierarchy was the aristocracy, consisting of those who owned land and received their income in the form of rent. The middle class or bourgeoisie, which included the new factory owners, possessed capital and derived their income from profits, whereas the working class owned nothing but their own labor and received their income from wages.

Historians and social scientists disagree over the extent to which men and women in the nineteenth century were actually conscious of their membership in these classes. Some historians claim that the growth of wage labor, the exploitation of

Friedrich Engels Deplores the Living Conditions of Industrial Workers

Since capital, the direct or indirect control of the means of subsistence and production, is the weapon with which this social warfare is carried on, it is clear that all the disadvantages of such a state must fall upon the poor man. For him no one has the slightest concern. Cast into the whirlpool, he must struggle through as well as he can. If he is so happy as to find work, i.e. if the bourgeoisie does him the favour to enrich itself by means of him, wages await him which scarcely suffice to keep body and soul together; if he can get no work he may steal, if he is not afraid of the police, or starve, in which case the police will take care that he does so in a quiet and inoffensive manner....

Every great city has one or more slums, where the working class is crowded together...these slums are pretty equally arranged in all the great towns of England, the worst houses in the worst quarters of the towns; usually one or two-storied cottage in long rows, perhaps with cellars used as dwellings, almost always irregularly built....The streets are generally unpaved, rough, dirty, filled with vegetable and animal refuse, without sewer or gutters, but supplied with foul, stagnant pools instead. Moreover, ventilation is impeded by the bad, confused method of building of the whole quarter, and since many human beings here live crowded into a small space, the atmosphere that prevails in these working men's quarters may readily be imagined....

Liverpool, with all its commerce, wealth and grandeur yet treats its workers with the same barbarity. A full fifth of the population, more than 45,000 human beings, live in narrow, dark, damp, badly-ventilated cellar dwellings, of which there are 7,862 in the city. Besides these cellar dwellings there are 2,270 courts, small spaces built up on all four sides and having but one entrance, a narrow, covered passageway, the whole ordinarily very dirty and inhabited exclusively by proletarians....In Nottingham there are in all 11,000 houses, of which between 7,000 and 8,000 are built back to back with a rear party-wall so that no through ventilation is possible, while a single privy usually serves for several houses.

Source: Friedrich Engels, *The Condition of the Working Class in England* (1845).

For Discussion

1. Is it possible that these two accounts of working class life in the industrial age could both be accurate? Which account do you find more persuasive and why?

2. How do the political agendas of the two authors influence their assessments of the effects of industrialization?

3. In what ways do these descriptions of industrial working class reflect the optimistic and pessimistic interpretations of industrialization discussed in this chapter.

the working class, and conflicts between capital and labor encouraged workers to think of themselves not so much as individuals who occupied a position in a social hierarchy, but as members of a large class of workers who shared the same relationship to the means of production. These historians have pointed to the growth of trade unions, political campaigns for universal male suffrage, and other forms of working-class organization and communication as evidence of this awakening of **class consciousness.**

Other historians argue that people were less conscious of their class. True, at certain times in the early nineteenth century some workers thought of themselves as members of a class whose

JUSTICE IN HISTORY

The Sadler Committee on Child Labor

The widespread use of child labor in British factories and mines during the early decades of the Industrial Revolution led to efforts by social reformers and Members of Parliament to regulate the conditions under which children worked. Parliament passed legislation restricting the number of hours that all children could work in textile mills in 1819 and 1829, but neither of these laws was enforced effectively, and they did not apply to all industries. Complaints of inhumane treatment, moral degradation, and exploitation of child workers continued to surface. In 1831 Michael Sadler (1780–1835), a Tory member of the British Parliament, introduced a bill in Parliament to limit the number of hours that all children could work to ten hours per day. Like many social reformers, Sadler was inspired by what he considered his Christian duty to protect dependent members of the community.

Sadler chaired the committee to which his bill was referred. To muster support for the bill, Sadler held hearings in which child workers themselves came before the committee to report on the conditions under which they lived and worked. The success of his bill was by no means guaranteed. Many Members of Parliament were deeply committed to the policy of *laissez-faire,* according to which the government should not intervene in the operation of the economy, treating it instead as a self-regulating machine. Sadler had to convince his colleagues that they should modify that policy in the case

of children, on the grounds that the state was obliged to provide for the welfare of children when their parents were unable to do so. He also needed to make the Members of Parliament and the broader public aware of the brutality of the conditions under which the children worked.

The hearings that took place were not a trial in the strict sense of the word, but they possessed many of the features of a judicial investigation, not unlike those conducted by American grand juries in criminal cases. Sadler intended the committee's proceedings to expose, condemn, and ultimately remedy misconduct by the factory owners. Procedurally the committee members had more latitude than courts of law. Because such parliamentary committees were designed to extract information rather than to bring offenders to trial, they did not need to adhere to any established judicial guidelines. There was no cross-examination of witnesses, nor could factory owners present a

CHILD LABOR IN THE TEXTILE INDUSTRY
Factory girls operate machinery in a textile mill under the tight supervision of the factory owner.

defense. The witnesses in this investigation were chosen because Sadler knew they would reveal the evils of the factory system.

The testimony presented to the Sadler Committee produced abundant evidence of the exploitation and physical abuse of child workers. Some of the most harrowing testimony came from the examination of a 17-year-old boy, Joseph Hebergam, on July 1, 1832. Hebergam revealed that he had begun the work of worsted spinning at age 7, that he worked at the factory from 5 A.M. until 8 P.M., and that he had only 30 minutes for lunch at noon, leaving him to eat his other meals while standing on the job. In the factory there were three overlookers (supervisors), one of whom was responsible for greasing the machinery and another for disciplining the workers. The latter overlooker walked continually up and down the factory with whip in hand.

When asked where his brother John was working, Joseph replied that he had died three years before at age 16. Sadler then inquired into the cause of his brother's death. The boy responded, "It was attributed to this, that he died from working such long hours and that it had been brought on by the factory. They have to stop the flies [part of the textile machinery] with their knees, because they go so swift they cannot stop them with their hands; he got a bruise on the shin by a spindle-board, and it went on to that degree that it burst; the surgeon cured that, then he was better; then he went to work again; but when he had worked about two months more his spine became affected, and he died." The witness went on to explain that his own severe labor had damaged his knees and ankles so much so that he found it painful to walk. His brother and sister would help carry him to the factory, but when they arrived late, even by as little as five minutes, the overlooker beat all three of them "till we were black and blue."[4] At the request of the committee, Joseph then stood up to show the condition of his limbs. He reported the death of another boy who had sustained massive injuries when he was caught in the shaft of the machinery he was running. Joseph concluded his testimony by recounting how the factory owners had threatened him and his younger brothers with losing their jobs if they testified before the committee.

Although widely publicized, the hearings of the Sadler Committee fell short of realizing their original objective. The bill, which eventually was approved by Parliament as the Factory Regulations Act of 1833, prohibited the employment of children under age nine in all factories. Boys and girls were allowed to work up to nine hours a day from age nine until their thirteenth birthday, and up to twelve hours a day from age 13 until their eighteenth birthday. Nevertheless, the long-term effect of this legislation was to establish in Western industrialized countries the principle that early childhood was a period of life set aside for education rather than work.

For Discussion

1. This investigation was concerned with the achievement of social justice rather than the determination of criminal culpability. What were the advantages of using legislative committees in such an undertaking?

2. Child labor was not a new phenomenon in the early eighteenth century. Why did the Industrial Revolution draw attention to this age-old practice?

Taking It Further

Pamela Horn. *Children's Work and Welfare, 1780–1890.* 1996. An examination of the scale and nature of child employment in Britain and changing attitudes toward the practice.

interests conflicted with those of factory owners and financiers. It was much more common, however, for them to think of themselves primarily as practitioners of a particular craft, as members of a local community, or as part of a distinct ethnic minority, such as the Irish in Britain. When they demanded the right to vote, workers based their claim on their historic constitutional rights, not the interests of all wage earners. When they demonstrated in favor of the ten-hour working day, they did so to improve the conditions in which they worked, not to advance the struggle of all workers against the middle class. The work experiences of laborers were too varied to sustain a widespread awareness that they belonged to one homogeneous group. Consequently, appeals for working-class solidarity to a large extent fell on deaf ears.

It is true that on certain occasions workers took violent action against their employers. In 1812 groups of hand loom weavers in the highly industrialized Midland region of England engaged in a determined campaign to destroy the new power looms that they blamed for rising unemployment and low wages. Often disguised

and operating at night, these "Luddites," who took their name from their mythical leader Ned Ludd, smashed the new textile machinery that factory owners had introduced. (Even today people who object to the introduction of new technology are referred to as Luddites.) These men, however, did not identify with other British workers, especially those tending textile machinery in the factories.

Nevertheless, occasional encounters between workers and bourgeoisie did heighten an awareness of class divisions in British society. In August 1819, 60,000 workers gathered in St. Peter's Field in Manchester to demand the right to vote and better working conditions. Frightened by the size of the demonstration and opposed to the workers' demands, the volunteer cavalrymen of the city, who belonged to the middle class, attacked the crowd, killing eleven people and injuring another 400. This violent confrontation, known as the Peterloo Massacre, did not lead to revolution or sustained class warfare, but it did contribute to the perception, shared by an increasingly large number of people, that British

THE PETERLOO MASSACRE, 1819

This drawing of the Peterloo Massacre shows the mounted yeomen of Manchester, with swords drawn, attacking the demonstrators, who had gathered to hear the speeches by the reformers on the platform above.

society was divided into large groups of people based on their economic position in society.

The Industrial Landscape

As industry spread throughout Europe, urban and rural areas underwent dramatic changes. The most striking of these transformations took place in the new industrial towns and cities, some of which had been little more than country towns before the factories were built. Manchester, for example, grew from a modest population of 23,000 people in 1773 to a bustling metropolis of 105,000 by 1820. Large factories with their smokestacks and warehouses, ringed by long rows of houses built to accommodate the armies of new industrial workers, gave these cities an entirely new and for the most part a grim appearance.

Cities experienced the most noticeable changes in physical appearance, but the countryside also began to take on a new look, mainly as a result of the transport revolution. The tunnels, bridges, and viaducts that were constructed to accommodate the railroad and the canals that were built to improve inland water transportation made an indelible imprint on the countryside. In many ways this alteration of the landscape demonstrated the mastery over nature that human beings had achieved at the time of the Scientific Revolution. The Industrial Revolution finally fulfilled the technological promise of that earlier revolution, and one of its effects was the actual transformation of the physical world.

The advent of modern industry also brought about a change in attitudes toward the landscape. The destruction of natural beauty in the interest of economic progress stimulated an appreciation of nature that had not been widespread during the medieval and early modern periods. Before the Industrial Revolution many features of the countryside, especially mountains, were viewed as obstacles to either travel or human habitation, not as objects of aesthetic appreciation. Urbanization and industrialization changed those perceptions, triggering a nostalgic reaction that became one of the sources of the romantic movement, which we shall consider in greater detail in the next chapter.

Industry did not always blight the landscape or offend artistic sensibilities. Some of the new industrial architecture, especially the viaducts and aqueducts that traversed valleys in the mountainous regions of the country, were masterpieces

**JOSEPH M. W. TURNER,
RAIN, STEAM AND SPEED: THE GREAT WESTERN RAILWAY
(1844)**

This was one of the first oil paintings that had the railroad locomotive as its theme.

of modern engineering and architecture. Sir Walter Scott (1771–1832), the Scottish romantic novelist, claimed that the cast-iron Pont Cysyllte aqueduct in Wales, which carried the waters of the Caledonian Canal 127 feet above the River Dee, was the most beautiful work of art he had ever seen. The railroad also had the ability to inspire the artistic imagination, as it did in Joseph Turner's (1775–1851) romantic painting *Rain, Steam and Speed,* which captured the railroad's speed and beauty.

INDUSTRY, TRADE, AND EMPIRE

■ **What was the relationship between the growth of industry and Britain's dominance in trade and imperial strength during the middle years of the nineteenth century?**

In the middle of the nineteenth century, Britain towered above all other nations in the volume of its industrial output, the extent of its international trade, and the size of its empire. In industrial production it easily outpaced all its competitors, producing two-thirds of the world's coal, about half of its cotton cloth, half of its iron, and 40 percent of its hardware. Little wonder that Britain became known as "the workshop of the world." Britain controlled about one-third of the world's trade, and London emerged as the undisputed financial center of the global economy. Britain's overseas empire, which included colonies in Canada, the Caribbean, South America, India, Southeast Asia, and Australia, eclipsed those of all other European powers and continued to grow during the second half of the century.

These three great British strengths—industry, trade, and empire—were closely linked. Britain's colonies in both Asia and the Americas served as trading depots, while the promotion of trade led directly to the acquisition of new imperial possessions. Even when Britain did not formally acquire territory, it often established exclusive trading relationships with those countries, thereby creating an informal "empire of trade." Trade and empire in turn served the purposes of industry. Many of the raw materials used in industrial production, especially cotton, came from Britain's imperial possessions. Those possessions also provided markets for Britain's mass-produced manufactured goods. Such imperial markets proved immensely valuable when France blockaded its ports during the Napoleonic wars and thereby cut into British trade with the entire European continent.

The great challenge for British industrialists during the nineteenth century was to find new markets for their industrial products. Domestic demand had been strong at the beginning of the Industrial Revolution, but by the 1840s British workers did not possess sufficient wealth to purchase the increasingly large volume of hardwares and textiles manufactured in the mills and factories. Britain had to look overseas to find markets in which to sell the bulk of its industrial products. One possibility was to market them in other European countries, such as France and Germany, where demand for manufactured goods was high. These countries, however, were in the midst of their own industrial revolutions, and their governments had often legislated high protective tariffs against British goods to encourage the growth of their own industries. British industrialists, therefore, marketed their goods in less economically developed parts of the world, including British colonies. In all these areas, moreover, British military power and diplomatic influence advanced the interests of industry, trade, and empire.

East Asia: The Opium War, 1839–1842

British conflict with China provides the best illustration of the way in which the British desire to promote trade led to the acquisition of new colonies. For three centuries the Chinese had tightly controlled their trade with European powers. By 1842, however, British merchants, supported by the British government, managed to break down these barriers and give Britain a foothold in China, allowing it to exploit the East Asian market.

The conflict arose over the importation of opium, a narcotic made from poppy seeds and produced in great quantities in India. This drug, which numbed pain but also had hallucinogenic effects and could cause profound lethargy, was in widespread use in Europe and had an even larger market in Asia. In China opium had became a national addiction by the middle of the eighteenth century. The situation became much worse when British merchants increased the volume of illegal imports from India to China in the early nineteenth century. The Chinese government prohibited the use of opium, but because it had difficulty enforcing its own edicts, it decided to put an end to the opium trade.

Chinese efforts to stop British merchants from importing opium led to an increase in tensions between China and Britain. The situation reached a climax in 1839, when the Chinese seized 20,000 chests of opium in the holds of British ships and spilled them into the China Sea. It is unknown what effect the opium had on the fish, but the incident led to a British attack on Chinese ports. In this conflict, the first Opium War (1839–1842), the British had the advantage of superior naval technology, itself a product of the Industrial Revolution. The first iron-clad, steam-driven gunboat used in combat, the *Nemesis,* destroyed Chinese batteries along the coast, and an assault by 75 British ships on Chinkiang forced the Chinese to come to terms. In a treaty signed in 1842 China ceded the island of Hong Kong to the British, reimbursed British merchants for the opium it had destroyed, and opened five Chinese ports to international trade. As part of this settlement, each of these ports was to be governed by a British consul who was not subject to Chinese law. In this way Britain expanded its empire, increased its already large share of world trade, and found new markets for British manufactured goods in East Asia.

India: Annexation and Trade

The interrelationship of industry, trade, and empire became even clearer in India, which became known as the jewel in Britain's imperial crown. As we saw in Chapter 18, Britain gained control of the Indian province of Bengal in the eighteenth century and subsequently acquired other Indian states. After the Sepoy Mutiny of 1857 the British government brought all of India under its direct control.

Political control of India during the nineteenth century served the interests of British trade in two ways. First, it gave British merchants control of the trade between India and other Asian countries. Second, Britain developed a favorable balance of trade with India, exporting more goods to that country than it imported. Taxes paid to the British government by Indians and interest payments on British loans to India increased the flow of capital from Calcutta to London. The influx of capital from India was largely responsible for the favorable balance of payments that Britain enjoyed with the rest of the world until World War I. The capital that Britain received from these sources as well as from trade with China was funneled into the British economy or invested in British economic ventures throughout the world.

Control of India also served British interests by supplying British industries with raw materials while giving them access to the foreign markets they needed to make a profit. This promotion of British industry came at the expense of the local Indian economy. The transportation of cotton grown in India to British textile mills only to be returned to India in the form of finished cloth certainly retarded, if it did not destroy, the existing Indian textile industry. Resentment of this economic exploitation of India became one of the main sources of Indian nationalism in the late nineteenth century.

Latin America: An Empire of Trade

British policy in Latin America developed differently from the way it had in China and India, but it had the same effect of opening up new markets for British goods. Great Britain was a consistent supporter of the movements for independence that erupted in South America between 1810 and 1824 (see Chapter 18). Britain supported these movements not simply because it wished to undermine Spanish and Portuguese imperialism, but also because it needed to acquire new markets for its industrial products. Britain did not need to use military force to open these areas to British trade, as it did in China. Once the countries became independent, they attracted large volumes of British exports. In 1840 the British cotton industry shipped 35 percent of its exports to Latin American countries, especially to Argentina, Brazil, Uruguay, Mexico, and Chile. British financiers also exported large amounts of capital to these Latin American countries by investing vast sums of money in their economies. Britain thus established an informal "empire of trade" in Latin America. Britain did not govern these countries, but they developed the same economic relationship with Britain as other parts of the British Empire.

British investment and trade brought the newly independent states of Latin America into the industrial world economy. These countries, however, assumed a dependent position in that economy, not unlike the position India acquired about the same time. One effect of this dependence was to transform the small, self-sufficient village economies that had developed alongside the large plantations in Central and South America. Instead of producing goods themselves and selling them within their own markets, these villages now became suppliers of raw materials for British industry. This transformation made the Latin American population more dependent upon British manufactured goods, retarded or destroyed native Latin American industry, and created huge trade deficits for Latin American countries by the middle of the nineteenth century.

Ireland: The Internal Colony

Of all the imperial possessions with which Britain engaged in trade, the position of Ireland was the most anomalous. Despite its proximity to England, Ireland had always been treated as a colony. In 1801, after the unsuccessful Irish rebellion of 1798 discussed in Chapter 18, the British government incorporated Ireland into the United Kingdom and abolished the Irish parliament. Although a small minority of Irishmen elected their representatives to sit in the

British Parliament, and although Ireland thus became a part of the British state, Britain nonetheless continued to treat the country as an imperial possession.

Throughout the nineteenth century Ireland remained almost entirely agricultural. Industrialization occurred only in the northern province of Ulster, which produced ready-to-wear undergarments for women and shirts for men. Ireland's vast agricultural estates, many of them owned by absentee British landlords, provided Britain with large imports of grain. Unable to afford the high cost of grain, which British protectionist legislation priced artificially high, and without the opportunity to find employment in industry, Irish tenants eked out an existence on the land, relying on a diet consisting almost entirely of potatoes. When a blight destroyed the potato crop in 1845, the country experienced a devastating famine that killed more than one million people and forced another million to emigrate—many of them to the United States and Canada—between 1845 and 1848. The famine occurred despite the fact that Irish lands produced enough grain to feed the entire population. As the Lord Mayor of Dublin complained in 1845, British commercial policy inflicted on the Irish "the abject misery of having their own provisions carried away to feed others, while they themselves are left contemptuously to starve."[5] Thus, even in this internal colony, the British government's policy of promoting industry at home while importing resources from its imperial possessions served British economic interests at the expense of the countries under its control.

CONCLUSION

Industrialization and the West

By 1850 the Industrial Revolution had initiated some of the most dramatic changes in human life recorded in historical documents. Not since the Neolithic Age, when people began to live in settled villages, cultivate grains, and domesticate animals, did the organization of society, the patterns of work, and the landscape undergo such profound changes. In many ways the Industrial Revolution marked the watershed between the old way of life and the new. It gave human beings unprecedented technological control over nature, made employment in the home the exception rather than the rule, and submitted industrial workers to a regimen unknown in the past. It changed family life, gave cities an entirely new appearance, and unleashed new and highly potent political forces, including the ideologies of liberalism and socialism, which we discuss in the next chapter.

Industrialization changed the very definition of the West. In the Middle Ages Christianity shaped the predominant cultural values of Western countries, while in the eighteenth century the rational, scientific culture of the Enlightenment became central to the idea of the West. Now, in the nineteenth century, industrialization—and the system of industrial capitalism it spawned—increasingly defined the West. In discussing the prospects of industrialization in the Ottoman Empire in 1856, a British diplomat wrote that "Europe is at hand, with its science, its labor, and its capital," but that the Qur'an and other elements of traditional Turkish culture "are so many obstacles to advancement in a Western sense."[6] The Industrial Revolution thus created new divisions between the West and the non-Western world.

Until the late nineteenth century, industrialization took place only in nations that had traditionally been a part of the West. Beginning in the 1890s, however, countries that lay outside the West or on its margins began to introduce industrial technology and methods. Between 1890 and 1910 Russia and Japan underwent a period of rapid industrialization, and in the second half of the twentieth century many countries in Asia, the Middle East, and Latin America followed suit. This process of industrialization and economic development is often described as one of Westernization, and it has usually led to conflicts within those countries between Western and non-Western values. Whether those countries that have industrialized should be considered Western is not clear. Industrialization outside Europe and the United States reveals once again that the composition of the West changes from time to time and that its boundaries are often difficult to define.

KEY TERMS

domestic system
division of labor
enclosure
capital
supply

demand
Malthusian population
    trap
industrial capitalism
class consciousness

CHAPTER QUESTIONS

1. What do historians mean when they refer to the Industrial Revolution of the late eighteenth and nineteenth centuries? (page 655)
2. What social and economic changes made industrial development possible? (page 662)
3. How did industrialization spread from Great Britain to the European continent and America? (page 665)
4. What were the economic, social, and cultural effects of the Industrial Revolution? (page 670)
5. What was the relationship between the growth of industry and Britain's dominance in trade and imperial strength during the middle years of the nineteenth century? (page 680)

TAKING IT FURTHER

1. Why did the Industrial Revolution begin in Great Britain?
2. What are the strengths and weaknesses of the optimistic view of the Industrial Revolution?
3. What was the relationship between the growth of the population and the Industrial Revolution?
4. How did the Industrial Revolution change the definition of the West?

✓•⃞Practice on MyHistoryLab

22

Ideological Conflict and National Unification, 1815–1871

■ New Ideologies in the Early Nineteenth Century ■ Ideological Encounters in Europe, 1815–1848 ■ National Unification in Europe and America, 1848–1871 ■ International Conflict and Domestic Politics, 1853–1871

ON MARCH 18, 1871, THE PRESIDENT OF THE FRENCH GOVERNMENT, Adolphe Thiers, sent a small unit of troops to Paris to seize cannons that had been used against Prussian forces during their siege of the city a few months before. The cannons were in the possession of the National Guard, the citizen militia of Paris. The members of the National Guard felt that Thiers's government had abandoned them by recently concluding an armistice with the Prussians, who were still camped outside the city. They also believed that Thiers was determined to gain control of the city, which had refused to comply with the orders of the national government. When the troops reached the city, they encountered a hostile crowd of Parisians, many of whom were armed. The crowd surrounded the two generals who led the detachment, placed them up against a wall, and executed them.

This action led to a full-scale siege of Paris by government troops. In the city a committed group of radicals formed a new municipal government, the Paris Commune, a revival of the commune established during the French Revolution in 1792. The Commune took steps to defend the city against the government troops, and it implemented several social reforms. The Communards, as the members were known, set up a central employment bureau, established nurseries for working mothers, and recognized women's labor unions. For many decades the Commune served as a model of working-class government.

Yet the Paris Commune itself lasted only a few weeks. On May 21 the troops of the provisional government poured through the gates of the city, and during the "bloody week" that followed they took the city street by street, demolishing the barricades and executing the Communards. The Communards retaliated by executing a number of hostages, including the archbishop of Paris. They also burned down the Tuileries Palace, the hall of justice, and the city hall. During this one week at least 25,000 Communards were killed.

The short life of the Paris Commune marked the climax of a tumultuous period of European history. Between 1815 and 1871 Europe witnessed numerous movements for reform, periodic uprisings, and several revolutions. The people who participated in these momentous developments were inspired in large part by **ideologies,** theories of society and

EUGÈNE DELACROIX, *LIBERTY LEADING THE PEOPLE* (1830)

The romantic representation of Liberty carrying the French tricolor during the Paris revolution of 1830 conveys the ideological inspiration and the violence of that armed uprising.

Source: Eugene Delacroix (1798–1860) "July 28th, 1830; Liberty Guides the People," oil on canvas, 260 × 325 cm. Louvre, Dept. des Peintures, Paris, France. © Photograph by Erich Lessing/Art Resource, NY

government that lay at the basis of political programs. The ideologies that developed during this period—liberalism, conservatism, socialism, and nationalism—endowed the West with a distinctive political culture. This chapter will address the following question: How did these four ideologies affect the political and social history of the West from 1815 until 1871?

NEW IDEOLOGIES IN THE EARLY NINETEENTH CENTURY

■ What were the main features of the ideologies that inspired people to political action during the period from 1815 to 1871?

The transformations of the West discussed in the last two chapters, the French Revolution and the Industrial Revolution, influenced the formation of the four new ideologies of the early nineteenth century.

Liberalism: The Protection of Individual Freedom

Liberalism is anchored in the belief that the main function of government is to promote political, social, and economic freedom. The primary objective of nineteenth-century liberals was to establish and protect individual rights, such as the freedom of the press, freedom of religion, and freedom from arbitrary arrest and imprisonment. Liberals sought to guarantee these rights in written constitutions. Opposed to aristocratic privilege, they supported the principle of equality before the law. They also tended to be anticlerical, a position that led to frequent tension between them and the Roman Catholic Church. As defenders of individual freedom, they often campaigned to end slavery and serfdom.

The second objective of liberals was the extension of the franchise (the right to vote) to all property owners, especially the middle class. Liberals were usually opposed to giving the vote to the working class on the grounds that poor people, with little property of their own, could not be trusted to elect representatives who would protect property rights. Liberals also were opposed to giving the vote or any other form of political power to women. They believed that the proper arena for female activity was the home, where women occupied their natural domain. Liberals thus subscribed to the theory of separate spheres, which held that women were different in nature from men and that only male property holders should be allowed to participate in public affairs.

The third objective of liberals was to promote free trade with other nations and to resist government regulation of the domestic economy. This economic dimension of liberal ideology is usually referred to as *laissez-faire,* which means "let (people) do (as they choose)." Advocates of *laissez-faire* held that the government should intervene in the economy only to maintain public order and protect property rights. As merchants and manufacturers, liberals favored a policy of *laissez-faire* because it offered them the freedom to pursue their own self-interest without governmental interference and thereby realize greater profits.

One of the most influential proponents of liberal economic theory was David Ricardo (1772–1823), a British economist and stockbroker who argued that government efforts to regulate wages and prices would slow economic growth. In *Principles of Political Economy and Taxation* (1819), Ricardo argued that if wages were left to the law of supply and demand, they would fall to near subsistence levels, leading workers to limit the size of their families. Lower wages and fewer consumers would in turn keep prices low. Industrialists found Ricardo's laissez-faire theory appealing, but it was harder to convince workers that this "iron law of wages" would benefit them.

Liberalism found its greatest strength among the urban middle class. These people formed the group that felt most aggrieved by their exclusion from political life during the eighteenth and early nineteenth centuries and most eager to have government protect their property.

Conservatism: Preserving the Established Order

In the early nineteenth century the ideals of the Enlightenment and the radical changes ushered in by the French Revolution led to the formulation of a new ideology of **conservatism,** a set of ideas intended to prevent a recurrence of the revolutionary changes of the 1790s. The main goal of conservatives after 1815 was to preserve the monarchies and aristocracies of Europe against liberal movements.

The founder of modern conservative ideology was the Irish-born parliamentary orator Edmund Burke (1729–1797). In *Reflections on the Revolution in France* (1790), Burke insisted that rights did not derive from human nature, as

Enlightenment thinkers insisted, but were privileges that had been passed down through the ages and could be preserved only by a hereditary monarchy. Burke also contended that equality, so loudly proclaimed at the time of the French Revolution, was a dangerous myth that would undermine the social order. For Burke the social order was a partnership between the living, the dead, and those who had yet to be born. By introducing revolutionary change, the French Revolution had broken that partnership.

Early nineteenth-century conservatives justified the institution of monarchy on the basis of religion as well as history. The French writer Louis de Bonald (1754–1840) argued that Christian monarchies were the final creation in the development of both religious and political society. Only monarchies of this sort could preserve public order and prevent society from degenerating into the savagery witnessed during the French Revolution. De Bonald and his fellow French writer, Joseph de Maistre (1754–1821), rejected the entire concept of natural rights and reiterated the traditional doctrine of divine right, according to which kings received their power from God.

Socialism: The Demand for Equality

Socialism, the third new ideology of the early nineteenth century, arose in reaction against the development of industrial capitalism and the liberal ideas that justified it. Socialism calls for the ownership of the means of production (such as factories, machines, and railroads) by the community, with the purpose of reducing inequalities of income, wealth, opportunity, and economic power. In small communities, such ownership can be genuinely collective. In a large country, however, the only practical way to introduce socialism is to give the ownership of property to the state, which represents the people.

The main appeal of socialism was the prospect of remedying the deplorable social and economic effects of the Industrial Revolution. As we saw in Chapter 21, the short-term effects of industrialization included wretched working conditions, low wages, a regimentation of the labor force, and a declining standard of living. Socialists did not object to the mechanization of industry as such. Like liberals, they wanted society to be as productive as possible. They did, however, object to the system of industrial capitalism that accompanied industrialization and the liberal economic theory that justified it. (See *Different Voices* in this chapter.)

The earliest socialists, known as Utopian socialists, envisioned the creation of ideal communities in which perfect social harmony and cooperation would prevail. One of these Utopian socialists, the British industrialist and philanthropist Robert Owen (1771–1858), turned his mill in New Lanark, Scotland, into a model socialist community where he housed his workers and educated their children. In 1825 he established a similar community in New Harmony, Indiana. Utopian socialism was not particularly concerned with the granting of political rights to workers, nor did it encourage class consciousness or class tensions.

A second generation of socialists became more concerned with using the power of the state to improve their lot. The most influential of these socialists was the French democrat Louis Blanc (1811–1882), who proposed that the state guarantee workers' wages and employment in times of economic depression. He also wanted the state to support the creation of workshops where workers would sell the product of their labor directly without middlemen. The principle underlying Blanc's concept of the social order was "From each according to his abilities; to each according to his needs." Blanc's brand of socialism began a long tradition in which workers tried to improve their circumstances by influencing government. This initiative was closely related to the radical democratic goal of universal male suffrage, which became one of the main objectives of many socialists after 1840.

The German social philosopher Karl Marx (1818–1883) formulated the most radical form of nineteenth-century socialism. Marx was much more preoccupied than other socialists with the collective identity and political activities of the working class. Reading about working conditions

DIFFERENT VOICES LIBERALS AND SOCIALISTS VIEW THE MIDDLE CLASS

Nineteenth-century liberals, who stressed individual rights and free trade, extolled the virtues of the middle class, whom they regarded as the most progressive and productive members of society. Socialists, however, viewed the middle class or bourgeoisie as exploitative capitalists who oppressed the working class. In the first document, the liberal British economist and political philosopher James Mill (1773–1836), who supported the effort to give the middle class greater representation in the British Parliament, argues that the working class should follow the advice and example of the middle class. Karl Marx and Friedrich Engels were the leading philosophers of communism, the form of socialism that emphasized class warfare and called for a dictatorship of the proletariat. In the second document Marx and Engels condemn the middle class for their oppression and exploitation of the proletariat.

James Mill Praises the Wisdom and Leadership of the Middle Class

It is to be observed, that the class which is universally described, as both the most wise, and the most virtuous part of every community, the middle rank, are wholly included in that part of the community which is not the aristocratical. It is also not disputed, that in Great Britain the middle rank are numerous, and form a large proportion of the whole body of the people. Another proposition may be stated, with a perfect confidence of the concurrence of all those men who have attentively considered the formation of opinions in the great body of society, or, indeed, the principles of human nature in general. It is, that the opinions of that class of the people, who are

below the middle rank, are formed, and their minds are directed by that intelligent and virtuous rank, who come the most immediately in contact with them, who are in the constant habit of intimate communication with them, to whom they fly for advice and assistance in all their numerous difficulties, upon whom they feel an immediate and daily dependence, in health and in sickness, in infancy and in old age; to whom their children look up as models for their imitation, whose opinions they have daily repeated, and account it their honour to adopt. There can be no doubt whatever that the middle rank, which gives their most distinguished ornaments to science, to art, and to legislation itself, to every thing which exalts and refines human nature, is that part of the community of which, if the basis of representation were now so far extended, the opinion would ultimately decide. Of the people beneath them, a vast majority would be sure to be guided by their advice and example.

Source: From James Mill, *Essay on Government* (1820).

Karl Marx and Friedrich Engels Assail the Middle Class for their Exploitation of Workers

The modern bourgeois society that has sprouted from the ruins of feudal society has not done away with class antagonisms. It has but established new classes, new conditions of oppression, new forms of struggle in place of the old ones. Our epoch, the epoch of the bourgeoisie, possesses, however, this distinct feature: it has simplified class antagonisms. Society as a whole is more and more splitting up into two great hostile

in France during the early 1840s, he became convinced that workers in industrial society were the ultimate example of human alienation and degradation. Marx and his co-author Friedrich Engels began to think of workers as part of a capitalist system, in which they owned nothing but their labor, which they sold to capitalist producers for wages.

Marx and Engels worked these ideas into a broad account of historical change in which society moved inevitably and progressively from one stage to another. They referred to the process by which history advanced as the **dialectic.** Marx acquired the idea of the dialectic from the German philosopher Georg Wilhelm Friedrich Hegel (1770–1831), who

camps, into two great classes directly facing each other—bourgeoisie and proletariat....

The bourgeoisie, wherever it has got the upper hand, has put an end to all feudal, patriarchal, idyllic relations. It has pitilessly torn asunder the motley feudal ties that bound man to his "natural superiors," and has left remaining no other nexus between man and man than naked self-interest, than callous "cash payment." It has drowned the most heavenly ecstasies of religious fervor, of chivalrous enthusiasm, of philistine sentimentalism, in the icy water of egotistical calculation. It has resolved personal worth into exchange value, and in place of the numberless indefeasible chartered freedoms, has set up that single, unconscionable freedom—Free Trade. In one word, for exploitation, veiled by religious and political illusions, it has substituted naked, shameless, direct, brutal exploitation....

The bourgeoisie has through its exploitation of the world market given a cosmopolitan character to production and consumption in every country. To the great chagrin of Reactionists, it has drawn from under the feet of industry the national ground on which it stood. All old-established national industries have been destroyed or are daily being destroyed. They are dislodged by new industries, whose introduction becomes a life and death question for all civilized nations, by industries that no longer work up indigenous raw material, but raw material drawn from the remotest zones; industries whose products are consumed, not only at home, but in every quarter of the globe. In place of the old wants, satisfied by the production of the country, we find new

wants, requiring for their satisfaction the products of distant lands and climes. In place of the old local and national seclusion and self-sufficiency, we have intercourse in every direction, universal interdependence of nations. The bourgeoisie, by the rapid improvement of all instruments of production, by the immensely facilitated means of communication, draws all, even the most barbarian, nations into civilization. The cheap prices of commodities are the heavy artillery with which it batters down all Chinese walls, with which it forces the barbarians' intensely obstinate hatred of foreigners to capitulate. It compels all nations, on pain of extinction, to adopt the bourgeois mode of production; it compels them to introduce what it calls civilization into their midst, i.e., to become bourgeois themselves. In one word, it creates a world after its own image.

Source: From Karl Marx and Friedrich Engels, *The Communist Manifesto* (1848).

For Discussion

1. How do the authors of these two documents differ in their descriptions of the relationships between the middle class and the working class?

2. What is the basis of Mill's praise for the middle class and Marx and Engels' condemnation of it?

3. How might a liberal like Mill have responded to the publication of the *Communist Manifesto*? How might a conservative have responded?

---

believed that history advanced in stages as the result of the conflict between one idea and another. Marx disagreed with Hegel on the source of historical change, arguing that material or economic factors rather than ideas determined the course of history. Hence, Marx's socialist philosophy became known as **dialectical materialism.**

According to Marx and Engels, the first stage of the dialectic had taken place when the bourgeoisie, who received their income from capital, seized political power from the aristocracy, who received their income from land, during the English and French revolutions. Marx and Engels predicted that the next stage of the dialectic would be a conflict between the bourgeoisie and

KARL MARX

Karl Marx, the German social philosopher who developed the revolutionary socialist doctrine of communism.

the working class or **proletariat,** which received its income from wages. This conflict, according to Marx and Engels, would result in the triumph of the working class. Led by a committed band of revolutionaries, the proletariat would take control of the state, establish a dictatorship so that they could implement their program without opposition, and usher in a classless society.

Marx and Engels issued this call to action in *The Communist Manifesto* (1848), which ended with the famous words, "Working men of all countries unite!" Marx's brand of socialism, **communism,** takes its name from this book. Communism is a revolutionary ideology that advocates the overthrow of "bourgeois" or capitalist institutions and the transfer of political power to the proletariat. Communism differs from other forms of socialism in its call for

revolution, its emphasis on class conflict, and its insistence on complete economic equality. Communism belongs to a tradition that originated among members of the extreme wing of the democratic movement at the height of the French Revolution. One of those radicals, François-Noël Babeuf (1760–1797), demanded economic and political equality, called for the common ownership of land, and spoke in terms of class warfare. Marx's achievement was to place Babeuf's radical ideas in the framework of dialectical materialism in his monumental three-volume work, *Capital* (1867–1894).

Nationalism: The Unity of the People

Nationalism, the fourth new ideology of the early nineteenth century, also took shape during and after the French Revolution. A **nation** in the nineteenth-century sense of the word refers to a large community of people who believe that they have a common homeland and share a similar culture. The ideology of **nationalism** is the belief that the people who form this nation should have their own political institutions and that the interests of the nation should be defended and promoted at all costs.

The geographical boundaries of nations, however, do not often correspond to the geographical boundaries of states, which are administrative and legal units of political organization. For example, in the early nineteenth century Germans often referred to their nation as comprising all people who spoke German. At that time there were more than a dozen German states, including Prussia, Bavaria, and Baden, and there were also many German speakers living in non-German lands, such as Bohemia. A primary goal of nationalists is to create a **nation-state,** a single political entity that governs all the members of a particular nation. The doctrine that justifies this goal is **national self-determination,** the claim that any group that considers itself a nation has the right to be ruled only by members of its own nation and to have all the members of the nation included in this state.

The ideology of nationalism had roots in the French Revolution. Most of the revolutionary steps taken in France during the 1790s were undertaken in the name of a united French people—the French *nation.* Article 3 of the *Declaration of the Rights of Man and Citizen* (1789) declared that "the principle of all authority rests essentially in the nation." The French Republic was constructed as the embodiment of the French nation. It gave an administrative unity to the French people and encouraged them to think of themselves as sharing a common cultural bond. Instead of a collection of regions, France had become *la patrie,* or the people's native land.

Nationalists emphasized the antiquity of nations, arguing that there had always been a distinct German, French, English, Swiss, or Italian people living in their respective homelands. This claim involved a certain amount of fiction, because in the past the people living in those lands possessed little cultural or linguistic unity. There was little uniformity, for example, in the languages spoken by people whom nineteenth-century nationalists identified as German, French, or Italian. Until the eighteenth century most educated Germans wrote in French, not German. Only a small percentage of Italians spoke Italian (the language spoken in Tuscany), and the main language of many Italian nationalists of the nineteenth century was French. Even after nation-states were formed, a large measure of linguistic, religious, and ethnic diversity persisted within those states, making true cultural unity impossible. The nation is, therefore, something of a myth—an imagined community rather than an objective reality.

The ideal of the nation-state has proved almost impossible to realize. The boundaries of nations and states have never fully coincided. Patterns of human settlement are too fluid to prevent some members of a particular cultural group from living as a minority in a neighboring state. Some Poles, for example, have always lived in Germany, Spaniards in Portugal, and Italians in Switzerland. France at the time of the French Revolution probably came closest to realizing the ideal of a nation-state, claiming jurisdiction over most French people. Nevertheless, different cultural identities, such as those of the Basques in southwest France and the Flemish in the far northeast, both of whom spoke their own language, prevented the emergence of a powerful sense of national identity in all parts of France until the late nineteenth or early twentieth century.

In Britain the creation of a nation-state was a complicated process. **National consciousness,** which is a people's belief that they belong to a nation, developed earlier in England than in any other country in Europe. In the sixteenth century almost all English people spoke the same language, and they were also subject to the same common law. In 1536, however, the principality of Wales was united to the kingdom of England, thereby including two nations, the English and the Welsh, in the same state. In 1707 England and Scotland were united in a new state, the United Kingdom of Great Britain, and in 1801 Ireland was brought into the United Kingdom as well. Thus, the United Kingdom in the nineteenth century included four nations: the English, the Welsh, the Scots, and the Irish. In this multinational state, the task of building a British nation, as opposed to an English or a Scottish nation, has taken time. To this day, Britons are more accustomed to think of themselves as English, Welsh, or Scottish than as British.

Other peoples faced even more daunting obstacles in constructing nation-states. Many nations were subsumed within large empires, such as Hungarians and Croatians in the Austrian Empire and Greeks and Serbs in the Ottoman Empire. In those empires, nationalist movements often took the form of separatist revolts or wars of independence, in which a nationalist group attempted to break off and form a nation-state of its own. A very different situation prevailed in Germany and Italy, where people who shared some linguistic and cultural traditions lived under the control of many different states. In these cases, nationalist movements sought to unite the smaller states into a larger nation-state.

One of the great paradoxes of nationalism is that the acquisition of colonies overseas often strengthened nationalist sentiment at home. The military conquest of these lands became a source of pride for the people in the metropolis, and also gave them a sense of cultural superiority. The main source of British national pride was the rapid spread of British control over one-quarter of the world's surface during the eighteenth and nineteenth centuries. Nationalism could also promote the supremacy of one's own nation over others. The French revolutionaries who conquered a large part of the European continent in the early nineteenth century justified their expansion on the grounds that they were superior to the rest of the human race. In 1848 a fervent German nationalist declared his support for "the preponderance of the German race over most Slav races." The Italian national leader Giuseppe Mazzini (1805–1872) preferred to be called a patriot rather than a nationalist on the grounds that nationalists were imperialists who sought to encroach on the rights of other peoples.

Nationalism was often linked to liberalism during the early nineteenth century, when both movements supported revolutionary programs to realize the goal of national self-determination. Liberals believed that representative government and a limited expansion of the franchise would provide a firm foundation for the establishment of the nation-state. The two ideologies, however, differed in emphasis. Liberalism stressed individual freedom, whereas nationalism was more concerned with political unity. At times those different ideals came into conflict with each other. The liberal doctrine of free trade, for example, ran into conflict with the doctrine of economic nationalism, which encouraged the protection of national industries.

Nationalism was just as capable of supporting conservatism as liberalism in the early nineteenth century. Because nationalists viewed the nation as having deep roots in the distant past, some of them glorified the monarchical and hierarchical political arrangements that prevailed in the Middle Ages. In 1848 conservative Prussian landlords rallied around the cause of "God, King, and Fatherland." Later in the nineteenth century, nationalism became identified almost exclusively with conservatism when the lower middle classes began to prefer the achievement of national glory, either in warfare or in imperialistic pursuits, to the establishment of individual freedom.

Culture and Ideology

The four new ideologies of the early nineteenth century were influenced by two powerful cultural traditions: scientific rationalism and romanticism. These two traditions represented sharply divergent sides of modern Western culture.

SCIENTIFIC RATIONALISM Scientific rationalism originated in the Scientific Revolution and reached its full flowering in the Enlightenment. This tradition has provided a major source of Western identity ever since the late eighteenth century. It stresses the powers of human reason and considers science superior to all other forms of knowledge. Scientific rationalism is essentially a secular tradition, in that it does not rely on theology or Christian revelation for its legitimacy. The effort to construct a science of human nature, which was central to Enlightenment thought, belongs to this tradition, while the Industrial Revolution, which involved the application of scientific knowledge to production, was one of its products.

During the nineteenth century, scientific rationalism continued to influence Western thought and action. As scientific knowledge expanded, and as more people received a scientific education, the values of science and reason were proclaimed more boldly. Scientific knowledge and an emphasis on the importance of empirical data (that which can be tested) became essential components of much social thought. The clearest statement that science was the highest form of knowledge and would lead inevitably to human progress was the secular philosophy of **positivism.**

The French philosopher Auguste Comte (1798–1857) set forth the main elements of positivism. Like many thinkers in the Enlightenment tradition, Comte argued that human society passed through a succession of historical stages, each leading to a higher level. It had already passed through two stages, the theological and the metaphysical, and it was now in the third, the positive or scientific stage. The word *positive* in this context means that which has substance or concrete reality, as opposed to that which is abstract or speculative. Comte predicted that in the final positive stage of history the accumulation of factual or scientific knowledge would enable thinkers, whom we now call sociologists, to discover the laws of human behavior and thus make possible the improvement of society. This prediction of human progress, and Comte's celebration of the liberation of knowledge from its theological shackles, had particular appeal to liberals, especially those who harbored hostility to the Roman Catholic Church.

The values of science and the belief in its inevitable advance also influenced the social thought of Karl Marx. Friedrich Engels called Marx's ideology of communism scientific socialism, in that it too offers a vision of history determined solely by positive, in this case material or economic, developments. Marxism rejects the metaphysical, idealistic world of Hegel and the theology of all Christian religion and thus fits into the same scientific tradition to which positivism and earlier Enlightenment thought belongs.

ROMANTICISM The cultural tradition that posed the greatest challenge to scientific rationalism was **romanticism**. This tradition originated as an artistic and literary movement in the late eighteenth century, but it soon developed into a more general worldview. The artists and writers who identified themselves as romantics recognized the limits of human reason in comprehending reality. Unlike scientific rationalists, they used intuition and imagination to penetrate deeper levels of being and to comprehend the entire cosmos. Romantic art, music, and literature therefore appealed to the passions rather than the intellect.

Romantics did not think of reality as being simply material, as did the positivists. For them it was also spiritual and emotional, and their purpose as writers and artists was to communicate that nonempirical dimension of reality to their audiences. Romantics also had a different view of the relationship between human beings and nature. Instead of standing outside nature and viewing it objectively, in the manner of a scientist analyzing data derived from experiments, they considered themselves part of nature and emphasized its beauty and power.

As an art form, romanticism was a protest against classicism and, in particular, the classicism that prevailed in the late eighteenth century. As we discussed in Chapter 19, classicism reflects a worldview in which the principles of orderliness and rationality prevail. Classicism is

CASPAR DAVID FRIEDRICH, *THE WANDERER ABOVE THE SEA OF FOG* (1818)
This early nineteenth-century painting of a man observing a landscape covered by fog conveys the mystery and majesty of nature, which was a main theme of romantic art. It is unclear, however, whether the man, whose back is turned to the viewer, was awestruck by what he observed or was contemplating the difficult task of achieving human mastery over nature.

a disciplined style that demands adherence to formal rules that govern the structure and the content of literature, art, architecture, and music. By contrast, romanticism allows the artist much greater freedom. In literature the romantic protest against classicism led to the introduction of a new poetic style involving the use of imagery, symbols, and myth. One example of this style is "Rime of the Ancient Mariner" (1798) by the English poet Samuel Taylor Coleridge (1772–1834). The poem uses the sun and moon as powerful symbols in describing a nightmarish sea voyage.

Many romantic works of literature, such as the novels of the Scottish author Sir Walter Scott (1771–1832), were set in the Middle Ages, which they saw not as a dark age of superstition but as an era that fostered spiritual and artistic pursuits. To emphasize the limits of scientific rationalism, other romantics explored the exotic, the weird, the mysterious, and even the satanic elements in human nature. Mary Shelley's introspective novel, *Frankenstein* (1818), an early example of science fiction, incorporated many of these themes. The novel, which tells the story of the creation of a large, ugly monster by the idealistic Swiss scientist Victor Frankenstein, reveals the preoccupation of romantic literature with the exotic and the mysterious. Frankenstein's rejection of the monster leads this freak of nature to kill the scientist's brother, his friend, his wife, and, ultimately, Frankenstein himself. Filled with self-loathing, this creature of modern science sets off to throw himself on his own funeral pyre.

Within the visual arts, romanticism also marked a rebellion against the classicism that had dominated eighteenth-century culture. Classicism emphasized formality and symmetry in art, and it celebrated the culture of an ideal Greek and Roman past. By contrast, romantic painters depicted landscapes that evoked a mood and an emotion rather than an objective pictorial account of the surroundings. Romantic paintings sought to evoke feeling rather than to help the viewer achieve intellectual comprehension. Some of their works conveyed the power of nature while others depicted its majesty and grandeur.

Romantic music, which also appealed to the emotions, marked a similar but more gradual departure from formal classicism. The inspirational music of Ludwig van Beethoven (1770–1827), the son of a German court musician from Bonn, marked the transition from classical to romantic forms. Beethoven's early work conformed to the conventions of classical music, but some of his later compositions, which defied traditional classical harmonies, were intended to evoke an emotional response. His famous "Ode to Joy" in his ninth and final symphony remains unequaled in its ability to rouse the passions. Another early romantic composer, Franz Schubert (1797–1828), who was born in Vienna, blended classical forms with romantic themes by incorporating Hungarian and gypsy folk music into his compositions. The emotionally powerful operas of the German composer Richard Wagner (1813–1883), many of which were set in the mythical German past, marked the height of the romantic movement in music. That style attained its greatest popularity during the second half of the nineteenth century with the lyrical symphonies and concertos of Johannes Brahms (1833–1897) in Germany and the symphonies, ballets, and operas of Peter Tchaikovsky (1840–1893) in Russia.

Romanticism, like the rational and scientific culture it rejected, had powerful political implications, leaving its mark on the ideologies of the modern world. In the early nineteenth century, romanticism appealed to many liberals because it involved a protest against the established order and emphasized the freedom of the individual. The French romantic author Victor Hugo (1802–1885), whose epic novels *The Hunchback of Notre Dame* (1831) and *Les Misérables* (1862) depicted human suffering with great compassion, identified romanticism as "liberalism in literature." For Hugo a relationship existed between liberty in art and liberty in society. Romanticism could, however, support conservatism by idealizing the traditional social and political order of the Middle Ages and the central importance of religion in society.

Romanticism has a closer association with nationalism than with any other ideology. In the most general sense romanticism invested the idea of "the nation" with mystical qualities, thus inspiring devotion to it. Romantics also had an obsessive interest in the cultural, literary, and historical roots of national identity. The German philosopher and literary critic Johann Gottfried von Herder (1744–1803), for example, promoted the study of German language, literature, and history with the explicit purpose of giving the German people a sense of national unity.

In other parts of Europe, especially in Poland and the Balkans, romantic writers and artists gave nationalists the tools necessary to construct a common culture and history of their nations. The Polish romantic composer Frédéric Chopin (1810–1849), who emigrated to Paris in 1831, inspired Polish nationalists by drawing on native Polish dances in his works for the piano. At the same time the romantic poet Adam Mickiewicz (1798–1855), another Polish exile in Paris, wrote *The Books of the Polish Nation* (1832), exalting his country as the embodiment of freedom and predicting that by its long suffering it would eventually liberate the human race.

IDEOLOGICAL ENCOUNTERS IN EUROPE, 1815–1848

■ How did the encounters among the people who espoused these ideologies shape the political history of Europe between 1815 and 1848?

The four new ideologies of the nineteenth century—liberalism, conservatism, socialism, and nationalism—interacted in a variety of ways, sometimes reinforcing each other and at other times leading to direct and violent political conflict. During the years between 1815 and 1831 the main ideological encounters occurred between liberalism, sometimes infused with nationalism, and conservatism. In 1815, at the time of the Congress of Vienna, it appeared that conservatism would carry the day. The determination of the major European powers to suppress any signs of revolutionary activity made the future of liberalism and nationalism appear bleak. The power of the new ideologies, however, could not be contained. Liberal and nationalist revolts took place in three distinct periods: the early 1820s, 1830, and 1848. During the latter two periods the demands of workers, sometimes expressed in socialist terms, added to the ideological mixture. In all these encounters conservatives had their say, and in most cases, they emerged victorious.

Liberal and Nationalist Revolts, 1820–1825

Between 1820 and 1825 a sequence of revolts in Europe revealed the explosive potential of liberalism and nationalism and the determination of conservatives to crush those ideologies. These revolts also reflected the strength of movements for national self-determination. The three most significant revolts took place in Spain, Greece, and Russia.

THE LIBERAL REVOLTS OF 1820 IN SPAIN AND PORTUGAL   The earliest clash between liberalism and conservatism occurred in Spain, where liberals ran into determined opposition from their king, Ferdinand VII (r. 1808–1833). Ferdinand had been restored to power in 1814 after his forced abdication in 1808. In 1812, during the rule of Joseph Bonaparte, the Spanish *Cortes*—the representative assembly in that kingdom—had approved a liberal constitution. This constitution provided a foundation for a limited monarchy and the protection of Spanish civil liberties. In keeping with the ideas of the French Revolution, it also declared that the Spanish nation, not the king, possessed sovereignty. The tension began when King Ferdinand declared that he would not recognize this constitution. Even worse for disheartened liberals, Ferdinand decided to reestablish the Spanish Inquisition, invited exiled Jesuits to return, and refused to summon the *Cortes*. In 1820, when the Spanish

Empire in the New World had already begun to collapse (see Chapter 18), liberals in Madrid, in alliance with some military officers, seized power.

This liberal revolt proved to be a test for the **Concert of Europe,** the mechanism established at the Congress of Vienna to preserve the balance of power in Europe and prevent further revolution wherever it might arise. Klemens von Metternich, the Austrian foreign minister who had been responsible for proposing this cooperation of the major powers, urged intervention in Spain, and although the British refused because they wanted to protect their trading interests with the Spanish colonies, Austria, Prussia, and Russia agreed. These conservative powers restored Ferdinand to the throne, and again he renounced the liberal constitution of 1812. The liberals not only lost this struggle, but they also suffered bitter reprisals from the government, which tortured and executed their leaders. The situation became only marginally better in 1833, when Ferdinand died and the liberal ministers of his young daughter, Queen Isabella II (r. 1833–1868), drew up another constitution. Her reign was marked by civil war, instability, and factional strife in which liberals made few substantial gains.

Shortly after the Spanish revolt of 1820, a similar rebellion based on liberal ideas took place in Portugal. The royal family had fled to Brazil during the Napoleonic wars, leaving Portugal to be governed by a regent. A group of army officers removed the regent and installed a liberal government, which proceeded to suppress the Portuguese Inquisition, confiscate church lands, and invite King John (r. 1816–1826) to return to his native land as a constitutional monarch. After the king returned in 1822, his enthusiasm for liberal government waned. His granddaughter, Maria II (r. 1826–1853), kept the liberal cause alive, relying on support from Portugal's traditional ally, Britain, but she struggled against the forces of conservatism and had only limited success.

THE NATIONALIST REVOLT OF 1821 IN GREECE   A revolt in Greece in 1821, inspired more by nationalism than liberalism, achieved greater

success than did the rebellions of 1820 in Spain and Portugal. It succeeded because other members of the Concert of Europe, not just Britain, lent their support to the revolt. Greece had long been a province in the sprawling Ottoman Empire, but a nationalist movement, organized by Prince Alexander Ypsilantis (1792–1828), created a distinct Greek national identity and inspired the demand for a separate Greek state. In 1821 a series of revolts against Ottoman rule took place on the mainland of Greece and on some of the surrounding islands. These rebellions received widespread support in Europe from scholars who considered Greece the cradle of Western civilization and from religiously inspired individuals who saw this as a struggle of Christianity against Islam. Hundreds of European volunteers joined the Greek rebel forces. Thus, the insurrection became not only a liberal and national revolt, but also a broad cultural encounter between East and West. The English romantic poets George Lord Byron (1788–1824) and Percy Shelley (1792–1822) became active and passionate advocates for Greek independence, while the romantic painter Eugène Delacroix (1798–1863) depicted the horror of the Turkish massacre of the entire population at the island of Chios in 1822. The link between nationalism and romanticism could not have been more explicit.

The Greek revolt placed the powers allied in the Concert of Europe in a quandary. On the one hand, they were committed to intervene on behalf of the established order to crush any nationalist or liberal revolts, and they condemned the insurrection on those grounds when it first erupted. On the other hand, they were Western rulers who identified the Ottoman Turks with everything that was alien to Christian civilization. Moreover, Russia wanted to use this opportunity to dismember its ancient enemy, the Ottoman Empire. The European powers eventually took the side of the Greek rebels. In 1827 Britain, France, and Russia threatened the Turks with military intervention if they did not agree to an armistice and grant the Greeks their independence. When the Turks refused, the combined naval forces of those three

EUGÈNE DELACROIX, *THE MASSACRE AT CHIOS* (1824)

In 1821 the Greeks on the Aegean Islands rebelled against their Turkish rulers, and in April 1822 Turkish reprisals reached their peak in the massacre of the inhabitants of Chios. Romantic paintings were intended to evoke feelings, in this case horror, at the genocide perpetrated by the Turks against the Greek rebels. The painting reveals the close association of romantic art with the causes of liberalism and nationalism.

Nicholas I (r. 1825–1855) on the first day of his reign. The officers, together with other members of the nobility, had been meeting for almost a decade in political clubs, such as the Society of True and Faithful Sons of the Fatherland in St. Petersburg. In these societies they articulated their goals of establishing a constitutional monarchy and emancipating the serfs.

The rebels, known as **Decembrists** for the month in which their rebellion took place, could not agree on the precise form of government they wished to institute. That disagreement, coupled with a reluctance to take action at the critical moment, led to their failure. When Tsar Alexander I died suddenly in 1825, the Decembrists hoped to persuade his brother Constantine to assume the throne and establish a representative form of government. Their hopes were dashed when Constantine refused to tamper with the succession and accepted the reign of his brother Nicholas. The reactionary Nicholas had no difficulty suppressing the revolt, executing its leaders, and leaving Russian liberals to struggle against police repression for the remainder of the nineteenth century.

countries destroyed the fleet of the Turks' main ally, Egypt, at Navarino off the Greek coast. This naval action turned the tide in favor of the Greeks, who in 1833 finally won their independence and placed a Bavarian prince, Otto I (r. 1833–1862), on the throne. Thus, the Greek war of independence effectively ended the Concert of Europe. Originally intended to crush nationalist and liberal revolts, the Concert in this case helped one succeed.

THE DECEMBRIST REVOLT OF 1825 IN RUSSIA The least successful of the early liberal revolts took place in Russia, where a number of army officers, influenced by liberal ideas while serving in western Europe during the Napoleonic wars, staged a rebellion against the government of Tsar

Liberal and Nationalist Revolts, 1830

A second cluster of early-nineteenth-century liberal and national revolts in 1830 achieved a greater measure of success than the revolts of the early 1820s. These revolutions took place in France, the kingdom of the Netherlands, and the kingdom of Poland.

THE FRENCH REVOLUTION: THE SUCCESS OF LIBERALISM The most striking triumph of liberalism in Europe during the early nineteenth century occurred in France, where a revolution took place 15 years after the final defeat of Napoleon at Waterloo. This liberal success did not come easily. During the first few years of the restored monarchy, conservatives had their way, as they did elsewhere in Europe. Louis XVIII had approved a Charter

CHRONOLOGY: LIBERAL AND NATIONALIST REVOLTS, 1820–1833

1820   Liberal revolt in Spain; liberal army officers seize power in Portugal
1821   Beginning of Greek revolt against the Ottoman Empire
1825   Decembrist revolt in Russia against Nicholas I
1829   Liberals gain majority in French Chamber of Deputies
1830   Revolution in Paris, Louis-Philippe I becomes king of France; Belgium becomes independent and adopts a liberal constitution; beginning of the Polish rebellion against Nicholas I of Russia
1833   Greece becomes independent; Otto I becomes king

of Liberties in 1814, but he was hardly receptive to any further liberal reforms. Between 1815 and 1828 ultraroyalists dominated French politics. These reactionaries sponsored a "white terror" (so called because they displayed the white flag of the Bourbon monarchy) against liberals and Protestants. Two men nicknamed Three Slices and Four Slices, indicating the number of pieces into which they butchered their Protestant enemies, were the main instigators of this terror.

In 1824, when the conservative Charles X (r. 1824–1830) ascended the throne and took steps to strengthen the Church and the nobility, there appeared to be little hope for liberalism. Nevertheless, liberal opposition to the monarchy gained support from merchants and manufacturers, as well as from soldiers who still kept the memory of Napoleon alive. Fears that Charles would claim absolute power and a serious economic crisis in 1829 helped liberals gain a majority in the Chamber of Deputies, the French legislature.

Charles then embarked upon a perilous course. In what became known as the July Ordinances he effectively undermined the principles of the 1814 Charter of Liberties. These ordinances dissolved the new Chamber of Deputies, ordered new elections under a highly restrictive franchise, and censored the press. The public reaction to this maneuver caught the king by surprise. Thousands of students and workers, liberals and republicans alike, poured onto the streets of Paris to demonstrate. Unable to restore order,

the king abdicated in favor of his grandson, but the liberals offered the crown instead to the Duke of Orléans, who was crowned as Louis-Philippe I (r. 1830–1848).

Louis-Philippe accepted a revised version of the Charter of 1814 and doubled the franchise, giving the vote to middle-class merchants and industrialists. The king catered to this bourgeois constituency by encouraging economic growth and restricting noble privilege. His reign, which is often referred to as the "bourgeois monarchy," also achieved a measure of secularization when the Chamber of Deputies declared that Roman Catholicism was no longer the state religion. In keeping with liberal ideals, however, he did nothing to encourage republicanism or radical democracy, much less socialism. Efforts to depict him as the heir to the French Revolution did not persuade the bulk of the population. When the government brought the ashes of Napoleon from St. Helena to Paris, thousands of French men and women turned out to pay homage to the former emperor. Much to his disappointment, Louis-Philippe gained little political benefit from the move. France had acquired a liberal monarchy, but it stood on a precarious foundation.

THE BELGIAN REVOLUTION: THE SUCCESS OF NATIONALISM The French Revolution of 1830 triggered the outbreak of a liberal and nationalist revolution in the neighboring country of Belgium. In 1815 the Congress of Vienna had united the Austrian Netherlands and the Dutch Republic in a new kingdom of the Netherlands. This union of the Low Countries did not work out; soon after the formation of the new kingdom, the Belgians began pressing for their independence as a nation. With a Dutchman, William I, as king and with the seat of government in Holland, the Dutch were the dominant partner in this union, a situation that caused considerable resentment in Belgium. Moreover, most Belgians were Catholics, whereas the majority of Dutch people were Protestants. With their own history and culture, Belgians thought of themselves as a separate nation. They also were more liberal than their Dutch neighbors, advocating free trade and the promotion of industry, while resenting the high tariffs imposed by the Dutch government.

The two main political parties in Belgium, the Liberals and the Clericals, joined forces to achieve national independence. When the news of the revolution in Paris reached Brussels, fighting broke out between workers and government troops. A Belgian national congress gathered to write a new constitution, and when the Dutch tried to thwart the rebellion by bombarding the Belgian city of Antwerp, Britain assembled a conference of European powers to devise a settlement. The powers agreed to recognize Belgium's independence, and they arranged for a German prince, Leopold of Saxe-Coburg, uncle of the future British Queen Victoria, to become king. The Dutch, however, refused to recognize the new government, and they renewed their military attacks on Belgium. Only in 1839 did all sides accept the new political arrangement.

THE POLISH REBELLION: THE FAILURE OF NATIONALISM
The French Revolution of 1830 triggered a second uprising, this one unsuccessful, in the kingdom of Poland (see **Map 22.1**). Poland had suffered many partitions at the hands of European powers during the eighteenth century, and in 1815 the Congress of Vienna had redefined its borders once again. The congress established a separate Polish kingdom, known as Congress Poland, with Warsaw as its capital and the Russian tsar, Alexander I (r. 1815–1825), as its king. The western part of Poland, the Duchy of Poznan, went to the kingdom of Prussia, while Cracow became a free city.

With a Russian king the independence of Poland was mere fiction, but Alexander had approved a liberal Polish constitution in 1815. He grew to regret this decision, and his rule as king of Poland gradually alienated Polish liberals within the national legislature, the *sejm*. The accession of Nicholas in 1825 aggravated those tensions. An uncompromising conservative, Nicholas accused the Polish opposition of complicity with the Russian Decembrist rebels. He brought them to the brink of rebellion when he made plans to send the Polish army, together with Russian troops, to suppress the French Revolution of 1830 and prevent the Belgians from receiving their independence.

The revolt began when army cadets in the officers' school in Warsaw attacked the residence of the Grand Duke Constantine, the governor-general of Poland, but it quickly gained the support of the entire army and the urban populace. The revolt appealed to both liberals and nationalists, and it drew inspiration from a group of romantic poets who celebrated the achievements of the Polish past. The rebels established a provisional Polish government at Warsaw, but the liberal members of the *sejm* were unwilling to enlist the peasantry in the conflict, fearful that they would rise against Polish landlords rather than the Russians. When the powers of western Europe refused to intervene on behalf of this liberal cause, Nicholas was able to crush the rebellion, abolish the *sejm*, and deprive the kingdom of Poland of its autonomous status. Nicholas visited a terrible revenge upon the leaders of the revolt, confiscated the lands of those who had emigrated, and shut down the University of Warsaw. His brutal repression set back the cause of liberalism and nationalism in Poland for another two generations.

Liberal Reform in Britain, 1815–1848
The challenges that liberals faced in Britain were somewhat different from those they confronted in most other European countries. Having maintained the status quo during the era of the French Revolution, the forces of British conservatism,

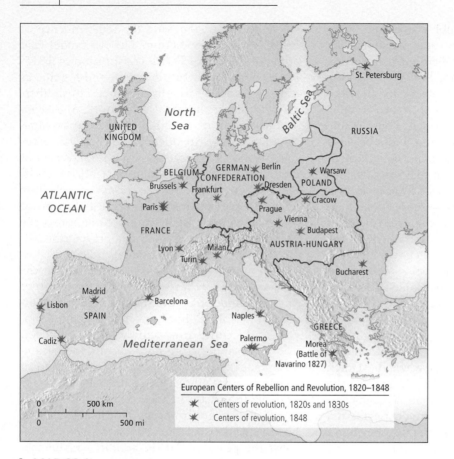

MAP 22.1

European Centers of Rebellion and Revolution, 1820–1848

All these political disturbances were inspired by ideology.

which bore the ideological stamp of Edmund Burke, remained formidable. At the same time, however, Britons already enjoyed many of the rights that liberals on the European continent demanded, such as freedom of the press and protection from arbitrary imprisonment. The power of the British monarchy was more limited than in almost any other European country. The ideology of liberalism, which had deep roots in British political and social philosophy, defined the political creed of many Whigs, who formed the main opposition to the ruling Conservative or Tory party after 1815.

In this relatively favorable political climate, British liberals pursued three major goals that amounted to a program for reform rather than

revolution. The first was the repeal of legislation that denied political power to Catholics and "nonconformist" Protestants who did not attend the services of the Anglican Church. Liberals were opposed on principle to religious discrimination, and many of them belonged to nonconformist congregations. The Tory prime minister, the Duke of Wellington, who had defeated Napoleon at Waterloo, eventually agreed to liberal demands. The Protestant nonconformists were emancipated in 1828 and the Catholics one year later.

The second liberal cause was the expansion of the franchise, which was realized when the Whigs, who came to power in 1830, passed the Great Reform Bill of 1832. The legislation expanded the franchise to include most of the urban middle class, created a number of new parliamentary boroughs (towns that elected representatives to sit in the House of Commons) in regions where industrial growth had led to an increase in population, and established a uniform standard for the right to vote throughout the country. In keeping with the principles of liberalism, however, the bill restricted the vote to property owners. It rejected the demands of radicals for universal male suffrage and denied all women the vote.

The third liberal cause was free trade. The target of this campaign was a series of protective tariffs on the import and export of hundreds of commodities, including raw materials used in production. The most hated protective tariff was on grain (known in Britain as corn), which kept the price of basic food commodities high to protect the interests of landlords and farmers. In 1837 a group of industrialists and radical reformers formed the Anti-Corn Law League with the purpose of bringing about the repeal of the Corn Law of 1815, which greatly restricted the importation of foreign grain into Britain. This campaign against protectionism did not succeed until 1845, when the Conservative prime minister, Sir Robert Peel, brought about repeal by securing the votes of some of his own party and combining them with those of the Whigs, all of whom favored free trade. Peel took this action only after the potato famine in Ireland, which was discussed in Chapter 21, had begun to cause widespread starvation.

Unlike the liberals, socialists and radical democrats achieved little success in Britain during the first half of the nineteenth century. In 1837 workers and middle-class radicals drew up a

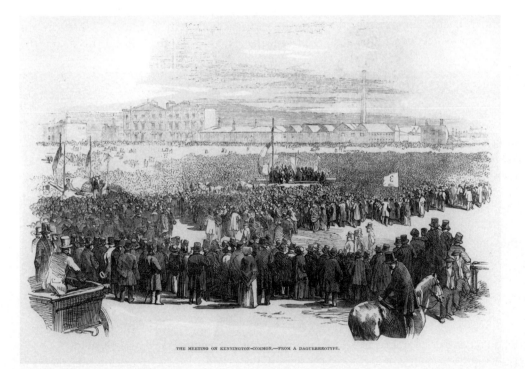

THE MEETING ON KENNINGTON-COMMON.—FROM A DAGUERREOTYPE.

THE LAST GREAT CHARTIST RALLY IN BRITAIN, APRIL 10, 1848

Government precautions, including the appointment of special constables to handle the crowd, and rain kept the number of demonstrators in London lower than anticipated. The government ordered the leader of the movement, Feargus O'Connor, to stop the planned march to Parliament.

People's Charter, demanding universal male suffrage, annual parliaments, voting by secret ballot, equal electoral districts, the elimination of property qualifications for Members of Parliament, and the payment of salaries to those same members. These **Chartists,** as they were known, gained widespread popular support when economic conditions deteriorated, but British workers showed little inclination to take to the streets. The government's reduction of indirect taxes during the 1840s, coupled with the effective use of the police force and the strict enforcement of the criminal law, also helped prevent Britain from experiencing revolution in 1848. The price of this failure was that further liberal reforms, such as the extension of the franchise to include workers, did not take place in Britain for another two decades.

The Revolutions of 1848

Unlike Britain, almost every country on the European continent experienced revolution in 1848. The revolutions took place during a period of widespread economic discontent. European countries had suffered bad harvests in 1845 and 1846 and an economic recession in 1847, leading to a decline in the standard of living for both industrial and agricultural workers. Discontent took the form of mass protests and demonstrations, which increased the likelihood of violent confrontation. The revolutions of 1848 were more widespread than the revolts of the 1820s and 1830, and more people participated. These revolutions also gave more attention to both nationalist and socialist issues.

THE FRENCH REVOLUTIONS OF 1848   The first of the revolutions of 1848 took place in France, where the liberal government of Louis-Philippe faced mounting criticism. Declining economic conditions led to a series of demonstrations in Paris for the right of workers to vote and receive state assistance for their trades. When troops from the Paris National Guard fired on the

CHRONOLOGY: THE REVOLUTIONS OF 1848

1848

February	Revolution in Paris
March	Insurrection in Berlin, peasant unrest in the countryside, formation of liberal governments in Prussia and other German states; revolutions in Milan and Venice; Ferdinand II issues a new constitution in Naples
April	Elections for a new National Assembly in France
May	Meeting of the Frankfurt Parliament; meeting of the Prussian Assembly
June	Suppression of working-class resistance in Paris; Pan-Slav Congress in Prague; suppression of the rebellion in Prague
October	Suppression of revolution in Vienna
December	Election of Louis-Napoleon as president of the Second French Republic; Frankfurt Parliament issues *Declaration of the Basic Rights of the German People;* Frederick William dissolves Prussian Assembly

1849

March	King Frederick William rejects the German crown offered by the Frankfurt Parliament
April	Frankfurt Parliament promulgates a new constitution; Hungarian Diet proclaims Magyar independence
May–June	Fall of the liberal ministries in German states
August	Venetian Republic surrenders to Austrian forces; suppression of the Hungarian movement for independence

demonstrators and killed 40 people, the barricades once again appeared in the streets and the rebels seized government buildings. France experienced its third revolution in 60 years. To save his regime, Louis-Philippe abdicated in favor of his grandson, but the revolutionaries abolished the monarchy and declared the Second French Republic.

The Chamber of Deputies selected a provisional government that included republicans, liberals, and radical democrats. It also included two socialists, Louis Blanc and a worker who preferred to be called by the single name of Albert. The French Revolution of 1848 offered the socialists their first opportunity to realize the goal of a democratic and socialist republic. Many of the 200 clubs formed in Paris at this time, some of which were exclusively female, were either republican or socialist in their orientation. The socialist agenda included not only universal male suffrage, which the government granted immediately, but also active support for unemployed workers. Blanc secured the establishment of national workshops to give the unemployed jobs on public projects. Ordinances reduced the length of the workday to ten hours in the city and twelve hours in rural areas.

These bold socialist initiatives did not last long. By the summer the euphoria of the revolution had dissipated and the aspirations of workers had been crushed. The elections held in April 1848 to constitute a new National Assembly and write a new constitution seated an overwhelming majority of conservative monarchists and only a small minority of republicans and socialists. Resentment of the provisional government's assistance to urban workers and anger at the levying of a surtax to pay for government programs revealed the lack of broad popular support for radical political programs. Tension between the new conservative assembly and the forces of the left mounted when the government closed the workshops and sent Parisian workers either into the army or exile in the provinces.

These newly adopted policies led to further working-class violence in Paris in June 1848. When General Louis Cavaignac, known as "the butcher," was called in to restore order, regular army troops killed at least 1,500 insurgents and sent another 4,000 into exile in French colonies. These confrontations appeared to Karl Marx to constitute class warfare, a prelude to the proletarian revolution he predicted for the future. Louis Blanc, who was implicated in these uprisings, fled to England, where Marx himself would soon arrive and spend the rest of his life.

The revolution ended with the election of Napoleon's nephew, Louis-Napoleon Bonaparte (1808–1873), as the president of the Second French Republic in December 1848. As president, Louis-Napoleon drew support from conservatives, liberals, and moderate republicans. He also benefited from the legend that his uncle had created and the nationalist sentiment it inspired. Because the first Napoleon had become emperor, even those who preferred an empire to a republic could vote for his nephew. The younger Napoleon followed in his uncle's footsteps, dissolving the National Assembly in December 1851 and proclaiming himself emperor of the French one year later. This step brought the Second Republic to an end and established the Second Empire. The new emperor called himself Napoleon III, in deference to the uncrowned Napoleon II, the son of Napoleon I who had died in 1823.

THE REVOLUTIONS OF 1848 IN GERMANY, AUSTRIA, HUNGARY, AND BOHEMIA   Before 1848, liberalism and nationalism had achieved little success in Germany. German university students, inspired by the slogan "Honor, Freedom, Fatherland," had staged a number of large rallies during the early years of the nineteenth century, but the forces of conservatism had kept them in check. The Carlsbad Decrees of 1819, intended to suppress university radicalism, inaugurated a period of severe repression throughout Germany. The only success achieved by German liberals and nationalists prior to 1848 was the establishment of the *Zollverein*, a customs union of the various German states, in 1834. Even that project, which promoted free trade within German lands, did not attract support from all liberals.

A major opportunity for the liberal cause in Germany came in 1848 in the immediate wake of the February Revolution in France. As in France, however, radical demands from democrats and socialists for universal suffrage, including equal rights for women, competed with the more moderate liberal agenda. German radicals also demanded government assistance for artisans and workers who had suffered economic hardship as a result of industrialization. In Berlin, the capital of Prussia, these discontents led radicals to barricade the streets. The protests escalated after troops fired into the crowd, killing some 250 people. The violence spread to the countryside, where peasants demanded that landlords renounce their privileges and grant them free use of their lands. In response to these pressures, King Frederick William IV summoned an assembly, elected by universal male suffrage, to write a new Prussian constitution. Other German states also yielded to liberal pressure, establishing liberal governments known as the "March ministries."

As these events were unfolding, the contagion of revolution spread to Austria, the other major German kingdom, which formed the nucleus of the sprawling Austrian Empire. News of the revolution in Paris led to demonstrations by students and workers in Vienna. An assortment of Austrian liberal aristocrats, middle-class professionals, and discontented workers demanded an end to the long rule of the conservative minister, Klemens von Metternich. In response to the demands of these groups, Emperor Ferdinand I (r. 1835–1848) summoned a constitutional assembly and installed a moderate government. A conservative Prussian observer feared that these concessions had broken "the most secure dam against the revolutionary tide."

The main difference between the revolutions of 1848 in Austria and the other German lands was that events in Vienna awakened demands of Hungarians and Czechs for national autonomy within the empire. In Hungary the nationalist leader Lajos Kossuth (1802–1894) pushed for a program of liberal reform and national autonomy. This initiative created further tensions between the Magyars and the various national minorities

within the kingdom of Hungary. Similar problems arose in Bohemia, where a revolution in Prague led to demands from the Czechs for autonomy within the Austrian Empire. In June 1848 the Czech rebels hosted a Pan-Slav Congress in Prague to advance a nationalist plan for achieving unity of all Slavic people. This idealistic proposal could not be realized, for there were many distinct Slavic nationalities, each of which had a desire to establish its autonomy. In addition, there was a large German-speaking population within Bohemia that identified with other German territories in the Confederation.

The most idealistic and ambitious undertaking of the revolution in central Europe was the meeting of the Frankfurt Parliament in May 1848. Some 800 middle-class liberals, most of whom were lawyers, officials, and university professors, came from all the German states to draft a constitution for a united Germany. The parliament produced powerful speeches in support of both liberal and nationalist ideals, and in December 1848 it promulgated a *Declaration of the Basic Rights of the German People*. This document recognized the equality of all German people before the law; freedom of speech, assembly, and religion; and the right to private property. (See *Justice in History* in this chapter.) Like so many liberal assemblies, however, the Frankfurt Parliament failed to address the needs of the workers and peasants. The delegates rejected universal male suffrage as a "dangerous experiment" and refused to provide protection for artisans who were being squeezed out of work by industrialization. For these reasons, the parliament failed to win broad popular support.

In April 1849 the Frankfurt Parliament drafted a new constitution for a united Germany, which would have a hereditary "emperor of the Germans" and two houses of parliament, one of which would be elected by universal male suffrage. Austria, however, voted against the new plan, and without Austrian support the new constitution had little hope of success. The final blow to German liberal hopes came when King Frederick William of Prussia refused the Frankfurt Parliament's offer of the German crown, which he referred to as coming from the gutter and "reek-

THE REVOLUTION OF 1848 IN GERMANY
The revolutionaries, positioned behind the barricades and displaying the first flag of a united Germany, are battling government troops at Alexanderplatz in Berlin on the night of March 18-19, 1848. Plans to unite Germany in 1848 failed, but this flag, consisting of equal widths of black, red, and gold, was officially adopted in 1919 and again in 1990, when East and West Germany were reunited.

ing of the stench of revolution." At that point the Frankfurt Parliament disbanded and the efforts of German liberals to unite their country and give it a new constitution came to an inglorious end.

By the middle of 1849, conservative forces had triumphed in the various German territories and the Austrian Empire. In Prussia the efforts of the newly elected assembly to restrict noble privilege triggered a reaction from the conservative nobles known as Junkers. Frederick William dismissed his liberal appointees, sent troops to Berlin, and disbanded the assembly. A similar fate befell the other German states, such as Saxony, Baden, and Hanover, all of which had installed liberal governments in the early months of the revolution. In Austria Prince Alfred Windischgrätz, who had crushed the Czech rebels in June, dispersed the rebels in Vienna in October. When Hungary proclaimed its independence

from the empire in April 1849, Austrian and Russian forces marched on the country and crushed the movement.

THE REVOLUTIONS OF 1848 IN ITALY The revolutions of 1848 also spread to Austrian possessions in the northern Italian territories of Lombardy and Venetia. In Milan, the main city in Lombardy, revolutionary developments followed the same pattern as those in Paris, Berlin, and Vienna. When the barricades went up, some of the Milanese insurgents used medieval pikes stolen from the opera house to fight off Austrian troops. Their success triggered rebellions in other towns in Lombardy, in Venice, and in the southern Kingdom of the Two Sicilies. In that kingdom the Spanish Bourbon king, Ferdinand II (r. 1830–1859), after suppressing a republican revolt in January, was forced to grant a liberal constitution. The spread

JUSTICE IN HISTORY

Prostitution, Corporal Punishment, and Liberalism in Germany

In March 1822 municipal authorities in the northern German city of Bremen arrested Gesche Rudolph, a poor, uneducated 25-year-old woman for engaging in prostitution without registering with the police. Ever since the days when troops from five different European states had occupied her neighborhood, Rudolph had been selling her sexual services as her only form of livelihood. After her arrest she was not given a formal trial, but was summarily expelled from the city and banned from ever returning. Unable to earn a living through prostitution in a village outside the city, where she resided with a brother who physically abused her, Rudolph returned to the city, where she was arrested once again for prostitution. This time she was sentenced to 50 strokes of the cane and six weeks in jail, after which she was once again expelled from the city. Returning again to Bremen, she was arrested in a drunken stupor in a whorehouse and subjected to a harsher sentence of three months' imprisonment and 150 strokes before another expulsion. This pattern of arrest, punishment, expulsion, and return occurred repeatedly during the next two decades, with the number of strokes rising to 275 and the period of imprisonment to six years. During a portion of her prison sentence she was given only bread and water for nourishment.

Rudolph's arrest in 1845 at the end of a six-year imprisonment and her subsequent expulsion and return to Bremen led to the appointment of a liberal lawyer, Georg Wilhelm Gröning, to represent her. After reviewing her case and calculating that she had been whipped a total of 893 times and imprisoned for a cumulative period of 18 years, Gröning appealed her sentence to the senate of Bremen on the grounds that her treatment was not only futile but immoral. His appeal addressed an issue that went far beyond this particular case or even the prosecution of the crime

of prostitution. Gröning's action raised the controversial issue of the legitimacy and value of corporal punishment, an issue that divided liberals and conservatives, who had different notions of justice.

Until the eighteenth century the penal systems of Europe had prescribed corporal punishments, administered publicly, for most crimes. These punishments ranged from whippings and placement in the stocks for minor offenses to mutilation, hanging, and decapitation for felonies. They were justified mainly on the grounds that they provided retribution for the crime and deterred the criminal and those who witnessed the punishment from committing further crimes. These two main functions of retribution and deterrence are the same functions that capital punishment allegedly serves today. Corporal punishments were also intended to humiliate the criminal by violating the integrity of the body and subjecting the prisoner to the mockery and sometimes the maltreatment of the crowd. The torture of suspects to obtain evidence also served some of these functions, although judicial torture took place during the trial, not as part of the sentence.

The entire system of corporal punishment and torture came under attack during the eighteenth century. Prussia abolished torture in 1754, and the Prussian General Law Code of 1794 eliminated many forms of corporal punishment. This code reflected the concern of Enlightenment thinkers that all such assaults on the body were inhumane and denied the moral dignity of the individual. Because most of the people who incurred corporal punishment were poor, the system also violated the liberal principle of equality before the law.

Despite these efforts at reform, the illegal administration of corporal punishment by public and private authorities continued in Prussia and the other German states. Conservatives,

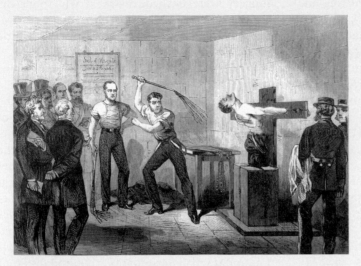

CORPORAL PUNISHMENT IN THE NINETEENTH CENTURY

A man receives the sixth of thirty lashes in 1872.

who had a different notion of justice from that of liberals, defended these sentences. For them any reference to natural rights and human dignity were "axioms derived from abstract philanthropic speculation." The president of the Prussian police, Julius Baron von Minutoli, expressing the conservative position on the issue, claimed that corporal punishment was more effective than imprisonment in preventing crime, as it alone could instill terror in the criminal.

It was apparent that in the case of Gesche Rudolph, 893 strokes had not instilled terror in her or deterred her from her crime. The Senate made the young woman Gröning's ward and suspended her sentence. Gröning arranged for Rudolph to live in the countryside under the strict supervision of a competent countryman. This compromise solution at least broke the cycle of expulsion, return, and punishment that had failed to reform her. We do not know whether she gave up her life of prostitution.

Soon after Gesche Rudolph became Gröning's ward, the liberal critics of corporal punishment in Germany celebrated a victory. King Frederick William IV of Prussia formally abolished the practice in May 1848. Shortly thereafter the Frankfurt Parliament included freedom from physical punishment by the state in its *Declaration of the Basic Rights of the German People.* Most German states and municipalities, including Bremen, wrote this right into law in 1849. The failure of the Frankfurt Parliament, however, and the more general failure of liberalism in Germany after 1849 led to a strong conservative campaign to reinstate corporal punishment in the 1850s. They succeeded only in maintaining corporal punishment within the family, on manorial estates, and in the prisons. Liberalism had not succeeded in completely establishing its standard of justice, but it did end exposure to public shame as a punishment for crime.

For Discussion

1. Why did liberals object to corporal punishment?

2. In addition to inflicting physical pain, corporal punishment produces social shame. What is the difference between social shame and legal guilt? In what ways does shame still play a role in punishments today?

Taking It Further

Evans, Richard. *Tales from the German Underworld: Crime and Punishment in the Nineteenth Century.* 1998. Provides a full account of the prosecution of Gesche Rudolph.

of these revolts inspired the hope of unifying all Italian people in one nation-state.

This Italian nationalist dream had originated among some liberals and republicans during the first half of the nineteenth century. Its most articulate proponent was Giuseppe Mazzini, a revolutionary from Genoa who envisioned the establishment of a united Italian republic through direct popular action. In 1831 Mazzini founded Italy's first organized political party, Young Italy, which pledged to realize national unification, democracy, and greater social equality. Mazzini combined a passionate commitment to the ideals of liberalism, republicanism, and nationalism.

Yet in 1848 an Italian prince, not Mazzini or Young Italy, took the first steps toward Italian unification. King Charles Albert ruled Piedmont-Sardinia, the most economically advanced of the Italian states. In 1848 his army, which included volunteers from various parts of Italy, marched into Lombardy and defeated Austrian forces. Instead of moving forward against Austria, however, Charles Albert decided to consolidate his gains, hoping to annex Lombardy to his own kingdom. This decision alienated republicans in Lombardy and in other parts of Italy. The rulers of the other Italian states feared that Charles Albert's main goal was to expand the limits of his own kingdom at their expense. By August 1848 the military tide had turned. Fresh Austrian troops defeated the Italian nationalists outside Milan. The people of that city turned against Charles Albert, forcing him to return to his own capital of Turin. The Italian revolutions of 1848 had suffered a complete defeat.

THE FAILURE OF THE REVOLUTIONS OF 1848 The revolutions of 1848 in France, Germany, the Austrian Empire, and Italy resulted in victory for conservatives and defeat for liberals, nationalists, and socialists. All the liberal constitutions passed during the early phase of the revolutions were eventually repealed or withdrawn. The high hopes of national unity in Germany, Italy, and Hungary were dashed. Workers who built the barricades in the hope of achieving improvements in their working conditions gained little from their efforts.

The revolutions failed because of divisions among the different groups that began the revolutions, particularly the split between the liberals who formulated the original goals of the revolution and the lower-class participants who took to the streets. Liberals used the support of the masses to bring down the governments they opposed, but their ideological opposition to broad-based political movements and their fear of further disorder sapped their revolutionary fervor. Divisions also emerged between liberals and nationalists, whose goals of national self-determination required different strategies from those of the liberals who supported individual freedom.

NATIONAL UNIFICATION IN EUROPE AND AMERICA, 1848–1871

■ How did liberal and conservative leaders use the ideology of nationalism as a tool to unite the people of various territories into nation-states between 1848 and 1871?

Prior to 1848 the forces of nationalism, especially when combined with those of liberalism, had little to show for their efforts. Besides the Greek rebellion of 1821, which succeeded largely because of international opposition to the Turks, the only successful nationalist revolution in Europe took place in Belgium. Both of these nationalist movements were secessionist in that they involved the separation of smaller states from larger empires. Efforts in 1848 to form nations by combining smaller states and territories, as in Italy and Germany, or by uniting all Slavic people, as proposed at the Pan-Slav Congress, had failed. Between 1848 and 1871, however, movements for national unification succeeded in Italy, Germany, and the United States, each in a different way. In the vast Austrian Empire a different type of unity was achieved, but it did little to promote the cause of nationalism.

Italian Unification: Building a Fragile Nation-State

The great project of Italian nationalists, the unification of Italy, faced formidable obstacles. Austrian military control over the northern territories, which had thwarted the nationalist movement of 1848, meant that national unification would not be achieved peacefully. The dramatic economic disparities between the prosperous north and the much poorer south posed a challenge to any plan for economic integration. A long tradition of local autonomy within the kingdoms, states, and principalities made submission to a strong central government unappealing. The unique status of the papacy, which controlled its own territory and which influenced the decisions of many other states, served as another challenge. Despite these obstacles, however, the dream of a resurgence of Italian power, reviving the achievements of ancient Rome, had great emotive appeal. Hatred of foreigners who controlled Italian territory, which dated back to the fifteenth century, gave further impetus to the nationalist movement.

The main question for Italian nationalism after the failure of 1848 was who could provide effective leadership of the movement. It stood to reason that Piedmont-Sardinia, the strongest and most prosperous Italian kingdom, would be central to that undertaking. Unfortunately its king, Victor Emmanuel II (r. 1849–1861), was more known for his hunting, his carousing, and his affair with a teenage mistress than his statesmanship. Victor Emmanuel did, however, appoint a nobleman with liberal leanings, Count Camillio di Cavour (1810–1861), as his prime minister. Cavour displayed many of the characteristics of

nineteenth-century liberalism. He favored a constitutional monarchy, the restriction of clerical privilege and influence, and the development of a capitalist and industrial economy. He was deeply committed to the unification of the Italian peninsula, but only under Piedmontese leadership, and preferably as a federation of states. In many ways, Cavour was the antithesis of the republican Mazzini, the central figure in Italian unification. Mazzini's idealism and romanticism led him to think of national unification as a moral force that would lead to the establishment of a democratic republic, which would then undertake an extensive program of social reform. Mazzini often wore black, claiming that he was in mourning for the unrealized cause of unification.

Mazzini's strategy for national unification involved a succession of uprisings and invasions. Cavour, however, adopted a diplomatic course of action intended to gain the military assistance of France against Austria. In 1859 French and Piedmontese forces defeated the Austrians at Magenta and Solferino and drove them out of Lombardy. One year later Napoleon III signed the Treaty of Turin with Cavour, allowing Piedmont-Sardinia to annex Tuscany, Parma, Modena, and the Romagna, while ceding to France the Italian territories of Savoy and Nice. This treaty resulted in the unification of all of northern and central Italy except Venetia in the northeast and the Papal States in the center of the peninsula (see **Map 22.2**).

The main focus of unification efforts now turned to the Kingdom of the Two Sicilies in the south. A rebellion against the Bourbon monarch Francis II, protesting new taxes and the high price of bread, had taken place there in 1860. At that point the third figure in the story of Italian unification, the militant republican adventurer Giuseppe Garibaldi (1807–1882), intervened with decisive force. Garibaldi, who was born in Nice and spoke French rather than Italian as his main language, was determined no less than Cavour and Mazzini to drive all foreigners out of Italy and achieve its unification. Originally a supporter of Mazzini's republican goals,

MAP 22.2

The Unification of Italy, 1859–1870

The main steps to unification took place in 1860, when Piedmont-Sardinia acquired Tuscany, Parma, Modena, and the Romagna and when Garibaldi seized control of the Kingdom of the Two Sicilies in the name of King Victor Emmanuel of Piedmont-Sardinia.

Garibaldi gave his support in the 1860s for Italian unification within the framework of a monarchy. A charismatic military leader, Garibaldi put together an army of volunteers, known as the Red Shirts for their colorful makeshift uniforms. In 1860 he landed in Sicily with an army of 1,000 men, took the main Sicilian city of Palermo, and established a dictatorship on behalf of King Victor Emmanuel. Garibaldi then landed on the mainland and took Naples. Shortly thereafter the people of Naples, Sicily, and most of the Papal States voted their support for union with

Piedmont-Sardinia. In March 1861 the king of Sardinia assumed the title of King Victor Emmanuel of Italy (r. 1861–1878). Complete unification was achieved when Austria ceded Venetia to Italy in 1866 and when French troops, which had been protecting a portion of the Papal States, withdrew from Rome in 1870.

The achievement of Italian unification did not fully realize the lofty nationalist goals of creating a culturally unified people or a powerful central state. Economic differences between northern and southern Italy became even greater after unification than before. The overwhelming majority of the people continued to speak their local dialects or even French rather than Italian. Traditions of local political autonomy and resentment against the concentration of wealth in the north retarded the development of loyalty to the new Italian state and inspired a series of bloody rebellions in the former Kingdom of the Two Sicilies during the 1870s and 1880s.

The widespread practice of banditry in the southern mainland aggravated this instability. Bandits were peasants who, in the hope of preserving a world that appeared to be vanishing, swept through towns, opened jails, stole from the wealthy, and sacked their houses. Closely related to banditry was the growth in Sicily of the **Mafia,** organizations of armed men who took control of local politics and the economy. The Mafia originated during the struggle for unification in the 1860s and strengthened their position in Sicily once the country had been unified. Their power, the prevalence of banditry, and the enduring strength of Italian loyalty to the local community all made it difficult for the new Italian state to flourish. The movement for national unification had driven the French and the Austrians out of the peninsula, but it had failed to create a model nation-state.

German Unification: Conservative Nation-Building

Like Italy, Germany experienced a successful movement for national unification after the

GIUSEPPE GARIBALDI

The uniform he is wearing was derived from his days as a guerilla fighting in the civil war in Uruguay (1842–1846). Garibaldi also spent two years in asylum in the United States.

disappointments of 1848. The German movement, like the Italian, benefited from the actions of crafty statesmen and the decisions made by other states. Unlike Italy, however, Germany achieved unification under the direction of highly conservative rather than liberal forces.

The kingdom of Prussia, with its largely German-speaking population, its wealth, and its strong army, assumed leadership of the nationalist movement. The key figure in this process was Count Otto von Bismarck (1815–1898), a lawyer and bureaucrat from an old Junker family whom King William I of Prussia appointed as his prime minister in 1862. By birth, training, and instinct,

Bismarck was an inflexible conservative, determined to preserve and strengthen the Prussian nobility and monarchy and make the Prussian state strong and powerful. To achieve his goals, Bismarck did not hesitate to make alliances with any political party, including the liberals. This subordination of political means to their ends, and Bismarck's willingness to use whatever tactics were necessary, regardless of any moral considerations, made him a proponent of *Realpolitik,* the adoption of political tactics solely on the basis of their realistic chances of success.

Bismarck pursued the goal of national unification through the exercise of raw military and political power. "The great questions of the day," he said in 1862, "will not be settled by speeches and majority decisions—that was the error of 1848 and 1849—but by iron and blood." Bismarck did not share the romantic devotion of other German nationalists to the Fatherland or their desire to have a state that embodied the spirit of the German people. His determination to achieve German national unification became synonymous with his goal of strengthening the Prussian state. This commitment to the supremacy of Prussia within a united Germany explained his steadfast exclusion of the other great German power, Austria, from his plans for national unification.

Bismarck achieved German unification mainly through Prussian success in three wars (see **Map 22.3**). The first, a war against Denmark in 1864, gave Prussia and Austria joint control of the Danish duchies of Schleswig and Holstein, which had large German-speaking populations. The second war, the Austro-Prussian War of 1866, resulted in the formation of a new union of 22 German states, the North German Confederation. This new political structure replaced the German Confederation, the loose association of 39 states, including Austria, established in 1815. The North German Confederation had a central legislature, the *Reichstag.* The king of Prussia became its president and Bismarck its chancellor. Most significantly, it did not include Austria.

The third war, which completed the unification of Germany, was the Franco-Prussian War of 1870–1871. This conflict began when Napoleon III, the French emperor, challenged Prussian efforts to place a member of the Prussian royal family on the vacant Spanish throne. Bismarck welcomed this opportunity to take on the French, who controlled German-speaking territories on their eastern frontier and who had cultivated alliances with the southern German states. Bismarck played his diplomatic cards brilliantly, guaranteeing that the Russians, Austrians, and British would not support France. He then used the army that he had modernized to invade France and seize the towns of Metz and Sedan. The capture of Napoleon III during this military offensive precipitated the end of France's Second Empire and the establishment of the Third French Republic in September 1870.

As a result of victory over France, Prussia annexed the predominantly German-speaking territories of Alsace and Lorraine. Much more important, the war led to the proclamation of the German Empire, with William I of Prussia as emperor. The empire, which included many German states, was formally a federation, just like the North German Confederation that preceded it. In practice, however, Prussia dominated this political structure, and the new German imperial government, just like that of Prussia, was highly autocratic. The government won the support of the middle class by adopting policies supporting free trade, but the ideologies that the imperial government promoted were those of conservatism and nationalism, which encouraged devotion to "God, King, and Fatherland."

Unification in the United States: Creating a Nation of Nations

At the same time that Italy and Germany were achieving national unification by piecing together disparate kingdoms, provinces, and territories, the United States of America engaged in a process of territorial expansion

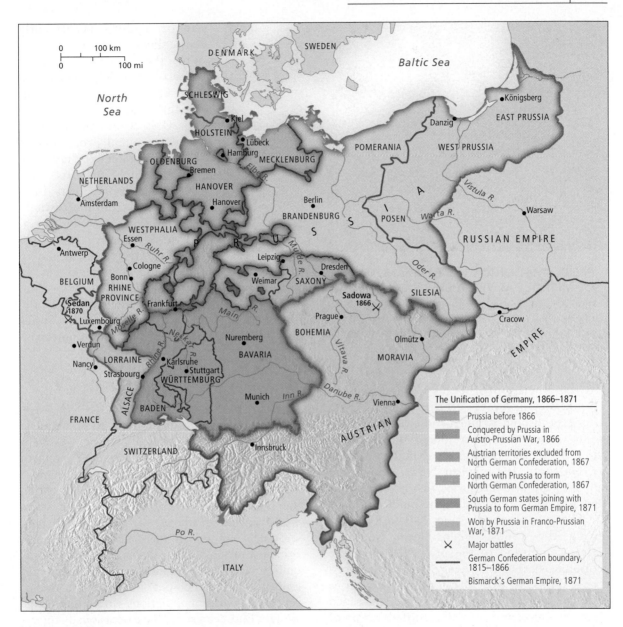

MAP 22.3

The Unification of Germany, 1866–1871

Prussia assumed leadership in uniting all German territories except Austria. Prussia was responsible for the formation of the North German Confederation in 1866 and the German Empire in 1871.

that brought lands acquired by purchase or conquest into the union as states. This process of unification, which proceeded in a piecemeal fashion, took much longer than the unifications of Italy and Germany in the 1860s. It included the annexation of Florida in 1819

PROCLAMATION OF THE GERMAN EMPIRE IN THE HALL OF MIRRORS AT VERSAILLES, JANUARY 21, 1871

King William I of Prussia, standing on the dais, is being crowned emperor of Germany. At the center of the picture, dressed in a white uniform jacket, is Otto von Bismarck, the person most responsible for the unification of all German territory in one empire.

cannot endure permanently half slave and half free." When the war ended and slavery was abolished, that union was not only preserved but strengthened. Amendments to the U.S. Constitution provided for equal protection of all citizens under the law. The South, which had its own regional economy, was integrated into the increasingly commercial and industrial North. Gradually, the people of the United States began to think of themselves as a united people, drawn from many different nations of the world. The United States became "a nation of nations."

and the admission of Texas, an independent republic for nine years, to the union in 1845. After establishing its independence from Mexico in 1846, California joined the union in 1850. This process of gradual unification did not end until 1912, when New Mexico and Arizona, the last territories in the contiguous 48 states, were admitted to the union.

The great test of American unity came during the 1860s, when eleven southern states, committed to the preservation of the economic system of slavery, and determined that it should be extended into new territories acquired by the federal government, seceded from the union and formed a confederation of their own. The issue of slavery had helped to polarize North and South, creating deep cultural and ideological divisions that made the goal of national unity appear remote. The constitutional issue underlying the Civil War was the preservation of the union. In a famous speech President Abraham Lincoln (1861–1865) declared that "a house divided against itself cannot stand...this government

Nationalism in Eastern Europe: Preserving Multinational Empires

The national unifications that took place in Germany and Italy formed part of a *western* European pattern in which the main units of political organization would become nation-states. Ethnic minorities would always live within the boundaries of these states, but the states would encourage the growth of national consciousness among all their citizens. In France, Britain, and Spain, all of which achieved national unification by the beginning of the nineteenth century, the state played a central role in this process. Minority populations within these large western European states have occasionally threatened to establish a separate political identity as nations, but with the one notable exception of Ireland, the southern portion of which became independent of Britain in the twentieth century, the large states of western Europe have maintained their unity and promoted nationalist sentiment to sustain it.

In *eastern* Europe a very different pattern prevailed, especially in the Austrian and Russian

Empires. Instead of becoming unified nation-states, these two empires remained large, multinational political formations, embracing many different nationalities. This pattern was most obvious in the large, sprawling Austrian Empire, which encompassed no fewer than 20 different ethnic groups, each of which thought of itself as a nation (see **Map 22.4**). The largest of these nationalities were the Germans in Austria and the Bohemians and the Magyars in Hungary, but the Czechs, Slovaks, Poles, Slovenes, Croats, Rumanians, Ukranians, and Italians (before 1866) all formed sizable minority populations. Map 22.4 charts this diversity. The various nationalities within the empire had little in common except loyalty to the Austrian emperor, who defended the Catholic faith and the privileges of the nobility. National unification of the empire presented a much more formidable task than those that confronted Cavour and Bismarck.

The ideology of nationalism threatened to tear apart this precariously unified empire. It awakened demands of Hungarians, Czechs, and others for national autonomy and also spawned a movement for the national unity of all Slavs. The emperor, Francis Joseph (r. 1848–1916), recognized the danger of nationalist ideology. He also feared that liberalism, which was often linked to nationalism, would at the same time

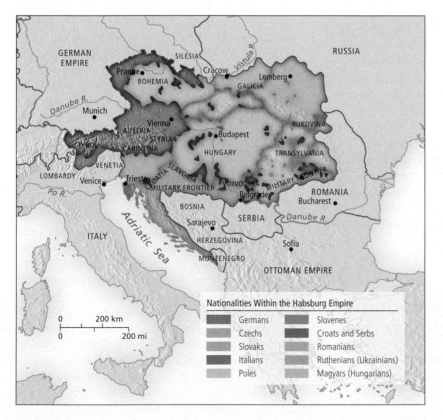

MAP 22.4

Nationalities within the Austrian Empire

The large number of different nationalities within the Austrian Empire made it impossible to accommodate the demands of all nationalities for their own state.

undermine his authority, which he had reasserted with a vengeance after the failure of the revolutions of 1848. He therefore repressed these nationalist aspirations at every turn. This policy had disastrous consequences for the future history of Europe, as Slavic nationalism and separatism have remained a source of political instability in southeastern Europe until the present day.

During this volatile period Francis Joseph made only one major concession to nationalist sentiment within his sprawling empire. In 1867 he agreed to create the Dual Monarchy of Austria-Hungary, in which he would be both king of Hungary and emperor of Austria. Each monarchy would have its own parliament and bureaucracy, although matters of foreign policy and finance would be handled in Vienna. This *Ausgleich* (settlement) represented a concession to the Magyars, the dominant ethnic group in Hungary and the second largest nationality in the empire. It gave very little, however, to all the other nationalities within the two kingdoms of Austria and Hungary. The *Ausgleich* officially recognized the equality of all nationalities within the Dual Monarchy and allowed schooling to be conducted in the local language, but it permitted only Germans in Austria and Magyars in Hungary to acquire their own political identity. Instead of a unified nation-state, the emperor now presided over two multinational monarchies.

INTERNATIONAL CONFLICT AND DOMESTIC POLITICS, 1853–1871

■ How did warfare contribute to political change in Russia and France during the second half of the nineteenth century?

Between 1853 and 1871 two wars between European powers, one on the boundaries of the West and the other at its center, had a significant effect on domestic politics. The Crimean War of 1853–1856 led to a reluctant adoption of liberal reforms in Russia, while the Franco-Prussian War of 1870–1871 set back the cause of both liberalism and socialism in France for the remainder of the nineteenth century.

Russia and the Crimean War, 1853–1856

The Crimean War was the direct result of Russian imperial expansion. It began when Russia occupied the principalities of Moldavia and Wallachia (present-day Romania) in the Ottoman Empire to gain access to the Straits of Constantinople. Russians justified this incursion by claiming they were protecting Orthodox Christians in the Balkans from their Muslim Turkish oppressors. They also claimed that they were promoting the national unity of all Slavic people under Russian auspices. This Russian version of Pan-Slavism was, in effect, an extreme form of Russian imperialism that opposed the claims of individual Slavic minorities to their own national identity.

When Russia occupied Moldavia and Wallachia, the Turks responded by declaring war on Russia. Britain joined the conflict on the side of the Turks, ostensibly to preserve the balance of power in Europe, but also to prevent Russia from invading India, Britain's most important colony. The French joined the British, and both powers sent large armies to begin a siege of the port of Sebastopol on the Black Sea.

The poorly trained British forces, commanded by officers who had purchased their commissions and who had no sound knowledge of military tactics, suffered staggering losses, more of them from disease than from battle. The most senseless episode of the war occurred when a British cavalry unit, the Light Brigade, rode into a deep valley near Balaklava, only to be cut down by Russian artillery perched on the surrounding hills.

Nevertheless, Britain, France, and Turkey, together with Piedmont-Sardinia, which entered the war in 1855, prevailed, and Russia suffered its most humiliating defeat of the nineteenth century. The defeat contributed to a crisis that led to a number of liberal reforms during the rule of Tsar Alexander II (1855–1881). Alexander, an indecisive man who had inherited the throne in the middle of the Crimean War, was hardly a liberal (he once referred to the French system of government as "vile"), but he did yield to mounting liberal pressure to emancipate 50 million serfs in 1861, a step that occurred two years before the emancipation of slaves in the United States. Alexander also established elected local assemblies in which 40 percent of peasants had the vote, implemented a new judicial system, and instituted educational reforms.

France and the Franco-Prussian War, 1870–1871

The defeat of France in the Franco-Prussian War of 1870–1871 had a negative effect on the fortunes of both liberalism and socialism in France. When Napoleon III established the Second Empire in 1852, he tried to mask his usurpation of power by preserving the tradition of universal male suffrage and by submitting his rule to popular ratification. During the 1860s his government became known

as "the Liberal Empire," a strange mixture of conservatism, liberalism, and nationalism. "The little Napoleon" gradually allowed a semblance of real parliamentary government, relaxed the censorship of the press, and encouraged industrial development. To this mixture he added a strong dose of nationalist sentiment by evoking the memory of his uncle, Napoleon I.

Military defeat, however, destroyed the regime of Napoleon III. The emperor himself was taken captive at the Battle of Sedan—a personal and national humiliation. The Second Empire collapsed. The establishment of the Third Republic in September 1870 led to a major ideological shift in French politics. The following January Adolphe Thiers (1797–1877), a veteran French statesman who hoped to establish a conservative republican regime or possibly a restoration of the monarchy, negotiated an armistice with Bismarck. This prospect gained strength when elections to a new National Assembly returned a majority of monarchists The National Assembly then elected Thiers as president of a provisional government.

The provisional government was determined to assert its authority over the entire French nation.

CHRONOLOGY: FRENCH POLITICS, 1848–1871

1848

February 25	Establishment of the Second Republic
December	Election of Louis-Napoleon as president of the Second Republic

1851

December 2	Louis Napoleon dissolves the National Assembly

1852

November	Establishment of the Second Empire under Napoleon III

1870

July 19	Beginning of the Franco-Prussian War
September 2	Surrender of Napoleon III to Prussia at Sedan
September 4	End of the Second Empire and proclamation of the Third Republic

1871

February	National Assembly meets at Bordeaux
March	Rising of the Paris Commune
May 10	End of the Franco-Prussian War
May 21–27	"Bloody Week"; suppression of the Paris Commune

EXECUTION OF PARIS COMMUNARDS, MAY 1871
Troops of the provisional French government killed at least 25,000 Parisians during the uprising.

In particular, it wanted to curb the independence of the city of Paris. Parisians, however, were just as determined to carry on the struggle against Prussia and keep alive the French radical tradition that had flourished in the city in 1792 and again in 1848. The socialist and republican ideals of the new Paris Commune, coupled with its determination to preserve the independence of the city, culminated in the bloodshed described at the beginning of this chapter. The crushing of the Commune marked a bitter defeat for the forces of French socialism and radicalism. The Third French Republic endured, but its ideological foundation was conservative nationalism, not liberalism or socialism.

CONCLUSION

The Ideological Transformation of the West

The ideological encounters that took place between 1815 and 1871 resulted in significant changes in the political cultures of the West. As the early nineteenth-century ideologies of liberalism, conservatism, socialism, and nationalism played out in political movements and revolutions, the people who subscribed to these ideologies often redefined their political objectives. Many British and French socialists, for example, recognizing the necessity of assistance from liberals, abandoned their call for creating a classless society and sought instead to increase wages and improve working conditions of the lower classes. The demands of socialists for greater economic equality pressured liberals to accept the need for more state intervention in the economy. The realities of conservative politics led liberal nationalists in Germany and Italy to accept newly formed nation-states that were more authoritarian than they had originally hoped to establish. Recognizing the strength of the ideologies to which they were opposed, conservative rulers such as Emperor Napoleon III and Tsar Alexander II agreed to adopt liberal reforms. Liberals, conservatives, socialists, and nationalists would continue to modify and adjust their political and ideological positions during the period of mass politics, which began in 1870 and which will be the subject of the next chapter.

The Western ideologies that underwent this process of adaptation and modification had a broad influence on world history. In the twentieth century, three of the four ideologies discussed in this chapter have inspired political change in parts of the world that lie outside the geographical and cultural boundaries of the West. Liberalism has provided the language for movements seeking to establish fundamental civil liberties in India, Japan, and several African countries. In its radical communist form, socialism inspired revolutions in Russia, a country that for many centuries had straddled the boundary between East and West, and in China. Nationalism has revealed its explosive potential in countries as diverse as Indonesia, Thailand, and the Republic of the Congo. Ever since the nineteenth century, Western ideologies have demonstrated a capacity both to shape and to adapt to a variety of political and social circumstances.

KEY TERMS

ideologies
liberalism
laissez-faire
conservatism
socialism
dialectic
dialectical materialism

proletariat
communism
nation
nationalism
nation-state
national
   self-determination

national consciousness
positivism
romanticism
Concert of Europe
Decembrists

Chartists
Junkers
Mafia
Realpolitik

CHAPTER QUESTIONS

1. What were the main features of the ideologies that inspired people to political action during the period from 1815 to 1871? (page 685)
2. How did the encounters among the people who espoused these ideologies shape the political history of Europe between 1815 and 1848? (page 695)
3. How did liberal and conservative leaders use the ideology of nationalism as a tool to unite the people of various territories into nation-states between 1848 and 1871? (page 708)
4. How did warfare contribute to political change in Russia and France during the second half of the nineteenth century? (page 716)

TAKING IT FURTHER

1. Why did liberals and socialists, both of whom opposed conservatives, disagree with each other?
2. How did romanticism provide support for liberalism, nationalism, and conservatism?
3. Why did the revolutions of 1848 fail?
4. Why did the pattern of national unification succeed in western Europe and America but fail in eastern Europe?

✓•┤**Practice** on **MyHistoryLab**

23

The Coming of Mass Politics: Industrialization, Emancipation, and Instability, 1870–1914

- Economic Transformation ■ Defining the Political Nation
- Broadening the Political Nation
- Outside the Political Nation? The Experience of Women

IN THE SPRING OF 1881, A HARROWING SCENE TOOK PLACE IN ST. PETERSBURG, capital of the Russian Empire. A 28-year-old woman, Sofiia Perovskaia, was scheduled to be executed for her part in the assassination of Tsar Alexander II. Although born into wealth and privilege, Perovskaia had joined the revolutionary socialist movement. She became a leader of the People's Will, a small revolutionary group that sought to undermine the tsarist regime through sabotage and assassination. On March 1, 1881, led by Perovskaia, six People's Will members (all under age 30) stationed themselves along the streets of St. Petersburg. At Perovskaia's signal, they released their bombs and assassinated one of the most powerful men in Europe.

Yet the death of the tsar did not destroy the tsarist regime. The assassins were arrested and sentenced to hang. On the day of Perovskaia's execution, she mounted the scaffold calmly, but when the noose was placed around her neck, she grabbed hold of the platform below with her feet. It took the strength of two men to pry her feet loose so that she could hang.

The image of Sofiia Perovskaia clinging to the platform with her bare feet while her executioners strained to push her to her death captures the ferocity of political struggle in Europe at the end of the nineteenth century. As we discussed in Chapter 22, the ideological conflict among liberals, conservatives, socialists, and nationalists shaped the political culture of the West in the nineteenth century. After 1870, industrial expansion intensified and widened these conflicts. Individuals and groups that had traditionally been excluded from power demanded a voice in political affairs. Neither economic modernization nor the coming of mass politics ensured the victory of democracy, however. Like Sofiia Perovskaia's executioners, the governing classes often struggled to pry newcomers off the platform of political power—and they often succeeded. Examination of these encounters answers a key question: How did the new mass politics reshape definitions of the West by the beginning of the century?

MASS SOCIETY AT PLAY

Pierre Auguste Renoir, *Le Moulin de la Galette* (1876). On Sunday afternoons in Paris, young working-class men and women dance at a popular café. Urbanization offered ordinary people new opportunities for leisure and relaxation.

Source: Pierre Auguste Renoir. Le Moulin de la Galette, 1876. Oil on canvas. © 2004 Artists Rights Society (ARS), New York. Louvre Museum/Art Resource, NY

ECONOMIC TRANSFORMATION

■ How did the economic transformation of the West after 1870 help shape the encounters between established political elites and newcomers to the political process?

Three economic developments helped shape Western actions and attitudes between 1870 and 1914: the economic depression that began in 1873, the expansion and transformation of the Industrial Revolution, and accelerated urbanization and immigration. The violent social encounters often produced by these developments helped transform the political structures and ideologies of the West.

Economic Depression

In 1873, Europe's economy tilted downward— prices, interest rates, and profits all fell

721

and remained low in many regions until the mid-1890s. Agriculture was hit hardest. By the 1890s, the price of wheat was only one-third of what it had been in the 1860s. Farmers across Europe found it difficult to make a living. Industry and commerce fared better than agriculture but declining prices for manufactured goods—often by as much as 50 percent—squeezed business profit margins.

What caused this depression? Ironically, the very success of the Industrial Revolution spawned it. The development of the steamship and the expansion of railway lines across Europe and the United States reduced the cost of transporting agricultural and industrial goods. Cheap grain and other agricultural products from the American Midwest and Ukraine forced European farmers to accept lower prices for their products. More generally, as regions and nations industrialized, they produced more goods. Yet

many industrial workers, agricultural laborers, and landowning peasants had little money to spend on industrial products. In other words, by the 1870s, a mass consumer society had not yet emerged. Thus, in many parts of Europe production exceeded consumption, and the result was long-term agricultural and industrial depression.

Industrial Expansion and Development

The economic depression was, then, closely linked to the second important economic development of this period—the continued expansion of the Industrial Revolution. As we saw in Chapter 21, between 1760 and 1860 economic production changed dramatically, first in Britain, then in parts of western Europe. After 1860, the Industrial Revolution spread across the European continent. Railways increasingly linked

PRE-INDUSTRIAL CONTINUITIES
This photograph of a French peasant family taking time off for a meal highlights the patchy nature of industrialization even in western Europe. Not until the 1880s and 1890s did many rural regions come within the embrace of the modern industrial economy.

Europe's diverse regions into a single economic network. From 1870 to 1914, the world's rail network grew by 500 percent.

Russia provides a telling example of the expansion of the Industrial Revolution. In the 1890s, Russia underwent dramatic industrialization under the leadership of Sergei Witte (1849–1915), Tsar Alexander III's finance minister. Before entering the tsar's administration, Witte had a successful career in the railway industry. He used this experience to carry out a program of planned economic development. The state-owned railway network doubled in size. This impressive engineering achievement, which included the 5,000-mile trans-Siberian railway, accelerated the movement of goods and laborers across the vast expanse of Russian territory. Witte also placed Russia on the gold standard. This move made the Russian ruble easily convertible into other currencies and so fostered international trade. Foreign capital poured into Russia. By 1900, only Britain, Germany, and the United States produced more steel than Russia— and Russia supplied 50 percent of the industrialized world's oil. Coal mines and steel mills dotted Ukraine, and huge state-run factories dominated Moscow and St. Petersburg.

The expansion of the Industrial Revolution across Europe and the United States coincided with a new phase in the techniques and technologies of production and consumption—what some historians call the **Second Industrial Revolution.** The development of synthetic dyes and new techniques for refining petroleum made the chemical industry into an important economic sector, while by the late 1870s, a series of technological innovations enabled manufacturers to produce steel cheaply and in huge quantities. This in turn expanded production in railroads, shipbuilding, and construction.

The construction industry itself was transformed. Advances in the production of steel, iron, cement, and plate glass, combined with the inventions of the mechanical crane and stonecutter, allowed builders to reach to the skies. Cityscapes changed as these new constructions thrust upward. The engineering firm of Gustave Eiffel (1832–1923) built an iron and steel tower to celebrate the Paris World's Fair of 1889. Modeled on the structural supports of railway viaducts, the Eiffel Tower was ridiculed by critics as a "truly tragic street lamp" and a "half-built factory pipe," but it soon came to symbolize both Paris and the new age of industrial modernity.

This same era saw the development of electric power. In 1866 the English scientist Michael Faraday (1791–1867) designed the first electromagnetic generator. In 1879, the American Thomas Edison (1847–1931) invented the lightbulb. These developments created a huge energy-producing industry. They also accelerated the production and distribution of other industrial goods as factories, shops, and the train and tram lines that serviced them were linked to city power grids.

Industrial organization changed as well. Businesses became larger and more complex. To control production costs in a time of declining profits, business owners developed new organizational forms, including *vertical integration*— buying the companies that supplied their raw materials and those that bought their finished products—and *horizontal integration,* linking up with companies in the same industry to fix prices, control competition, and ensure a steady profit (often called trusts or cartels). The Standard Oil Company exemplifies both trends. Formed in 1870 by John D. Rockefeller (1839–1937), Standard Oil monopolized 75 percent of the petroleum business in the United States by the 1890s, and controlled iron mines, timberland, and manufacturing and transportation businesses.

Within these new, huge, often multinational companies, organization grew more complex and impersonal. The small family firm run by the owner became rarer as layers of managers and clerical staff separated worker from owner. Even identifying "the owner" grew difficult. The need for capital to fuel these huge enterprises drove businesses to *incorporate*—to sell "shares" in the business to numerous stockholders, each of whom now shared ownership in the company.

The marketing of goods also changed. During these decades, a revolution in retailing occurred, one that culminated in a new type of business aimed at middle-class customers—the department store. In a traditional shop, the retailer (who was often also the producer) offered a small selection of products in limited quantities at fairly high prices. In contrast, in the new department stores—Bon Marché in Paris, Macy's in New York, Whiteley's in London—a vast array of products in huge quantities confronted the consumer. These new enterprises made their profits from a quick turnover of a large volume of low-priced goods. To stimulate sales, they sought to make shopping a pleasant experience by providing huge, well-lighted expanses filled with appealing goods sold by courteous, well-trained clerks. In-store reading rooms and restaurants pampered shoppers. Another innovation, mail-order catalogs, offered the store's delights to distant customers. Advertising became a crucial industry as business sought to persuade potential customers of new needs and desires.

On the Move: Emigration and Urbanization

Economic depression and the expansion and transformation of the Industrial Revolution accelerated patterns of urbanization and immigration. The depression hit agricultural regions particularly hard, just when population growth exerted greater pressure on land and jobs. In addition, industrial expansion undercut rural manufacturing and handicraft production. As a result, men and women from traditional villages sought new economic opportunities in the industrializing cities of Europe, the Americas, and Australia.

European cities grew dramatically after 1870. In 1800, only 23 European cities had more than 100,000 inhabitants. By 1900, there were 135 cities of such a size. The European population as a whole continued to expand in this period, but the cities increased at a much faster pace. For example, in 1800 the city of Odessa in Ukraine held 6,000 inhabitants. By 1914, Odessa contained 480,000 people.

Seeking opportunities, inhabitants of industrially underdeveloped regions migrated to more economically advanced areas. Italians headed to France and Switzerland, while the Irish poured across the Irish Sea into Liverpool and Glasgow. Some immigrants headed not for the nearest city, but for a different continent. Between 1860 and 1914, more than 52 million Europeans crossed the oceans in quest of a better life. Over 70 percent of these transoceanic immigrants traveled to North America, 21 percent to South America, and the rest to Australia, New Zealand, or colonies in Asia and Africa.[1] Emigrants from eastern Europe accounted for an ever-larger share of those bound for America. In the 1880s 100,000 Poles moved to the United States. By the 1900s, however, between 130,000 and 175,000 Poles were heading to the United States *each year*.

Growing Social Unrest

Rapid economic change, combined with accelerated urbanization and immigration, heightened social tensions and destabilized political structures. The freefall in prices that characterized the depression eroded capitalist profit margins. In response, businessmen sought to reduce the number of their employees and to increase labor productivity. Workers reacted angrily. Reduced prices did mean that the living standards of *employed* workers rose, but so, too, did unemployment and underemployment. Heightened class hostilities thus characterized these decades.

In rural regions such as Spain and Ireland, the collapse in agricultural prices fostered social and economic crises. Agricultural laborers and peasants turned to violence to enforce their calls for a fairer distribution of land. The spread of industrialization into southern and eastern Europe also led to unrest as handicraft producers and independent artisans fought to maintain their traditional livelihoods.

The flow of immigrants into Europe's cities raised social tensions. Cities were often unable to cope with their dramatic increases in population. Newcomers battled with established residents

Costume original des dames au concours de vélocipèdes, à Bordeaux. (D'après le croquis de M. Guinn-Marie Priest) 1868

THE BICYCLE REVOLUTION

The bicycle revolutionized daily life for ordinary Europeans. The introduction of equal-sized wheels in 1886 and of pneumatic tires in 1890 allowed for a far more comfortable ride than had been the case with the bone-breaking cycles built earlier. Mass industrial production made the bicycle affordable. For the first time, ordinary individuals, far too poor to afford a horse or automobile, could dare to purchase their own private means of transportation that would get them where they wanted to go in one-quarter of the time that walking required. No longer confined to their village for work opportunities or social contacts, bicycle owners discovered that their daily world had widened fourfold. As this engraving shows, the bicycle also contributed to the expansion of the woman's sphere.

for jobs and apartments. The mixture of nationalities and ethnic groups often proved particularly explosive.

DEFINING THE POLITICAL NATION

- How did Western ruling classes respond to the threats and opportunities of mass political participation?

Economic and social changes helped create **mass politics**—a new political culture characterized by the participation of men (but not yet women) outside the upper and middle classes. Mass politics redefined the **political nation**: those with a voice in political affairs who participated in the political process or who voiced political opinions. Because industrial expansion broke down local and regional cultures, loyalties, and mindsets, it cleared the way for the development of new national political identities and interests. The railroads, telegraph, and telephone shattered the barriers of distance, while new printing technologies made newspapers cheap and available to ordinary people. With access to information, they could now form opinions and participate in national and international debate as never before. The dramatic expansion of cities also created the environments in which mass political movements could grow.

Faced with the challenge of this new political culture, political leaders sought to quell social discontent and ensure the loyalty of their populations. They did so in the context of the turbulent international climate created by the national unification of Italy and Germany and the continuing decline of the Ottoman Empire (see Chapter 22). As the European balance of power shifted, governments scrambled to strengthen their states at home and abroad.

Nation-Making

After 1870, all but the most authoritarian European leaders recognized the importance of "nation-making," of creating a sense of national identity to overcome the conflicting regional, social, and political loyalties that divided their citizens and subjects. But while European political elites sought to make ordinary men feel a part of political life, they also tried to retain their dominant social and political position. As socialism challenged both liberal and conservative regimes, those in power had to figure out how to stay there.

FRANCHISE EXPANSION   One way to stay in power was to share it, as the British example proved. In the first half of the nineteenth century, Britain's landed elite had accommodated middle-class demands for greater influence without relinquishing its own dominance. Aristocrats and landed gentlemen played leading roles in both major political parties—the Liberals and the Conservatives (also called "Tories")—but both parties encouraged industrial growth and policies that benefited the middle classes. In the last third of the century, this system expanded to include working-class men. In 1867, many urban working men won the right to vote, and in 1884 this right was

extended to rural male laborers. Although Britain did not achieve universal male suffrage until after World War I, this gradual expansion of the franchise convinced many British working-class men that there was no need for revolution.

Similar patterns emerged across Europe in this era as aristocratic and middle-class politicians extended the vote to lower-class men. These political leaders regarded franchise reform as a way to avoid socialist revolution by incorporating potential revolutionaries within the system.

SOCIAL REFORM   New voters, however, had to be wooed and wowed. They had to be persuaded to vote the way their leaders wished. Political parties thus turned to social welfare legislation. Both liberal and conservative politicians used social welfare reform to convince working-class voters that they had a stake in the existing political system—and thus to reduce the appeal of socialism.

In the 1880s, for example, German Chancellor Otto von Bismarck introduced some of the most thoroughgoing social welfare measures yet seen in Europe. Bismarck, a fiercely conservative aristocrat, sought to ensure German stability and national unity. Alarmed by the popularity of the socialist German Social Democratic Party (SPD), Bismarck outlawed it in 1878, and then enacted laws to attract working-class voters. He initiated sickness benefits in 1883, coverage for industrial accidents in 1884, and old-age pensions and disability insurance in 1889.

Like their conservative opponents, liberal politicians also saw social reform as a way to stay in power and create national unity. In 1906, British trade unionists and socialists formed the Labour Party. Alarmed by this socialist threat, Britain's Liberal government enacted welfare measures, including state-funded lunches for schoolchildren, pensions for the elderly, and sickness and unemployment benefits for some workers. A similar process occurred in Italy. Frightened by the growing appeal of revolutionary socialist parties, the Liberal Party leader Giovanni Giolitti (1842–1928) tried to improve workers' lives and convince them that real change did not require revolution. Giolitti legalized trade unions, established public health and life insurance programs, cracked down on child labor, and established a six-day workweek.

SCHOOLING THE NATION Like social welfare programs, state elementary schools served as important tools in the effort to build internally united (and therefore externally competitive) nation-states. During the late nineteenth century, most of the nations of western and central Europe established free public elementary education systems. Such schools helped foster loyalty to the nation and its leaders. In the 1880s, for example, French student teachers were instructed that "their first duty is to make [their pupils] love and understand the fatherland."[2]

Schools helped forge a national identity in three ways. First, they ensured the triumph of the national language. Required to abandon their regional dialect (and sometimes brutally punished if they did not), children learned to read and write in the national language. Second, history and geography lessons taught children versions of the past that strengthened their sense of belonging to a superior people and often served a specific political agenda. For example, French classrooms continued to display wall maps of France that included the provinces of Alsace and Lorraine, even though Germany had seized these regions after the Franco-Prussian War. Finally, the schools, with their essentially captive populations, participated fully in nationalistic rituals, including singing patriotic songs such as *Deutschland Über Alles* ("Germany Over All") or *Rule Britannia*, and observing special days to commemorate military victories or national heroes.

MASS SCHOOLING

Jean Jules Henri Geoffroy, *The Junior Class,* 1889. Geoffroy presented this painting at the World's Fair of 1889 in celebration of the 100th anniversary of the French Revolution. In France, supporters of the Republic saw the state school system as one of the Revolution's central achievements and the state school teacher as an embodiment of republican (as opposed to religious or monarchical) ideals. In keeping with these revolutionary and republican ideals, Geoffroy's classroom contains both middle-class boys (wearing white collars) and their lower-class peers.

INVENTING TRADITIONS Nationalistic ritual was not confined to the schoolroom and playground. Making nations often meant *inventing* traditions to capture the loyalty of the mass electorate. German policymakers, for example, invented "Sedan Day." This new national holiday celebrated the victory over France in the Franco-Prussian War that helped create the new German Empire. It featured parades, flag raisings, and special services to foster a sense of German nationalism among its citizens.

Inventing a set of traditions around the monarchy and making the royal family the center of the nation were also effective nation-making tools. When the German states united in 1871, the king of Prussia, William I, became the new German emperor. William I, however, tended to identify himself more as a Prussian than a German. It was his grandson, William II (r. 1888–1918), who used personal appearances and militaristic pageantry to make the monarchy a symbolic center of the new nation. In Britain,

the anniversaries of Queen Victoria's accession to the throne (the Silver Jubilee of 1887 and the Diamond Jubilee of 1897) were elaborately staged and orchestrated to make ordinary Britons feel close to the queen and therefore part of a powerful, united nation. Mass printing and production helped support this new mass politics of nationality. At the Jubilees, participants could purchase illustrated commemorative pamphlets, plates etched with the queen's silhouette, teapots in the shape of Victoria's head, or even an automated musical bustle that played *God Save the Queen* whenever the wearer sat down.

Nation-Making: The Examples of France, Russia, and Ireland

By the late nineteenth and early twentieth centuries, political leaders recognized that fostering a sense of national identity among their citizens or subjects would both lessen the appeal of socialism and strengthen the nation-state in war

4523

Der Kaiser mit seinen 6 Söhnen.

Phot. B. I. G. Berl

GERMAN EMPEROR WILLIAM II AND HIS ENTOURAGE

William preferred to wear military regalia when he appeared in public. In this way, William himself symbolized the link between the German state and Germany's military might.

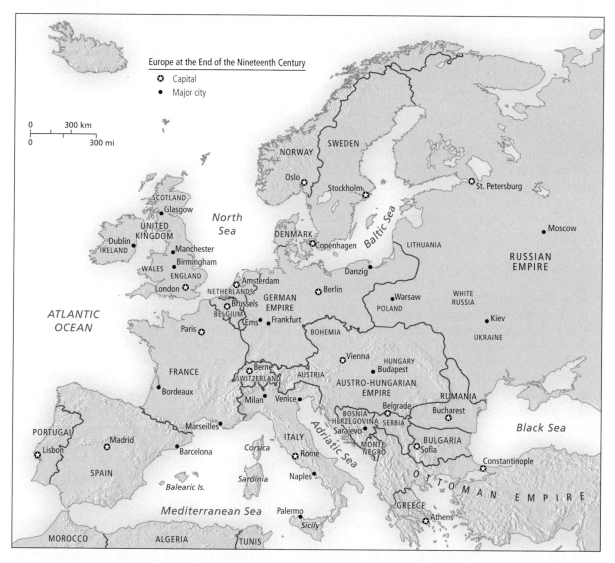

MAP 23.1

Europe at the End of the Nineteenth Century

A comparison of this map with Map 20.3 ("Europe After the Congress of Vienna in 1815," page 650) shows the impact of modern nationalism on European political geography. The most striking change is the formation of the new states of Italy and Germany (the German Empire). In addition, nationalist movements succeeded in carving away large chunks of the Ottoman Empire's European territories.

with competitors. The examples of France, Russia, and Ireland, however, demonstrate the complexities of nation-making.

FRANCE: A CRISIS OF LEGITIMACY After France's defeat in the Franco-Prussian War of 1870–1871,

the French returned to a republican form of government, based on universal manhood suffrage (see Chapter 22). This "Third Republic" faced a crisis of legitimacy. Many Frenchmen argued that the Republic was the product of military defeat and therefore not worth their loyalty or support.

These opponents of the Third Republic included monarchists who wanted a king, Bonapartists longing for a Napoleonic empire, Catholics disturbed by republican efforts to curb the political power of the Church, and aristocrats opposed to democracy.

To understand the opposition to the Third Republic in France after 1871, it is essential to remember that "republicanism" in France meant more than "no king, no emperor." Rooted in the radical Jacobin Republic of 1792 (see Chapter 20), republicanism rested on a vision of an ideal France of male equals—small shopkeepers and independent artisans—governed by reason, not religion. Such a vision clashed with the interests and ideals of monarchists, Bonapartists, and Catholics. The clash of these rival ideologies generated chaos in French politics.

The **Dreyfus Affair** revealed the lack of consensus about the nature of France. (See *Justice in History* in this chapter.) In 1894, a French military court wrongly convicted Captain Alfred Dreyfus (1859–1935) of espionage. French intellectuals took up Dreyfus's case, and supporters and opponents of Dreyfus battled in the streets and the legislature. Support for Dreyfus, who was Jewish, became equated with support for the secular ideals of the Republic. The anti-Dreyfusards, in contrast, saw the affair as a symptom of everything wrong with the Republic. They believed that true French nationalism should center on Catholicism and respect for the military.

In some ways, the supporters of Dreyfus—and therefore of the Republic—won. Dreyfus was declared "not guilty" in 1906, and the government placed the army under civilian control and removed the Catholic Church from its privileged position. With these measures politicians aimed to separate citizenship from religious affiliation and unite the nation around the ideal of a secular Republic. In 1914, on the eve of World War I, the Third Republic was thus stronger than it had been two decades earlier.

It had not yet, however, gained the approval of all of French society. Royalist and Catholic opposition remained strong, and working-class disaffection was growing. The Radical Party, which represented the interests of small store-owners and independent craftsmen, not industrial workers, dominated political life and drew its support from rural and small-town constituencies. The Radicals opposed the high taxes necessary to establish social welfare programs and dragged their feet on social legislation such as the ten-hour workday (not passed until 1904) and old-age pensions (not established until 1910). As a result, French workers increasingly turned to violence.

RUSSIA: REVOLUTION AND REACTION In the sprawling Russian Empire, the task of nation-making was immense, but well underway by 1914. The "Great Reforms" of the 1860s—including the emancipation of 50 million serfs, the creation of a new judicial system, and the vesting of local governmental authority in elected assemblies (for which 40 percent of the peasantry was able to vote)—energized Russian provincial and press culture and enlivened local politics. As new opportunities arose for lawyers, clerks, shopkeepers, accountants, journalists, and the like, the middle classes expanded. The industrialization program of Tsar Alexander III (r. 1881-1894) accelerated the pace of change by creating a small but significant industrial working class which had, by 1895, a literacy rate approaching 70 percent and thus access to the liberal and socialist political ideas that many in the middle classes promoted.

Such ideas clashed with the absolutist convictions of the tsarist regime. Convinced that God had appointed them to rule, Alexander III and Nicholas II (r. 1894–1917) clung to absolutism. To catch up with the West, the tsarist regime adopted Western industrialization but had no intention of accepting Western ideas of representative government. It could not, however, completely block the flow of these ideas into the Russian Empire. Nor could it stamp out the social upheaval created by economic change. Rapid state-imposed industrialization produced cities simmering with discontent. Factory workers labored eleven hours a day in poor conditions,

JUSTICE IN HISTORY

The Dreyfus Affair: Defining National Identity in France

On September 27, 1894, French counterespionage officers examined a disturbing document—an unsigned, undated cover letter for documents containing information on French military equipment and training. The officers concluded that the letter was intended for the German military attaché in Paris. This torn piece of paper was evidence of treason. Someone in the French officer corps was selling military secrets to the Germans.

After a brief investigation and a cursory comparison of handwriting samples, the French investigators concluded that the traitor was Captain Alfred Dreyfus, a candidate officer on the General Staff. An unlikely traitor, Dreyfus had compiled a strong record during his military career and, by all accounts, was a staunch French patriot. Moreover, because his wife was wealthy, he had no need to sell his country for money. He was, however, an aloof and arrogant man, disliked by most of his fellow officers. He was also a Jew.

Despite the lack of solid evidence, Dreyfus was convicted of treason and exiled in 1895 to Devil's Island, a former leper colony twelve miles off the coast of French Guyana in the Caribbean. Many believed he had gotten off too lightly. Public and press clamored for his execution.

The case seemed closed. But some months later, the new chief of the Intelligence Bureau, Major Marie-Georges Picquart, discovered that someone was continuing to pass military secrets to the Germans. Ignoring his superiors' instructions to leave the Dreyfus case alone, Picquart set out to trap the man he believed to be Dreyfus's accomplice. The evidence he uncovered, however, convinced him that Dreyfus was innocent.

Picquart's efforts created a national crisis. On January 13, 1898, one of France's most famous authors, Émile Zola, alleged in a Paris newspaper that the French military was engaged in a cover-up. In an article headlined *"J'accuse!"* ("I accuse!"), Zola charged that the General Staff had deliberately convicted an innocent man. Over the next six weeks, riots broke out in French cities.

Retried before a second military court in 1899, Dreyfus was again found guilty—this time "with extenuating circumstances," a ridiculous verdict (there were no extenuating circumstances for treason) concocted to salvage the military's position despite Dreyfus's obvious innocence. In the subsequent riots in Paris, 100 people were wounded and 200 jailed. Ten days later, the French president pardoned Dreyfus to heal the divisions opened by the trial. Finally, in 1906, a French high court exonerated Dreyfus. Not until 1995, however, did the French military acknowledge his innocence.

The Dreyfus Affair drew international attention, polarized French politics, and tore apart Parisian society. It sparked violent protests, duels, and trials for assault, defamation, and libel. To uphold Dreyfus's conviction, high-ranking military officials falsified evidence and forged documents. The question "Are you for or against Dreyfus?" divided families and destroyed friendships. During the height of the controversy, for example, the painter Edgar Degas ridiculed Camille Pisarro's paintings. When reminded that he had once admired these same works, Degas said, "Yes, but that was before the Dreyfus Affair." Degas was a passionate anti-Dreyfusard; Pisarro believed Dreyfus was innocent.[3]

Why did the Dreyfus Affair change one painter's perception of another's work? Why was this trial not simply a case, but an *affair,* a matter of public debate and personal upheaval, rioting and political turmoil?

To comprehend the Dreyfus Affair, we must understand that it was less about Captain Alfred Dreyfus than about the very existence of the Third Republic, founded in 1871 in the wake of military defeat in the Franco-Prussian War and the collapse of Napoleon III's empire. The intellectuals and politicians who supported Dreyfus were defending the Republic. These men and women linked monarchy and empire to national disaster rather than national glory. They sought to limit the army's involvement in France's political life and upheld a secular definition of the nation that treated Catholics no differently from Protestants, Jews, or atheists.

Dreyfus's opponents, in contrast, regarded the Third Republic as a betrayal of the true France. They wanted a hierarchical, Catholic, imperial state, steeped in military traditions. By defending the military conviction of Dreyfus, they supported the army and the authoritarian traditions that the Republic had jettisoned. The Dreyfus Affair was thus an encounter between competing versions of French national identity.

The question "What is France?" however, could not be answered without considering a second question: "Who belongs in France?"—or more specifically, "What about Jews?" France's small Jewish community (less than 1 percent of the population) had enjoyed the rights of full citizenship since 1791—much longer than in most of Europe. Yet the Dreyfus Affair showed that even in France, the position of Jews in the nation remained uncertain. Although anti-Semitism played little role in the initial charges against Dreyfus, it quickly became a dominating feature of the affair. Anti-Semitic politicians and publications led the anti-Dreyfus forces and more than 70 anti-Semitic riots ravaged France. For many anti-Dreyfusards, Dreyfus's Jewishness explained everything. The novelist and political theorist Maurice Barrès insisted, "I have no need to be told why Dreyfus committed treason. . . . That Dreyfus is capable of treason I conclude from his race."[4]

Anti-Semites such as Barrès regarded Jewishness as a kind of hereditary disease that made Jews unfit for French citizenship. To the anti-Semitic nationalist, the Jew was a person without a country, unconnected by racial or religious ties to the French nation—the opposite of a patriot. A symbol of rootlessness, "the Jew" represented the forces of economic and political change that appeared to be weakening France. Anti-Semites pointed to the successes of assimilated Jews such as Dreyfus—in the army, the universities, the professions, and business—as evidence of what they saw as the threat of Jewish "domination" of French culture.

Dreyfus survived to serve his country with distinction in the First World War. Like Dreyfus, the Third Republic survived the Dreyfus Affair. It was probably even strengthened by it. Outrage over

THE DREYFUS AFFAIR
Captain Alfred Dreyfus before his judges, 1899.

the army's cover-up led republican leaders to limit the powers of the military and so lessened the chances of an anti-republican coup. Anti-Semitism, however, remained pervasive in French politics and cultural life well into the twentieth century.

For Discussion

1. What does the Dreyfus Affair reveal about definitions of national identity in late-nineteenth-century Europe?

2. Once Dreyfus was convicted, many French men and women believed that for the sake of the national interest, his conviction had to be upheld—whether he was actually guilty or not. In what situations, if any, should "national interest" override an individual's right to a fair trial?

Taking It Further

Begley, Louis. *Why the Dreyfus Affair Matters.* 2009. Begley, a novelist and a lawyer, uses the history of the Dreyfus Affair to reflect on contemporary political and legal issues.

Burns, Michael. *France and the Dreyfus Affair: A Documentary History.* 1999. An accessible collection of primary documents.

Kleeblatt, Norman, ed. *The Dreyfus Affair: Art, Truth, and Justice.* 1987. This richly illustrated collection of essays explores the cultural, political, and legal impact of the case.

---

but both strikes and unions were illegal. In the countryside, heavy taxation and rapid population growth increased competition for land and intensified peasant discontent.

In 1905, popular discontent flared into revolution. That year Japan trounced Russia in a war sparked by competition for territory in Asia. The military disaster of the Russo-Japanese War revealed the incompetence of the tsarist regime and provided an opening for reformers to demand political change. On a day that became known as "Bloody Sunday" (January 22, 1905), 100,000 workers and their families attempted to present to the tsar a petition calling for higher wages, better working conditions, and political rights. Troops fired on the unarmed crowd. At least 70 people were killed and more than 240 wounded. The massacre strengthened the call for revolution. Across the empire, workers went on strike and demanded economic and political rights. In June, parts of the navy mutinied. By the fall, Russia was in chaos and in October, Tsar Nicholas II gave in to demands for the election of a national legislative assembly, the Duma. Yet the revolution

continued. In December a military mutiny sparked an uprising in Moscow. As buildings burned and street battles raged, revolutionary socialists controlled parts of the city.

By the time the first Duma met in April of 1906, however, tsarist forces had regained the offensive and terrorized much of the opposition. Because most of the army remained loyal, the tsarist regime was able to quell the Moscow uprising by December 17 and then move to suppress revolutionary forces across the empire. But just as importantly, the violence and radicalism of the Moscow uprising horrified middle-class liberals, who now refused to cooperate with revolutionary or socialist groups. Nicholas succeeded in limiting the Duma's legislative role and, by 1907, regained many of his autocratic powers.

The Revolution of 1905, then, did not overthrow the tsarist regime or transform it into a limited monarchy. Yet it was not a complete failure. Trade unions, strikes, and political parties remained legal. The Duma, limited as it was, did exist. Although not an independent legislative branch of government, it helped

THE REVOLUTION OF 1905 IN THE MOVIES

On Bloody Sunday, January 22, 1905, Russian troops opened fire on more than 100,000 citizens who had gathered in St. Petersburg to present a petition to the tsar. Rather than subduing the revolt, the massacre sparked a revolution. This photograph, supposedly of the moment when the tsar's troops began to shoot the demonstrators, is one of the most familiar images of the twentieth century—yet it is *not* in fact a documentary record. Instead, it is a still taken from *The Ninth of January*, a Soviet film made in 1925.

connect the still-thriving provincial and urban political cultures with the central state. The revolution's most important success, however, was the loosening of censorship. The already influential local press expanded further, as did the numbers of all sorts of publications. Public opinion now became a crucial force in Russian politics.

Nicholas, however, did not recognize the power or legitimacy of public opinion and ignored the Duma whenever possible. Growing popular interest in Russian history and culture in the decade after the revolution revealed a strengthened sense of "Russianness," at least among the Russian peoples of the empire. Yet

Nicholas's commitment to autocracy prevented him from effectively cementing the bonds

CHRONOLOGY: INSTABILITY WITHIN THE RUSSIAN EMPIRE

1881	Assassination of Tsar Alexander II; accession of Alexander III
1882	May Laws reimpose restrictions on Russian Jews
1890s	Industrialization accelerates under Witte
1894	Accession of Nicholas II
1904	Outbreak of Russo-Japanese War
1905	Revolution

between this emerging national identity and the tsarist regime, even when the celebrations marking the 300 years of Romanov rule in 1913 revealed a surprising amount of pro-monarchy sentiments among Russians at all social levels.

THE IRISH IDENTITY CONFLICT   In France, competing notions of "Frenchness" erupted into the Dreyfus Affair. In Russia, the Revolution of 1905 challenged the tsarist definition of Russia as a divinely ordained hierarchical order. In Ireland, two different forms of national identity led to the brink of civil war.

Theoretically, Ireland since 1801 was part of the United Kingdom of England, Wales, Scotland, and Ireland. In reality, as we saw in Chapter 21, a chasm yawned between the first three overwhelmingly Protestant and industrialized nations, and the largely Roman Catholic, largely peasant culture of Ireland. While the English, Scottish, and Welsh economies prospered, the Irish economy stagnated. The economic grievances of Irish Catholic peasants fused with their sense of political and religious repression and convinced many of the need for independence from Britain.

Faced with growing Irish Catholic nationalism, the British resorted to military rule, accompanied by attempts to resolve grievances through land reform. Such reform measures were always too little, too late. In 1898 Irish nationalists organized themselves as Sinn Fein (pronounced "shin fane"—Gaelic for "Ourselves Alone"), a political movement devoted to complete independence for Ireland. By 1914 Sinn Fein had a paramilitary force of 180,000 fighters. Its success demonstrated that Irish Catholics had developed their own sense of nationhood, which refused to be subordinated to or absorbed by Britain.

But Irish *Protestants* refused to consider themselves as anything but British. The descendants of English and Scottish settlers in Ireland, these Protestants constituted a minority of the Irish population as a whole, but made up the majority in the northernmost province of Ulster. Frightened by the idea of belonging to a Catholic state, the Ulster Protestants opposed the British government's plans to grant Ireland "Home Rule," or limited autonomy, by 1914. The Ulstermen, or "Unionists," made it clear that they would fight to preserve the union of Ireland with Britain. By 1914, they too were setting up secret paramilitary organizations. Only the outbreak of war in Europe postponed civil war in Ireland.

BROADENING THE POLITICAL NATION

■ What forms did mass politics assume during this time of industrial expansion and the spread of modern nationalist ideology?

By expanding the franchise, passing social welfare legislation, and inventing nationalist traditions, liberal and conservative political leaders sought to win the loyalty of the lower classes. Mass support for socialist and racist-nationalist political parties, however, challenged traditional elites.

The Politics of the Working Class

The rise of working-class socialist political parties and the emergence of more radical trade unionism reflected an escalation of class hostilities. Workers often rejected the political authority of their bosses and landlords and sought power on their own terms.

THE WORKERS' CITY   In the decades after 1870, the impact of agricultural crisis and industrial expansion created large working-class communities in the rapidly growing industrial cities. At the same time, technological developments such as electrified tram lines and the expansion of the railway system enabled wealthy Europeans to retreat from overcrowded, dirty, disease-ridden city centers to the new suburbs. Increasingly isolated from the middle and upper classes, industrial workers developed what sociologists call "urban villages," closely knit neighborhoods in which each family had a clear and publicly acknowledged place.

Sharply defined gender roles played an important part in ordering this world. The home became the woman's domain (although many working-class women also worked outside the home). Wives often controlled the family income and made most decisions about family life. Men built their own cultural and leisure institutions, free from middle-class (and female) participation and control—the corner pub, the music hall, the football club, the brass band. These institutions provided an escape from the confines of work and home. They also secured the bonds of male working-class identity, one that rested on a sharp distinction between "Us"—ordinary men, workers, neighbors—and "Them," bosses, owners, landlords, those with privilege and power.

WORKING-CLASS SOCIALISM AND THE REVOLUTIONARY PROBLEM   The emergence of working-class socialist political parties embodied this class identity. By 1914, 20 European countries had socialist parties.

Why socialism? As we saw in Chapter 22, by 1870 Karl Marx had published his economic and political theory of revolutionary socialism. Not many workers had the time, education, or energy to study Marx's complex ideas. But Marx's basic points, presented to workers by socialist activists and organizers, resonated with many workers. Quite simply, these laborers had already identified their boss as the enemy, and Marx assured them that they were right. His insistence that class conflict was inherent within the industrial system accorded with workers' own experience of social segregation and economic exploitation. The onset of economic depression in the 1870s also appeared to confirm Marx's prediction that capitalism would produce economic crises until it finally collapsed.

The most dramatic socialist success story was in Germany. In the elections of 1912, the socialist SPD won 35 percent of the national vote and became the largest party in the German Reichstag or parliament. German socialism was, however, more than just party politics. The SPD provided German workers with an alternative community. They could send their children to socialist day care centers and bury their parents in socialist cemeteries. They could spend their leisure time in socialist bicycling clubs and chess teams. They could read socialist newspapers, sing socialist songs, save their money in socialist banks, and shop at socialist cooperatives.

By the 1890s, the rapid growth of socialist parties such as the SPD persuaded many activists that working-class revolution was just around the corner. In 1885 the SPD leader August Bebel (1840–1913) declared, "Every night I go to sleep with the thought that the last hour of bourgeois society strikes soon."[5]

Yet Bebel was wrong. Ironically, the immediate success of socialist parties ensured their long-term failure to foment a working-class revolution. To continue to attract voters, socialist parties needed to pass legislation that would appeal to workers. But minimum wage laws, pension rights and the like improved workers' lives within a *non-socialist* system—and so made socialist revolution more remote. Why resort to violent revolution when participation in parliamentary politics was paying off? Why overthrow capitalism when workers were benefiting from it?

In Germany, the quest for an answer to these questions led to **socialist revisionism,** a set of political ideas most closely associated with Eduard Bernstein (1850–1932). Bernstein rejected the Marxist faith in inevitable violent revolution and argued instead for the gradual and peaceful evolution of socialism through parliamentary politics. He called for German socialists to form alliances with middle-class liberals and carry out social and economic reforms.

In 1899, the SPD condemned Bernstein's revisionism and reaffirmed its faith in the inevitability of capitalism's collapse and working-class revolution. Bernstein had lost the battle—but he won the war. For, in practice, the SPD acted like any other parliamentary party. It focused on improving the lot of its constituency through legislative change. As a result, the German political system grew more responsive to workers' needs, and revolution in Germany grew less likely.

Socialist parties across Europe tended to follow the pattern of the SPD: They voiced the rhetoric of revolution while working for gradual change through parliamentary politics. Despite the almost hysterical fears of many middle- and upper-class Europeans, the successes of socialist political parties probably worked less to stir up revolution than to strengthen parliamentary politics.

RADICAL TRADE UNIONS AND THE ANARCHIST THREAT Much of the support for socialist parliamentary parties came from the trade union movement. As we have seen, the onset of economic depression in the 1870s shattered middle-class confidence and shrank capitalists' profit margins. Looking to cut costs, businessmen sought to reduce the number of laborers, increase production, and decrease wages. To protect workers from this onslaught, unions grew more radical.

While the unions of the 1850s and 1860s had tended to be small, craft-based groupings of skilled workers, the new unions aimed to organize all the male workers in an entire industry—for example, all male textile workers, rather than just the skilled weavers. This more radical approach resulted in larger unions. In Britain between 1882 and 1913, for example, union membership increased from 750,000 to 4,000,000. But these new unions were also more willing to resort to strikes and violence. Unionized workers in barbershops were even encouraged to "inflict nonfatal cuts on the clients of their capitalist masters."[6]

The ideology of **syndicalism** further radicalized the union movement. Syndicalists sought to use the economic clout of the working class to topple capitalism and create a worker-controlled, egalitarian society. In the syndicalist vision, if every worker in a nation went on strike—a **general strike**—the resulting disruption of the capitalist economy would lead to working-class

ANARCHISM AND ASSASSINATION

The anarchist Luigi Luccheni assassinated Empress Elizabeth of Austria-Hungary in 1898. Luccheni targeted the empress not for anything she had done, but simply for who she was. He wrote in his diary, "How I would like to kill someone, but it must be someone important so it gets in the papers."

revolution. Although the French syndicalist Georges Sorel (1847–1922) did not believe that a general strike was possible, he argued that the *idea* of the general strike was crucial. In Sorel's view, the general strike served as an essential myth, an inspirational idea that would give workers the motivation and self-confidence to make a revolution.

In their rejection of parliamentary politics and their willingness to use violence to achieve their revolutionary ends, syndicalists were influenced by **anarchism**. Anarchists shunned politics and opted for direct action such as street fighting and assassination. Whereas Marxists sought working-class control of the state, anarchists aimed to destroy the state entirely. The Russian anarchist Mikhail Bakunin (1814–1876) insisted that the great obstacle to a just and egalitarian society was the state itself, not capitalism or the industrial middle class.

The combined impact of both syndicalism and anarchism created a climate of social unrest and political turmoil in much of Europe before 1914. In the 1890s anarchists carried out a terrorist campaign in Paris that began with a series of bombings and culminated in the fatal stabbing of President Sadi Carnot. Other anarchist victims included Empress Elisabeth of Austria in 1898, King Umberto I of Italy in 1900, and U.S. President William McKinley in 1901.

The Politics of Race and Nation

Mass politics were not limited to socialism, syndicalism, and anarchism. Members of the lower middle class, for example, rarely joined socialist parties or trade unions: Fighting to protect their middle-class status, these clerks, shop assistants, and small store-owners regarded the socialist vision of working-class rule as a nightmare. Socialism also possessed little appeal in areas just beginning to industrialize, such as much of eastern Europe, which still contained many independent artisans and peasants threatened by the modernization that socialism represented. Many within these social groups turned to political parties based on ethnic identity or racism.

Part of the appeal of **nationalist-racist politics** lay in its radical style. Possessing only a basic education, most of the newly enfranchised had little time for reading or sustained intellectual work. They worked long hours and needed to be entertained. They needed a new style of politics— one based more on visual imagery and symbolism than on the written word. Nationalist politics fit the bill perfectly. Unlike socialists, who placed faith in education and rational persuasion, nationalist-racist politicians relied on emotional appeals. By waving flags, parading in historical costumes or military uniforms, and singing folk songs, they tapped into powerful personal and community memories to persuade voters of their common identity, based not on shared economic interests but on ethnic, religious, or linguistic ties— and a mistrust of those who did not share those ties.

NATIONALISM IN THE OTTOMAN EMPIRE AND AUSTRIA- HUNGARY: THE POLITICS OF DIVISION Nationalist mass politics proved powerful in the multiethnic, industrially underdeveloped Ottoman and Austro- Hungarian empires. These regions possessed a diversity of ethnic, linguistic, and religious groups. Nationalist ideology taught these groups to identity themselves as nations and demand independent statehood.

By the 1870s, as we saw in Chapter 22, nationalism had already weakened the Ottoman Empire's rule over its European territories. Determined to hold on to his empire, the Ottoman sultan in 1875 and 1876 suppressed nationalist uprisings in Bosnia-Herzegovina and Bulgaria with ferocity. But this repression gave Russia the excuse it needed to declare war on behalf of its Slavic "little brothers" in the Balkans. As a result of this Russo-Turkish War (1877–1878), the Ottomans lost most of their remaining European territories. **Map 23.2** shows that Montenegro, Serbia, and Romania became independent states, while Austria-Hungary took Bosnia-Herzegovina. Bulgaria received autonomy, which the Bulgarians widened into full independence in 1908.

Ottoman weakness appeared to make Austria-Hungary stronger. The appearance of strength, however, was deceptive. Straining under the pressures of late industrialization, Austria-Hungary's numerous ethnic and linguistic groups competed for power and privileges (see Map 22.4, page 715). In the age of mass politics, these divisions shaped political life.

Language became a key battleground in this political competition. In a multilingual empire, which language would be taught in the schools, be used in official communications, guarantee career advancement? Not surprisingly, politicians agitated for the primacy of their native language and pushed for the power needed to ensure it. In the Hungarian half of the empire, for example, the ruling Magyar-

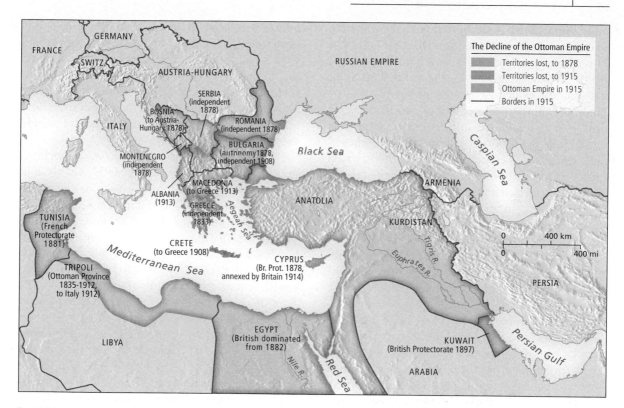

MAP 23.2

The Disintegration of the Ottoman Empire

The disintegration of the Ottoman Empire was a slow process that began at the end of the seventeenth century. By 1870, the Ottoman regime had already lost territory and political control over much of its once-mighty empire to both nationalist independence movements and to rival European powers. From the 1870s on, mass nationalism accelerated Ottoman disintegration. By the 1880s, Bosnia and Herzegovina were under Austrian administration, and Greece, Serbia, Montenegro, Rumania, and Bulgaria had all achieved independence. The Ottoman Empire would finally disappear as a consequence of the peace settlement of World War I.

speaking Hungarian landlords redrew constituency boundaries to give maximum influence to Magyar speakers in parliament and undercut the power of other ethnic groups. "Magyarization" in governmental offices and schools bred resentment among non-Hungarians. They formed their own political parties and began to dream of political independence. Similarly, in the Austrian half of the empire, the struggle between Germans and Czechs over language laws became so intense that no party could establish a majority in parliament, and in 1900 Emperor Francis Joseph (r. 1848–1916) resorted to ruling by decree.

ANTI-SEMITISM IN MASS POLITICS Anti-Semitism played a central role in the new nationalist mass politics. Across Europe, anti-Semitic parties emerged, while established conservative parties adopted anti-Semitic rhetoric to attract voters. To explain this heightened anti-Semitism, we need to understand three developments: the increased emphasis on racial identity, the numbers of Jewish immigrants into western cities, and Jewish integration into the new industrial economy.

Nationalism raised the question, "Who does *not* belong to the nation?" For many Europeans and Americans, race provided the answer. Concepts such as "the English race" or the "racial heritage" of the French had no scientific basis, but the perception of the racial roots of nationhood nonetheless was powerful. As the "nation" came to be defined in racial terms, so did "Jewishness." This shift from a religious to a more racial definition of Jewishness strengthened anti-Semitism. If national identity grew from racial roots, then for many, Jews were foreign plants, outsiders who threatened national unity.

Growing immigrant Jewish populations in much of Europe and the United States in the 1880s and 1890s heightened the perception of Jews as outsiders. Events in Russia help explain this upsurge in Jewish immigration. Tsar Alexander III believed that a Jewish conspiracy was responsible for his father's assassination. In 1882 the May Laws reimposed restrictions on Jewish economic and social life. **Pogroms**—mass attacks on Jewish homes and businesses, sometimes organized by local officials—escalated. Fleeing this persecution, Jews from the Russian Empire settled in Paris, London, Vienna, and other European cities.

The encounter between these immigrant Jewish communities and their hosts was often hostile. Extremely poor, the immigrants spoke Yiddish rather than the language of their new home, dressed in distinctive clothing, and sometimes practiced an ardently emotional style of Judaism that resisted assimilation. As the numbers of Jews rose in Europe's cities, these clearly identifiable immigrants were blamed for unemployment, disease, crime, and any other difficulty for which desperate people sought easy explanations.

Many anti-Semites, however, associated Jews not with poverty, but with wealth and power. A few Jewish families, such as the Rothschild banking dynasty, did possess spectacular fortunes and political clout. Far more important in explaining the outburst of anti-Semitism, however, is what one historian has labeled the "rise of the Jews,[7] a development linked to Jewish emancipation and assimilation. At the start of the nineteenth century, most European Jews had few political rights and were often confined to specific economic roles and required to live in restricted territories or city districts. In the second half of the century, most European Jews were *emancipated*: They gained civil and political rights. Many Jews assumed new economic roles and moved into new regions. And significantly, as newcomers, they often took up positions in the newest sectors of the industrial economy. They became department store owners or newspaper editors rather than farmers

THE RESULTS OF ANTI-SEMITISM

In this 1905 painting by Samuel Hirszenberg, Hasidic Jews in Russian-governed Poland bury the victim of a pogrom. Hirszenberg called his painting *The Black Banner* in reference to both "The Black Hundreds," armed thugs who belonged to the anti-Semitic "Union of the Russian People," and *The Russian Banner,* the Union's newspaper that was partially funded by the tsar.

or small craftsmen. Many Jews also *assimilated* into European societies: They dropped distinctive dress styles, stopped speaking Yiddish, and discarded or modernized their practice of Judaism. Because many assimilated Jews secularized the traditional Jewish emphasis on studying the Torah into an emphasis on educational and artistic excellence, they also moved into professional and cultural fields.

As a result, Jewish communities became significant in European economic and artistic life. In Budapest in 1900, for example, Jews formed 25 percent of the population, yet they accounted for 45 percent of the city's lawyers, more than 40 percent of its journalists, and more than 60 percent of its doctors. In Germany, Jews owned almost all the large department stores, and in Frankfurt, Berlin, and Hamburg, Jews owned all the large daily newspapers. Many prominent artists, musicians, and intellectuals were Jewish.

Jewish success in emerging areas of the industrial economy meant that many Europeans linked Jewishness to modernity. For independent shopowners, traditional artisans, and small farmers with much to lose from modernization, Jews became the symbol of the world they feared. Like Tsar Alexander III, ordinary men and women blamed Jews for their own personal disasters.

ZIONISM: JEWISH MASS POLITICS The heightened anti-Semitism of the late nineteenth century convinced some Jews that the Jewish communities of Europe would be safe only when they gained their own state. The ideology of Jewish nationalism was called **Zionism** because many Jewish nationalists called for the establishment of a Jewish state in "Zion," the biblical land of Palestine. Most Jews in western nations such as France and Britain viewed Zionism with skepticism, but it had a potent appeal in eastern Europe, home to more than 70 percent of the world's Jewish community—and to the most vicious anti-Semitism.

Zionism became a mass movement under the guidance of Theodor Herzl (1860–1904), an Austrian Jewish journalist. Herzl reported on the Dreyfus Affair. This display of anti-Semitism in a prosperous, industrialized, western European society convinced him that Jews would always be outsiders in Europe. In 1896, Herzl published *The Jewish State,* a call for Jews to build a nation-state of their own.

By 1914 some 90,000 Jews had settled in Palestine, where they hoped to build a Jewish state. Zionism, however, faced strong opposition. Many Jewish leaders argued that Herzl played into the hands of anti-Semites by insisting that Jews did not belong in Europe, while many ultra-orthodox Jews, who believed that only God could accomplish the Jewish return to Zion, condemned Zionism as blasphemy. Marking out Palestine as the Jewish "homeland" also clashed with Arab nationalism. By the 1890s, Arab leaders had begun to dream of independence from the Ottoman Empire. Their vision of an independent Arab state included Palestine, home to 700,000 Arabs.

OUTSIDE THE POLITICAL NATION? THE EXPERIENCE OF WOMEN

■ How did the emergence of feminism in this period demonstrate the potential and the limits of political change?

As more men from the laboring classes received the vote, middle-class women demanded that they, too, be made part of the political nation. The campaign for women's suffrage, however, was only part of a multifaceted international middle-class **feminist movement.** For feminists, the vote was a way to transform cultural values and expectations. Nineteenth-century feminism rejected the liberal ideology of separate spheres— the insistence that both God and biology destined middle-class men for the public sphere of paid employment and political participation, and women for the private sphere of the home. In seeking political rights, feminists sought not just to enter the public, masculine sphere, but to obliterate many of the distinctions between the public and private spheres altogether.

Changes in the Position of Middle-Class Women

Changing economic and social conditions provided the context for the emergence of the feminist movement. In 1850, the unmarried middle-class woman who had to support herself had little choice but to become a governess or a paid companion to a widow. But by the 1870s, the expansion of the Industrial Revolution and the widening of state responsibilities created new opportunities. Middle-class women became typists, telephone and telegraph operators, sales clerks, and bank tellers. During the 1860s in England, the number of women working as commercial clerks and accountants increased tenfold.

The same period saw governments assume greater responsibility for the welfare and education of the poor. Middle-class women, who had served as volunteers and charity workers, quickly claimed both paying and elected positions in the new local and state bureaucracies. Women served on school and welfare boards, staffed government inspectorates, and managed poorhouses. In some states, they voted in local (but not national) elections and were elected to local (but not national) office. Compulsory mass education also created a voracious demand for teachers and thus a new career path for unmarried women.

Expectations also began to change for married middle-class women. As we have already seen, they moved into a new public role as consumers. It was the woman who was the principal target of the new advertising industry, the woman whom the new department stores sought to entice with their window displays and courteous clerks, the woman who rode the new tram lines and subways to take advantage of sales.

The largest change for married middle-class women was much more basic, however. In the last third of the nineteenth century, middle-class couples began to limit the size of their families. In Britain, for example, the average middle-class family in the 1890s had fewer than three children. In contrast, at mid-century, the typical family had had six children. This enormous change was in part a response to new economic realities. As economic depression cut into business profits, middle-class families looked to cut expenses and yet maintain their lifestyle. Limiting births, through already well-known methods such as abstinence, withdrawal, and abortion, provided the answer. Married women no longer spent much of their adult life pregnant or nursing and were thus free to pursue other interests, including feminist activism.

In working-class families, however, children left school by age eleven or twelve and so began to contribute to the family income much earlier. In contrast to middle-class families, more children meant more income for working-class families, which remained large. The difference in the size of families meant the gap between middle-class and working-class women's experience widened. Perhaps it was not surprising, then, that the feminist movement remained largely middle class. To most poor women struggling to survive, the vote seemed irrelevant. Moreover, politically active working-class women tended to agree with Karl Marx that class, not gender, was the real dividing line in society. To better their lives, they turned to labor unions and socialism. The British activist Selina Cooper (1868–1946), for example, fought hard for women's rights, but within the British Labour movement. Cooper, who was sent to work in a textile mill at age ten, viewed the widening of women's opportunities and the achievement of working-class political power as two sides of the same coin.

As middle-class women's opportunities widened, they confronted the legal, political, and economic disabilities that they still faced. An international feminist movement emerged and campaigned on four fronts: the legal impediments married women faced, employment opportunities and higher education for girls and women, the double standard of sexual conduct enshrined in European laws, and national women's suffrage.

Women and the Law

European legal systems strongly reinforced the liberal ideology of separate spheres for men

MIDDLE-CLASS WOMEN MOVING INTO THE PUBLIC SPHERE

Julius LeBlanc Stewart, *The Goldsmith Girls in a Peugeot Voiturette in the Bois de Boulogne in 1897*, 1901. As this turn-of-the-century painting testifies, new leisure opportunities for women challenged the middle-class ideal of the "Angel in the House." No longer passive or confined to the domestic sphere, middle-class women began to move onto not only the roads, but also ski slopes, billiards halls, tennis courts, and many other public arenas.

and women. Law codes often classified women with children, criminals, and the insane. Article 231 of the Napoleonic Code, the legal system of France and the basis of the legal codes of much of Europe, declared that "the husband owes protection to his wife; the wife owes obedience to her husband." In Russia a woman could not travel without her father's or husband's permission, and the husband was also the legal guardian of all children. He alone picked their schools, determined their punishments, and approved their marriage partners. In Prussia only the husband could decide when his baby should stop breastfeeding. According to English common law, "the husband and wife are one person in law," and that person was the husband. Most property brought into

a marriage, given to a woman, or earned by her while married, became the property of her husband.

From the mid-nineteenth century on, women's groups fought to improve the legal rights of married women. The results were uneven. By the end of the 1880s, English married women could own their own property, control their own income, and keep their children. Two decades later, French women could claim similar rights. In contrast, the German Civil Code of 1900 granted all parental authority to the husband—even over his stepchildren. While married women could keep money they earned, all property owned by the wife before marriage or given to her after marriage became the husband's.

Finding a Place: Employment and Education

Feminists also worked to widen women's educational and employment opportunities. Even girls from privileged families rarely received rigorous educations before 1850. The minority who did go to school spent their time learning ladylike occupations such as fancy embroidery, flower arranging, and piano playing. Posture was more important than literature or science. Widening the world of women's education, then, became a crucial feminist aim and an area in which they achieved considerable, but limited, success.

Feminists' educational campaigns had three main emphases: improving the quality of girls' secondary education, expanding the number of girls' secondary schools, and opening universities to women. The fight to upgrade the quality of girls' secondary education was difficult. Many parents opposed an academic curriculum for girls, a position reinforced by medical professionals who argued that girls' brains could not withstand the strain of an intellectual education. Dorothea Beale (1831–1906) established one of the first academic high schools for girls in London in the 1850s, but she faced an uphill battle persuading parents to allow her to teach their daughters mathematics. In France, feminists achieved their goal of a state system of secondary schools for girls in the 1880s. They lost the battle for a university-preparatory curriculum, however, which made it difficult for girls to pass the exams necessary to enter the French university system.

Not surprisingly, few women entered French universities in this period. Opportunities for university education for women varied. In the United States, one-third of all students in higher education were women by 1880, while in Germany, women were not admitted as full-time university students until 1901. In Russia, full-time university study became available to women in Moscow in 1872, and by 1880 women in Russia had some of the best opportunities for higher education in Europe. But the involvement of Sofiia Perovskaia—an educated woman—in the assassination of Tsar Alexander II in 1881 convinced the authorities that revolutionary politics and advanced female education went hand in hand. Most educational avenues for Russian women were blocked for more than two decades after the assassination.

Despite such limitations and reverses, the range of jobs open to women broadened. In 1900, French women won the right to practice law, and in 1903 a French woman lawyer presented a case in a European court for the first time. In 1906, the Polish-born physicist and Nobel Prize winner Marie Curie became the first woman to hold a university faculty position in France. By the early twentieth century, women doctors, although still unusual, were not unheard of. In Russia, women accounted for 10 percent of all physicians by 1914.

No More Angels

The campaigns for women's legal rights and the expansion of employment and educational opportunities helped women move into the public sphere. But the third goal of feminist activity—eradicating the double standard of sexual conduct—posed a more radical challenge to separate-sphere ideology. By arguing that the same moral standards should apply to men and women, feminists questioned whether separate spheres should exist at all.

The ideology of separate spheres glorified women's moral purity and held that the more aggressive, more animal-like natures of men naturally resulted in such pastimes as heavy drinking and sexual adventurism. The laws and the wider culture reflected these assumptions. For example, in France, a woman with an illegitimate child could not institute a paternity suit against the father: Premarital sex was a crime for the woman, but not for the man. Similarly, the English divorce legislation of 1857 declared that a woman's adultery was sufficient for a husband to sue for divorce, but for a wife to divorce her husband, she had to prove that he had committed not just adultery, but bigamy, incest, or bestiality.

To feminists, applying different moral standards to men and women degraded men and blocked women's efforts to improve their own lives and society as a whole. As the French feminist leader Maria Desraismes explained, "To say that woman is an angel is to impose on her, in a sentimental and admiring fashion, all duties, and to reserve for oneself all rights....I decline the honor of being an angel."[8]

To erase the moral distinctions between men and women, feminists fought on several fronts. One key struggle was over the regulation of prostitution. By the 1870s, many European countries, as well as the United States, had established procedures that made it safer for men to hire prostitutes, while still treating the women involved as criminals. In England, the Contagious Diseases Act, passed in 1870 to address the problem of venereal disease, declared that the police could require any woman suspected of being a prostitute to undergo a genital exam. Feminists such as Josephine Butler (1857–1942) contended that such legislation made it easier for men to indulge their sexual appetites, while punishing the impoverished women who had to sell their bodies to feed themselves and their children. For almost 20 years Butler led a campaign both to repeal the legislation that regulated prostitution and focus public attention on the lack of employment opportunities for women.

Abuse of alcohol was another battleground for the women's movement. Feminists argued that the socially accepted practice of heavy male drinking impoverished families and caused domestic violence. The temperance or prohibitionist cause thus became a women's rights issue. Temperance organizations spread across much of the western world and, between 1916 and 1919 succeeded in pushing through prohibitionist legislation in Iceland, Finland, Norway, the United States, and many Canadian provinces. "Prohibition," however, did little to transform gender relations, proved difficult to enforce, and was fairly rapidly repealed.

Other feminist moral reform campaigns achieved only limited success. The regulation of prostitution did end in England in 1886 and in the United States, France, and the Scandinavian countries by 1914, but remained in effect in Germany. By 1884 in France, a husband's adultery, like a wife's, could end a marriage; but in England, the grounds for divorce remained differentiated by gender until 1923. In all European countries and in the United States, the sexual double standard remains embedded in much of middle- and working-class culture.

The Fight for Women's Suffrage

The slow pace and uneven progress on both the legal and moral fronts convinced many feminists that they needed the political clout of the *national* suffrage to achieve their goals. In 1867 the National Society for Women's Suffrage was founded in Britain. Over the next three decades, suffrage societies emerged on the Continent. The French suffragist Hubertine Auclert (1848–1914) described the vote as "the keystone that will give [women] all other rights." She refused to pay taxes on the grounds of "no taxation without representation" and was the first woman to describe herself as a "feminist," a word that entered the English language from French around 1890.

Auclert and other **suffragists** had little success. Only in Finland (1906) and Norway (1913) did women gain the national franchise in this period. The social upheaval of World War I brought women the vote in Russia (1917), Britain (1918), Germany (1918), Austria (1918), the Netherlands (1919), and the United States (1920). But women in Italy had to wait until 1945, in France until 1944, and in Greece until 1949. Swiss women did not vote until 1971.

Feminists faced significant obstacles in their battle for the national franchise. (See *Different Voices* in this chapter.) In Catholic countries such as France and Italy, the women's suffrage movement failed to become a political force not only because the Church opposed the women's vote, but also because in Catholicism—in its veneration of the Virgin Mary and other female saints, in its exaltation of family life, in the opportunity it offered for religious vocation as a nun—women found many avenues for emotional expression and intellectual satisfaction.

DIFFERENT VOICES THE DEBATE OVER WOMEN'S SUFFRAGE

The debate over a woman's right to vote did not divide along gender lines. Many men supported women's suffrage, and many women, including Britain's Queen Victoria, regarded it as a violation of the natural order. The excerpts below present arguments in the women's suffrage debate. The best-selling British novelist Mary Ward—or, as she always presented herself, Mrs. Humphry Ward (1851–1920)—wrote the first document, a letter to the editor of an influential magazine, in 1889. Many well-known and influential women signed the letter. The second excerpt comes from a French suffragist pamphlet published in 1913.

An Anti-Suffrage Argument: Mrs. Humphry Ward

We, the undersigned, wish to appeal to the common sense and the educated thought of the men and women of England against the proposed extension of the Parliamentary suffrage to women.

While desiring the fullest possible development of the powers, energies and education of women, we believe that their work for the State, and their responsibilities towards it, must always differ essentially from those of men, and that therefore their share in the working of the State machinery should be different from that assigned to men....To men belong the struggle of debate and legislation in Parliament; the working of the army and navy; all the heavy, laborious, fundamental industries of the State, such as those of mines, metals, and railways; the lead and supervision of English commerce, the service of that merchant fleet on which our food supply depends.

At the same time we are heartily in sympathy with all the recent effort which have been made to give women a more important part in those affairs of the community where their interests and those of men are equally concerned; where it is possible for them not only to decide but to help in carrying out, and where, therefore, judgment is weighted by a true responsibility, and can be guided by experience and the practical information which comes from it. As voters for or members of School Boards, Boards of Guardians, and other important public bodies, women have now opportunities for public usefulness which must promote the growth of character, and at the same time strengthen among them the social sense and habit. But we believe that the emancipation process has now reached the limits fixed by the physical constitution of women, and by the fundamental difference which must always exist between their main occupations and those of men. The care of the sick and the insane, the treatment of the poor; the education of children: in all these matters, and others besides, they have made good their claim to larger and more extended powers. We rejoice in it. But when it comes to questions of foreign or colonial policy, or of grave constitutional change, then we maintain that the necessary and normal experience of women does not and can never provide them with such materials for sound judgment as are open to men.

In conclusion: nothing can be further from our minds than to seek to depreciate the position or the importance of women. It is because we are keenly alive to the enormous value of

---

The failure of British suffragists to win the national franchise persuaded some activists to adopt more radical tactics. Led by the imposing mother-and-daughters team of Emmeline (1858–1928), Christabel (1880–1958), and Sylvia Pankhurst (1882–1960), the **suffragettes** formed a breakaway women's suffrage group in 1903. The suffragettes argued that male politi-cians would never simply give the vote to women; instead, they had to grab it by force. Adopting as their motto the slogan "Deeds, Not Words," suffragettes disrupted political meetings, chained themselves to the steps of the Houses of Parliament, shattered shop windows, burned churches, destroyed mailboxes, and even, in a direct attack on a cherished

their special contribution to the community, that we oppose what seems to us likely to endanger that contribution. We are convinced that the pursuit of a mere outward equality with men is for women not only vain but demoralizing. It leads to a total misconception of women's true dignity and special mission. It tends to personal struggle and rivalry, where the only effort of both the great divisions of the human family should be to contribute the characteristic labour and the best gifts of each to the common stock.

A Pro-Suffrage Argument: The French Union for Womens' Suffrage

We are going to try to prove that the vote for women is a just, possible and desirable reform....

A woman has responsibility in the family; she ought to be consulted about the laws establishing her rights and duties with respect to her husband, her children, her parents.

Women work—and in ever greater numbers; a statistic of 1896 established that...the number of women workers was 35 percent of the total number of workers, both male and female.

If she is in business, she, like any businessman, has interests to protect....

If a woman is a worker or a domestic, she ought to participate as a man does in voting on unionization laws, laws covering workers' retirement, social security, the limitation and regulation of work hours, weekly days off, labor contracts, etc.

....

Finally, her special characteristics of order, economy, patience and resourcefulness will be as useful to society as the characteristics of man and will favor the establishment of laws too often overlooked until now.

The woman's vote will assure the establishment of important social laws.

All women will want:

To fight against alcoholism, from which they suffer much more than men;

To establish laws of health and welfare;

To obtain the regulation of female and child labor;

To defend young women against prostitution;

Finally, to prevent wars and to submit conflicts among nations to courts of arbitration.

For Discussion

1. How does the argument of Mrs. Humphrey Ward reflect the liberal ideology of separate spheres for men and women?

2. What is the basic argument presented by the French Union for Women's Suffrage? Why did the suffragists argue that the women's vote would create a better world?

3. How does this argument in the pro-suffrage pamphlet reflect rather than reject separate sphere ideology?

Source: 1. Mrs. Humphry Ward. "An Appeal against Female Suffrage," Nineteenth Century 147 (June 1889): 781–785. 2. A report presented to Besançon Municipal Council by the Franc-Comtois Group of the Union Française pour le Suffrage des Femmes. Besançon, March 1913, 6–9.

citadel of male middle-class culture, vandalized golf courses.

In opting for violence, suffragettes assaulted a central fortification of middle-class culture—the ideal of the passive, homebound woman. Their opponents reacted with fury. Police broke up suffragette rallies with sexually focused brutality: They dragged suffragettes by their hair, stomped on their crotches, punched their breasts, and tore off their blouses. Once in jail, hunger-striking suffragettes endured the horror of forced feedings. Jailers pinned the woman to her bed while the doctor thrust a tube down her throat, lacerating her larynx, and pumped in food until she gagged.

CONCLUSION

The West in an Age of Mass Politics

The clash between the suffragettes and their jailers was only one of a multitude of encounters, many of them violent, among those seeking access to political power and those seeking to limit that access, between 1870 and the start of World War I in 1914. Changing patterns of industrialization and accelerated urbanization gave rise to other sorts of encounters—between the manager seeking to cut production costs and the employee aiming to protect his wages, for example, or between newly arrived immigrants in the city and long-established residents who spoke different languages.

Out of such encounters emerged key questions about the definition of "the West." Where, for example, did the West end? Did it include Russia? "Yes," replied the small revolutionary groups who embraced Karl Marx's socialist theories and argued that Russia would follow Western patterns of economic and political development. Other Russian revolutionaries, however, sought a revolutionary path unique to Russia. The expansion of the franchise and the processes of making nations raised even more fundamental questions. Did democracy define the West? Should it? Was the West synonymous with white, western European men or could people with olive-colored or black skin—or women of any color—participate fully in Western culture and politics? Was "the West" defined by its rationality? In the eighteenth century, Enlightenment thinkers had looked to reason as the path to social improvement. The rise of a new style of politics, based on emotional appeal or racist hatred, challenged this faith in reason. But at the same time, developments in industrial organization and technology, which helped expand European national incomes, pointed to the benefits of rational processes.

As we will see in the next chapter, the expansion of Western control over vast areas of Asia and Africa in this period led many Europeans and Americans to highlight economic prosperity and technological superiority as the defining characteristics of the West. Confidence, however, was accompanied by anxiety as these years also witnessed a far-reaching cultural and intellectual crisis. Closely connected to the development of mass politics and changes in social and gender relations, this crisis eroded many of the pillars of middle- and upper-class society and raised questions about Western assumptions and values.

KEY TERMS

Second Industrial Revolution
mass politics
political nation
Dreyfus Affair
socialist revisionism
syndicalism
general strike

anarchism
nationalist-racist politics
pogrom
Zionism
feminist movement
suffragists
suffragettes

CHAPTER QUESTIONS

1. How did the economic transformation of the West after 1870 help shape encounters between established political elites and newcomers? (page 721)
2. How did the ruling classes of the Western powers respond to the new threats and opportunities provided by mass political participation? (page 725)
3. What forms did mass politics assume during this time of industrial expansion and the spread of modern nationalist ideology? (page 735)
4. How did the emergence of feminism demonstrate the potential and the limits of political change? (page 741)

TAKING IT FURTHER

1. How did the economic transformation of the West after 1870 contribute to changes in middle-class women's roles—and in at least some women's expectations?

2. How do you explain the successes—and the limitations—of socialism after 1870?

3. Why did anti-Semitism emerge as a powerful political force after 1870?

✓●–[Practice on **MyHistoryLab**

The West and the World: Cultural Crisis and the New Imperialism, 1870–1914

■ Scientific Transformations ■ Cultural Crisis: The *Fin-de-Siècle*
and the Birth of Modernism ■ The New Imperialism

IN THE SUMMER OF 1898, BRITISH TROOPS INVADED THE SUDAN IN NORTHEAST AFRICA. On September 2, 40,000 Sudanese soldiers retaliated against British defenses at Omdurman. The Sudanese soldiers possessed a reputation for military fierceness, but they attacked with swords, spears, and outdated firearms. Equipped with repeating rifles and Maxim guns (a type of early machine gun), British troops simply mowed them down. After only five hours of fighting, 11,000 Sudanese lay dead. The British lost just 40 men. According to one soldier—the future prime minister Winston Churchill—the biggest danger to the British troops was boredom: "The mere physical act [of loading, firing, and reloading] became tedious." In contrast, Churchill recalled, "all the time out on the plain on the other side bullets were shearing through flesh, smashing and splintering bone; blood spouted from terrible wounds; valiant men were struggling through a hell of whistling metal, exploding shells, and spurting dust—suffering, despairing, dying."[1]

The lopsided Battle of Omdurman was one episode in the story of new imperialism, the final phase in the Western conquest of the globe. This often violent encounter between the West and the rest of the world was closely connected to the political and economic upheavals examined in Chapter 23. An understanding of new imperialism, however, also demands a close look at scientific, intellectual, and cultural developments between 1870 and 1914. As Western adventurers risked life and limb to chart Africa's rivers and exploit Asia's resources, artists and scientists explored new worlds of thought and perception that challenged the social order and even the meaning of reality itself. This chapter examines the scientific, artistic, and physical explorations that characterized these decades and asks: In what ways did these explorations redefine the West and its relationship with the rest of the world?

SCIENTIFIC TRANSFORMATIONS

■ How did scientific developments during this period lead to both optimism and anxiety?

Scientific advances after 1870 improved the health and hygiene of the Western world. Yet these changes also deepened the cultural anxiety of Europeans and Americans in this period

PAUL GAUGUIN, *MATAMOE* ("PEACOCKS IN THE COUNTRY"), 1892

Like many of Paul Gauguin's works, this painting reflects both his own and the wider modernist fascination with the non-Western world during an era of renewed imperial conquest. Gauguin fled Europe for Tahiti in an effort to restore to his art the vitality that he observed in the island culture.

as they pushed men and women into new encounters with the human body and the wider physical universe. In the crowded cities, the threat of contagious disease forced policymakers, physicians, and scientists to rethink the way the human body interacted with other bodies, human and microscopic. The work of biologists highlighted the way bodies had evolved to meet the challenges of survival, while the experiments of chemists and physicists exposed key flaws in the accepted model of the physical world.

Medicine and Microbes

In the nineteenth century, a series of developments transformed the practice of Western medicine. Before this time, physicians assumed that bad blood caused illness and so relied on practices such as leeching (attaching leeches to the skin) and bloodletting (slicing open a vein). Ignorant of the existence of bacteria and viruses, doctors attended one patient after another without bothering to wash their hands or surgical instruments. The only anesthetic available was alcohol. Patients and doctors regarded pain as inevitable, something to be endured rather than eased.

Urbanization overwhelmed such traditional medical practices. Expanding urban populations served as seedbeds for contagious diseases. Cholera outbreaks first forced doctors and public officials to pay attention to the relationship between overcrowding, polluted water, and epidemic disease. In 1848, for example, a cholera epidemic persuaded British officials to build the sewer system that still serves London today.

Neither officials nor doctors, however, understood the causes of disease until the 1860s, when

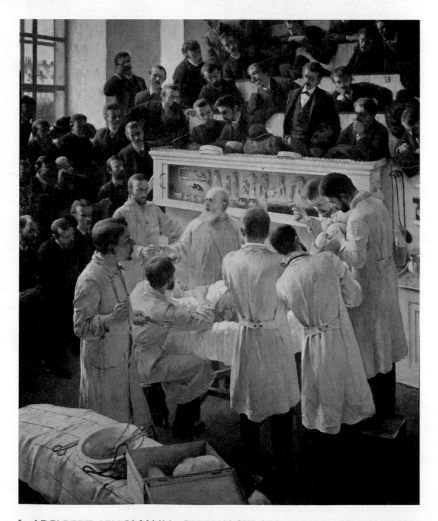

ADELBERT SELIGMANN, *GERMAN SURGEON THEODOR BILLROTH AT WORK IN VIENNA* (1890)

Modern surgery in the making: The patient has been anesthetized, but the modern operating room does not yet exist, nor are the doctors wearing gloves or masks. Billroth, the director of the Second Surgical Clinic in Vienna, pioneered surgical techniques for gastrointestinal illnesses and cancer.

the chemist Louis Pasteur (1822–1895) discovered the source of contagion to be microscopic living organisms—bacteria. Building on this discovery, Pasteur developed vaccines against anthrax, rabies, and many other diseases. (His process of purifying milk and fermented products is still known as pasteurization.) Following Pasteur, Robert Koch (1843–1910), professor of public health in Berlin, isolated the tuberculosis bacillus in 1882 and the bacteria that cause cholera in 1883. The work of Pasteur, Koch, and other scientists in tracing the transmission of disease improved Western medical practice. Between 1872 and 1900, the number of European deaths from infectious diseases dropped by 60 percent.

The use of anesthetics marked another important medical advance. In 1847 a Scottish physician first delivered a baby using chloroform to dull the mother's pain. Although condemned by theologians (who regarded pain as a necessary part of sinful human existence), the use of anesthetics spread quickly. Britain's Queen Victoria, who gave birth to nine children, expressed the feelings of many patients when she greeted the use of anesthetics in the delivery room with delight: "Oh blessed chloroform!"

These medical advances gave Europeans genuine confidence that the scientific conquest of nature would create a healthier environment. But the widespread awareness of germs also heightened anxiety. After the 1870s, Europeans were aware that they lived in a world populated by potentially deadly but invisible organisms, carried on the bodies of their servants, their employees, their neighbors, and their family members. Isolation of the bacilli that caused an illness did not immediately translate into its cure, and viral infections such as measles continued to be killers. Those who could afford to isolate themselves from danger often did so. As wealthy Europeans fled from urban centers of contagion, suburbs and seaside resorts multiplied.

The Triumph of Evolutionary Science

Developments in geology and biology also led to both confidence and anxiety. Evolutionary science provided a scientific framework in which educated Europeans could justify their own superior social and economic positions. Yet it challenged basic religious assumptions and depicted the natural world in new and unsettling ways.

Christians had long relied on the opening chapters of the Bible to understand the origins of nature and humanity, but nineteenth-century geologists challenged the biblical account. Although a literal reading of the Bible dated the Earth at 6,000 years old, geologists such as Charles Lyell (1797–1875) argued that the Earth had formed over millions of years. In *Principles of Geology*—a best-seller that went through eleven editions—Lyell refuted the orthodox Christian position that the biblical account of Noah's Flood and other divine interventions explained geological change and the extinction of species. He argued that the material world must be seen as the product of natural forces still at work, still observable today.

But how did natural processes explain the tremendous variety of plant and animal species in the world? The British scientist Charles Darwin (1809–1882) answered this question in a way that proved satisfying to large numbers of educated Europeans—and horrifying to others. In the 1830s Darwin participated in a global expedition. On this trip he observed that certain species of animal and plant life, isolated on islands, had developed differently from related species on the coast. After returning to Britain, Darwin read the population theory of Thomas Malthus (see Chapter 21). Malthus argued that all species produce more offspring than can actually survive. Putting together Malthus's theory with his own observations, Darwin concluded that life is a struggle for survival, and that small biological variations can help an individual member of a species win this struggle. From this understanding came the **Darwinian theory of evolution.**

Darwin's evolutionary hypothesis rested on two ideas: *variation* and *natural selection*. Variation refers to the biological advantages that assist in the struggle for survival. A bird with a slightly longer beak, for example, might gain easier

DARWIN'S DISTURBING MIRROR
Simplified and often ridiculous versions of Darwin's ideas almost immediately entered popular culture. Here a monkey version of Darwin holds up a mirror to his fellow creature, who seems surprised by his reflection.

access to scarce food supplies. Over generations, the individuals with the variation displace those without. Variation, then, provides the means of natural selection, the process by which new species evolve.

Darwin provided an explanation for evolutionary change, but two factors remained problematic. First, the process of variation that he described required many, many generations. Could it account for the multitude of variations apparent in the biological world? Second, how

did variations first emerge and how are they inherited?

The answers lay embedded in the research of an Austrian monk, Gregor Mendel (1822–1884). Experimenting in his vegetable garden, Mendel developed the laws of genetic heredity. Mendel's work, however, was ignored until the end of the nineteenth century, when the Dutch botanist Hugo DeVries (1848–1935) used Mendel's data to hypothesize that evolution occurred through radical mutations in the reproductive cells of an organism, which pass on to offspring at the moment of reproduction. Mutations that offer an advantage in the struggle for existence enable the mutated offspring to survive—and to produce more mutant offspring. Thus, evolution can proceed by leaps, rather than over a very long period of time.

Long before these genetic underpinnings of evolution were understood, however, Darwin's theories proved influential. Published in 1859, *The Origin of Species* aroused immediate interest and debate. Controversy intensified when, in 1871, Darwin published *The Descent of Man*, in which he argued that human beings, like other species, evolved over time. This denial of humanity's special place within the universe horrified many Christians. They found the Darwinian view of nature even more troubling. According to orthodox Christian theology, the beauty of nature reveals God to the believer. In the Darwinian universe, however, nature does not display God's hand at work. Instead, it is a blood-filled arena in which organisms compete for survival—"nature red in tooth and claw," as the British poet Alfred Lord Tennyson put it. In such a universe, ideas of purpose and meaning seemed to disappear.

Nevertheless, many Europeans and Americans welcomed Darwin's evolutionary theory because it seemed to confirm their faith in the virtues of competition and in the inevitability of progress. As Darwin himself wrote, because "natural selection works solely by and for the good of each being, all [physical] and mental development will tend to progress toward perfection."

Social Darwinism and Racial Hierarchies

While Darwin used his theory of evolution to explain biological change, the British writer Herbert Spencer (1820–1902) insisted that evolutionary theory should be applied to social policy as well. A champion of *laissez-faire* economics (see Chapter 22), Spencer coined the phrase "the survival of the fittest." He argued that charity or government assistance for the poor slowed the evolution of a better society by enabling the weak—the less fit—to survive.

Social Darwinists applied Spencer's concept of the survival of the fittest to entire races. They argued that the nonwhite races in Africa and Asia stood below white Europeans on the evolutionary ladder. Hence, G. A. Henty, a novelist and Social Darwinist, insisted that the "intelligence of the average negro is about equal to that of a European [male] child of ten years old."[2] Social Darwinists used such pseudoscientific arguments to justify Western imperialism. Evolutionary backwardness, they argued, doomed the nonwhite races to conquest and even extinction. These lines from a bestselling British novel sum up the Social Darwinist worldview: "Those who are weak must perish; the earth is to the strong.... We run to place and power over the dead bodies of those who fail and fall; ay, we win the food we eat from out the mouths of starving babes. It is the scheme of things."[3]

Social Darwinists used evolution to justify not only racial but also gender hierarchies. Arguing that the bodies of women were less evolved than those of men, they identified women as mentally and physically inferior. Such ideas spread throughout Western culture in the late nineteenth century. Leading intellectuals such as the psychiatrist Sigmund Freud, for example, argued that "the female genitalia are more primitive than those of the male," while the French social theorist Gustave LeBon compared the average female brain to that of a gorilla.

Wrenched out of its biological framework and misapplied to social and international affairs, evolutionary theory thus justified the central assumptions of nineteenth-century society: the benefits of competition, the rightness of white rule and male dominance, and the superiority of Western civilization. Yet evolutionary science also worked to undermine Western confidence because with the idea of evolution came the possibility of *regression*: Was the traffic on the evolutionary ladder all one-way, or could species descend to a lower evolutionary level? Could humanity regress to its animal origins?

The concept of the "inheritance of acquired characteristics," associated with the work of the French scientist Jean-Baptiste Lamarck (1744–1829), strengthened these fears of regression. More than 50 years before Darwin published his *Origin of Species*, Lamarck theorized that "acquired characteristics"—traits that an individual developed in response to experience or the environment, such as the stooped back of a miner, the poor vision of a lace maker, or the promiscuity of a prostitute—could be "acquired" by the individual's children. Because the process of genetic reproduction was not yet understood, Lamarck's theories remained influential throughout the nineteenth century. Middle-class Europeans and Americans feared that the impoverished masses in the expanding city slums were acquiring undesirable characteristics, ranging from physical deformity to sexual immorality and violent criminality. Using Lamarck's theories, they concluded that if growing numbers of poor children inherited these traits, the evolutionary ascent of the West could slow or even reverse.

The Revolution in Physics

A revolution in physics also began in this era. Although its most dramatic consequences—atomic weapons and nuclear energy—would not be realized for another half century, this revolution contributed to both the exhilaration and the uncertainty that characterized Western intellectual and cultural history after 1870.

At the core of the revolution in physics lay the question, "What is matter?" The triumph of the theories of Isaac Newton had ensured that for 200 years, educated Westerners had a clear, certain answer: Matter was what close observation and measurement showed it to be (see Chapter 17). Three-dimensional material bodies, made up of the building blocks called atoms, moved against a fixed backdrop of space and time. Like a machine, nature was predictable. Using reason, observation, and common sense, then, human beings could understand, control, and improve the material world.

A series of discoveries and experiments challenged this commonsense view of the universe and offered in its place a more mysterious and unsettling vista. The discovery of the X-ray in 1895 disrupted prevailing assumptions about the solidity of matter. These assumptions crumbled further when the Polish chemist Marie Curie (1867–1934) found a new element, radium, which did not behave the way matter was supposed to behave: Continually emitting subatomic particles, radium did not possess a constant atomic weight. Two years later, the German scientist Max Planck (1858–1947) theorized that a heated body radiates energy not in the continuous, predictable stream most scientists envisaged, but rather in irregular clumps, which he called *quanta*. Most scientists dismissed Planck's hypothesis as contrary to common sense, but soon his "quantum theory" helped shape a new model of a changeable universe.

These scientific discoveries provided the context for the work of Albert Einstein (1879–1955), the most famous scientist of the twentieth century. Bored by his job as a patent clerk, Einstein passed the time speculating on the nature of the cosmos. In 1905, he directly challenged the Newtonian model of the universe by publishing his **theory of relativity**. With this theory, Einstein offered a model of a four rather than three-dimensional universe. To height, width, and depth, Einstein added *time*. He theorized that time and space are not fixed. They shift, relative to the position of the observer. Similarly, matter itself shifts because the mass of a material object changes with its motion. In the Einsteinian model, then, time, space, and matter intermingle in a universe of relative flux. Einstein used his

own everyday experiences to explain his model. He noticed that as the streetcar in which he was traveling passed a fixed object, like a house, the object appeared to narrow. The faster the streetcar, the more the object narrowed. In other words, the dimension of width varies according to the speed and position of the viewer.

Despite such efforts at everyday explanation, the revolution in physics made much of science incomprehensible to ordinary men and women. Most importantly, the new science challenged the basic assumptions that governed nineteenth-century thought by offering a vision of the universe in which what you see is *not* what you get, in which objective reality might well be the product of subjective perception.

Social Thought: The Revolt Against Positivism

Just as the revolution in physics presented a new and unsettling picture of the physical universe, so troubling theories about the nature of human society surfaced in "social thought" (the research and publications that lay the foundations for disciplines such as sociology, psychology, and anthropology). As Chapter 22 explained, the mainstream of nineteenth-century thought was **positivist**: It placed great faith in human reason. At the end of the century, however, social thinkers revolted against positivism by emphasizing the role of nonrational forces in determining human conduct.

Gustave LeBon (1841–1931), for example, developed his theory of crowd or collective psychology by studying how appeals to emotion, particularly in the form of symbols and myths, influenced group actions. For Le Bon, the new mass politics (see Chapter 23) was a form of such crowd behavior: Uneducated voters made choices on the basis of emotion, not logical argument. Le Bon concluded that democracy relinquished political control to the irrational masses and so would lead only to disaster.

While LeBon focused on the crowd, the German social theorist Max Weber (1864–1920) explored the "bureaucratization" of modern life—the tendency of political and economic institutions to become standardized and impersonal. Weber saw the triumph of bureaucracy as generally positive, the victory of reason and science over tradition and prejudice. But he also recognized that bureaucracies could crush ideals and individuals and so threaten personal freedom.

Troubled by the vision of individuals trapped within "the iron cage of modern life," Weber in 1898 suffered a nervous breakdown. According to his wife, "an evil something out of the subterranean unconscious…grasped him by its claws."[4] This view of the individual as a captive of the unconscious was central to the revolt against positivism and reached its fullest development in the influential work of the Viennese scientist and physician Sigmund Freud (1856–1939). Freud's effort to treat patients suffering from nervous disorders persuaded him that the conscious mind plays a limited role in shaping an individual's actions. In *The Interpretation of Dreams* (1900), Freud argued that beneath the rational surface of each human being surge all kinds of hidden desires, including such irrational drives as the longing for death and destruction. Freud believed that he could understand human behavior (and treat mental illness) by diving below the rational surface and exploring the submerged terrain of unconscious desire. The emergence of Freudian psychology, however, convinced many educated Western individuals not that the irrational could be uncovered and controlled, but rather that the irrational was *in* control.

CULTURAL CRISIS: THE *FIN-DE-SIÈCLE* AND THE BIRTH OF MODERNISM

- Why did many Europeans in this period believe they were living in a time of cultural crisis?

The recognition of the power of the irrational contributed to a growing cultural crisis. The French phrase *fin-de-siècle,* literally translated as "end of the century," served as a shorthand term

for the mood of uneasiness that characterized much of Western society in this era. Fast-moving economic and social changes, coupled with new scientific theories, convinced many that old solutions no longer worked. The quest for new answers fostered the birth of **modernism,** a broad label for a series of unsettling developments in thought, literature, and art. Many Europeans and Americans celebrated modernism as a release from restraining middle-class codes. Others, however, responded fearfully.

The *Fin-de-Siècle*

The sense that the West was in a state of decline fostered *fin-de-siècle* anxiety. Urbanization aroused fears of degeneration. As cities spread, so did perceptions of rising crime rates. Such perceptions went hand in hand with the reality of increasing drug and alcohol use. Diners in high society finished their sumptuous meals with strawberries soaked in ether, and respectable bourgeois men offered each other cocaine as a quick "pick-me-up" at the end of the working day. Middle-class mothers fed restless babies opium-laced syrups, while workers bought enough opium-derived laudanum on Saturday afternoon to render them unconscious until work on Monday morning. Using Lamarck's theory of the inheritance of acquired characteristics, scientists contended that criminality and drug addictions would be passed on from generation to generation, thus contributing to social decline.

Popular novels also contributed to the fear of degeneration by depicting Western culture as diseased or barbaric. In *Nana* (1880), the French novelist Émile Zola (1840–1902) used the title character, a prostitute, to embody his country. Watching as French soldiers march to defeat in the Franco-Prussian War, Nana is dying of smallpox, her face "a charnel-house, a heap of pus and blood, a shovelful of putrid flesh."[5] Works such as *Dr. Jekyll and Mr. Hyde* (1886) and *Dracula* (1897) showed that beneath the cultured exterior of a civilized man lurked a primitive, bloodthirsty beast.

EDGAR DEGAS, *ABSINTHE* (1876–1877)

Parisian café-goers often indulged in absinthe, a strong alcoholic drink flavored with anise. Degas' portrait of one such absinthe drinker is a picture of deterioration: This woman's lined face, weary posture, and isolation provide an evocative image of the *fin-de-siècle*.

Source: Edgar Degas, "The Glass of Absinthe," 1876. Oil on canvas, 36 × 27 in. Musee d'Orsay, Paris. Scala/Art Resource, NY

The writings of the German philosopher and poet Friedrich Nietzsche (1844–1900) epitomized the mood of the *fin-de-siècle*. Nietzsche dismissed most members of modern society as little more than sheep, penned in by outdated rules and beliefs. Middle-class morality, rooted in Christianity, had sapped Western culture of its vitality. "Christianity has taken the side of everything weak," Nietzsche insisted.

Nietzsche traced the weakness of Western culture beyond Christianity, however, back to the ancient Greek emphasis on rationality. He argued that by overemphasizing rational thought, Western

societies repressed powerful instinctive and emotional forces. Even the style of his publications reflected Nietzsche's impatience with reason. Rather than write carefully constructed essays that proceeded logically from one fact to another, he adopted an elusive, poetic style characterized by disconnected fragments, more accessible to intuitive understanding than to rational analysis.

Nietzsche's call to "become what you are" attracted young enthusiasts throughout Europe in the 1890s. These Nietzsche fans embraced his conviction that the confining codes of middle-class morality held back the individual from personal liberation. "God is dead," Nietzsche proclaimed, "and we have killed him." If God is dead, then "there is nobody who commands, nobody who obeys, nobody who trespasses." Such declarations alarmed other readers, who viewed Nietzsche's work as a cause rather than a critique of Western decay.

Tightening Gender Boundaries

Fear of degeneration also expressed itself in late-nineteenth century efforts to strengthen the boundaries that separated "maleness" from "femaleness." The feminist and the homosexual joined the criminal, the drug addict, and the prostitute in the list of dangerous and degenerate beings. (See *Justice in History* in this chapter.)

In the decades after 1870, as middle-class women began to move into the public spheres of university education and paid employment, feminism emerged as a political force (see Chapter 23). Many Europeans and Americans viewed these developments with alarm. They argued that the female body and brain could not withstand the strains of public life. In the antifeminist view, a woman who pursued higher education or a career not only risked her own physical and mental breakdown, she also tended to produce physically and morally degenerate children and so threatened the evolutionary advance of Western societies.

Like feminists, homosexuals were singled out as threats to the social order in this period. Before 1869, *homosexual* was not a word: Coined by a

Hungarian scientist seeking a new label for a new concept, it entered the English language in 1890. Traditionally, Europeans and Americans had viewed same-sex sexual practice as a form of immoral behavior, indulged in by morally lax—but otherwise normal—men. (Few considered the possibility of female homosexual behavior.) In the later nineteenth century, however, the emphasis shifted from *actions* to *identity*, from condemning a type of behavior to denouncing a type of person: the homosexual.

Three developments heightened the fear of homosexuality. First, the anonymity and mobility of urban life offered homosexuals space in which they could express a more confident homosexual identity. Throughout Western cities, homosexual subcultures became more numerous and more visible—and, therefore, more threatening.

Second, the rise of corporate capitalism (see Chapter 23) undercut the liberal masculine ideal. Liberal ideology depicted middle-class men as aggressive, self-reliant initiators. Now these men found themselves bound to desks and taking orders. No longer masters of their own fates, they were now bit players in the drama of corporate capitalism. Condemnation of not only homosexuality but also feminism provided a way to redefine and strengthen masculine identity.

Finally, a new science of sexuality contributed to new fears. During the final decades of the nineteenth century, scientists made important breakthroughs in the understanding of human reproduction and sexual physiology. In 1879, for example, scientists first witnessed, with the aid of the microscope, a sperm cell penetrating an egg. Greater understanding of sexual *physiology*, however, went hand in hand with the effort to define normal sexual *practice* and to the medical condemnation of homosexuality as pathology.

Heightened concern about gender boundaries pervaded not only the science, but also the art of the late-nineteenth-century West. In the visual arts, women often appeared as elemental forces, creatures of nature rather than civilization, who threatened to trap, emasculate, engulf, suffocate, or destroy the unwary man. The Austrian Gustav Klimt (1862–1918) frequently painted women as creatures of nature, often provocatively sexual. Such images recur even more graphically in the work of Klimt's student, Egon Schiele (1890–1918). In his short life Schiele created more than 3,000 works on paper and 300 paintings, many of these depictions of dangerous women. Works such as *Black-Haired Girl with Raised Skirt* (1911) used harsh colors and brazen postures to present an unsettling vision of female sexuality.

GUSTAV KLIMT, *WATER SERPENTS* (1904–1907)
Klimt's paintings often featured women as alluring but engulfing elemental forces. Here he uses the mythological imagery of sea serpents to depict women as unabashedly sensual, even as creatures on the prowl—quite a contrast to the passive woman of separate-sphere ideology.

JUSTICE IN HISTORY

The Trial of Oscar Wilde

In March 1895 the Marquis of Queensberry left a message with the porter of a gentleman's club in London. The message, written on Queensberry's calling card, read "To Oscar Wilde, posing as a *somdomite.*" What Queensberry meant to write was *sodomite,* a common term for a man who engaged in sexual relations with other men. By handing the card to the porter, Queensberry publicly accused Wilde, a famous novelist and playwright, of homosexual—and therefore criminal—activity. Ten years earlier the British Parliament had declared illegal all homosexual activity, even consensual relations between adults in a private home. Queensberry's accusation, then, was serious. Oscar Wilde responded by suing Queensberry for libel—and set in motion a legal process that led to Wilde's imprisonment, and indirectly, to his early death.

Wilde made a reckless mistake when he chose to sue for libel, for in fact Queensberry had not libeled him. Wilde was a homosexual. He and Queensberry's son, Lord Alfred Douglas, were lovers. Why, then, did Wilde dare to challenge Queensberry? Perhaps he thought that the fact that he was married, with two children, shielded him against the charge. Or perhaps his professional successes gave Wilde a sense of invulnerability. With two of his plays then appearing on the London stage to favorable reviews, he stood at the pinnacle of his career in the spring of 1895.

Wilde had built that career by flouting middle-class codes of morality. He saw himself as an artist and insisted that art should be freed from social convention and moral restraint. His "High Society" comedies about privileged elites living scandalous lives and exchanging witty epigrams were far from the morally uplifting drama expected by middle-class audiences.

Wilde also used his public persona to attack the conventional, the respectable, and the orthodox. Widely recognized for his outrageous clothing and conversation, he had consciously adopted the mannerisms of what nineteenth-century Britons called a "dandy"—a well-dressed, irreverent, artistic, leisured, and effeminate man. Before his trial, such effeminacy did not serve as a sign of, or a code for, homosexual inclinations, but it did signal to many observers a lavish—and loose—lifestyle. Oscar Wilde, then, was a man many British men and women loved to hate.

Even so, when his trial opened Wilde appeared to be in a strong position, the prosecutor rather than the defendant. Because Wilde had Queensberry's card with the "sodomite" charge written on it, Queensberry faced certain conviction unless he could show that Wilde had engaged in homosexual activity. Wilde knew that Queensberry would not risk shining the legal spotlight on his own son's homosexuality.

At first, Queensberry's attorney, Edward Carson, focused on Wilde's published works, trying to use Wilde's own words against him. It proved an ineffective strategy. On the witness stand, Wilde reveled in the attention and made Carson seem like a man of little culture and no humor.

On the second day of the libel trial, however, Carson interrogated Wilde about his frequent visits to a male brothel and his associations with young, working-class male prostitutes. Suddenly the issue was no longer the literary merit or moral worth of Wilde's published writings, but rather his sexual life. At this point, Wilde withdrew his libel charge against Queensberry, and the court declared the marquis not guilty.

If Queensberry was innocent of libel in calling Wilde a sodomite, then by clear implication, Wilde was guilty of homosexual activity and therefore a criminal. Within days, Wilde was charged with "gross indecency" with another male. The jury failed to reach a verdict, but the state was determined to obtain a conviction and brought the charges again. Refused bail, Wilde returned to court for a new trial.

On May 25, 1895—just three months after Queensberry had left his misspelled message with the club porter—Wilde's promising literary career ended. He was found guilty of seven counts of gross indecency with other men. The presiding judge, Sir Alfred Wills, characterized the trial as "the worst case I have ever tried," and declared, "I shall under the circumstances be expected to pass the severest sentence the law allows. In my judgment it is totally inadequate for such a case." He sentenced Wilde to two years at hard labor. The physical punishment took its toll. Wilde died in 1900 at age 46.

In sentencing Wilde, Wills described him as "the centre of a circle of extensive corruption of the most hideous kind." How do we account for the intensity of Wills's language and the severity of Wilde's sentence? Homosexual activity had long been condemned on religious grounds, but this condemnation grew harsher in the closing decades of the nineteenth century. In a time of rapid and threatening change, the marking of gender boundaries became a way to create and enforce social order. Wilde crossed those boundaries and so seemed to threaten social stability.

Moreover, by the end of the nineteenth century, the state had assumed new responsibilities. Desperate to enhance national strength in a period of heightened international competition, Western governments intervened in areas previously considered to be the domain of the private citizen. To strengthen their nation's economic productivity and military viability, governments now compelled parents to send their children to school, regulated the hours adults could work, supervised the sale of food and drugs, set new standards for housing construction—and policed sexual boundaries.

The policing of sexual boundaries became easier after the Wilde trial because it provided a homosexual personality profile, a "Wanted" poster to hang on the walls of Western culture. For many observers of his well-publicized trial, Wilde became the embodiment of The Homosexual, a particular and peculiar type of person, and a menace to cultural stability. The Wilde trial linked "dandyism" to this new image. Outward stylistic choices such as effeminacy, artistic sensibilities, and flamboyant clothing and conversation became, for many observers, the telltale signs of inner corruption. Thus, the Wilde case marked a turning point in the construction and the condemnation of a homosexual identity.

OSCAR WILDE AND LORD ALFRED DOUGLAS
Although the British government pursued its case against Wilde, it made no effort to put together a case against Douglas.

For Discussion

1. How does this trial illustrate the role of medical, legal, and cultural assumptions in shaping sexual identity in the late nineteenth century?

2. Did the trial of Oscar Wilde achieve justice? If so, what kind and for whom?

Taking It Further

An Ideal Husband. 1999. This film adaptation of Oscar Wilde's hilarious play exemplifies his lighthearted but devastating critique of conventional manners and morals.

Ellman, Richard. *Oscar Wilde.* 1988. An important biography of Wilde.

McLaren, Angus. *The Trials of Masculinity: Policing Sexual Boundaries, 1870–1930.* 1997. Places the Wilde trial within a wider cultural context.

The Real Trial of Oscar Wilde: The First Uncensored Transcript of The Trial of Oscar Wilde vs. John Douglas (Marquess of Queensberry), 1895. 2003. Includes an introduction by Wilde's grandson Merlin Holland.

The Birth of Modernism

Schiele's disturbing paintings exemplify the new **modernist movement.** In the final decades of the nineteenth century, modernist artists such as Schiele tossed aside the rules and embarked on a series of bold experiments. No single style characterized modernism, but modernist artists, musicians, and writers shared an impatience with the middle-class liberal worldview.

In that worldview, the arts served a useful purpose in civilized society. Visiting art galleries was a popular activity, rather like going to the movies today. Respectable workers and middle-class men and women crowded into exhibitions where they viewed paintings that told an entertaining story and had a clear moral message. Modernism shattered this community between artist and audience by rejecting the idea of art as an instrument of moral or emotional uplift. Modernists declared "art for art's sake." The value of art rests in itself, not on its social impact. Modernist painters did not seek to tell a story or to preach a sermon, but rather to experiment with line, color, and composition.

In addition to rejecting the idea that art must be useful, modernists also challenged middle-class liberalism by insisting that history was irrelevant. The middle class viewed history as an important source of moral lessons and as a key to understanding the present and improving the future. In contrast, modernists argued that fast-moving industrial and technological change shattered the lines connecting past, present, and future. Painters such as the Futurists in Italy (one of the many artistic movements that clustered under the modernist umbrella) reveled in the new machine age, a world cut off from anything that had gone before. In their paintings they depicted human beings as machines in motion, moving too fast to be tied down to history. The Futurists also challenged traditional ways of living, epitomized in their declaration of war on spaghetti.

New musical styles emerging in popular and high culture in these decades also demonstrated this modernist sense of discontinuity. Ragtime, for example, combined syncopation with unexpected rhythms and sudden stops, while jazz, which developed around the turn of the century in black urban neighborhoods in the United States, created a musical universe of constant spontaneous change. In Europe, symphonic musicians such as Russian composer Igor Stravinsky (1882–1971) and his Austrian counterpart Arnold Schoenberg (1874–1951) shocked their audiences with pieces that broke all the rules. In Stravinsky's ballet, *The Rite of Spring* (1913), the meter shifts 28 times in the final 34 bars of the central dance. Similarly, Schoenberg eliminated repetition from his works and used rapid tempo changes.

Modernists also rejected the middle-class faith in the power of human reason and observation, and instead emphasized the role of individual experience and intuition in shaping human understanding. In Paris, for example, a group of artists centered on the Spaniard Pablo Picasso (1881–1973) juxtaposed different perspectives and points of view on a single canvas. They called themselves **Cubists**. In one cultural historian's apt description, "Cubists cracked the mirror of art."[6] Their fragmented, jagged, energetic works no longer reflected the world "out there," but instead revealed the artist's fluid and contradictory vision. (See *Encounters and Transformations* in this chapter.)

This emphasis on art as a personal expression is also seen in the **Expressionist** movement, centered not in France as was Cubism, but in central and eastern Europe. Expressionists such as Egon Schiele argued that art should express the artist's interior vision, not the exterior world. In nude self-portraits, Schiele depicted himself as ugly and emaciated, a graphic expression of his tormented internal universe. His fellow Expressionist, the Russian painter Wassily Kandinsky (1866–1944), went further in shattering artistic boundaries and splashing his emotions all over the canvas. Kandinsky sought to remove all form from his painting, to create a universe of pure color. In the process, he produced the first purely abstract paintings in Western art.

Audiences tended to greet modernist works with incomprehension and outrage. At the first performance of Schoenberg's *Five Orchestral Pieces* in London in 1912, one listener reported that "the audience laughed audibly all through...and hissed vigorously at the end." The next year in Vienna, the performance of a different Schoenberg piece had to be abandoned after the audience rioted. Reviewers routinely condemned modernist painting as sick, pornographic, or simply insane. One London reviewer dismissed the painter Paul Cézanne (1869–1954) as "an artist with diseased retinas."

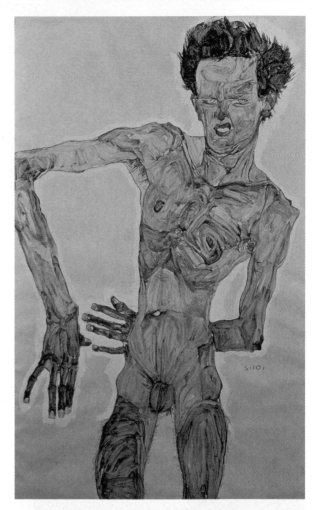

EGON SCHIELE, *NUDE SELF-PORTRAIT WITH OPEN MOUTH* (1910)

Schiele's paintings exemplify the Expressionist movement with their bold use of color and their no-holds-barred exploration of human emotion and sexuality.

Source: Egon Schiele (1890–1918), "Standing Nude, Facing Front (Self Portrait), 1910." Graphische Sammlung Albertina, Vienna, Austria/The Bridgeman Art Library

Most audiences remained firmly within a cultural milieu in which paintings revealed pretty scenes, novels told a moral tale, and music offered harmonious charm. In the early twentieth century, one of the most popular pieces of art in the English-speaking world was *The Light of the World* by William Holman Hunt (1827–1910). This moralistic piece with

WILLIAM HOLMAN HUNT, *THE LIGHT OF THE WORLD* (1903)

In this devotional painting, Jesus, the light of the world, stands knocking at the closed door of a lost soul. The overgrown weeds and fallen fruit symbolize sin and the lantern stands for Christ's illuminating power. The stars and crescents on the lantern represent Holman Hunt's hope for the conversion of Jews and Muslims to Christianity. The popularity of this work highlights the limited appeal of modernist art in the pre-1914 era.

Source: William Holman Hunt (1827–1910), "The Light of the World", c. 1852, oil on canvas. © Manchester Art Gallery, UK/The Bridgeman Art Library

its easy-to-understand and uplifting story, at odds with every modernist principle, triumphantly toured the British Empire from 1905 to 1907. Enthusiastic crowds jostled for tickets and hailed the painting as a religious and artistic masterpiece.

Popular Religion and Secularization

As the response to Holman Hunt's depiction of Jesus shows, religious belief remained a powerful force in the decades after 1870. In Britain, Sunday worship continued to be a central aspect of middle-class culture, and the still-strong Sunday School movement and religious instruction in state schools ensured that working-class children were taught the fundamentals of the Christian faith. On the Continent, many Europeans connected revolutionary anarchy with unbelief after revolutionaries executed the Archbishop of Paris in 1871 (see Chapter 22). The excesses of the Paris Commune thus contributed to a religious revival. Popular Catholic religiosity often focused on the cult of the Virgin Mary: By the 1870s, the shrine at Lourdes, the site of Mary's miraculous appearance in 1858, was attracting hundreds of thousands of Catholic pilgrims.

Three additional factors contributed to the religiosity of late-nineteenth-century Europe. First, the high rate of immigration meant that many people found themselves searching for something familiar in foreign cities. They often turned to the religious cultures of the homeland. In English cities, for example, Irish immigrants looked to the local Roman Catholic Church for spiritual solace, material support, and social contacts. Second, in many regions nationalism strengthened religious belief and practice. Hence, for Polish nationalists dreaming of independence from Russian rule, Roman Catholicism was a key part of a separate national identity. Finally, as we shall see in the next section, the expansion of Western empires across the globe appeared to provide clear evidence of the ongoing triumph of Christianity.

Yet this triumphalism met growing anxiety as Christians faced new challenges. As we saw in our discussion of Darwin, developments in biology undermined the orthodox Christian view of nature as harmonious and divinely directed. Medical advances also narrowed the appeal of traditional religion. People had once accepted diseases such as cholera as "acts of God," but now they understood their natural causes. Scientists, in other words, seemed able to answer questions previously thought the province of theologians. Finally, the emergence of the social sciences directly challenged Christianity by dismissing the question of religious truth and asking instead, what is the function of religious belief in a society? Emile Durkheim (1858–1917), one of the founders of French sociology, dared to lump Christianity with "even the most barbarous and the most fantastic rites and the strangest myths." Durkheim insisted that no religion was more true than any other—each filled a social need.[7]

The Christian response to these challenges varied. Many Protestants embraced the scientific method as a gift from God. They argued that the study of the Bible as a historical and literary document—as a collection of divinely inspired texts produced by all-too-human writers—promised to free Christians *from* antiquated beliefs impossible to sustain in the new scientific age and *for* a more relevant, reform-oriented religious life. Protestant fundamentalists, however, insisted on retaining a belief in the literal, historical, and scientific accuracy of the Christian scriptures, a stance that led them to oppose science as the enemy of religion.

The Roman Catholic papacy also adopted a defiant pose in the face of modern challenges. In 1864, Pope Pius IX (r. 1846–1878) issued a *Syllabus of Errors,* which condemned the notion that the pope should "harmonize himself with progress, with liberalism, and with modern civilization." Six years later, a church council—the first called since the sixteenth-century Catholic Reformation—proclaimed the doctrine of **papal infallibility**. According to this doctrine, when the pope issues a decree that concerns matters of faith and morality, that decree is free from error and valid for all time and all places. The proclamation of papal infallibility rebuked those Catholic theologians who argued that Christianity had to adapt to the modern world.

The Roman Catholic Church also faced important political challenges in these decades. The spread of socialism provided European workers with a belief system and source of communal life outside of, and opposed to, the Church. Moreover, in countries with a large Catholic population, the Church's alliance with conservatism pushed **anticlericalism** to a dominant position on the liberal agenda. In France, Catholics dominated the political parties that demanded a return to monarchical or authoritarian rule, and liberal Frenchmen who wanted the Third Republic to survive fought to reduce the Church's influence.

The most significant challenge faced by religious institutions after 1870, however, emerged not from parliamentary assemblies, socialist rallies, or scientific laboratories, but rather from the department stores and sports fields. In the growing industrial cities, working- and middle-class individuals enjoyed new, secular sources of entertainment, inspiration, and desire. Energies once focused on religious devotion centered increasingly on the activities of consumption and recreation. Whereas shared religious worship had once cemented community life, the rituals of spectator sports now forged new bonds of loyalty and identity. The ever-changing array of colorful products displayed in shop windows promised fulfillment and satisfaction in the here and now, an earthly paradise rather than a heavenly reward.

THE NEW IMPERIALISM

■ **What were the causes and consequences of the new imperialist ideology for the West and non-Western societies?**

Many of those items on display behind the new plate-glass shop windows were the products of imperial conquest. **New imperialism** intertwined with many of the developments we have already examined in this chapter and in Chapter 23. Telegraphs ensured rapid communication from far-flung empires and mass printing technologies guaranteed that illustrated tales of imperial achievement made their way into homes and schools. Social Darwinism supplied a supposedly scientific justification for the conquest of peoples deemed biologically inferior, while swift military victories over other societies helped quell anxiety about European degeneration. For many Europeans—particularly the British, who presided over the largest empire in the world—imperialist domination served as reassuring evidence of the apparent superiority of Western civilization.

Understanding the New Imperialism

Imperialism itself was not new. In the fifteenth century, Europeans had embarked on the first phase of imperialism, with the extension of European control across coastal ports of Africa and India, and into the New World of the Americas (see Chapter 13). In the second phase, which began in the late seventeenth century, European colonial empires in Asia and the Western Hemisphere expanded as governments sought to increase their profits from international trade (see Chapter 18).

As in these earlier phases of imperialism, trade motivated much of the imperial activity after 1870 as well. The need to protect existing imperial interests also impelled further conquests. The desire to protect India—the "Jewel in the Crown" of the British Empire—explains much of British imperial acquisition throughout the nineteenth century. Britain's annexation of Burma and Kashmir, its establishment of spheres of influence in the Middle East, and its interests along the coast of Africa were all linked to its empire in India.

Defense of existing empires and commercial considerations, however, does not fully explain new imperialism. After 1870 and particularly after 1880, the West's expansion became much more aggressive. In just 30 years, European control of the globe's land surface swelled from 65 to 85 percent. In addition, new players joined the expansionist game. Recently formed nation-states such as Germany and Italy jostled for colonial territory in Africa, the United States began to extend its control over the Western Hemisphere, and Japan initiated its imperialist march into China and Korea. What factors lay behind this new imperialism?

TECHNOLOGY, ECONOMICS, AND POLITICS   Part of the answer lies in the economic developments examined in Chapter 23. Because of the Second Industrial Revolution, European and American economies increasingly depended on raw materials available only in regions such as Asia, Africa, and South America. Rubber insulated the electrical and telegraph wires now encircling the globe. Palm oil from Africa provided the lubricant needed for industrial machinery. The slaughter of Africa's once-plentiful elephant herds provided the ivory for many of the new consumer goods now decorating middle-class parlors, such as piano keys and billiard balls. Relying on these primary resources, Western states were quick to respond to perceived threats to their economic interests. The Germans even coined a word to describe this fear of losing access to essential raw materials: *Torschlusspanik,* or "fear of the closing door."

Competition for markets also accelerated imperial acquisition. With the onset of economic depression in the 1870s (discussed in Chapter 23), industrialists faced declining demand for their products in Europe. Imperial expansion seemed to provide a solution, with annexed territories seen as captive markets. As a French newspaper editorial explained in

1891, "every gunshot opens another outlet for French industry."[8]

By the mid-1890s, however, the depression had ended in most regions—yet the pace of imperialist expansion did not slow. Instead, a global investment boom ensured continuing imperialist expansion. European capital financed railway lines, mines, and public utilities across the world. With each railroad or coal mine or dam, European interests in non-European regions expanded, and so did the pressure on European governments to assume formal political control should outside competitors or local political instability threaten those interests.

In addition to these economic factors, domestic political pressures encouraged imperialist acquisition. In the age of mass politics, political leaders needed to find issues that would appeal to new voters. Tales of dangerous explorations and decisive military victories proved popular. Imperialist conquest assured ordinary men that they were part of a superior, conquering people.

As the *Different Voices* feature in this chapter illustrates (see page 770), international competition also fostered imperialism. Newly formed nations such as Italy and Germany sought empires outside Europe as a way to gain power and prestige within Europe. The nineteenth-century German historian Heinrich von Treitschke explained, "All great nations in the fullness of their strength have desired to set their mark on barbarian lands and those who fail to participate in this great rivalry will play a pitiable role in time to come."[9] Similar concerns about status and strategic advantages motivated nations such as Britain and France to defend and expand their empires.

THE IMPERIAL IDEA   New imperialism functioned as a belief system that permeated middle-class and mass culture in the decades after 1870. To educate viewers in the "imperial idea," exhibitions and fairs displayed goods and peoples from conquered regions. Images of empire appeared in boys' adventure stories, glossy ads for soap and chocolates, picture postcards, cookie tins, and cheap commemorative china plates and mugs. In the music halls and theaters, imperialist songs and dramas received popular applause.

W w   𝒲 𝓌

W   is   the   Word
Of an Englishman true:
When given, it means
What he says, he will do.

A LESSON IN THE IMPERIAL IDEA

As this alphabet reader makes clear, education in imperial ideology began early.

ENCOUNTERS AND TRANSFORMATIONS

Picasso Goes to the Museum

After months of work and more than 800 preparatory sketches, Pablo Picasso judged the painting finished at last. But when he showed *Les Demoiselles d'Avignon* to his friend and rival Matisse, the Frenchman thought the work a joke. Another friend and fellow painter, Georges Braques, found it appalling. Picasso did not exhibit the painting for several years and it remained largely unknown until 1939 when it went on display at the Museum of Modern Art in New York City. Today, *Demoiselles* is one of the most well-known modernist works of art in the Western world, "the amazing act on which all the art of our century is built."[10] It helped transform the history of Western art and even, perhaps, the history of perception itself.

With its in-your-face sexuality, *Demoiselles* retains its ability to shock. Five naked whores (*demoiselles* means "prostitutes") advertise for trade, twisting their bodies into erotic, even pornographic poses. The painting's eroticism alone, however, does not explain its impact.

The painting as we now know it resulted from a specific encounter that occurred when Picasso went to a museum in Paris. Some time in 1906 or 1907, when he was already deeply involved in this painting, Picasso viewed African tribal masks on exhibit at the Ethnographic Museum in the Trocadero. This museum visit profoundly excited and upset the Spanish painter. His girlfriend Fernande Olivier reported, "Picasso is going crazy over Negro works and statues."[11] In Picasso's view, these "Negro works and statues" possessed the vitality and authenticity missing from Western art. Picasso and many modernists believed that Western civilization, with its urbanization and industrialism, its organizations and academies, its codes and regulations, had stifled artistic

expression. They saw most modern art as weak and lifeless—the tired-out product of a worn-out society. In contrast, they argued, African art resembled the pictures drawn by children: energetic, playful, creative, colored outside the lines.

This notion of African culture as childlike, of course, reflected the imperialist idea of "backward peoples." Picasso and other modernists rejected the imperialist notion of Western superiority and criticized Western empires, yet they could not escape imperialist stereotypes. Within the limits of these stereotypes, however, modernists turned the cultural relationship of the West and Africa upside down. Picasso went to African art to learn, not to conquer.

PABLO PICASSO, *LES DEMOISELLES D'AVIGNON* (1907)

Source: Pablo Picasso, "Les Demoiselles d'Avignon." 1907. Oil on canvas. 8' × 7'8" (2.44 × 2.34 m). Acquired through the Lillie P. Bliss Bequest. Digital Image © The Museum of Modern Art/Licensed by Scala-Art Resource, NY. © 2008 ARS Artists Rights Society, NY

Picasso's encounter with the African masks transformed this specific painting and modern art itself. After his Trocadero visit, Picasso reconfigured the faces of the two women on the right so that their masklike appearances now clash awkwardly with those of the three other prostitutes. This step destroyed any unity of narrative or composition in the painting: The five figures are no longer part of a single story or share a single point of view. Picasso also fragmented each of the bodies, flattening them and reducing them to jutting geometric forms. Thus, *Demoiselles* pushed Picasso toward Cubism, one of the most influential artistic styles of the twentieth century (see page 763).

As the art historian John Golding has written, "In the *Demoiselles* Picasso began to shatter the human figure.... He spent the rest of his artistic life dissecting, reassembling, and reinventing it."[12] After Picasso, Western artists spent the rest of the twentieth century dissecting, reassembling, and reinventing the way we see and depict our world.

For Discussion

How did Picasso use the art of a different culture to explain and challenge his own? Did *Demoiselles* challenge or did it affirm Western imperialist ideas?

At the center of the imperial idea stood the assumption that Western dominance over the world was a good thing. Europeans would not have sought to remake the world in the European image had they not been convinced of the superiority of that image. What led them to believe they had the right and the responsibility to take charge of other cultures and continents?

One key factor was the perceived link between Western Christianity and "civilization." Christian missionaries served as a vanguard of Western culture throughout the nineteenth century. The celebrated Scottish explorer David Livingstone (1813–1873), who mapped out much of central and southern Africa, was a Protestant missionary (although not a very successful one— his only convert eventually renounced the Christian faith). Missionary society publications introduced their readers to exotic territories, while the societies themselves lobbied for Western territorial expansion to promote the spread of Christian missions.

Technology also seemed to justify Western imperialism. Before the eighteenth century, the technological gap between the West and other societies had not loomed large. In some cases, such as China, non-Western societies had held the technological advantage. Industrialization, however, gave the West the technological edge. Thus, the British adventurer Mary Kingsley (1862–1900) wrote, "....[W]hen I come back from a spell in Africa, the thing that makes me proud of being one of the English is...a great railway engine.... [I]t is the manifestation of the superiority of my race."[13]

Finally, Social Darwinism seemed to provide scientific authority for the imperial idea. Thus, the British Lord Milner (1854–1925) explained in a speech in South Africa in 1903: "The white man must rule, because he is elevated by many, many steps above the black man; steps which it will take the latter centuries to climb, and which it is quite possible that the vast bulk of the black population may never be able to climb at all."

Imperialists believed that empire—whether ordained by God or by biology—was a moral duty: Men and women in the West were obliged to bring the benefits of their civilization to the rest of the world. The British poet Rudyard Kipling (1865–1936) famously articulated this

DIFFERENT VOICES ADVOCATES OF NEW IMPERIALISM

New imperialism resulted from a variety of fears and ambitions, as these two documents illustrate. While some advocates of imperial expansion sought to convert the world's populace to Christianity, others insisted that overseas possessions strengthened a nation's ability to compete with its rivals, not only in the economic but also in the military, diplomatic, and even cultural arenas.

Jules Ferry, Speech Before French National Assembly, July 1883

Jules Ferry (1832–1893), who served two terms as premier (prime minister) of France, supported French imperial expansion. As the interruptions and objections to his speech reveal, Ferry faced opposition, particularly from socialist politicians.

M.* JULES FERRY: Gentlemen....I believe that there is some benefit in summarizing...the principles, the motives, and the various interests by which a policy of colonial expansion may be justified.

In the area of economics, I will allow myself to place before you...the considerations which justify a policy of colonial expansion from the point of view of that need, felt more and more strongly by the industrial populations...of our own rich and hard working country: the need for export markets....Why? Because next door to us Germany is surrounded by barriers, because beyond the ocean, the United States of America has become protectionist...because not only have these great markets...become more difficult of access for our industrial products, but also these great states are beginning to pour products not seen heretofore onto our own markets....

Gentlemen, there is a second point...the humanitarian and civilizing side of the question. On this point the honorable M. Camille Pellatan [an anti-imperialist opponent of Ferry's] has jeered in his own refined and clever manner; he jeers, he condemns, and he says "What is this civilization which you impose with cannonballs?

What is it but another form of barbarism? Don't these populations, these inferior races, have the same rights as you? Aren't they masters of their own houses? Have they called upon you? You come to them against their will, you offer them violence, but not civilization."...

Gentlemen, I must speak from a higher and more truthful plane. It must be stated openly that, in effect, superior races have rights over inferior races. *[Movement on many benches on the far left.]*

M. JULES MAIGNE [a socialist opponent]: Oh! You dare to say this in the country which has proclaimed the rights of man!

....

FERRY: I repeat that superior races have a right, because they have a duty. They have the duty to civilize inferior races.... *[Approbation from the left. New interruptions from the extreme left and from the right.]*...

Gentlemen, there are certain considerations which merit the attention of all patriots. The conditions of naval warfare have been profoundly altered. ["Very true! Very true!"][†] At this time, as you know, a warship cannot carry more than 14 days' worth of coal...and a ship which is out of coal is a derelict on the surface of the sea, abandoned to the first person who comes along. Thence the necessity of having on the oceans provision stations, shelters, ports for defense and revictualling. *[Applause at the center and left. Various interruptions.]* And it is for this that we needed Tunisia, for this that we needed Saigon and the Mekong Delta, for this that we need Madagascar...and will never leave them! *[Applause from a great number of benches.]* Gentlemen, in Europe as it is today, in this competition of so many rivals which we see growing around us,...in a Europe, or rather in a universe of this sort, a policy of peaceful seclusion or abstention is simply the highway to decadence!...

---

*"M."= abbreviation for "Monsieur" ("Mister").

[†]These words were shouted out in the assembly by other legislators.

France…cannot be merely a free country…she must also be a great country, exercising all of her rightful influence over the destiny of Europe…she ought to propagate this influence throughout the world and carry everywhere that she can her language, her customs, her flag, her arms, and her genius. *[Applause at center and left.]*

Friedrich Fabri, *Does Germany Need Colonies?* (1879)

A pastor and theology professor, Friedrich Fabri (1824–1891) directed an interdenominational German missionary society that worked in southern Africa and the East Indies. In 1879, Fabri published Does Germany Need Colonies? *His answer was unequivocal.*

In looking for colonial possessions Germany is not prompted by the desire for expanding its power; it wants only to fulfill a national, we may even say a moral duty….

The German nation has long experience on the oceans, is skilled in industry and commerce, more capable than others in agricultural colonization, and furnished with ample manpower like no other modern highly cultured nation. Should it not also enter successfully upon this new venture?…There is much bitterness, much poisonous partisanship in our newly united Germany; to open a promising new course of national development might have a liberating effect, and move the national spirit in a new direction.

Even more important is the consideration that a people at the height of their political power can successfully maintain their historic position only as long as they recognize and prove themselves as the bearers of a cultural mission. That is the only way which guarantees the stability and growth of national prosperity, which is the necessary basis for an enduring source of power. In past years Germany has contributed only its intellectual and literary work to this century; now we have turned to politics and become powerful. But if the goal of political power becomes an end in itself, it leads to

hardness, even to barbarism, unless that nation is willing to undertake the inspirational, moral, and economic leadership of the times….[L]ook around the globe and assess the ever-increasing colonial possessions of Great Britain, the strength which it draws from them, the skills of its administration, and the dominant position which the Anglo-Saxon stock occupies in all overseas countries….It would be well if we Germans began to learn from the colonial destiny of our Anglo-Saxon cousins and emulate them in peaceful competition. When, centuries ago, the German empire stood at the head of the European states, it was the foremost commercial and maritime power. If the new Germany wants to restore and preserve its traditional powerful position in future, it will conceive of it as a cultural mission and no longer hesitate to practice its colonizing vocation.

Sources: Jules Ferry, Speech before French National Assembly, 1883, in Ralph A. Austin (ed.), *Modern Imperialism: Western Overseas Expansion and Its Aftermath, 1776–1965* (Lexington, Mass.: D.C. Heath, 1969), 70–73. Friedrich Fabri, *Does Germany Need Colonies?* (Gotha, Germany: Perthes, 1879). Translated by Theodore von Laue. In Perry et al., *Sources of the Western Tradition*, 4th ed, Vol. 2. (New York: Houghton Mifflin, 1999), 235–237. Copyright © 1999 Wadsworth, a part of Cengage Learning, Inc. Reproduced by permission. www.cengage.com/permissions

For Discussion

1. What are the four reasons Ferry gives for imperial expansion? Do they differ from Fabri's?

2. Which sections of these documents might any nineteenth-century imperialist of any nationality have articulated? Which sections make sense only within the specific French and German contexts?

3. The "imperial idea" played an important role in shaping Western identities at the end of the nineteenth century. How would Ferry and Fabri have defined the West? How would Ferry's parliamentary opponents?

idea in 1899, in a poem urging American policy-makers to conquer the Philippines:

> *Take up the White Man's burden—*
> *Send forth the best ye breed—*
> *Go bind your sons to exile,*
> *To serve your captives' need;*
> *To wait in heavy harness*
> *On fluttered folk and wild—*
> *Your new-caught sullen peoples,*
> *Half devil and half child.*[14]

Not all Europeans and Americans embraced the idea of the "White Man's burden," and many rejected the imperialist assumption of Western superiority. As the example of Picasso makes clear (see *Encounters and Transformations* in this chapter), some modernist artists looked to non-Western cultures for artistic inspiration. The

Fauves ("wild beasts"), a Paris-based circle of artists that included Henri Matisse (1869–1954) and Paul Gauguin (1848–1903), condemned most Western art as artificial, and sought in their own brilliantly colored works to rediscover the vitality that they found in non-Western cultures.

Critics of empire often focused on its domestic political and economic implications. The British economist J. A. Hobson (1858–1940) charged that overseas empires benefited only wealthy capitalists while distracting public attention from the need for political and economic reform at home. Hobson argued that unregulated capitalism led almost inevitably to imperialist expansion: While impoverishing the masses, the capitalist system generates huge surpluses in capital for a small

MAP 24.1A

(a) Africa Before the Scramble, 1876 and (b) Africa After the Scramble, 1914

A comparison of these two maps reveals the dramatic impact of the new imperialism on African societies. Indigenous empires such as the Sokoto Caliphate in West Africa came under Western rule, as did tribal societies such as the Herero. Even indigenous states ruled by whites of European descent came under European rule, as the examples of the Transvaal and the Orange Free State in South Africa illustrate. Only Ethiopia and Liberia remained independent.

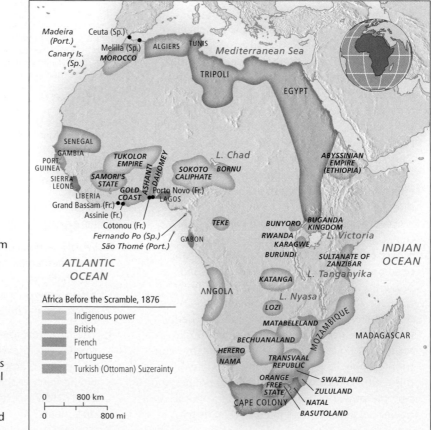

elite, who must then find somewhere to invest these surpluses. Hobson's ideas influenced European socialists, who condemned imperialism along with capitalism.

The Scramble for Africa

New imperialism reached its zenith in Africa. As maps 24.1a and 24.1b show, in just 30 years, between 1875 and 1905, Europeans established 30 new colonies and protectorates encompassing ten million square miles of territory and controlling 110 million Africans. By 1905, 90 percent of Africa was under European control. The conquest of the African continent was so rapid and dramatic that as early as 1884 mystified Europeans began to talk about the **Scramble for Africa.**

OVERCOMING THE OBSTACLES When the nineteenth century began, Europeans knew little more about the continent of Africa than the ancient Greeks had known. A profitable trading network between European merchants and Africa's coastal regions existed, but European efforts to establish settlements in the African interior faced three key obstacles: the climate, disease, and African resistance.

Africa was known as "the white man's grave." Over 75 percent of the white soldiers sent to West Africa in the early nineteenth century died there, and another 20 percent became invalids. Temperatures of more than 100 degrees Fahrenheit in some regions and constant rainfall in others made travel extremely difficult. The mosquito and the tsetse fly made it deadly. Mosquito bites brought malaria, while the tsetse fly carried trypanosomiasis, or sleeping sickness, an infectious illness that ended in a deadly paralysis. Sleeping sickness killed livestock as well as people. In regions with endemic trypanosomiasis, such as equatorial, southern, and eastern Africa, the use of horses and oxen was impossible. Despite such difficulties, Europeans did endeavor to establish inland settlements in Africa, but then faced the obstacle of African resistance. In the seventeenth century, for example, the Portuguese set up forts and trading centers in modern Zimbabwe but were driven out by local African populations.

Beginning around 1830, however, a series of developments altered the relationship between Europe and Africa and made European conquest possible. First, European explorers changed the

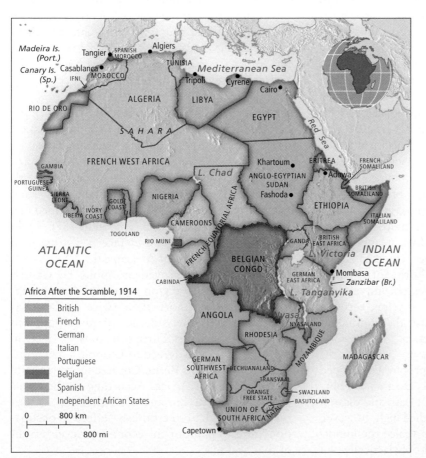

Africa After the Scramble, 1914

	British
	French
	German
	Italian
	Portuguese
	Belgian
	Spanish
	Independent African States

0   800 km
0   800 mi

I MAP 24.1B

Western understanding of Africa. Between 1830 and 1870, adventurers mapped out the chief geographical features of Africa's interior and so illuminated the "Dark Continent" for Europeans. They discovered that central Africa was not the empty desert that Europeans had assumed, but rather a territory with abundant agricultural and mineral resources—and lots of people, all of them potential consumers of European goods.

The shift in the European vision of Africa—from desert to treasure house—coincided with important political changes within Africa itself. Many of these political shifts were the unintended consequences of Western efforts to abolish the slave trade. We saw in Chapter 18 that in the 1830s, Britain and other European powers, pressured by humanitarian and missionary groups, sought to wipe out the West African slave trade. They succeeded—and the slave trade shifted to central and eastern Africa. This shift caused great political instability. African slaving nations relied on frequent military raids to obtain their human merchandise. These raids—carried out by Africans against Africans—disrupted agricultural production, shattered trade networks, and undermined the authority of existing political rulers. With political systems in disarray, many African regions were vulnerable to European encroachment.

Finally, three specific techno-scientific developments—the steamship, the "quinine prophylaxis," and the repeating, breech-loading rifle—shifted the balance of power in the West's favor. The steam revolution began in 1807 when the *Clermont,* a ship powered by a steam engine, chugged its way along the Hudson River between Albany and New York City. Steam proved crucial in enabling Western imperialists to overcome the obstacles to traveling through Africa by allowing them to use the continent's extensive but shallow river system.

Steam enabled Westerners to penetrate the African interior. The quinine prophylaxis helped them survive once they got there. Doctors had long prescribed quinine for malaria. Death and disability rates from the disease remained high, however, until some chance discoveries revealed the importance of taking quinine prophylactically—of

saturating the system with quinine *before* any infection. By the 1860s, Westerners routinely ingested quinine in preparation for postings in Africa—and their death rates dropped dramatically.

African death rates, however, soared because of the third crucial technology of imperialism—the repeating, breech-loading rifles Europeans carried from the 1870s on. Before the invention of these rifles, Europeans used muskets or muzzle-loading rifles. These weapons fouled easily, particularly in damp weather, and could be loaded only one ball at a time—usually while the rifleman was standing up. The musket-armed European did not gain a significant military advantage, even over spears. With the repeating rifle, however, "any European infantryman could now fire lying down, undetected, in any weather, 15 rounds of ammunition in as many seconds at targets up to half a mile away." As we saw at the beginning of this chapter, the repeating breech-loader and its descendant, the machine gun, made the European conquest of regions such as the Sudan "more like hunting than war."[15]

SLICING THE CAKE: THE CONQUEST OF AFRICA   In the decades after 1870, convinced that the conquest of African territories would guarantee commercial prosperity and strengthen national power, European states moved quickly to beat out their rivals and grab a piece of the continent. As King Leopold II of Belgium (1865–1909) explained in a letter to his ambassador in London in 1876, "I do not want to miss a good chance of getting us a slice of this magnificent African cake."[16]

Leopold's slice proved enormous. He wanted the Congo, a huge region of central Africa comprising territory more than twice as large as central Europe. After a decade of quarreling, representatives of the European powers met in Berlin in 1884 and agreed to Leopold's demands. They also used this **Berlin Conference** to regulate the Scramble for Africa. According to the terms established in Berlin, any state claiming a territory in Africa had to establish "effective occupation" and to plan for the economic development of that region.

But as the history of the Congo Free State demonstrated, such economic development served European, not African, interests. Leopold's personal mercenary army turned the Congo into a hellhole of slavery and death. By claiming all so-called vacant land, Leopold deprived villagers of the grazing, foraging, and hunting grounds they needed to survive. He levied rubber quotas for each village, forcing villagers to harvest wild rubber for up to 25 days each month while their families starved. Brutal punishments ensured compliance: Soldiers chopped off the hands of villagers who failed to meet their quota. The Belgians also forced Africans to serve as human mules, a practice that spread sleeping sickness from the western coast into the interior. As an estimated three million people died from the combined effects of forced labor, brutal punishments, starvation, and disease, Leopold II's enormous profits from the Congo enabled him to indulge his hobby of building elaborate tourist resorts on the Riviera.

King Leopold's brand of imperialism proved so scandalous that in 1908 the Belgian government replaced Leopold's personal rule with state control over the Congo. Yet the king's exploitation of the Congo differed only in degree, not in kind, from the nature of European conquest elsewhere in Africa. Forced labor was common throughout European-controlled areas, as were brutal punishments for any Africans who dared resist. Faced with tribal revolt in Southwest Africa, the German colonial army commander in 1904 ordered the extermination of the entire Herero tribe. His soldiers drove 20,000 men, women, and children from their villages into the desert to die of thirst.

AFRICAN RESISTANCE As the Herero rebellion demonstrated, Africans frequently resisted imperial regimes, but to no avail. The only successful episode of African resistance to European conquest occurred in northern Africa, in the kingdom of Ethiopia (also called Abyssinia). By the time of the European Scramble for Africa, Ethiopia had developed not only a modern standing army, but also an advanced infrastructure and communications system. In 1896 these

factors enabled the Ethiopian nation to defeat the Italian army at the Battle of Adowa.

Adowa, however, was the exception. The technological gap between the indigenous peoples and their European conquerors doomed most African resistance. Africans did have guns, the result of a booming arms trade between European rifle manufacturers and African states. Frequently, however, the arms shipped to Africa were inferior models—muskets or single-firing muzzle-loaders rather than the up-to-date and deadly efficient repeating rifles and early machine guns possessed by the European invaders. African military leaders who did obtain advanced weaponry often failed to make the strategic leap necessary to adapt their military tactics to new technologies. (As we will see in Chapter 25, European military leaders made similar mistakes in World War I.)

Asian Encounters

Unlike most of Africa, many of the diverse states of Asia had already been woven into the web of the Western economy well before 1870 as a part of the eighteenth-century mercantilist empires established by Dutch, British, Portuguese, and French trading companies (see Chapter 18). Throughout the nineteenth century, European governments strengthened their control over many of these regions, primarily to protect trade routes or to ensure access to profitable commodities such as rubber, tin, tobacco, and sugar. The Dutch, for example, expanded their East Indies empire, moving from control of the island of Java in 1815 to domination over almost the entire archipelago several decades later (see **Map 24.2**).

Four factors accelerated the pace of imperialist acquisition in Asia after 1870. First, in the age of steam, Western powers needed Pacific islands to serve as coaling stations for their commercial and naval fleets. Second, new industrial processes heightened the economic value of many of these regions. The development of a process for producing dried coconut, for example, made Samoa so valuable that Germany, Britain, and the United States competed for

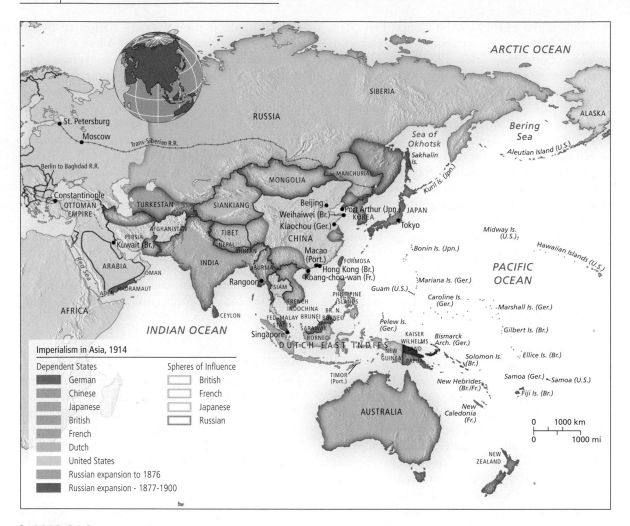

MAP 24.2

Imperialism in Asia, 1914

The impact of the new imperialism on Asia was not as dramatic as in Africa, but the spread of Western rule is significant nonetheless. This map shows a key development: the entry of non-European powers—Japan and the United States—into the imperialist game. What it does not show is the extent of Western and Japanese influence in China. Profoundly destabilized by foreign intervention, China in 1914 was in the midst of revolution.

control over the tiny islands. Third, as in Africa, international competition accelerated imperialism. Territorial gains by one power led to anxiety and a quicker pace of expansion by its rivals.

Finally, the steady erosion of Chinese political stability—itself a result of encounters with the West—intensified this "scramble for Asia." As Western powers competed for access to Chinese

markets, Western empires expanded throughout Asia. The quest for a protected trade route to China, for example, impelled the French to extend their control over neighboring Indochina. By 1893, the Union of French Indochina included the formerly independent states of Laos, Cambodia, Annam, and Tonkin—the latter two better known by their contemporary name of Vietnam.

EXPANDING THE WEST: THE UNITED STATES AND AUSTRALIA In the latter half of the nineteenth century, the United States and Australia established themselves as extensions of the West. As these states expanded and consolidated their territories and subdued indigenous populations, race-based versions of national identity that had justified European imperialist adventures came to be applied to all peoples of color.

For the United States, the acquisition of an empire in Asia followed consolidation of control over most of North America. After emerging victorious from a war with Mexico in 1846, the United States gained the territories of California, Nevada, Utah, Arizona, New Mexico, and southern Colorado. The completion of the transcontinental Union Pacific railroad in 1869 accelerated the pace of westward settlement. The conquest of the continent, however, depended on the defeat of its indigenous peoples. A series of "Indian wars" punctuated the decades from 1860 through 1890 as the United States expanded westward.

Once its borders reached the Pacific Ocean, the United States quickly emerged as an imperialist power in Asia. In 1853, Commodore Matthew Perry used his squadron of four warships to open Japan to American commerce; during the 1860s and 1870s the United States participated with the European powers in chipping away at China's national sovereignty to ensure favorable terms of trade there. By the end of the century, the United States had annexed Hawaii and part of Samoa, and as a result of the Spanish-American War had acquired Guam, the Philippines, Cuba, and Puerto Rico.

American acquisition of empire in Asia heightened anti-Asian sentiment within the United States. The Chinese Exclusion Act of 1882 (renewed in 1902) prohibited Chinese immigration. In 1913, the Alien Land Law, which outlawed land ownership by noncitizens, sought to restrict the property rights of Japanese immigrants.

These efforts paralleled attempts in the American South to construct a version of national identity confined to whites. Southern legislators used literacy tests, poll taxes, and violent intimidation to deprive blacks of their right to vote, while **Jim Crow** or segregation laws defined blacks as second-class citizens.

Australia's territorial expansion and its emergence as a Western state resembled the United States' development in many respects. After Captain James Cook discovered and claimed Australia for the British Crown in 1770, the British government used it as a dumping ground for convicts. But with the expansion of the wool industry in the decades after 1830, the six British colonies established in Australia became a center of British immigration. In 1901, these colonies joined together in the Commonwealth of Australia, part of the British Empire but a self-governing political entity—and a self-defined "Western" nation, despite its geographical location in the Eastern Hemisphere. Many Australians, including the first prime minister, Edmund Barton, identified the "West" as "white." Barton campaigned on a platform calling for a "White Australia."

As in the United States, the process of extending Western civilization demanded the defeat of the indigenous population. At the start of Britain's occupation of Australia, King George III had forbidden anyone to "wantonly destroy [the Aboriginal peoples] or give them any unnecessary interruption in the exercise of their several occupations."[17] But the settlement of whites intent on building cities, planting farms, and fencing in land for pastures interrupted the nomadic way of life for the estimated 500,000 inhabitants of Australia, living in scattered tribal groupings.

The British divided over how to treat the Aborigines. Many British settlers, and as the decades passed, many in the growing group of Australia-born whites, regarded the Aborigines as a threat to white settlements. Massacres of Aborigines resulted. Christian and humanitarian groups, and the British government in London, denounced this violence and insisted that the Aborigines should be westernized and Christianized, rather than exterminated. From the 1820s on, mission stations housed and educated Aboriginal children. Forcibly removed from their homes, these children were schooled in British ways and then at age 15 placed in employment as apprentices and domestic servants. Despite these missions, few Aborigines assimilated to the Western way of life. In the final decades of the nineteenth century, official policy shifted from assimilation to "protection." The Australian government declared Aborigines and mixed-race individuals to be legal wards of the state and required them to live on reserves. Aborigines did not receive Australian citizenship until 1967.

Many white Australians perceived not only Aborigines but also Asian immigrants as threats to their Western identity. By the 1850s, tens of thousands of Chinese had migrated to Australia. Arriving as indentured servants, they worked under brutal conditions. Many labored in the gold mines, where they received one-twelfth of the wages paid to a European. As the numbers of Chinese immigrants grew, so, too, did anti-Chinese sentiment.

One newspaper editor noted, "The Chinese question never fails. At every meeting…visions of millions of the barbarians swooping upon the colony…rise in the mental horizons of every man present."[18] In 1888, the Australian government turned back ships containing Chinese immigrants. Legislation to restrict Chinese immigration soon followed.

THE CONTINUED EXPANSION OF THE RUSSIAN EMPIRE   As in the United States and Australia, imperial expansion in nineteenth-century Russia took the form of territorial consolidation across a continent. As **Map 24.3** shows, by 1914, the Russian Empire stretched from Warsaw in central Europe to Vladivostok on the Sea of Japan—one-seventh of the global land surface. Ethnic Russians accounted for only 45 percent of the population of this empire.

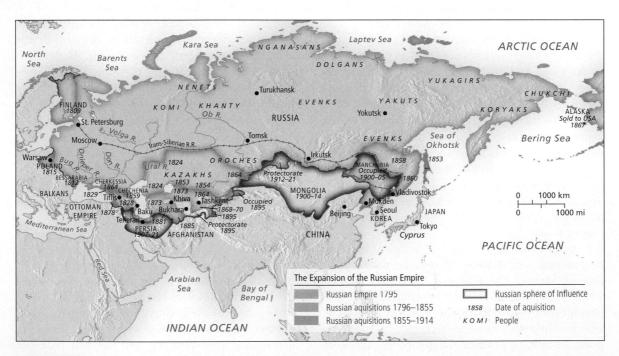

MAP 24.3

The Expansion of the Russian Empire

Throughout the nineteenth century, the Russian empire expanded to the west and south. After Russia's acquisition of territories in the Caucasus and Black Sea region, more Muslims lived under tsarist rule than in the Ottoman Empire.

The colonization of Siberia began in the sixteenth century when Russian serfs fled eastward in search of land and freedom. The end of serfdom actually accelerated the flow to Siberia, because peasants now needed to escape the debts imposed on them by the emancipation legislation of 1861 (see Chapter 22). The tsarist policy of exiling political dissenters to Siberia added to the outflow, while the completion of the trans-Siberian railway in the 1890s made the journey easier. Between 1800 and 1914, seven million Russians settled in or were deported to Siberia.

Just as American expansion westward and the British conquest of Australia dramatically depleted Indian and Aboriginal numbers, so Russian migration into Siberia displaced that region's original population. Until 1826 Russians could trade Siberians as slaves and many died because of brutal treatment. In addition, the immigrants brought with them new epidemic diseases and the booming fur trade depleted the animal herds that served as the Siberians' main food source. Disease and famine decimated the Siberian population.

Russia also expanded southward into central Asia, primarily as a preemptive response to the growth of British power in India. Fearing that the British might push northward, the Russians pushed south. By 1885, the Black Sea region, the Caucasus, and Turkestan had all fallen to Russian imperial control, and Muslims constituted a significant minority of the tsar's subjects. Over the next three decades the oil fields of the Caucasus became a crucial part of the Russian industrial economy.

The expansion of the Russian empire eastward encroached upon Chinese territory and thus helped destabilize China. It also led to growing hostilities between Russia and Japan, as both regimes coveted Chinese Manchuria. We saw in Chapter 23 that the growing antagonism between Russia and Japan led to the Russo-Japanese War in 1904 and that defeat in this war helped provoke the Russian Revolution of 1905. Imperialism could be a risky business.

JAPANESE INDUSTRIAL AND IMPERIAL EXPANSION

Japan's victory over Russia in 1905 signaled its rise to global power and its emergence as an imperialist player. In the 1630s the Japanese emperor sealed Japan from the West by closing Japanese ports to all foreigners except a small contingent of Dutch and Chinese traders confined to the city of Nagasaki. The Japanese government rebuffed all Western overtures until 1853, when, as we have seen, Commodore Perry forced Japan to open two of its ports to American ships. Over the next 15 years, Western powers pushed to expand their economic influence in Japan, and Japanese elites fought over how to respond. Anti-Western terrorism became endemic, civil war broke out, and a political revolution ensued.

Japan emerged from this turbulent time with a new government. For more than 200 years effective political control had rested in the hands not of the Japanese emperor, but rather of the "Shogun," the military governor of Japan. In 1868, however, Japan's warrior nobility tossed the Shogun from power and restored the young Emperor Mutsuhito (1867–1912) to effective rule—the Meiji Restoration.

Japan's new government determined that the only way to resist Western conquest was to adopt Western industrial and military technologies and techniques. Over the next four decades, a revolution from the top occurred, as a modern centralized state, modeled on France, replaced Japan's feudal political system. Funds poured into building a modern navy, modeled on Britain's, and a powerful conscript-based army, modeled on Germany's.

Beginning in the 1890s, Japan pushed its way into the imperialist game. Wars with China in 1894 and Russia in 1904 led to the Japanese seizure of Taiwan and Korea, and to expanded Japanese economic influence in Manchuria. One writer, Tokutomi Soho (1863–1957), proclaimed that Japan's imperial conquests showed that "civilization is not a monopoly of the white man."[19] Certainly imperialist violence was not a white man's monopoly: The Japanese brutally punished Koreans and Taiwanese who dared to protest against their new rulers.

SCRAMBLING IN CHINA While Japan used its encounter with the West to modernize and militarize its society, China proved less successful in withstanding Western hegemony. Throughout the nineteenth century, Chinese national sovereignty slowly eroded as European powers, the United States, and Japan jostled for access to China's markets and resources. In 1899, European states with interests in China did agree to back the American "open door" policy, which opposed the formal partitioning of China (as had just occurred in Africa). This policy, however, actually increased rather than blocked Western interference in Chinese economic and political affairs.

Many Chinese resented Western encroachment, and in 1900, a secret society devoted to purging China of Western influence began attacking foreigners. Because members of the society practiced the martial arts, this event was called the Boxer Rebellion. With the covert support of the Chinese government, the rebels attacked European diplomatic headquarters in Beijing and killed more than 200 missionaries and several thousand Chinese Christians. The West responded in fury. A combined military force, drawing 16,000 soldiers from Russia, Germany, Austria-Hungary, France, Britain, Japan, and the United States, crushed the rebellion and sacked Beijing. Required to grant further trade and territorial concessions to its invaders, the Chinese central government was fatally weakened. In 1911, revolution engulfed China and propelled it into four decades of political and social tumult.

THE BOXER REBELLION QUELLED

Although never formally controlled by Western powers, China was, by the end of the nineteenth century, a Western "sphere of influence," as the aftermath of the Boxer Rebellion of 1900 made clear. At the insistence of the Western powers, the Chinese government publicly executed the Boxer ringleaders in front of the foreign troops who had defeated the rebels.

CHRONOLOGY: ASIA ENCOUNTERS THE WEST

1853	Commodore Matthew Perry forces Japan to open its markets to the United States
1868	The Meiji Restoration in Japan; Japan begins rapid modernization
1885	Russia establishes control over Central Asia
1893	Union of French Indochina includes Laos, Cambodia, Tonkin, and Annam
1894–1895	The Sino-Japanese War: China defeated
1898	Spanish-American War; United States annexes Puerto Rico, Philippines, Hawaii, and Guam; establishes protectorate over Cuba
1899	"Open door" policy in China proclaimed by United States
1900–1903	Boxer Rebellion in China
1901	Commonwealth of Australia formed
1904–1905	Russo-Japanese War: Russia defeated
1911	Revolution in China: Overthrow of Manchu Dynasty

A Glimpse of Things to Come: The Boer War

In the 1840s, a British journalist in China urged the Chinese to accept what he regarded as the crucial lesson of history: "Ever since the dispersion of man, the richest stream of human blessings has, in the will of Providence, followed a western course." To many Europeans, Australians, and Americans, the rapid expansion of Western imperial control across the globe after 1870 confirmed this lesson. At the end of the nineteenth century, however, the British found themselves embroiled in a conflict that challenged this complacency. The Boer War of 1899–1902 shook British self-confidence and foreshadowed the total warfare and the crumbling of empires that marked the experience of the West in the twentieth century.

The Boer War was the culmination of a century of hostility among British imperialists, Dutch settlers (called Boers, the Dutch word for "farmer"), and indigenous Africans in the southern triangle of Africa. Germany's move into Southwest Africa in 1884 worsened this conflict: The British in the Cape Colony (see **Map 24.4**) feared that the Boers would work with Germany against British interests. The discovery in 1886 of diamonds and gold in the Transvaal, an independent Boer republic, intensified the conflict.

British investors in the profitable diamond and gold mines resented Boer taxation and labor policies, and pressed the British government to invade the Boer republics and place them under British rule.

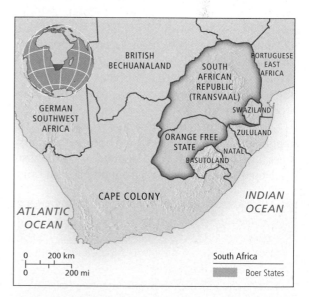

MAP 24.4

South Africa

After the defeat of the Boer states—the Transvaal and the Orange Free State—in the Boer War in 1902, the Union of South Africa comprised the Cape Colony and the two Boer republics.

In 1899, these imperialists got the war they had demanded, but it turned out to be different from what they expected. The Boers proved formidable enemies, skilled riflemen who knew the land and were fighting for their homes. Mired in a guerilla war, the British command decided to smoke out the Boer fighters through a scorched-earth policy. British troops burned more than 30,000 farms to the ground and confined Boer women and children, and their black African servants, in poorly provisioned concentration camps. Diseases such as diphtheria and typhus soon took their toll. Almost 20,000 Boer women and children, and at least 14,000 blacks, died in these camps.

The British finally defeated the Boers in April 1902, but two factors limited this victory. First, the Boer states came under British control, but the Boers (or Afrikaners) outnumbered other whites in the newly created Union of South Africa. After South Africa received self-government in 1910, the Afrikaners dominated the political system and created a nation founded on racial segregation. Second, Britain emerged from the Boer War with its military and its humanitarian reputation severely tarnished. The war aroused strong opposition inside Britain and showed that popular support for imperialism would rapidly disappear if the costs proved too high.

The sort of conflict between imperialism's opponents and supporters would be repeated many times over the next several decades as nationalist challenges against imperial rule multiplied and the

CHRONOLOGY: THE STRUGGLE FOR CONTROL IN SOUTH AFRICA

1806	Britain takes control of the Cape Colony from the Dutch
1837	Boers establish independent republics of Transvaal and Orange Free State
1884	German annexation of Southwest Africa
1886	Gold discovered in the Transvaal
1899	Anglo-Boer War begins
1910	Self-government granted to South Africa

imperial idea grew less and less persuasive. More ominously, the sight of noncombatants confined—and dying—in concentration camps would soon become all too familiar. The Boer War thus served as a prophetic opening to the twentieth century.

CONCLUSION

Reshaping the West: Expansion and Fragmentation

Africans and Asians who saw their political and social structures topple under the imperialist onslaught would probably have agreed with the Austrian poet Hugo von Hoffmansthal (1874–1929) when he wrote in 1905 that "what other generations believed to be firm is in fact sliding." Hoffmansthal, however, was not commenting on Africa or Asia. He was describing the Western cultural and intellectual landscape that, like colonial political boundaries, underwent enormous and disturbing change in the decades after 1870. In this era, matter itself began to slide, as the Newtonian conception of the world gave way to a new, more unsettling picture of the physical universe. Changes in medical practice, the triumph of Darwin's evolutionary theory, and the revolt against positivism helped undermine established assumptions and contributed to the sense that the foundations of Western culture were shifting. So, too, did the birth of modernism and broader changes, such as middle-class women's move into the public sphere and the redefinition of sexual boundaries, push Western culture in a new direction.

In the later nineteenth century, then, a series of encounters reshaped the West. Its geographic boundaries expanded as non-European regions such as the United States emerged as significant economic and imperial powers. With Australians claiming Western identity, "the West" even spilled over into the Eastern Hemisphere. Yet fragmentation as well as expansion characterized the Western experience after 1870. At the same time that social thinkers proclaimed white cultural superiority,

European artists such as Gauguin and Picasso embraced the artistic styles of non-European, nonwhite societies in an effort to push open the boundaries of Western culture. While scientific and technological achievements convinced many Europeans and Americans that the West would conquer the globe, others regarded these developments with profound uneasiness.

The next chapter will show that the sense that old certainties were slipping led some Europeans to welcome war in 1914 as a way to restore heroism and moral purpose to Western society. The trenches of World War I, however, provided little solidity. Many nineteenth-century political, economic, and cultural structures slid into ruin under the impact of total war.

KEY TERMS

Darwinian theory of
    evolution
Social Darwinism
theory of relativity
positivism
fin-de-siècle
modernism, modernist
    movement

Cubism
Expressionism
papal infallibility
anticlericalism
new imperialism
Scramble for Africa
Berlin Conference
Jim Crow

CHAPTER QUESTIONS

1. How did scientific developments during this period lead not only to optimism but also to anxiety? (page 750)
2. Why did many Europeans in this period believe they were living in a time of cultural crisis? (page 757)
3. What were the causes and consequences of the new imperialist ideology for the West and non-Western societies? (page 765)

TAKING IT FURTHER

1. How did Social Darwinism contribute to the mood of cultural uneasiness that characterized the *fin-de-siècle*? How did Social Darwinism and the sense of crisis inherent in the *fin-de-siècle* help shape the new imperialism?
2. What factors strengthened religious beliefs and allegiances in late-nineteenth-century Europe? Given these factors, why did many Western Christians feel that Christianity was under attack in this era?
3. Compare the patterns of territorial and political expansion in the United States, Australia, and Russia. How did these developments change the definition and power of the West?

✓●┤Practice on MyHistoryLab

25

The First World War

■ The Origins of the First World War ■ The Experience of Total War
■ The Home Fronts ■ War and Revolution

ON THE MORNING OF JULY 1, 1916, IN THE FIELDS OF NORTHERN France near the Somme River, tens of thousands of British soldiers crawled out of ditches and began to walk across a muddy expanse filled with shards of metal and decomposing human bodies. Weighed down with 60-pound backpacks, they trudged forward. The soldiers expected little opposition. For a week British heavy artillery had pummeled the Germans who lay on the other side of the mud. But the German troops had waited out the bombardment in the safety of "dugouts"—fortified bunkers scooped from the earth beneath the trenches. When the attack began, they raced to their gunnery positions and raked the evenly spaced lines of British soldiers with machine-gun fire. More than 20,000 British soldiers died that day, thousands within the first minutes of the attack. Another 40,000 were wounded. Yet the attack went on. Between July 1 and November 18, 1916, when the Battle of the Somme finally ended, almost 420,000 soldiers from Britain and the British Empire were killed or wounded. Their French allies lost 200,000 men to death or injury. German casualties are estimated at 450,000.

Such carnage became commonplace during the First World War. Between 1914 and 1918, European commanders sent more than eight million men to their deaths in a series of often futile attacks. The total number of casualties—killed, wounded, and missing—reached more than 37 million. These casualty figures were in part the products of the Industrial Revolution, as the nations of the West used their factories to churn out ever more efficient tools of killing. The need for machine guns, artillery shells, poison gas canisters, and other implements of modern warfare meant that World War I was the first **total war,** a war that demanded that combatant nations mobilize their industrial economies and their armies, and thus a war that erased the distinction between civilian and soldier. In total war, victory depended on the woman in the munitions factory as well as the man on the front lines.

This first total war redefined the West. By shattering the authoritarian empires of eastern and central Europe and integrating the United States more fully in European affairs, the war ensured that commitment to democratic values became central to one dominant twentieth-century definition of "the West." But the war also strengthened antidemocratic forces: It catapulted into power a communist regime in Russia, intensified eastern Europe's ethnic and nationalist conflicts, and undermined many of the economic structures on which Western stability and prosperity rested. This chapter explores a key question: How did the encounter with total war transform Western cultures?

THE ORIGINS OF THE FIRST WORLD WAR

■ What factors led Europe into war in 1914?

On June 28, 1914, ethnic Serbian terrorists assassinated Archduke Franz Ferdinand (1863–1914), the heir to the throne of the Austro-Hungarian Empire. One month after the archduke's death, Austria declared war on Serbia. One week later,

THE BATTLE OF THE SOMME

This movie still comes from *The Battle of the Somme,* a documentary filmed during the actual battle and watched by an estimated 20 million British viewers in 1916 and 1917.

Europe was at war. Germany entered the war on Austria's side. These two **Central Powers** squared off against not only small Serbia, but also the colossal weight of the **Allies,** the combined forces of Russia, France, and Britain. By the time the war ended in late 1918, it had embraced states from around the globe.

Why did the murder of one man on the streets of a Balkan city lead to the deaths of millions? To understand the origins of World War I, we need to examine four interlocking factors: the destabilizing impact of eastern European nationalism, the creation of rival alliance systems, the

requirements of an industrialized military, and the "will to war"—the conviction among both policymakers and ordinary people that war provided a resolution to social and cultural crisis.

Nationalism in Eastern Europe: Austria-Hungary and the Problem of Serbia

In eastern Europe, where ethnic, religious, or linguistic identities rather than political citizenship defined the "nation," nationalism served as an explosive force. For the Czechs, Slovenians, Serbs, Poles, Ukrainians, and many other groups, translating national identity into political identity—creating a "nation-state"—demanded the breakup of empires and a redrawing of political boundaries.

The divisive impact of nationalism in eastern Europe explains why officials within the Austro-Hungarian Empire regarded the small state of Serbia as a major threat. A multiethnic, multilinguistic empire, Austria-Hungary's survival depended on damping down the fires of nationalism wherever they flamed up. Yet Serbian politics centered on fanning the nationalist flame. In 1903, a group of Serbian army officers had shot Serbia's despised king and queen, chopped their bodies into bits, and threw the pieces out the window. To remain in power and avoid such a

grisly fate, the new king catered to the demands of radical nationalists who sought the unification of all Serbs into a Greater Serbian state. Because more than seven million Serbs lived not in Serbia, but in Austria-Hungary, the Austrian monarchy regarded this call for Serbian unification as a serious threat to the Austro-Hungarian Empire.

The hostile relations between Serbia and Austria-Hungary led directly to the outbreak of World War I. In 1908 Austria annexed Bosnia, a region with a large Serbian population. The Serbian government responded by encouraging Bosnian Serb separatist and terrorist groups. One such group, the Black Hand, assassinated Archduke Franz Ferdinand in the summer of 1914. That assassination convinced Austrian officials to declare war on Serbia.

ARREST OF GAVRILO PRINCIP

Princip was only 18 years old when he assassinated Archduke Franz Ferdinand and set into motion the sequence of events that led to the First World War. Because of his age, he did not receive the death penalty but instead received a sentence of 20 years in prison. He died at age 22 of tuberculosis.

International Competition and Rival Alliance Systems

To understand what transformed this Austro-Serbian conflict into a European war, we need to look at the rival alliance systems that emerged in response to heightened international competition. These alliances helped escalate a regional conflict into a European and then a global war.

The unification of Germany in 1871 upset the balance of power by creating a military and economic powerhouse in the middle of Europe. Until 1890, however, the diplomatic maneuvers of Otto von Bismarck, the new Germany's chancellor, ensured stability. Bismarck recognized that the Franco-Prussian War of 1870 (which brought about German unification) had made antagonism toward Germany central to French foreign policy. He also recognized that Germany's position in the center of Europe made it vulnerable to encirclement, should France succeed in forming an anti-German alliance with another European state. To avoid such encirclement, Bismarck maintained alliances with Russia, Austria, and Italy. The Dual Alliance between Germany and the Austro-Hungarian Empire in 1879 became the **Triple Alliance** of 1882, which joined Germany, Austria, and Italy in a defensive treaty. With the **Reinsurance Treaty** of 1887, Russia and Germany agreed to remain neutral if either was attacked.

But in 1888, a new emperor, Kaiser William II (r. 1888–1918), ascended the German throne. William, an ambitious and impatient young man, dismissed Bismarck in 1890 and launched Germany down a more dangerous path. The new kaiser broke with Bismarck's policies in two areas. First, William let the Reinsurance Treaty with Russia lapse, thus allowing anti-German France to join with Russia in the Franco-Russian Alliance of 1894. Germany now faced exactly the sort of encirclement by hostile powers, and the resulting threat of a two-front war, that Bismarck had sought to avoid.

Second, William favored a new "world policy" (*Weltpolitik*) for Germany that alienated Britain. Whereas Bismarck had confined Germany's interests to Europe, William and many prominent Germans wanted to see Germany claim its "place in the sun" as a global power: Germany needed a mighty overseas empire and a navy to defend it. Such policies were guaranteed to aggravate the British. As an island state dependent on its overseas empire, Britain based its defense on its naval supremacy. From the British point of view, a strong German navy challenged British national security and an expanding German empire conflicted with British imperial interests.

Hostility toward German ambitions overcame Britain's long tradition of "splendid isolation" from continental entanglements. In the first decade of the twentieth century, a series of military and economic arrangements formed ever-tighter links between Britain and Russia and France, clearing the way for the formation of the **Triple Entente** among these three powers. An informal association rather than a formal alliance, the Triple Entente did not *require* Britain to join in a war against Germany. Many British officials, however, viewed Germany as the major threat to British interests.

In this situation, German policymakers placed heavy emphasis on the alliance with Austria-Hungary. Strengthening this crucial ally became paramount. In July 1914, then, when Austrian officials debated their response to the assassination of Franz Ferdinand, the German government urged a quick and decisive blow against Serbia. Kaiser William assured the Austrian ambassador that Germany would stand by Austria no matter what the cost.

Both German and Austrian policymakers recognized that the cost might well be war with Russia. Eager to expand its influence in the Balkan region (and so gain access to the Mediterranean Sea), the Russian imperial regime had for decades positioned itself as the champion of Slavic peoples in the Balkans and as the protector of independent Slavic states such as Serbia. Thus, if Austria attacked Serbia, Russia might well mobilize in Serbia's defense.

German officials gambled, however, that Russia was not yet strong enough to wage war on Serbia's behalf. A decade earlier, Russia's defeat in the Russo-Japanese War (see Chapter 23) had exposed its military weakness. Yet if Russia did choose war, then, the German chancellor Theobold von Bethmann-Hollweg explained, Germany's chances of victory were "better now than in one or two years' time."[1] Bethmann-Hollweg and his advisors knew that the tsarist government, in response to its loss to Japan, had implemented a military reform and rearmament program. Russia would only grow stronger.

Mobilization Plans and the Industrialized Military

The alliance system helps explain the beginnings of World War I: Germany's alliance with Austria emboldened Austrian policymakers to attack Serbia, while the links between Serbia and Russia made it likely that this attack would pull in the Russian Empire—and Russia was allied with France. Alliances alone, however, did not transform the Austro-Serbian conflict into a European war. No alliance *required* either Russia or Britain to enter the fray. Moreover, Italy, a member of the Triple Alliance, did not join Germany and Austria in August 1914. In fact, when Italy entered the war in 1915, it fought *against* Germany and Austria. (See **Map 25.1.**)

To understand the origins of World War I, then, we need to look not only at the impact of nationalism and rival alliance systems, but also at a third factor—the widening gap between the expectations of traditional diplomacy and the requirements of an industrialized military. This growing gap ensured that when preparations for war began in the summer of 1914, control of the situation slipped out of the hands of the diplomats and their political superiors and into the grasp of the generals. The generals had planned for a European war. Once set in motion, their plans dictated events.

An important factor in these plans was the railroad, which enabled military planners to move large numbers of men quickly to precise locations. The speed with which governments could now throw armies into battle muddled the distinction between mobilization and actual war. *Mobilization* refers to the transformation of a standing army into a fighting force—calling up reserves, requisitioning supplies, enlisting volunteers or draftees, moving troops to battle stations. Traditionally, mobilization meant preparation for a possible fight, a process that took months and could be halted if the diplomats succeeded in avoiding war. But the railroads accelerated the mobilization process and thereby altered military planning. Aware that the enemy could also mobilize quickly, planners stressed the importance of preventive attacks, of striking before being struck. Once a state mobilized, the momentum toward war seemed almost irresistible.

These developments help explain the **Schlieffen Plan,** the military blueprint that structured German actions—and Allied reactions—in the summer of 1914. After the creation of the Franco-Russian Alliance in 1894, German military planners had to prepare for a two-front war. They devised the Schlieffen Plan for just that eventuality. The plan assumed that Russia's mobilization would take time: The vastness of its territory and the underdevelopment of its industrial infrastructure (including railroads) would slow its military mobilization and so guarantee that Russian troops would not pose an immediate threat to German borders. According to the Schlieffen Plan, then, the smaller Austrian army would hold off the slowly mobilizing Russians while the German army moved with lightning speed against France (see **Map 25.2**). After a quick knock-out blow against France, the Germans would concentrate on defeating Russia.

The Schlieffen Plan's need for speed thus pressured German politicians to treat a Russian declaration of mobilization as a declaration of war itself. As soon as Russia began to mobilize, German military leaders pushed their political counterparts to break off diplomatic negotiations so that the troop-laden trains could set off. Only two days elapsed between Russia's order of mobilization and the German declaration of war.

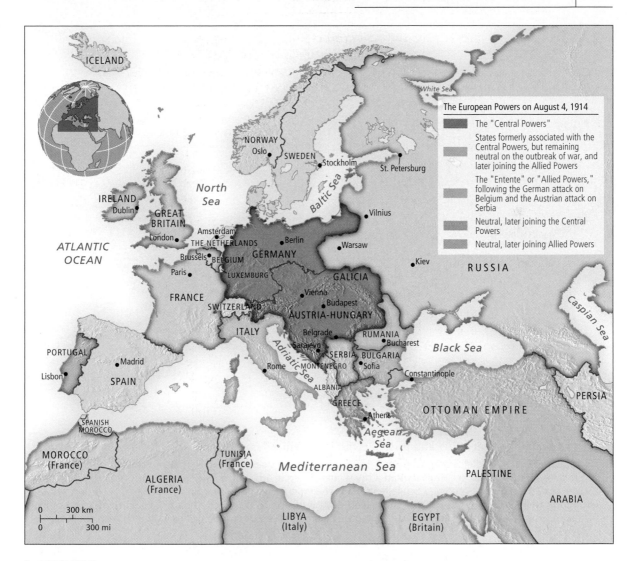

MAP 25.1

Europe, August 1914

In August 1914 each of the Central Powers faced the challenge of war on two fronts, but the entry of the Ottoman Empire into the war on the side of the Central Powers in November 1914 blocked Allied supply lines to Russia through the Mediterranean.

The need for speed also dictated that the attack against France would proceed via Belgium. Because German planners knew that the French expected any German attack to come through Alsace and Lorraine (the provinces that the Germans had taken from France after the Franco-Prussian War), the Schlieffen Plan called for the bulk of the German army to avoid France's fortified northeastern border (see **Map 25.2**) and instead swing to the west. Moving in a wide arc, the German army would flood into France through Belgium, encircle Paris, and scoop up the French forces before their generals knew what had hit them. With France out of the fight, the German

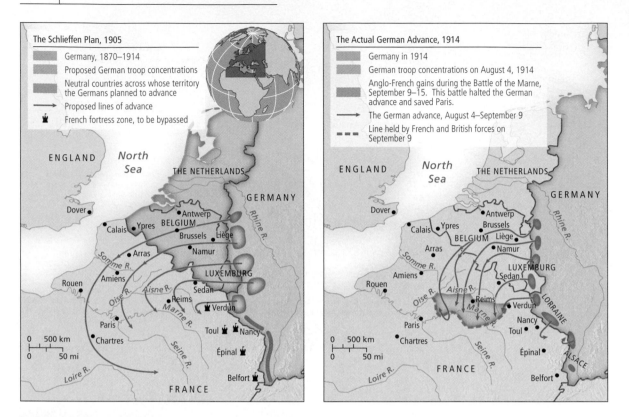

MAP 25.2

(a) The Schlieffen Plan, 1905 and (b) The Actual German Advance, 1914

Count Alfred von Schlieffen's original plan of 1905 called for the sleeves of the German soldiers on the right flank to brush the English Channel: The German army would sweep in a huge arching movement west. In the fall of 1914 Helmut von Moltke modified Schlieffen's plan: The crucial right flank was only three times as strong as the left, rather than eight times as strong as Schlieffen stipulated, and Moltke moved his troops north and east of Paris instead of south and west. Military historians today still argue over whether Schlieffen's original plan could have succeeded.

troops would then board trains and speed back to the Eastern Front to join their Austrian allies.

By invading Belgium, German policymakers knew they risked bringing Britain into the war, as a longstanding international agreement appointed Britain Belgium's protector. Yet German policymakers gambled that Britain would stay out of the conflict. Again their gamble failed. Convinced that Germany threatened British economic and imperial interests, Britain's policymakers regarded the German invasion of Belgium as the pretext they needed to enter the war with mass support. Thus, just six weeks after a Serbian terrorist shot

an Austrian archduke in Bosnia, British and German soldiers were killing each other in the mud of northern France.

The Will to War

The needs of an industrialized military outweighed traditional diplomacy and pushed those soldiers into that mud. Similarly, new pressures from public opinion constrained diplomats in the summer of 1914. This public pressure, or the "will to war," constituted the fourth factor in the outbreak of World War I.

Still drawn largely from the aristocracy, diplomats sought to maintain the balance of power in a Europe unbalanced by the forces of not only nationalism and industrial change, but also mass politics. The widening of the franchise meant that public opinion now played a role in international relations. Most new voters relied on the popular press—cheap newspapers marketed to a semiliterate public—for their understanding of foreign affairs. The banner headlines, large photographs, and short, simplified stories in these newspapers transformed the dense complexities of foreign relations into a compelling drama of Good Guys versus Bad Guys. Well-schooled in national identity, ordinary Europeans by 1914 tended to view foreign affairs as a giant nationalistic competition. They wanted evidence that "we" were ahead of "them."

In the last weeks of July 1914, pro-war crowds gathered in large cities, but not all Europeans welcomed the prospect of war. In Berlin, for example, 30,000 middle-class men and women paraded through the streets on the evening of July 25, singing patriotic songs and massing around statues of German heroes, while in working-class neighborhoods antiwar demonstrations received solid support. The declaration of war, however, silenced these demonstrations. Opposition to the war muted after August 1914, even among working-class socialists. National loyalty proved stronger than class solidarity.

What made the idea of war so appealing to so many in 1914? Some Europeans saw war as a powerful cleanser that would scour society of corruption. As Chapter 24 explained, fears of racial degeneration and gender confusion marked the years before 1914. War seemed to provide an opportunity for men to reassert their virility and their superiority. It also offered them the chance to be part of something bigger than themselves—to move beyond the boundaries of their often-restricted lives and join in what was presented as a great national crusade. Carl Zuckmayer, a German playwright and novelist who volunteered to fight, later explained that men like him welcomed the war as bringing "liberation…from…the saturation, the stuffy air, the petrifaction of our world."[2]

For political leaders, war provided the opportunity to mask social conflicts and to displace domestic hostilities onto the battlefield. We saw in Chapter 23 that violent trade unionism, socialist politics, anarchist-inspired assassinations, ethnic terrorism, and feminist protests characterized the decades before 1914. To many European elites, their society seemed on the verge of disintegration. But, as the future British prime minister Winston Churchill explained, war united societies with "a higher principle of hatred."

The war for which university students cheered, politicians schemed, and generals planned was not anything like the war that happened, however. Most people anticipated a short war. Theorists argued that the cost of waging an industrial war was so high that no state could sustain a conflict for long. The men who marched off to war in August 1914 expected that they would be home by Christmas. Instead, if they survived, which few of them did, they would spend not only that Christmas, but the next three, in the midst of unprecedented horror.

CHRONOLOGY: THE OUTBREAK OF THE FIRST WORLD WAR, 1914

June 28	Assassination of Archduke Franz Ferdinand
July 28	Austro-Hungarian declaration of war against Serbia
July 30	Russian mobilization
July 31	French, Austrian, and German mobilization
August 1	German declaration of war on Russia
August 3	German declaration of war on France
August 4	German invasion of Belgium; British declaration of war against Germany

THE EXPERIENCE OF TOTAL WAR

■ When, where, and how did the Allies defeat the Central Powers?

Counting on *élan*, the French military spirit, to see them to victory, French troops swung into battle sporting bright red pants and flashy blue tunics. At their head rode the cream of the French military education system, the graduates of the Saint-Cyr military academy, who charged wearing their parade dress of white gloves and plumed hats. All that color and dash made easy targets for the German machine guns. As one military historian wrote, "Never have machine-gunners had such a heyday. The French stubble-fields became transformed into gay carpets of red and blue." Those "gay carpets," colored with the blood and broken bodies of young French men, signaled that this would be a war of unexpected slaughter.[3]

The Western Front: Stalemate in the Trenches

Implementing a modified version of the Schlieffen Plan (see **Map 25.2**), German troops swept through Belgium into France. By the first week of September they seemed poised to take Paris. This rapid advance, however, overstretched German supply lines, allowing French and British forces to turn back the Germans at the Marne River. In an episode that signaled the importance of the internal combustion engine—and the oil that fueled it—in modern warfare, an ingenious French commander exploited a gap in the German lines by moving troops rapidly from Paris to the front in the only vehicles available: taxicabs. (The army paid the drivers full fare for the trip.)

Taxicabs saved Paris, but the Allied forces failed to push the Germans out of France. By the middle of October, German, British, and French soldiers huddled in trenches that eventually extended more than 300 miles from the Belgian coast to the borders of Switzerland. There they stayed for the next four years.

LIFE AND DEATH IN THE TRENCHES
The dead, the dying, and the surviving jostle one another in a French trench.

HOLES AND DITCHES Siegfried Sassoon, a British poet and a World War I veteran, insisted that "when all is said and done, this war was a matter of holes and ditches."[4] From the strategic point of view, these holes and ditches—the trenches—were defensive fortifications, and the long stalemate on the Western Front shows that they worked well. Attacking infantry units walked forward against an enemy armed with machine guns and sheltered behind wide barbed-wire fences and a thick wall of dirt and sandbags. Despite numerous attempts between the fall of 1914 and the spring of 1918, neither side was able to break through the enemy line.

A discussion of trench strategy, however, conveys nothing of the appalling misery summed up by the term "trench warfare." Imagine standing in a ditch about seven or eight feet deep and about three or four feet wide. The walls of the ditches are packed mud, propped up with sandbags. Wooden boards cover the floor, but the mud squelches between them. Piles of sandbags and barbed-wire barricades on the enemy's side of the ditch deepen your sense of being underground. Moreover, the trenches do not run in tidy straight lines. Instead, they zigzag at sharp angles, restricting the range of fire for enemy snipers and limiting the impact of explosives, but also ensuring that everywhere you look you see a wall of mud. Because you are in northern France, it is probably raining. Thus, you are standing not on but *in* mud—if you are lucky. In some parts of the line, soldiers stand in muddy water up to a foot deep. On the other side of your sandbag defenses stretches **no-man's-land,** the territory dividing the British and French trench systems from the German. Pocked with deep craters from heavy shelling, often a sea of mud churned up by the artillery, no-man's-land is littered with stinking corpses in various states of decomposition—all that is left of the soldiers who died during previous attacks. Your constant companions are lice (the term *lousy* was

A BATTERY SHELLED BY PERCY WYNDHAM LEWIS (1919)

The mechanical nature of this war dominated many soldiers' accounts. Seeking the chance to be heroes, men volunteered to fight and found themselves reduced to interchangeable parts in a colossal war machine. In works such as *A Battery Shelled*, British artist Percy Wyndham Lewis (1882–1957) used modernist techniques to represent the reality of mechanized war. Lewis served in a British artillery unit and, in 1917, became an "Official War Artist," charged with recording and memorializing the war through painting. In this work, a burial party digs a grave for a gunner killed by enemy shells but the three soldiers in the foreground seem utterly detached, as distanced from the death as the men who fired the shells.

DIFFERENT VOICES THE CULTURAL IMPACT OF THE WESTERN FRONT

Many of the upper- and middle-class officers fighting on the Western Front volunteered out of love for their country, an idealistic view of war as a heroic mission, and a longing for adventure. British recruiting posters described the war as the "Greatest Game of All." Trench warfare defied these expectations. The following poems, written by two young upper-middle class British officers, illustrate the shift from the initial enthusiasm for the war to later disillusionment and despair. Neither man survived the war: Rupert Brooke died of blood-poisoning on his way to Gallipoli in 1915. Wilfred Owen was killed in battle in 1918, just days before the war ended.

In the sonnet series "1914," written just as the war began, Rupert Brooke not only welcomed the war but, as his first subtitle indicates, linked the outbreak of war to the coming of internal or personal peace.

1914. I. Peace

Now, God be thanked Who has matched us with His hour,
And caught our youth, and wakened us from sleeping,
With hand made sure, clear eye, and sharpened power,
To turn, as swimmers into cleanness leaping,
Glad from a world grown old and cold and weary
Leave the sick hearts that honor could not move,

And half-men, and their dirty songs and dreary,
And all the little emptiness of love.

Oh! we, who have known shame, we have found
  release there,
Where there's no ill, no grief, but sleep is mending,
Naught broken save the body, lost but breath;
Nothing to shake the laughing heart's song peace there
But only agony, and that has ending;
And the worst friend and enemy is but Death.

1914. III. The Dead

Blow out, you bugles, over the rich Dead!
There's none of these so lonely and poor of old,
But, dying, has made us rarer gifts than gold.
These laid the world away; poured out the red
Sweet wine of youth; gave up the years to be
Of work and joy, and that unhoped serene,
That men call age; and those who would have been,
Their sons, they gave, their immortality.
Blow, bugles, blow! They brought us, for our dearth,
Holiness, lacked so long, and Love, and Pain.
Honour has come back, as a king, to earth,
And paid his subjects with a royal wage;
And Nobleness walks in our ways again;
And we have come into our heritage.

Owen composed this piece, one of the most famous poems written during World War I, in several drafts between October 1917 and March

coined on the Western Front) and rats. For the rats, the war is an endless feast as they grow enormously fat, nibbling their way through the piles of dead.

From 1915 on, the horror of the Western Front escalated with the introduction of a new killing tool—poison gas, first deployed by the Germans in the spring of 1915. The Allies condemned the use of poison gas as inhumane, but within months the British and French, too, were firing poison gas canisters across the lines. The consequences were appalling: blinded eyes, blistered skin, seared lungs, death by asphyxiation. By 1916, with the gas mask a standard part of every soldier's uniform, military companies resembled hordes of insects. And, like insects, they were easily squashed. In the summer of 1915 an average of 300 British men became casualties on the Western Front every day, not because they were wounded in an attack, but because they were picked off by snipers, felled by an exploding shell, or wasted by disease brought on by living in the mud amid putrefying corpses.

THE OFFENSIVES The offensives, the attacks launched by both sides on the Western Front, sent the numbers of dead and wounded soaring.

1918. The poem flatly describes a soldier being asphyxiated by poison gas while Owen and the rest of the company watch.

Dulce et Decorum Est by Wilfred Owen

Bent double, like old beggars under sacks,
Knock-kneed, coughing like hags,
we cursed through sludge,
Till on the haunting flares we turned our backs
And towards our distant rest began to trudge.
Men marched asleep. Many had lost their boots
But limped on, blood-shod. All went lame; all blind;
Drunk with fatigue; deaf even to the hoots
Of tired, outstripped Five-Nines that dropped behind.
Gas! Gas! Quick, boys!—An ecstasy of fumbling,
Fitting the clumsy helmets just in time;
But someone still was yelling out and stumbling
And flound'ring like a man in fire or lime...
Dim, through the misty panes and thick green light,
As under a green sea, I saw him drowning.
In all my dreams, before my helpless sight,
He plunges at me, guttering, choking, drowning.
If in some smothering dreams you too could pace
Behind the wagon that we flung him in,
And watch the white eyes writhing in his face,
His hanging face, like a devil's sick of sin;
If you could hear, at every jolt, the blood
Come gargling from the froth-corrupted lungs,
Obscene as cancer, bitter as the cud
Of vile, incurable sores on innocent tongues,—

My friend, you would not tell with such high zest
To children ardent for some desperate glory,
The old Lie: "*Dulce et decorum est
Pro patria mori.*"*

For Discussion

1. Why did Brooke see the war as a path to some sort of personal peace? How might his enthusiasm for war reflect the power of what Owen labeled "The old Lie"?

2. Compare the language and imagery in the two poems. How do the words themselves demonstrate a shift in the view of war?

3. Did disillusionment of soldiers on the Western Front differ from the disillusionment experienced by most soldiers, regardless of time or place? Isn't the experience of combat always a rude awakening from innocence into brutal knowledge?

Sources: From "Peace" from *"1914" Five Sonnets* by Rupert Brooke. London: Sidgwick & Jackson, 1915; "Dulce et Decorum Est" from *Poems* by Wilfred Owen, with an Introduction by Siegfried Sassoon. London: Chatto and Windus, 1920.

*"It is good and right to die for one's country."

None of the elderly commanders—the Germans Helmut von Moltke and Erich von Falkenhayn, the French Joseph Joffre and Ferdinand Foch, and the British Douglas Haig and John French— knew what to make of trench warfare. Schooled to believe that war was about attacking, they sought vainly to move this conflict out of the ditches by throwing masses of both artillery and men against the enemy lines. But time and time again the machine gun foiled these mass attacks.

The Battle of the Somme, described in the opening of this chapter, illustrates a typical offensive on the Western Front. By the end of 1917, the death tolls on the Western Front rose to astonishing levels, yet neither side had gained much ground. Many soldiers, who enlisted not for a specific term or tour of duty but "for the duration"—until the war ended— became convinced that only the dead escaped from the trenches. (See *Different Voices* in this chapter.)

The War in Eastern Europe

The Western Front was only one of several theaters of war. Floundering in the snows of the Italian Alps, the Italian and Austrian armies fought along a stationary front for two brutal

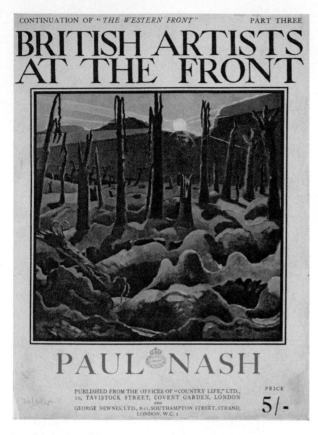

CONTINUATION OF *"THE WESTERN FRONT"*   PART THREE

BRITISH ARTISTS AT THE FRONT

PAUL NASH

PUBLISHED FROM THE OFFICES OF "COUNTRY LIFE," LTD., 20, TAVISTOCK STREET, COVENT GARDEN, LONDON
AND
GEORGE NEWNES, LTD., 8-11, SOUTHAMPTON STREET, STRAND, LONDON, W.C. 2

PRICE
5/-

WE ARE MAKING A NEW WORLD

During World War I, many modernists abandoned "art for art's sake" (see Chapter 24). Paul Nash (1889–1940), a British artist and army volunteer, explained, "I am a messenger who will bring back word from the men who are fighting to those who want the war to go on forever...may it burn their lousy souls."[5] In *We Are Making a New World* (1918), Nash transformed the landscape's pastoral tranquility into a cry of pain.

years after Italy, enticed by the promise of territorial gain, joined the war on the Allies' side. Characterized by futile offensives and essential immobility, the war in Italy mirrored the conflict on the Western Front. In eastern Europe, however, a different plot unfolded. For three years, massive armies surged back and forth, as the plains and mountains of eastern Europe echoed with the tumult of spectacular advances, headlong retreats, and finally, political revolution.

THE EASTERN FRONT: A WAR OF MOVEMENT   Much of the movement in eastern Europe consisted of Russians running—running forward in surprising advances, running back in terrifying retreats. When the war began in August 1914, Russia shocked its enemies by mobilizing quickly. As **Map 25.3** shows, Russian troops headed in a two-pronged onslaught against the Germans in East Prussia and against the Austrians in Galicia, the northeastern region of the Austro-Hungarian Empire. Surprised by the speed of the Russian advance, German troops in East Prussia fell back. Skillful maneuvering by the German commanders Paul von Hindenburg (1847–1934) and Erich von Ludendorff (1865–1937), however, turned the Russian tide at the Battle of Tannenberg at the end of August. Within two weeks the Germans had shoved the Russian troops back across the border. In the subsequent months, the Germans advanced steadily into Russian imperial territory. At the same time, a combined German and Austrian assault forced the Russian army to retreat from Galicia—and more than 300 miles into its own territory. Russian casualties in the offensive stood at 2.5 million. Over the next two years the pattern of Russian advances and retreats continued. Russian soldiers pushed into Austria-Hungary in June 1916, but could not sustain the attack. They advanced again in the summer of 1917, but it too soon disintegrated into a retreat.

These retreats revealed that Russia's economic and political structures could not withstand the pressures of total war. Russian supply lines were so overextended that the poorly fed and inadequately clothed Russian troops found themselves without ammunition and unable to press ahead. Demoralized, they began to desert in large numbers. On the home front workers and peasants grew impatient with wartime deprivations and demands. This disaffection led to the Russian Revolution. As we will explore in detail later in this chapter, revolution forced the tsar to abdicate in February 1917. In October, the Bolsheviks, a small group of socialist revolutionaries, seized control and moved quickly to pull Russia out of the war.

The Bolshevik military withdrawal freed Germany from the burden of waging a two-front war.

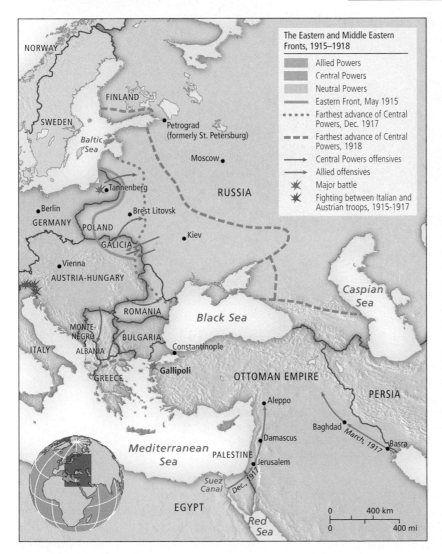

MAP 25.3

The Eastern and Middle Eastern Fronts, 1915–1918

Unlike the Western Front, the Eastern Front was far from stationary. By 1918, the Central Powers occupied Serbia, Romania, and parts of European Russia. The entry of the Ottoman Empire on the side of the Central Powers in November 1914 extended the conflict into the Middle East. In 1915 Ottoman forces repelled an initial British advance toward Baghdad and threatened Egypt. By the end of 1917, however, Arab nationalists helped the British defeat the Central Powers in the Middle East.

commit large numbers of troops to controlling this new territory, Germany reaped less advantage from this victory than might have been expected.

THE FORGOTTEN FRONT: THE BALKANS In southeastern Europe, World War I was in many ways the "Third Balkan War," yet another installment in an ongoing competition for territory and power. In 1912 and again in 1913, Greece, Bulgaria, Romania, and Serbia had fought each other in the First and Second Balkan Wars. Hence, in 1915 Bulgaria allied with the Central Powers to gain back the territory it had lost in the Second Balkan War while Romania joined the Allies in 1916 to protect its hold on that territory.

For most of the war, the Central Powers controlled the Balkans. A joint Bulgarian, German, and Austro-Hungarian invasion crushed Romania. The Serbian experience was even bleaker. In the first year of the war Austrian and Serbian troops jostled back and forth for control of the country, but in October 1915 Bulgarian, German, and Austrian forces advanced into Serbia from three directions. By November, the Ser-

Signed in March 1918, the **Treaty of Brest-Litovsk** ceded to Germany all of Russia's western territories, containing one-third of the population of the prewar Russian Empire. But because it had to bian army had been pushed to the Albanian border. Some 200,000 Serbian soldiers fled over the snow-swept mountains of Albania to the Adriatic Sea in the disastrous "Winter March."

"A WHOLE EMPIRE WALKING"
This hand-colored slide features a group of refugees in wartime Russia. In 1915, as its army retreated on the Eastern Front, the Russian High Command ordered a "scorched earth" policy: the destruction of buildings, crops, and livestock. This policy led to a massive wave of refugees—what the historian Peter Gatrell termed "a whole empire walking." By 1917, approximately seven million refugees wandered the Russian empire, subject to months or years of hunger, cold, disease, rape, looting, and beatings.

Austrian troops occupied Serbia and placed the country under military rule. By the war's end, approximately 25 percent of Serbian citizens lay dead.

The World at War

The imperialist expansion of the later nineteenth century ensured that as soon as the war began, it jumped outside European borders. The British and French Empires supplied the Allies with invaluable military and manpower resources. Australia, New Zealand, Canada, India, South Africa, and Ireland supplied no less than 40 percent of Britain's military manpower during the war. More than 650,000 men from Indochina,

Algeria, and French West Africa assisted the French war effort.

Fighting fronts multiplied around the globe as combatants struggled for imperial and European supremacy (see **Map 25.4**). Portugal joined the Allies largely because it hoped to expand its colonial possessions in Africa. Japan seized the opportunity to snatch German territories in China while using its navy to protect Allied troop and supply ships. By the end of 1914, Japanese, Australian, and New Zealander troops occupied most of Germany's island colonies in the Pacific as well.

The Middle East also became a key theater of war. Once the Ottoman Empire joined the Central Powers, Britain's Middle Eastern economic and

A WORLD AT WAR: SIKH CAVALRY OFFICERS

Sikh cavalry officers from India patrol the Western Front. India provided 1.3 million men to assist the British war effort. Indian troops fought—and more than 49,000 Indian soldiers died—in battles in the Middle East, in East Africa, and on the Western Front. Similarly, black Senagalese soldiers fought for France on various fronts; 30,000 Senagalese died during the war.

military interests lay vulnerable. Britain was desperate to protect Allied access to the Suez Canal—a vital link to the soldiers and supplies of India, Australia, and New Zealand—and to Persian oil fields, an important source of fuel for the British navy. In a move with far-reaching consequences for twentieth-century geopolitics, the British joined forces with Arab nationalists. Led by a British soldier named T. E. Lawrence (1888–1935)—better known as "Lawrence of Arabia"—and inspired by promises of postwar national independence, Arab nationalists used guerilla warfare to destroy what remained of Ottoman rule in the Middle East. By 1917 the Ottomans had lost control of almost the entire coastal region of the Arabian Peninsula bordering the Red Sea, and Lawrence and his Arab allies had captured Jerusalem.

THE WAR AT SEA AND THE ENTRY OF THE UNITED STATES While infantrymen rotted in trenches and froze in mountain passes, the German and British navies fought a critical war at sea. German submarines sought to cut Britain's imperial lifeline and starve out its civilian population by sinking ships before they could reach British ports. Almost 14,000 British sailors and civilians died in these submarine attacks. In turn, British destroyers stretched a blockade across all ocean and sea passageways to Germany and its allies.

The Allied blockade prevented food and other essential raw materials from reaching Germany, Austria-Hungary, and their associates. Food shortages sparked riots in more than 30 German cities in 1916. When the potato crop that year failed and eliminated one of the only

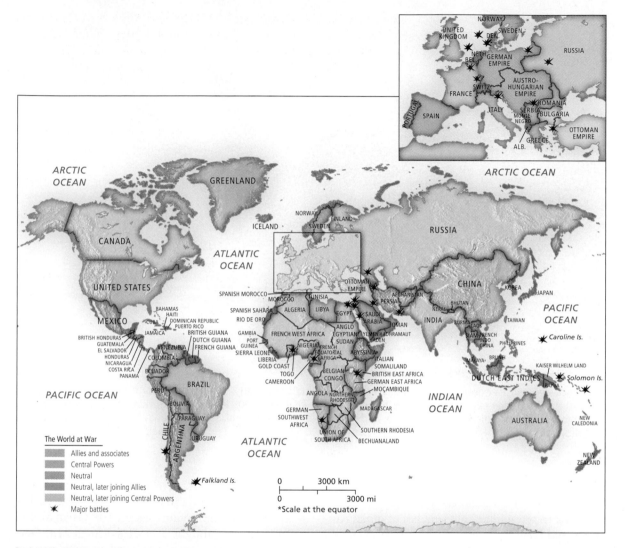

MAP 25.4

The World at War

Imperialist relationships and global economics ensured that a European conflict became a world war. In Africa, Portuguese and South African troops fought a bush war against German and native soldiers. Japan, the first non-European power to enter the war, occupied German colonial territories in Asia and the Pacific region. When the United States joined the Allies in April 1917, several Latin American countries also declared war on Germany.

remaining sources of nutrition, children's rations fell to *one-tenth* of their actual needs.

Desperate to win the war quickly, German policymakers in 1917 decided to escalate their submarine war against Britain. Suspecting (correctly) that supposedly neutral American passenger ships were delivering essential war materiel to Britain, the German government ordered its submarines to sink without warning any ship heading for British shores. The Germans recognized that this unrestricted submarine warfare would probably pull the United States into the war. But Germany stood on the brink of economic collapse, and German policymakers decided they had no choice. They gambled that they would defeat the Allies in a last-ditch effort before the United States' entry into the war could make much of a difference.

The United States declared war on Germany in April 1917. Outrage over American deaths at sea served as the most immediate cause of American entry into the war. Four other factors also played a role. First, Franco-British news stories about German atrocities during the invasion of Belgium persuaded many Americans that right rested on the Allied side. Second, the Russian Revolution removed an important obstacle to American cooperation with the Allies—the tsarist regime. Americans had balked at the idea of allying with the repressive government of Tsar Nicholas II, but the February Revolution, which overthrew Nicholas, offered American policymakers a more acceptable wartime partner. Third, by the time President Woodrow Wilson asked the U.S. Congress for a declaration of war, the American economy was intertwined with that of the Allies. Trade between the United States and the Allied states had grown from $825 million in 1914 to more than $3 billion in 1916, and American bankers had loaned more than $2 billion to the Allied governments. Finally, the German government committed a serious blunder in the spring of 1917 when it offered to assist Mexico in recovering New Mexico, Arizona, and Texas in exchange for Mexican support should war break out between Germany and the United States. The interception of a telegram sent by the German foreign minister Arthur Zimmermann exposed this offer and inflamed anti-German sentiment in the United States. The German policy of unrestricted submarine warfare, then, put flame to kindling that was already in place.

The U.S. declaration of war (followed by those of Brazil, Costa Rica, Cuba, Guatemala, Haiti, Honduras, Nicaragua, and Panama) provided an immediate psychological boost for the Allies, but several months passed before American troops arrived on the battlefield in significant numbers. By July 1918, however, the United States was sending 300,000 fresh soldiers to Europe each month. The Allies now had access to an almost unlimited supply of materiel and men. Eventually nearly two million American soldiers were sent to Europe and almost 49,000 American soldiers died in battle.

BACK IN MOTION: THE WESTERN FRONT IN 1918   Faced with the prospect of having to fight fresh American forces, German policymakers decided to gamble one more time. On March 2, 1918—before the bulk of the U.S. army had been deployed—the German army launched an overwhelming ground assault against British and French lines. The gamble almost succeeded. In just 30 minutes the German troops broke through the British front line. By April the German army stood just 50 miles from Paris.

What explains this sudden shift on the Western Front from a conflict characterized by stalemate to a war of decisive movement? As we have seen, in the first years of the war commanders remained committed to offensive techniques suited to an age of preindustrial warfare—the mass charge, the cavalry attack—even though industrial technologies such as the machine gun had transformed the power of defensive war. Certainly, Western commanders were well-acquainted with the killing potential of the machine gun. In the imperial conflicts discussed in Chapter 24, the machine gun enabled small European forces to defeat larger indigenous armies. But on the Western Front, both sides possessed the machine gun. In other words, both sides were good on defense but poor on offense.

In 1918, however, the Germans came up with new offensive strategies. Instead of a frontal assault dictated by commanders sitting well behind the lines, Germany's offensive of 1918 consisted of a series of small group attacks aiming to cut behind British and French positions rather than straight on against them. In addition, the Germans in 1918 scrapped the preliminary artillery barrage that signaled when and where an attack was about to begin. In place of the barrage they employed sudden gas and artillery bursts throughout the offensive. The rapid German

CHRONOLOGY: THE END OF THE WAR, 1917–1918

1917	Stalemate continues on the Western Front
February	Collapse of the Russian imperial government
April	U.S. declaration of war on Germany
October	Bolshevik Revolution in Russia
December	Bolsheviks sign armistice with Germany; capture of Jerusalem by British troops
1918	
March	Treaty of Brest-Litovsk
March–July	German offensive on Western Front, rapid gains
July–November	Allied counteroffensive begins
September	Bulgaria and Allies sign armistice
November 3	Austria-Hungary sues for peace with Allies
November 9	Kaiser William abdicates
November 11	Fighting ends on Western Front at 11:00 A.M.

advance in the spring of 1918 showed that technique had caught up with technology.

In July, however, the Allies stopped the German advance. In August they broke through the German lines and began to push the German army backward. Throughout the summer the push continued. By September the Western Front, which had stood so stationary for so long, was rolling eastward at a rapid clip. The final German gamble failed for three reasons: First, the rapidity of the advance overstrained German manpower and supply lines. Second, the Allies learned from their enemies and adopted the same new offensive strategies. And third, the Allies figured out how to make effective use of a new offensive technology—the tank. Developed in Britain, the tank obliterated the defensive advantages of machine-gun-fortified trenches. A twentieth-century offense met a twentieth-century defense, and the war turned mobile.

Reinforced with fresh American troops and the promise of more to come, the Allied forces surged forward against the hungry and demoralized Germans. When the Bulgarian, Ottoman, and Austrian armies collapsed in September and October, Germany stood alone. On November 11, 1918, German leaders signed an armistice and the war ended.

THE HOME FRONTS

■ How did total war structure the home fronts?

The term *home front* was coined during World War I to highlight the fact that this conflict was fought not only by soldiers on the front lines, but also by civilians at home. Total war demanded the mobilization of a combatant state's productive capacity. Total war recast and in some cases revolutionized not only the economies, but also the political, social, and gender relations of the states involved.

Industrial War

World War I was the first industrial war. Poison gas and machine guns, barbed wire and shovels, canned foods and mass-produced uniforms—all poured out of factories and helped shape this war. Industrialization made it possible for governments to deploy the masses of men mobilized in this conflict. While 170,000 men fought in the Battle of Waterloo in 1815 and 300,000 soldiers in the Battle of Sedan in 1870, *one million* combatants were swept up in the Battle of the Marne in 1914. Only industrialized production could keep these huge armies supplied with weapons, ammunition, and other necessities.

THE EXPANSION OF THE STATE

At first, no government realized the crucial role that industrial labor would play in this war. Both military and political leaders believed that the war would end quickly and that success depended on throwing as many men as possible into the front lines. In France, even munitions factories were shut down and their workers sent to the front. Governments practiced "business as usual"—letting the free market decide wages, prices, and supply—with disastrous results. Soaring inflation, growing black markets, public resentment over war profiteering (the practice of private businessmen making huge profits off the war), and, most crucially, shortages of essential military supplies, including ammunition, proved that a total war economy needed total regulation.

Beginning in 1915, both the Allied and Central Powers' governments gradually assumed the power to requisition supplies, dictate wages, limit profits, and forbid workers to change jobs. In Germany, the increasing regulation of the economy was called "war socialism," a misleading term because it was big business that benefited. The German army worked in partnership with large industrial firms to ensure the supply of war materiel to the front lines, while the Auxiliary Service Law of 1916 drafted all men age 17 to 60 for war work. Measures such as these greatly expanded the size and power of the central governments in the combatant states. For example, in 1914 the British office in charge of military purchases employed 20 clerks. By 1918, it had become the Department of Munitions, a bureaucratic empire with 65,000 employees overseeing more than three million workers in government-owned and -operated munitions plants.

This expansion of governmental power corresponded with restricted individual freedom, even in traditionally liberal states such as Britain. Flying in the face of tradition, in 1916 Britain's government imposed the draft—a clear example of the requirements of the state overriding the desires of the individual. By the war's end, the British government had also restricted the hours that pubs could be open (as a way of encouraging workers to show up for work sober) and tampered with time itself by inventing Daylight Saving Time as a means of maximizing war production.

THE POLITICS OF TOTAL WAR

The war's reliance on industrial production greatly empowered industrial producers—the workers. In 1915 both France and Britain abandoned political party competition and formed coalition governments that included socialist and working-class representatives. In return, French and British union leaders agreed to a ban on labor strikes and accepted the temporary "deskilling" of certain jobs—a measure that allowed unskilled laborers, particularly women, to take the place of skilled workers at lower rates of pay.

Nevertheless, the number of labor strikes rose in Britain and France in 1916 and in 1917. Faced with the potential of disintegration on the home front, British and French political leaders reacted similarly. They formed war governments committed to total victory. In Britain, David Lloyd George (1863–1945) became prime minister at the end of 1916. A Welsh artisan's son who had fought hard to reach the top of Britain's class-bound, English-dominated political system, Lloyd George was not a man to settle for a compromise peace. One year later, Georges Clemenceau (1841–1929) became prime minister of France. Nicknamed "the Tiger," Clemenceau demanded victory. When asked to detail his government's program, he replied simply, "*Je fais la guerre!*" ("I make war!").

But making war, French and British officials realized, demanded public support. They cultivated this support in two ways. First, they sought to depict the war as a struggle between democracy and authoritarianism—a crusade not for national power or economic gain, but for a better world. Second, they recognized that if they failed to meet the basic needs of ordinary citizens, civilian morale would plummet. Both governments intervened regularly in the economy to ensure that workers received higher wages, better working conditions, and a fair distribution of food stocks. In state-owned munitions factories, workers for the first time received benefits such as communal kitchens and day care. Food rationing actually improved the diets of many poor families. Living standards among employed workers in France and in Britain rose during the war.

The situation in Germany differed significantly. Until the last weeks of the war German political leadership remained in the hands of the conservative elite. Increasingly, the aristocratic generals Hindenburg and Ludendorff—the heroes of the Battle of Tannenberg—called the political shots. The army and big industrial firms seized control of German economic life. Given the power to set prices and profit margins, industrialists—not surprisingly—made a killing. Their incomes soared, while escalating inflation and chronic food shortages ground down ordinary workers. In 1917, industrial unrest slowed German war production, civilian discontent reached dangerous levels, and the success of the Allied blockade meant Germans were starving.

The World Turned Upside Down

By the war's end, changes in the relations among classes and between men and women caused many Europeans to feel as if their world had turned upside down. European workers grew more radical as they realized the possibilities of their own collective power and the potential of the state as an instrument of social change. The fact that by 1917 many of these workers were women also had revolutionary implications. In the work world and in society at large, gender roles, like class relations, underwent a marked shift.

THE WAR'S IMPACT ON SOCIAL RELATIONS   In the trenches and on the battlefields, World War I had a leveling effect. For many young, middle- and upper-class soldiers, the war provided their first sustained contact with both manual labor and manual laborers. In letters home, they testified to a newfound respect for both, as the horrors of the war experience broke down rigid class barriers.

On the home front, however, social relations grew more rather than less hostile. During the war years, inflation eroded the savings of

middle-class men and women and left them scrambling to maintain their social and economic status. In Germany and throughout eastern Europe, food shortages and falling wages produced a revolutionary situation. By contrast, in Britain and France, a rising standard of living demonstrated to workers the benefits of an interventionist state. Yet class hostilities rose in western Europe, too. Working-class activists demanded that the state continue to regulate the economy in peacetime to improve the standard of living of ordinary workers. Having finally tasted the economic pie, workers fought for a bigger piece, while the middle class struggled to defend its shrinking slice.

THE WAR'S IMPACT ON GENDER RELATIONS   By 1916, labor shortages in key military industries, combined with the need to free up as many men as possible for fighting, meant that governments on both sides actively recruited women for the paid workforce. Women were suddenly visible in the public sphere as bus drivers, elevator operators, and train conductors. In eastern Europe, the agricultural labor force came to consist almost entirely of women. In western Europe, women took on dangerous positions in munitions factories, worked just behind the front lines as ambulance drivers and nurses, and in 1917 and 1918, often led the way in walking off the job to demand better conditions.

The impact of the war on women's roles should not be exaggerated, however. Throughout the war, more women continued to work in domestic service—as cooks, maids, nannies—than in any other sector of the economy. The great majority of the women who did move into skilled industrial employment were not new to the paid workforce. Before 1914 they had worked in different, lower-paying jobs. And they certainly were not treated as men's equals. In government-run factories in Britain, women received as little as 50 percent of men's wages for the same job.

Nevertheless, for many women, the war was a liberating experience. With their husbands away, many wives made decisions on their own for the first time. Female munitions workers in Britain received wages three times higher than their prewar earnings. But middle- and upper-class women experienced the sharpest change. Despite the rise, from 1870 on, of feminist challenges to the ideology of separate spheres (detailed in Chapter 23), the predominant idea remained that women were biologically suited for the private domestic sphere. In the prewar years, immobility and passivity continued to mark the lives of many middle-class girls—sheltered within the family home, subject to paternal authority, waiting for a marriage proposal. The war threw women into the public space. The middle-class girl who before 1914 was forbidden to travel without a chaperone might be driving an ambulance, splashing through the mud and blood, or washing the bodies of naked working-class soldiers.

At the same time that the war smashed many of the boundaries that had restricted women, it narrowed the world of the middle-class male soldier. While women were on the move—driving buses, flying transport planes, ferrying the wounded—men were stuck in the mud, confined to narrow ditches, waiting for orders. Expecting to be heroic men of action, they found themselves instead living the sort of immobile, passive lives that had characterized the prewar middle-class woman's experience. In total war, even gender roles turned upside down.

Yet when the war ended, many of these radical changes proved to be only temporary. The wartime movement of women into skilled factory jobs and public positions such as bus drivers and train conductors was rapidly reversed. For example, by the terms of the British Restoration of Pre-War Practices Act (1919), women who had taken up skilled factory jobs received two weeks' pay and a train ticket home.

Other changes appeared more permanent. France in 1919 possessed ten times as many female law students and three times as many female medical students as it had in 1914. British women over age 30 received the vote on a limited basis while in the United States, Germany, and most of the new states in eastern

ROLE REVERSAL

The imagery in this British Red Cross poster infantilized the soldier while making the nurse into a figure of saintly power. Many men found the forced confinement and passivity of trench warfare profoundly unsettling, while many women experienced the war as a time of liberation.

Europe, the achievement of female suffrage was more complete. Cultural changes also seemed to signal a gender revolution. Women smoked in public, raised their hemlines, cut their hair, and threw away their corsets.

Identifying the Enemy: From Propaganda to Genocide

Many of the changes in gender and class relations resulted from government efforts to regulate the economy for total war. To ensure that their citizens remained committed to the war effort, governments also sought to regulate the production and distribution of ideas. Pacifists and war objectors faced prison sentences and even execution. In France, journalists and rival politicians—even the former prime minister—who dared suggest negotiations with Germany were thrown in prison.

Wartime governments worked to create ideas that would encourage a total war mentality. Propaganda emerged as a crucial political tool. By censoring newspapers and doctoring photographs, politicians ensured that the public viewed the war positively. In Germany, the government paraded giant wooden statues of the war hero Hindenburg to rally war enthusiasm, while in all the combatant states, poster campaigns using new techniques developed in the advertising industry aroused patriotic fervor.

Fostering a total war mentality also required stirring up hatred for those labeled as the Enemy. In words that were soon set to music and became a popular wartime song, poet and army private Ernst Lissauer (1882–1937) urged Germans to "hate [England] with a lasting hate....Hate of seventy millions, choking down."[6] Meanwhile in Britain, anti-German feeling ran so high that the royal family changed its name from Hanover to Windsor in an effort to erase its German lineage. In the ethnic cauldron of eastern Europe, hatred of the enemy often fed hostility toward ethnic minorities, perceived as the enemy within. In Austria-Hungary, for example, more than 500 Bosnian Serbs and hundreds of Ukrainians were shot without trial because they were seen as Russian sympathizers.

The most horrific result of the tendency to look for the enemy at home occurred in the

THE HARVEST OF WAR
The Turkish massacre of more than one million Armenians illustrates the destructive consequences of combining nationalist hatred with total war. This criminal horror is often seen as foreshadowing the Jewish Holocaust during World War II.

Ottoman Empire, where suspicion of the Armenian minority resulted in mass murder. The brutal "solution" to the so-called "Armenian question" began in April 1915. After arresting Armenian elites (and thus removing potential resistance leaders from Armenian communities), Turkish troops rounded up and killed Armenian men. In some cases, soldiers marched the men outside their town or village and then shot them. In other instances, they were pushed into caves and asphyxiated by fires blocking the entrances. The Ottoman government then ordered the women, children, and the elderly deported to Syria. Driven from their homes on short notice, they marched through mountain and desert terrain without food or water. Rapes and executions were commonplace. Between 1915 and 1918, more than one million Armenian men, women, and children died in this attempt at **genocide,** the murder of an entire people.

WAR AND REVOLUTION

■ What were the consequences of this war for the European and the global political and international order?

Total war tore at the social and political fabric of European societies. As seams began to fray and gaping holes appeared, many welcomed the opportunity to tear apart the old cloth and weave something new. Some of these revolutionaries were Marxists, aiming to build a socialist Europe. Others were nationalists, determined to assert the rights of their ethnic or linguistic group, or to overthrow their colonial rulers. Not all revolutionaries belonged to underground or terrorist groups. The president of the United States, Woodrow Wilson, also demanded a new world order. The peace settlement, however, failed to realize these revolutionary expectations.

The Russian Revolutions

Tsarist Russia began the war already divided. In regions such as Latvia, Lithuania, Poland, and Ukraine, anti-Russian sentiment flared high, and nationalists saw the war as opening the door to independent statehood. Even within Russia itself, as we saw in Chapter 23, the clash between Tsar Nicholas II's vision of Russia as a divine autocracy and the political demands of the growing middle and working classes created an explosive situation.

The war brought political chaos to the Russian Empire. Nicholas, a man with a remarkable capacity for self-delusion, insisted on going to the front and commanding his army. He left political affairs in the hands of his wife Alexandra (1872–1918) and her spiritual mentor Grigorii Rasputin (1869–1916). Rasputin is one of the more intriguing characters in twentieth-century history. An illiterate, unwashed faith healer from a peasant background, he possessed a well-documented and still-unexplained ability to stop the bleeding of Alexei, the young hemophiliac heir to the throne. Many high-ranking Russians, however, argued that Rasputin was not a miracle worker but a traitor. Because Rasputin opposed the war against Germany, they perceived him as a voice of treason whispering in the German-born tsarina's ear. In 1916 Russian noblemen murdered Rasputin, in hopes of restoring authority and stability to the tsarist government.

THE FEBRUARY REVOLUTION Rasputin's removal achieved little. The French ambassador in Russia wrote in January 1917, "I am obliged to report that, at the present moment, the Russian Empire is run by lunatics."[7] Almost two million Russian soldiers had died and many more had been wounded or taken prisoner. Economic and communications networks had broken down, bread prices were rising, and people were hungry. Even members of the tsarist government began to ask not *if* revolution would occur, but *when*.

The answer came on February 24, 1917 (March 8 on the western calendar). A group of women workers in Petrograd (formerly St. Petersburg) demonstrated to protest inadequate food supplies. Over the course of the

THE REVOLUTIONARY SPARK

On March 8, 1917, thousands of women took to the streets of Petrograd to protest the imposition of bread rationing. Their cries for "Peace and Bread" sparked the Russian Revolution.

next few days, similar demonstrations flickered across the city. On February 27, they coalesced into revolutionary fire when the troops who were ordered to put down the protest joined it instead. Governmental orders lost all authority, and on March 2 Tsar Nicholas was forced to abdicate. The Russian Revolution had begun.

Who now controlled Russia? Two competing centers of power emerged: the Provisional Government and the Petrograd Soviet. On March 12, the Duma, or Russian parliament, created a Provisional Government from among its members. Like the Duma, the new Provisional Government was dominated by members of the gentry and middle classes: professionals, businessmen, intellectuals, bureaucrats. These men tended to be liberals who

believed that Russia was now moving along the path toward a parliamentary democracy. They quickly enacted important reforms such as universal suffrage, the eight-hour workday, and civic equality for all citizens. The Provisional Government, however, was exactly what its name indicated: provisional. Its members believed they should not take any drastic measures. Their task was to serve as a caretaker government until an elected Constituent Assembly wrote a constitution for the new Russia.

But at the same time that the Provisional Government was struggling to bring order to the chaos of revolutionary Russia, across the empire socialists, industrial workers, and soldiers formed **soviets,** or councils, to articulate their grievances and hopes. The Petrograd Soviet, led by revolutionary socialists, soon became a powerful political rival to the less radical Provisional Government.

But neither the liberals in the Provisional Government nor the socialists in the Petrograd Soviet could control the revolution. A *popular* revolution—a revolution *of the people*—had overthrown Nicholas II, and at the core of this popular revolution stood a simple demand: "Peace, Land, Bread." Soldiers—and most Russians—wanted an immediate end to a war that had long ceased to make any sense to them. Peasants, as always, wanted land, their guarantee of survival in a chaotic world. And city dwellers wanted bread—food in sufficient quantities and at affordable prices.

The Provisional Government could not satisfy these demands. It did promise the gradual redistribution of royal and Church lands, but peasants, unconstrained by the liberal regard for law and the rights of private property, wanted land immediately. More important, by the summer of 1917 no Russian government could have provided bread without providing peace. Russia no longer had the resources both to continue its war effort and to reconstruct its economy. The urban population dwindled as food disappeared from the shops, factories ceased operation because of shortages of raw materials, and the currency lost all value. Peace appeared impossible, however. Not only did Russia have commitments to its allies, but German armies stood deep within Russian territory. A separate peace with Germany would mean huge territorial losses. Only a constitutionally elected government would have the legitimacy to take such a drastic step, most Provisional Government members believed. And so the war continued.

And so, too, did the revolution. Peasants made their own land reform by seizing the land they wanted. Soldiers declared their own peace by deserting. (Of every 1,000-man Russian troop sent to the front, fewer than 250 men made it into combat. The rest deserted.) The Provisional Government grew more unpopular. Not even the appointment of the well-liked socialist and Petrograd Soviet member Alexander Kerensky (1881–1970) as prime minister stabilized the government's position.

THE OCTOBER REVOLUTION This tumultuous situation created the opportunity for the **Bolsheviks,** one of the socialist factions in the Petrograd Soviet, to seize control. In April 1917, the Bolshevik leader, Vladimir Lenin (1870–1924), returned from almost 20 years in exile. While still in his teens, Lenin had committed himself to revolution after his older brother was executed for trying to assassinate Tsar Alexander III. Iron-willed and ruthlessly pragmatic, Lenin argued that a committed group of professional revolutionaries could force a socialist revolution on Russia.

By the fall of 1917, Bolshevik membership had grown from 10,000 to 250,000, and the party held a majority in the Petrograd Soviet. Lenin now demanded the immediate overthrow of the Provisional Government. On October 25 (November 7 on the western calendar), Bolshevik fighters captured the Winter Palace in Petrograd, where the Provisional Government was meeting.

The *second* Russian Revolution was underway. The Bolsheviks declared a policy of land and peace—land partition with no compensation to estate owners and an immediate peace with Germany, regardless of the cost. (As we have seen, the cost was high: According to the terms of the Treaty of Brest-Litovsk, signed with Germany in 1918, Russia lost its western territories.)

Promises of peace and land did not win over everyone in Russia, however. Civil war erupted as rival socialists, liberals, and tsarist supporters resisted Bolshevik rule. These "Whites" (distinguished from "Red" Bolsheviks) received assistance from foreign troops. Fearing the spread of communist revolution, 14 countries (including the United States, Britain, France, and Japan) sent 100,000 soldiers to Russia. Non-Russian nationalists fighting for independent statehood joined in the conflict. (See *Justice in History* in this chapter.)

The civil war killed off more combatants than had World War I, but by 1922 the Bolsheviks emerged victorious over the Whites and most of the nationalist uprisings. Only Poland, Finland, and the Baltic states (Estonia, Latvia,

JUSTICE IN HISTORY

Revolutionary Justice: The Nontrial of Nicholas and Alexandra

On July 16, 1918, Bolshevik revolutionaries shot and killed Nicholas II, tsar of Russia; his wife, the tsarina Alexandra; his heir, 14-year-old Alexei; their four daughters—Olga (age 23), Tatiana (age 21), Maria (age 19), and Anastasia (age 17); their three servants; and their physician. When leaders in other states heard the news of the deaths, they condemned the killings as murders. The Bolsheviks, however, termed them executions, acts of revolutionary justice.

Faced with counterrevolutionary challenges on all sides in the months following the October Revolution, the Bolsheviks feared that Nicholas would become a rallying symbol for their enemies. They decided that the tsar and his family—already under house arrest outside Moscow—must be moved about 900 miles to the east, to Ekaterinburg, a region controlled by the Bolshevik Ural Regional Soviet. Meanwhile,

the Bolshevik government prepared to try Nicholas publicly for crimes against the Russian people.

But the trial never happened. By July of 1918, an anti-Bolshevik army was approaching Ekaterinburg. If these troops freed the imperial family, they would score a crucial victory. Told that the city might fall to the enemy within days, the Ural Soviet decided—probably with Lenin's approval—to execute the tsar and his family immediately.

Pavel Medvedev, one of the tsar's guards, later recounted the events of the evening of July 16. His interviewer recorded what Medvedev had told him:

> [He said,] The Tsar, the Tsaritsa [Tsarina], the Tsar's four daughters, the doctor, the cook and the lackey came out of their rooms. The Tsar was carrying the heir [Alexei] in his arms..... In my presence there were no tears, no sobs and no questions....

TSAR NICHOLAS II AND FAMILY
Tsar Nicholas II, the Tsarina Alexandra, and their family.

Medvedev then testified that his officer ordered him to leave. When he returned a few minutes later:

> ....he saw all the members of the Tsar's family lying on the floor with numerous wounds to their bodies. The blood was gushing. The heir was still alive—and moaning. [The commander] walked over to him and shot him two or three times at point blank range. The heir fell still.[8]

Medvedev's understated account did not relate the more gruesome details of the execution. Trying to preserve part of the family fortune, the tsar's daughters wore corsets into which they had sewn diamonds. When they were shot, the bullets, in the words of one eyewitness, "ricocheted, jumping around the room like hail."[9] Even after several pistols were emptied, one of the girls remained alive. The guards resorted to bayonets.

The killing of not just the tsar but also his wife and children was a startling act, as the Bolsheviks themselves recognized. The Ural Regional Soviet announced the tsar's execution, but said nothing about his family, while the official statement from Moscow reported that "the wife and son of Nicholas Romanov were sent to a safe place."[10]

These lies reveal the Bolsheviks' own uneasiness with the killings. Why, then, did they shoot the family? Determination to win the civil war provides part of the answer. According to Trotsky, Lenin "believed we shouldn't leave the Whites [the anti-Bolshevik forces] a live banner to rally around."[11] Any member of the royal family could have become such a banner. But Trotsky also viewed the killings as an essential and absolute break with the past. In his words, "the execution of the Tsar's family was needed not only to frighten, horrify, and to dishearten the enemy, but also in order to shake up our own ranks, to show them that there was no turning back, that ahead lay either complete victory or complete ruin."[12]

The killing of Tsar Nicholas and his family thus formed part of the pattern of escalating violence that characterized World War I and its revolutionary aftermath. But in the blood of these killings we can also see reflected two ideas that shaped Bolshevik politics: the subordination of law to the revolutionary state and the concept of collective guilt.

The Bolsheviks rejected the liberal democratic ideal of impartial justice. They argued that justice was never blind, that it always served the interests of the ruling classes. In a discussion of the tsar's killing, a Bolshevik pamphlet admitted, "Many formal aspects of bourgeois justice may have been violated." But, the pamphlet argued, such a violation of "bourgeois" standards of justice did not matter because "worker-peasant power was manifested in the process, making no exception for the All-Russian murderer, shooting as if he were an ordinary brigand.... Nicholas the Bloody is no more."[13] In the Bolshevik model, the law was not separate from, but rather subordinate to the state. "Worker peasant power," embodied in the revolutionary state, trumped such "formal aspects of bourgeois justice" as legal rights.

While this concept of the law as subordinate to the state helps us understand the tsar's execution without trial, the concept of collective guilt provides a context for the killing of his children. The Bolshevik model of socialism assumed that *class* constituted objective reality. Simply by belonging to a certain social class, an individual became an enemy of the revolution. Hence, the Bolshevik constitution denied the vote to individuals who lived off investment interest or bore other marks of tsarist-era privilege. Aristocratic and middle-class origins served as an indelible ink, marking a person permanently as an enemy of the revolutionary state—regardless of that person's own actions or inclinations. From the Bolshevik perspective, then, royal origins tainted the tsar's children. When their continuing existence threatened the revolution, they were shot. Over the next four decades, the concept of collective guilt contributed to millions of deaths in the former Russian Empire.

When World War I ended and the Allied victors met in Paris in 1919 to build the postwar world, they sought to establish democracies in which the rule of law would guarantee the rights of individuals. These two interlinked concepts of law and individual rights became for many the defining features of "the West," of democracy, and of civilization itself. The Bolsheviks challenged this definition. They offered instead a definition of democracy based on class and an understanding of the law resting on the demands of continuing revolution.

For Discussion

1. How was the murder of the Russian royal family the by-product of total war rather than the result of any revolutionary ideals?

2. Were the Bolsheviks correct in arguing that "justice" is never blind, that legal systems reflect the interests of a society's dominant groups? Is there such a thing as impartial justice?

Taking It Further

Kozlov, Vladimir, and Vladimir Khrustalëv. *The Last Diary of Tsaritsa Alexandra.* 1997. A translation of Alexandra's diary from 1918.

Rosenberg, William, ed. *Bolshevik Visions: First Phase of the Cultural Revolution in Soviet Russia.* 1990. The section on "Proletarian Legality" explores the Bolsheviks' effort to develop a legal system that embodied their revolutionary ideals.

Steinberg, Mark, and Vladimir Khrustalëv. *The Fall of the Romanovs.* 1999. A detailed account of the last two years of the tsar and his family, based on archives opened only after the collapse of the Soviet Union.

---

and Lithuania) retained their hard-won independence. Formally, states such as Ukraine and Georgia were republics with their own constitutions and communist parties, joined together with Russia in the "Union of Soviet Socialist Republics" (USSR, or the Soviet Union). In reality, power remained centralized in Moscow.

CHRONOLOGY: REVOLUTION IN RUSSIA, 1917–1922

1917

February 24	St. Petersburg/Petrograd women's protest; revolution begins
March 2	Establishment of Provisional Government and abdication of tsar
October 25	Bolshevik overthrow of the Provisional Government
1918–1922	Civil war

THE SPREADING REVOLUTION The victory of the Russian Bolsheviks inspired socialists across Europe and around the world. In January 1919, communists in Buenos Aires, Argentina, led by Russian immigrants, controlled the city for three days until they were crushed by the Argentine army. British dockworkers struck in support of the Bolshevik Revolution, and in French cities general strikes caused chaos. In Austria, revolutionaries attempted to take control of government buildings in Vienna but were quickly defeated by the Austrian army. In Hungary, Bela Kun, a journalist who had come to admire the Bolsheviks while a prisoner of war in Russia, established a short-lived soviet regime in the spring of 1919.

Revolution also swept through defeated Germany. In October 1918, its military commanders recommended that the German government enter into peace negotiations, but the Allies refused to negotiate until the Germans democratized their political system. As a result, representatives of left-wing and centrist parties—including the SPD, the largest socialist party in Europe—joined the German government.

This "revolution from above" coincided and competed with a "revolution from below." Inspired by the Bolshevik Revolution, many German socialists condemned the SPD as too moderate; instead, they supported the more radical Spartacists (named after Spartacus, the gladiator who led a slave revolt against Rome in the first century B.C.E.). Directed by Karl Liebknecht (1871–1919) and Rosa Luxemburg (1870–1919), the Spartacists demanded an immediate communist revolution. By November 8, German communists declared the establishment of a Soviet republic in the province of Bavaria and the Red Flag—symbol of communism—flew over eleven German cities.

On November 9, the kaiser abdicated and the head of the SPD, Friedrich Ebert (1871–1925), became chancellor of Germany. From the window of the Reichstag building in Berlin, one of Ebert's colleagues in the SPD proclaimed that Germany was now a parliamentary democracy. Almost at that very moment, Karl Liebknecht stood at another window in Berlin (in the occupied royal palace) and announced that Germany was now a revolutionary communist state. With two opposing versions of revolution on offer, civil war raged until the spring of 1919, when the SPD defeated the communists.

THE REVOLUTION HALTED Even after this defeat, however, Lenin hoped that the communist revolution would spread throughout western Europe. The Polish-Soviet War of 1919–1921 inspired and then crushed this hope of a European communist revolution.

Partitioned among Prussia, Austria, and Russia in the eighteenth century, Poland was reconstructed after World War I. Its eastern borders, however, remained unclear because of the ongoing civil war and nationalist conflicts in Bolshevik Russia. Poland's newly elected president, Josef Pilsudski (1867–1935), aimed to create a federation consisting of Poland and independent Ukraine, Belarus, and the Baltic states, a kind of twentieth-century version of the early modern Polish-Lithuanian Commonwealth. Nationalists within these states, however, refused to cooperate and although by May 1920, Pilsudski's army controlled much of this territory, a Soviet counterattack in June forced the Poles to retreat.

This successful Soviet push into Poland led Lenin to believe that the revolution was unstoppable, even though Polish workers rejected Lenin's call for a working-class uprising. Once the Soviets conquered Poland, Lenin argued, they could use it as "a base against all the contemporary states."[14] Thus, Lenin termed the Battle of Warsaw of August 1920 a "turning point for the world."[15] Instead, Pilsudski and his forces held Warsaw and drove the Red Army back. The Peace of Riga of 1921 granted to Poland most of the pre-partition territory Pilsudski had demanded and blocked Lenin's plan of moving west.

The Failure of Wilson's Revolution

At the beginning of 1919, representatives of the victorious Allies gathered in Paris to draw up the peace treaties. These officials aimed for more than ending the war. They wished to construct a new Europe. At the center of this high endeavor was the American college professor-turned-president Woodrow Wilson. Wilson based his version of revolutionary change on the ideal of national self-determination—a world in which "every people should be left free to determine its own polity, its own way of development, unhindered, unthreatened, unafraid, the little along with the great and powerful." Wilson foresaw a new map of Europe, with independent, ethnically homogenous, democratic nation-states replacing the old authoritarian empires.

Wilson envisioned that these new nation-states would interact differently from the empires of the past. In what he called his **Fourteen Points,** Wilson demanded a revolution in international relations. He argued that "Points" such as freedom of the seas, freedom of trade, and open diplomacy (an end to secret treaties) would break down barriers and guarantee peace and prosperity for all peoples. The cornerstone of this new world order would be an international organization, the **League of Nations.** By overseeing the implementation of the Fourteen Points and resolving disputes between states through negotiation, the League would guarantee that World War I was "the war to end all wars." Because all states—big and small, European and non-European—would have an equal voice in the League, the systems of secret diplomacy and Great Power alliances that had led to total war would disappear.

Wilson's vision, however, went unrealized. In Paris in 1919 and 1920, the Allies and their defeated enemies signed a series of treaties, the most important of which was the Treaty of Versailles with Germany. The treaty writers sought to create a new international order based on three features: a democratic Germany, national self-determination in eastern Europe, and a viable system of international arbitration headed by the League of Nations. They failed in all three.

THE TREATY OF VERSAILLES AND GERMAN DEMOCRACY

At the center of the new Europe envisioned by Woodrow Wilson was to be a new democratic Germany, but the French leader, Georges Clemenceau, did not share this vision. After surviving two German invasions of his homeland, he wished to ensure that Germany could never again threaten France. Clemenceau proposed the creation of a Rhineland state in Germany's industrialized western region as a buffer zone between France and Germany and as a way to reduce Germany's economic power. The British leader David Lloyd George promised his people that he would squeeze Germany "until the pips squeak" and publicly supported Clemenceau's hardline approach. In private, Lloyd George feared that this approach would feed the flames of German resentment and undermine the structures of German democracy.

Lloyd George's fears proved well-grounded. The German people bitterly resented the **Versailles Treaty,** which they perceived as unjustly punitive. By the terms of the treaty, Germany lost all of its overseas colonies, 13 percent of its European territory, 10 percent of its population, and its ability to wage war. The treaty limited the German army to a defensive force of 100,000 men, with no aircraft or tanks. Clemenceau failed to create a separate Rhineland state, but the Rhineland was demilitarized, emptied of German soldiers and fortifications. In addition, the Versailles Treaty ceded the coalfields of the Saar region to France for 15 years (see **Map 25.5**).

Most significantly, the treaty declared that German aggression had caused the war and therefore that Germany must recompense the Allies for their costs. In 1921, the Allies presented Germany with a bill for **reparations** of 132 billion marks ($31.5 billion). As Chapter 26 details, this reparations clause helped set up an economic cycle that proved devastating for both global prosperity and German democratic politics.

THE FAILURE OF NATIONAL SELF-DETERMINATION

The peace settlement sought to redraw eastern Europe on national lines. Map 25.5 shows that the old multinational empires of eastern and central Europe disappeared, replaced with independent nation-states. Poland again became a state, with pieces carved out of the German, Austro-Hungarian, and Russian Empires. One entirely new state—Czechoslovakia—was formed out of the rubble of the Austro-Hungarian Empire. Romania, Greece, and Italy all expanded as a result of serving on the winners' side, while Serbia became the heart of the new Yugoslavia. The defeated

MAP 25.5

The Struggle over Boundaries: The Redrawing of Central and Eastern Europe after World War I

A comparison of this map with Map 25.1 on page 799 illustrates that the war redrew the political map of eastern Europe. By the terms of the Versailles Treaty, Germany lost 13 percent of its prewar territory and 10 percent of its prewar population. France regained Alsace and Lorraine; the industrialized Rhineland became a demilitarized zone; and reconstructed Poland was given a corridor to the sea. Poland also gained Austrian Galicia and part of what had been the Russian Empire. Although the Bolsheviks were able to beat back nationalist secession movements in Belarus and Ukraine, Finland and the Baltic states of Estonia, Latvia, and Lithuania all split from what had been the Russian Empire. Serbia gained a big chunk of the former Austro-Hungarian Empire to become Yugoslavia. The former Austro-Hungarian Empire also lost territory to an expanded Romania and to the new state of Czechoslovakia. All that remained of the Ottoman Empire was the new state of Turkey.

states shrank, some dramatically. Austria, for example, became a mere rump of what had been the mighty Habsburg Empire, and Hungary was reduced to one-third of its prewar size. All that remained of the Ottoman Empire was Turkey.

President Wilson heralded these changes as the victory of "national self-determination."

But as Wilson's own secretary of state complained, "This phrase is simply loaded with dynamite. It will raise hopes which can never be realized." Wilson had called for "every people" to be left free to determine its political destiny—but who constituted "a people"? Did the Macedonians? Should there be an independent Macedonia? Macedonians said yes, but the Paris peace negotiators answered no. Macedonia was enveloped by Yugoslavia and Greece, and in consequence, throughout the 1920s and 1930s Macedonians waged a terrorist campaign in the Balkans.

The Macedonians were not the only dissatisfied ethnic group in eastern Europe. Even after the peace settlements redrew the map, 30 million eastern Europeans remained members of minority groups. Less than 70 percent of Hungarians, for example, lived in Hungary—more than three million were scattered in other states. Over nine million Germans resided outside the borders of Germany. In the newly created Czechoslovakia, one-third of the population was neither Czech nor Slovak. The new state of Yugoslavia contained an uneasy mixture of several ethnic groups, most resentful of the dominant Serbs. Rather than satisfying nationalist ambitions, the peace settlements served to inflame them, thus creating a volatile situation for the post-World War I world.

THE LIMITS OF THE LEAGUE True to Wilson's vision of a new international order, the treaty makers included the Covenant of the League of Nations in each of the treaties. The League, however, never fulfilled Wilson's hopes of making war obsolete. When the League met for the first time in 1920, three significant world powers had no representative present: Germany and Russia were excluded, and, in a stunning defeat for President Wilson, the U.S. Senate rejected membership. The failure of these three states to participate in the League at its beginning stripped the organization of much of its potential influence.

Two additional factors weakened the League. First, it had no military power. Although the League could levy economic sanctions against states that flouted its decisions, it could do nothing more. Second, the will to make the League work was lacking. With Wilson removed from the picture, European leaders pursued their own more traditional visions of what the League should be. French

politicians, for example, believed that its primary reason for existence was to enforce the provisions of the Versailles Treaty—in other words, to punish Germany rather than to restructure international relations.

The Making of the Modern Middle East

In the Middle East, the end of World War I meant an entirely new map, but not the end of European dominance. As **Map 25.6** shows, under terms set by the new League of Nations, the Allies carved the Ottoman territory in the Middle East into separate and nominally independent states. The League, however, judged these states as "not yet able to stand by themselves under the strenuous conditions of the modern world" and so placed them under French or British control (or "Mandate"). Syria and Lebanon fell to the French, while Britain

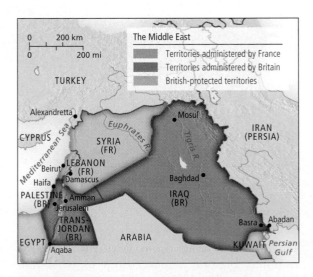

MAP 25.6

The Middle East after World War I

The hopes of Arab and Jewish nationalists for independent states were put on hold by the League of Nation's creation of European mandates in the Middle East.

claimed Iraq (Mesopotamia), Palestine, and Transjordan (later called Jordan). Britain also continued to exercise its influence over Egypt, Iran (Persia), and what would become Saudi Arabia.

This remaking of the Middle East failed to effect a lasting settlement in the region. The new map violated wartime promises and so created a long-lasting legacy of mistrust and resentment against the West. In addition, the new states imposed on the region were artificial, the creation of the Allied victors rather than a product of historical evolution or of the wishes of the inhabitants themselves. And finally, Western mandatory supervision (which in actual practice differed little from old-fashioned imperial rule) brought with it Western practices and concepts that destabilized regional social and economic structures.

The early history of Iraq exemplifies these three developments. In 1915, Sharif Husayn (Hussein) ibn Ali, head of the Hashemite dynasty that guarded the Islamic holy sites, agreed to fight the Central Powers in exchange for British support of an independent Arab state. The British argued they fulfilled this promise when they placed Husayn's son Faisal on the throne of the newly created Iraq. Huseyn and his supporters, however, felt betrayed. They believed that the British had reneged on the promise of an independent Arab kingdom centering on what became Syria and including Palestine.

The artificiality of Iraq also created a revolutionary situation. In creating Iraq, the Allies glued together three provinces—Basra, Baghdad, and Mosul—that the Ottomans had never treated as a single political or economic unit. The population of this new state consisted of a volatile mixture of ethnicities (including Arab, Kurd, and Assyrian) and religions (including Shia and Sunni Muslims, Christians, Jews, and Zoroastrians). These groups did not identify as "Iraqi" nor did they feel any sense of allegiance to their new ruler. They regarded Faisal as an imperialist puppet, jumping as British "advisers" pulled the strings.

Finally, the British inadvertently destabilized Iraq's social structures by introducing British legal and economic concepts that destroyed indigenous traditions. For example, by applying the concept of private land ownership to Iraqi customary relations, the British transformed the traditional tie between tribal sheikh and tribesmen into an economic arrangement between landowner and tenants—one that tended to enrich the landowner while impoverishing the tenants.

The settlement of Palestine destabilized the Middle East even further. Huseyn and his supporters believed that the British government had promised them an independent Arab kingdom that would include Palestine. Yet during the war British officials also pledged support for a Jewish state in Palestine. Influenced by the anti-Semitic myth of a powerful Jewish elite wielding influence over world affairs, British policymakers believed (wrongly) that Jewish influence could determine whether the United States entered and Russia remained in the war. Desperate to ensure both, the British government in 1917 issued the **Balfour Declaration,** which announced that Britain favored the Zionist goal of a Jewish national homeland in Palestine.

After the war, Palestine passed into British hands as a United Nations mandate. The British remained formally committed to the Balfour Declaration. Some 90 percent of the inhabitants of Palestine in 1920, however, were Arabs (both Christians and Muslims). They viewed the Balfour Declaration as an effort to take away their land and give it to Europeans. Arab protests and riots in Palestine erupted, and by 1922 the British government decided to slow the pace of Jewish immigration into the region to alleviate Arab fears. Over the next two decades the British faced continuous pressure from both Arab and Jewish nationalist forces. Like the remaking of eastern Europe, the remaking of the Middle East ushered in decades of political turmoil and violence.

CONCLUSION

The War and the West

The idea of "the West" changed as a result of World War I. The entry of American forces in the final year of the war signaled that in the twentieth century, the United States would feature in any definition of "Western culture" or "Western civilization." At the same time, the spread of the war to the Middle East and Africa and the significant role played by soldiers from imperial territories such as Tunisia, India, and Australia demonstrated the global framework that complicated and constrained Western affairs.

The war's revolutionary aftermath also had consequences for formulations of "Western identity." With the triumph of the Bolshevik Revolution, two versions of modernity now presented themselves—one associated with the United States and capitalism, and the other represented by Russia and its communism. The Bolshevik Party's intellectual roots lay in Marxism, a Western ideology shaped by Western ideals of evolutionary progress and the triumph of human reason. But after the Russian Revolution, communism was viewed in the West as the "Other" against which the West identified itself.

The carnage of World War I challenged the faith of many Europeans that industrial development ensured the West's continual moral and material progress. In the final decades of the nineteenth century, European and American soldiers had used repeating rifles and machine guns to conquer huge sections of the globe in the name of Western civilization. In 1914, European and American soldiers turned their machine guns on each other. The world the war created was one of unprecedented destruction. Millions lay dead, with millions more maimed for life. Vast sections of northern France and eastern Europe became giant cemeteries filled with rotting men and rusting metal. Across central and eastern Europe, starvation continued to claim thousands of victims, while a worldwide influenza epidemic, spread in part by the marching armies, ratcheted up the death tolls even higher. In the new world shaped by relentless conflicts such as the Battle of the Somme, the pessimism and sense of despair that had invaded the arts in the decade before the war became more characteristic of the wider culture. For many Europeans, the optimism and confidence of nineteenth-century liberalism died in the trenches.

Yet, paradoxically, the war also fostered high hopes. Wilson declared that this had been the war to end all wars. The fires of revolution burned brightly and many in the West believed that on top of the ashes of dismantled empires, they would now build a better world. The task of reconstruction, however, proved immense. Seeking stability, many Europeans and Americans did their best to return to prewar patterns. The failure of the peace settlement ensured that the "war to end all wars" set the stage for the next, more destructive total war.

KEY TERMS

total war	genocide
Central Powers	soviets
Allies	Bolsheviks
Triple Alliance	Fourteen Points
Reinsurance Treaty	League of Nations
Triple Entente	Versailles Treaty
Schlieffen Plan	reparations
no-man's-land	Balfour Declaration
Treaty of Brest-Litovsk	

CHAPTER QUESTIONS

1. What factors led Europe into war in 1914? (page 784)
2. When, where, and how did the Allies defeat the Central Powers? (page 792)
3. How did total war structure the home fronts? (page 802)
4. What were the consequences of this war for the European and the global political and international order? (page 807)

TAKING IT FURTHER

1. Compare and contrast the Eastern, Western, and Middle Eastern Fronts in World War I: Who was involved, where, and why? How and why did the experiences of ordinary soldiers in these war zones differ? Which front was more important for shaping the postwar West?
2. What do the phrases "total war politics" and a "total war mentality" mean? How did total war politics and mentalities affect European women? The working class? National minorities?
3. How did the Wilsonian and Leninist visions of postwar Europe differ? Which was more "Western" and why? Which was more successful and why?

✓●─[Practice on **MyHistoryLab**

26

Reconstruction, Reaction, and Continuing Revolution: The 1920s and 1930s

■ Cultural Despair and Desire ■ Out of the Trenches: Reconstructing National and Gender Politics in the 1920s ■ The Rise of the Radical Right ■ The Polarization of Politics in the 1930s ■ The West and the World: Imperialism in the Interwar Era

ON SEPTEMBER 14, 1927, A CONVERTIBLE ACCELERATED DOWN A STREET in Nice in southern France. In its passenger seat sat Isadora Duncan, who let her long silk shawl whip in the wind. One of the most famous dancers in the Western world, Duncan had pioneered a revolutionary style of dance that replaced toe shoes and tutus with bare feet and simple tunics. Attacking classical ballet as an artificial form that deformed the female body, the American-born Duncan created dances that did not impose movement on the body, but instead flowed from the body itself. Speeding down the streets in a convertible, Duncan provides a fitting image for Western culture after World War I. She was an American, and in these decades American culture came to represent for many Europeans the limitless future. Like Duncan in her car, Americans and Europeans in the postwar era wanted to move in new directions, break traditional barriers, and push toward greater liberation. Even Duncan's clothing—loose tunics, free-flowing scarves, fluid shawls—symbolized a love of freedom and mobility.

Yet freedom is sometimes dangerous and movement can be violent. On that autumn day in 1927 Duncan's scarf became entangled in the wheel of the car and strangled the dancer. Gruesome as it is, this image, too, symbolizes the West in the turbulent interlude between two world wars. The American president Woodrow Wilson hailed World War I as the "final war for human liberty." Many Europeans agreed. They thought that the war would propel their society down a new road. In much of Europe, however, the drive toward freedom ended with the triumph of ideologies that viewed human liberty as an illusion and mass murder as a tool of the state.

The strangulation of democracy in eastern and southern Europe during these decades highlights a central theme of this book: the contested definition of "the West." In the Wilsonian vision, the West promoted individual freedom through democratic politics and capitalist economics. But in the 1920s and 1930s, antidemocratic and anticapitalist ideologies defined the West differently. Examination of the aftermath of World War I answers the question: why was the link between "Western" and "democratic" so fragile?

OTTO DIX, *FLANDERS* (1934–1935)
In this painting, the bodies of soldiers shape the Flanders landscape. Like these soldiers—and much of postwar European culture—Dix, a veteran, could not escape the war. His paintings reveal a man permanently wounded.

CULTURAL DESPAIR AND DESIRE

■ **What was the impact of the war on European cultural life?**

After World War I, many in the West turned from the future in despair. Others, however, dreamed of building a new world.

The Waste Land

Within a few years of the war's end, war memorials dotted cities and villages throughout France and Britain. These memorials rarely celebrated the Allies' victory. They focused instead on dead soldiers—on slaughter, not success. At Verdun, for example, the memorial was an ossuary, a gigantic receptacle for the skulls and bones of 130,000 men. In some ways, European culture after the war took the form of an ossuary, as intellectuals and artists looked at the death tolls from the war and concluded that the end product of human reason and scientific endeavor was mass destruction.

In the English-speaking world, "The Waste Land" (1922), a poem by the American expatriate poet T. S. Eliot (1888–1965), supplied an evocative portrait of postwar disillusion. Like a Cubist painting, this lengthy poem contains no straightforward narrative. Instead, it comprises fragments of conversation, literary allusions, disjointed quotations, and mythological references, all clashing in a modernist cry of despair:

> White bodies naked on the low damp ground
> And bones cast in a little low dry garret,
> Rattled by the rat's foot only, year to year.

Pessimism also marked theology and philosophy. In the nineteenth century, theologians and philosophers emphasized humanity's progressive evolution, but World War I raised doubts about the moral progress of human society. In his writings, the Swiss theologian Karl Barth (1886–1968) emphasized human sinfulness and argued that an immense gulf separated humanity from God. Human intellectual effort could not bridge the gap. Reaching God demanded a radical leap of faith.

Barth's German colleague Rudolf Bultmann (1884–1976) made the leap of faith even more radical. Bultmann argued that the Jesus Christ depicted in the New Testament—the foundation of Christianity—was largely fictional. In Bultmann's view, the New Testament resembled Eliot's "Waste Land" in its layered fragments originating from myth and folk tale, capable of multiple interpretations. Bultmann, a Lutheran pastor, argued that in this Christian mythology persons can find spiritual—although not scientific or historical—truth.

Bultmann's form of Christianity is often called Christian **existentialism** because Bultmann put a Christian twist on the existentialist philosophy that emerged in the interwar era. Existentialists such as Jean-Paul Sartre (1905–1980) taught that existence has no built-in meaning—no religious purpose or moral value. It just *is*. To overcome the fear, alienation, even *Nausea* (the title of one of Sartre's novels, published in 1938) of mere existence, a person must consciously choose actions that create meaning and a sense of self. As Sartre put it, each person is "condemned to be free."

Building Something Better

In *Flanders,* painted in 1934, the war veteran Otto Dix (1891–1969) depicted a nightmare of trench soldiers, rotting like blasted trees. Stuck in the mud, Dix's soldiers provide a haunting image of interwar culture. A different vision, however, takes shape when we examine the work of Dix's contemporaries in the *Bauhaus*. Established in Berlin in 1919 as a school for architects, craftsmen, and designers, the Bauhaus epitomized postwar Western idealism rather than despair. Its members sought to eliminate the barriers between "art" (what we put on our walls or see in museums) and "craft" (what we actually use in daily life: furniture, textiles, dishes, and the like). By making daily living more effective, efficient, and beautiful, the Bauhaus' founder Walter Gropius (1883–1969) and his students hoped to become "the architects of a new civilization."[1] Like Gropius, many artists abandoned the prewar modernist ideal of "art for art's sake" and produced work steeped in political passion and the hope of radical social change.

Faith in technology characterized this optimistic side of interwar culture. Having demonstrated the destructive power of machines during World War I, human beings would now use their mechanical powers to reconfigure modern society. Architecture illustrated this mechanical faith. A house, explained the Swiss architect Le Corbusier (1887–1965), was "a machine for living in." Le Corbusier and his fellow modernist architects stripped their buildings of ornamentation and exposed the machinery—the supporting beams, the heating ducts, the elevator shafts. Concrete, steel, and glass became the building materials of choice as modernist skyscrapers—glittering rectangles—transformed urban skylines and testified to the triumph of the human-made.

This enthusiasm for the mechanical also influenced interwar popular culture. In the Charleston, a dance of the 1920s, the dancers' arms and legs fired like pistons, the entire body a fast-moving machine. Another American import, Hollywood's "moving pictures," presented European audiences with an appealing, if unrealistic, picture of the United States as a land of technological modernity and unlimited mobility.

THE CHARLESTON: THE BODY AS MACHINE

The Charleston grabbed Western imaginations in the 1920s and became the decade's most popular dance. In this photograph, a couple dances the Charleston on stage in London in 1926, during a performance of the musical *Just a Kiss*.

Appropriately, the car and the airplane symbolized this new sense of technological possibilities. The export of the assembly line from the United States to Europe cut the cost of automobile manufacturing: The rich man's toy became a middle-class necessity. The airline industry also took off in this era, with air passenger service between London and Paris beginning in 1919. In 1927, when the American Charles Lindbergh (1902–1974) completed the first solo flight across the Atlantic, he became an international hero, a symbol of human resourcefulness and technological mastery.

Scientific Possibilities

The ongoing scientific revolution also offered new possibilities. As Chapter 24 explained, from the 1890s on, a new model of the universe began to take shape. By the 1920s, Albert Einstein's concept of matter as "frozen energy" engaged scientists from all over the world. In theory, if the energy could be "thawed out," then this energy could be released. But could this theory become reality? In 1936, the British scientist Ernest Rutherford (1871–1937), head of one of the most important research laboratories in the West, dismissed the idea of unlocking the atom to release energy as "moonshine."

Four years earlier, however, a scientist working in Rutherford's laboratory had in fact found the key to unlocking the atom, although no one realized it at the time. In 1932, James Chadwick (1891–1974) discovered that atoms contain not only positively charged protons and negatively charged electrons, but also neutrons. Because neutrons possess no electrical charge, neither the protons nor electrons repel them. Thus, a bombardment of heavy neutrons could, in theory, split an atom's nucleus—a process called nuclear fission. The split nucleus itself would then emit neutrons, which would burst open other atoms, which in turn would emit further neutrons...and on and on in a nuclear chain reaction. The result: a colossal burst of energy that could be harnessed for industrial production—or for military destruction.

Such possibilities remained theoretical until 1938 when German scientists Otto Hahn (1879–1968) and Fritz Strassmann (1902–1980) broke open the uranium atom. Within a year, more than 100 articles on the implications of this discovery appeared in scientific journals. As one historian noted, "Physicists viewed the discovery of nuclear fission like the finding of a lost treasure map."[2]

OUT OF THE TRENCHES: RECONSTRUCTING NATIONAL AND GENDER POLITICS IN THE 1920s

■ In what ways did retrenchment rather than revolution characterize the postwar period?

Chapter 25 argued that after World War I Europe stood on the brink of revolutionary change. Gender roles turned upside down, imperial patterns shattered, and social expectations heightened. Yet retrenchment rather than revolution characterized the immediate postwar period as Europeans sought to reconstruct the structures toppled by total war.

The Reconstruction of Imperial Russia: The Soviet Union

Even in revolutionary Russia, important prewar patterns reemerged. We saw in Chapter 25 that after four years of bitter fighting, the Bolsheviks reestablished Russian authority over most of the former tsarist empire, including Ukraine, Georgia, Armenia, Azerbaijan, and most of Byelorussia (Belarus). This reassertion of the empire accompanied the return of a second prewar pattern: authoritarian rule. Once in power, Lenin imposed single-party rule, silenced

debate, and used intimidation and murder to crush dissent.

Bolshevik dictatorship emerged in part as a pragmatic response to the Russian civil war of 1918–1922. As the war raged, transportation systems shut down, the water supply ceased to run, and furniture became the only source of fuel. When the furniture ran out, entire families froze to death inside apartment blocks. Urban areas emptied as their inhabitants fled to the countryside. By 1921, Moscow had lost half its residents and Petrograd (formerly St. Petersburg) lost two-thirds. Yet rural conditions were also brutal, a consequence of the Bolshevik policy of "War Communism": requisitioning (stealing) food and seed stores from peasants. The peasants resisted—actively, with violence, and passively, by refusing to plant crops. Famine resulted. The need to impose order on this chaotic situation led Lenin and his supporters to adopt authoritarian measures. Like the Jacobins in 1792 during the French Revolutionary Wars, the Bolsheviks turned to terror to defeat their domestic and foreign enemies.

Authoritarianism, however, was also inherent in Leninist ideology, an adaptation of Marxism. In a largely peasant society such as Russia, Lenin argued, the agent of revolutionary change could not be the urban industrial working class (as Karl Marx had theorized). The masses could not make the revolution, and so the Bolshevik or Communist Party, the revolutionary "vanguard," made it for them. The rule of the tsar gave way not to democracy, but to the rule of the commissar, the Communist Party functionary. Party bureaucrats became a privileged upper class, with access to the best jobs, food, clothing, and apartments.

A third area of pre- and postwar continuity lay in the economic sphere. Famine and peasant unrest forced Lenin to abandon socialist dogma for the **New Economic Policy (NEP)**. Under NEP, peasants were allowed to sell their produce for profit. Although the state continued to control heavy industry, transport, and banking, NEP encouraged small private businesses and farms—just as the tsar's economic policymakers had done before the war. The Soviet Union thus replicated many of the authoritarian features of the tsarist regime: violent coercion, a highly centralized state, a bureaucratic elite living in conditions of privilege that cut it off from ordinary people, and a peasant economy.

The Reconstruction of National Politics in Eastern and Central Europe

In his plans for postwar Europe, American president Woodrow Wilson envisioned a new international order based on national self-determination and democratic politics. But in the new states of eastern Europe, democracy proved fragile because much of old Europe survived the war intact.

THE DEFEAT OF DEMOCRACY IN EASTERN EUROPE **Map 26.1** shows that after the peace negotiations concluded by 1921, postwar eastern Europe certainly *looked* markedly different from its prewar counterpart. The Russian, Austro-Hungarian, and Ottoman Empires had all disappeared, replaced by a jigsaw puzzle of small independent states. But lines on the map did not change key political realities. Few of these regions had any democratic traditions or history, and few political leaders had mastered the give-and-take of parliamentary rule.

Two additional threads tied the new states to their prewar past. First, despite the Allied commitment to the ideal of national self-determination in drawing the new state boundaries, in many of these states nationalist divisions in fact worsened in the 1920s and 1930s. In Poland, for example, Jewish, Ukrainian, and German minorities made up one-third of the population, and 25 different parties contended for control. In Yugoslavia, Croats and Slovenes expected a federal system that would grant them local autonomy; instead, they found themselves in a centralized state dominated by Serbs.

These unsteady political structures rested on underdeveloped economies, the second thread linking the new states to prewar conditions. Much of eastern Europe remained a world of peasants and aristocratic landlords. In Romania, Poland, and Hungary, at least 60 percent of the population worked the land. In Bulgaria and Yugoslavia, the figure was 80 percent—versus 20 percent in industrialized Britain. With little industrial growth in these regions and few cities to absorb labor, unemployment rates rose.

Nationalist conflicts and economic weakness helped destabilize and then destroy eastern Europe's new democratic political systems. As the chronology table shows, in every eastern European state except Czechoslovakia, democracy gave way to authoritarian government during the 1920s or 1930s.

THE WEAKNESS OF THE WEIMAR REPUBLIC In Germany, as in the new states of eastern Europe, the appearance of radical change masked crucial continuities between the pre- and postwar eras. The kaiser's empire gave way to the **Weimar Republic,** led by a democratically elected parliamentary government. This democratic political structure, however, sat uneasily atop antidemocratic foundations.

The survival of authoritarian attitudes and institutions resulted in part from the civil war that raged throughout Germany in the fall of 1918 and the first months of 1919 (see Chapter 25). In this struggle, German communists, inspired by the Bolshevik revolution, fought their one-time colleagues in the more moderate socialist party (the SPD). Anxious to impose order, the SPD leaders who governed Germany chose to work with rather than replace the existing civil service dominated by aristocrats who had served the kaiser. To put down the communist threat, they also abandoned their longstanding loathing of the German military

MAP 26.1

Europe and the Middle East in the 1920s and 1930s

The map shows the consequences of World War I and its successor conflicts. 1. War between Ireland and Britain (1920–21): Northern Ireland remained a part of Britain while the rest of the island became independent Eire (see p. 847); 2. Civil war in Bolshevik Russia (1918–1922): Poland, Latvia, Lithuania, Estonia, and Finland became independent states but the Soviet Union reclaimed Ukraine and the Caucasus region (see p. 809); 3. The Turkish uprising blocked Allied plans to create an independent Kurdistan and an independent Armenia (see p. 850); and 4. The French army blocked Arabian nationalist plans for an independent Arab state centered on Damascus. Instead, as we saw in Chapter 25, the League of Nations recast former Ottoman territories in the Middle East as "Mandates" under French and British control.

and deployed regular army units and the "Free Corps" (volunteer paramilitary units, often comprising demobilized soldiers addicted to violence).

By the spring of 1919, this strange alliance of moderate socialists, traditional aristocrats, soldiers, and thugs had triumphed. In January 1919, Free Corps officers murdered the communist leaders Karl Liebknecht and Rosa Luxemburg in Berlin. Three months later, an equally savage repression crushed the communist soviet in Munich, with the Free Corps killing more than 600 people.

The SPD had won. Yet it lost. By allying with the aristocratic civil service, the army, and the Free Corps, the SPD crushed not only the communist revolution, but also its own chances of achieving significant social change. Many of the officers in the army and aristocrats in the civil service opposed democracy. Continuing in positions of power and influence, they constituted an authoritarian force at the heart of the new Germany. The approximately 400,000 men who made up the Free Corps also regarded democracy with contempt—"an attempt of the slime to govern."[3] Its slogan summed up the Free Corps attitude: "Everything would still have been all right if we had shot more people."[4]

The antidemocratic sentiments that characterized the Free Corps also flourished among Weimar judges and prosecutors. In 1923, a former army corporal named Adolf Hitler and a small group of followers tried to overthrow the Weimar government by force. This attempted coup, called the "Beer Hall Putsch" (because it originated in a beer hall) did not succeed. The light sentences imposed on its participants, however, made clear that opposition to Weimar democracy ran deep within the power structures of postwar Germany. (See *Justice in History* in this chapter.)

Suspicions of democracy fed on resentment of the Versailles Treaty. Many Germans could not separate the birth of the Weimar Republic from the national humiliation imposed by Versailles. They blamed the moderate socialist government that signed the treaty for this humiliation. Army officers encouraged the idea that Germany could have kept on fighting had the SPD not "stabbed it in the back." This "stab-in-the-back" legend helped undermine support not only for the SPD's moderate socialism, but for democracy itself.

Hyperinflation further weakened Weimar democracy. In 1923, the German mark collapsed completely and paper money ceased to have any value. The German mark, which in 1914 could be traded for the American dollar at a rate of 4:1, plummeted by October 1923 to an exchange rate of 440,000,000:1. Families who had scrimped for years found they had only enough savings to buy a loaf of bread.

Hyperinflation resulted from the Weimar government's effort to force the Allies to reconsider the reparations payments demanded by

CHRONOLOGY: THE RETURN OF AUTHORITARIAN RULE TO EASTERN EUROPE

1923	Boris III establishes a royalist dictatorship in Bulgaria
1926	May: Marshal Josef Pilsudski establishes a military dictatorship in Poland; December: Smetona establishes dictatorship in Lithuania
1928	A new constitution gives King Zog in Albania almost unlimited powers
1929	Alexander I establishes a royal dictatorship in Yugoslavia
1932	Fascist leader Gyula Gömbös appointed prime minister in Hungary
1934	Dictatorships established in Latvia and Estonia
1938	King Carol establishes a royal dictatorship in Romania

the Versailles Treaty. In 1922, the government halted payments and requested a new economic agreement. When the French retaliated by sending troops into Germany's Ruhr Valley to seize coal as a form of reparations, German miners went on strike. To pay the striking workers, the German government began printing money with abandon. The inflation rate surged upward—and then out of control.

Faced with the potentially disastrous collapse of the German economy, Allied and German representatives drew up the Dawes Plan in 1924, which renegotiated reparations. By the end of 1924, the German economy had stabilized. But the hyperinflation seriously eroded support for the Weimar Republic. Many Germans concluded that democracy meant disorder and degradation.

The Reconstruction of Gender

Many of the patterns that shaped interwar national politics also characterized the politics of gender in these years. Because the demands of total war meant that women moved into economic areas previously designated as "men only," World War I seemed an important turning point in the history of Western women. But here, too, continuity with prewar patterns is a dominant theme.

THE NEW WOMAN   At first sight, the postwar period seemed to be an era of profound change for women. In the films, magazines, novels, and popular music of the 1920s, the "New Woman" took center stage. Living, working, and traveling on her own, sexually active, she stepped out of the confines of home and family. Women's dress and hairstyles reinforced the sense of change. Whereas nineteenth-century women's clothing had accentuated the womanly body while restricting movement, the clothing of the 1920s ignored a woman's curves and became less confining. Sporty new "bobs" replaced the long hair that had long been a sign of proper femininity.

GEORGE GROSZ, *THE PILLARS OF SOCIETY* (1926)

A World War I veteran like Otto Dix (see page 822), the Expressionist artist and communist George Grosz used his art to criticize the Weimar Republic. In this painting, a drunken military chaplain preaches while soldiers rampage behind his back. In the foreground sits a lawyer, supposedly a modern professional, but out of his head bursts a cavalry officer bent on destruction. To the lawyer's right, a publisher with a chamber pot on his head clutches the newspapers that guarantee his fortune and delude the masses. To the lawyer's left totters an SPD politician. His pudgy, drink-reddened cheeks, the steaming pile of excrement on his head, and the pamphlet he presses to his chest (headlined "Socialism is Work") indicate Grosz's contempt for reformist socialism.

Source: George Grosz (1893–1959), "Stuetzen der Gesellschaft (Pillars of Society)". 1926. Oil on canvas, 200,0 × 108,0 cm. Inv.: NG 4/58. Photo: Joerg P. Anders. Nationalgalerie, Staatliche Museen zu Berlin, Berlin, Germany. Art © Estate George Grosz/Licensed by VAGA, New York, New York

JUSTICE IN HISTORY

The Trial of Adolf Hitler

On February 24, 1924, Adolf Hitler appeared in court in Munich on a charge of high treason. The trial marked a turning point in Hitler's career. It gave him a national platform and convinced him of the futility of an armed offensive against the state. From 1925 on, Hitler would work through the parliamentary system to destroy it. But the trial of Adolf Hitler was also significant in what it revealed about the power of antidemocratic forces in the new Germany. The trial made clear that many in positions of authority and responsibility in the Weimar Republic shared Hitler's contempt for the democratic state. By treating Hitler not as a traitorous thug, but rather as an honorable patriot, his prosecutors helped weaken the already fragile structures of German democracy.

Hitler's attempt to overthrow the Weimar Republic by force occurred at the height of hyperinflation. By November 8, 1923, when Hitler took up arms, the German mark was worth only one-trillionth of its prewar value. As the currency eroded, the Weimar government saw its political legitimacy seeping away as well. Separatist movements in several states threatened the sovereignty of the central government in Berlin. Separatist politics attracted many men from aristocratic backgrounds, members of the conservative elite who viewed Weimar democracy as a foreign and unwelcome import.

Hitler had little interest in the separatist movement, but he believed he could channel its antidemocratic sentiments into a national revolution. His supporters included one of the most important men in Germany, the World War I hero, General Erich von Ludendorff. Seeking to avoid the blame for Germany's defeat in 1918, Ludendorff insisted that his army could have won the war had it not been stabbed in the back by the Social Democratic politicians who now ran the government. Like many German conservatives—and like Hitler—Ludendorff viewed the Weimar Republic as illegitimate.

On November 8 Hitler made his move. His men surrounded a Munich beer hall where 2,000 supporters of Bavarian separatism had gathered. Hitler declared that the Bavarian regional government and the German federal government had been overthrown and that he was now the head of Germany, with Ludendorff as his commander-in-chief. Around noon the next day, Hitler, Ludendorff, and several thousands of their followers marched toward the regional government buildings on one of Munich's main squares. Armed police blocked their passage and the ensuing firefight killed 17 men. Despite the bullets whizzing through the air, Ludendorff marched through the police cordon and stood in the square awaiting arrest. Hitler ran away. Police found him two days later, cowering in a supporter's house outside Munich.

The Beer Hall Putsch had failed. In jail awaiting trial, Hitler contemplated suicide. Yet later he described his defeat as "perhaps the greatest stroke of luck in my life." The defeat meant a trial and a trial meant a national audience—and an opportunity for Hitler to present his case against the Weimar Republic. During the trial Hitler admitted that he had conspired to overthrow the democratically elected Weimar government. He insisted, however, that he was not guilty of treason. To Hitler, the real treason occurred in November 1918, when the Social Democratic government surrendered to the Allies: "I confess to the deed, but I do not confess to the crime of high treason. There can be no question of treason in an action which aims to undo the betrayal of this country in 1918.... I consider myself not a traitor but a German."

Hitler also argued that he did not care about power: "In what small terms small minds think!...What I had in mind from the very first day was a thousand times more important than becoming a [Cabinet] minister. I wanted to become the destroyer of Marxism." Hitler depicted himself as a patriot, a nationalist motivated by love of Germany and hatred of communists and socialists. "The eternal court of history" would judge him and his fellow defendants "as Germans who wanted the best for their people and their Fatherland, who were willing to fight and to die."[5]

Despite Hitler's admission of conspiring against the government, the presiding judge could persuade the three lay judges (who took the place of a jury) to render a guilty verdict only by arguing that Hitler would soon be pardoned. The reluctance of the judges to convict Hitler highlights the extraordinary sympathy shown to him and to his political ideas throughout the trial and during his imprisonment. The chief prosecutor offered a rather surprising description of an accused traitor: "Hitler is a highly gifted man, who has risen from humble beginnings to achieve a respected position in public life, the result of much hard work and dedication.... As a soldier he did his duty to the utmost. He cannot be accused of having used the position he created for himself in any self-serving way." In delivering the verdict, the judge emphasized Hitler's "pure patriotic motives and honorable intentions." Rather than being deported as a foreign national convicted of a serious crime (Hitler was still an Austrian citizen), he was given a slight sentence of five years, which made him eligible for parole in just six months. Prison officials treated Hitler like a visiting dignitary—they exempted him from work and exercise requirements, cleaned his rooms, and provided a special table decorated with a swastika banner in the dining hall. When Hitler was released in September, his parole report described him favorably as "a man of order."[6]

Hitler's gentle treatment revealed the precarious state of democratic institutions in Germany after World War I. Many high-ranking Germans in positions of power and influence (such as judges and prosecutors) loathed parliamentary democracy. The trial also revealed the willingness of conservative aristocrats to ally with Radical Right groups such as the Nazis. Not yet strong, the Nazis in 1923 were easily reined in. A decade later, however, the conservatives who thought they could ride Hitler to power found that they were no longer in control.

HITLER IN LANDSBERG PRISON, 1924
This photo of Hitler during his short imprisonment was made into a postcard, to be purchased by his supporters.

For Discussion

1. Imagine you are a German war veteran reading about this case in the newspaper in 1924. Why might you be attracted to the party of Adolf Hitler?
2. Hitler appealed to the "eternal court of history." What do you think he meant? How would Hitler have defined "justice"?

Taking It Further

The Hitler Trial Before the People's Court in Munich, trans. H. Francis Freniece, Lucie Karcic, and Philip Fandek (3 vols.). 1976. An English translation of the court transcripts.

Kershaw, Ian. *Hitler 1889-1936: Hubris.* 1999. A compelling (and massive) account of Hitler's early life and rise to power.

THE "NEW WOMAN"

Almost every aspect of the "New Woman" (captured in this 1927 French magazine illustration) offended traditionalists: The bobbed hair, manly fashions, and aggressive strutting crossed the border into masculine terrain.

This perception of the New Woman rested on changing political and economic expectations. By 1920 women in the United States and many European countries had received the right to vote in national elections and to hold national office. In all the industrialized countries, expansion of the health care and service sectors meant new jobs for women as nurses, social workers, secretaries, telephone operators, and clerks. Women's higher education opportunities also widened in this period.

The biggest change affecting the lives of ordinary women, however, was more intimate: the spreading practice of family limitation. We saw in Chapter 23 that by the 1870s middle-class women in Western countries were practicing birth control. In the 1920s and 1930s, an increasing number of working-class women began to do so as well. Fewer pregnancies and fewer mouths to feed improved women's health and living standards.

THE RECONSTRUCTION OF TRADITIONAL ROLES Despite these important changes, however, women's *roles* altered little in the two decades after World War I. Governments and ordinary citizens recoiled from wartime gender upheaval and worked to reconstruct nineteenth-century masculine and feminine ideals.

The war's lengthy casualty lists and the drop in the average family size provoked widespread fear about declining populations—and thus declining national strength. Governments, religious leaders, and commercial entrepreneurs joined together to convince women that their destiny lay in motherhood. Sales and purchases of birth control devices became illegal during the 1920s in France, Belgium, Italy, and Spain. France outlawed abortions in 1920. In Britain after 1929, a woman who had an abortion could be sentenced to life imprisonment. To encourage population growth, governments expanded welfare services. By providing family allowances, subsidized housing, school lunches, health insurance, and prenatal and well-baby care, politicians and policymakers hoped to ensure that married women stayed at home and produced large families.

Eugenics (the effort to improve the physical and intellectual capacities of the population by encouraging individuals with "desirable" traits to reproduce) played an important role in this legislation. National leaders wanted to increase not only the quantity, but the quality of the population. On the positive side, this meant improving the health of babies and mothers. More ominously, welfare policy rhetoric often focused on separating the "fit" from the "unfit," with class and race used to designate who was "fit" to produce children for the nation.

Despite the calls for women to remain at home, many women had to work in paid employment. In the work world, just as in the family, traditional roles strengthened after World War I. Most working women returned to jobs in domestic service or to factory positions labeled unskilled and therefore low-paying. Because employers still tended to bar women from management positions, assign them to the most repetitive tasks, and pay them by piecework, the wage gap between male and female laborers remained wide. The numbers of women employed in the clerical and service sectors did rise in this era, but the movement of women into these positions meant such jobs were reclassified as "women's work," a guarantee of low pay and little power.

WOMEN AND THE BOLSHEVIK REVOLUTION   In contrast to these efforts to reinforce traditional family structures, in Russia the Bolsheviks promised

to revolutionize gender roles. Lenin believed that the family was a middle-class institution doomed to "wither away." He declared that in the ideal communist society, marriage would be a mutually beneficial—and in many cases temporary—arrangement between two equally educated and equally waged partners, and housework and child care would move from the private domestic household into the public

"WORKING WOMEN IN THE STRUGGLE FOR SOCIALISM AND THE STRUGGLE AGAINST RELIGION"

This Soviet propaganda poster proclaims a new age of liberation for Soviet women. The light of socialism, reached through Lenin's writings (top left) and visible in clean, modernist design (top right), penetrates the darkness of superstition and patriarchal abuse (bottom left and right). The woman who dominates the poster, an architect designing the socialist future, represents the ideal Soviet woman.

sphere of paid employment. Nevertheless, in revolutionary Russia, too, continuities linked the pre- and postwar experience of women.

One month after seizing power, the Bolsheviks legalized divorce and civil marriages. In 1918, a new family legal code declared women and men equal under the law and abolished the distinction between legitimate and illegitimate children. To free women from housework—described by Lenin as "barbarously unproductive, petty, nervewracking, and stultifying drudgery"[7]—the Bolsheviks promised communal child care centers, laundries, and dining rooms. In 1920, just as other states were outlawing abortion, the practice became legal in Bolshevik Russia. A Women's Bureau instructed women in their new rights, challenged the traditional patriarchy of peasant households, and encouraged Muslim women to remove their veils.

But by 1922, as we have already seen, Lenin retreated from communist ideology by instituting the New Economic Policy. NEP also meant reversals in the gender revolution. By 1923, the dining halls had closed and more than half of the day care centers shut down. Throughout the 1920s, Soviet women's wages averaged 65 percent of men's. Moreover, in rural and Islamic regions, the Bolshevik attempt at gender revolution aroused strong and sometimes violent resistance. The majority of Soviet women remained in subordinate roles.

THE RISE OF THE RADICAL RIGHT

■ What circumstances explain the emergence of the Radical Right?

As the revolution in gender roles was reversed, as Lenin's communist revolution shifted into a lower gear, and as Wilson's democratic revolution ran out of fuel, a different sort of revolution occurred in Italy. The **fascist** revolution introduced Europe to the politics of the Radical Right. Like conservatism, the new Radical Right ideologies—**fascism** and its younger cousin, Nazism—dismissed equality as a socialist myth and emphasized the importance of authority. Yet unlike conservatism, fascism and Nazism sought radical political change.

The Fascist Alternative

Conceived in the coupling of wartime exhilaration and postwar despair, fascism offered an alternative to the existing political ideologies. Fascism was more than a set of political ideas, however. As presented by its creator, Benito Mussolini (1883–1945), fascism was an ongoing performance, a spectacular sound-and-lights show with a cast of millions.

MUSSOLINI'S RISE TO POWER Fascism originated in Italy as a product of World War I. When Italy entered the war on the side of the Allies in 1915, many Italians welcomed the war as a cleansing force, a powerful disinfectant that would purify Italian society. Mussolini, a socialist journalist, shared these views. Because the Socialist Party opposed Italy's entry into the war, Mussolini broke with the socialists, joined the army, and fought until he was wounded in 1917. When the war ended, he sought to create a new politics that would build on the camaraderie and exhilaration of combat.

In March 1919, Mussolini and about 100 men and some women gathered in Milan and declared themselves the fascist movement. Like Mussolini, many of these "fascists of the first hour" were war veterans. A number had served in the *arditi*, elite commando units that fought behind enemy lines. The arditi uniform, a black shirt, became the fascist badge of identity. The arditi slogan, *me ne frego* ("I don't give a damn") became the blackshirts' creed, a fitting expression of their willingness to throw aside conventional standards and politics.

Just three and a half years after the first fascist meeting in Milan, Mussolini became prime minister of Italy. His rise to power occurred against a backdrop of social turmoil. In 1919 and 1920, more than one million workers were on strike and a wave of socialist-inspired land seizures spread across the countryside. Fearing that communist revolution would engulf Italy just as it had destroyed tsarist Russia, landowners and industrialists looked to Mussolini's fascists for help. Fascist squads disrupted Socialist Party meetings, broke up strikes, beat up trade unionists, and protected aristocratic estates from attack. By 1922, the fascists were a powerful political force with 35 parliamentary seats. In October, King Victor Emmanuel III (r. 1900–1946) asked Mussolini to become prime minister. Fascists from all over Italy converged in the "March on Rome," a piece of street theater designed to demonstrate the disciplined might of Mussolini's followers.

THE FASCIST REVOLUTION IN ITALY   Over the next four years Mussolini used legal and illegal methods, including murder, to eliminate his political rivals and remake Italy as a one-party state. By 1926, he had succeeded. Party politics, an independent press, and the trade union movement disappeared. Victor Emmanuel remained on the throne, the official head of state, but power lay in Mussolini's hands. The restored death penalty and a strong police apparatus stood ready to crush dissent and fortify the fascist state. But what was fascism? As a political ideology, fascism was, first, intensely *nationalistic*. The interests of the nation took precedence over any tradition, class, or individual. Fascism was also *statist* and *antidemocratic*. A centralized state, governed by a single party and led by an authoritarian leader, protected the nation's interests. Finally, fascism was *militaristic*. It exalted violence and military action. Influenced by Social Darwinism (see p. 755), Mussolini believed that nations, like species, competed for survival in a hostile world. Only the strong would—and should—survive.

Mussolini also saw fascism as the politics of change. With a strong leader at the wheel, with violent action as its fuel, the fascist state would crash through social and economic barriers and transport the nation into the modern age. Yet Mussolini's supposedly radical revolution in fact reinforced traditional upper-class interests. Early fascist promises of land redistribution were never realized. In theory, fascism promised to replace capitalist competition and the profit motive with **corporatism:** Committees (or "corporations") made up of representatives of workers, employers, and the state would direct the economy for

the good of the nation. In actuality, workers' rights disappeared while industrialists' profits remained untouched.

Although Mussolini had no intention of giving *genuine* political power to ordinary people, he did recognize the importance of giving them the *illusion* of power. Fascism made individuals feel a part of a mighty nation. "After-work" recreational groups connected ordinary people to the fascist state by serving as a channel for fascist propaganda and occupying their leisure hours.

The "Cult of the Duce" also fostered a sense of national community. Mussolini insisted, "I am Fascism." Choreographed public appearances gave ordinary Italians the chance to see, hear, and adore their Duce ("Leader"), and through contact with his person, to feel a part of the new Italy. Mussolini paid careful attention to his public image. He ordered the press to ignore his birthdays and the births of his grandchildren: The Duce could not be seen to age. Instead, Mussolini appeared as a man of action. Depicted in planes, trains, and racing cars, he was always on the move, always pressing forward. (See *Different Voices* in this chapter.)

Mussolini combined up-to-date advertising and mass media technologies with age-old rituals inspired largely by the Catholic Church. Huge public rallies set in massive arenas, carefully staged with lighting and music, inspired his followers. A popular fascist slogan summed up the leadership cult: "Believe, Obey, Fight." Italians were not to think or question. They were to *believe*. What were they to believe? Another slogan provided the answer: "Mussolini is always right."

THE GREAT DEPRESSION AND THE SPREAD OF FASCISM AFTER 1929   The key factor in the spread of fascism outside Italy was the **Great Depression**. On October 24, 1929, the U.S. stock market collapsed. Over the next two years, the American economic crisis evolved into a global depression. Banks closed, businesses collapsed, and unemployment rates rose to devastating levels.

CHRONOLOGY: MUSSOLINI'S RISE TO POWER

1915–1917	Serves in the Italian army
1919	Participates in the creation of the fascist movement
1921	Fascist Party wins 35 seats in parliament
1922	Becomes prime minister
1925–1926	Abolishes party politics and establishes himself as dictator

The Depression spread so quickly because World War I shifted the world's economic center from Europe to the United States. To pay for the war, European states had sold off their assets and borrowed heavily. By the end of 1918 Allied states owed the United States more than $9 billion. New York's stock market rivaled London's, and the United States moved from the position of debtor to creditor.

The problem of wartime indebtedness soon became entangled with the issue of German reparations. Britain, France, and Italy could pay off their debts to the United States only if Germany paid reparations to them. American credit became the fuel that kept the European economy burning. From 1925 on, American investors loaned money to Germany, which used the money to pay reparations to the Allies, which in turn used the money to pay back the United States. The system worked for a short time. Fueled by loans, the German economy kicked into gear. Currencies stabilized, production rose, and American money flowed not only into Germany, but into all of Europe. If these loans dried up, however, Europe faced disaster.

In 1929 that disaster struck. With the collapse of the U.S. stock market, savings portfolios lost between 60 and 75 percent of their value almost overnight. Scrambling to scrape up any assets, American creditors liquidated European investments, and European economies tumbled. Germany's industrial output fell by 46 percent and its number of jobless grew to more than six million.

The political and social disarray that accompanied the Great Depression enhanced the appeal of fascist promises of stability, order, and national strength. Over the next decade fascist movements emerged across Europe and existing authoritarian regimes adopted fascist trappings to stay in power. For example, Romania's King Carol II (r. 1930–1940) faced a strong challenge to his rule from the Iron Guard, the first mass fascist movement in the Balkans. To compete with the Guard, Carol embraced fascist features such as uniformed paramilitaries, a youth group, and mass rallies. In 1938 he abolished all political parties, placed the judicial system under military control, and declared himself a royal dictator. He then dissolved the Iron Guard and had its leader strangled.

The Nazi Revolution

In Germany, the Nazi Party offered a different version of Radical Right ideology. Just as the emergence of fascism was inextricably linked to Benito Mussolini, so **Nazism** cannot be separated from Adolf Hitler (1889–1945). To understand the Nazi revolution in Germany, we need first to explore Hitler's rise to power and then to examine the impact of Nazi rule on ordinary people.

HITLER'S RISE TO POWER Hitler, a German nationalist, was not a citizen of Germany for most of his life. Born in the Austrian half of the Austro-Hungarian Empire, Hitler came of age in Vienna, where he made a meager living as a painter while absorbing the anti-Semitic German nationalism that permeated this capital city. By the time World War I broke out, however, Hitler had settled in Germany. Delighted by the chance to fight the war in a German rather than an Austrian uniform, Hitler regarded army life as "the greatest of all experiences." He served as a German soldier until he was temporarily blinded by poison gas in 1918. Hitler then returned to Munich, home to large bands of unemployed war veterans and a breeding ground for nationalist and racist groups.

The Nazi Party began as one of these groups, with Hitler quickly emerging as its leader. *Nazi* is shorthand for National Socialist German Workers' Party, but this title, like all of Nazi ideology, was an empty promise. Nazism opposed socialism, communism, and trade unionism. Like fascism, Nazism was a nationalistic, statist, anti-democratic, and militaristic ideology. In Nazism, however, racism, particularly anti-Semitism, played the central role. To Hitler, all history was the history of racial struggle, and in that racial struggle, the Jews were always the principal enemy. Hitler regarded Jewishness as a biological rather than a religious identity, a toxic infection that threatened "Aryans," a linguistic term that Hitler misused to identify the "racially pure"—white northern Europeans.

In Hitler's distorted vision, Jewishness and communism formed two parts of the same evil whole. He saw the Bolshevik victory in Russia as part of a wider struggle for Jewish world domination, and he promised his followers that the Aryan race would defeat the forces of "Judeo-Bolshevism" and establish a mighty empire encompassing all of eastern Europe, including the Soviet Union.

In its early days Nazism appealed to men like Hitler, individuals without power or, apparently, much chance of getting it—unemployed ex-soldiers, small shopkeepers wiped out by postwar inflation, lower middle-class clerks anxious to preserve their shaky social status, and workers who had lost their jobs. Nazism offered a simple explanation of history, a promise of future glory, and someone to blame for personal and national woes. By the time of the Beer Hall Putsch in November 1923, party membership stood at about 55,000. (See *Justice in History* in this chapter.)

Although the Beer Hall Putsch failed in its aim to overthrow the Weimar Republic, it brought Hitler before a national audience. His speeches during the ensuing trial for treason and *Mein Kampf* ("My Struggle"), the book he wrote while in prison, publicized his racialized view of German political history. After Hitler emerged from prison, he concentrated on transforming the Nazis into a persuasive political force. To infiltrate German society at all levels, Nazis formed university and professional groups, labor unions, and agrarian organizations, while the Nazi paramilitary organization, the SA (*Sturmabteilung*), terrorized opponents. The party held meetings and rallies incessantly, not just during election periods, and so ensured that Germany was saturated with its message. Even so, in the elections of 1928, Nazi candidates won only 2.6 percent of the vote.

CHRONOLOGY: HITLER'S RISE TO POWER

1914–1918	Serves in the German army
1919–1923	Establishes himself as a right-wing activist in Munich
1923	Fails to overthrow the government with the Beer Hall Putsch
1929	Collapse of the U.S. stock market; onset of Great Depression
1930	Nazis win 107 seats in German parliament
1932	Nazis win 230 seats; become largest party in German parliament
1933	
January	Becomes chancellor
February	Uses Reichstag fire as pretext to gain emergency powers
March	Uses the Enabling Act to destroy democracy in Germany

The Great Depression gave the Nazis their chance at power. After 1929, unemployment rates skyrocketed and the Weimar political system began to collapse. No German political leader could put together a viable governing coalition. In all of 1932 the federal parliament met for only 13 days. As the mechanisms of parliamentary democracy faltered, political polarization accelerated. By July 1932, the Nazis were the largest party in the parliament, winning 37 percent of German votes. Support for their communist rivals also continued to grow.

In this unstable climate, Chancellor Heinrich Bruning turned to an emergency measure in the German constitution—rule by presidential decree. This practice meant that power shifted from parliament to the president, the World War I hero General Paul von Hindenburg. Already in his 80s, Hindenburg was a weak man easily manipulated by a small circle of aristocratic advisors. These men, terrified of communism and convinced that the Nazis could be easily controlled, persuaded Hindenburg to offer Hitler the position of chancellor in January 1933. One of the group, Baron Franz von Papen, reassured a friend that Hitler posed "no danger at all. We have hired him for our act. In two months' time we'll have pushed Hitler so far into the corner, he'll be squeaking."[8]

Within six months Hitler established a Nazi dictatorship in Germany. Almost as soon as he took office he persuaded Hindenburg to pass an emergency decree ordering the seizure of all Communist Party presses and buildings. Then in February a fire destroyed the German parliament building. Declaring (wrongly) that the fire was part of a communist plot against the state, Hitler demanded the power to imprison without warrant or trial. Arrests of more than 25,000 of his political opponents followed—communists, socialists, and anyone who openly opposed him. At the end of March, German politicians, cowed by Nazi threats of imprisonment, passed the Enabling Act, giving Hitler the power to suspend the constitution and pass legislation without a parliamentary majority. By the summer of 1933, Hitler had destroyed German democracy.

Often presented as a model of authoritarian efficiency, the Nazi dictatorship was actually a confusing mass of overlapping bureaucracies, in which ambitious officials competed with each other for power and influence. This planned chaos ensured that none of Hitler's deputies acquired too much authority. It also enhanced the mystery of the state. The individual citizen attempting to make a complaint or resolve a problem would soon feel as if he were engaged in a battle with a multilimbed monster.

This monster, however, had only one head: Adolf Hitler. Like Mussolini, Hitler realized the importance of personalizing his rule. In his early years of power, he was constantly on the move, using cars and planes to visit city after city, to deliver speech after speech, to touch person after person. Leaders of the Hitler Youth swore this oath: "Adolf Hitler is Germany and Germany is Adolf Hitler. He who pledges himself to Hitler pledges himself to Germany."[9]

NATIONAL RECOVERY When the Nazis seized control in 1933, depression gripped the German economy. The rules of economic orthodoxy dictated that in times of depression, a government should cut spending and maintain a balanced budget. Hoping to jump-start the stalled economy, Hitler's immediate predecessors in office had set aside these rules and begun to plan programs based on deficit spending. Hitler took these plans and ran with them. He invested heavily in public works and after 1936 poured money into rearmament. These programs created thousands of jobs. Unemployment dropped from 44 percent in 1932 to 14.1 percent in 1934 to less than 1 percent in 1938—while unemployment rates in the double digits persisted in democratic states such as Britain and France.

Germans and non-Germans alike hailed Nazi Germany as an economic success, yet under Nazi rule, real wages fell and workers' rights disappeared. Emphasis on rearmament led to shortages in food supplies and in consumer goods. Still, many Germans *believed* themselves to be much better off. The expansion of social welfare assistance (for those considered "Aryan") helps explain this perception, as does the establishment of the "Strength through Joy" program that provided workers with cheap vacations, theater and concert tickets, and weekend outings. But most important, under the Nazis, Germans were working. The abundance of jobs—despite the low wages, despite the disappearance of workers' rights, despite the food shortages—made Hitler an economic savior to many.

Many Germans also viewed him as a national savior who restored Germany's pride and power. German payments of war reparations halted in 1930 because of the global economic crisis. Hitler never resumed payment. He also ignored the treaty's military restrictions and rebuilt Germany's armed forces. By 1938, parades featuring row after row of uniformed troops signaled the revitalization of German military might. For many ordinary Germans, traumatized and shamed by the sequence of national disasters—military defeat, loss of territory, hyperinflation, political and fiscal crises, unemployment—the sight of troops goosestepping under the German flag meant personal and national renaissance. As one Nazi song proclaimed, "And now the me is part of the great We."[10] (See *Different Voices* in this chapter.)

CAMPAIGNS OF REPRESSION AND TERROR The creation of the "great We" depended on the demonization and repression of the "not Us," those defined as outside or opposed to the nation. Hitler used the existing German police force and his own paramilitary troops—the brownshirted SA and the blackshirted SS (*Schutzstaffel*)—to terrorize those he defined as enemies of the nation. The Nazis first targeted political opponents. By 1934 half of the 300,000 German Communist Party members were in prison or dead and most of the rest had fled the country. The Nazis also persecuted specific religious groups on the basis of their actual or presumed opposition to the Nazi state. Roman Catholics faced constant harassment and about half of Germany's 20,000 Jehovah's Witnesses were sent to concentration camps.

The groups that the Nazis deemed biologically inferior suffered most severely. Beginning in 1933, the Nazi regime forced the sterilization of the mentally and physically handicapped and mixed-race children (in most cases, the offspring of German women and black African soldiers serving in the French occupation force in the Rhineland). The campaign was soon extended to the Roma (Gypsies). By 1939, 370,000 men and women had been sterilized.

The Jewish community—less than 1 percent of the German population—bore the brunt of Nazi racial attacks. To Nazi anti-Semites, Hitler's accession to the German chancellorship was like the opening of hunting season. They beat up Jews in the streets, vandalized Jewish shops and homes, threatened German Christians who associated with Jews, and violently enforced boycotts of Jewish businesses. Anti-Jewish legislation piled up. In 1933, the Nazi government dismissed "non-Aryans" (Jews) from the civil service and the legal profession, and restricted the number of Jewish students in high schools and universities. Every organization in Germany—youth clubs, sports teams, labor unions, charitable societies—underwent "Nazification," which meant the dismissal of all Jewish members and the appointment of Nazis to leadership roles. In 1935, the "Nuremberg Laws" deprived German Jews of their citizenship and declared marriage or sexual relations between German Jews and non-Jews a serious crime.

Women and the Radical Right

Fascism and Nazism promised to restore order to societies perceived to be on the verge of disintegration. Restoration of order meant the return of women to their proper place. According to Nazi propaganda, "the soil provides the food, the woman supplies the population, and the men make the action."[11] Hitler proclaimed, "The Nazi Revolution will be an entirely male event." Mussolini agreed: "Woman must obey.... In our State, she must not count."[12]

The Nazi government offered financial and cultural incentives to encourage women to stay at home and produce babies. These measures ranged from marriage loans (available only if the wife quit her job) and income tax deductions for

"*HEIL* (HAIL) *HITLER!*"

An enthusiastic crowd salutes Hitler at a Nazi party rally. The women in the traditional costumes illustrate a key aspect of the Nazis' appeal: their promise to restore women to their traditional domestic roles. The men in military uniform indicate a second source of Nazi popularity: the restoration of military strength and national pride.

families to the establishment of discussion, welfare, and leisure groups for housewives. The Nazis also used disincentives. One of the first actions of Hitler's government was to restrict women's employment in the civil service and to rule that female physicians could work only in their husbands' practices. By 1937, female physicians and women with Ph.D.s had lost the right to be addressed as "Doctor" or "Professor." Women could no longer work as school principals. Coeducational schools were abolished. Birth control became illegal and penalties for abortion increased while prosecutions doubled.

In fascist Italy, Mussolini's government focused its legislation on both men and women. Unmarried men over age 30 had to pay double income tax (priests were exempt) and fatherhood became a prerequisite for men in high-ranking public office. Quotas limited the number of women employed in the civil service and in private business, while women found themselves excluded entirely from jobs defined as "virile," a list that included boat captains, diplomats, high school principals, and history teachers. A wide-ranging social welfare program that included family allowances, maternity leaves, and marriage loans sought to strengthen the traditional family. Despite these provisions, birth rates in Italy actually declined because low wages meant families could not afford more children.

THE POLARIZATION OF POLITICS IN THE 1930s

■ **What factors led to the polarization of European politics in the 1930s?**

The apparent successes of fascist Italy and Nazi Germany appealed to many Europeans and Americans disenchanted with democracy in the era of the Great Depression. During this period, the Soviet Union also seemed a success story. While the capitalist states struggled with high unemployment rates and falling industrial output, the Soviet Union appeared to be performing economic miracles. As politics in the West became polarized between communism on the radical left and fascism and Nazism on the radical right, politicians and policymakers in the United States and in western Europe sought to maintain the middle ground, to retain democratic values in a time of extremist ideologies.

The Soviet Union: Revolution Reconstructed, Terror Extended

During the 1930s, the Soviet economy finally took off into full-scale industrialization. This economic transformation, however, rested on dead bodies, millions of dead bodies. During the 1930s, mass murder became even more an integral part of the Soviet regime under Joseph Stalin (1879–1953).

STALIN'S RISE TO POWER   By 1928, Stalin was the uncontested head of the Soviet Union, yet when Lenin died in 1924, few observers would have predicted Stalin's success. Although a stalwart Bolshevik, he stood in the shadow of more charismatic, intellectually able colleagues such as Leon Trotsky (1879–1940) and Nikolai Bukharin (1888–1938). Two factors explain how Stalin was able to seize control of the Communist Party and the Soviet state.

First, as party secretary from 1922 on, Stalin processed party membership applications and decided who got promoted to what and where. Thus, throughout the 1920s he built a base of support within the party. Vast numbers of ordinary communists owed their party privileges and their livelihoods to Stalin. Unlike the original Bolsheviks, most of the new members were not well educated or well versed in Marxist theory—25 percent were functionally illiterate.

Second, while Stalin expanded his support at the grassroots, an ideological struggle at the highest levels of the Communist Party distracted his rivals for the party leadership. To launch the Soviet economy into industrialization, Trotsky urged the abandonment of Lenin's NEP, which had encouraged small private farms. Bukharin, however, insisted that agricultural development should precede industrialization. By playing one side against the other, Stalin was able to seize control of the party and the state by 1928.

THE "REVOLUTION FROM ABOVE": COLLECTIVIZATION AND INDUSTRIALIZATION, 1928–1934   Stalin aimed to catapult the Soviet Union into the ranks of the industrialized states. The first step in what Stalin called "the revolution from above" was **collectivization,** the replacement of private and village farms with large cooperative agricultural enterprises run by communist managers according to directives received from the central government. Collectivization had economic and

CHRONOLOGY: STALIN'S RISE TO POWER

1917	Bolshevik revolution
1918–1921	Russian civil war
1921	New Economic Policy (NEP) begins
1922	Stalin appointed general secretary of the Central Committee of the Communist Party
1924	Death of Lenin
1925–1928	Leadership disputes; Stalin emerges as the head of the Communist Party
1929	NEP ended; collectivization begins
1934	The Congress of Victors
1934–1938	The Great Purge

"PEOPLE'S DREAMS HAVE COME TRUE!"

Whereas Lenin had allowed modernist experimentation, Stalin demanded that artists adhere to traditional, nationally oriented styles. Artists knew that their literal survival depended on their conforming to the principles of "Socialist Realism": *Partinost* (loyalty to the state), *Ideinost* (correct ideology and content), and *Narodnost* (easy accessibility to ordinary viewers). The abstract experiments of the early Soviet period gave way to pretty pictures of happily collectivized peasants and portraits of Stalin in heroic poses. In this typical example of "Socialist Realism," an older Soviet citizen points proudly to the achievements of Stalinist industrialization while the young boy, in the uniform of the Pioneers, the Stalinist youth organization, listens eagerly.

political aims. Regarded as more modern and efficient, collective farms were expected to produce an agricultural surplus and thereby raise the capital needed for industrialization. In addition, collectivization would realize communist ideals by eradicating the profit motive, abolishing private property, and transforming peasants into modern state employees.

Peasants resisted this transformation, however. They burned their crops and slaughtered their livestock. Famine followed. The numbers of deaths resulting from collectivization and the famine of 1931–1932 remain controversial, but the available evidence points to death figures between five and seven million. Ukraine and

Kazakhstan were hardest hit. Almost 40 percent of the Kazakh population died from starvation or typhus and the number of dead in Ukraine reached into the millions. Millions more were deported to forced labor camps.

While class war raged in the countryside, city dwellers embarked on the second stage of the "revolution from above"—industrialization. In 1931 Stalin articulated the task facing the Soviet Union: "We are fifty or a hundred years behind the advanced countries. We must catch up this distance in ten years. Either we do it or we go under."[13] "Doing it" demanded, first, fierce labor discipline. If fired, a worker was automatically evicted from his or her apartment and deprived of a ration card. "Doing it" also demanded reducing personal consumption. Eighty percent of all investment went into heavy industry, while domestic construction and light industry—clothing, furniture, dishes, appliances, and the like—were ignored. Scarcity became the norm, long lines and constant shortages part of every citydweller's existence. Soviet citizens endured an estimated 40 percent fall in their already low standard of living between 1929 and 1932.

While millions starved in the countryside, young communists acclaimed these years of hardship and horror as an era of heroism. They volunteered to organize collective farms, to work in brutal conditions at construction sites, to labor long hours in factories and mines. Propaganda campaigns aimed at persuading laborers to work harder kept this enthusiasm at a fever pitch. The most productive workers earned medals and material gifts. Publicity focused on gargantuan engineering achievements—the cities built atop swampland, the hydroelectric projects with their enormous dams and power plants, the Moscow subway system. Such publicity made party members feel part of a mighty endeavor. A popular song announced, "We were born to make fairy tales come true."[14]

No propaganda campaign and no amount of effort from enthusiastic communists, however, could provide the Soviet Union with the labor it needed to catch up with the West in ten years. Forced labor was crucial. Throughout the 1930s, approximately five million men, women, and children toiled in prison camps.[15] Many of the huge engineering triumphs of the decade rested on the backs of prisoners and deportees.

By the end of the 1930s, Stalin's "revolution from above" had achieved its aim. The pouring of resources into heavy industry and the wringing of every ounce of labor out of an exhausted, cold, and hungry populace succeeded in building the foundations of an industrial society. This society would stand the test of total war in the 1940s.

Stalin's revolution, however, failed to convert Soviet agriculture into a modern, prosperous sector of the economy. Rural regions remained backward. Peasant villages, for example, were not electrified until the later 1950s. Under Stalin, peasants were second-class citizens. Ineligible for internal passports, they could not leave their farms and so had little access to the meager benefits of Soviet industrialization. Like their ancestors under serfdom, peasants who survived collectivization found themselves tied to a particular village, saddled with forced labor obligations, and compelled to spend the bulk of their time farming for someone else's profit. Most peasants viewed the communist state as another in a long line of harsh landlords, to be ignored when possible, tricked if necessary, and endured no matter what.

STALIN'S CONSOLIDATION OF POWER: THE GREAT PURGE AND SOVIET SOCIETY, 1934–1939 The 17th Communist Party Congress in 1934 called itself the "Congress of Victors," as the party celebrated its industrial successes and the achievement of collectivization. But within five years, half of the 2,000 delegates had been arrested. Of the 149 elected members of the Congress's Central Committee, 98 were shot dead. These Congress delegates, and hundreds of thousands of other Soviet citizens, fell victim to the "**Great Purge**."

The early victims of the Great Purge were top-ranking Communist Party officials, many of whom had opposed Stalin during the 1920s. By charging these powerful men with conspiring against the communist state, Stalin reduced the chances that any competitor might oust him. The purge, however, quickly spread beyond the top ranks of the party. Anxious and hungry, Soviet citizens were eager to find someone to blame for the inevitable breakdowns and failures of an overly centralized economy. The purge made it easy to point the finger, to charge this manager with deliberately failing to order tractors or that engineer with sabotaging production. Thus, the Great Purge quickly spun out of control to embrace low-level party members, managers in state agencies, factory directors, and engineers—and their families and friends. Many were killed without trial, others executed after a legal show, and still others deported to labor camps to be worked to death on Stalin's construction projects. Death estimates vary widely but at least 750,000 people were killed, with the numbers of those arrested, imprisoned, or deported running into the millions.[16]

The Great Purge consolidated Stalin's hold on the Soviet Union. It not only eliminated all potential competitors, it also gave many people a reason to believe in their leader. The Purge focused mostly on urban managers. These managers had reprimanded, fined, insulted, and assaulted ordinary citizens, who now tended to believe that the purge's victims got what they deserved. Moreover, the purge functioned as a huge job creation program. Individuals who moved into the positions left vacant by the purge's victims had a material and psychological stake in believing that these victims were guilty and that the purge was justified.

STALIN, THE FAMILY, AND THE NATION A personality cult also reinforced Stalin's power. Innumerable posters and statues ensured that Stalin's figure remained constantly in front of Soviet citizens. Textbooks rewrote the history of the Bolshevik revolution to highlight Stalin's contribution and linked every scientific, technological, or economic advance in the Soviet Union to him. The scores of letters personally addressed to Stalin testify to the success of this cult. To many Soviet citizens, Stalin personified the nation. (See *Different Voices* in this chapter.)

And it was the Russian *nation*—not the worker, not socialism, not the revolution—that assumed the central role in Soviet propaganda in the 1930s. Lenin had condemned nationalism as a middle-class ideology to be eradicated along with capitalism. The working class, not the nation, mattered. But Stalin reversed this aspect of Lenin's revolution. The tsarist imperial anthem resounded again, while films and books praised strong Russian leaders such as Peter the Great. Although this resurgence of Russian nationalism was popular with many Russians, it meant that the 50 percent of the Soviet population who were not Russian had to repress their own sense of national identity.

Just as Stalin resurrected Russian nationalism in the 1930s, so he sought to resurrect the Russian family. Lenin had viewed the family as a middle-class institution that would wither away, but Stalin promoted the family as vital to national strength. In 1936, the Soviet government outlawed abortion and made divorce more difficult. Like Western leaders, Stalin also tried to increase birth rates by granting pregnant women maternity stipends and improving prenatal care. He made no effort to pull women out of the workforce, however. Of the more than four million new workers entering the labor force between 1932 and 1937, 82 percent were women. Soviet women continued to have access to higher education and professional jobs—working as doctors, engineers, scientists, and high-ranking government officials—and, like men, they were deported and executed in huge numbers.

The Response of the Democracies

The apparent economic successes of fascism and Nazism on the right and Stalinism on the left polarized European politics. Many in the West concluded that democracy had failed. Yet in western Europe and the United States, governments took important steps to ensure that democracy survived.

A THIRD WAY? THE SOCIAL DEMOCRATIC ALTERNATIVE The effort to meet the challenge of the depression without embracing either Nazism or Stalinism accelerated the development of the political model that would dominate western Europe after World War II: **social democracy.** In a social democracy, a democratically elected government accepts the responsibility of ensuring a decent standard of living for its citizens. To achieve this goal, the government assumes two functions—first, regulating an economy containing both private enterprise and nationalized,

DIFFERENT VOICES THE CULT OF THE LEADER

Stalinism stood on the extreme left of the political spectrum; Nazism and fascism, on the extreme right. Mussolini's fascists came to national prominence by beating up socialists, and Hitler ranked communists alongside Jews as enemies of the German nation. Yet Radical Right and Radical Left states resembled each other in many ways. Fascist Italy, Nazi Germany, and the Stalinist Soviet Union shared contempt for individual rights and a willingness to use violence as an instrument of the state. These states also all relied on the cult of personality (or the leadership cult). Searching for a way to mobilize the masses without granting them actual political power, Mussolini, Hitler, and Stalin used their own images to personify and personalize the state and to make their authoritarian rule more extensive and more acceptable. The following excerpts illustrate the cults of personality that helped shape the West in the 1930s.

I. Description of Mussolini's Visit to Trieste in 1938

Finally we have seen and heard Him!...These first reactions, expressed with indescribable joy, eyes moved to tears and an ineffable, agonizing joy....It is not easy to describe the expression on most faces, on those of the little people as on those of the educated, of the mass as a whole. Expressions of wonderful contentment and pride among those who saw Him pass close by— especially among the dockworkers He visited yesterday—and those whose eyes He met, those who caught His eye. "Never such eyes! The way he looks at you is irresistible! He smiled at me...

I was close, I could almost touch him.... When I saw him my legs trembled"...and a thousand other similar statements show and confirm the enormous fascination exercised by his person.

II. Description of an Early Nazi Rally by Louise Solmitz, Schoolteacher

The April sun shone hot like summer and turned everything into a picture of gay expectation. There was immaculate order and discipline...the hours passed.... Expectations rose. There stood Hitler in a simple black coat and looked over the crowd. Waiting. A forest of swastika pennants swished up, the jubilation of this moment was given vent in a roaring salute.... How many look up to him with a touching faith! As their helper, their savior, their deliverer from unbearable distress—to him who rescues the Prussian prince, the scholar, the clergyman, the farmer, the worker, the unemployed, who leads them from the parties back into the nation.

III. Letter from a Nazi Party member, a "party comrade," to Hitler, 1936.

My Führer!...I feel compelled by unceasing love to thank our creator daily for, through his grace, giving us and the entire German people such a wonderful Führer, and in a time...where our beautiful dear Fatherland was threatened with the most horrible destruction through Jewish bolshevism. It does not bear thinking about what floods of tears, what blood after the scarcely healed wounds of the World War, would have flowed, if you, my beloved Führer, in all your anguish for such a

or state-controlled, businesses, and second, overseeing a welfare state, which guarantees citizens access to unemployment and sickness benefits, pensions, family allowances, and health services. Although social democracy did not triumph in the West until after a second total war, interwar Western societies took important steps on this third path, an alternative to the extremes

of the Radical Right (fascism and Nazism) and the Radical Left (Stalinism).

One of the most striking experiments in changing the relationship between democratic governments and the economy occurred in the United States. Franklin Delano Roosevelt (1882–1945) was elected president in 1932 at the height of the Great Depression, when unemployment stood at

great people had not found the courage, with at that time a small band of seven men, to win through as the saviour of 66 million Germans, in that through your great love of every individual, from the smallest child to the most aged, you captured all, all, women, men, and the whole of German youth.... It is a pleasure for me, not a compliment, not hypocrisy, to pray for you, my Führer, that the Lord God who has created you as a tool for Germany should keep you healthy, that the love of the people towards you should grow, firm and hard like the many oak trees which have been planted in love and honour to you, my Führer, even in the smallest community in Germany.... A Heil to the Führer for victory with all the former front-line fighters who still remain today devoted to the Führer to death. For Germany must live even if we must die.

IV. Speech by a Woman Delegate at a Workers' Conference in the Soviet Union

Thank you comrade Stalin, our leader, our father, for a happy, merry kolkhoz* life!

He, our Stalin, put the steering-wheel of the tractor in our hand.... He, the great Stalin, carefully listens to all of us in this meeting, loves us with a great Stalinist love (*tumultuous applause*), day and night thinks of our prosperity, of our culture, of our work....

Long live our friend, our teacher, the beloved leader of the world proletariat, comrade Stalin! (*Tumultuous applause, rising to an ovation. Shouts of "Hurrah!"*)

*kolkhoz = collective farm

For Discussion

1. Why did Radical Right and Radical Left movements include cults of personality? Do these excerpts reveal any differences between the leadership cults of these states?

2. How and why did the cult of personality take on religious dimensions? Should we view modern nationalism as a secular religion?

3. Can we take these documents at face value? In a dictatorial state, where any dissent risks punishment and even death, people often hide their true feelings and beliefs. How do we know that the individuals speaking here were not putting on an act to survive or to get ahead?

Sources: I. "Description of Mussolini's Visit to Trieste in 1938," reprinted by permission of the publisher from *The Sacralization of Politics in Fascist Italy* by Emilio Gentile, translated by Keith Botsford, p. 147, Cambridge, Mass.: Harvard University Press. Copyright © 1996 by the President and Fellows of Harvard College. II. "Description of an Early Nazi Rally by Louise Solmitz, Schoolteacher," copyright © 1988 by Claudia Koonz. From *Mothers in the Fatherland: Women, the Family, and Nazi Politics* by Claudia Koonz. New York: St. Martin's Press, 1987. III. Quoted in Ian Kershaw, *The Hitler Myth*, Oxford: Oxford University Press, 1987, p. 81. By permission of Oxford University Press. Copyright © 1987 by Ian Kershaw. IV. "Speech by a Woman Delegate at a Worker's Conference in the Soviet Union," from *Stalin's Peasants: Resistance and Survival in the Russian Village After Collectivization* by Sheila Fitzpatrick. Copyright © 1996 by Oxford University Press, Inc. Published by permission of Oxford University Press.

24 percent and federal troops in Washington, D.C. fought rioting unemployed veterans. Promising a "New Deal" of "Relief, Recovery, Reform," Roosevelt tackled the depression with an activist governmental policy that included agricultural subsidies, public works programs, and the Social Security Act of 1935, which set the foundations of the U.S. welfare program.

Yet even with this sharp upswing in government activity, unemployment in the United States remained high—ten million workers were without jobs in 1939—and the gross national product (GNP) did not recover to 1929 levels until 1941. In the view of some economists, Roosevelt failed to solve the problem of unemployment because he remained committed to the ideal of a balanced budget. In contrast, the British economist John Maynard Keynes (1883–1946) insisted that in times of depression the state should not reduce spending and endeavor to live within its budget, but instead should adopt a program of deficit spending to stimulate economic growth. Only when prosperity returned, Keynes advised, should governments increase taxes and cut expenditures to recover the deficits.

The experience of Sweden appeared to confirm **Keynesian economics.** The Swedish Social Democratic Party took office in 1932 with the intention of using the powers of central government to revive the economy. The government allowed its budget deficit to climb while it financed public works and increased welfare benefits, ranging from unemployment insurance to maternity allowances to subsidized housing. By 1937 unemployment was shrinking rapidly as the manufacturing sector boomed.

Throughout most of western Europe, however, governments proved reluctant to embrace new policies. For example, Britain's limited economic recovery in the later 1930s stemmed largely from the emergence of new private industries aimed at domestic consumption (such as radios and other small electronics). In the areas hardest hit by depression—northern British cities, home to export industries such as coal, shipbuilding, textiles, and steel—the lack of government intervention meant continuing unemployment and widespread poverty throughout the 1930s.

POPULAR FRONTS IN FRANCE AND SPAIN The limited success of democratic governments in addressing the problems of the Great Depression meant that many experienced the 1930s as a hard, hungry decade. The examples of France and Spain illustrate the political polarization occurring in Europe in the 1930s, as well as the sharp limits on governments seeking both to maintain democratic politics and to improve living conditions.

The Great Depression hit France later than most other European states, but in 1931 the French economy plummeted. Social unrest grew, and so, too, did the appeal of fascism. The fascist threat, combined with the deepening national

emergency, led to the formation of the **Popular Front,** a coalition comprising radicals, socialists, and communists. In 1936, the Popular Front won the national elections and Socialist Party leader Léon Blum (1872–1950) took office as prime minister. Over the next year, Blum nationalized key industries and gave workers pay increases, paid holidays, and a 40-hour workweek.

Many conservative French voters saw Blum's policies of social reform as the first step on the road to Stalinism. They cried, "Better Hitler than Blum!"—in other words, better the Radical Right than the Stalinist Left. The global business community pulled capital out of France, which brought on a major financial crisis and the devaluation of the French franc. Dependent on foreign loans, Blum's government tried to retreat from its social and economic reforms. Its working-class constituency responded with riots, and the Popular Front in France disintegrated.

In Spain, the Popular Front was defeated not by economic pressures, but by civil war. In 1931, a democratically elected republican government replaced the Spanish monarchy, and in 1936, a Popular Front government, comprising socialists and communists, took office. Army officers, led by General Francisco Franco (1892–1975), rebelled and civil war began.

The struggle between the left-wing Republican government and the right-wing rebels quickly became an international issue. Fascist Italy and Nazi Germany supported the rebellion. The Republic of Spain appealed to the democracies for aid, but the only state that came to its assistance was the Soviet Union. Unnerved by Soviet involvement, the French, British, and American governments remained neutral, although 15,000 of their citizens joined the International Brigades to fight for Spanish democracy. All total, over 59,000 volunteers from 55 countries fought in these brigades.

The Spanish Civil War raged until March 1939, when the last remnants of the Republican forces surrendered to Franco. At least 400,000 men and women died in the war, and Franco executed another 200,000 after he took power and established an authoritarian state.

THE SPANISH CIVIL WAR

The Spanish Civil War mobilized women as well as men. These soldiers, fighting in the uniform of the anarchist militia, are defending the barricades of Barcelona against rebel attack.

THE WEST AND THE WORLD: IMPERIALISM IN THE INTERWAR ERA

■ How did the interaction between the West and the world outside change after World War I?

During World War I the Allies championed national self-determination in Europe, but they had no intention of allowing the nations under their imperial rule to determine their own government. Britain and France emerged from the war with their empires greatly expanded: They divided up Germany's overseas colonies in Africa and Asia, and as we saw in Chapter 25, became the dominant powers in the Middle East. Belgium and Portugal retained their African colonies, while in Asia, some of the spoils went to Japan, Australia, and New Zealand. Popular imperialism reached its zenith after the war as well, as filmmakers and novelists found that imperial settings formed the perfect backdrop for stirring tales of individual heroism and limitless adventure.

The Irish Revolution

In this period, however, important challenges to the imperial idea emerged. The most successful of these challenges occurred in Ireland. Many Irish men, Catholic and Protestant, fought for Britain during World War I, but a small group of revolutionary Catholic nationalists saw the war as an opportunity for revolt. They mounted an armed rebellion on Easter Monday in 1916. Although quickly and brutally suppressed, the "Easter Rising" became for Irish nationalists a key moment in the fight for an independent Ireland. The executed leaders of the rising became martyrs for the sacred cause of nationhood, while the ease with which the British crushed the revolt convinced Irish nationalist leaders of the necessity of employing guerilla tactics rather than open military assault to defeat their powerful foe.

In 1921, ground down by more than two years of guerilla warfare waged with consummate skill by the Irish Republican Army (IRA), the British government offered Ireland independence. The offer, however, came with strings attached: Independent Ireland was to retain its membership within the British Empire, and the six northern counties within the province of Ulster, dominated by Protestants who opposed Irish independence, were to remain under British rule. The independent state of Ireland (Eire) finally severed its ties with the British Empire in 1937. Northern Ireland today retains its constitutional links to Britain. (See **Map 26.2.**)

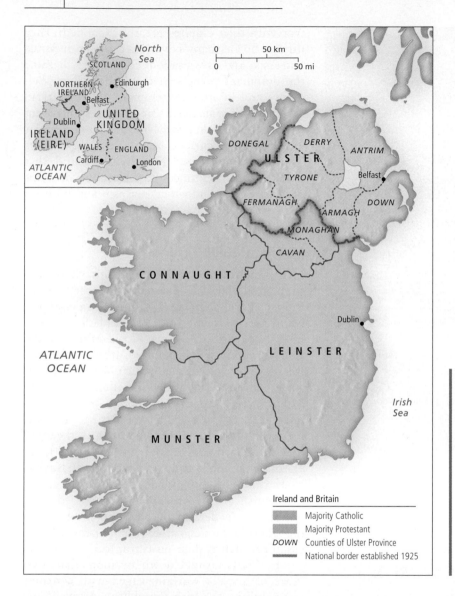

MAP 26.2

Ireland and Britain

The treaty of 1921 that ended the Anglo-Irish War partitioned the Irish island. Six northern counties (or "Ulster") remain part of the British state. The rest of Ireland became the Irish Free State, an independent state within the British Empire. In 1937, a new constitution declared Ireland (Eire) to be a republic and cut most ties to Britain.

Changing Power Equations: Ideology and Economics

Ireland's revolt against British imperial rule, while unusual in its success, revealed the growing power of anti-imperialist forces across the world. Shifting global economic relationships and communist ideology accelerated the spread of mass nationalist movements and so eroded imperial control.

World War I and the Great Depression strained the economic links between European states and their imperial territories. The demands of total war forced Europe's imperial powers to utilize fully their colonial resources. This strategy brought with it unintended social changes, including the migration of workers, the expansion of cities, and the enveloping of once-isolated villages in the global economic web. These unsettling changes provoked anti-Western agitation and strengthened nationalist resistance to imperial rule.

Then the Great Depression brought a sharp fall in the prices of primary products, which spelled disaster for many colonial regions that relied on the production of cash crops for export. The depression also diminished the benefits of imperial governance. Looking for ways to reduce expenditures, European governments cut funds to colonial schools, public services, and health care. Direct taxation rates rose while unemployment rates soared. In response, nationalist movements exploded.

Communist ideology also played a role in the spread of nationalism throughout European empires. Lenin argued that capitalist competition for markets led inevitably to imperialism and thus that anticapitalism and anti-imperialism went hand in hand. Under Lenin, the Soviet Union declared itself the defender of oppressed nationalities everywhere and provided ideological and material assistance to nationalist independence movements in Indonesia, Indochina, Burma, and most significantly, China, where Soviet advisers helped form the Communist Party in 1921.

Postwar Nationalism, Westernization, and the Islamic Challenge

Anti-Western sentiment in imperial territories also took religious form. In Africa, for example, a revival of animist religion expressed an explicit rejection of the Christian teachings brought by European and American missionaries and an implicit refusal of Western cultural and political styles. Throughout many African regions, however, Islam possessed the most potent appeal. In the growing cities, immigrants cut off from their villages and traditional religious practices found that Islam provided an alternative cultural identity to the one offered by their European rulers.

The end of World War I marked the beginning of a new era in Islamic history. The Ottoman Empire had symbolized a unified Islam: As caliph, the Ottoman sultan claimed religious authority over all Muslims, even those not under Ottoman political rule. The collapse of the Ottoman Empire and the abolition of the Ottoman caliphate in the wake of World War I created a new religious and political environment for Muslims. Many followed Western secular models and turned to ethnic nationalism. Others, however, found spiritual solace and political identity in Islamic revival movements.

THE EMERGENCE OF PAN-ARABISM In the Middle East, **pan-Arabism** emerged as a powerful form of nationalism. Just as pan-Slavism promoted the ideal of a single Slavic state (see page 694), so pan-Arabism insisted that all Arabs—including the minority who were not Muslim—should unite in an Arab state. Three postwar developments nourished pan-Arabism. First, the collapse of the Ottoman Empire shattered traditional loyalty to the caliphate. Second, the new postwar map of the Middle East placed Arabs in states they regarded as artificial, unrelated to dynastic or tribal identities. Thus, nationalist movements centering on these new states—Iraqi nationalism, for example—possessed little popular appeal. And finally, as Chapter 25 explained, the postwar system of "Mandates" continued imperial rule in a new form and thereby strengthened anti-Western resentments and the pan-Arabist movement.

STATE NATIONALISM ON THE WESTERN MODEL Not all Arab nationalists, however, embraced pan-Arabism. In states such as Egypt, with a national identity not imposed by Western imperialists or World War I, nationalism tended to coalesce around the state itself. Hence, in Egypt, the nationalist political party, *Wafd,* called for Egyptian national freedom, not for pan-Arabic unity. Wafd fought the British-backed Egyptian monarchy and sought to modernize Egypt along Western lines.

For nationalists such as those in Wafd, the successful nationalist revolution in Turkey provided a source of inspiration. After World War I, the Allies forced the defeated Ottoman government to sign the humiliating Treaty of Sèvres, which not only dispossessed the

Ottoman government of its Middle Eastern empire, but also gave territories in the Turkish heartland to Greece, Italy, an autonomous Kurdistan, and an independent Armenia. In addition, Sèvres gave the Allies the right to intervene in Turkey's economic, military, and foreign affairs. Turkish nationalists, led by Mustafa Kemal Pasha, rejected the treaty and rebelled against the government that signed such a document. Kemal's nationalist rebellion overthrew the Ottoman sultan, repelled a Greek invasion, and forced the Allies to draw up a new settlement. In 1923, the Treaty of Lausanne restored to Turkey most of its territory and full national sovereignty.

But while Kemal had no intentions of letting Western powers govern in Turkey, he was not anti-Western. Kemal viewed the West as modern—and he wanted to modernize Turkey. Thus, Kemal declared Turkey a secular republic, outlawed polygamy, granted women civil and legal rights, and required all Turks to take surnames. He became known as Kemal "Ataturk" ("Father of the Turks"). A mass literacy program aimed to teach Turks how to read and write using the Latin alphabet. Schoolmasters who dared use Arabic lettering were arrested. Ataturk even condemned the traditional form of Turkish headwear, the fez, as "an emblem of ignorance, negligence, fanaticism, hatred of progress and civilization."[17] To represent Turkey's new Western orientation, Turkish men were ordered to wear Western suits and English bowler hats.

Ataturk was less enthusiastic about English political freedom. Despite setting up a parliament elected by universal suffrage, he used executive power to govern with an iron grip over a one-party state. He also continued the Ottoman policies of repression toward Turkey's Armenian minority.

Kemal Ataturk's secularist, Westernized model of nationalism proved alluring. During the 1920s and 1930s nationalists in the Middle East, Africa, and Asia tended to embrace Western models, even as they rejected Western (or Western-imposed) rulers. They formed parliamentary political parties, advocated Western political ideologies such as liberalism and communism, regarded the state as secular, and saw political independence as a crucial step toward industrial modernization and economic prosperity.

THE ISLAMIC CHALLENGE   Beneath the surface of political life, however, different movements with different aims were coalescing. Throughout the new states of the Middle East, soaring sales of popular biographies of the Prophet Muhammad and the proliferation of Islamic leagues and clubs hinted that many ordinary people found secular nationalism as alien as the faces of their Western-imposed rulers and as meaningless as the boundaries on the new map. These sentiments did not harden into political movements until the 1940s, but the Wahhabi religious revival in central Arabia during the 1920s and 1930s and the foundation of the Muslim Brotherhood in Egypt in 1928 set a new direction for Islam's relationship to the West.

Founded by Muhammad Abd al-Wahhab (1703–1787) in the eighteenth century, **Wahhabism** sought to purify Islam by returning to a strict interpretation of the *Sharia,* or Islamic law. Wahhabism revived in the tumultuous period after World War I because its reassertion of fundamental truths and practices proved reassuring in times of unsettling political change. Moreover, the postwar Wahhabi revival had a powerful patron: Abd al-Aziz Ibn Saud (ca. 1888–1953), the head of the Saudi dynasty whose conquests on the Arabian Peninsula became the basis for the kingdom of Saudi Arabia.

Like Wahhabism, the Islamic Brotherhood (or *Ikhwan*) rejected modernizing interpretations of Islam and reasserted the universal jurisdiction of Islamic law. For the Brotherhood, Islam governed not just religious belief, but all areas of life. Working through youth groups, educational institutes, and business enterprises, the Brotherhood spread from its Egyptian base throughout the Middle East during the 1930s.

Moral Revolution in India

During this same era, a different sort of anti-Western protest movement took shape in India under the leadership of Mohandas Gandhi (1869–1948). Gandhi had spent 20 years in South Africa fighting to improve the lot of indentured Indian laborers under British imperial rule and developing his commitment to social and political change through nonviolent protest and civil disobedience.

After he returned to India in 1916, Gandhi transformed Indian nationalism into a mass movement by appealing to traditional Indian customs and religious identities. He did not oppose modernization, but he argued that modernization did not mean Westernization. India could—and should—follow its own path. Gandhi rejected Western dress and presented himself in the role of the religious ascetic, a familiar and honored figure in Indian culture. In his insistence that the nationalist struggle be one of "moral force" rather than a physical fight, Gandhi drew on the Hindu tradition of nonviolence. He was careful, however, not to equate "Indian" with "Hindu." Gandhi strove to incorporate the minority Muslim community into the nationalist movement, and he broke with the traditional Hindu caste system by campaigning for the rights of those deemed "untouchable." (*See Encounters and Transformations* in this chapter.)

Unable to decide whether to arrest Gandhi as a dangerous revolutionary or to negotiate with him as a representative of the Indian people, the British did both. In 1931, Gandhi and the viceroy of India (literally the "vice-king," the highest British official in India) met on equal terms for a series of eight meetings. A few months later Gandhi was in prison, along with 66,000 of his nationalist colleagues. Successive British governments passed a series of measures granting Indians increasing degrees of self-government, but Gandhi and the Indian National Congress demanded full and immediate national independence. The resulting impasse led to escalating unrest and terrorist activity, despite Gandhi's personal commitment to nonviolence.

India remained the jewel in Britain's imperial crown, but the glue holding it in place was deteriorating rapidly by the end of the 1930s.

The Power of the Primitive

When asked what he thought of "Western civilization," Gandhi replied, "I think it would be a very good idea." Just as nationalists outside of the West such as Gandhi began to challenge the equation of the West with civilization, so too did Westerners themselves. In the nineteenth century, imperialists insisted that "civilization" gave the West the right to rule the "barbarians" in the rest of the world. But by 1918, in the wake of the war, at least some Europeans asked, "Who is the barbarian now?"

Developments in psychology further eroded the boundaries between barbarian or "primitive" and modern cultures. In his postwar writings, Sigmund Freud emphasized that human nature was fundamentally aggressive, even bestial. Freud's three-part theory of personality, developed in the 1920s, argued that within each individual the *id*, the unconscious force of primitive instinct, battles against the controls of the *ego*, or conscious rationality, and the *superego*, the moral values imposed by society. Although Freud taught that the continuity of civilization depended on the repression of the id, many Freudian popularizers insisted that the individual should allow his or her primitive self to run free.

The work of Freud's onetime disciple Carl Jung (1875–1961) also stressed the links between the primitive and the modern. Jung contended that careful study of an individual's dreams will show that they share common images and forms—"archetypes"—with ancient mythologies and world religions. These archetypes point to the existence of the "collective unconscious," shared by all human beings, regardless of when or where they lived. Thus, in Jung's analysis the boundary between "civilized" and "primitive," "West" and "not West," disappeared.

ENCOUNTERS AND TRANSFORMATIONS

From Mohandas to Mahatma: Gandhi's Transformation

In April 1893, a young, well-dressed Indian lawyer purchased a first-class train ticket from Durban to Pretoria (South Africa). The first part of the journey proceeded uneventfully, but then another traveler, a white man, entered the first-class compartment. He turned around and returned with two guards, who demanded that the Indian man sit in third class, with the other "colored" passengers. The young lawyer refused and so was thrown off the train at the next stop.

Mohandas Gandhi's experience on the train to Pretoria was not unusual. The Indian immigrant community in South Africa had long endured legal discrimination, economic exploitation, and frequent violence, while the black African community suffered far worse. But the 24-year-old Gandhi knew little about such things. Growing up as the spoiled youngest son in an upper-caste family in India, he had known privilege rather than prejudice. Even the three years he spent in London studying law did not expose him to racial discrimination. Gandhi, in fact, felt that when he left Britain he was leaving "home." He returned to India in 1891 convinced of the superiority of British law and culture. He banned Indian-style clothing from his household, insisted that his illiterate young wife learn English, and decreed that his children eat porridge and cocoa for breakfast. He saw himself as a successful British lawyer.

But others did not see him that way. When Gandhi asked a British official for a favor for his brother, he was humiliated, actually pushed out the door by a servant. "This shock changed the course of my life," Gandhi later noted.[18] Offered a job in South Africa, he went—and on that train to Pretoria encountered further humiliation. By the time Gandhi finally reached Pretoria, he had decided to fight. He became the leader of the Indian civil rights movement in South Africa.

Gandhi lived in South Africa for 21 years. During these decades, the westernized, Britain-loving lawyer became a Hindu holy man. Mohandas became Mahatma, the "great-souled one." This transformation occurred in part because of Gandhi's sense of betrayal as he encountered the racial discrimination embedded in British imperialism. His time in London had taught Gandhi that Britain epitomized the Western ideals of impartial justice and individual rights. But the British colonial regime he encountered in South Africa violated those ideals. Disillusioned, Gandhi turned back to his Hindu roots.

Western culture also, however, played a positive role in Gandhi's transformation. During his

THE MAHATMA
Gandhi drew on Hindu and Western traditions in formulating his moral protest.

time in South Africa, Gandhi read widely in Christian and Western texts, including the New Testament, and books by nineteenth-century European social and cultural critics that exposed the spiritual and material failures of industrial society. Gandhi's intellectual encounter with these texts helped him formulate the idea of *Satyagraha* ("Truth-Force"). In its most specific sense, Satyagraha is a political tool. Through nonviolent mass civil disobedience, the powerless persuade the powerful to effect political change. But Satyagraha is also a spiritual act, the victory of goodness over violence and evil.

Gandhi's specific encounters with the injustice of imperial rule, first in the home of a British official in India and then on his South African train ride, forced him to embark on a different sort of spiritual and political journey, an exploration of both Western and Hindu thought. This journey transformed Gandhi from Mohandas into Mahatma and led him to Satyagraha—and the transformation of Indian nationalism into a mass movement. By 1948, this movement made it impossible for the British to govern India.

For Discussion

Encounters with Western ideas and Western people helped transform Gandhi "from Mohandas to Mahatma." How have Gandhi's ideas transformed Western culture and politics?

THE POWER OF THE PRIMITIVE

When the American dancer Josephine Baker first hit the stage in Paris in 1925, her audience embraced her as the image of African savagery, even though Baker was a city kid from Philadelphia. A Parisian sensation from the moment she arrived, Baker's frenetic and passionate style of dancing—and her willingness to appear on stage wearing nothing but a belt of bananas—epitomized for many Europeans the freedom they believed their urbanized culture had lost, and that the United States and Africa retained. Baker's belt of bananas, designed by her white French employer, shows that racist stereotypes shaped this idealization of the primitive. Yet Baker's blackness and her Americanness represented a positive image of liberation to many Parisians.

In the work of other thinkers and artists, that boundary remained intact, but Western notions of cultural superiority turned upside down. The German novelist Herman Hesse (1877–1962) condemned modern industrial society as spiritually barren and celebrated Eastern mysticism as a source of power and wisdom. Many writers agreed that the West needed to look to outside its borders for vibrancy and vitality. The belief that Western culture was anemic, washed out, and washed up also led to a new openness to alternative intellectual and artistic traditions. As the energetic rhythms of African American jazz worked their way into white musical traditions, they transformed popular music.

Similarly, the *Négritude* movement stressed the history and intrinsic value of black African culture. Founded in Paris in 1935 by French colonial students from Africa and the West Indies, Négritude condemned European culture as weak and corrupted and called for blacks to recreate a separate cultural and political identity. The movement's leading figures, such as Leopold Senghor (1906–2001), who later became the first president of independent Senegal, opposed Western imperialism and demanded African self-rule. Drawing together Africans, Afro-Caribbeans, and black Americans, Négritude assumed the existence of a common black culture that transcended national and colonial boundaries. The movement stole the white racists' stereotype of the "happy dancing savage" and refigured it as positive: Black culture fostered the emotion, creativity, and human connections that white Western industrial society destroyed.

CONCLUSION

The Kingdom of Corpses

In 1921, the Goncourt Prize, the most prestigious award in French literature, was awarded not to a native French writer, but to a colonial: René Maran, born in the French colony of Martinique. Even more striking than Maran's receiving the prize was the content of the novel for which he was honored. In *Batouala,* Maran condemned Western culture: "Civilization, civilization, pride of the Europeans and charnel house of innocents.... You build your kingdom on corpses."[19]

For many in the West, Maran's description of Europe as a kingdom of corpses appeared apt in the aftermath of total war. During the 1920s and 1930s Soviet communism on the left and Nazism and fascism on the right rejected such key Western ideals as individual rights and the rule of law. These extremist ideologies seemed persuasive in the climate of despair produced not only by the war, but also by the postwar failure of democracy in eastern Europe and the collapse of the global economy after 1929. As a result, the kingdom of corpses grew: in Nazi Germany, in Spain, and most dramatically in the Soviet Union. The kingdom of corpses was, however, a particularly expansionist domain. As the 1930s ended, the West and the world stood on the brink of another total war, one in which the numbers of dead spiraled to nearly incomprehensible levels.

KEY TERMS

existentialism	Nazism
New Economic Policy (NEP)	collectivization
Weimar Republic	Great Purge
hyperinflation	social democracy
eugenics	Keynesian economics
fascism	Popular Front
corporatism	pan-Arabism
Great Depression	Wahhabism

CHAPTER QUESTIONS

1. What was the impact of the war on European cultural life? (page 821)
2. How did retrenchment rather than revolution characterize the postwar period? (page 824)
3. What circumstances explain the emergence of the Radical Right? (page 833)
4. What factors led to the polarization of European politics in the 1930s? (page 839)
5. How did the interaction between the West and the world outside change after World War I? (page 847)

TAKING IT FURTHER

1. Was Stalinism the logical conclusion of the Bolshevik Revolution and Leninism? Or did Stalinism reject or redirect Lenin's revolution?
2. What were the key developments in governmental policies toward women, welfare, and the family in the interwar era? How can we explain the similarities in Radical Right, democratic, and Radical Left policies?

✓•⎯Practice on MyHistoryLab

27

World War II

■ The Coming of War ■ Europe at War, 1939–1941
■ The World at War, 1941–1945 ■ The War Against the Jews
■ The Home Front: The Other Wars

IN THE FINAL WEEKS OF WORLD WAR II IN EUROPE, MANY ALLIED SOLDIERS faced their most difficult assignment yet. Combat veterans, accustomed to scenes of slaughter, broke down and cried as they encountered a landscape of horror beyond their wildest nightmares: the Nazi concentration and death camps. As one American war correspondent put it, "We had penetrated at last to the center of the black heart, to the very crawling inside of the vicious heart."[1] The American soldiers who opened the camp in Mauthausen, Austria, never forgot their first sight of the prisoners there: "By the thousands they came streaming.... Hollow, pallid ghosts from graves and tombs, terrifying, rot-colored figures of misery marked by disease, deeply ingrained filth, inner decay.... squat skeletons in rags and crazy grins."[2]

Similarly, the sights they saw at Bergen-Belsen in Germany left an indelible mark on the British troops who liberated that camp. Bergen-Belsen had become the dumping ground for camp inmates from eastern Europe as the German army retreated in front of the advancing Soviet army. Sick and starving, these prisoners were packed, 1,200 at a time, into barracks built to accommodate a few hundred. By March 1945, drinking water and food had disappeared, excrement dripped from bunk beds and coated the floors, and dead bodies piled up everywhere. In these conditions, the only living beings to flourish were the microorganisms that caused typhus. Floundering in this sea of want, British soldiers, doctors, and nurses did what they could. Even so, 28,000 of Bergen-Belsen's 60,000 inmates died in the weeks following liberation.

In Mauthausen and Bergen-Belsen, in the piles of putrefying bodies and among the crowds of skeletal survivors, American and British soldiers encountered the results of Adolf Hitler's effort to redefine the West. In Hitler's vision, Western civilization comprised ranks of white, northern Europeans, led by Germans, marching in step to a cadence dictated by the all-powerful state. To realize this vision, Hitler turned to total war and mass murder.

This quest to reconfigure the West as a race-based German empire led Hitler to join hands with an ally outside the West: Japan. The German-Japanese alliance transformed a European war into a global conflict. Understanding World War II thus demands that we look not only at the results of Nazi racial ideology, but also at global power relations and patterns of economic dependency. The Pacific war constituted the most brutal in a long series of encounters between Japanese elites and the West. Like Hitler, Japan's governing elites longed for an empire—in their case, an Asian empire to ensure access to the resources and domination over the peoples of the Pacific region. With such access and such domination, they hoped to insulate Japan's economic and political structures from Western influence or control.

As we examine both the European and the Pacific theaters of war, we will need, then, to ask how competing definitions of "the West" helped shape this conflict. We will also confront the question of results: How did the cataclysm known as World War II redefine the West?

THE MASS GRAVES AT BERGEN-BELSEN
British soldiers liberated the Nazi concentration camp of Bergen-Belsen on April 15, 1945. For many prisoners, however, death provided their only "liberation."

THE COMING OF WAR

■ What were the expectations concerning war in the 1920s and 1930s, and how did these hopes and fears lead to armed conflict in both Europe and Asia?

World War I was supposed to be the "war to end all wars." Instead, a little more than 20 years later, total war again engulfed Europe and then the world. Hitler's ambitions for a German empire in eastern Europe account for the immediate outbreak of war in September 1939. But a complete explanation of the origins of World War II extends beyond Hitler's aims and actions.

An Uneasy Peace

The Second World War originated in the settlement of the First. As we saw in Chapters 25 and 26, the treaties negotiated after 1918 created an uneasy peace. Three factors account for the fragility of the peace settlement. First, the Versailles Treaty created great resentment among Germans, helped weaken postwar Western economies, and enhanced Hitler's appeal. Second, the League of Nations, created to replace the alliance systems that many blamed for starting World War I, could not realize the high hopes of its planners. Lacking military power, boycotted by the United States, and at various times excluding the key states of Germany and the Soviet Union, the League proved too weak to serve as the basis of a new international order. Finally, the redrawing of the map of eastern and central Europe failed to fulfill the nationalist ambitions of many groups. Hungarians, for example, mourned the loss of lands to Czechoslovakia, Romania, and

Yugoslavia, while Italians argued that their nation's contribution to the Allies' victory had earned the reward of territories granted instead to Yugoslavia, Austria, and Albania.

The onset of the Great Depression in 1929 further destabilized the peace. Economic nationalism intensified as governments erected tariff walls to protect their own industries. Some sought to escape economic difficulties through territorial expansion. Japan, threatened by the collapse of export markets for raw silk and cotton cloth, invaded Manchuria (in eastern China) in 1931 and Italy invaded Ethiopia in 1935. The Ethiopians endured many of the horrors soon to come to the European continent, including the saturation bombing of civilians, the use of poison gas, and the establishment of concentration camps. At the end of June 1936, Ethiopia's now-exiled Emperor Haile Selassie (1892–1975) addressed the Assembly of the League of Nations and warned, "It is us today. It will be you tomorrow."[3]

One year after Italian troops invaded Ethiopia, civil war broke out in Spain. As Chapter 26 explained, the victory of General Francisco Franco's rebels seemed to signal that aggressors could act with impunity. While the Spanish Civil War raged, the Japanese resumed their advance in China. In what became known as the Rape of Nanking (Nanjing), soldiers used babies for bayonet practice, gang-raped as many as 20,000 young girls and women, and left the bodies of the dead to rot in the street.

The Expansion of Nazi Germany

Against this backdrop of military aggression and the democracies' inaction, Hitler made his first moves to establish a German empire in Europe (see **Map 27.1**). In 1933, he withdrew Germany from the League of Nations and two years later announced the creation of a German

THE PRELUDE TO WORLD WAR II
The Japanese resumption of their war in China in 1937 added to the horrors of the 1930s. Here a photographer captured the agony of a baby separated from its parents in the railway station in Shanghai.

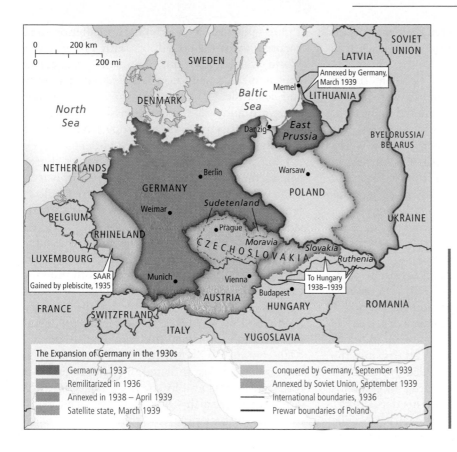

MAP 27.1

The Expansion of Germany in the 1930s

Beginning with the remilitarization of the Rhineland in 1936, Hitler embarked on a program of German territorial expansion. This map also indicates the expansion of the Soviet Union into Poland as a result of the secret terms of the German-Soviet Non-Aggression Pact.

air force and the return of mass conscription—in deliberate violation of the terms of the Versailles Treaty. In 1936, Hitler allied with Mussolini in the **Rome-Berlin Axis** and again violated his treaty obligations when he sent German troops into the Rhineland, the industrially rich region on Germany's western border. Yet France and Britain did not respond. Two years later, in March 1938, Germany broke the Versailles Treaty once more by annexing Austria.

After the successful *Anschluss* ("joining") of Germany and Austria, Hitler demanded that the Sudetenland, the western portion of Czechoslovakia inhabited by a German-speaking majority, be joined to Germany as well. He seemed finally to have gone too far. With France and the Soviet Union pledged to protect the territorial integrity of Czechoslovakia, Europe stood on the brink of war. The urgency of the situation impelled Britain's prime minister Neville Chamberlain

(1869–1940) to board an airplane for the first time in his life and fly to Munich to talk with Hitler. After negotiations that excluded the Czech government, Chamberlain and French prime minister Edouard Daladier agreed to grant Hitler the right to occupy the Sudetenland immediately. Assured by Hitler that this **Munich Agreement** satisfied all his territorial demands, Chamberlain flew home to an enthusiastic welcome. Crowds cheered when he declared "peace in our time." (See *Different Voices* in this chapter.)

"Peace in our time" lasted for six months. In March 1939, Hitler's promises were proven worthless as German troops occupied the rest of Czechoslovakia. Hitler then took out an insurance policy against fighting a two-front war by persuading Stalin to sign the **German-Soviet Non-Aggression Pact.** The pact publicly pledged the two powers not to attack each other. It also secretly divided Poland between them and promised Stalin substantial territorial gains in eastern Poland and the Baltic regions.

On September 1, 1939, German troops invaded Poland and within weeks were implementing racial policies that murdered millions of Poles. The British and French declared war against Germany on September 3. Two weeks after German troops crossed Poland's borders in the west, the Soviets pushed in from the east and imposed a regime characterized by mass deportations and death. World War II had begun.

Evaluating Appeasement

Could Hitler have been stopped before he catapulted Europe into World War II? The debate over this question has centered on British policy during the 1930s. With France weakened by economic and political crises, the United States remaining aloof from European affairs, and the communist Soviet Union regarded as a pariah state, Britain assumed the initiative in responding to Hitler's rise to power and his demands.

British policymakers—particularly Neville Chamberlain, who was prime minister in the late 1930s—pursued a policy of conciliation and negotiation in their dealings with Hitler. After World War II broke out, that policy was called **appeasement,** a word now equated with passivity and cowardice. Chamberlain, however, was not a coward and was far from passive. Convinced he had a mission to save Europe from war, he actively sought to accommodate Hitler.

For Chamberlain, and many other Europeans, the alternative to appeasement was a total war that would destroy Western civilization. They remembered the last war with horror and agreed that the next war would be even worse, for it would be an air war. The years after 1918 saw the aviation industry take off in Europe and the United States, and both military experts and ordinary people recognized the disastrous potential of airborne bombs. Stanley Baldwin (1867–1947), Chamberlain's predecessor as prime minister, told the British public, "The bomber will always get through." The civilian casualties inflicted by the Italian air force in Ethiopia and by the bombing of Spanish cities in the Spanish Civil War convinced many that Baldwin was right, and that war was, therefore, unacceptable.

CHRONOLOGY: ON THE ROAD TO WORLD WAR II

1919	Versailles Treaty
1929	Onset of the Great Depression
1931	Japan invades Manchuria
1933	Hitler becomes chancellor of Germany
1935	Hitler announces a German air force and military conscription; Italy invades Ethiopia
1936	German troops occupy the Rhineland; civil war breaks out in Spain; Hitler and Mussolini form the Rome-Berlin Axis
1937	Japan advances against China; Rape of Nanking
1938	
March	Germany annexes Austria (the *Anschluss*)
September	Munich Conference: Germany occupies the Sudetenland
1939	
March 15	Germany invades Czechoslovakia
August 23	German-Soviet Non-Aggression Pact
September 1	Germany invades Poland
September 3	Great Britain and France declare war on Germany

Motivated by the desire to avoid another horrible war, appeasement rested on two additional pillars—the assumption that many of Germany's grievances were legitimate and the belief that only a strong Germany could neutralize the threat posed by Soviet communism. During the 1920s, many scholars and policymakers studied the diplomatic records concerning the outbreak of World War I. They concluded that the treaty makers at Versailles were wrong in blaming Germany for starting the war. Convinced that the Versailles Treaty had treated Germany unjustly, British leaders sought to renegotiate reparations, to press the French into softening their anti-German policies, and to draw Germany back into the network of international diplomatic relations. Hitler's rise to power gave added impetus to a policy already in place. British leaders argued that they could rob Hitler of much of his appeal by rectifying legitimate German grievances. Fear of communism reinforced this desire to stabilize Germany. Many politicians applauded Hitler's suppression of German communists and welcomed a remilitarized Germany as a strong barricade against the threat posed by Soviet Russia. The startling announcement of the German-Soviet Non-Aggression Pact in the summer of 1939, however, revealed this barricade to be hollow.

EUROPE AT WAR, 1939–1941

■ How did Nazi Germany conquer the continent of Europe by 1941?

Within just two years, Hitler appeared to have achieved his goal of establishing a Nazi empire in Europe. By the autumn of 1941, almost all of continental Europe was either allied to or occupied by Nazi Germany.

A New Kind of Warfare

The four-year stalemate on the Western Front in World War I demonstrated that an entrenched defense, armed with machine guns, could easily withstand an infantry assault. Postwar German military strategists, seeking to avoid the stalemate of trench warfare, theorized that the airplane and the tank could together act as an "armored fist" strong and swift enough to break through even the most well-fortified enemy defenses. The bomber plane would provide a mobile bombardment to shatter fortifications, break communication links, and clog transport routes. Simultaneously, motorized infantry and tank formations would punch through enemy lines.

Germany's successes in the first years of World War II illustrated the effectiveness of a mobile, mechanized offensive force. Germany's only defeat during these years came in the Battle of Britain, when Germany confronted a mobile, mechanized defense. Like Germany's victories, this defeat highlights a crucial theme of this chapter: the central role of industrial production in modern war.

BLITZKRIEG   During the invasion of Poland, most of the German army moved on foot or horseback, as soldiers had done for centuries. Motorized divisions, however, bludgeoned through the Polish defenses, penetrated deep into enemy territory, and secured key positions. While these units wreaked havoc on the ground, the Luftwaffe—the German air force—rained ruin from the air. Over 1,300 planes shrieked across the Polish skies and destroyed the Polish air force.

Western newspaper reporters christened Nazi Germany's offensive techniques **blitzkrieg**—lightning war. Western Europeans experienced blitzkrieg firsthand in the spring of 1940 when the German army invaded Denmark and Norway in early April and moved into western Europe in May. The Netherlands fell in four days. Belgium, supported by French and British units as in World War I, held out for two weeks.

By the end of May, the Germans had trapped the British army and several divisions of the French force in a small pocket on the northern French coast called Dunkirk. While the British Royal Air Force (RAF) held off the Luftwaffe, the British navy and a flotilla of fishing and

DIFFERENT VOICES APPEASEMENT AND THE MUNICH AGREEMENT

After World War I the victorious Allies redrew the map of central Europe and assigned the Sudetenland, a crescent-shaped region on the edge of what had been the Austro-Hungarian province of Bohemia, to Czechoslovakia. During the 1920s and 1930s, ethnic German Sudetenlanders experienced discrimination in education, employment, and political life, while German nationalist politicians fanned the flames of discontent and, in some cases, worked secretly with Hitler to prepare the ground for a Nazi takeover. In 1938, following his successful annexation of Austria, Hitler demanded the Sudetenland. After a series of meetings, Hitler, the British prime minister Neville Chamberlain, and the French premier Eduard Daladier announced the "Munich Agreement," which gave the Sudetenland to Germany. On his return to Britain, Chamberlain made his infamous proclamation of "peace in our time." The majority of British citizens cheered the Munich Agreement. One who did not was Winston Churchill, a member of Chamberlain's Conservative Party, but a critic of Chamberlain's appeasement policy.

In the first excerpt, Chamberlain defends appeasement in a speech before the House of Commons. In the second excerpt, Churchill attacks the Munich Agreement.

I. Neville Chamberlain in the House of Commons, 1938

War today...is a different thing...from what it used to be....When war starts today, in the very first hour, before any professional soldier, sailor or airman has been touched, it will strike the workman, the clerk, the man-in-the-street or in the 'bus, and his wife and children in their homes....[Y]ou cannot ask people to accept a prospect of that kind...unless you feel yourself, and can make them feel, that the cause for which they are going to fight is a vital cause—a cause that transcends all the human values....

Since I first went to Berchtesgaden* more than 20,000 letters and telegrams have come to No. 10, Downing Street.†...the people who wrote did not feel that they had such a cause for which to fight.... That is my answer to those who say that we should have told Germany weeks ago that, if her army crossed the border of Czechoslovakia, we should be at war with her....

What is the alternative to this bleak and barren policy of the inevitability of war?...we should seek by all means in our power to avoid war, by analysing possible causes, by trying to remove them, by discussion in a spirit of collaboration and good will....even if it does mean the establishment of personal contact with dictators....

I am asked how I can reconcile an appeal to the country to support the continuance of [the rearmament program]‡ with...my belief that we might have peace for our time...I never meant to suggest that we should [secure peace] by disarmament, until we can induce others to disarm too. Our past experience has shown us only too clearly that weakness in armed strength means weakness in diplomacy....

II. Winston Churchill in the House of Commons, October 5, 1938

[W]e have sustained a total and unmitigated defeat....The utmost my right hon. Friend the Prime Minister has been able to secure...has been that the German dictator, instead of snatching the victuals from the table, has been content to have them served to him course by course....

After [Germany's] seizure of Austria in March...I ventured to appeal to the

---

*"Berchtesgarden": Hitler's mountain retreat where the political leaders met.
†"No. 10, Downing Street"—the address of the British prime minister's residence.
‡British governments adopted a policy of increased expenditure on armaments from 1934 on.

Government...to give a pledge that in conjunction with France and other Powers they would guarantee the security of Czechoslovakia while the Sudeten-Deutsch [Sudeten-German] question was being examined either by a League of Nations Commission or some other impartial body.... Between submission and immediate war there was this third alternative, which gave a hope not only of peace but of justice. It is quite true that such a policy in order to succeed demanded that Britain should declare straight out and a long time beforehand that she would, with others, join to defend Czechoslovakia against an unprovoked aggression....

All is over. Silent, mournful, abandoned, broken, Czechoslovakia recedes into the darkness.... I think you will find that in a period of time which may be measured by years, but may be measured only by months, Czechoslovakia will be engulfed in the Nazi regime....

It must now be accepted that all the countries of Central and Eastern Europe will make the best terms they can with the triumphant Nazi power.... Many of those countries...have already got politicians, Ministers, Governments, who were pro-German, but there was always an enormous popular movement in Poland, Rumania, Bulgaria, and Yugoslavia which looked to the Western democracies and loathed the idea of having this arbitrary rule of the totalitarian system thrust upon them, and hoped that a stand would be made. All that has gone by the board....

The Prime Minister desires to see cordial relations between this country and Germany. There is no difficulty at all in having cordial relations between the peoples.... But never will you have friendship with the present German Government. You must have diplomatic and correct relations, but there can never be friendship between the British democracy and the Nazi power....

I do not grudge our loyal, brave people...the natural, spontaneous outburst of joy and relief when they learned that the hard ordeal would no longer be required of them at the moment; but they should know the truth. They should know that there has been gross neglect and deficiency in our defences; they should know that we have sustained a defeat without a war...

And do not suppose that this is the end. This is only the beginning of the reckoning. This is only the first sip, the first foretaste of a bitter cup which will be proffered to us year by year unless by a supreme recovery of moral health and martial vigour, we arise again and take our stand for freedom as in the olden time.

Sources: I. *Parliamentary Debates.* Fifth Series. Volume 339. House of Commons Official Report (London, 1938), 544–552. II. http://www.winstonchurchill.org/i4a/pages/index.cfm?pageid=1189. Accessed 12-12-07.

For Discussion

1. How did Chamberlain defend the Munich Agreement? What was he trying to achieve?

2. What alternatives did Churchill offer to the Munich Agreement? How realistic were these alternatives?

3. At the end of 1918, ethnic German delegates from Bohemia and Moravia rejected inclusion in Czechoslovakia and instead declared the union of German-majority regions (such as the Sudetenland) with Austria. In response, the new Czech government mobilized its army to enforce its boundaries—even though these boundaries contained over three million ethnic Germans. Does awareness of this history change your assessment of the Munich Agreement? If so, how and why?

recreational boats piloted by British civilians evacuated the troops. By June 4, 110,000 French and almost 240,000 British soldiers had been brought safely back to Britain. But, as the newly appointed British prime minister, Winston Churchill (1874–1965), reminded his cheering people, "Wars are not won by evacuation."

On June 14, German soldiers marched into Paris. The French Assembly voted to disband and to hand over power to the World War I war hero Marshal Philippe Pétain (1856–1951), who established an authoritarian government. On June 22 this new **Vichy regime** (named after the city Pétain chose for his capital) signed an armistice with Germany and pledged collaboration with the Nazi regime. Theoretically, Pétain's authority extended over all of France, but in actuality the Vichy regime was confined to the south (and to the French colonial regions), with Germany occupying France's western and northern regions, including Paris, as well as the Atlantic seaboard. Germany, with its allies and satellites, held most of the continent.

THE BATTLE OF BRITAIN   After the fall of France, Hitler hoped that Britain would accept Germany's domination of the continent and agree to a negotiated peace, but his hopes went unrealized. The failure of appeasement and the subsequent military disasters had thoroughly discredited Prime Minister Neville Chamberlain. A member of Chamberlain's own party spoke for the nation, "In the name of God, go!" Chamberlain went. The British parliament suspended party politics for the duration of the war, and power passed to an all-party coalition headed by Churchill, a critic of Britain's appeasement policy since 1933. Never a humble man, Churchill wrote that when he accepted the position of prime minister, "I felt as if I were walking with Destiny, and that all my past life had been but a preparation for this hour and this trial...I was sure I should not fail." In his first speech as prime minister, Churchill promised, "Victory— victory at all costs."

Faced with the British refusal to negotiate, Hitler ordered his General Staff to prepare for a land invasion of Britain. But placing German troops in the English Channel while the RAF still controlled the skies would be a certain military disaster. The destruction of Britain's air power had to come first. On July 10, German bomber raids on English southern coastal cities opened the Battle of Britain, a battle waged in the air and in the factories, and Germany's first significant defeat.

The British had three important advantages in the Battle of Britain. First, RAF pilots were flying in the skies above Britain—which meant that pilots who survived crashes could be rescued to fight again, whereas German survivors sat out the rest of the war as prisoners. Second, the rearmament program begun in 1934 had constructed a chain of anti-aircraft gun installations and radar stations that protected the British Isles and increased German losses. And finally, and most significantly for the future course of the war, Britain's industrial productivity outweighed Germany's. In the summer of 1940, British factories each month produced twice the number of fighter aircraft coming out of German plants. On September 17, 1940, Hitler announced that the invasion of Britain was "postponed."

The Invasion of the Soviet Union

War against Britain had never been one of Hitler's central goals, however. His dreams of the **Third Reich,** a German empire that was to last a thousand years, centered on capture of the agricultural and industrial resources of the Soviet Union. But Hitler sought far more than resources. He envisioned war with the Soviet Union as an apocalyptic clash of Good versus Evil: the superior German race against the twin evils of "Judeo-Bolshevism." The Soviet Union was, of course, the center of global "Bolshevism," or communism, while the majority of European Jews lived in Soviet-controlled eastern Polish lands or in the Soviet Union itself.

A CRUCIAL POSTPONEMENT   In July 1940, as the Battle of Britain began, Hitler ordered his military to plan a Soviet invasion. By December the plan was set: German troops were to invade the Soviet Union in April 1941. But they did not. Hitler postponed the invasion for two crucial months because the ambitions of an incompetent ally—Mussolini—threatened to undermine the economic base of the Nazi war machine.

Hoping to expand his Mediterranean empire, Mussolini ordered Italian troops into British imperial territories in North Africa in July 1940, followed by an invasion of Greece in October. But with a military budget one-tenth the size of Germany's, outdated tanks and aircraft, no aircraft carriers or anti-aircraft defenses, and a limited industrial base, Italy was ill-equipped to fight a total war. By the spring of 1941, the British army had pushed the Italians back into Libya while the Greeks mounted a strong resistance.

Hitler feared the consolidation of British power in Africa and was even more terrified of a British advance into eastern Europe. If Britain were able to build air bases in Greece, the Balkans would lie open to British bombing runs that could cripple the German war effort. Germany received 50 percent of its cereal and livestock from the Balkan region, 45 percent of its aluminum ore from Greece, 90 percent of its tin from Yugoslavia—and most of its oil from. Romania. Without oil, there would be no *blitz* in *blitzkrieg*.

These considerations led Hitler to delay the invasion of the Soviet Union while the German army mopped up Mussolini's mess in the Balkans and North Africa. In April 1941, German armored units punched through Yugoslavian defenses and encircled the Yugoslav army. Greece came next. Meanwhile, in North Africa German troops recaptured all the territory taken by the British the previous year. As **Map 27.2** shows, by the summer of 1941, Germany stood triumphant, with dramatic victories in North Africa and the Balkans. But these victories came at a high price: the postponement of the German invasion of the Soviet Union from April to June.

EARLY SUCCESS At first, that postponement seemed to matter little. On June 22, 1941, the largest invading force the world had yet seen began to cross the Soviet borders. Three million German soldiers, equipped with 2,770 modern aircraft and 3,350 tanks, went into battle. In a matter of days, most of the Soviet air force was destroyed. By October, the Germans had taken Kiev, besieged Leningrad, and stood 80 miles from Moscow. Almost 45 percent of the Soviet population was under German occupation, and the Germans controlled access to much of the Soviet Union's natural and industrial resources, including more than 45 percent of its grain and 65 percent of its coal, iron, and steel. On October 10, Hitler's spokesman announced to the foreign press corps that the destruction of the Soviet Union was assured. German newspapers proclaimed, "CAMPAIGN IN THE EAST DECIDED!"[4]

Why was Germany so successful at the start of the invasion? Blitzkrieg provides part of the answer. Germany's spearhead force of tank and motorized infantry divisions shattered the Soviet defensive line and seized key targets. Stalin's stubborn refusal to believe that Hitler would violate the Non-Aggression Pact also weakened Russian defenses. Soviet intelligence sources sent in more than 80 warnings of an imminent German attack. Stalin classified these messages as "doubtful" and ordered the messengers themselves punished. Moreover, the initial German advance occurred in territories where Soviet rule had brought enormous suffering and where, therefore, the population had little reason to defend the Soviet state. Ukraine, for example, was still recovering from the Stalinist-inflicted famine of the 1930s, while eastern Poland and the Baltic states, which Stalin had gained through the German-Soviet Non-Aggression Pact, were still bleeding from the Soviet takeover in 1939.

THE FATAL WINTER Yet in the winter of 1940–1941, the German advance stalled. Leningrad resisted its besiegers, and Moscow remained beyond the Germans' reach. Three obstacles halted the German invasion. First, German atrocities strengthened local

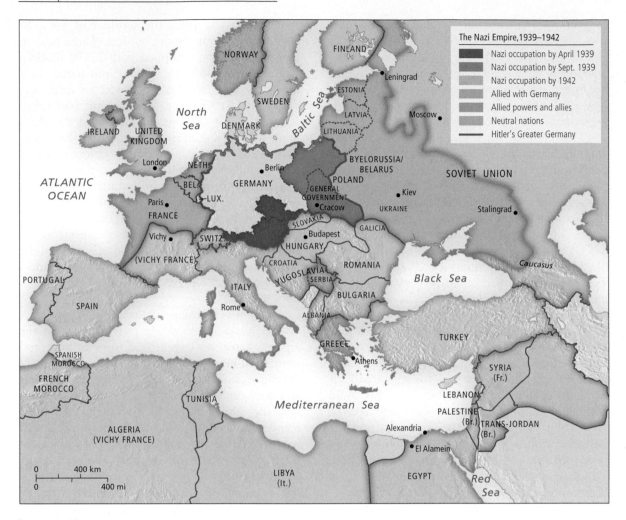

MAP 27.2

The Nazi Empire, 1939–1942

By 1942, Nazi Germany occupied or was allied to not only most European countries but also much of North Africa and the Middle East. Spain, Portugal, Ireland, Iceland, Sweden, and Switzerland remained neutral. Great Britain and the Soviet Union east of Moscow remained unconquered.

resistance against the occupiers. The troops in occupied Soviet territory treated the local populations with utter cruelty. Like a plague of locusts, SS and army units moved through Soviet lands, seizing all livestock, grain, and fuel. The Nazi governor of Ukraine insisted, "I will pump every last thing out of this country."[5] By 1941, human-made famine devastated Ukraine and Galicia. As partisan units worked behind the German lines, sabotaging their transportation routes, hijacking their supplies, and murdering their patrols, they found the Germans vulnerable to guerilla attack because of the second factor in halting the invasion: Germany's overstretched lines. Since June the German army had advanced so far so fast that it overstrained its supply and communication lines.

GERMAN MASSACRE AT KERCH

In one of the most famous Soviet photographs taken during the war, relatives try to identify their dead after German troops massacred all the men in the village of Kerch. Such atrocities as this strengthened the will of the Polish, Baltic, and Soviet peoples to resist their German occupiers.

The weather, the third and most crucial obstacle for the Germans, worsened these logistical problems. Had the Germans invaded in April, as originally planned, they might have captured Moscow and pushed even further east well before winter set in. Instead, the crucial postponement forced German troops to confront the fatal conditions imposed by Russia's brutal climate. An early October snowfall, which then melted, turned Russia's dirt roads to impassable mud. By the time the ground froze several weeks later, the German forces, like Napoleon's army 130 years earlier, were fighting the Russian winter. Subzero temperatures wreaked havoc with transportation lines. Horses froze to death, and machinery refused to start. Men fared just as badly. Dressed in lightweight spring uniforms, German soldiers fell victim to frostbite. By the end of the winter, the casualty list numbered more than 30 percent of the German East Army.

At the start of 1942, this army still occupied much of the Soviet Union and controlled the majority of its agricultural and industrial resources. More than three million Soviet soldiers had been killed and another three million captured. But the failure to deal the Soviets a quick death blow in 1941 gave Stalin and his high command a crucial advantage—*time*. During the German advance, Soviet laborers dismantled entire factories to transport them east, to areas out of German bombing range. Between August and October 1941, 80 percent of the Soviet war industry was in pieces. The *time* gained in the winter of 1941–1942 allowed the Soviets to put these pieces back together: They rebuilt their factories and focused the colossal productive power of the Soviet Union on the war effort. By 1943, Russia was outproducing Germany: 24,000 tanks versus 17,000; 130,000 artillery pieces versus 27,000; 35,000 combat aircraft versus 25,000. In a total war, in which victory occurs on the assembly line as well as on the front line, these statistics threatened Hitler's dreams of a German empire.

REBUILDING THE INDUSTRIAL MIGHT OF THE SOVIET UNION

The stalling of the German offensive in the winter of 1941–1942 gave the Soviet Union the essential advantage of time: time to rebuild their industrial strength. Thousands of factories were dismantled and shipped to safety east of the Urals. In this photo, workers begin the massive job of putting their factory back together. Before the war, they made railway cars. Now they would build tanks.

CHRONOLOGY: EUROPE AT WAR

1939

September	German-Soviet conquest of Poland

1940

April 9	German blitzkrieg against Denmark and Norway begins
May 10	Germans attack western Europe
June 22	Fall of France
July 10	Battle of Britain begins
September 7	London Blitz begins
September 17	Hitler cancels plans for invasion of Britain

1941

March	U.S. Congress passes Lend-Lease Act
April	German invasion of the Soviet Union postponed; German offensives in Yugoslavia, Greece, and North Africa
June 22	German invasion of the Soviet Union begins
December	German advance halted outside Moscow

THE WORLD AT WAR, 1941–1945

■ Why did the Allies win in 1945?

In December 1941, as the German advance slowed in the Soviet Union, Japanese expansionism in the Pacific fused with the war in Europe and drew the United States into the conflict. Over the next four years, millions of soldiers, sailors, and civilians lost their lives in a gargantuan and complicated conflict waged around the world.

The Globalization of the War

Even before 1941, Europe's imperialist legacy ensured that World War II was not confined to Europe. Mussolini's desire to expand his Mediterranean empire pushed the fighting into North Africa, while Britain would never have been able to stand alone in 1940 against the German-occupied continent without access to the manpower and materials of its empire. German efforts to block British access to these resources spread the war into the Atlantic, where British merchant marines battled against German submarines to keep open the sea lanes to Britain.

Those sea lanes provided a crucial connection between Britain and the still-neutral United States, on whose resources Britain drew heavily. In March 1941, the U.S. Congress passed the **Lend-Lease Act,** which guaranteed that the United States would supply Britain with necessary military supplies, with payment postponed until after the war ended. The passage of Lend-Lease was one of the most important decisions in all of World War II. It gave first Britain and then the Soviets access to American industrial might.

As the United States drew closer to Britain, its relations with Japan grew more hostile. In 1941 the Japanese occupied Indochina, and the United States responded by placing an embargo on trade in oil with Japan. Japanese policymakers viewed the embargo as tantamount to an act of war. Japan's imperial ambitions demanded that it move decisively before its oil ran out. The South Pacific, a treasure house of mineral and other resources, beckoned.

Between December 7 and 10, 1941, Japanese forces attacked American, British, and Dutch territories in the Pacific—Hong Kong, Wake and Guam Islands, the Philippines, Malaya, and the American naval base at Pearl Harbor, Hawaii. After an attack that lasted only a few hours, the U.S. Pacific fleet lay gutted. Guam fell immediately, while Wake Island held out until December 23 and Hong Kong surrendered on Christmas Day. February saw both Malaya and Singapore in Japanese hands. By May, Japanese forces had conquered Indonesia, Burma, and the Philippines. As **Map 27.3** illustrates, in just a few months, the Japanese established themselves as imperial overlords of the South Pacific, with its wealth of raw materials.

The audacity of the Japanese attack impressed Hitler. Although he had long feared American industrial power, he joined Japan by declaring war on the United States on December 11, 1941. In Europe Germany now faced an alliance of Britain, the Soviet Union, and the United States. Yet even against this alliance, Germany appeared to occupy a strong position. By January a spectacular offensive in North Africa brought German forces within 200 miles of the strategically vital Suez Canal. In June the German army resumed its advance in the Soviet Union and soon threatened Russia's oil fields in the southern Caucasus. With Germany on the offensive in the Middle East and the Soviet Union, and Japan controlling the Pacific, the Allies looked poised to lose the war.

The Turning Point: Midway, El Alamein, and Stalingrad

Twelve months later the situation had changed, and the Allies were on the road to eventual victory. The second half of 1942 proved the turning point as three very different battles transformed the course of the war. In the Pacific, victory at the Battle of Midway gave the U.S. forces a decisive advantage. In North Africa, British forces experienced their first battlefield victory at El Alamein. And in Europe, the Battle of Stalingrad dealt Germany a blow from which it never recovered.

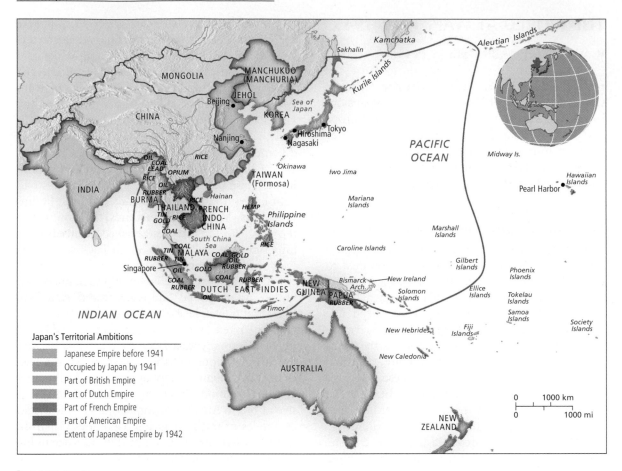

MAP 27.3
Japan's Territorial Ambitions

Lacking its own supply of natural resources, Japan embarked on imperial conquest.

THE BATTLE OF MIDWAY   The Battle of Midway resulted from the Japanese effort to ensure its air supremacy by destroying U.S. aircraft carriers. To do so, the Japanese attacked Midway Island, a U.S. outpost, on June 4, 1942. By mid-morning the Japanese had shot down two-thirds of the American planes. But then an American dive-bomber group, which had gotten lost, suddenly found itself above the main Japanese carriers. Their decks cluttered with gas lines and bombs, these ships were caught in the act of refueling and rearming the strike force. In five minutes, three of Japan's four carriers were destroyed. The fourth sank later in the day. The destruction

of the Japanese carriers dealt Japan a blow from which it could not recover. The United States possessed the industrial resources to rebuild its lost ships and airplanes. Japan did not. In five explosive minutes at Midway the course of the Pacific war changed.

THE BATTLE OF EL ALAMEIN   In contrast, the Battle of El Alamein marked the culmination of over two years of fighting in North Africa. As we have already seen, in the spring of 1941 German troops came to the aid of retreating Italian forces in Libya, and by June 1941, had muscled the British back into Egypt. For more than a year the two armies pushed each other back and forth across the desert. But finally the British caught the Germans by surprise at El Alamein in October 1942.

One month later combined British and American forces landed in Morocco and Algeria. Over the next six months they pushed Germany out of North Africa and secured a jumping-off point for their invasion of southern Italy in July 1943. El Alamein thus marked a turning point in the war. Churchill said of it, "It is not the beginning of the end, but it may be the end of the beginning."[6]

THE BATTLE OF STALINGRAD Churchill's apt description also fits the third turning point of 1942, the Battle of Stalingrad. In July the German army was sweeping south toward the oil-rich Caucasus. Hitler ordered the southern offensive split into two, with one arm reaching up to conquer Stalingrad on the Volga River. The conquest of Stalingrad would give the Germans control over the main waterway for the transport of oil and food from the Caucasus to the rest of the Soviet Union. But by dividing his offensive, Hitler widened his front from 500 to 2,500 miles. When the Germans reached Stalingrad on August 23, their resources were overstretched.

Stalin's generals assured him they could destroy the exposed German army—but only if Stalingrad could hold on for almost two months while they assembled the necessary men and machinery. An epic urban battle ensued, fought street by street, house by house, room by room. By November, Soviet troops had surrounded the Germans. When the German commander, General Friedrich von Paulus (d. 1953), requested permission to surrender, Hitler replied, "The army will hold its position to the last soldier and the last cartridge."[7] Paulus disobeyed orders and surrendered on January 30, 1943, but by then his army had almost ceased to exist. The Germans never made up the losses in manpower, material, or morale they suffered at Stalingrad.

The Allied Victory in Europe

The Allies moved to the offensive as **Map 27.4** illustrates. From 1943 on, the Soviet army pushed the Germans back toward the west and in mid-1944, British and American troops opened an effective "Second Front" with a successful invasion of German-occupied France.

THE DECISIVE FRONT On July 10, 1943, British and American forces landed in Sicily, prepared to push up the Italian peninsula, described by Churchill as the "soft underbelly" of German-controlled

CHRONOLOGY: 1942: THE TURNING POINT

1941

December 7	Japan bombs Pearl Harbor
December 11	Germany declares war on United States

1942

January 21	German offensive begins in North Africa
February 15	Surrender of British forces to Japan at Singapore
April 22	British retreat from Burma
May 6	Japan completes conquest of the Philippines
June 4	Battle of Midway
August 7	First U.S. Marine landing on Guadalcanal
August 23	German Sixth Army reaches Stalingrad
October 23	Battle of El Alamein begins
November 8	Anglo-American landing in North Africa begins
November 23	German Sixth Army cut off at Stalingrad

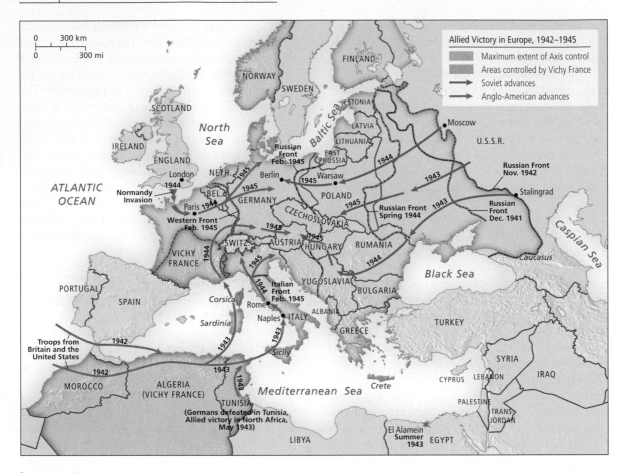

MAP 27.4
Allied Victory in Europe, 1942–1945
Beginning in late 1942, Allied forces moved onto the offensive.

Europe. The Italian offensive, a response to Stalin's pleas that Britain and the United States relieve the pressure on Russian troops by opening a "Second Front" in Europe, at first appeared a success. Within just 15 days, Mussolini had been overthrown and his successor opened peace negotiations with the Allies. But the German army then occupied Italy. Ridged with mountains and laced with rivers, Italy formed a natural defensive fortress. In an eight-month period, Allied forces advanced only 70 miles.

The European war was thus decided not in the mountains of Italy, but on the Eastern Front. Beginning in the summer of 1943, the Russians steadily pushed back the Germans. In the spring of 1944 the Red Army reached the borders of Poland. In August Soviet troops turned south into Romania and Hungary. By February 1945 they were within 100 miles of Berlin (see Map 27.4).

The Soviet advance showed that the Red Army had by 1943 learned important lessons from being on the receiving end of blitzkrieg. It multiplied its number of radios and field telephones to avoid the organizational chaos that had greeted the invasion of 1941, and it concentrated its tanks into forces that combined motorized infantry regiments, tanks, antitank battalions, and mobile anti-aircraft artillery.

Such mobile armored forces depended on factories churning out steel, rubber, oil, and all the various machine parts needed by a modern army. Achievements in industrial production thus constituted a second key factor in the Soviet victory. While Lend-Lease supplied the Soviet Union with the basics needed to keep its army moving—aircraft and tanks, rails and locomotives, trucks and gasoline, and 15 million pairs of boots—the Soviets did not rely on imports alone. In 1943, Russia manufactured four times as many tanks as it imported, and Soviet production of tanks and antitank guns doubled Germany's.

THE FALL OF GERMANY   As the Red Army closed in on Germany from the east, the British and Americans pushed in from the west. On June 6, 1944, the Allies carried out the largest amphibious operation in history. Five seaborne divisions (two American, two British, and one Canadian) and three airborne divisions (two American and one British) crossed the English Channel and landed on the coast of northern France. The **D-Day** landings illustrated the Allied advantage in manpower and material. Against the Allies' eight divisions, the Germans had four and against the Allies' 5,000 fighter planes, the Germans could send up 169.

Yet the strength of the German resistance—particularly on Omaha Beach, where U.S. troops sustained more than 4,000 casualties—signaled that the road to Berlin would not be easy. The Allies faced the task of uprooting the Germans from territory where they had planted themselves five years earlier. For ten months, American, British, and other Allied troops fought a series of hard-won battles.

In the same time period on the Eastern Front, the Soviets launched Operation Bagration, a colossal offensive involving 2 million Soviet soldiers against 165 German divisions. (For comparison: the Germans had 30 divisions in the west to fight the D-Day invasion.) German losses in Operation Bagration reached 1.5 million. Hitler's dreams of a 1,000-year Reich crumbled. By March 1945, as the Russian army approached Berlin from the east, the British and American armies reached Germany's Rhine border and by mid-April stood within 50 miles of Berlin.

The Allies agreed to leave the conquest of Berlin to the Soviet Army. In this climactic battle of the European war, 320,000 Germans, many of them young boys, fought three million Soviet troops. Even so, it took eleven days before the city's commander surrendered on May 2. Two days earlier, Hitler took a cyanide

CHRONOLOGY: THE LONG MARCH TOWARD ALLIED VICTORY

1943

February	German surrender at Stalingrad; Red Army goes on the offensive; Allied round-the-clock bombing of Germany begins
May	German surrender in North Africa
July 10	Allied invasion of Italy begins

1944

January	Lifting of the siege of Leningrad
June 4	Allies liberate Rome
June 6	D-Day landings; Allied offensive in France begins
June 22	Operation Bagration begins
August 24–26	Allied liberation of Paris
September	Allies liberate the Netherlands, Belgium, and Luxembourg
October	U.S. invasion of Philippines

THE BATTLE FOR BERLIN

On April 20, 1945, Hitler celebrated his fifty-sixth birthday and made a rare visit out of his Berlin bunker to visit with the troops defending his city. As this photograph shows, these "soldiers" were just children. Ten days later, Hitler committed suicide.

capsule and then shot himself. On May 7, 1945, General Alfred Jodl (1890–1946) signed the unconditional surrender of German forces.

In the months after the war ended, Allied leaders struggled to bring Nazi leaders to trial to account for their crimes. What one participant called "the greatest trial in history" opened in November 1945. For eleven months, a four-man tribunal—American, British, French, and Soviet—sat in a courtroom in the German city of Nuremberg to judge 19 prominent German military, political, and industrial leaders. The **Nuremberg trials** introduced the category of "crimes against humanity" into international law. The participation of the Soviets, however, undercut the trials' effectiveness. The judges carefully avoided any mention of the Soviets' own war crimes, such as the mass murder of 22,000 Polish officers and other Polish prisoners in the forest of Katyn and nearby prisons in March 1940.

The Air War, the Atom Bomb, and the Fall of Japan

When Germany surrendered in the spring of 1945, the war in the Pacific still raged. After the Midway battle of 1942, the United States steadily, but slowly, agonizingly, pushed the Japanese back island by island. Japanese industry could not make up for the weapons and ammunition expended in these battles. In contrast, American factories were just gearing up. Whereas in 1940 American assembly lines produced only a little more than 2,000 aircraft, by 1944 they had manufactured over 96,000 bombers and fighters. American productivity per worker hour was five times that of Japan.

While U.S. troops moved closer to the Japanese mainland, British and Indian troops rebuffed a Japanese attempt to invade India and pushed the Japanese out of Burma. Australian forces, with American assistance, held the line at

New Guinea and forestalled a Japanese invasion of Australia. By February 1945, then, when American marines landed on the small island of Iwo Jima, just 380 miles from Japan's home islands, the Japanese war effort was in tatters and an Allied victory ensured.

Obtaining this final victory, however, was not easy. In the month of fighting on Iwo Jima, one-third of the American landing force died or suffered injury. The April conquest of Okinawa was even more hard-won. Outnumbered two to one, the Japanese endured staggering losses— 110,000 of the 120,000 soldiers on the island died. Yet they still inflicted serious damage on the attacking force, killing or wounding 50,000 Americans before the fight was over. Nobody counted how many Okinawans died in a battle they had done nothing to provoke, although estimates ranged as high as 160,000.

THE AIR WAR After the capture of Iwo Jima and Okinawa, American forces had the bases needed to bomb Japanese cities. This air war utilized tactics and technologies the Allies developed over the previous five years in the war against Germany. Their victory in the Battle of Britain in 1940 shielded the British from an invasion but not from bombing. By May 1941, German planes had bombed almost every major industrial city in Britain, killing 43,000 noncombatants. But from January 1941 on, British bombers retaliated in kind, and as the war wore on, developed new techniques of airborne destruction. In May 1942, for example, British planes destroyed Cologne with the world's first 1,000-bomber raid. One year later, the British bombing of Hamburg created the world's first **firestorm.** In this human-made catastrophe, incendiary bombs causefires, which then combine with winds to suck the oxygen out of the air and raise temperatures to combustible levels. As one survivor of the Hamburg bombing recalled, "The smallest children lay like fried eels on the pavement."[8] More than 500,000 German civilians died in Allied bombing attacks. Twenty percent of those were children.

To defeat Japan, the U.S. air command adopted the tactics that the British had perfected in the skies over Germany. On a single March evening, American bombs and the ensuing firestorm killed 85,000 residents of Tokyo. Over the next five months, American bombers hit 66 Japanese cities, burned 180 square miles, and killed approximately 330,000 Japanese. At the same time, a U.S. naval blockade cut Japan off from its supply lines.

THE MANHATTAN PROJECT While American bombers pulverized Japanese cities during the spring and summer of 1945, a multinational group of scientists fought a different battle in a secret military installation in New Mexico. The **Manhattan Project,** the code name for the joint British-American-Canadian effort to construct an atom bomb, was an extraordinary endeavor, the biggest and most expensive weapons development project up to that point in history. Yet even American vice president Harry Truman did not know about the project until after President Roosevelt died.

The Manhattan Project originated as part of the war against Nazi Germany. When the European war began, a number of scientists—many of them eastern and central European émigrés who had fled the Nazis and many of them Jewish—feared that Germany might develop an atom bomb. They pressured the British and American governments to build the Bomb before Hitler did. Britain took the initial lead by creating a committee to oversee atomic research in the spring of 1940. British research persuaded the Americans that an atom bomb could be constructed and in October 1941—two months *before* Japan bombed Pearl Harbor—Roosevelt and Churchill created an atomic partnership. For three years the Manhattan Project scientists labored to unlock the atom's power. They succeeded on July 16, 1945, when the world's first atomic explosion—the Trinity test— detonated over the desert of New Mexico. But by the time of the Trinity test, Nazi Germany had already fallen. The threat of a Nazi atom bomb disappeared.

The Pacific War, however, raged on. The decision to use atom bombs against Japan generated immediate controversy. Many of the scientists on the Manhattan Project opposed the decision as a step across a crucial moral dividing line, as did important American military officials such as General Dwight Eisenhower (1890–1969), supreme commander of the Allied forces in Europe, and General Douglas MacArthur (1880–1964), supreme Allied commander in the Pacific. Those in favor of the decision argued that if atom bombs were not used, the Allies would have to invade Japan. U.S. Army planners warned that if casualty rates were as high as those on Okinawa, the numbers of Americans killed in the first phase of the invasion could reach 50,000. Admiral William Leahy (Truman's Chief of Staff) and others, however, argued that if the Allies maintained the naval blockade and continued to attack Japanese cities with conventional bombs, Japan would surrender by the end of the year—without an invasion.

In 1946, the U.S. Strategic Bombing Survey, which studied the effects of U.S. conventional bombing on Japan, concluded that "in all probability prior to 1 November 1945, Japan would have surrendered... even if no invasion had been planned or contemplated" and no atom bomb had been dropped. But President Truman could not have known this in August 1945. From his perspective, continuing the war—with or without an invasion of Japan—meant continuing to put Allied soldiers in harm's way. The Bomb promised to end the war quickly and bring Allied servicemen home.

A LIGHT BRIGHTER THAN A THOUSAND SUNS At 8:15 A.M. on August 6, 1945, an American plane named the *Enola Gay* (after the pilot's mother) dropped an atom bomb above the city of Hiroshima (see Map 27.3). A light "brighter than a thousand suns" flashed in the sky. Temperatures at the site of the atomic explosion reached 5,400 degrees Fahrenheit. All those exposed within two miles of the center suffered primary thermal burns—their blood literally

boiled and their skin peeled off in strips. Scientists calculated that the atom bomb produced casualties 6,500 times more efficiently than an ordinary bomb. Of Hiroshima's wartime population of 400,000, 140,000 died by the end of 1945, with another 60,000 dying in the next five years.

The Japanese reacted to the atomic bombing of Hiroshima with incomprehension and

THE MUSHROOM CLOUD
The detonation of the atomic bomb over Hiroshima on August 6, 1945, produced what would become one of the most familiar images of the post–World War II age.

confusion. They did not know what had hit them. Within the high levels of the Japanese government, gradual realization of the atomic bomb's power strengthened the position of those officials who recognized that Japan must now give up. A hard-line faction of the military, however, wished to fight on.

Then, on August 8, the Soviet Union declared war on Japan. The next day American forces dropped an atom bomb on the city of Nagasaki and killed 70,000 outright (with another 70,000 dying over the next five years). On August 10, Emperor Hirohito (1901–1989) told his military leaders to surrender. Viewed in the West as an implacable warlord, Hirohito actually possessed fairly limited political power and had been pressing for peace since June. Negotiations between the Allies and the Japanese continued until August 15, when the war ended.

In Hiroshima and Nagasaki, however, another war was raging, this time against an unseen and at first unrecognized enemy—radiation. The lingering horror of radiation sickness, which many Americans and British first dismissed as Japanese propaganda, signaled that the atom bomb was not just a bigger weapon. In the months after the war's end, both policymakers and ordinary people came to recognize that the revolutionary new force

of atomic power had introduced the world to new possibilities—and new horrors.

THE WAR AGAINST THE JEWS

- How and why did the war against the Jews take place, and what were its consequences?

In the months following the war's end, the world also confronted a very different sort of horror, as people began to piece together the story of the **Holocaust** or the Shoah, Hitler's war against the Jews. For European Jews, World War II brought unprecedented terror and, for millions, death. In total, the Holocaust claimed the lives of approximately six million Jews. Children were especially vulnerable. Of the Jewish children living in 1939 in the regions already or soon to be under German control, only 11 percent survived. The Nazis' genocidal fury also targeted the Roma (Gypsies). Somewhere between 200,000 and 600,000 died in what the Roma call the *Porajmos*—the Devouring. Jews and Gypsies were the only groups singled out for genocide. But Hitler's drive to create his new Germany claimed three to five million other victims as well. Five thousand to

CHRONOLOGY: THE END OF WORLD WAR II

1945

March 16	American victory on Iwo Jima
April	Red Army encircle Berlin
April 11	American troops reach Elbe River in Germany
April 30	Hitler commits suicide
May 7	VE Day: Official German surrender
June 22	American victory at Okinawa
August 6	United States drops atomic bomb on Hiroshima
August 8	Soviet Union enters war against Japan
August 9	United States drops atomic bomb on Nagasaki
September 2	V-J Day: Formal Japanese surrender

15,000 homosexuals perished. So, too, did at least three million Poles.

From Emigration to Extermination: The Evolution of Genocide

The German occupation of Poland marked the first step toward the Nazi construction of a new racial order in Europe. As **Map 27.5** shows, Germany annexed much of western Poland and began a program of deporting Poles from and encouraging German migration to this area. The remainder of German-held Poland became the "General-Government" under German military rule. As specified in the secret clauses of the Nazi-Soviet Non-Aggression Pact, the Soviet Union occupied eastern Poland. In all three sections, Poles endured government by thugs, with mass arrests and executions now a part of "ordinary" life.

Hitler intended the Slavic populations, defined in his racist hierarchy as biologically inferior, to serve as a labor pool for their German superiors. To reduce the Polish people to slaves, the Nazis attempted to destroy Polish society and culture. They seized businesses and bank accounts, replaced Polish place names with German names, closed universities and high schools, and murdered Polish intellectuals and professionals. By the time the war ended in 1945, more than 20 percent of Poland's population had died.

The Nazi effort to "eliminate" the Jews from Poland occurred within this context of racial reordering. We saw in Chapter 26 that during the 1930s, Nazi policies focused on forcing German Jews to emigrate. The conquest of western Poland in September 1939, however, brought almost two million more Jews under German control. Pushing Jews to emigrate no longer seemed a workable "solution" to what the Nazis defined as the "Jewish Problem." But even more important, the fact of war itself made a turn toward murderous violence more acceptable.

The German policy toward the Jews in Poland initially focused on ghettoization. The Nazis expelled Jews from their homes and confined them in ghettos sealed off from their

MAP 27.5

Poland during World War II

In September 1939, the Germans and Soviets invaded and divided Poland between them. Each set up murderous regimes in the territories they occupied. The Germans split their territory in two. Western Poland became part of Greater Germany, with the Polish and Jewish residents displaced to make room for new German settlers. The rest of German-occupied Poland became the General Government, a vast forced labor zone. When the Germans invaded the Soviet Union in June 1941, the first territories they entered were, in fact, the Polish lands that the Soviets had occupied in 1939. The Nazis set up a vast network of concentration and labor camps across Europe, but built death camps only in Poland, closest to the heartland of European Jewry.

non-Jewish neighbors. Packed into over-crowded apartments, with inadequate food and sanitation, the ghetto populations lived in a nightmare of disease, starvation, and death. In the almost two-year period between the invasion of Poland and the invasion of the Soviet Union, an estimated 30,000 Jews died, killed outright by German soldiers or dead from starvation and disease as a result of deportation and ghettoization. Yet the suffering had only begun.

In the summer of 1941, the Nazis decided on what they termed the **Final Solution:** genocide. The German invasion of the Soviet Union provided the opportunity to implement this "Solution." Alongside the regular army marched special units of the SS called *Einsatzgruppen* ("strike forces"). With the army providing logistical support, these small motorized units (about 3,000 men in all) took on the task of murdering those Hitler designated as enemies of the Nazi Reich: Soviet communists and every Jew that they could find.

Most of these murders followed the same general pattern: SS soldiers—often aided by local populations—rounded up all of the Jewish men, women, and children in a town or village and marched them in batches to a field or woods. They ordered the first batch to dig a large ditch. They stripped their victims of their clothing, lined them up on the edge of the ditch, and shot them at point-blank range. They then lined up subsequent batches and shot them as well, so that by the end of a day's worth of killing, dead and dying bodies filled the ditch. A thin layer of soil thrown on top transformed the ditch into a mass grave. Estimates of the final death count of the Einsatzgruppen actions range from 1.5 to 2 million.

EINSATZGRUPPEN **ACTION**
A soldier shoots the last remaining Jew in a Ukrainian village.

Genocide by Assembly Line

On January 20, 1942, senior German officials met in a villa in Wannsee, outside Berlin, to finalize plans for killing every Jew in Europe. SS lieutenant colonel Adolf Eichmann (1906–1962) listed the number of Jews in every country. Even the Jewish populations in neutral countries such as Sweden and Ireland showed up on the target list. The Wannsee Conference marked the beginning of a more systematic approach to murdering European Jews.

This systematic approach built on the experience in mass murder gained by the Einsatzgruppen. By trial and error, these squads discovered the most efficient ways of identifying and rounding up Jews, shooting them, and burying the bodies. But the Einsatzgruppen actions also revealed the limits of conventional methods of killing. Shooting took time, used up valuable ammunition, and required many men. Moreover, even well-trained and indoctrinated soldiers cracked under the strain of shooting unarmed women and children at close range. The Nazis needed a technological approach, one that would provide a comfortable distance between the killers and the killed. The death camp filled this need. (See *Justice in History* in this chapter.)

THE DEATH CAMPS

Death camps were specialized concentration camps. From 1933 on, Hitler's government sentenced communists, Jehovah's Witnesses, the Roma, and anyone else defined as an enemy of the regime to forced labor in concentration camps. After the war began, the camp system expanded dramatically throughout German-controlled Europe. Concentration camps became an essential part of the Nazi war economy. Important German businesses set up factories inside or right next to camps, to have ready access to their supplies of slave labor. Concentration camp inmates died in huge numbers from brutal physical labor, torture, and diseases linked to malnutrition, inadequate shelter, and poor sanitation. Yet death in these camps was a byproduct rather than central aim. In contrast, death camps had only one purpose: murder, primarily the murder of Jews.

In early 1942 trains conveying Jews to death camps began to rumble across Europe. Jewish ghettos emptied as individuals selected for extermination received orders to gather at the railway station for deportation to "work camps" farther east. Soldiers packed them into cattle cars, more than 100 people per car, all standing up for the entire journey. Deprived of food and water, with hardly any air, often for several days, many died en route.

The survivors stumbled off the trains into a vast machine of death. At some camps, SS guards culled stronger Jews from each transport to work as slave laborers before being killed. Most, however, walked straight from the transport trains into a reception room. Forced to undress, they were then herded into a fake communal shower—actually a gas chamber. After the poison had done its work, Jewish slaves emptied the chamber and burned the bodies in crematoria, modeled after industrial bake ovens. The death camps thus used the techniques and technologies of industrial production for human destruction. Along a murderous assembly line the human raw material moved from arrival through selection to the undressing rooms to the gas chamber to the crematoria.

THE EXAMPLE OF AUSCHWITZ-BIRKENAU

Auschwitz-Birkenau was the largest component in the Nazis' death machine. Auschwitz originated in 1940 as a concentration camp for Polish, then Soviet, prisoners of war. It became an industrial complex covering several square miles, with barracks for 70,000 prisoners who slaved in its coal mines, synthetic rubber and oil factories, and several smaller military industries. Its inmate population soon included not only Poles and Russians, but also a cross section of peoples from across Europe. A special section of the camp was reserved for the Roma. Given just enough food for survival (the official diet permitted a prisoner to remain alive for an average of three months), Auschwitz's inmates endured daily hard labor and the constant, indiscriminate brutality of their captors.

With the "Final Solution" underway, Auschwitz's cruel empire expanded to encompass a death camp: Birkenau. In the summer of 1942, trainloads of Jews began arriving in Birkenau. Jews deemed strong enough (never more than 20 percent of a typical transport) were selected for hard labor in the main camp. The rest perished in Birkenau's gas chambers. The writer Elie Wiesel, deported to Auschwitz with his family when he was 15, recalled the selection process:

> 'Men to the left! Women to the right!' Eight words spoken quietly, indifferently, without emotion. Eight short, simple words. Yet that was the moment when I parted from my mother.[9]

Wiesel's mother and younger sister, and hundreds of thousands of others, died in the gas chamber. Their bodies were burnt in one of five crematoria. At least one million people were gassed at Auschwitz, most of them Jews.

The Allies' Response

Allied leaders had access to accurate information about the Holocaust from very early on. In July 1939, before the war had begun, Polish

JUSTICE IN HISTORY

The Trial of Adolf Eichmann

On May 23, 1960, David Ben-Gurion (1886–1973), the prime minister of Israel, made a spectacular announcement: Israeli secret service agents had kidnapped Adolf Eichmann, a wanted Nazi war criminal, and smuggled him into Israel to await trial. During World War II Eichmann, the head of the Gestapo's Jewish Affairs unit, implemented Nazi policies on Jewish emigration and deportation. His office sorted through the complicated bureaucratic procedures to ensure that the trains laden with Jews kept to their schedules and delivered their human cargo to the gas chambers on time. For many Jews, Eichmann represented German power and personified Nazi evil. He had disappeared in the chaotic final days of World War II and eventually made his way to Argentina, where, as "Ricardo Klement," he lived a quiet, respectable life with his wife and children—until 1960.

From the moment of Ben-Gurion's sensational announcement, the Eichmann case occupied the attention of the world. Six hundred foreign correspondents attended the trial, which was one of the first to be filmed by television cameras. More than 1,500 documents were submitted and 120 witnesses testified in the 114 sessions held between April 11 and August 14, 1961. Three judges, each of whom had been born in Germany and had migrated to Palestine in 1933, heard the evidence. On December 15, they sentenced Eichmann to death. He died by hanging on May 31, 1962, the first execution in Israel, which had abolished capital punishment for all crimes except genocide.

The Eichmann trial told the story of Jewish suffering during World War II to the widest possible audience. Both Ben-Gurion and the chief prosecutor, Gideon Hausner, stated publicly that the trial aimed to construct "a living record of a gigantic human and national disaster" and so educate both young Israelis and the entire world in the causes and consequences of the Holocaust.[10] As Hausner explained in his emotional opening statement, he saw himself as the spokesman for "six million accusers...[whose] ashes were piled up in the hills of Auschwitz and in the fields of Treblinka, or washed away by the rivers of Poland."[11] Hausner (who, like many Israelis, had lost most of his relatives in the Nazi death camps) called more than 100 witnesses, many of them death camp survivors. Their testimony, published or broadcast throughout the world, painted a detailed picture of genocide.

By the time the prosecution rested its case, no one could doubt that Eichmann had played an

I EICHMANN ON TRIAL

essential role in the murder of millions. Yet the Eichmann trial attracted an enormous amount of criticism and continues to arouse great controversy. Critics charged that to achieve moral justice for Holocaust victims and survivors, the Israeli court committed a legal injustice against Eichmann. The trial, which a violation of international law (Eichmann's kidnapping) made possible, was filled with irregularities, including the introduction of testimony that did not pertain to the specific crimes charged. Critics also disputed Israel's legal right to try Eichmann: The crimes had not occurred in Israeli territory, nor were Eichmann's victims Israeli citizens. (The state of Israel did not exist until 1948.)

In reply to these critics, Hausner and other supporters of the prosecution insisted that justice demanded that Eichmann be brought to trial and that the Israeli government had pursued the only course of action open to it. In the Eichmann trial, then, we confront a case in which what was legal on the one hand and what was just on the other appeared very much at odds. There is no doubt that Eichmann was guilty of horrendous crimes. There is also no doubt that the Israeli government stepped beyond established legal boundaries in trying and condemning Eichmann.

The Eichmann trial also raised important questions about the nature of the Holocaust. Was it a crime perpetrated by a few evil men, or did the evil penetrate deep into German, and European, society? The prosecution's case sought to depict Eichmann as a monster, a demonic mastermind responsible for the deaths of millions of Jews. As Hausner contended, "it was [Eichmann's] word that put gas chambers into action; he lifted the telephone, and railway trains left for the extermination centers; his signature it was that sealed the doom of tens of thousands."[12] Such a depiction provided a comforting explanation for the Holocaust—monstrous devils rather than ordinary human beings perpetrated this colossal crime.

Yet many trial observers and subsequent historians argued that such a depiction was wrong. This argument structured the most well-known critique of the prosecution—Hannah Arendt's *Eichmann in Jerusalem: A Report on the Banality of Evil,* published in 1963. Arendt (1906–1975), a Jewish philosopher who had fled Nazi Europe in 1941, argued that the trial showed Eichmann to be a plodding bureaucrat obsessed with trivial details—an ordinary man, capable of extraordinary evil.

Should ordinary men be held responsible for following evil orders? Defense attorney Robert Servatius insisted that the Holocaust was an "act of state," a crime carried out by a political regime, for which no civil servant could bear the blame. Eichmann only followed orders. Servatius concluded his arguments by asking Eichmann how he viewed "this question of guilt." Eichmann replied,

> Where there is no responsibility, there can be no guilt....The questions of responsibility and conscience are for the leadership of the state....I condemn and regret the act of extermination of the Jews which the leadership of the German state ordered. But I myself could not jump over my own shadow. I was a tool in the hands of superior powers and authorities.[13]

Eichmann's judges disagreed. In declaring Eichmann guilty of genocide, they argued,

> We reject absolutely the accused's version that he was nothing more than a "small cog" in the extermination machine....He was not a puppet in the hands of others. His place was among those who pulled the strings.[14]

For Discussion

1. What if Eichmann really was only "a tool in the hands of superior powers and authorities"? Would he still have been responsible for his actions?

2. In the Eichmann case, the letter of the law and justice appeared at odds. In what situations—if any—must we break the law

to ensure that justice prevails? Who has the authority to make such a judgment?

Taking It Further
Laqueur, Walter. "Hannah Arendt in Jerusalem: The Controversy Revisited," in Lyman H. Legters, ed., *Western Society After the*

Holocaust. 1983. Examines the impact of Arendt's critique of the trial.
The Trial of Adolf Eichmann: Record of Proceedings in the District Court of Jerusalem. Vols. 1–9. 1993–1995. The basic primary source.

Intelligence provided the British government with a copy of "Enigma," the German coding machine, and thus throughout the war British code breakers translated German military radio transmissions. In the summer of 1941, as the German army and the Einsatzgruppen moved into the Soviet Union, British officials intercepted messages such as this one from August 27: "Regiment South shot 914 Jews; the special action staff with police battalion 320 shot 4,200 Jews." By June 1942, Allied leaders knew that death camps existed.

Such information quickly became accessible to ordinary people. British and American newspaper readers and radio listeners received numerous reports about Jewish massacres. After 1942, these reports told about the death camps. But this information had to compete with other war news and many of these articles were written in a skeptical tone. Reporters, editors, and readers had a difficult time believing that even the Nazis could commit such atrocities, although in December 1942 the British and American governments issued an inter-Allied declaration that described and condemned Hitler's efforts to murder European Jews.

Despite this public acknowledgment, the Allies did not act directly to stop the killings. Should the Allies then be considered bystanders in the crime of the Holocaust? Some historians contend that anti-Semitism in both British and American societies prevented their leaders from exploring ways to stop the Holocaust (such as sending in commando units, bombing the rail lines into the death camps, or even bombing the camps

themselves). Other historians argue that these alternatives were not militarily feasible and that the Allies did the only thing they could do for Europe's Jews: Win the war as quickly as possible.

THE HOME FRONT: THE OTHER WARS

■ What did total war mean on the home front?

As the Holocaust made clear, for many Europeans during World War II the home front was not a place of safety, but a place where other wars were fought. The spreading resistance against the Nazi regime, as well as bombing raids and forced labor obligations, obliterated the distinction between combatant and noncombatant, blurred gender roles, and provoked calls for radical social change.

The Limits of Resistance
Throughout the war men and women in occupied Europe participated in the **Resistance,** the struggle against Nazi rule. Resistance movements hid Jews and others on the run, disrupted transportation systems, assassinated Nazi officials, and relayed secret information to the Allies. In Poland, the Resistance developed into a secret "state within a state" that included an underground parliament, school system, printing

press, and an army of 350,000 men and women. In areas where the terrain offered shelter for guerillas (such as parts of the Soviet Union and the mountainous regions of Yugoslavia Italy, and southern France), the Resistance formed partisan groups that attacked German army units.

The story of the Resistance is one of great heroism, yet only a minority of Europeans joined. The Germans' military strength and ruthlessness made resistance seem futile. In one of the best-known cases, for example, Jews in the Warsaw ghetto rose up in the spring of 1943 and—armed with only one or two submachine guns and a scattering of pistols, rifles, hand grenades, and gasoline bombs—held off the Germans for more than a month. But in the end, the Germans leveled the ghetto and deported its survivors to death camps.

The German policy of exacting collective retribution also undercut mass support for anti-German efforts. In 1942, for example, British intelligence forces parachuted Czech agents into German-held Czechoslovakia. The agents assassinated the chief SS official in the region, Reinhard Heydrich (1904–1942), but they were immediately betrayed. In retaliation, the Germans massacred the entire population of the village of Lidice. Similarly, an assassination attempt against Hitler led to the executions of 5,000 Germans in 1944.

In Germany and in countries allied to rather than conquered by the Germans, potential resisters had to convince themselves that patriotism demanded working against their own government. In France until 1943, resistance meant opposing the lawfully instituted collaborationist Vichy government of Marshal Pétain. In the early years of the war, then, many French men and women viewed Resistance fighters as traitors, not heroes. By 1943, however, an alternative focus of national loyalty had emerged: the Free French headed by General Charles De Gaulle (1890–1970). De Gaulle had gone into exile rather than accept the armistice with Nazi Germany. After the Anglo-American landings in North Africa in November 1942, De Gaulle claimed Algeria as a power base, declared himself the head of a Free French provisional government, and called on all loyal French men and women to resist Nazi rule and Vichy collaboration.

A genuine spirit of unity characterized the Resistance struggle in many areas, with socialists, communists, and Catholics working together not only to defeat the Nazis, but also to create the foundations of a better society. In France, for example, the Resistance Charter of 1944 demanded the construction of a "more just social order" through the nationalization of key industries, the establishment of a comprehensive social security system, and the recognition of the rights of workers to participate in management.

In other areas, however, divisions within the Resistance limited its impact. In the German-occupied regions of the Soviet Union, Ukrainian, Lithuanian, and other nationalist guerilla groups fought not only the German army but also Soviet partisans. In Greece, the communist-dominated National Liberation Front battled a rival Resistance group that fought for the return of the Greek monarchy. There was, then, no single "Resistance," and fighting among Resistance groups often shaded into civil war.

Civil War in Yugoslavia

The fiercest such struggle occurred in Yugoslavia, which experienced a bloodletting unmatched anywhere in Europe except in Poland and the Soviet Union. The violence peaked in the fascist state of Croatia, formed after Germany invaded Yugoslavia in 1941 and divided it into smaller states. Created by and allied to the Nazis, the new state of Croatia terrorized and murdered Jews, Muslims, and Serbs. Serbian guerilla bands, called *Chetniks,* supported the exiled Yugoslav monarchy and fought the Croatian fascists and the Nazis. But as ardent Serbian nationalists, the Chetniks also slaughtered Muslims and Jews because they were not Serbs.

In the midst of this bloody free-for-all, a second Resistance group emerged: the communist Partisans. Led by Josip Broz (1892–1980), alias "Tito," the Partisans saw the war as a chance for communist revolution and promised equality for all ethnic groups in a reunited Yugoslavia. Tito's Partisans focused on fighting Germans—and succeeded in diverting ten German divisions from the Eastern Front. But they, too, fought fellow Yugoslavs, as both fascist Croats and royalist Chetniks opposed Tito's aim of a state based on communist ideology rather than ethnic identity.

Tito's Partisans won this civil war. In 1944 they fought alongside the Soviet army and liberated Yugoslavia from German control. With 90 percent of the vote in the first postwar election, Tito assumed control of communist Yugoslavia, a position he held for the next 35 years. Beneath the uniform surface created by communist ideology, however, the jagged edges of ethnic division in Yugoslavia remained sharp.

Under Occupation

In occupied Europe, Nazi racial ideals determined ordinary people's reality. The Nazis drew a sharp line between western Europeans—the Dutch, Norwegian, Danes, and Flemish, all considered of racially superior "Germanic stock"—and the Slavs of eastern Europe. The Nazis believed that "Germanic" peoples could be taught to become good Nazis and therefore spared them the extreme violence that characterized German occupation in the east.

The German treatment of prisoners of war (POWs) illustrates the gap between the western and eastern European experience of World War II. By the end of 1941, 2.5 million Soviet soldiers had been captured. Within a few months, two million of these had died from starvation or the epidemic diseases nurtured by camp conditions. In contrast, of more than one million French soldiers captured by the Germans in 1940, 19 out of 20 returned home at the end of the war.

Yet German occupation in the west, although less brutal than in the east, remained harsh. Anyone who spoke out against the Nazis faced imprisonment or death. The Nazis forced occupied countries to pay exorbitant sums to cover the costs of their own occupation and to sell manufactured products and raw materials to Germany at artifi-

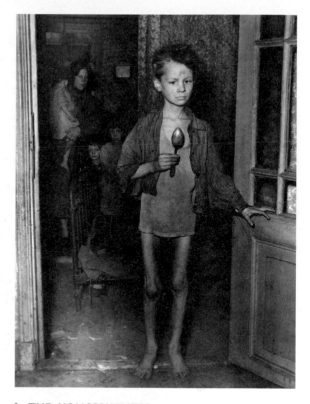

THE *HONGERWINTER*

By the fall of 1944, the southern provinces of the Netherlands were liberated, but the north remained under German occupation. After Dutch railway employees refused to transport any more German troops, the Germans retaliated by blocking all food shipments to the north. Twenty thousand Dutch civilians died in the resulting "Hunger Winter."

Source: Marius Meijboom/Nederlands Fotomuseum

cially low prices. The occupation grew even more harsh after 1943 as German military losses piled up, stocks of food and other supplies dwindled, and German demands for civilian labor increased.

For millions of European men and women, the war meant forced labor in Germany. With the need to free up men for the front lines, the Nazis faced labor shortages in almost every economic sector. Placing the economy on an all-out war footing would have meant imposing unpopular measures such as conscripting women for industrial labor, lengthening working hours, and prohibiting holidays. The Nazis chose instead to "recruit" labor from conquered territories. By August 1944, German farmers and factory owners employed over 5.7 million foreign civilian laborers (one-third of whom were women) and almost two million POWs. These foreign workers accounted for more than half the labor in German agriculture and munitions plants and one-third of the labor force in key war industries such as mining, chemicals, and metals.

Foreign labor not only fueled the German war machine, it also maintained German civilian morale. Foreign labor cushioned Germans on the home front from the impact of total war and reassured them that they belonged to a superior race. Nazi regulations stipulated that German workers regard themselves as the masters of the foreigners working alongside them. Many German factory owners were relieved to find they now employed laborers with few political rights. The director of one aircraft manufacturing firm explained, "The great advantage of employing foreigners…is that we only have to give orders. There is no refusal, no need to negotiate."[15]

The Women's War

Throughout Europe women tended to bear the brunt of home front deprivation, as they were usually the ones who had to get a meal on the table and clothe their children in the face of severe rationing. Basic household goods such as frying pans, toothbrushes, bicycle tires, baby bottles, and batteries almost disappeared. Food was in short supply and clothing had to be recycled. Women became experts at "make do and mend," as British government pamphlets advised.

British women were fully mobilized. They did not serve in combat, but they were drafted for service in civilian defense, war-related industry, or the armed forces. Women accounted for 25 percent of the civilians who worked in Britain's Air Raid Protection services as wardens, rescuers, and telephone operators. The numbers of women employed in male-dominated industries such as metals and chemicals rose dramatically.

Only the Soviet Union mobilized women more fully than Britain. Soviet women constituted 80 percent of the agricultural and 50 percent of the industrial labor force. All Soviet adult men and women under age 45 who were not engaged in essential war work were required to work eleven hours a day constructing defenses. Soviet women also served in combat. By 1944, 246,000 women were in front-line units. For all Soviet citizens, male and female, life on the home front meant endless labor, inadequate food supplies, and constant surveillance under martial law.

Until 1943, the German home front contrasted sharply with that of Britain and the Soviet Union. The Nazi policy toward female employment rested on Hitler's conviction that Germany had lost World War I in part because of the collapse of morale on the home front. In the first years of the war, then, the Nazi government did not dramatically cut consumption levels. Moreover, Hitler believed that the future of the "German race" depended on middle-class women being protected from the strains of paid labor so that they could bear healthy Aryan babies. The use of foreign labor took the place of the full-scale mobilization of women, until military necessity undercut Nazi gender ideology. The fall of Stalingrad marked the turning point for German women. With losses on the Eastern Front averaging 150,000 men per month, the German army needed more men. Hitler's deputy Joseph Goebbels (1897–1945) ordered a total mobilization of the home front and the final, desperate year of the war saw a concentrated use of female labor in Nazi Germany.

Of all the combatant states, the United States stood out as unique with regard to the home front. More than 70 percent of American women remained outside the paid workforce. Rationing was comparatively minimal and consumption levels high. In fact, for many families, the war years brought prosperity after years of economic depression. American cities were never bombed, and thus the United States was able to maintain a clear distinction between soldier and civilian, man and woman—a distinction that was blurred in other combatant nations.

What Are We Fighting For?

To mobilize their populations for total war, governments had to convince their citizens to support the war effort. Maintaining morale and motivating civilians and soldiers to endure deprivation and danger demanded that leaders supply a persuasive answer to the question: What are we fighting for?

MYTH AND MORALE All nations—democratic or authoritarian—rely on *myths,* on stories of national origins and identity, to unify disparate individuals, classes, and groups. In times of total war, such myths become crucial. During World War II, state agencies responsible for propaganda institutionalized the process of mythmaking. In Britain, the newly formed Ministry of Information (MOI) took on the task of propping up civilian morale. Staffed by upper-class men, the MOI's efforts often betrayed its class composition: Many of its posters and leaflets adopted a hectoring tone, subjecting ordinary citizens to a barrage of do's and don'ts. Far more effective were the speeches of Prime Minister Winston Churchill, whose romantic vision of Britain as a still-great power destined to triumph was exactly the myth that the beleaguered British needed.

In all the combatant nations, governments enlisted artists, entertainers, and the technologies of the mass media for mythmaking and morale-building. In Britain, for example, Henry Moore's (1898–1986) drawings of ordinary people in air raid shelters (completed under an official commission) evoked the survival of civilized values in the midst of unspeakable degradation. In Germany, strict censorship before the war had already subordinated the arts and entertainment industries to the demands of the Nazi state. The war heightened this control as censorship tightened even further, paper shortages limited the production of books and periodicals, and the threat of being drafted for the Eastern Front kept artists in line.

During the war, film came into its own as an artistic form capable of creating important myths of national unity. Laurence Olivier's version of Shakespeare's *Henry V* (1944) comforted British moviegoers with its classic story of a stirring English military victory against huge odds. In Italy, a group of filmmakers known as the Neo-Realists created a set of films that dramatized the Resistance spirit of national unity. Shot on location, with amateur actors and realistic sets, movies such as Roberto Rossellini's *Open City* (1945) depicted lower-class life with honesty and respect and called for the creation of a better society from the rubble of the old.

PLANNING FOR RECONSTRUCTION Rossellini's call for the creation of a new society was echoed throughout Europe during the war. A consensus emerged on the need for **social democracy,** a society in which the state intervenes in economic

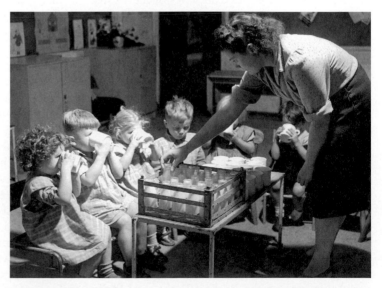

WARTIME GAINS

British children began enjoying free school milk during the war, as part of the state's efforts both to ensure equitable distribution of resources and to shore up the health of the population. Popular sentiment demanded that such communal efforts be continued in peacetime as well.

life to ensure both public welfare and social justice. As early as December 1942, a British government committee set out a radical plan for postwar society. In rather unusual language for an official document, the committee's report identified "five giants on the road to reconstruction": Want, Disease, Ignorance, Squalor, and Idleness. To slay these giants, the committee recommended that the state assume responsibility for ensuring full employment and a minimum standard of living for all through the provision of family allowances, social welfare programs, and a national health service. The Beveridge Report (named after the committee's chairman) became a best-seller in Britain and the basis for a number of postwar European social welfare plans.

Three factors explain this radical reorientation of European politics. First, and most important, as the war dragged on and the death tolls mounted, European men and women demanded that their suffering be worthwhile. They wanted to know that they were fighting not to rebuild the depressed and divided societies of the 1930s, but to construct a new Europe. Second, the war (and the ongoing revelations of Nazi atrocities) discredited the politics of the far right. This sort of politics, whether fascist, Nazi, or conservative-authoritarian, disappeared from legitimate political discussion. But in Europe (although less so in the United States) the liberal ideal of the free and self-interested individual competing in an unregulated economy also lay in ruins, the victim of the prewar Great Depression. The new Europe, then, had to be built along different lines.

Finally, both the Resistance and the experience of wartime mobilization taught that the power of the state could be used to improve the well-being of its citizens without trampling on the rights of the individual. In the 1930s, Hitler and Mussolini on the Radical Right, and Stalin on the Radical Left, had persuaded many that the individual was not important, that only the state mattered. But the Resistance reasserted the essential significance of the individual and the choices he or she makes. At the same time, the combatant nations' success in mobilizing their economies for total war indicated the positive possibilities of state action. If governments could regulate economies to fight wars, why could they not regulate economies for peacetime prosperity and greater social justice? In the postwar era, then democracy reclaimed the activist state from fascism and Nazism on the one hand and Stalinism on the other.

CONCLUSION

The New West: After Auschwitz and the Atom Bomb

The wartime encounter with the Nazi vision of the West as a race-based authoritarian order was crucial. From it emerged a sharpened commitment within the West to the processes and values of democracy. But to present the Second World War as a conflict between democracy and Nazism is to oversimplify. To defeat Nazi Germany, the democracies of Britain and the United States allied with Stalin's Soviet Union, a dictatorial regime that matched Hitler's Germany in its contempt for democratic values and human rights and that surpassed it in state-sanctioned mass murder.

The Soviet Union emerged from the war as the dominant power in eastern Europe. As we will see in the next chapter, the presence of the Soviet Army obliterated any chance to establish democratic governments in this region. The tensions inherent in the Anglo-American alliance with the Soviets led directly to the Cold War, the ideological and political conflict that dominated the post-World War II world and that again forced a redefinition of the West. From 1949 until 1989, drawing the West on any map was easy: One shaded in the United States and the countries allied to it—and against the Soviet Union. At the same time, however, a new division emerged. World War II marked the beginning of the end of European imperial control over the non-European world. The postwar era would thus see growing tensions between "North" and

"South"—between the industrially developed nations and the underdeveloped regions seeking to shrug off their colonial past.

Much of the impetus for imperial control over non-European regions had come from the conviction of Western supremacy. During World War II, however, Japanese victories had exposed the illusion of Western military invincibility. And after the war, the gradual realization of the full horror of the Holocaust demolished any lingering claim to Western cultural superiority. What sort of superior position could be claimed by a culture in which educated, supposedly civilized men sent children into gas chambers disguised as showers? The atomic bombings of Hiroshima and Nagasaki added more questions to the ongoing debate about the meaning of the West. With the best of intentions, some of the greatest minds in the Western world had produced weapons designed to kill and maim tens of thousands of civilians within seconds. Had Western technology outdistanced Western ethics? And what about the implications of such technologies in a democratic society? For example, would the need to control such weapons lead to measures that eroded individual freedom?

Thus, the assembly-line techniques of mass murder developed by the Nazis and, in very different ways, the sheer efficiency of the atom bomb in obliterating urban populations forced both individuals and their political leaders to confront the destructive potential of Western industrialism. For centuries, the use of the methods of scientific inquiry to uncover truth and achieve both material and moral progress had supported Westerners' self-identification and their sense of cultural superiority. But World War II demonstrated that the best of science could produce the worst of weapons, that technology

and technique could combine in the death factory. The task of accepting this knowledge, and facing up to its implications, helped shape Western culture after 1945.

KEY TERMS

Rome-Berlin Axis
Munich Agreement
German-Soviet Non-Aggression Pact
appeasement
blitzkrieg
Vichy regime, Vichy France

Third Reich
Lend-Lease Act
Nuremberg trials
firestorm
Holocaust
Final Solution
the Resistance
social democracy

CHAPTER QUESTIONS

1. What were the expectations concerning war in the 1920s and 1930s, and how did these hopes and fears lead to armed conflict in both Europe and Asia? (page 857)
2. How did Nazi Germany conquer the continent of Europe by 1941? (page 861)
3. Why did the Allies win in 1945? (page 869)
4. How and why did the war against the Jews take place, and what were its consequences? (page 877)
5. What did total war mean on the home front? (page 883)

TAKING IT FURTHER

1. Why do historians assert that World War II in Europe was won on the Eastern Front?
2. How did the home fronts of World War I differ from those in World War II? What explains the similarities? The differences?

✔•─[Practice on MyHistoryLab

28

Redefining the West After World War II

■ A Dubious Peace, 1945–1949 ■ The West and the World:
Decolonization and the Cold War ■ The Soviet Union and Eastern Europe
in the 1950s and 1960s ■ The West: Consensus, Consumption, and Culture

ON AN APPARENTLY ORDINARY DAY IN AUGUST 1961, WESTERN European television viewers witnessed an extraordinary sight. While the news cameras rolled, policemen from East Berlin—the section of Berlin controlled by East Germany's communist government—played tug-of-war with firemen from West Berlin, the half of the city that belonged to the democratic state of West Germany. Between them, however, was not the usual length of rope, but rather a middle-aged woman. As East Berlin policemen tried to pull this woman back into an apartment building, West Berlin firemen struggled to pull her out.

The construction of the Berlin Wall set this bizarre contest in motion. During the 1950s a growing number of East Germans sought to flee communist rule by crossing into (free) West Berlin. Finally in 1961, the East German and Soviet authorities took action. In the early morning hours of Sunday, August 13, they erected a barbed-wire fence along Berlin's east-west dividing line and blocked anyone from crossing this fence into West Berlin. In some cases, however, the dividing line ran right through apartment buildings and so, for the next few weeks, these apartments provided literal "windows to the west." West Berlin firemen waited with blankets ready to catch anyone willing to jump out of a window—and out of communist eastern Europe. These windows closed quickly. The communist authorities first bricked up windows facing West Berlin. Later they leveled entire apartment buildings. The barbed-wire fence became a concrete wall buttressed by gun towers, lit by searchlights, and patrolled by armed guards with "shoot to kill" orders.

The unidentified woman dangling out of the window, literally caught between West and East, symbolizes Europe during the 1950s and 1960s. In these decades, the Cold War between the United States and the Soviet Union helped shape European politics, culture, and society. As the woman's desperation to reach the West indicates, American influence in western Europe did not parallel Soviet domination of eastern Europe. Nevertheless, many Europeans in the West as well as the East felt that they no longer fully controlled their own societies.

The Cold War was in part an encounter of two clashing ideologies, as much a battle of ideas and values as weapons and warriors. Both sides laid claim to universal cultures—to have achieved a way of life that would benefit *all* human societies. This ideological encounter forced a redefinition of "the West." Previous chapters have described the way in which this cultural construct shifted over time. By the late nineteenth century, Christianity, although still important, played a less central role in defining "the West" than did such factors as industrial technology, the illusion of white racial superiority, and faith in

TUG-OF-WAR AT THE BERLIN WALL

Caught by the television cameras, this woman sought to escape through her window into West Berlin. She succeeded.

capitalist economics and liberal political values. The Cold War added fears of the Soviet Union and communist ideology to the mix. These fears at times eroded the Western commitment to democracy, particularly within the developing world.

Significantly, the Cold War turned "hot" not in Europe, but in places such as Korea, Cuba, and Vietnam. This era witnessed a widening economic gap between "North" and "South"—between the industrialized nations, largely located in the Northern Hemisphere, and economically underdeveloped regions, many south of the equator, many now shrugging off colonial rule. As the Cold War moved

beyond Europe's borders to the developing regions two different contests—North versus South and West versus East—intertwined. How, then, did these contests shape the ever-evolving idea of the West?

A DUBIOUS PEACE, 1945–1949

■ Why and how did the world step from World War II to the Cold War?

World War II ended in the spring and summer of 1945, but the killing did not. Postwar purges, deportations, and civil wars ensured that the death totals continued to mount. As the "hot" war waned, the Cold War began between the Soviet Union and the countries it controlled on the one hand and the United States and its Western allies on the other.

Devastation, Death, and Continuing War

Germany's surrender in May 1945 did not bring immediate peace to Europe. Many regions in southern and eastern Europe experienced civil war while in other areas victors turned with vengeful fury against the vanquished. Those left alive in post-World War II Europe faced the overwhelming task of reconstruction. Intensive bombing rendered most highways, rail tracks, and waterways unusable. With laborers, seed, fertilizer, and basic equipment all in short supply, agricultural production in 1945 stood below 50 percent of prewar levels. Less visible, but just as devastating, was the destruction of the financial system. Few European currencies were worth much. In defeated Germany, cigarettes replaced marks as the unit of exchange.

Map 28.1 indicates one of the most serious problems facing postwar Europe: that of the refugees or displaced persons (DPs). The DP problem stemmed, first, from the war itself, with millions made homeless by invasions and mass bombing. Second, Hitler's attempts at racial reordering also caused DP numbers to skyrocket, as concentration camp survivors now stumbled through the wreckage of war-torn Europe. A third factor in the worsening DP problem was the peace settlement itself. Acquiescing to the Soviet annexation of eastern Poland, the Allies shifted the borders of Poland 200 miles to the west, and in the process pushed millions of Poles and Germans out of their homes. Germans were also expelled from Czechoslovakia, Romania, Yugoslavia, and Hungary. Often forced on the road with no food or supplies, approximately two million Germans died in this postscript to World War II.

From Hot to Cold War

The conflict that posed the greatest threat to the dubious peace after 1945 was the **Cold War,** the struggle for global supremacy between the United States and the Soviet Union. Within just a few years of the defeat of Germany and Japan, the allies became enemies, and what Winston Churchill called the **"Iron Curtain"** dropped between eastern and western Europe.

THE DELICATE FABRIC OF THE WARTIME ALLIANCE   A common wartime enemy rather than shared postwar aims wove together the alliance of Britain, the Soviet Union, and the United States. To ensure Soviet (and his own) security and power, Joseph Stalin demanded that Soviet boundaries extend westward and that the Soviet "sphere of influence" include the states along the Soviet Union's western borders. He noted bluntly, "The more you've got, the safer you are."[1] Stalin's demands for "friendly" and therefore communist-dominated governments in eastern Europe conflicted with American and British aims. The American president, Franklin D. Roosevelt, saw the establishment of democracies throughout Europe—including along the Soviet borders—as essential to international security and American prosperity. One American official explained to Congress, "If you create good governments in foreign countries, you will have better markets for ourselves."[2] The third Allied leader, Winston Churchill, the British prime minister, regarded the extension of Soviet influence westward as a threat to the European balance of power. He saw Stalin's plans for Poland as a particular problem: Britain had gone to war in September 1939 because of the Nazi invasion of Poland and over 200,000 Polish soldiers were fighting for the Allies.

Poland was very much on the agenda in November 1943 when the **Big Three**—Stalin, Churchill, and Roosevelt—met together for the first time in the Tehran Conference. Stalin insisted on the restoration of the *1940* Polish-Soviet border—the boundary line drawn by the secret clauses of the German–Soviet Non-Aggression

MAP 28.1

After World War II: Shifting Boundaries, Shifting Populations

World War II and its aftermath resulted in the movements of millions. Political ambitions and military concerns fused with racial and ethnic hatreds and the emerging Cold War to create new state boundaries that resulted in the exchange of entire populations. The Allies once again divided Germany and Austria, returned the Sudetenland to Czechoslovakia, divided East Prussia between the Soviet Union and Poland, and extended the Polish borders westward to embrace Silesia and Pomerania. The human suffering involved in such large-scale transformation is almost incomprehensible. One boundary line, shifted one-quarter inch on a map, meant hundreds of thousands of men, women, and children were forced out of their homes and into strange new cities or villages, in the midst of postwar economic breakdown and social upheaval.

Pact. Churchill and Roosevelt recognized that if they agreed, they would be affirming the brutal Soviet invasion of eastern Poland in 1939. Yet they also knew that Soviet soldiers were dying by the millions on the Eastern Front and they were eager to retain Stalin's full commitment to the alliance. At Tehran, then, they agreed—secretly—that Poland's postwar borders would shift hundreds of miles westward.[3]

By February 1945, when the Big Three met in the Crimean seaside town of Yalta, Stalin stood in an even stronger negotiating position. As he said, "Everyone imposes his own system as far as his armies can reach"—and in 1945, the Soviet army had a long reach, with its soldiers occupying Poland, Romania, Bulgaria, Hungary, and much of Czechoslovakia. Roosevelt's desire to obtain Stalin's commitment to enter the war against Japan also strengthened Stalin's hand. The **Yalta Conference** thus produced a contradictory compromise. Stalin promised free and democratic elections in eastern Europe while Roosevelt and Churchill agreed that such freely elected democratic governments should be pro-Soviet. They

did not, however, define "free" or "democratic," and made no arrangements to oversee or regulate the elections. Stalin noted privately, "A freely elected government in any of these countries would be anti-Soviet, and that we cannot allow."[4]

The Big Three also differed on the fate of Germany. Stalin hoped to wring every available resource out of Germany to pay for Soviet reconstruction. Roosevelt, however, became convinced that the economic revival of Europe depended on a prosperous Germany. He and Churchill also feared that a weak or partitioned German state would invite Soviet expansion into central Europe. At Yalta, the Big Three did not resolve the issue of Germany's future, but they agreed to divide Germany and the symbolically and strategically vital city of Berlin into occupation zones controlled by the U.S., the Soviet Union, France, and Britain (see **Map 28.1**).

Reluctant to place too much pressure on the alliance's fraying seams, Roosevelt opted for postponing the hard decisions at Yalta. He hoped that a new international body, the United Nations (UN), would settle the controversial questions after the war. If the Soviet Union refused to participate, however, the UN, like the interwar League of Nations, would be a failure. Therefore, Roosevelt sought to avoid confrontations that might give Stalin a reason to block Soviet membership.

Roosevelt also hoped that new international economic structures would stabilize the postwar order. In 1944 leading American and European economists had gathered in New Hampshire to construct a system for postwar economic revival. Aware of the economic chaos that had followed World War I and desperate to avoid a repeat of the Great Depression of the 1930s, they drew up the **Bretton**

THE BIG THREE I (YALTA, FEBRUARY 1945)
From 1941 until April 1945, the Big Three meant Churchill, Roosevelt, and Stalin. At the very end of the war, however, the composition of the Big Three suddenly changed, as Harry Truman replaced Roosevelt and Clement Attlee replaced Churchill.

Woods Agreement, the framework for the Western postwar economic order. To keep the global economy running smoothly, Bretton Woods recognized the American dollar as the world's reserve currency and fixed currency exchange rates. It also established two new international economic institutions—the International Monetary Fund (IMF), to maintain the stability of member currencies, and the World Bank, to encourage global economic development.

FRAYING SEAMS, 1945–1946 The final Big Three conference in the German city of Potsdam in July 1945 did not bridge the gap between the Soviet Union and its allies. Stalin faced two unfamiliar negotiating partners. The new American president Harry Truman (1884–1972) replaced Roosevelt, who had died in April, and midway through the summit, the new British prime minister, the Labour Party leader Clement Attlee, arrived to take Churchill's place. The changes made little difference. Stalin demanded control over the territories occupied by his armies, while the British and Americans increasingly saw this demand as a threat to democratic ideals and the European balance of power.

Two additional factors heightened the hostility between the Allied leaders during the **Potsdam Conference.** First, the British foreign secretary, Ernest Bevin (1881–1951), the man who largely determined foreign policy in Attlee's government, had a history of fighting communist efforts to control British unions. A fierce anti-Stalinist as well as an ardent British nationalist, Bevin believed that a stronger Soviet Union threatened Britain's status as a Great Power. He urged the United States to stand tough against Soviet demands.

The second factor was more dramatic. During the summit Truman received a telegraph informing him of the successful Trinity test of the atomic bomb in New Mexico (see Chapter 27). This news meant that the war against Japan would soon be over—and that the Americans and British no longer needed or wanted Stalin to join the war in the Pacific. An important Western incentive for placating Stalin disappeared.

Yet the wartime alliance remained intact after Potsdam. Truman resisted the idea of a permanent American military presence in Europe and so for the next few months sought to resolve the conflicts that divided the Allied leaders. Stalin, too, was unwilling to push too far. He feared American military might and hoped to reduce military expenditures to revive the Soviet economy. Thus, in regions that he viewed as part of the Western sphere of influence, Stalin adopted a policy of passivity. He refused to assist communists seeking to overthrow the British-backed monarchy in Greece, and he ordered communist parties in western Europe to participate with non-communists in coalition governments.

TORN IN TWO, 1946–1949 Stalin, however, adopted no such policy of passivity in eastern Europe. Throughout 1945 and 1946 communists in these states used legal and illegal methods—including intimidation, torture, and kidnapping—to expand their power base and to co-opt, silence, or expel noncommunist leaders. In Poland, for example, Stalin ordered topranking members of the wartime underground government secretly arrested, flown to Moscow, and thrown into prison. Those Poles who had fought in the Home Army against German rule were shipped to Soviet labor camps.

Disagreements over the fate of Germany also helped tear apart the alliance. At Yalta the Allies had agreed to share the postwar occupation, and at Potsdam, Truman and Attlee gave in to Stalin's demand for German reparations: The British, American, and French occupying governments shipped manufactured goods and machines from the more industrialized western regions of Germany to the largely agricultural Soviet zone in the east. In exchange, the Soviets agreed to provide food and raw materials from their zone to the western territories. The Soviets, however, proved more interested in plundering their zone than in establishing a workable joint economic policy. By 1946, British and American authorities recognized that Germans faced starvation. Convinced that economic recovery must be made an immediate priority, they combined their zones into a single economic unit and stopped reparations deliveries to the Soviets. With all pretense of a united Allied policy in Germany now dropped, Truman reversed his initial plan to withdraw American troops from Germany as soon as possible. "We are staying here," declared Secretary of State James Byrnes in September 1946. And stay they did: As of 2010, American forces remain in Germany.

The announcement of the **Truman Doctrine** in 1947 exposed the widening rift between Stalin and the West. An American policy, the Truman Doctrine evolved in response to British actions. In February 1947 the British government informed Truman's administration that it could not afford to continue to assist the Greek government in its fight against communist rebels. The United States immediately assumed Britain's role in Greece. More important, Truman used this development to issue the Truman Doctrine, which committed the U.S. to the policy of **containment**: resisting communist expansion wherever in the world it occurred.

The **Marshall Plan**—and more particularly, Stalin's rejection of it—reinforced the division of Europe into two hostile camps. In 1947, U.S. Secretary of State George Marshall (1880–1959) toured Europe and grew alarmed at the devastation and despair that he observed. Fearing that hungry Europeans might turn to communism, Marshall proposed that the United States underwrite Europe's economic recovery. Marshall's proposal at first received little attention, but in Britain Foreign Secretary Ernest Bevin heard a report of it on the radio. Convinced that an ongoing American presence in Europe would serve British interests, Bevin hailed the Marshall Plan as "a lifeline to sinking men."

Bevin's French counterpart, Foreign Minister Georges Bidault (1899–1983), shared his enthusiasm, and together they helped make the Marshall Plan a reality. With representatives from twelve other European states, Bevin and Bidault devised a four-year plan for European economic reconstruction that accelerated western Europe's leap into postwar prosperity. Eventually the United States sent $17 billion to Europe, and a new international body, the Organization for European Economic Cooperation (OEEC), worked to eliminate trade barriers and stabilize currencies.

By some estimates, the wealth that the Soviet Union siphoned from eastern Europe roughly equaled the amount of Marshall aid that the United States injected into western Europe. The United States offered aid to every European state, but if a state did accept aid, it also had to join the OEEC. Because Stalin viewed the OEEC as an instrument of American domination, he banned eastern European governments from receiving Marshall funds. When the Czechs tried to do so, Stalin engineered a communist coup in February 1948 that destroyed what remained of democracy in Czechoslovakia—and the last remnant of parliamentary democracy in eastern Europe. Over the next few years, eastern Europeans endured what Soviet citizens had suffered in the 1920s and 1930s: the extension of Communist Party control over the armed forces and the state bureaucracy, forced collectivization, the sacrifice of the standard of living to fuel heavy industrialization—and Stalinist terror.

Stalin's tightening grip over eastern Europe solidified American and western European suspicions of Soviet aims. Yet the spread of Stalinism in eastern Europe originated in part from Stalin's *loss* of control over a key eastern European state. In 1948, the Yugoslav communist leader, Tito, broke with Stalin. Alarmed by Tito's independence, Stalin cracked down across the rest of eastern Europe. He first purged eastern European Communist Parties of any potential "titoists"—leaders who might threaten his dominance. Between 1948 and 1953 more communists were killed by their own party members than had died at the hands of the Nazis during World War II. (See *Justice in History* in this chapter.) The terror then spread beyond communist ranks. Labor and prison camps dotted the eastern European landscape.

Only Stalin's death in 1953 caused the wave of persecution to recede.

Stalin's break with Tito and the resulting spread of terror throughout eastern Europe coincided with the first "battle" of the Cold War. In June 1948, Stalin ordered the western sectors of the city of Berlin—those areas controlled by the U.S., France, and Britain—blockaded. Stalin hoped to force the Western powers to resume the delivery of reparations payments from western Germany or at the very least, to give up control of West Berlin. Instead, the British and Americans responded with the Berlin Airlift. For almost a year, planes landed in West Berlin every three minutes, day and night, delivering 12,000 tons of daily supplies. In May 1949 Stalin recognized defeat and called off the blockade. The city of Berlin, like Germany itself, remained divided for the next 40 years.

In 1949, three additional developments wove the final threads into the basic Cold War pattern. First, the British and American zones of occupied Germany, joined with the French zone, became the Western-allied state of West Germany, while the Soviet zone became communist East Germany. Second, in April 1949 nine western European nations allied with the United States and Canada in the **North Atlantic Treaty Organization** (**NATO**), a military alliance specifically aimed at repelling a Soviet invasion of western Europe. And third, on August 29, 1949, the Soviet Union tested its own atomic bomb. Over the next few years, Stalin forced his eastern European satellites into an anti-Western military alliance (finalized as the **Warsaw Pact** in 1955), and the United States and the Soviet Union developed hydrogen or thermonuclear bombs, weapons with far more destructive might than their atomic predecessors. Europe stood divided into two hostile military blocs, each dominated by a superpower in possession of a nuclear arsenal.

CHRONOLOGY: THE OUTBREAK OF THE COLD WAR

1944

August	Soviet Army advances into Balkans

1945

January	Soviet Army advances into Poland
February	Yalta Conference
July	Potsdam Conference
August	United States drops atomic bombs on Hiroshima and Nagasaki

1946

March	Churchill gives his "Iron Curtain" speech in Missouri

1947

February	Truman Doctrine announced
June	Marshall Plan announced

1948

February	Communist coup in Czechoslovakia destroys last democracy in eastern Europe
June	Split between Yugoslavia's communist leader Tito and Stalin, Stalinist terror throughout eastern Europe widened; Soviet blockade of West Berlin, Berlin Airlift

1949

April	Formation of North Atlantic Treaty Organization (NATO)
May	Official formation of West Germany (Federal Republic of Germany)
August	Soviet atomic bomb test

JUSTICE IN HISTORY

Show Time: The Trial of Rudolf Slánský

On the night of July 31, 1951, Rudolf Slánský, general secretary of the Communist Party of Czechoslovakia (CPC), left his fiftieth birthday party and headed home, a frightened man. Outwardly, nothing was wrong. The CPC had celebrated the day in style. The communist president, Klement Gottwald, presented Slánský with the medal of the Order of Socialism, the highest honor awarded in Czechoslovakia. Congratulatory telegrams poured in from all over the country. But Slánský knew he was in trouble: Stalin had not acknowledged his birthday. In the upper ranks of Czechoslovakia's Communist Party in 1951, signs of Stalin's approval or disapproval were literally matters of life or death. The Stalinist purge of eastern Europe was well underway, with thousands arrested, tortured, imprisoned, or killed.

Slánský knew he was vulnerable on three counts. First, he held a rank high enough to ensure a spectacular show trial. As the Soviet Great Purge of the 1930s had demonstrated, trials and executions of leading communists worked not only to terrorize Stalin's potential rivals, but also to cement mass loyalty to the regime by rousing ordinary citizens to perpetual vigilance. For a trial to be a genuine show, the defendant had to be worth showing. Any trial with Slánský, the CPC general secretary, as defendant would be the perfect show.

Second, Slánský was a Czech, and Stalin viewed his Czech colleagues with particular suspicion. Czechoslovakia was the only state in eastern Europe with a history of successful democracy. Moreover, the CPC had participated with noncommunists in a coalition government longer than any other eastern European communist party. Such differences linked the CPC to the ideology of "national communism," which taught that each state should follow its own route to communism, that the Soviet path was not the only way. After the Yugoslav communist leader Tito had dared to defy Stalin's leadership in 1948 and led Yugoslavia down a different road, Stalin became obsessed with rooting out "national communism" and punishing any potential "titoists." To save his own skin, CPC leader Klement Gottwald needed to demonstrate his willingness to eradicate titoism from his party and his government. Slánský became that demonstration.

Finally, Slánský knew that he occupied a vulnerable position because he was a Jew. When the purges in eastern Europe began in 1948, anti-Semitism played no prominent role, but by 1950 the intersection of Middle Eastern power plays, Cold War hostilities, and the still-powerful tradition of Jew-hating in eastern European culture made Jewish communists targets for Stalin's paranoia. Aiming to establish a Soviet presence in the Middle East after the war, Stalin had tried to persuade the new state of Israel to align with the Soviet Union by offering the new Israeli government diplomatic recognition and arms deals. But Stalin's efforts failed. By 1950, Israel had become an ally of the United States. In response, Stalin regarded all Jews as potential "Zionists" (that is, as pro-Israel and therefore pro-Western and anti-Soviet in their allegiances).

Slánský's fears turned out to be correct. In the months following his birthday, Soviet advisers and homegrown Czech torturers pressured prisoners already caught in the net of the purge to confess that they were part of a Slánský-led conspiracy to overthrow the communist government and to turn Czechoslovakia against the Soviet Union. These torture-induced confessions were then used to prepare a flimsy case against Slánský and 13 other men (11 of them Jews).

Shortly before midnight on November 24, 1951, security agents arrested Slánský at his home. A lifelong atheist, Slánský could say nothing except "Jesus Maria." He knew what was coming. Instrumental in initiating the Stalinist terror in Czechoslovakia, Slánský had approved the arrests and torture of many of his colleagues.

Ironically, he had drafted the telegram asking Stalin to send Soviet advisers to assist in the Czech purge—the very same advisers who decided to target Slánský.

For the next year, Slánský endured mental and physical torture, directed by these advisers. Common torture tactics included beatings and kickings; prolonged periods in a standing position and/or without sleep, food, or water; and all-night interrogation sessions. One interrogator recalled, "Instead of getting evidence, we were told that they were villains and that we had to break them."[5] Breaking Slánský took six months. His torturers spent the remaining months defining and refining the details of Slansky's imaginary crimes against the communist regime, and rehearsing with Slánský for the all-important show trial.

Before the show began on November 20, 1952, party officials had already determined the trial verdict and sentences. Prosecutors, defense attorneys, judges, and the accused spoke the lines of a script written by security agents. One year after his arrest, Slánský stood up in court and pleaded guilty to the crimes of high treason, espionage, and sabotage. A founding member of the CPC, he said he had conspired to overthrow the communist government. A resistance fighter during World War II, he confessed to working with the Nazis against the communists. A zealous Stalinist, he announced that he was a titoist-Zionist who had plotted to hand Czechoslovakia to the United States.

Why did Slánský make such a ludicrous confession? Fear of further torture was clearly one motive, but other factors also came into play. Communists such as Slánský believed that the interests of the party always came first, ahead of individual rights, ahead of abstractions such as "truth." Slánský may have believed that his confession, false though it was, served the party. As one experienced interrogator noted about a different defendant, "He'll confess; he's got a good attitude toward the party."[6] In addition, Slánský may have been promised, as were other show trial defendants, that his life would be spared and his family protected if he confessed.

In his closing statement Slánský said, "I deserve no other end to my criminal life than that proposed by the state prosecutor."[7] The prosecutor demanded the death penalty. Slánský hanged on December 3, 1952. Ten of his co-accused were also executed. Their families were stripped of their

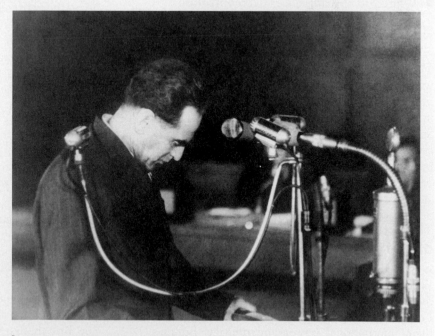

RUDOLF SLÁNSKÝ ON TRIAL
Slánský, already a broken man, bows his head as he hears his death sentence on November 27, 1952.

party memberships and privileges, deported with only the barest essentials to designated districts, and assigned to manual labor.

For Discussion

1. How did Cold War concerns shape Slánský's trial?

2. Slánský supervised the start of the Terror in Czechoslovakia. Did he, then, "get what he deserved"? What sort of justice was served in the trial of Rudolf Slánský?

Taking It Further

Lukes, Igor. "The Rudolf Slánský Affair: New Evidence." *Slavic Review* 58, 1 (Spring 1999): 160–187. Illuminating study of the role of Cold War intrigue in determining Slánský's fate.

Kaplan, Karel. *Report on the Murder of the General Secretary.* 1990. Kaplan emigrated from Czechoslovakia to West Germany in the late 1970s, with a stack of hidden documents, and wrote this report.

THE WEST AND THE WORLD: DECOLONIZATION AND THE COLD WAR

■ What was the impact of decolonization and the Cold War on the global balance of power?

The conflict between East and West soon blended with a very different struggle, one between the peoples of the developing nations and European imperialism. The Soviet Union and the United States used economic and military aid, as well as covert action, to cajole and coerce newly independent nations into choosing sides in what became the global Cold War conflict.

The End to the Age of European Empires

In the economic hard times following World War II, European governments regarded their empires as more crucial than ever. States such as Britain and France looked to their imperial possessions to give them international power and prestige. Britain's Foreign Minister Ernest Bevin, for example, saw the British Empire as the means "to develop our own power and influence to equal that of the U.S. of A. and the U.S.S.R."[8] The war, however,

strengthened colonial independence movements, with nationalists highlighting the inherent contradiction between the Allies' fight for democracy in Europe and the denial of democratic rights to the imperial subjects of European states.

When the war ended, these nationalists resisted European efforts to reimpose imperial rule, and a series of bloody colonial conflicts resulted. In Indonesia, war raged from 1945 to 1949 as the Dutch fought to keep hold of a region they viewed as vital to their economic survival. They lost the fight, and in 1949 the nationalist Ahmed Sukarno (1949–1966) led his country into independence. Similarly, nationalists in Indochina rose up against the return of French rule and began a lengthy war for independence.

The British, too, found much of their empire in revolt in the postwar period at precisely the moment when the economic and military demands of total war significantly weakened Britain's ability to control its far-flung possessions. To retain Britain's hold on its essential imperial territories, the first postwar prime minister, Clement Attlee, adopted a policy of jettisoning those regions that Britain no longer needed—or could no longer afford.

The British first jettisoned the Indian subcontinent. During World War II, the refusal of Indian nationalists to cooperate with the war effort made clear that Britain could no longer control India. After the war, therefore, Attlee's

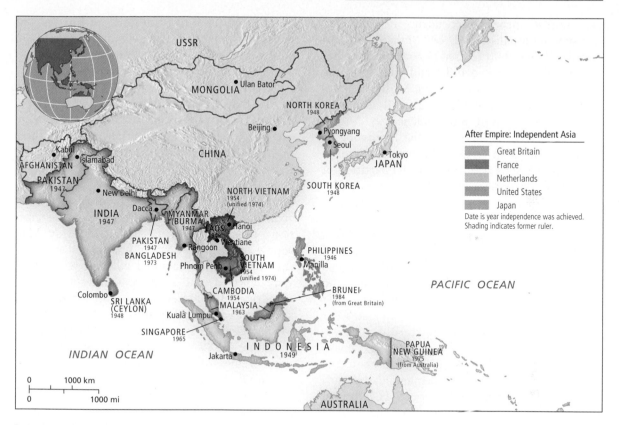

MAP 28.2

After Empire: Asia

Dates of national formation often give no indication of the continuing political upheaval and violence that afflicted the countries of Asia in the postwar period. The formation of the nations of Vietnam, Laos, and Cambodia in 1953–1954, for example, did not mean an end to warfare in Indochina.

CHRONOLOGY: THE END TO EUROPEAN EMPIRE

1946	French colonial war in Indochina begins
1947	India, Pakistan, and Burma achieve independence from Britain
1948	State of Israel established
1949	Indonesia achieves independence from Dutch rule
1952	Mau Mau rebellion begins in Kenya
1954	Defeat of French forces in Indochina; partition of Vietnam; beginning of Franco-Algerian War
1955	Bandung Conference: the "Third World" is born
1957	Ghana becomes the first black-ruled African state in the British Empire to achieve independence
1960	Congo, Nigeria, and most French colonies in Africa become independent
1962	Algeria achieves independence from French rule
1963	Jomo Kenyatta becomes first prime minister of Kenya

government opened independence negotiations. Muslim nationalists led by Muhammad Ali Jinnah (1876–1948) refused to accept citizenship in a Hindu-dominated India and won from the British the creation of a separate Muslim state— Pakistan. India and Pakistan, as well as Burma (Myanmar), received independence in August 1947 (see Map 28.2). Just as the redrawing of boundary lines in eastern Europe resulted in mass deportations and death, so the partition of the Indian subcontinent sparked widespread devastation. More than ten million people fled their homes and became refugees—Muslims fearing Hindu rule, Hindus fearing Muslim rule, Sikhs fearing both. Mahatma Gandhi begged for an end to the killing, but the death tolls reached 250,000—and included Gandhi himself, who was shot by an assassin just six months after India achieved independence.

In Palestine, too, British retreat led to bloodshed. After the war in Europe ended, Jewish refugees, persuaded by Hitler that a Jew could be safe only in a Jewish state, demanded that they be allowed to settle in Palestine. The British, however, sought to limit Jewish immigration to maintain regional political stability (and protect their own interests). But faced with mounting violence as well as growing international pressure to grant Jewish demands for statehood, the British announced they would leave Palestine and turned the problem over to the new United Nations. At the end of 1947, the UN announced a plan to partition Palestine into a Jewish and an Arab state. Arab leaders rejected the plan, however, and British troops left in May 1948 without transferring authority to either party. Jewish leaders proclaimed the new state of Israel, and the region erupted into war. After nine months of fighting, an uneasy peace descended, based on a partition of Palestine among Israel, Jordan, and Egypt (see Map 28.4). Approximately 750,000 Palestinian Arabs became stateless refugees.

By withdrawing from hot spots such as India and Palestine, the British hoped to preserve what remained of the British Empire. During the 1950s, successive British governments sought to diminish the force of nationalism by diverting it

down channels of constitutional reform and systems of power sharing—and stomping on nationalists who broke out of these channels. But neither compromise nor coercion stemmed the nationalist tide.

In Kenya, for example, Britain offered a gradual process of constitutional reforms leading toward eventual self-government, but these reforms were too slow and limited to satisfy Kenyan nationalists. The result, in 1952, was the "Mau Mau" rebellion, actually a combined peasant uprising, nationalist insurgence, and civil war. Britain imposed a brutal "villagization" program, intended to cut off Mau Mau supply lines. British forces imprisoned much of the population in enclosed villages, where they were deprived of adequate food and shelter, commandeered for forced labor, and often beaten and tortured. Yet all of this bloodshed did little to stop Kenyan independence. In 1963, Jomo Kenyatta (1889–1978), imprisoned for seven years because of his role in the uprising, became Kenya's first elected leader.

Many African leaders followed Kenyatta on the path from a British prison cell to a prime ministerial or presidential office (see **Map 28.3**). By the end of the 1960s, the British Empire had been reduced to an assortment of small island territories.

France, too, saw its empire disintegrate in the postwar decades despite efforts to resist nationalist movements. In Indochina, the nationalist leader Ho Chi Minh (1890–1969) adopted the U.S. Declaration of Independence for his model when he proclaimed independence in September 1945. The stirring rhetoric failed to convince the French, who fought for almost a decade to retain their hold in southeast Asia. But in 1954, the French army suffered a decisive defeat at Dien Bien Phu in Vietnam, and French rule in Indochina ended.

Humiliated by this defeat, French army officers responded ferociously to the outbreak of a nationalist revolt in Algeria that same year. Many French men and women shared the army's view that France had been pushed too far and had to stand fast. The result was the Franco-Algerian War. By the time Algeria claimed independence in

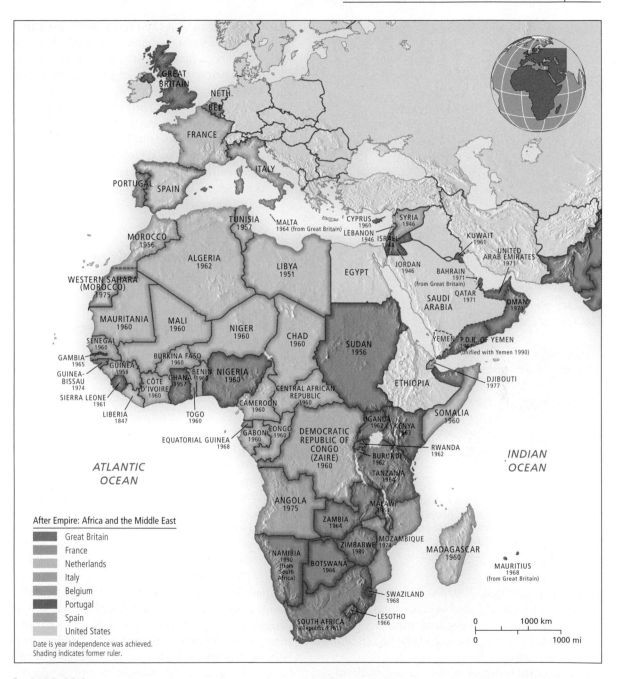

MAP 28.3

After Empire: Africa

We saw in Chapter 24 that in just three decades, between 1880 and 1910, European nations divided up between them almost the entire African continent in the notorious "Scramble for Africa." African nationalists effected an even more dramatic scramble of European imperial regimes *out* of sub-Saharan Africa. In the ten years after Ghana (formerly the British Gold Coast) became independent in 1957, 32 independent African states were formed.

DIEN-BIEN-PHU

...ILS SE SONT SACRIFIÉS POUR LA LIBERTÉ

PAIX et LIBERTÉ

PAUL COLIN

IMPERIAL SACRIFICE

This poster reminded French men and women of the sacrifice made by their army at the Battle of Dien Bien Phu in Vietnam: "They sacrificed themselves for your liberty." The memory of the army's defeat at Dien Bien Phu helped strengthen French determination to hold on to Algeria.

the evidence that the French army used torture against its enemies, argued that the war threatened to corrupt French society. (See **Different Voices** in this chapter.) By 1958 France teetered on the brink of civil war, with French army officers preparing for an assault on Paris. The World War II hero Charles De Gaulle forced through a new constitution, which sharply tilted the balance of power in French domestic politics toward the president (conveniently De Gaulle himself).

The Globalization of the Cold War

The process of **decolonization** often became entangled with Cold War rivalries, and in many regions, superpower influence replaced imperial control. Despite fears of World War III and a Europe devastated by nuclear weapons, the Cold War actually turned hot only in the developing nations, at the intersection of superpower rivalries and nationalist conflicts.

THE KOREAN WAR, 1950–1953 The first such intersection occurred in Korea. Once part of the Japanese Empire, Korea, like Germany, was divided after World War II. A Soviet-linked communist regime assumed power in North Korea, and an anticommunist state propped up by the United States controlled the south (see Map 28.2, p. 901). In 1950, North Korean troops invaded South Korea in an attempt to unite the country under communist rule. This civil war, a struggle between rival groups of Korean nationalists, soon became a new theater of the Cold War. A UN-sponsored, largely American army fought alongside South Korean troops, while the Soviet Union supplied arms and Communist China provided soldiers to support North Korea.

The Korean War accelerated the globalization of the Cold War. Convinced that communism was on the march, Truman's administration supported France's struggle against the nationalists in

1962, approximately 200,000 Algerian nationalist fighters had been killed or imprisoned. Fifteen thousand French soldiers and auxiliary forces were dead, as were almost 23,000 Algerian and French civilians.

The Franco-Algerian War seriously divided French society, called into question the meaning of French democracy, and transformed France's political structure. Supporters of the French army in Algeria saw it as a force fighting on behalf of Western civilization against barbarism (Muslim and communist). Critics, pointing to

Indochina, thus drawing the United States onto the path that would lead to its war in Vietnam. The conflict in Korea also welded Japan firmly into the Western alliance. As the U.S. army turned to the Japanese for vital military supplies, more than $3.5 billion poured into and rejuvenated the Japanese economy. (American military orders for trucks guaranteed the success of a struggling new Japanese firm called Toyota.) Transformed from an occupied enemy to a staunch ally and an economic powerhouse, Japan became the dam holding back "the red tide that threatens to engulf the world."[9] Thus, in a curious way, Japan—geographically as far "East" as one can get—became a part of the "West."

The Korean War also solidified the Cold War within Europe. The escalating costs of the war led Truman's administration to demand that its European allies strengthen their own military forces and permit the rearmament of West Germany. With the trauma of German conquest so recently behind them, many Europeans were horrified by the second demand. Britain's prime minister Attlee warned, "The policy of using Satan to defeat Sin is very dangerous." But after four years of controversy, West Germany rearmed under the NATO umbrella.

CHANGING TEMPERATURES IN THE COLD WAR, 1953–1960 In 1953, both sides in the Cold War changed leaders. Stalin died in March, just a few months after a new Republican administration headed by President Dwight Eisenhower (1890–1969) took office in the United States. This change of leadership heralded a new phase in the Cold War. When Eisenhower took office, he condemned Truman's policy of *containing* communism as defeatist, a "negative, futile and immoral policy...which abandons countless human beings to a despotism and Godless terrorism."[10] Instead, Eisenhower committed the United States to *roll back* communism and insisted that communist aggression would be met with massive nuclear retaliation. The term **brinkmanship** entered the Cold War vocabulary when Eisenhower's Secretary of State John Foster Dulles (1888–1959) warned, "If you try to run away from [nuclear war], if you are scared to go to the brink, you are lost."[11]

This newly aggressive American stance was matched on the other side of the Cold War divide. After a period of uncertainty following Stalin's death in 1953, Nikita Khrushchev (1955–1964) emerged in 1955 as the new Soviet leader. Loud and boisterous, given to off-the-cuff remarks and spontaneous displays of emotion, Khrushchev contrasted sharply with the reserved Stalin. (It is hard to imagine Stalin taking off his shoe and beating it on a table, as Khrushchev did in front of the television cameras at an assembly

CHRONOLOGY: THE COLD WAR, 1950–1968

1950	Outbreak of the Korean War
1953	First American and Soviet hydrogen bomb tests; death of Joseph Stalin; end of the Korean War
1955	First Geneva summit
1956	Hungarian uprising and its repression by Soviet troops
1957	Launch of *Sputnik*
1959	Khrushchev's visit to the United States
1961	Berlin Wall built
1962	Cuban Missile Crisis
1963	Nuclear Test Ban treaty signed
1964	Khrushchev ousted; beginning of the Brezhnev era
1965	U.S. bombing of North Vietnam begins

DIFFERENT VOICES TORTURE AND TERRORISM IN THE FRENCH-ALGERIAN WAR

The French-Algerian War shattered France's post-war political system, and raised troubling question about French identity. Much of the controversy aroused by the war centered on the revelations that French police and the French military routinely used torture to interrogate captured Algerian rebels. In the excerpts below we hear the voices of soldiers—the first a high-ranking officer, the second, a volunteer paratrooper.

I. War Against Terrorism

Roger Trinquier (1908–1985) served in both World War II and Indochina before becoming commander of the 3rd Colonial Airborne Regiment in Algeria. In Modern Warfare: A French View of Counterinsurgency, *Trinquier identified terrorism—and the fight against it—as the quintessential form of modern warfare.*

The goal of modern warfare is control of the populace, and terrorism is a particularly appropriate weapon, since it aims directly at the inhabitant.... What characterizes modern terrorism, and makes for its basic strength, is the slaughter of generally defenseless persons.... The terrorist should not be considered an ordinary criminal. Actually, he fights within the framework of his organization, without personal interest, for a cause he considers noble and for a respectable ideal, the same as the soldiers in the army confronting him. On the command of his superiors, he kills without hatred individuals unknown to him, with the same indifference as the soldier on the battlefield. His victims are often women and children.... But during a period of history when the bombing of open cities is permitted, and when two Japanese cities were razed to hasten the end of the war in the Pacific, one cannot with good cause reproach him. The terrorist has become a soldier, like the aviator or the infantryman.

But the aviator... knows that anti-aircraft shells can kill or maim him.... It never occurs to [the infantryman]... to ask... that his enemy renounce the use of the rifle, the shell, or the bomb.... [The terrorist] must be made to realize that, when he is captured, he cannot be treated like an ordinary criminal.... No lawyer is present for such an interrogation. If the prisoner gives the information requested, the examination is quickly terminated; if not, specialists must force his secret from him.... The terrorist must accept this as a condition inherent in his trade and in the methods of warfare that, with full knowledge, his superiors and he himself have chosen....

Interrogations in modern warfare should be conducted by specialists perfectly versed in the techniques to be employed.... The interrogators must always strive not to injure the physical and moral integrity of individuals. Science can easily place at the army's disposition the means for obtaining what is sought. But we must not trifle with our responsibilities. It is deceitful to permit artillery or aviation to bomb villages and slaughter women and children, while the real enemy usually escapes, and to refuse interrogation specialists the right to seize the truly guilty terrorist and spare the innocent.

If... our army refused to employ all the weapons of modern warfare, it could no longer fulfill its mission. We would no longer be defended. Our national independence, the civilization we hold dear, our very freedom would probably perish.

II. The Torture Room

In 1954 Pierre Leuillette enlisted in the French Army. After he finished his tour of duty in Algeria, he wrote St. Michael and the Dragon: Memoirs of a Paratrooper, *published in France in 1961.*

A volunteer paratrooper is never at the start anything but a grown-up little boy, at best an enthusiastic boy scout, dreaming of cuts and bruises, of bursts of machine-gun fire, of his parachute spread in the wind, and of the glamorous uniform, red beret, jungle-green combat suit, and commando dagger slipped into the boot.... He leaves everything, parents, friends, school, work, for "adventure." It's his first free act. It will be his last, too, for a long time: the enlistment is for three years....

I shall speak of the torture room of the 1st Company of the 2nd R. P.C., my company.... Every day, the lieutenant on duty, assisted by Sergeant T., of the Signal Corps, and another sergeant, a very muscular Alsatian, spends several hours there. They have plenty to do.... With interrogation for a pretext, their work really amounts to torturing naked, bound prisoners, one after another, from morning to night. *[Leuillette describes the various torture methods ranging from the basic slap to simulated drowning to crushing the genitals in a vise.]* Our principal implement did not, however, exist in the Middle Ages. This refinement of civilization presents at first glance a quite innocuous appearance: simply an electric wire attached to a floor plug.... Besides being efficacious, [*torture by electricity*] has the added advantage of leaving no marks....

Even if the great majority of those we interrogate are criminals of the most evil sort, there are also among them men only suspected—of, for example, harboring [rebels], or of collecting money for them; and there are some completely innocent, who, like most innocent people, cannot possibly prove it....

To civilians ... I tell about what I see every day. They have always had a lofty idea of the greatness of France. They listen politely. But I sense their unbelief. They are thinking, "This isn't possible. We'd have known about it." Will they ever know about it? The German people, after the war, never stopped saying, and it was probably true, "We didn't know." ... Have they ever realized that not knowing is also a way of being guilty?

[His tour of duty complete, Leuillette sails back to France.] On the boat my joy is so great that all night long I whistle and sing.... The [ship] comes into Marseilles and my excited joy suddenly dissolves. For there on the dock several hundred soldiers are waiting to leave, just as I was three years ago. I am afraid, afraid for them.... For I now know that they risk more than death. They risk the loss of everything that could make them men.

Sources: *Modern Warfare: A French View of Counterinsurgency* by Roger Trinquier, translated from the French by Daniel Lee; with an introduction by Bernard B. Fali; Foreword by Eliot A. Cohen. (New York: Frederick Praeger, 1964), 16, 17, 20–21, 23, 115. Copyright © 1964, 2006 by Praeger Security International. Pierre Leuillette, *St. Michael and the Dragon: Memoirs of a Paratrooper*. Trans. John Edmonds (Boston: Houghton Mifflin, 1964), 1–2; 286–288, 298–299, 334. Originally published in French as *Saint Michel et le dragon*. Copyright © 1961 by Les Editions de Minuit. Reprinted by permission of Georges Borchardt, Inc., for Les Editions de Minuit.

For Discussion

1. Why was the French-Algerian War so divisive in France? What issues did it raise about French national identity?

2. The controversy over French police and military tactics in Algeria raised a question that is much debated today: Does the fight against terrorism demand the use of torture, or is the turn to torture as much a threat to Western values as terrorism itself? Can we use the history of the French-Algerian War to answer this question? How do we "learn from history," given the uniqueness of each historical event?

of the United Nations.) Khrushchev played a dangerous game of nuclear bluff, by which he convinced allies and foes alike that the Soviet Union possessed a stronger nuclear force than it actually did.

Khrushchev and Eisenhower recognized, however, that nuclear weapons made total war unwinnable. Thus, the period from 1953 until 1964 witnessed thawing superpower relations followed by the icy blasts of renewed hostilities. In 1955, for example, representatives of Britain, France, the United States, and the Soviet Union met in Geneva for the first summit of the Cold War. This initial thaw ended one year later when Khrushchev sent tanks into Hungary to crush an anti-Soviet rebellion.

The Soviets' successful launch of the first human-made satellite, *Sputnik*, in 1957 was even more chilling. Khrushchev claimed—falsely—that the Soviets possessed an advanced intercontinental ballistic missile (ICBM) force and that Soviet factories were producing rockets "like sausages from a machine."[12] *Sputnik* had ominous implications, especially for western Europeans. If the Soviets could launch a satellite into space, they seemed capable of delivering a nuclear bomb to American as well as European cities. If the Soviets invaded western Europe with conventional forces, would the Americans defend Europe—and so open their own cities to nuclear retaliation? Would the United States risk Chicago to save Paris?

Yet in the late 1950s, the Cold War ice seemed to be breaking once again. In 1958 the Soviet Union announced it would suspend nuclear testing. The United States and Britain followed suit and nuclear test ban talks opened in Geneva. The next year Khrushchev spent twelve days touring the United States. (Much to his regret, security concerns kept him from visiting Disneyland.) The communist leader impressed Americans as down-to-earth, a man rather than a monster. Khrushchev ended his U.S. visit with the promise of another four-power summit in 1960.

ON THE BRINK: THE BERLIN WALL AND THE CUBAN MISSILE CRISIS   These warming relations, however, turned frosty in 1960 after the Soviet Union announced it had shot down an American spy plane and captured its pilot. This announcement aborted the planned summit and initiated one of the most dangerous periods in the post–World War II era, one that saw the construction of the **Berlin Wall** and an escalation of the arms race. As we saw at the beginning of this chapter, the continuing outflow of East Germans to the West through Berlin led the East German communist leader Walter Ulbricht (1893–1973) and Khrushchev to erect the wall. Two weeks later, the Soviet Union resumed nuclear testing. The new American president John F. Kennedy (1961–1963) increased military spending and called for an expanded civil defense program to prepare for nuclear war. Across Europe, men and women feared that their continent would become a nuclear wasteland.

Such a war was narrowly avoided in the fall of 1962 as once again the Cold War intersected with a nationalist struggle. In 1959, a nationalist revolutionary movement led by Fidel Castro (b. 1926) toppled Cuba's pro-U.S. dictator. Castro aligned Cuba with the Soviet Union. In 1962, Kennedy learned that the Soviets were building missile bases in Cuba. What he did not know was that the Soviet forces in Cuba were armed with nuclear weapons—and with the power to use these weapons if U.S. forces attacked. Some of Kennedy's advisers urged just such an attack, but instead the president used secret diplomatic channels to broker a compromise. Khrushchev removed the missiles and in exchange, Kennedy withdrew NATO's nuclear missiles from Turkey and guaranteed that the United States would not invade Cuba.

In the aftermath of the Cuban Missile Crisis, the United States and the Soviet Union backed off from brinkmanship. In 1963, the superpowers agreed to stop above-ground nuclear testing with the Nuclear Test Ban treaty and set up between them the "hotline," a direct communications link to encourage immediate personal consultation in the event of a future crisis.

The retreat from brinkmanship did not, however, slow the globalization of the Cold

War. The superpowers served as magnetic poles, attracting competing nationalist and regional forces. Many newly independent nations resisted being drawn in, as the Bandung Conference of 1955 made clear. Bandung brought together "nonaligned" states who sought to establish themselves as a collective force separate from both superpowers. French journalists at the conference gave these nations a collective label—neither the first (Western, capitalist) nor the second (Eastern, communist), but rather the **Third World.** Genuine independence, however, proved difficult to retain.

COLD WAR ARENAS: VIETNAM AND THE MIDDLE EAST Increasingly the superpowers replaced European empires as global powerbrokers, as the transformation of the Vietnam War from a struggle against French imperial rule into a Cold War conflict illustrates. After the defeat of French forces at Dien Bien Phu in 1954, rival Vietnamese nationalists fought to control the Indochinese peninsula. Ho Chi Minh and his communist regime in North Vietnam relied on the Soviet Union and China for support, while American military and economic aid propped up an anticommunist (but not democratic) government in South Vietnam. Under the Kennedy presidency (1961–1963), the number of military advisers in Vietnam expanded rapidly, as did American involvement in South Vietnamese politics. When Kennedy's successor, Lyndon Johnson (1908–1973), took office, he issued a clear order, "Win the war!" In 1964, the U.S. Congress granted Johnson the authority to take "all necessary measures" to do so. By 1968, more than 500,000 American soldiers were fighting in Vietnam. About 58,000 GIs died during the war—as did well over one million Vietnamese.

Like Vietnam, the Middle East became a Cold War arena in the 1950s. Events in Egypt proved pivotal. In 1954 the revolutionary nationalist Gamal Abdel Nasser (1918–1970) overthrew the British-dominated Egyptian monarchy. The United States immediately sought to woo Nasser to the West by offering aid to build the Aswan Dam, a huge hydro-electric project on the Nile River. But when Nasser arranged a weapons deal with Czechoslovakia, outraged American policymakers denied him funds for the dam. The Egyptian leader retaliated by aligning with the Soviet Union and by nationalizing the Suez Canal.

This series of events set off what is known as the Suez Crisis, a dramatic demonstration of the waning power of European empires and of the rising dominance of the superpowers. Angered by Nasser's seizure of the canal, the British and French governments conspired with Israel to topple him from power. Israeli forces invaded Egypt, according to plan, on October 31, 1956. Posing as peacekeepers, the British and French demanded that both sides pull back from the Canal Zone. When, as they expected, Nasser refused, British and French troops invaded. But then the plan unraveled under Superpower pressure. With the Soviet Union threatening a nuclear strike against the invading forces, President Dwight Eisenhower telephoned the British prime minister, Anthony Eden, and exploded, "Is that you, Anthony? Well, this is President Eisenhower, and I can only presume you have gone out of your mind!" Eisenhower's administration blocked Britain's IMF loan application and pushed Britain to the edge of financial collapse. Eden's government had no choice but to declare a ceasefire and withdraw British troops.

While the Suez Crisis highlighted superpower dominance in the Middle East, the Six-Day War of 1967 marked a clear Cold War division of the region. In six days of fighting, Israel gained possession of the Sinai Peninsula from Egypt, the West Bank from Jordan, the Golan Heights from Syria—and one million stateless Palestinian refugees (see **Map 28.4**). In the wake of the war, American foreign policy shifted to decisive support for Israel. In turn, Egypt, Syria, Iraq, Sudan, and Libya aligned with the Soviet Union.

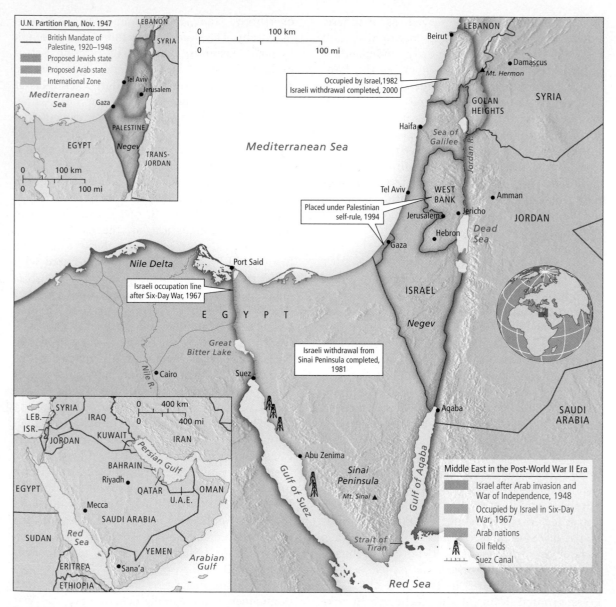

MAP 28.4

The Middle East in the Post-World War II Era

The map inset outlines the United Nations' plan to partition Palestine into Jewish and Arab states, with Jerusalem as an international zone. This plan was not implemented; instead, Israel carved out its own boundaries as a result of war with the surrounding Arab powers. The Six-Day War in 1967 greatly expanded those boundaries. Israel withdrew from western Sinai in 1975 and from the whole of the peninsula in 1981. The West Bank and the Gaza Strip were placed under Palestinian self-rule in 1994.

THE SOVIET UNION AND EASTERN EUROPE IN THE 1950s AND 1960s

■ **What patterns characterized the history of the Soviet Union and eastern Europe after the death of Stalin?**

Divided by the Cold War, the peoples of western and eastern Europe in the 1950s and 1960s followed separate paths (see **Map 28.5**). For the citizens of eastern Europe and the Soviet Union, Stalin's death in 1953 inaugurated a period of political reform and hope for prosperity. By the

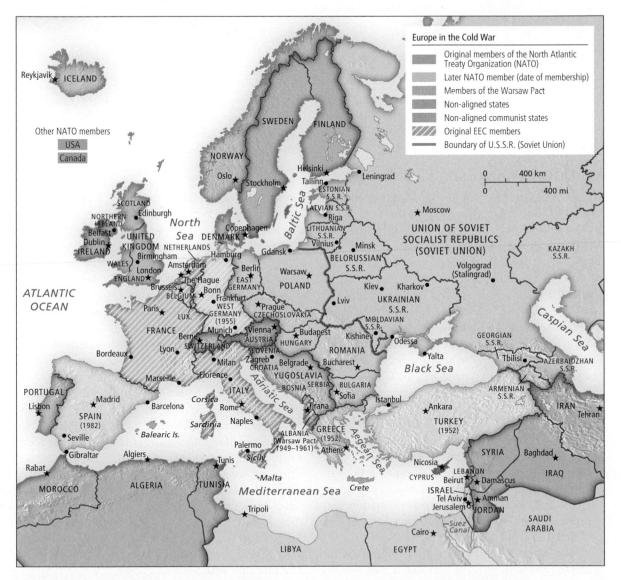

MAP 28.5

Europe in the Cold War

As this map shows, during the Cold War the "West" was defined culturally and politically, rather than in geographic terms. Greece and Turkey stand far to the east in Europe, yet their membership in NATO placed these states within the "West."

CHRONOLOGY: THE SOVIET BLOC AFTER STALIN

1953   Death of Stalin; relaxation of terror in eastern Europe and Soviet Union
1955   Khrushchev emerges as new Soviet leader
1956   Khrushchev's "Secret Speech," de-Stalinization accelerates; unrest in Poland results in new regime under Gomułka; Hungarian Revolution crushed by Soviet forces
1964   Khrushchev ousted; Brezhnev era begins
1968   Prague Spring crushed

end of the 1960s, however, economic stagnation and political discontent characterized life in the Soviet bloc.

De-Stalinization under Khrushchev

By 1955 Nikita Khrushchev had triumphed over his rivals and claimed control of the post-Stalin Soviet Union. A true communist success story, Khrushchev was born to illiterate peasants and began work as a coal miner at age 14. Recognized as a man with talent by the Communist Party, he trained as an engineer and helped build the Moscow subway system. Khrushchev owed everything to the Communist Party, and he never forgot it. Confident in the moral and material superiority of communism, Khrushchev believed that the Soviet Union would win the Cold War on the economic battlefield. But this victory would occur only if Soviet living standards substantially improved and only if the Stalinist systems of terror and rigid centralized control were dismantled. Khrushchev's accession to power thus ushered in the era of **de-Stalinization,** a time of greater openness in the Soviet bloc as governments lifted many of the controls on speech and publication, and for the first time in years, dissent and debate reappeared in public life.

The most dramatic sign of de-Stalinization was the release of at least four and a half million prisoners from slave labor camps. As one Soviet citizen recalled, their return was disturbing: "In railway trains and stations, there appeared survivors of the camps, with leaden grey hair, sunken eyes, and a faded look; they choked and

dragged their feet like old men."[13] These survivors often returned to find their spouses remarried, their children embarrassed by their presence, their world destroyed. Some, such as the writer Alexander Solzhenitsyn, wrote horrifying accounts of their experiences. Solzhenitsyn's books narrated the daily degradation of prison life and provided a detailed map of the network of slave labor camps that he christened "The Gulag Archipelago."

Yet in 1959, four years after the start of de-Stalinization, the Gulag still held at least one million prisoners. De-Stalinization did not end political and religious repression or artistic control. Under Khrushchev, Soviet Jews continued to suffer harassment and imprisonment while Orthodox Christians experienced an intensified anti-Christian campaign, which destroyed churches, imprisoned clergy, closed seminaries and monasteries, and in some cases removed children from Christian homes. Artists who dared challenge the standards of Socialist Realism (see Chapter 26) also suffered. An exhibition of long-hidden works by Picasso inspired many Soviet artists to experiment with abstract art, but when Khrushchev saw their work on show, he thundered, "What's hung here is simply anti-Soviet. It's immoral."[14] Within days, the artists in the show were censured, expelled, or unemployed.

De-Stalinization was also limited in its economic impact. In agriculture in particular, the Soviet Union continued to lag behind the West. Refusing to retreat from collectivization, Khrushchev instead implemented a series of

DE-STALINIZATION

On October 31, 1956, Hungarian demonstrators pulled down a huge statue of Joseph Stalin and then dragged it two miles through the city center. Stalin's head still sits at an intersection in Budapest.

poorly planned reforms, including rapid mechanization, a massive chemical fertilizer program, and the plowing of virgin lands. The fundamental productivity problem remained unsolved—and worsened in the long term because of the ecological damage inflicted on the Soviet countryside. Soil erosion increased exponentially, nitrogen runoff from fertilized fields contaminated water supplies, and soil fertility declined. The full force of these problems would not be felt until the 1980s, but as early as 1963 the Soviet Union had to import Western grain, a humiliating admission of failure for Khrushchev's regime.

Re-Stalinization and Stagnation: The Brezhnev Era

De-Stalinization unsettled many high-ranking communists who forced Khrushchev out of office in 1964. After a short period of collective leadership, Leonid Brezhnev (1906–1982) emerged as the new Soviet leader. A polite man with no interest in original ideas, Brezhnev was far more reassuring to Soviet bureaucrats than the flamboyant Khrushchev, whose boisterous embrace of ambitious schemes had proven destabilizing. Fifty-eight years old and already physically ailing when he assumed the party leadership, the increasingly decrepit Brezhnev matched his era.

Under Brezhnev the Soviet economy stagnated. Growth rates in industrial production and labor productivity slowed during the second half of the 1960s and almost disappeared in the 1970s. Improving living standards, however, masked this economic stagnation. Brezhnev continued Khrushchev's policies of free higher education and rising wages, while accelerating the expansion of consumer goods. State subsidies ensured that the cost of utilities, public transport, and rents remained far lower than in the West (although apartments were in short supply), and an extensive welfare system eased pressures on ordinary people.

By the middle of the 1960s, the Soviet Union appeared to have achieved a sort of stability. It was, however, a stability relying on repression. Judging de-Stalinization to be too risky, Brezhnev and his colleagues withdrew the limited cultural and intellectual freedoms introduced under Khrushchev. Those who expressed dissident views soon found themselves denied employment and educational opportunities, imprisoned, sent to the Gulag, or confined indefinitely in psychiatric wards.

Yet dissent did not disappear. Soviet society may have resembled a stagnant pond by the 1970s, but beneath the surface churned dangerous currents that, in the late 1980s, would engulf the entire communist system. Nationalism among the non-Russian populations served as the source of much discontent, as did resentment about political repression. Reviving a practice employed by reformers under the tsarist regime, dissidents evaded the censors by *samizdat* or "self-publishing." Novels, plays, poetry, political treatises, and historical studies were circulated privately, copied by hand or duplicated on treasured (and often confiscated) typewriters and photocopiers and distributed more widely. Nonconformist artists, banned from official exhibitions, used private apartments to show their work.

Diversity and Dissent in Eastern Europe

Despite the uniformity imposed by Soviet-style communist systems during these decades, the nations of eastern Europe developed in different ways. De-Stalinization accelerated this diversification. In his "Secret Speech" of 1956, Khrushchev declared, "it is ridiculous to think that revolutions are made to order"[15] and so indicated that communist nations could follow paths diverging from the road traveled by the Soviet Union.

1956 AND AFTER But just how far from the Soviet road could those paths go? The contrasting fates of Poland and Hungary in 1956 provided the answer. In Poland, protests against Stalinist controls proved strong enough to bring back into power Władisław Gomułka (1905–1982). An influential Polish communist who had been purged in the Stalinist terror in 1951, Gomułka succeeded in establishing a uniquely Polish brand of communism, one that abandoned collective farming and gave a certain amount of freedom to the Roman Catholic Church in Poland, yet remained loyal to the Warsaw Pact.

Hungary also pursued a de-Stalinizing "New Course" under the leadership of the reformist communist Imre Nagy (1896–1958). Unlike Gomułka, however, Nagy gave in to popular demands for a break with the Soviet Union. On October 31, 1956, Hungary withdrew from the Warsaw Pact—or tried to. A few days later, Khrushchev sent in the tanks. At least 4,000 Hungarians died as the Red Army crushed all resistance. Nagy was executed in 1958.

The smashing of the Hungarian revolt defined the limits of de-Stalinization in eastern Europe: The satellite states of the Soviet Union could not follow paths that led out of the Warsaw Pact. Within the confines of this structure and of the one-party state, however, the governments of eastern Europe pursued different courses. Poland held onto its small family farms, with less than one-eighth of farmland collectivized by 1960, in contrast to collectivization rates of 84 percent in Romania, and 87 percent in Czechoslovakia. In Hungary, the post-1956 government of János Kádár (1912–1989)—who had survived torture and imprisonment during the Stalinist terror of the early 1950s—instituted the New Economic Mechanism in the second half of the 1960s. This "mechanism" sharply reduced the state's control of the economy. In contrast, Romanians endured the reign of the "mini-Stalins," Gheorghe Gheorghiu-Dej (1901–1965) and Nicolae Ceauşescu (1918–1989), who imposed not only one-party but one-man control over the country through Stalinist methods of terror.

Within the diverse experiences of eastern Europeans, certain commonalities characterized the post-1956 era. Except in Romania and even more oppressive Albania, living standards improved, particularly in comparison with the hard times of the 1930s and 1940s. Educational opportunities expanded, the supply of consumer goods increased, and political repression became less overt. Even so, overcentralization, bureaucratic mismanagement, and political corruption ensured that living standards remained below those of the West. Moreover, the very consumer goods that were supposed to persuade eastern European citizens of the superiority of the communist system instead demonstrated its deficiencies. With a radio, a Hungarian teenager could tune into Radio Free Europe and hear of a livelier, more abundant society in the West. In East Germany, television watchers could view West German networks and catch a glimpse of Western prosperity.

THE PRAGUE SPRING Discontent simmered throughout the Eastern bloc during the 1960s and then, in 1968, boiled over in Czechoslovakia. During the 1960s, a reform movement emerged in the ranks of the Czechoslovakian Communist Party. It included Slovaks, who believed that the regime's centralized policies favored Czechs, and younger, university-educated managers and scientists who resented the power of uneducated party superiors. At the beginning of 1968, demands for reform fueled an intraparty revolution that brought to power the Slovakian communist Alexander Dubček (1921–1992). Dubček embarked on a program of radical reform aimed at achieving "socialism with a human face." This more humane socialism included freedom of speech, press, assembly, and travel; the removal of Communist Party controls from social and cultural life; and decentralization of the economy. Dubček's effort to reform the system from the top quickly merged with a wider popular protest

movement that had arisen among intellectuals, artists, students, and workers. The result was the "Prague Spring"—the blossoming of political and social freedoms throughout Czechoslovakia, but especially in the capital city of Prague.

Well aware of the fate of Hungary in 1956, Dubček reassured Brezhnev that his reforms would not lead Czechoslovakia out of the Warsaw Pact. But by the summer of 1968, word of the Prague Spring had reached other eastern European countries and the Soviet Union itself. In Ukraine, nationalist protesters looked to Prague for inspiration, while in Poland, student rioters waved placards reading "Poland is awaiting its own Dubček." Frightened communist leaders throughout the Eastern bloc demanded that Brezhnev stifle the Prague Spring.

On the night of August 20–21, 80,000 Soviet, Polish, Hungarian, and East German troops crossed the Czech border, and over the next several weeks crushed the Prague Spring. That fall, Brezhnev acknowledged that Soviet domination in eastern Europe rested on force alone when he articulated what came to be known as the "Brezhnev Doctrine." Formally a commitment to support global socialism, the Brezhnev Doctrine essentially promised to use the Red Army to destroy any effort to achieve fundamental change within the Soviet bloc.

THE WEST: CONSENSUS, CONSUMPTION, AND CULTURE

- What patterns characterized the history of western Europe in the 1950s and 1960s?

As in eastern Europe, in western Europe both World War II and the Cold War shaped the 1950s and 1960s. The desire to make the suffering of the war years worthwhile, and opposition to communism, fueled economic integration and strengthened political centrism. The dominant fact of the postwar years was, however, material prosperity as western European economies embarked on two decades of dramatic economic growth and consumer spending.

The Triumph of Democracy

In contrast to the interwar years, the parties in power in western Europe in the 1950s and 1960s and the voters who put them there agreed on the virtues of parliamentary democracy. The new constitutions of France, West Germany, and Italy guaranteed the protection of individual rights, and French and Italian women achieved suffrage. The democratic ideal of the universal franchise had finally been realized in most of western Europe.

Citizenship, though, meant more than the right to vote after 1945. With the triumph of *social democracy* throughout western Europe, the meaning of citizenship broadened to include the right to a decent standard of living. Through the nationalization of key industries, the establishment of public agencies to oversee and encourage investment and trade, and the manipulation of interest rates and currency supplies, governments assumed the task of ensuring full employment and material well-being for their citizens. A slogan of the German Social Democratic Party—"as much competition as possible, as much planning as necessary"—summed up an approach common to much of western Europe at this time.

Social democracy also meant the construction of comprehensive welfare states to guarantee citizens adequate incomes and medical care. By the end of the 1950s, the average western European working-class family received 63 percent of its income from wages. The substantial remaining income came from welfare benefits such as family allowances, national health services, sickness and disability insurance, and old-age pensions. In addition, state-run vaccination and inoculation programs, stricter sanitation regulation, and the development of policies to control communicable diseases all meant an improvement in the health of Europe's populations.

As we saw in Chapter 27, the victory of social democracy was rooted in the suffering of

World War II, when Europeans grew determined to create a better world out of the rubble of total war. This determination remained, but wartime radicalism receded as the Cold War constricted the parameters of political debate. The mainstream political parties—Christian Democrats or Conservatives on the right, Social Democrats or Socialists on the left—agreed in refusing to allow Communist Party members to participate in governing coalitions. In France and Italy, communist parties consistently drew 20 to 30 percent of the vote, but were effectively marginalized by their exclusion from office after 1948.

With the communists isolated, and with the ideologies of the extremist Right such as fascism and Nazism discredited by the horrors of the war, western European politics became more centrist. **Christian Democracy**—which has no American or British counterpart—flourished on the Continent. Drawing on a largely Roman Catholic base for support, Christian Democrats espoused a conservative social ideology combined with a progressive commitment to the welfare state. Christian Democrats dominated much of European politics in the 1950s and 1960s: They played significant roles in the political life of France and Belgium, governed West Germany between 1949 and 1969, and provided every prime minister except two in Italy between 1945 and 1993.

Three factors account for Christian Democracy's success. First, as anticommunists and advocates of the free market, Christian Democrats benefited from Cold War anxieties and more directly from American aid. Second, because they were based on religion (Roman Catholicism) rather than class, Christian Democratic parties appealed to middle-class and working-class voters, and particularly to women, who tended to be more religious and to vote more conservatively than men. Finally, the triumph of Christian Democracy rested on its transformation from a right-wing to a centrist political movement. In the interwar period, Christian Democracy, rooted in a religious and political tradition based on hierarchy and authoritarianism, had veered close to fascism. But during World War II, many Catholics served in the Resistance, where they absorbed progressive political ideas. The war-inspired desire to use the power of the state to improve the lives of ordinary people blended with traditional Catholic paternalism. After the war the Christian Democrats embraced democracy and supported the construction of comprehensive welfare states.

Prosperity in the West

These political developments unfolded against an economic backdrop of increasing prosperity. In the first half of the 1950s, Europeans moved rapidly from the austerity of the immediate postwar years to an age of affluence.

ECONOMIC INTEGRATION The greater coordination of western European economies contributed to this new prosperity. World War II provided the initial impetus for this economic integration. Fighting in conditions of unprecedented horror, Europeans looked for ways to guarantee a lasting peace. In July 1944, Resistance leaders from France, Italy, the Netherlands, and a number of other countries met in Geneva to declare their support for a federal Europe.

No such radical restructuring occurred, but Cold War concerns helped western Europeans see themselves as part of a single region with common interests. In addition, American policymakers required any state that received Marshall aid to develop transnational economic institutions. Looking back on this early stage of European economic integration, the Belgian prime minister (and ardent proponent of European union) Paul-Henri Spaak (1899–1972) wrote in the later 1960s, "Europeans, let us be modest. It is the fear of Stalin and the daring views of Marshall which led us into the right path."[16]

Efforts at European economic integration culminated with the formation of the **European Economic Community (EEC)** or **Common Market** in 1957. Consisting of Germany, France, Italy, and the "Benelux" states (Belgium, the Netherlands, and Luxembourg), the EEC sought to establish a free trade zone across member boundaries and to coordinate policies on wages, prices, immigration, and social security. Between 1958 and 1970, trade among its six member states increased fivefold. The rapid movement of goods, services, and even workers ensured that the economies of member states flourished. In contrast, Britain, which chose to remain outside the EEC to preserve its preferential trading relationships with its former and current colonies, struggled with growth rates below those of its continental competitors.

THE AGE OF AFFLUENCE By the mid-1950s, western Europe entered an age of consumption. After years of wartime rationing, Europeans went on a spending spree and did not stop. Climbing real wages—by 80 percent in England, for example, between 1950 and 1970—help explain why. So too does the construction of the welfare state. With full employment and comprehensive welfare services offering unprecedented financial security, Europeans shrugged off habits of thrift. Credit buying (what the British called "buying on the never-never") became commonplace and made possible even more consumption.

This spending spree transformed the interiors of European homes and their exterior environment. Housing construction boomed, and with new houses came new household goods. Items such as refrigerators and washing machines, once unaffordable luxuries, now became increasingly common in ordinary homes. In France, the stock of home appliances rose by 400 percent between 1949 and 1957. At the same time, the automobile revolutionized the rural and urban landscape. Highways, few and far between in 1950, cut across the countryside, and parking meters, unknown in Europe before 1959, dotted city streets. In 1964, the archbishop of Florence presided over a thanksgiving service in a gas station to celebrate the completion of a highway linking Milan and Naples. Out-of-town shopping centers, geared to the convenience of car owners, proliferated while city centers decayed.

Western Culture and Thought in the Age of Consumption

Cultural developments in Western society highlight the shift from an era structured by the austerity and suffering of World War II to an age of affluence and opportunity. By the second half of the 1950s, artists began to retreat from engagement with the horrors of war and instead produced works that commented on and reveled in the cascade of consumer abundance.

FINDING MEANING IN THE AGE OF AUSCHWITZ AND THE ATOM BOMB In the years immediately after 1945, existentialism (which first emerged in the despair of the 1930s) remained a powerful cultural force. Jean-Paul Sartre's conviction that existence has no intrinsic meaning and yet that the individual retains the freedom to act and therefore make meaning, resounded in a world that had experienced both the Holocaust and the Resistance. The existentialist emphasis on individual action as the source of meaning could lead to a life of political activism. Sartre, for example, worked with the French Resistance and became a prominent participant in left-wing political causes in the 1950s and 1960s. Yet existentialist anxiety also justified political disengagement. In the Irish-French playwright Samuel Beckett's (1906–1989) *Waiting for Godot* (1952), two tramps sit in an empty universe, waiting for someone who never comes. In this absurd void, politics has no relevance or resonance.

Existentialist themes echoed throughout the visual arts in the early 1950s. The sculptures of the Swiss artist Alberto Giacometti (1901–1966) embody existentialism—fragile, insubstantial, they appear ready to crack under the strain of being. While Giacometti's sculptures exemplify existentialist terror, the works of the preeminent British painter of the 1950s, Francis Bacon (1909–1992), evoke outright nausea. Bacon's canvases are case studies in the power of the subconscious. He painted the people he saw around him, but his perceptions were of a society disfigured by slaughter. Slabs

of meat, dripping in blood, figure prominently. Bacon explained, "When you go into a butcher's shop...you can think of the whole horror of life, of one thing living off another."[17]

The terrors of the nuclear age also shaped cultural consciousness in this period. Because figurative painting seemed utterly incapable of capturing the power and terror of the atomic age, the Bomb reinforced the hold of abstract

ALBERTO GIACOMETTI, *MAN POINTING* (1947)
Giacometti's sculptures embodied existentialist anguish. His account of this piece's creation seems to be lifted from a Samuel Beckett play or one of Jean-Paul Sartre's novels: "Wanting to create from memory [the figures] I had seen, to my terror the sculptures became smaller and smaller, they had a likeness only when they were small, yet their dimensions revolted me, and tirelessly I began again, only to end several months later at the same point."

Source: Alberto Giacometti (1901–1966), "Man Pointing." 1947. Bronze, 70 1/2 × 40 3/4 × 16 3/8", at base, 12 × 13 1/4". Gift of Mrs. John D. Rockefeller 3rd. (678.1954) The Museum of Modern Art, New York, NY, U.S.A. Digital Image. The Museum of Modern Art/Licensed by SCALA/Art Resource, NY. © 2010 ARS Artists Rights Society, NY

FRANCIS BACON, *FIGURE WITH MEAT,* 1954

Bacon's disturbing images resonated with a European public still struggling with the impact of total war. *Figure with Meat* is one of a series of paintings that Bacon modeled on Diego Velazquez's *Portrait of Pope Innocent X* (1649–1650). By replacing the draperies in Velazquez's masterpiece with slabs of meat, Bacon challenged the solace and authority of traditional religion.

Sources: Francis Bacon, English, born Ireland, 1909–1992, Figure with Meat, 1954. Oil on canvas, 129.9 × 121.9 cm (51 1/8 × 48 in.) Unframed, Harriott A. Fox Fund, 1956.1201. Photograph Bob Hashimoto. The Art Institute of Chicago. All Rights Reserved. Diego Rodriguez Velasquez (1599–1660), "Portrait of Innocent X", 1650. Araldo De Luca © ADP Management Fratelli Alinari/Art Resource, NY

art over the avant-garde. But abstract art itself changed. Before the war, formal geometric compositions predominated. After the war, a type of modernism, Abstract Expressionism, displayed more spontaneous styles. The Abstract Expressionist Jackson Pollock (1912–1956), for example, invented an entirely new way of painting. Placing the canvas on the ground, he moved around and in it, dripping or pouring paint. In Pollock's works (see p. 920), the canvas has no clear center, no focal point. Instead, it disintegrates, like matter itself. As Pollock explained, "New needs need new techniques.... The modern painter cannot express his age, the airplane, the atom bomb...in the old forms."[18]

Most people confronted their nuclear fears not in art galleries, but rather in movie theaters and popular fiction. In the movies, various nuclear-spawned horrors, such as giant spiders, ants, and turtles, wreaked weekly havoc on the Western world. Fittingly enough, many of these films were produced in Japan. Throughout the 1950s, nuclear war and the postnuclear struggle for survival also filled the pages of popular fiction. Probably the most important "nuclear" novel, however, confined mention of atomic bombs to a single sentence. In *Lord of the Flies* (1954), the British author William Golding (1911–1993) told the simple but brutal story of a group of schoolboys stranded on an island after they flee atomic attack. Their moral deterioration poses basic questions about the meaning of civilization, a question brought to the forefront of Western society by its use of advanced science and technology to obliterate civilian populations during World War II.

CULTURE AND IDEAS IN THE WORLD OF PLENTY In the later 1950s, artists began to turn away from such big questions and to focus instead on the material stuff of everyday existence.

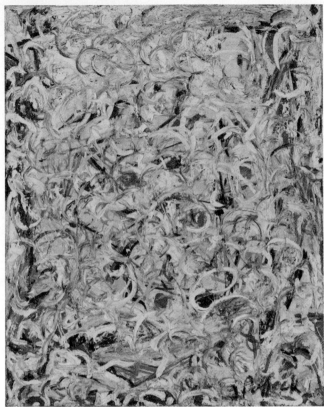

JACKSON POLLOCK, *SHIMMERING SUBSTANCE* (1946)
Many of Pollock's postwar works—huge paintings that pulse with power—show an obsession with heat and light, surely no coincidence in the dawn of the nuclear age.

Works such as the British artist Richard Hamilton's *Just What Is It That Makes Today's Homes So Different, So Appealing?* (1956) satirized and yet celebrated the plethora of material objects pouring off assembly lines. Hamilton was a leading force in the Independent Group, a loose association of British artists, designers, and architects that explored the "aesthetics of plenty"—the idea that consumer affluence had smashed the barriers between fine art and popular culture. The Independent Group, along with other movements such as "New Realism" in France and "Capitalist Realism" in West Germany, helped shape what became known as **pop art.**

Pop artists dismissed the anguish of Bacon and Giacometti as the concerns of an older generation still mired in World War II. Pop art looked outward rather than inward and focused on the material rather than the spiritual. Pop artists spoke in the vocabulary of mass materialism, relied on mass production and mass marketing, and challenged accepted ideas about the role of art and the artist in Western society. When Gerhard Richter (b. 1932) placed himself in the furniture display of a West German department store and called the resulting "piece" *Living with Pop* (1963) he turned the artist, as well as art, into a commodity, something to be bought and sold just like anything else. In the age of consumption, pop advocates declared, the individual artist's intentions were unimportant, and concepts such as artistic genius were irrelevant.

Similar themes also characterized developments in social thought. Existentialism had elevated the individual as the only source of meaning in an absurd universe. In the late 1950s, however, a new social theory, **structuralism,** pushed the individual off center stage. Structuralism, which French anthropologist Claude Lévi-Strauss (1908–2009) first introduced to a wide audience, transformed a number of academic disciplines, including literary criticism, political theory, sociology, and history. Lévi-Strauss argued that the stories that people told, whether medieval French peasants or contemporary Londoners, shared "deep structures," repeated patterns such as pairings and oppositions that shape the way individuals perceive the world. The stories themselves—and the storytellers—were unimportant.

SCIENCE AND RELIGION IN AN AGE OF MASS CONSUMPTION At the same time that structuralists depicted the individual as stuck within a cultural and linguistic web, breakthroughs in the biological sciences suggested that perhaps the web lay *inside* the individual. In 1953, the British biologist Francis Crick (1916–2004) and his American colleague

RICHARD HAMILTON, *JUST WHAT IS IT THAT MAKES TODAY'S HOMES SO DIFFERENT, SO APPEALING?* (1956)

British artist Richard Hamilton was one of the leading figures in the pop art of the 1950s. The image plays with the consumerism and domesticity that marked the postwar period.

James Watson (b. 1928) discovered the structure of DNA, the basic building block of genetic material. Crick and Watson's model of the "double helix," the intertwined spirals of chemical units that, in a sense, issue the instructions for an individual's development, caught the attention of the world. As biologists and geneticists furthered their investigations into human genetic inheritance, they raised exciting yet disturbing possibilities, such as the cloning of living organisms and genetic manipulation. These possibilities added a new dimension to the perennial debate about individual freedom.

Other scientific developments assured human beings more freedom from their physical environment than ever before. Motivated by the Cold War, the space race launched humanity beyond the confines of Earth, culminating in 1969 with American astronaut Neil

CHRONOLOGY: MEDICAL BREAKTHROUGHS

1950	First kidney transplant
1952	First sex-change operation
1952	Polio vaccine first produced
1953	Discovery of DNA
1957	CAT scan developed
1967	First heart transplant

Armstrong's moon walk. Large-scale production of penicillin transformed ordinary medical care, as did rapid development of vaccines against many childhood killers such as measles. In 1953, the American doctor Jonas Salk announced the first successful clinical trial of a polio vaccine. Blood transfusions became more commonplace, along with the development of organ transplants, following the first successful kidney transplant in Chicago in 1950. Like washing machines and television sets, a long and healthy life suddenly appeared accessible to many people in the West.

While scientists were claiming more control over the physical environment, the organized churches continued to offer spiritual authority and sustenance. Church attendance, which had declined in most Western countries in the interwar period, rose during the 1950s. In the United States between 1942 and 1960, church membership per capita grew faster than at any time since the 1890s. No European nation shared this dramatic religious upsurge. Nevertheless, except in Scandinavia, western Europe experienced a gentle religious revival. In Britain during the 1950s, church membership, Sunday school enrollment, and the numbers of baptisms and religious marriages all increased. In West Germany, the rate of churchgoing rose among Protestants from 1952 until 1967. Throughout Catholic Europe, the vibrancy of Christian Democratic politics reflected the vital position of the Roman Catholic Church in society.

In the 1960s, however, the situation changed as Europeans abandoned the church sanctuary in favor of the department store, the sports stadium, and the sofa in front of the television set. Declining rates of church attendance, a growing number of civil rather than religious marriage ceremonies, and an increased reluctance to obey Church teaching on issues such as premarital sexual relations all pointed to the secularization of European society. By the 1970s, churchgoing rates in both Protestant and Catholic countries were in freefall. In what had once been called "Christendom," the fastest-growing religious community was Islam.

The churches did not remain stagnant during this time of change. A number of Protestant theologians argued that Christianity could maintain its relevance in this more secular society by adapting the biblical message to a modern context. The British theologian (and Anglican bishop) John Robinson achieved great notoriety in 1963 when he proclaimed the "death of God." Most of those who jeered at or cheered for Robinson's statement missed his point—that Christians had to update the language in which they articulated their faith to make sense in the modern world.

The biggest change occurred in Roman Catholicism. In 1962 the Second Vatican Council—widely known as **Vatican II**—convened in Rome, the first Catholic council to meet since 1870. In calling the council, Pope John XXIII (r. 1958–1963) sought to modernize the Church, a process that, he recognized, would demand "a change in mentalities, ways of thinking and prejudices, all of which have a long history."[19]

John did not live to see this change in mentalities take place, but his successor Paul VI (r. 1963–1978) presided over a quiet revolution. The Church emerged from Vatican II less hierarchical, with local and regional councils sharing more power with the papacy. For ordinary Catholics, the most striking changes occurred in the worship service, where a number of reforms narrowed the gap between priest and people. The priest moved behind the altar, so that he could face the congregation; he spoke in the vernacular rather than in Latin; and all worshipers, not only the priest, received the wine at communion.

Vatican II was less revolutionary in its approach to sexual issues and gender roles. The council said nothing about homosexuality, reaffirmed the traditional doctrine of clerical celibacy, and insisted that only men could be ordained as priests. The council left open the question of birth control but three years later, the pope declared contraceptive use to be contrary to Catholic teaching. The issues of clerical celibacy, women's ordination, and contraceptive use would bedevil the Church for the rest of the century.

Social Encounters in the Age of Affluence

With the prosperity of the postwar years came a series of encounters—between Americans and Europeans, between immigrants and indigenous populations, between men and women, and between generations—that transformed Western cultures.

AMERICANIZATION, COCA-COLONIZATION, AND THE GAULLIST PROTEST   In the postwar decades, U.S.-based corporations scattered branch offices throughout western Europe, and American-produced goods filled the shelves of European shops. The American presence in science and technology was also formidable. The United States invested more in scientific research and development, produced more graduates in the sciences and engineering than all other Western countries combined, and came out on top in terms of numbers of papers published and patents registered.

American domination of popular culture was even more striking. Immediately after World War II, the U.S. government forced European states to dismantle quotas on American film imports by threatening to withhold much-needed loans. By 1951, American productions accounted for more than 60 percent of films showing in western Europe. American television, too, quickly established a central position in European mass culture. The popular *Lone Ranger* series, for example, appeared in 24 coun-

tries. Language itself seemed subject to American takeover. Words such as *babysitter* and *comics* entered directly into German, while French children coveted *les jeans* and *le chewing-gum*.

Europeans differed in their response to this American presence. Many enthusiastically embraced American culture, equating it with openness and freedom. Others, however, feared that American products such as Coca-Cola would degrade European tastes. They spoke with alarm about the "brain drain" of scientists and academics heading to the richer universities of the United States and argued that even as Europe was losing its colonial possessions, it was itself undergoing colonization, or at least "coca-colonization."[20]

One of the most powerful voices protesting "coca-colonization" belonged to Charles De Gaulle, France's president throughout the 1960s. De Gaulle combined anticommunism and traditional social values with a commitment to a strong state and centralized direction of the economy. Perhaps most of all, **Gaullism** championed France and Frenchness. In De Gaulle's imagination, France was "like the princess in the fairy stories or the Madonna in the frescoes, as dedicated to an exalted and exceptional destiny...France cannot be France without greatness."[21]

De Gaulle did not sympathize with the Soviet Union, but he believed that American "coca-colonization" posed the more immediate threat to the French way of life. Taken in 1960 to view a new highway in California, De Gaulle gazed somberly at the sight of cars weaving in and out on a traffic cloverleaf and commented, "I have the impression that all this will end very badly."[22] To reduce American influence in Europe, and thus to restore France to its rightful position of grandeur and glory, De Gaulle pursued independent foreign and military policies. He extended diplomatic recognition to communist China, made a state visit to Moscow, and withdrew French forces from NATO command (although France remained formally a part of the NATO alliance). In 1960 France exploded its own atomic bomb.

Like De Gaulle, Europeans across the political spectrum feared that their countries might become secondhand versions of the United States, yet the cultural history of this era was one of reciprocal encounters rather than one-way Americanization. Europeans consumed American products with gusto, but in the process they adapted these products to suit their own needs. In the late 1950s, for example, four young working-class men from the northern British seaport of Liverpool latched on to the new American rock-and-roll music, mixed in their own regional musical styles, and transformed popular music not only in Europe, but also in the United States. The impact of the Beatles testified to the power of European culture to remake American cultural products. Even McDonald's, when it arrived in European cities in the 1960s, made subtle changes to the composition of its fast food to appeal to the differing tastes of the new markets.

IMMIGRATION AND ETHNIC DIVERSITY Rising numbers of immigrants who brought with them new and, in many cases, non-Western cultural traditions also transformed European societies during this era. Two developments—decolonization and economic prosperity—explain the upsurge in immigration. With the collapse of European imperial control, white settlers retreated to their country of origin, and colonial "losers"—indigenous groups that had allied with the colonial powers—fled because they feared persecution and discrimination. At the same time, the soaring economies of western Europe created a voracious demand for labor that governments and business sought to fill by recruiting outside their state borders. By the beginning of the 1970s, approximately nine million immigrants had settled in western Europe. Half of these came from the less prosperous Mediterranean states of Portugal, Spain, Italy, and Greece and the other half from Turkey, Yugoslavia and countries in Asia, Africa, and the Caribbean.

These workers did the dirtiest, most dangerous, least desirable jobs. They worked the night

IMMIGRANTS ARRIVING IN BRITAIN, 1956
Many immigrants from regions within the British Empire had been taught that Britain was the "mother country" or "home." They were shocked to discover that once in Britain, they were regarded as foreign and as inferior.

shifts, emptied the bedpans, dug the ditches, and cleaned the toilets. They lived in substandard housing, often confined to isolated dormitories or inner-city slums, and accepted low, often illegally low, pay rates. The reason they did so is starkly presented in Table 28.1. Despite racial discrimination and economic exploitation, western Europe offered greater economic opportunities than were available in the immigrants' homelands.

The majority of the early immigrants were single men. They tended to see themselves, and were seen by their host countries, as "guestworkers," temporary laborers who would earn money and then return home to their native lands. In the mid-1960s, however, families began to join these

TABLE 28.1

ANNUAL PER CAPITA GROSS NATIONAL PRODUCT:
MID-1960S

Pakistan	$125
Jamaica	$520
Turkey	$353
Spain	$822
Italy	$1272
Britain	$1977
France	$2324

Source: Leslie Page Moch, *Moving Europeans: Migration in Western Europe Since 1650* (Bloomington: Indiana University Press, 1992), 177.

men, and a second generation of "immigrants" was born. This generation changed the face of Europe. By the 1980s European societies had become multiethnic.

The emergence of urban ethnic subcultures enlivened European cultures and economies (and diets). It also complicated domestic politics and raised challenging questions about the relationship between national and ethnic identity. Racism became more overt, first, because the white settler groups who returned "home" in the wake of decolonization often brought with them hardened racist attitudes and, second, because the presence of nonwhite minority groups, clustered in certain cities, sparked resentment in societies unused to cultural diversity.

THE SECOND SEX? A third area of encounters that shaped postwar western culture was that between men and women. In 1949, the French writer Simone de Beauvoir (1908–1986) published *The Second Sex*. In this influential critique of gender divisions in Western industrial society, de Beauvoir argued that women remained the "second sex"—that despite political and legal changes, a woman's relationship to men, rather than her own actions or achievements, still defined her. Over the next two decades, the new prosperity pushed women into higher education and the labor force and so, in the long run,

worked to undermine the traditional gender roles that de Beauvoir described. In the short run, however, affluence accentuated women's identity as the second sex.

Demographic changes reflected and reinforced postwar domesticity. Marriage rates rose and the marriage age dropped in the postwar years. In the United States between 1940 and 1957, the fertility rate rose by 50 percent. Europe experienced a baby "boomlet" rather than a baby boom with birth rates rising in the late 1940s but dropping in the 1950s.

By exalting women's maternal identity, both religion and popular culture provided a potent ideology for these demographic changes. The Roman Catholic Church of the 1950s placed renewed emphasis on Mary, the paragon of motherhood. Pope Pius XII (r. 1939–1958) particularly encouraged the growth of devotion to Mary. He proclaimed in 1950 that Mary had ascended bodily into heaven (the Doctrine of the Assumption) and designated 1954 as the Year of Mary. This Marian devotion encouraged women to regard motherhood as a holy calling. Popular culture reinforced this religious message, with its glossy images of what families should look like and how they should interact. In television programs and in the articles and advertisements of women's magazines, the woman stayed at home, presiding over an expanding array of household machines that, in theory, reduced her housework burden and freed her to focus on the satisfactions of motherhood.

Cold War concerns also accentuated the Western woman's domestic role. First, anticommunist propaganda hailed domesticity as a sign of Western superiority by contrasting the favorable lot of Western women to their Soviet counterparts, who combined their domestic duties with full-time outside employment, often in jobs involving heavy manual labor, and with the tiresome task of lining up for hours each day to purchase scarce goods. Second, the nuclear age made the nuclear family seem all the more important. Feeling increasingly helpless in a superpower-dominated world on the brink of nuclear annihilation, Europeans tended to withdraw for shelter to family life.

For some women, this shelter was more like a prison. In *The Feminine Mystique* (1963), the American journalist Betty Friedan (1921–2006) identified what she called "the problem that had no name," a crisis of identity and purpose among middle-class, educated women confined in the role of housewife and mother. The research of British sociologist Hannah Gavron (1936–1965) supported Friedan's argument. In *The Captive Wife*, (1966), Gavron used interviews and other sociological data to explore "the conflicts of housebound mothers." She asked, "Have all the great changes in the position of women in the last one hundred and fifty years come to nothing?" A 29-year-old wife and mother of two young sons, Gavron committed suicide the year before her work was published.

Whether a nightmare or a dream, the domestic ideal remained removed from the reality of many women's lives in the postwar era. In the poorer social classes, women by necessity continued to work outside the home, as they always had. At the same time, the new culture of consumption demanded that many women, clinging precariously to middle-class status, take on waged employment to pay for the ever-expanding list of household necessities.

A new pattern of employment emerged that reconciled renewed domesticity with the needs of expanding economies and ambitious consumers. Increasingly, single women worked until they married. Many continued to do so until the first child arrived and resumed paid employment after the last child had left home or at least started school. This work was regarded, however, as secondary to their main job—the making of a home and the rearing of children. Part-time employment, with lower wages and few or no benefits, expanded accordingly. Everywhere pay rates for men and women remained unequal.

THE PROTEST ERA   The unprecedented prosperity of the West in this era permitted a dramatic expansion of higher education systems. By the later 1960s, these universities became the center of powerful protests as political demonstrations exploded in almost every Western country and in the developing nations well. In France, a student demonstration blossomed into a full-scale social revolt. Within a few days, eight million French men and women were on strike. "Paris '68" came to symbolize the political and social discontent of many in the West, particularly the youth, during these years.

Much of this discontent focused on the **New Left** argument that ordinary people, even in democratic societies, possessed little power. Appalled by the inhumanity of Stalinism, New Leftists differed from the "old" Left in their suspicion of the state. New Left thinkers such as the German philosopher Herbert Marcuse (1898–1979) warned that expanding state power threatened the individuality and independence of the ordinary citizen. They argued that debate might seem open, but that experts and elites, not ordinary people, made the actual choices. Hence, the protesters demanded "participatory" rather than parliamentary democracy, the revitalization of citizenship through active participation in decision making.

Discarding orthodox political solutions went hand in hand with overturning traditional social rules. In their demand for "liberation," the students focused as much on cultural as on economic and political issues. As behaviors labeled immoral or bohemian in the 1950s became commonplace—for example, couples living together before marriage or individuals engaging in sexual relationships with a variety of partners—commentators began to talk about a sexual revolution.

The protests of the later 1960s were also linked to the wider context of decolonization and the Cold War. Protesters identified their struggle for more open politics with colonial independence movements. Rejecting both Soviet-style communism and free-market capitalism, protesters turned for inspiration to the newly emerging nations of Latin America and Asia. Seeking to break free from the confines of the Cold War, they fiercely criticized American involvement in Vietnam, in which they believed the United States served not as "the leader of the free world," but rather as an imperialist oppressor.

CONCLUSION

New Definitions, New Divisions

When Soviet tanks rolled through the streets of Budapest in 1956, they flattened not only the Hungarian Revolution, but also any illusions about the democratic nature of Soviet-style communism. Yet the hope that the communist system could be reformed, that Marx's original concern for social justice and political equality could be reclaimed, remained—until twelve years later when the tanks rolled again in an eastern European city. The crushing of the Prague Spring destroyed any hope of a democratic eastern Europe under Soviet domination.

In contrast, democracy took firm root in western Europe during the postwar era, even in nations with antidemocratic cultural traditions such as West Germany and Italy. Yet in 1968, protesters in Paris and in cities throughout the world challenged the easy linkage of "the West" with democracy. They pointed out that the increasing scale and complexity of industrial society deprived ordinary people of opportunities for genuine participation in political decision making. And they pointed to the way that Cold War divisions superseded democratic commitments. Within the Cold War context, "the West" sometimes seemed to mean simply "anti-Soviet."

By the early 1970s, the sharp bipolarities of West versus East had begun to break down. Over the next three decades, economic crisis, combined with revolutionary changes in eastern European and Soviet affairs, would reshape the contemporary world. By the early 1990s, the Cold War was over and nationalist conflicts, often fueled by vicious ethnic and religious hatreds, once again played front and center after 20 years of being upstaged by superpower hostilities.

KEY TERMS

Cold War
Iron Curtain
Potsdam Conference
Big Three
Yalta Conference
Bretton Woods Agreement
Truman Doctrine
containment
Marshall Plan
NATO (North Atlantic Treaty Organization)
Warsaw Pact
decolonization
brinkmanship
Berlin Wall
Third World
de-Stalinization
Christian Democracy, Christian Democratic parties
European Economic Community (EEC)
Common Market
pop art
structuralism
Vatican II
Gaullism
New Left

CHAPTER QUESTIONS

1. Why and how did the world step from World War II to the Cold War? (page 891)
2. What was the impact of decolonization and the Cold War on the global balance of power? (page 901)
3. What patterns characterized the history of the Soviet Union and eastern Europe after the death of Stalin? (page 911)
4. What patterns characterized the history of western Europe in the 1950s and 1960s? (page 915)

TAKING IT FURTHER

1. Was the Cold War inevitable? If so, why? If not, what event constituted the "point of no return" and why?
2. How did consumerism structure Western economies culture, and politics in the 1950s and 1960s?

✓• Practice on MyHistoryLab

The West in the Contemporary Era: New Encounters and Transformations

■ Economic Stagnation and Political Change: The 1970s and 1980s
■ Revolution in the East ■ In the Wake of Revolution ■ Rethinking the West

ON THE EVENING OF NOVEMBER 9, 1989, EAST GERMAN BORDER guards at the Berlin Wall watched nervously as thousands of East Berliners crowded in front of them and demanded to be allowed into West Berlin. This demand was extraordinary: In the 28 years that the Berlin Wall had stood, some 200 people had been shot trying to cross from east to west. But the autumn of 1989 was no ordinary time. A reformist regime had emerged in the Soviet Union and proclaimed that eastern European governments could no longer rely on the Red Army to crush domestic dissent. Poland and Hungary were in the process of replacing communist governments with pluralist parliamentary systems. And in East Germany, over one million disaffected citizens had joined illegal protest demonstrations.

In response to this overwhelming public pressure, the East German government had decided to relax the requirements for obtaining an exit visa to visit West Germany. But at a press conference on the morning of November 9, the East Berlin Communist Party boss Gunter Schabowski stated, wrongly, that anyone who wanted to head to the West could obtain an automatic exit visa at the border. As huge crowds gathered at the checkpoints that dotted the Berlin Wall, the border guards had no idea what to do. Panicked, they opened the gates. While television cameras broadcast the scene to an astonished world, tens of thousands of East Berliners walked, ran, and danced across the border that had for so long literally and symbolically divided West from East. Elated with their new freedom and energized with a sense of power and possibility, they jumped upon the Wall. An instrument of coercion and division became a platform for partying. Within a few days, and again without any official approval, ordinary Germans, equipped with hammers and chisels, began to dismantle the Wall erected almost three decades earlier.

The fall of the Berlin Wall has come to symbolize the dramatic events that closed the twentieth century: the collapse of communist regimes throughout eastern Europe, the end of the Cold War, the disintegration of the Soviet Union, and the onset of civil war

AND THE WALL CAME TUMBLING DOWN

Events in Hungary helped topple the Berlin Wall in East Germany. In the summer of 1989, the Hungarian government, already well along the road from communism to democracy, assisted the anti-communist movement in East Germany by opening Hungary's borders with Austria. The repressive East German communist regime did not permit its citizens to travel to the West; it did, however, allow them to vacation in Hungary. The new Hungarian border policy meant that East Germans seeking to escape communism had only to book a holiday in Hungary and then walk, drive, or take a train across the Hungarian border into Austria, and into freedom. In just three days in September, 13,000 East Germans did exactly that. This mass exodus forced the East German communist government to promise reforms—too little, too late.

in Yugoslavia and in many formerly Soviet regions. In the subsequent decades, governments and ordinary people—not only in Europe but across the globe—struggled to build new structures to suit the transformed geopolitical landscape. What, then, were the causes and consequences of these developments? And what were their implications for Western identity—and for the future of Western civilization?

ECONOMIC STAGNATION AND POLITICAL CHANGE: THE 1970s AND 1980s

■ How did economic and political developments in the 1970s and 1980s destabilize post-World War II national and international structures?

The 1970s and 1980s saw the post-World War II political settlement, in national and international terms, begin to collapse. The stark clarity—the "Them versus Us"—of the Cold War grew more opaque at the same time that economic crisis widened divisions within Western societies and eroded the social democratic political consensus.

The 1970s: A More Uncertain Era

In the early 1970s, the West entered a new era. **Détente,** the effort to stabilize superpower relations through negotiations and arms control, shifted the Cold War status quo while the easy affluence of the postwar period abruptly ended.

THE ERA OF DÉTENTE   West German diplomacy caused the first shift in Cold War relations. In 1969 the West Berlin mayor and Social Democratic Party (SPD) leader Willy Brandt (1913–1992) became chancellor. For the first time in its history, West Germany had a government not led by a Christian Democrat. Brandt proceeded to implement a new *Ostpolitik* or "Eastern policy"—the opening of diplomatic and economic relations between West Germany and the Soviet Union and its satellite states. Ostpolitik reached its climax when East and West Germany recognized the legitimacy of each other's existence in 1972 and both Germanys entered the United Nations in 1973.

Economic pressures led the leaders of the superpowers to embrace a much wider version of Ostpolitik: détente. By the end of the 1960s, the Soviet and the American economies were stagnating. With both states spending colossal sums on nuclear weapons, their leaders looked for a new approach to the Cold War. Thus, in November 1969 Soviet and American negotiators began the Strategic Arms Limitation Talks (SALT). Signed in 1972, the agreement froze the existing weapons balance. SALT left the superpowers with sufficient nuclear weaponry to destroy the globe several times over, but it helped slow the armaments spiral and ease Cold War tensions.

Détente also extended to U.S. relations with the other great communist power: China. In 1971 President Richard Nixon (1913–1994) announced the lifting of travel and trade restrictions with China and then visited China himself. "East versus West" had formed a basic building block of international relations throughout the 1950s and 1960s. In the era of détente, however, the shape of international politics became more fluid.

ECONOMIC CRISIS IN THE WEST   The economic outlook also blurred in this era as the 1970s brought an unprecedented combination of high inflation and high unemployment rates. Commentators labeled this new reality **stagflation**—escalating prices combined with the joblessness of a stagnant economy. Between 1974 and 1976 the average annual growth rate within western European nations dropped to zero.

War and oil helped create this economic crisis. In October 1973, the Yom Kippur War began when Egyptian and Syrian armies attacked Israel. In retaliation for American assistance to Israel, the oil-producing Arab states in OPEC (the Organization of Petroleum Exporting Countries) imposed an embargo on sales to the United States and quintupled the price of a barrel of oil. In 1979 political revolution in Iran doubled the price again. These two "oil crises" vastly accelerated the inflationary spiral.

Two other factors also contributed the economic crisis. First, in 1973 President Nixon acted to defend the weakening dollar by letting it "float." Market forces rather than fixed exchange rates now determined the dollar's value against other currencies. This decision gutted the Bretton Woods Agreement, which had governed international economic affairs since World War II (see Chapter 28), and introduced a less regulated, more volatile economic era. In the two decades after the collapse of Bretton Woods, 69 countries experienced serious banking crises as currency speculators destabilized national economies and the annual economic growth rates of the developing nations fell by one-third.

A second factor in the economic crisis of the 1970s was international competition as Asian, South American, and Latin American economies industrialized. Because Western societies possessed a politicized workforce that demanded relatively high wages and extensive social services, manufacturing firms began to move south and east to take advantage of the lack of labor regulation and protection in the developing world.

CONSEQUENCES OF THE CRISIS As the economic pie appeared smaller, competition for slices increased. The 1970s saw a resurgence of industrial unrest. Conflict with unions brought down three successive British governments in a decade. Throughout the West images of picketing workers, often fighting with police, dominated televised news broadcasts.

Racial conflict also escalated, with the nine million immigrants residing in northern and western Europe making easy targets for those individuals and groups who sought someone to blame for their economic hardships. By 1975 West Germany, France, the Netherlands, Britain, Belgium, Sweden, and Switzerland had all banned further immigration, but ironically, this legislation actually increased the size of immigrant communities. Foreign workers scrambled to get into western Europe before the doors shut, and those already established hastened to bring in family members. By 1991, 25 percent of the inhabitants of France were either immigrants or the children or grandchildren of immigrants.

The resulting encounters among peoples of different religious and ethnic traditions transformed European cultures and raised questions about national identities. In Britain, for example, Afro-Caribbean styles of dress and music reshaped white working-class youth culture. At the same time, however, journalists often described an individual born in Britain to British citizenship as a "third-generation immigrant," a label that revealed the "whiteness" of popular notions of British identity. At least in Britain, as well as in France, immigrants could become or already were legal citizens. In contrast, in West Germany, Switzerland, and the Scandinavian countries, immigrants remained "foreign," with no chance of obtaining citizenship. Thus, their children grew up in a society in which they had no political rights. These "foreigners" experienced widespread discrimination in education, housing, and employment.

Explicitly racist political parties capitalized on anti-immigration sentiment. The most important such party emerged in France in 1974 when Jean-Marie Le Pen (b. 1928) created the *Front National*. In Le Pen's view, "Everything comes from immigration. Everything goes back to immigration." Unemployment, rising crime rates, an increase in illegitimate births, crowded schools, AIDS—Le Pen blamed it all on nonwhite immigrants. Appealing particularly to young, male working-class voters, Le Pen's party remained a political presence in France for the next three decades.

The 1980s: The End of Political Consensus in the West

The economic crisis cracked the postwar political consensus. Two offshoots of the protests of the 1960s—new feminism and environmentalism—demanded a reorientation of social democratic politics, while New Conservatives rejected social democratic fundamentals.

NEW CHALLENGES AND NEW IDENTITIES: NEW FEMINISM **New feminism** (also called "Second Wave feminism") emerged directly out of the student protest movement of the 1960s, when female activists grew frustrated with their limited role—"We cook while the men talk of revolution."[1] Their efforts to liberate women from political and cultural limits gave birth to an international feminist movement.

Although new feminists worked for the election of female candidates and other such political goals, they refused to confine their efforts to parliamentary politics. Asserting that "the personal is political," new feminists attacked beauty pageants, critiqued the fashion industry, and demanded equal access for girls to sporting funds and facilities. They also sought to outlaw spousal rape and to legalize abortion. Abortions became legal first in northern Europe: in Britain in 1967, in Denmark in 1970. Catholic Europe followed: In Italy abortions became legally available in 1978, in France in 1979.

New feminism extended its critique of gender inequalities to the economic and educational spheres. Feminists demanded equal pay for equal work and greater access for women to professional opportunities. They pressed for more generous parental leave policies, family allowances, and child care provisions. With women accounting for approximately half of the university students in many Western countries, feminists also began to alter the content of the curriculum. Challenging the biases that had regarded women's contributions as irrelevant and women's lives as insignificant, feminists brought to light the "hidden history" of women.

NEW CHALLENGES AND NEW IDENTITIES: ENVIRONMENTALISM   Environmentalists added their voice to the political cacophony of the 1970s and 1980s. At the heart of environmentalism was the idea of natural limits, often conceptualized as "Spaceship Earth," the vision of the planet as a "single spaceship, without unlimited reservoirs of anything."[2] This vision led environmentalists to question the fundamental structures of industrial economies (capitalist and communist), particularly their inherent emphasis on "more, bigger, faster, now." The movement argued that quantitative measures of economic growth (such as the GNP) failed to factor in environmental destruction and social dislocation and that in many contexts, "small is beautiful."

The environmentalist movement's concern with ecological sustainability helped create "Green" political parties. **Green** politics drew on two other sources: new feminism and the New Left. The Greens contended that the degradation of the natural environment stemmed from the same root as discrimination against women—an obsession with physical power and an unwillingness to tear down hierarchical structures. Green politics also championed the key New Leftist goal of participatory democracy (see Chapter 28) and so articulated a basic challenge to the political status quo: "We are neither left nor right; we are in front." By the late 1980s Green Parties had sprouted in 15 western European countries. The Greens were the most successful in West Germany, where they sat in the legislature from 1983 and formed an important voting bloc.

THE NEW CONSERVATIVES   Discontented by the economic crisis and social unrest of the 1970s, voters throughout the West looked for new answers. In Spain, Portugal, and Greece, they turned to socialist parties. Throughout most of western Europe and in the United States, however, **New Conservatism** dominated political society. Three leaders epitomized the New Conservatism: the Republican Ronald Reagan in the United States (1911–2004), the Christian Democrat Helmut Kohl in West Germany (b. 1930), and the Conservative Margaret Thatcher in Britain (b. 1925). New Conservatives rejected the postwar emphasis on social improvement in favor of individual achievement. They argued that rising social expenditures, funded by rising taxes, bore the blame for surging inflation and declining economic growth rates. As Kohl demanded during his 1983 campaign, "Less state, more market; fewer collective burdens, more personal performance; fewer encrusted structures, more mobility, self-initiative, and competition."

The New Conservative agenda included lifting regulations on business, privatizing nationalized or state-owned industries, and reining in the welfare state. Most dramatically, New Conservatives abandoned the central feature of the postwar social democratic consensus: the conviction that the state has the responsibility to ensure full employment. By imposing high interest rates on their economies, New Conservative leaders such as Thatcher lowered damaging double-digit inflation rates. But high interest rates hurt domestic manufacturing and led to rising unemployment numbers. In Britain, 13 percent of the workforce was unemployed by 1984. In West Germany, too, Kohl's policies of holding down taxes and government expenditures accompanied unemployment rates over 9 percent in the mid-1980s.

THE END OF DÉTENTE   Like the emergence of New Conservatism, rising superpower tensions

NEW CONSERVATIVES AT WORK
British Prime Minister Margaret Thatcher and German Chancellor Helmut Kohl address the press after a meeting in London in 1988.

accelerated the breakdown of the post-World War II political consensus within Western societies. Those tensions had appeared to be receding in the early 1970s as the leaders of the superpowers embraced détente. In 1975 representatives of 32 European states, Canada, the United States, and the Soviet Union signed the **Helsinki Accords,** which ratified existing European borders, agreed to the joint notification of major military exercises (to reduce the chances of accidental nuclear war), and promised to safeguard human rights.

The Helsinki Accords came about because of détente—yet they helped destroy it. Eastern European and Soviet dissidents used the Helsinki human rights clauses to publicize the abuses committed by their governments and to demand justice. Dissident activities expanded throughout the Soviet bloc, as did efforts at repression. When U.S. president Jimmy Carter took office in

1976, he placed human rights at the center of his foreign policy. Carter's approach infuriated Soviet leaders. Détente finally died in December 1979, when Soviet troops invaded Afghanistan. Calling the invasion "the most serious threat to peace since the Second World War," Carter warned that if the Soviets moved toward the Middle East, he would use nuclear weapons.

The election of New Conservatives such as Thatcher in 1979 and Reagan in 1980 intensified the rejection of détente and the renewal of the Cold War. Reagan labeled the Soviet Union the "Evil Empire"—a reference to the popular *Star Wars* film series released in the 1970s—and revived the anticommunist attitudes and rhetoric of the 1950s. Thatcher strongly supported Reagan's decision to accelerate the arms buildup begun by Carter. Her hard-line anticommunism won her the nickname "Iron Lady" from Soviet policymakers.

THE GREENHAM COMMON PROTESTS

In the spring of 1983, protesters formed a 14-mile human chain across Greenham Common in England to protest against NATO's deployment of cruise missiles. The protest was part of a much wider movement in western Europe and the United States against the intensification of the Cold War after the collapse of détente. The Greenham Common protest also played a pivotal role in British feminism, as female activists established a women-only camp at the Greenham Common military base.

REVOLUTION IN THE EAST

■ What factors explain not only the outbreak but also the success of the revolutions of 1989–1991?

Between 1989 and 1991, revolution engulfed eastern Europe and the Soviet Union and set in motion a series of breathtaking changes: Soviet control over eastern Europe ended, the Cold War came to an abrupt halt, the Soviet Union itself ceased to exist. Mikhail Gorbachev (1985–1991), appointed Soviet Communist Party secretary in 1985, played a pivotal role in

these events. But Gorbachev did not control the story. Ordinary people developed their own plot lines. What the Czech dissident (and future president) Vaclav Havel called "the power of the powerless" proved powerful indeed.

The Crisis of Legitimacy in the East

While Western countries in the 1970s struggled with stagflation, the Soviet Union posted record-breaking production figures. But Soviet statistics ignored the quality of goods produced, the actual demand for a product, or the cost of producing it. And while Soviet leaders boasted that they had completed the heavy industrial expansion planned by Khrushchev in the early 1960s, microchips now counted for more than iron ore, and fiber optics, not steel, buttressed the new modernity. The rigid Soviet command economy could not keep up. By the 1980s, its only growth sectors were oil and vodka—and then the bottom dropped out of the oil market. After peaking in 1981, oil prices began a steady decade-long fall—and so, too, did the Soviet economy.

The Soviet Union's satellite states in eastern Europe also lurched from apparent prosperity into economic crisis during this period. During the 1970s, two factors cushioned eastern Europe from the economic crisis in the West. First, eastern governments could purchase Soviet oil at prices below market value. (In return these states had to sell their own products to the Soviets at similar discounts.) Second, loans from Western banks helped mask fundamental problems such as over-centralization and under-productivity. But in the 1980s, the Soviet Union, struggling with its own faltering economy, began charging higher oil prices at the same time that debt loads overwhelmed eastern European economies.

THE BEGINNING OF THE END: SOLIDARITY Events in Poland indicated the fragility of the communist system and initiated the process that led to the system's collapse. Faced with negative economic growth rates, the Polish government announced in July 1980 a rise in prices for meat and other essentials. Workplace strikes protesting the price rises spread throughout Poland. Then, workers at the Lenin Shipyard in Gdansk, led by a charismatic electrician named Lech Wałęsa (b. 1943), demanded the right to form a trade union independent of communist control. One month later, they did so—Solidarity was born. More than a trade union, Solidarity demanded the liberation of political prisoners, an end to censorship, and a rollback of governmental power. Within just a few months, more than eleven million Poles joined Solidarity.

How could Solidarity become such a powerful political and social presence so quickly? The answer rests in the concept of civil society: public organizations and activities separate from the state, commerce, or the family. Ranging from church and charitable groups to sports and hobby clubs, from theater companies to rock bands to radio stations, these organizations and activities help create community life—and in such communities, an individual creates his or her own sense of independent identity. In Soviet-style communism, where the state aimed to control not only public life but even private consciousness, such a self-identity, forged outside state control, threatened the entire political system. (See *Encounters and Transformations* in this chapter.)

In Poland, however, communist control had never entirely destroyed civil society, in part because of the key role of the Roman Catholic Church. Participation in the Church had long been a way for Poles to express not only their religious faith but also their Polishness—an identity not controlled by the communist government. The power of this Catholic identity became clear in 1979, when Pope John Paul II (r. 1978–2005) visited Poland. This visit marked the first time any pope traveled to a communist country–but John Paul II was not just any pope. Born Karol Wojtyła, he was the first non-Italian pope since 1523 and the first Polish pope ever. Twelve million people—one-third of the Polish population—greeted the pope during his visit. Many Solidarity members testified to the importance of this visit in empowering them to challenge the communist order.

Solidarity's growing popularity soon threatened communist control of Poland. In December 1981 Prime Minister Wojciech Jaruzelski declared martial law and arrested more than 10,000 Solidarity members (including Wałęsa). Like the Hungarian Revolution in 1956 and the Prague Spring of 1968, Solidarity seemed to be one more noble but defeated protest in eastern Europe.

But Solidarity refused to be defeated. It remained a political presence and a moral force in Polish society throughout the 1980s. Solidarity members met in small groups, published

THE MOMENT OF SOLIDARITY

Pope John Paul II greets Lech Wałęsa. The Polish pope's visit to his homeland in 1979 helped energize the anticommunist protests that coalesced into Solidarity the following year.

newspapers, and organized election boycotts. At the same time, activists throughout Hungary, Czechoslovakia, East Germany, and the Soviet Union itself drew on Solidarity for inspiration and practical lessons in resistance.

Before 1989 no other eastern European state experienced a protest movement as dramatic as Solidarity, yet throughout much of the region two important developments marked the later 1970s and the 1980s. First, economic hardship fed widespread political alienation and a deepening longing for radical change. And second, activists and ordinary people worked to create the structures of civil society.

ENVIRONMENTAL PROTEST For many eastern Europeans, environmental activism helped create at least the beginnings of civil society. For decades, the conquest of nature had been a key part of communist ideology: "We cannot wait for favors from nature; our task is to take from her."[3] Governments throughout the Soviet bloc ignored the most basic environmental precautions, dumping untreated sewage and nuclear waste into lakes and rivers and pumping poisons into the air. But because communist officials regarded the natural environment as insignificant, they tended to view environmentalist protest as unimportant, a "safe" outlet for popular frustration. Thus, by the later 1970s, many Soviet and eastern European citizens had joined environmentalist groups. Environmental activism worked like a termite infestation, nibbling away at communist structures. In Hungary, public outrage over a Czech-Hungarian collaboration to dam the Danube River resulted in the formation of environmentalist organizations that encouraged Hungarians to question not only the

Danube project, but also the priorities and policies of the entire communist system.

Environmentalism also fueled nationalist protest among the non-Russian peoples within the Soviet Union. The various national and ethnic groups of the Soviet empire watched their forests disappear, their lakes dry up, and their ancient cities bulldozed as a result of decisions made in faraway Moscow by men they regarded as foreigners—as *Russians* rather than *comrades* or fellow Soviets. By the 1980s, for example, with schools in Latvia forced to issue gas masks as a routine safety precaution because of the dangers of chemical spills, many Latvians concluded that they would be better off in an independent Latvia.

Gorbachev and Radical Reform

As these discontents simmered among the peoples of the Soviet bloc, a series of deaths ushered in an era of dramatic change. In 1982, the decrepit Leonid Brezhnev died—and so, in rapid succession, did his successors, Yuri Andropov (1914–1984) and Konstantin Chernenko (1911–1985). The time had come for a generational shift. When Mikhail Gorbachev succeeded Chernenko, he was 54 years old. Compared with his elderly colleagues on the Politburo, he looked like a teenager.

Gorbachev's biography encompassed the drama of Soviet history. Born in 1931 Gorbachev experienced Stalinism at its worst. One-third of the inhabitants of his native village in Stavropol were executed, imprisoned, or died from famine or disease in the upheavals of collectivization. Both of his grandfathers were arrested during the Great Purge. His father served in the Red Army during World War II and was wounded twice. Yet Gorbachev's family continued to believe in the communist dream. In 1948 Gorbachev and his father together won the Order of Red Banner of Labor for harvesting almost six times the average crop. This achievement, and his clear ability, won Gorbachev a university education. After earning degrees in economics and law, Gorbachev rose through the ranks of the provincial and then the national Communist Party.

Although an ardent communist, Gorbachev became convinced that the Soviet system was ailing, and that the only way to restore it to health was through radical surgery. What he did not anticipate was that such surgery would, in fact, kill the patient. Gorbachev's surgical tools were *glasnost* and *perestroika*, two Russian terms without direct English equivalents.

GLASNOST AND PERESTROIKA **Glasnost,** sometimes translated as "openness," "publicity," or "transparency," meant abandoning the deception and censorship that had always characterized the Soviet system for a policy based on open admission of failures and problems. According to Gorbachev, "Broad, timely, and frank information is testimony of faith in people...and for their capacity to work things out themselves."[4]

Soviet citizens remained wary of Gorbachev's talk of glasnost—until April 1986 and the Chernobyl nuclear power plant disaster. Operator error at the Ukrainian power plant led to the most serious nuclear accident in history. In the days following the accident, 35 plant workers died. Over the next five years the cleanup effort claimed at least 7,000 lives. The accident placed more than four million inhabitants of Ukraine and Belarus at risk from excess radiation and spread a radioactive cloud that extended all the way to Scotland. When news of the accident first reached Moscow, party officials acted as they had always done: They denied it. But after monitors in Western countries recorded the radiation spewing into the atmosphere, Gorbachev dared to release accurate information to the public. In 1986, 93 percent of the Soviet population had access to a television set and what they saw on their screens convinced them that glasnost was real. A powerful change had occurred in Soviet political culture.

Through glasnost Gorbachev aimed to overcome public alienation and apathy and so convince Soviet citizens to participate in

ENCOUNTERS AND TRANSFORMATIONS

Rock and the Velvet Revolution

In September 1968, less than one month after the armies of the Soviet Union and its satellite states had crushed the Prague Spring (see Chapter 28), a Czech bass player named Milan Hlavsa formed a rock band. The military invasion and the subsequent political crackdown throughout Czechoslovakia appalled Hlavsa, but it never occurred to him that he could do anything to change the harsh reality of life in the communist bloc. He certainly did not see forming a rock band as a political act. He and the other members of the band simply liked Western rock music (particularly the "psychedelic" music of Frank Zappa, the Velvet Underground, and the Doors), and they wanted to play in a rock band. Yet the encounter between the communist state and the anarchic energy of rock helped undermine communist rule and so contributed to the transformation of eastern Europe. Despite the efforts of many communist governments to block access to what they viewed as a Western and therefore subversive cultural form, rock music flourished in eastern Europe. It offered entertainment and escape—and also the chance to create an identity outside of communism.

Hlavsa and his friends called their band "The Plastic People of the Universe" (PPU), after a Frank Zappa song, and PPU quickly became the most popular psychedelic group in Prague. But almost as quickly the band ran into trouble. As part of the post-1968 crackdown, the Czech communist government insisted that rock bands conform to a set of official guidelines governing how, what, and where they performed. PPU refused and, in January 1970, lost its professional license. In the communist system, the state not only controlled broadcasting and recording, but even owned the distribution of musical instruments and electrical equipment. Without a license, PPU lost access to rehearsal and recording space and their instruments as well. But the band played on by repairing cast-off instruments and constructing

amplifiers from old transistor radios. Banned in 1972 from performing in Prague, PPU moved to the countryside. Banned in 1974 from playing anywhere, PPU dove underground. Fans alerted other fans when the band would be playing at some remote farm, while recordings made in houses and garages circulated illegally.

During this period PPU became more than just a rock band. It stood at the center of what artistic director and manager Ivan Jirous labeled the "Second Culture." An alternative to the official communist "First Culture," the "Second Culture" comprised musicians, fans, artists, writers, and anyone else who sought to carve out a space of individuality and integrity in a society based on conformity and lies.

On March 17, 1976, the Secret Police arrested 27 musicians, including every member of PPU. Six months later rock music went on trial. In response to international protests, the Czech government released most of the 27 rockers. But Jirous and the band's saxophonist, Vratislav Brabenec, as well as two musicians from other groups, were found guilty of "organized disturbance of the peace" and sentenced to between eight and 18 months in prison.

In the courtroom the day of the sentencing sat Václav Havel, an ardent Frank Zappa fan as well as a playwright who used drama to satirize the communist system. The imprisonment of Jirous and Brabenec infuriated Havel. For the next several years, he opened his farmhouse to PPU for illegal concerts and recording sessions.

More important, Havel walked out of the courtroom convinced that the time had come to challenge communism openly. On January 1, 1977, Havel and other artists and intellectuals announced the formation of Charter 77 to publicize human rights abuses under communism. Over the next decade many Charter members, including Havel, spent time in prison. Yet, by calling the state to account for its crimes, Charter 77 helped weaken the communist regime. When revolution came in 1989, that regime toppled with astounding ease.

ROCKING THE BLOC

In 1977, the Plastic People of the Universe play an illegal concert in Václav Havel's farmhouse.

PPU had split up two years before and so did not sing in the new era, but fittingly, one of the first individuals that President Václav Havel invited to the new free Czechoslovakia was an aging psychedelic rocker named Frank Zappa.

For Discussion

Imagine that the post-1968 Communist government in Czechoslovakia simply ignored the PPU. Would events have unfolded any differently? Why or why not?

reforming political and economic life—or **perestroika,** often translated as "restructuring" or "reconstruction." Gorbachev believed he could reverse Soviet economic decline by restructuring the economy through modernization, decentralization, and the introduction of a limited market. Gorbachev knew, however, that even limited economic reforms threatened the vested interests of communist bureaucrats and that these bureaucrats would block his reforms if they could. Thus, economic perestroika would not succeed without political perestroika—restructuring the political system, opening it up to limited competition to allow new leaders and new ideas to triumph. So in 1990 Gorbachev ended the Communist Party's monopoly on parliamentary power, and the

Soviet Union entered the brave new world of multiparty politics.

ENDING THE COLD WAR Restructuring Soviet economics and politics led almost inevitably to restructuring international relations—and to ending the Cold War. By the 1980s, the arms race absorbed at least 18 percent of the Soviet GNP, as the Soviets scrambled to keep pace with the Reagan military build-up. Gorbachev concluded that the Soviet Union could not afford the Cold War. To signal to the West his desire for a new international order, Gorbachev reduced Soviet military commitments abroad and asked to resume arms control negotiations. In December 1987, Gorbachev and Reagan signed the INF (Intermediate

GLASNOST
Mikhail Gorbachev meets with workers in Moscow in 1985.

Nuclear Forces) Treaty, agreeing to eliminate all land-based intermediate-range nuclear missiles. In 1991, the Soviets and Americans signed the Strategic Arms Reduction Treaty (START I), in which they pledged to reduce intercontinental ballistic missiles. The nuclear arms race was over.

Gorbachev also moved to restructure Soviet policies in eastern Europe. He realized, first, that western leaders would not end the Cold War as long as the Soviet Union sought to dictate eastern European affairs, and second, that the Soviet Union could no longer afford to control its satellite states. In his first informal meetings with eastern European communist leaders in 1985, Gorbachev told these aging communist stalwarts that the Red Army would no longer enforce their will on rebellious populations. By the time Gorbachev addressed the UN General Assembly at the end of 1988 and declared that the nations of eastern Europe

were free to choose their own paths, dramatic changes were underway.

Revolution in Eastern Europe

Hungary and Poland were the first states to jettison communist rule. Even before Gorbachev took power, economic crisis and public discontent had driven the Polish and Hungarian governments to embrace reform. In the early 1980s Hungary moved toward a Western-oriented, market-driven economy by joining the World Bank and the International Monetary Fund (IMF) and establishing a stock market. In 1985, independent candidates for the first time appeared on Hungarian ballots—and many won. In Poland, Jaruzelski's government also experimented with restoring some measures of a market economy and with limited political reform. Once martial law ended in 1983, censorship loosened. Newspapers published criticisms of

CHRONOLOGY: REVOLUTION IN EASTERN EUROPE

1980	Formation of Solidarity in Poland
1981	Martial law declared in Poland; Solidarity made illegal
1983	End of martial law in Poland, political and economic reforms begin; political reforms liberalize Hungarian elections
1985	Independents allowed to run for election in Hungary; Gorbachev becomes Soviet leader
1988	Gorbachev's address to UN: Eastern European nations free to choose their own paths
1989	
January	Noncommunist parties and unions legalized in Hungary
February	Roundtable talks between Polish government and Solidarity
June	Free elections in Poland
September	Solidarity forms government in Poland
November	Fall of Berlin Wall; reformist communists overthrow Zhivkov in Bulgaria
December	Collapse of communist government in Czechoslovakia and East Germany; execution of Ceaușescu in Romania
1990	
March	Free elections in East Germany and Hungary
October	Reunification of Germany
December	Wałęsa elected president of Poland
1993	Division of Czechoslovakia into the Czech Republic and Slovakia

governmental policy that would never have been permitted before 1980.

Once Gorbachev came to power, the pace of reform in these two states accelerated. In January 1989, Hungary legalized noncommunist political parties and trade unions. In February, Solidarity and Polish communist officials began "roundtable talks" aimed at restructuring Poland's political system. In June, Poland held the first free elections in the Soviet bloc. Solidarity swept the contest and formed the first noncommunist government in eastern Europe since 1948.

These remarkable events sparked revolutions throughout the Soviet bloc. In the fall of 1989, mass protests toppled communist governments in Czechoslovakia and East Germany. In November, as the introduction to this chapter detailed, East Berliners succeeded in tearing down the Berlin Wall. One month later the world watched in wonder as the dissident playwright Václav Havel became Czechoslovakia's president.

Quickly the revolutionary fire spread to Bulgaria and Romania. There, however, communism was reformed rather than overthrown. In Bulgaria, reform-minded Communist Party members ousted the government of Todor Zhivkov, who had been in power for 35 years. The Romanian revolution was similar in outcome—but much bloodier. In December 1989, Romania's dictator Nikolae Ceaușescu ordered his army to fire on a peaceful protest and hundreds died. In a matter of days, however, the soldiers turned against Ceaușescu. He and his wife went into hiding, but on Christmas Day they were caught and executed by a firing squad. A new government formed under Ion Iliescu (b. 1930), a communist reformer

"COMRADES, IT'S OVER!"
This Hungarian political poster sums up the revolutions of 1989.

The Disintegration of the Soviet Union

Western political leaders and ordinary people praised Gorbachev for ending the Cold War and removing the Soviet hold on eastern Europe. Gorbachev, however, regarded these changes as the international means to a domestic end—freeing the Soviet economy for prosperity and thereby saving the communist system. But prosperity eluded his grasp, and the system Gorbachev sought to save disintegrated. Economic perestroika proved a failure. By 1990, food and other essential goods were scarce, prices had risen by 20 percent since the year before, and productivity figures and incomes were falling. Dramatic increases in the number of prostitutes, abandoned babies, and the homeless population all signaled the economic and social breakdown of the Soviet Union.

As these problems escalated, Gorbachev faced growing opposition from hard-line communists and from reformers who wanted a thoroughly capitalist economy. These reformers found a spokesman in Boris Yeltsin (1931–2007), a charismatic, boisterous politician who became the president of Russia (as distinct from the Soviet Union) in 1991. When the hard-liners attempted to overthrow Gorbachev in August 1991, Yeltsin led the popular resistance that blocked the coup. From that point on, Yeltsin, not Gorbachev, dominated Soviet politics.

Yet nationalism rather than the hard-liners or Yeltsin's pro-capitalist movement toppled Gorbachev—and destroyed the Soviet Union. The success of eastern European nations in freeing themselves from Soviet domination encouraged separatist nationalist movements within the Soviet Union. Although Gorbachev deployed troops to quell nationalist rioting in Azerbaijan and Georgia and to counter independence movements in the Baltic states, the Soviet Union broke apart anyway. On December 25, 1991 Gorbachev resigned his office as president of a state that no longer existed (see **Map 29.1**).

who had attended Moscow University with Gorbachev.

The final chapter of the eastern European revolutions featured a redrawing of political borders—and a corresponding shift of political identities. In October of 1990, the line dividing West and East Germany disappeared; Germany was once again a single nation-state. But three years later, the nation-state of Czechoslovakia cracked apart, as President Havel was unable to satisfy the demands of Slovakian nationalists. Out of Czechoslovakia came two new states: the Czech Republic and Slovakia.

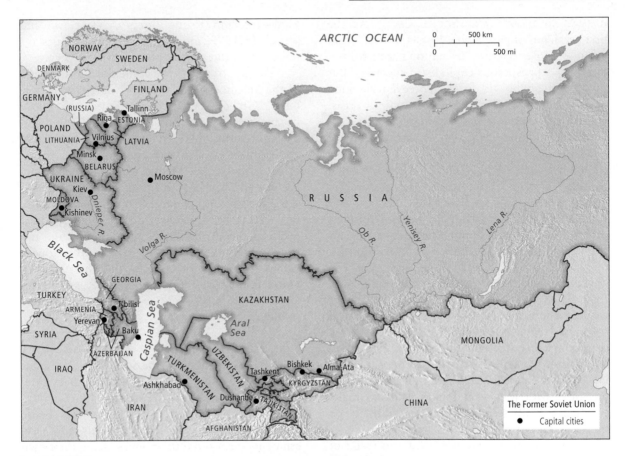

MAP 29.1

The Former Soviet Union

In December 1991, the Soviet empire disintegrated. In its place stood 14 independent republics, ranging from tiny and impoverished Moldova to relatively affluent and Europeanized Latvia to Russia itself, still the dominant power in the region.

IN THE WAKE OF REVOLUTION

■ **What were the consequences of the Revolutions of 1989–1990 for the societies of eastern Europe?**

The collapse of communist regimes in eastern Europe and the disintegration of the Soviet Union meant exhilarating yet exhausting change. Democracy-building proved to be a colossal task in societies burdened with the communist legacies of social division, political skepticism, and economic stagnation.

Russia After the Revolution

In contrast to states such as Poland, where the dismantling of communism came as the result of popular protests, in the Soviet Union change had been initiated from above. Moreover, unlike in eastern Europe, Russians could point with pride to at least some achievements of communism: They had created an industrial society, won World War II, and become a Superpower. In the 1990s, then, Russians struggled to come to terms with their unexpected—and for some, unwanted—revolution.

RUSSIA'S ECONOMIC AND SOCIAL CRISIS As the first president of post-Soviet Russia, Boris Yeltsin promised to accelerate his nation's transformation into a prosperous capitalist democracy. But he proved unable to do so. Three interlocking developments—continuing economic crisis, widening corruption and criminality, and growing socioeconomic inequality—characterized the Yeltsin era.

In January 1992, Yeltsin applied "shock therapy" to the ailing Russian economy. He lifted price controls, abolished subsidies, and privatized state industries. But the economy did not prosper. Prices climbed dramatically, and the closure of unproductive businesses worsened unemployment, at the same time that cuts in government spending severed welfare lifelines. By 1995, 80 percent of Russians were no longer earning a living wage. Food consumption fell to the same level as the early 1950s. The economic situation worsened in 1998 when Russia effectively went bankrupt. The value of the ruble collapsed, and the state defaulted on its loans. Even Russians with jobs found it difficult to make ends meet. Many resorted to barter and the black market to survive.

This economic crisis worsened as a result of widespread corruption and crime. In the 1990s Russians suddenly had the right to own private property, but they could not count on the state to protect that property. Russia's policing and judicial systems could not keep up with the new demands placed upon them. As a result, a new force appeared in Russian life—the "Russian Mafia," crime syndicates that offered "protection" at a high price and used extortion and intimidation to seize control of large sectors of the economy.

Economic crisis, combined with criminality and corruption, meant growing inequality. By 1997, *seven* individuals controlled an estimated *50 percent* of the Russian economy.[5] Clearly a minority of powerful and influential Russians experienced the 1990s as years of extraordinary opportunity and wealth accumulation. For many other Russians, however, the ending of the Soviet regime meant freedom of the worst

kind—freedom to be hungry, homeless, and afraid. In 1999, almost 40 percent of Russians fell beneath the official poverty line.

The end of the 1990s coincided with the end of the Yeltsin era. In December of 1999 the former KGB officer Vladimir Putin (b. 1952) became president of Russia. Well-manicured and austere, Putin provided stable and competent government—a welcome change to the roller-coaster ride of the Yeltsin years. The economy became stronger. Stabilization, however, came at a political price: the return to authoritarianism. Putin centralized political power and economic decision-making under his own control and ran roughshod over such key democratic touchstones as freedom of the press and the right to a fair trial. In 2008 Putin gave up the Russian presidency, but not executive power—he became prime minister instead.

NATIONALIST CHALLENGES IN THE FORMER SOVIET UNION The breakup of the Soviet Union did not bring an end to nationalist violence in the region. Popular nationalist movements vaulted states such as Georgia, Ukraine, and the Baltic republics to independence, but many new governments then found themselves facing their own nationalist challenges. Georgia, Armenia, and Azerbaijan all experienced civil war in the 1990s as regions within these new states sought to break away and form their own independent states.

Russia, too, faced continuing violent efforts to redraw its boundaries. Russia remained an enormous multinational federation—and not all of its national minorities wanted to remain part of Russia. The sharpest challenge came from Chechnya, one of 21 autonomous republics within the larger Russian Federation. When the Soviet Union broke up, Chechens saw no reason that Chechnya should not follow the path of Georgia or Azerbaijan toward independent nation-statehood. In 1991 Chechnya declared independence, but Russia refused to acknowledge this declaration. The dispute simmered until 1994 when Yeltsin sent in the Russian army to force Chechnya back within Russia's embrace. In the ensuing 20-month conflict, 80,000 died and 240,000 were wounded—80 percent of these Chechen civilians. Yeltsin negotiated a truce in the summer of 1996, but four years later Putin renewed the war. As of 2010, Russia retains control over Chechnya by military force, but Chechen nationalists continue to resist this control through terrorism.

Central and Eastern Europe: Toward Democracy?

Like the former Soviet Union, the states of eastern Europe found the path from communist rule to democracy strewn with obstacles. By the end of the 1990s, much of the region—but not all of it—had successfully negotiated that path and achieved political and economic stability.

STRUGGLES WITHIN THE REUNITED GERMANY   Almost half the population of East Germany crossed the border into West Germany in the first week after the fall of the Berlin Wall. They returned home dazzled by the consumer delights they saw in store windows and eager for a chance to grab a piece of the capitalist pie. The West German chancellor, Helmut Kohl, recognized the power of these desires and skillfully forced the pace of reunification. When the two Germanys united at the end of 1990, Kohl became the first chancellor of the new German state.

Kohl trusted that West Germany's economy was strong enough to pull its bankrupt new partner into prosperity, but he proved overly optimistic. The residents of the former East Germany soon found their factories closing and their livelihoods gone. These economic troubles leached over into the western regions of Germany. By 1997, German unemployment stood at 12.8 percent—the highest since World War II. Economic difficulties were most concentrated in the former East Germany, where over 20 percent of the population was out of work in the later 1990s.

The divide between "Wessies" (West Germans) and "Ossies" (East Germans) sometimes seemed unbridgeable. Women of the former East Germany, for example, often found it difficult to adjust to a culture in which more conventional gender roles and conceptions of sexual morality dominated. In communist East Germany, women had expected to work full time and to have access to state-provided day care, contraceptives, and abortion. In contrast, in West Germany the concept of the male breadwinner/head of household was enshrined in the legal code until the end of the 1970s and prominent in West German culture for a long time after.

In 2005, however, the election of Angela Merkel (b. 1954) as chancellor marked an important symbolic moment for united Germany. The first woman to head the German Christian Democrats (and a Protestant in a heavily Catholic party), Merkel was also the first East German to hold such a prominent political office in the new Germany. Under Merkel, the divide between East and West in Germany began to wane.

WINNERS AND LOSERS AFTER 1989   East Germany, of course, was unique among the former Soviet bloc states because of its rapid unification with West Germany, but peoples throughout the region experienced hard times immediately after 1989. Western advisers and the International Monetary Fund (IMF), which controlled access to much-needed loans, insisted that the new governments follow programs of "austerity" aimed at cutting government spending and curbing inflation. The result was economic hardship far beyond what any Western electorate would have endured.

In the second half of the 1990s, however, Poland, Hungary, the Czech Republic, and the Baltic countries saw their economies stabilize and their overall standard of living rise rapidly. In 2002, the average Pole's purchasing power was 40 percent higher than in 1989. But in countries such as Slovakia, Bulgaria, Romania, and Albania, the economies continued to flounder. In Albania, conditions were so dire that some 40 percent of Albanians of working age went abroad for jobs between 1994 and 1998. An important divide opened up in eastern Europe between the "winners" and the "losers" in the struggle to adjust to post-1989 conditions. The same divide appeared in political development. By the end of the 1990s, the "winners" had successfully negotiated the transition to stable democratic politics, while elsewhere power remained concentrated in the hands of a few.

Three factors explain this new divide between "winners" and "losers" in eastern and central Europe. First, Poland and Hungary already had begun moving toward market reforms well before 1989 and so were best prepared for the transition to capitalism, while Czechoslovakia and the Baltic states could look back to pre-World War II national independence. Second, proximity to markets in and investment from western Europe played an important role. But third and most significant of all is a factor we have already discussed: the construction of civil society. The states that floundered in the post-1989 world were those in which opposition to communist rule before 1989 had not yet coalesced in a vibrant civil society. The revolutions of 1989 in Bulgaria and Romania, for example, were carried out by reformers within the communist system, not by citizens with a sense of identity apart from—and opposed to—that system.

WHO WAS GUILTY? Many eastern Europeans wanted to draw a curtain on the communist era. Others, however, argued that those who participated in and benefited from what they regarded as a criminal regime should be punished. Yet who should be put on trial? Communism had been "normal" in eastern Europe for 40 years. Almost every citizen participated in some way or another with the communist regime just to get by.

For a solution, many of the former communist states considered **lustration,** a policy that banned anyone who had collaborated with the communist state from "public office," a category that often included jobs in state-run media and in universities. In Czechoslovakia and Germany, lustration became official policy and soon proved

controversial. Lustration did not distinguish between an informer whom the communist state had brutalized into collaboration and who did her best to avoid giving any usable information, and someone who had volunteered to inform and who benefited for years because of it. Concluding that lustration constituted vengeance rather than justice, lustration's opponents argued that it threatened to undermine democratic politics. Yet the disagreements over lustration occurred in public—in parliamentary debates, newspaper columns, television and radio talk shows, and political campaigns. Dissent was not driven underground or punished. In many ways, then, the controversy bore witness to the success of democracy-building in eastern and central Europe since 1989.

The Breakup of Yugoslavia

Across eastern and central Europe in the early 1990s, many had feared that hate-based nationalist politics and policies would fill the ideological vacuum left by communism's collapse. These concerns escalated as minority populations such as the Roma became targets of discrimination and violence and as neo-Nazi movements emerged. But while racism and the treatment of minority groups remained problematic (as was the case throughout the West), fears that eastern Europe might descend once again into the whirlwind of genocidal slaughter proved unfounded—except in Yugoslavia. There the revival of nationalist hostilities led to state-sanctioned mass murder and scenes of carnage not seen in Europe since the 1940s.

When the communist guerilla leader Tito seized control of the Yugoslav state after World War II, he sought to separate Yugoslavia from the divisive battles of its recent past. To construct a united nation, Tito utilized two tools—federalism and communism. A federal political structure comprising six equal republics prevented Serbia, or any other of the republics, from dominating Yugoslavia. Communism served as a unifying ideology, a cluster of ideas that transcended divisions of ethnicity, religion, and language. Tito declared ethnic identities and rivalries unacceptable, part of the bourgeois past that Yugoslavs left behind.

Yugoslavs often said, however, that their nation consisted of "six nationalities, five languages, four religions...and one Tito." According to this folk wisdom, Tito—not communism, not federalism—glued together this diverse state. In 1980, Tito died. Ominously, the year after his death saw the outbreak of riots between ethnic Albanians and Serbs in the province of Kosovo. Even more ominously, Tito's death coincided with the onset of economic crisis. Rising oil prices undercut the Yugoslav economy as did its debt load. By 1987, inflation was raging at 200 percent per year; two years later it had burst through into hyperinflation—200 percent *per month*.

Under pressure from this economic crisis, the federal structure Tito built began to collapse. The wealthier Yugoslav republics such as Croatia sought to loosen their ties to poorer republics such as Serbia. Then, in 1989, the revolutions that swept through the Soviet satellite states shattered the hold of communism on Yugoslavia as well. Ethnic nationalism, long simmering under the surface of Yugoslavian political life, poured into the resulting ideological void.

In Serbia, the former communist functionary Slobodan Milošević (1941–2006) transformed himself into a popular spokesman for aggressive Serbian nationalism. Milošević used rallies and the mass media, which he controlled, to convince Serbs that their culture was under attack and that he would defend it. To enhance Serbia's power, Milošević opposed the efforts of Croatian and other leaders to dismantle the Yugoslav federation. If Yugoslavia split apart, Serbia would be nothing but a small, poor, powerless state. As long as Yugoslavia remained intact, however, Serbia could continue to siphon the economic resources of the other, wealthier republics. And now, without Tito and as the largest and most populous of the Yugoslav republics, Serbia would dominate national politics and determine national policy.

Milošević possessed a powerful weapon to enforce his will: the Yugoslav army, the

CHRONOLOGY: THE SHATTERING OF YUGOSLAVIA

1989	Slobodan Milošević becomes president of Yugoslavian Republic of Serbia	
1991		
July	Civil war in Croatia begins	
1992		
April	Civil war in Bosnia begins	
1994		
April	NATO air strikes against Bosnian Serb positions begin	
1995		
December	Dayton Accords	
1998	Large-scale fighting in Kosovo between Albanians and Serbs	
1999		
March	NATO air strikes against Serbia	
June	Cease-fire in Kosovo	
2000		
October	Milošević defeated in Serbian elections	
2001		
June	Milošević extradited to the Hague to be tried for genocide	

fourth-largest fighting force in Europe and dominated by Serbs. Thus, when Croatia declared independence in June 1991, the Yugoslav army mobilized against the Croatian separatists and civil war began. In 1992 the war spread to Bosnia-Herzegovina after its government, too, declared independence. The war degenerated into an ethnic bloodbath, with memories of World War II shaping the conflict. Serbs viewed Croats as the heirs of the Nazi-backed Croatian fascists, responsible for the mass slaughter of Serbs and Jews in World War II. In turn, Croats called all Serbs "Chetniks," linking them to the anti-Croat Serbian guerilla bands of the war years (see Chapter 27). The presence of paramilitary forces also heightened the brutality of the war. With no military discipline and often possessing criminal records, the volunteers in these units plunged into a fury of plunder, murder, and rape.

This war introduced the world to **ethnic cleansing.** To create all-Serb zones within Croatia

and Bosnia, Serb paramilitary units embarked on a campaign of terror designed to force Muslims and Croats to abandon their homes and villages. They burned mosques, closed schools, vandalized houses, and imprisoned women and girls in special camps where they were subjected to regular, systematic rape. The brutality proved contagious: By 1994, all sides within the Bosnian war were practicing ethnic cleansing.

With Serbia assisting the Bosnian Serbs and Croatia assisting the Bosnian Croats, the Muslim community within Bosnia suffered the most intensely, and begged Western governments to abandon their positions of neutrality and to stop the atrocities. Finally, in 1994, NATO planes began bombing Serb positions, the first time in its history that NATO had gone into combat. One year later, the Dayton Accords, signed in Dayton, Ohio, brought an uneasy peace to Bosnia (see **Map 29.2**).

Peace eluded Serbia during this period, however. Milošević's brand of vicious nationalism

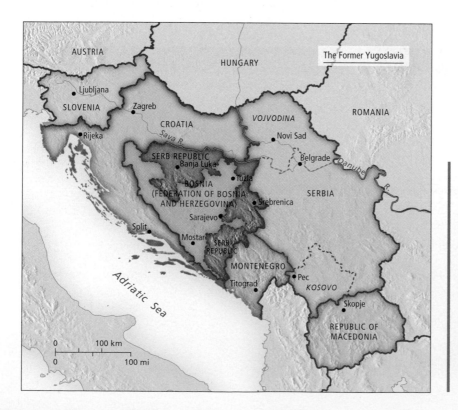

MAP 29.2

The Former Yugoslavia

The breakup of Yugoslavia began in June 1991 with the Slovenian and Croatian declarations of independence. Bosnia and Macedonia soon followed. Montenegro split from Serbia and became an independent nation-state in 2006. In 2008, Kosovo declared its independence but the Serbian government regards this declaration as illegal. As of 2009, the United Nations had not recognized Kosovo's independence.

demanded a constant supply of enemies and a continuous cycle of violence. In 1998, fighting between Serbs and ethnic Albanians erupted in the province of Kosovo. Ethnic cleansing, mass rape, and a huge exodus of refugees began again. After a NATO bombing campaign in Serbia, NATO and Russian troops moved into Kosovo, and in 2001, a police helicopter transported Milošević to the Netherlands to be tried for genocide before the International War Crimes Tribunal. Milošević, however, died before the tribunal came to a judgment. Kosovo declared its independence from Serbia in 2008.

RETHINKING THE WEST

■ How and why was the West redefined at the end of the twentieth century and the beginning of the twenty-first?

At the start of the 1990s, triumphalism characterized much of Western culture—at its simplest, expressed as "we won the Cold War." But who was "we"? For 40 years, the Cold War had provided a clear enemy and thus a clear identity: The West was anticommunist, anti-Soviet, anti-Warsaw Pact. The fall of communism thus demanded that the West revise itself. But so, too, did other important social, political, and cultural changes that occurred in the wake of the tumultuous events of the later 1960s and the economic downturn of the 1970s.

The European Union

With the ending of the Cold War, the nations of western Europe moved to take on a much more important role in global affairs. As **Map 29.3** shows, during the 1970s and 1980s the European Economic Community (EEC) widened its membership and became the European Community (EC), a political and cultural as well as economic organization. In 1979, Europeans voted in the first elections for the European Parliament, while the European Court of Justice gradually asserted the primacy of the European over national law.

Then, in 1991, the European *Community* (EC) became the **European *Union*** (EU), defined by France's President François Mitterrand as "one currency, one culture, one social area, one environment." The establishment of the EU meant visible changes for ordinary Europeans. They saw their national passports replaced by a common EU document and border controls eliminated. The creation of a single EU currency—the euro, which replaced many national currencies in 2002—tore down one of the most significant economic barriers between European countries. At the same time, the powers of the European Parliament expanded and member states moved toward establishing common social policies such as labor rights.

As these developments were underway, Europeans confronted the unexpected challenge posed by the ending of the Cold War. Should the European Union (often called simply "Europe") now include East as well as West? Attracted by the EU's prosperity, the nations of the former Soviet bloc answered "yes." Hesitant to join their countries to eastern Europe's shattered economies and divided societies, western European leaders drew up a list of qualifications for applicant nations. To belong to "Europe," nations had to meet financial requirements that demonstrated their economic stability and their commitment to market capitalism. Thus, the EU defined "Europe" first of all as capitalist. But a set of political requirements made clear that "Europe" also meant a commitment to democratic politics. Applicants' voting processes, treatment of minority groups, policing methods, and judicial systems were all scrutinized. Map 29.3 shows that in 2004 and again in 2007 the EU expanded so that it now embraces much of central and eastern Europe.

Many Europeans greeted the launch of the euro and the expansion of the EU as signs that the dream of a united Europe was being realized. Other Europeans, however, perceived this dream as a nightmare. They pointed out that throughout the 1990s, the U.S. economy outperformed that of the EU, and European unemployment rates were often much higher than in countries not aligned with the EU. Britain, Denmark, and Sweden refused to adopt the euro, fearing that their economies would

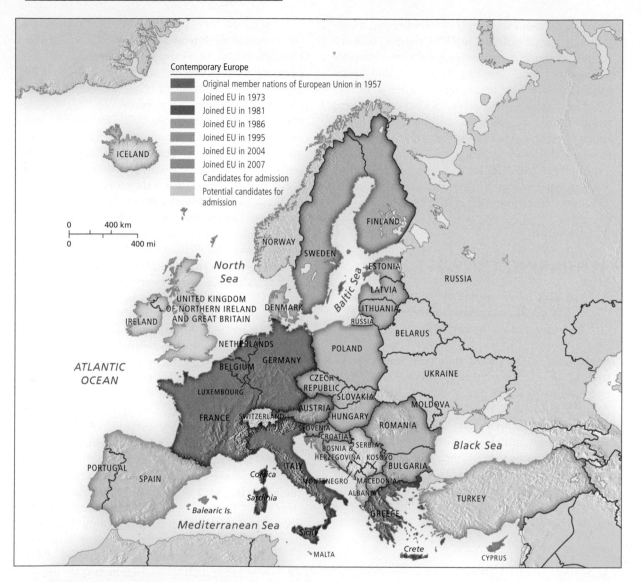

Contemporary Europe

- Original member nations of European Union in 1957
- Joined EU in 1973
- Joined EU in 1981
- Joined EU in 1986
- Joined EU in 1995
- Joined EU in 2004
- Joined EU in 2007
- Candidates for admission
- Potential candidates for admission

MAP 29.3

Contemporary Europe

The revolutions of 1989 and their aftermath mark a clear turning point in European history, as a comparison of this map and that of Map 28.5, "Europe in the Cold War" (p. 911) will show. Significant changes include the breakup of the Soviet Union and Yugoslavia, the replacement of Czechoslovakia by the Czech Republic and Slovakia, and the unification of Germany. The widening membership of the European Union reflected these changes.

be dragged down by slower-performing EU states. Small traders and independent producers felt overwhelmed by the EU bureaucracy, while many workers in western Europe feared having to compete for jobs with lower-paid eastern Europeans.

Islam, Terrorism, and European Identity

Significantly, the expansion of the EU in 2004 and 2007 did not include Turkey. A member of NATO since 1952, Turkey first applied for associate membership in the EU (then the EEC) in 1959, but did not succeed until 1991. Negotiations between the EU and Turkey on entry as a full member began in 2005. Opponents to full Turkish membership in the EU argued that if Turkey joined the EU, it would immediately become the most populous and the poorest member of the union. Could the European economy absorb the expected influx of impoverished Turkish migrant workers? Opponents also highlighted the clash between Turkey's repressive penal system and EU human rights legislation. The central obstacles on Turkey's path to full membership in "Europe," however, were not economic or political, but rather religious and cultural. Most Turks are Muslim, and for many Europeans, "European" and "Islamic" described opposing cultures.

The struggle over Turkish membership in the EU was just one of many controversies in contemporary Europe resulting from an ongoing battle to reconcile European identity with a growing Islamic cultural and political presence. In eastern European countries such as Bulgaria, Albania, and Bosnia, an Islamic population was nothing new: Muslims were part of the indigenous nation, the descendants of those who converted to Islam during the centuries of Ottoman rule. In western Europe, by contrast, most Muslims were immigrants or the children or grandchildren of immigrants, drawn to the West by greater economic and educational opportunities. As minarets began to rival church steeples in the skylines of European cities, questions about the definitions of and relationships between Islamic, European, and Western identities intensified.

TERRORISM, THE WEST, AND THE MIDDLE EAST

Terrorism deepened hostilities between Muslims and non-Muslims in the West—and made the resolution of these hostilities more urgent. Terrorism directly opposes what many now regard as the bedrock of Western culture—a commitment to democracy. Terrorism short-circuits the democratic process by shifting decision-making from the ballot box to the bomb. The equation of the West with democracy, however, conveniently ignores the history of the West and of terrorism itself. Terrorism grew out of late nineteenth-century anarchism, which advocated violence as a means of political change (see Chapter 23). Unable to achieve their goals through political persuasion (lobbying, campaigning, winning votes), terrorists endeavored to destabilize the societies they opposed through acts of violence and intimidation.

Thwarted nationalism provided especially fertile soil for terrorism's growth. In Northern Ireland, assassinations and bombings became commonplace from the 1970s on after the Irish Republican Army (IRA) turned to terror to pressure the British government to relinquish its control over the province. In Spain, the Basque separatist group Eta has for more than three decades waged a campaign of terror to achieve its aim of an independent Basque state.

Although the examples of the IRA and Eta demonstrate that terrorism is part of "Western civilization," by the 1990s, many in the West regarded terrorism as an outside threat, usually bearing an Arabic face and carrying a copy of the Qur'an. This textbook has traced the way in which "the West" changed meaning, often in response to places and peoples defined as "not West." With the ending of the Cold War, the West lost its main enemy, but a replacement stood readily at hand. In 1996, the American president Bill Clinton (b. 1946) identified terrorism as "the enemy of our generation." In the post–Cold War world, terrorism, usually linked to Islam, replaced communism as the new foe against which the West defined itself.

Terrorist activity arising out of the Palestinian-Israeli conflict helped create this perception. Frustrated by the failure of the United Nations to implement its 1947 resolution promising a

Palestinian state, Palestinian nationalists—most but not all of whom were Muslim—in 1964 formed the Palestine Liberation Organization (PLO). Like the IRA and Eta, the PLO saw violence as the only means to its nationalist ends. The PLO's commitment to terrorism deepened after the Six-Day War of 1967 led to Israel occupying East Jerusalem, the West Bank, and the Golan Heights. (See Map 28.4, p. 910.) During subsequent decades the PLO took its campaign of terror around the world, bombing airports, targeting tourists, and persuading many in the West that "Arab," "Muslim," and "terrorist" were interchangeable terms.

At the same time, American support for Israel convinced many Muslims that "the West" (often equated simply with the United States) was an enemy. Between 1949 and 1998, Israel received more American aid than any other country. Palestinians and their supporters argued that the United States was bankrolling a repressive regime and that Israel was a Western colonialist outpost.

ISLAMISM AND THE WEST   Western perceptions of a link between Islam and terrorism were further strengthened by the development of **Islamism** (as distinct from Islam). Also called Islamic fundamentalism or *jihadism* (after the Islamic idea of *jihad*, or holy war), Islamism is explicitly anti-Western—and is rejected by most Muslims as a corruption or negation of Islamic values. Islamism views Western culture as a threat to Islamic identity. It regards the United States as the standard-bearer of the West and thus as a particular enemy of Muslim interests; and it accepts violence, including the murder of civilians, as an acceptable means to its ends.

Four international developments helped nurture Islamism. First, the West's willingness during the Cold War to prop up autocratic governments (as long as they were anti-Soviet) turned the Western promise of democracy into a sham for many Muslims. Throughout much of the post-World War II period in Iran, for example, the United States supported the authoritarian but pro-Western regime of the Shah.

American and European support for antidemocratic regimes helped create the second important development in fostering Islamism: the appeal of Islamist leaders who promised relief from the corruption and oppression of Western-allied dictatorships. Iran again provides a compelling example. In 1979 a popular revolution in Iran vaulted the Ayatollah Khomeini (1901–1989) into power. Khomeini rapidly reversed the westernizing and modernizing policies of the Shah and condemned the United States as the "Great Satan." He became an international Islamist hero during the "Iranian hostage crisis" of 1979–1980, when Iranian students took over the U.S. Embassy in Tehran, kidnapped 66 Americans, and held most of them for over a year. Khomeini's decision ten years later to issue a death sentence against the British writer Salman Rushdie for what he considered to be a blasphemous portrayal of the prophet Muhammad widened the gap between his Islamist regime and the West and, once again, made him a popular hero among Islamists. (See *Justice in History* in this chapter.)

The Gulf War was the third important international development that strengthened Islamism. In 1991 American and British forces led a 28-country coalition in a military intervention to drive invading Iraqi forces out of tiny but oil-rich Kuwait. The war itself could not be construed as "the West versus Islam": One Islamic country had invaded another. But in the aftermath of the war, U.S. forces remained in American-controlled bases in Saudi Arabia, home to some of Islam's most holy sites. For Islamists, the presence of the United States in this region sullied Islamic purity and insulted Arab political independence.

Finally, the wars in Bosnia and Chechnya fed Islamist hatred of the West. The initial passivity of western Europe and the United States during the Bosnian war of 1992–1995 while Muslim men and boys were slaughtered and Muslim women and girls raped convinced many European Muslims that Western governments had an anti-Muslim agenda. This perception grew stronger when Western states refused to back the Chechens (who are Muslim) in what many viewed as the Chechen war of independence against Russian oppression.

9/11 AND AFTER   Significantly, many Islamists viewed Russia as part of the West. The

JUSTICE IN HISTORY

The Sentencing of Salman Rushdie

In February 1989, the Ayatollah Khomeini, political leader of Iran and spiritual head of the Shi'a Muslim community, issued a death sentence against the novelist Salman Rushdie and offered an award of $2.5 million to any faithful Muslim who killed him. Rushdie, a British citizen who had never been tried in any Iranian or Islamic court, immediately went into hiding, where he remained for several years. His death sentence ignited the "Satanic Verses Affair," a tumultuous international crisis caused by a resounding clash of cultural assumptions and expectations.

The crisis centered on a book. In the early autumn of 1988 Viking Penguin published Rushdie's *The Satanic Verses,* a difficult novel about the complexities and contradictions of the modern immigrant experience. Born in India and raised in an Islamic home, Rushdie wrote *The Satanic Verses* to describe "migration, metamorphosis, divided selves, love, death, London, and Bombay."[6] The novel received immediate critical acclaim, with reviewers praising it as an astonishing work of postmodernist fiction.

Other readers judged it differently. Many Muslims around the world regarded the book as a direct attack on the foundations of their religious faith. One scene in the novel particularly horrified devout Muslims. In this episode, the central character has a psychotic breakdown and falls into a dream: The prophet Muhammad appears as a corrupt businessman, and prostitutes in a brothel take on the names of the Prophet's wives.

The novel aroused controversy from the moment of its publication. The government of India banned it almost immediately. Within a matter of weeks, several other states followed suit. Anti-Rushdie demonstrations in India and Pakistan turned violent. Bookstores selling the novel received bombing and death threats. In western Europe, hostilities between Muslims and non-Muslims intensified. Then, on February 14,

1989, an announcer on Radio Tehran read aloud the text of a *fatwa,* or decree, issued by the Ayatollah Khomeini:

> I would like to inform all the intrepid Muslims of the world that the author of the book entitled *The Satanic Verses,* which has been compiled, printed and published in opposition to Islam, the Prophet and the Koran, as well as those publishers who were aware of its contents, have been sentenced to death. I call on all zealous Muslims to execute them quickly, wherever they find them....Whoever is killed on this path will be regarded as a martyr, God willing.

Western governments reacted quickly against Khomeini's call for Rushdie's death. The twelve nations of the European Community, the United States, Sweden, Norway, Canada, Australia, and Brazil all condemned Khomeini's judgment, recalled their ambassadors from Tehran, and cancelled high-level diplomatic contacts with Iran. British prime minister Margaret Thatcher provided police protection for Rushdie and dismissed British Muslim demands to ban the book: "It is an essential part of our democratic system that people who act within the law should be able to express their opinions freely."[7]

Large numbers of Muslims, including many who spoke out against Rushdie's book, also condemned Khomeini's fatwa. Some Muslim scholars contended that the Ayatollah's fatwa was a scholarly opinion, not a legally binding judgment. Others argued that Rushdie could not be condemned without a trial or that because Rushdie lived in a society without an Islamic government, he was not bound by Islamic law.

But many ordinary Muslims ignored these theological and legal arguments and greeted the Ayatollah's fatwa with delight. The news of the

CULTURE CLASH

In 2007, Britain's Queen Elizabeth awarded Salman Rushdie a knighthood for his services to literature. The award sparked protests within the Islamic world, including this one in Lahore, Pakistan, where demonstrators burned the British flag to express their outrage.

Ayatollah's fatwa brought crowds of cheering Muslims into city streets across Europe. In Manchester and Bradford, young British Muslim men insisted they would kill Rushdie if given the chance. In Paris, demonstrators marched to cries of "We are all Khomeinists!"

Why did Khomeini's fatwa arouse such popular enthusiasm within Western Muslim communities—particularly given the fact that the majority of Europe's Muslims were Sunni rather than Shi'a, and therefore not readily inclined to recognize Khomeini as a spiritual leader? A partial answer to this question is that many Muslims were frustrated with what they regarded as the unequal application of the laws of censorship. Faced with what they saw as a hate-filled, pornographic caricature of Islam, they demanded that Western governments use existing laws censoring pornography and banning hate crimes to block the publication of Rushdie's book. In Britain, Muslims were particularly outraged that the existing law against blasphemy protected only Christianity, the official state religion.

But the controversy was not simply a dispute about censorship. For some Muslims, Rushdie's *Satanic Verses* epitomized Western secular society with its scant regard for tradition or religious values. As Dr. Kalim Siddiqui of the pro-Iranian Muslim Institute in Britain proclaimed, "Western civilization is fundamentally an immoral civilization. Its 'values' are free of moral constraints."[8] From this perspective, Khomeini's fatwa condemned not just one book or one author, but an entire culture. Khomeini had already proven himself a forceful leader in the American-Iranian hostage crisis of 1979–1980, when he successfully thumbed his nose at U.S. power. Now once again he seemed willing to take on the West to defend Islam.

The anti-Western stance of some radical Muslims was mirrored by the anti-Islam position soon occupied by some Rushdie supporters. In all of his books, Rushdie condemned British racism and exposed the falsehood of Western claims to cultural superiority. Yet in an ironic twist, Rushdie found himself championed by individuals who articulated precisely the sort of Western cultural chauvinism against which he had written so passionately. For example, Robert Maxwell, a multimillionaire communications tycoon, offered $10 million to any individual "who will, not kill, but civilise the barbarian Ayatollah" by forcing him to recite publicly the Ten Commandments.[9] Many western Europeans agreed with the conclusion drawn in this letter to a British daily newspaper: "The lesson of the Rushdie affair is that it was unwise to let Muslim communities establish themselves in our midst."[10] The lines were drawn, with Islam standing for irrationalism, barbarity, intolerance, and ignorance, while the "West" was linked to democracy, reason, freedom, and civilization. At precisely the moment when the crumbling of communism and the ending of the Cold War deprived the West of one of its defining attributes, the Satanic Verses Affair offered up a new Other against which the West could define itself.

For Discussion

1. On what grounds are publications censored in secular, Western societies? Given the existence of this censorship, should Rushdie's book have been banned?

2. How does the Satanic Verses Affair illuminate the tensions within many European societies from the 1970s on, as communities struggled to adapt to the challenges of ethnic and religious diversity?

Taking It Further

Bowen, David G., ed. *The Satanic Verses: Bradford Responds.* 1996. This collection of essays and documents helps explains why many British Muslims viewed the British government's failure to censor Rushdie's book as an act of injustice.

Pipes, Daniel. *The Rushdie Affair: The Novel, the Ayatollah, and the West.* 2003. An informative overview by a controversial scholar.

---

predominantly Muslim states of the Caucasus had a long history of fighting against Russian rule, and Soviet communism was no more tolerant of Islam than it was of Judaism or Christianity. But the Soviet-Afghan War of 1979–1989 particularly intensified Islamist rage against Russia. To Islamists, the Afghan guerillas fighting Afghan communists and the Soviet army represented the wider struggle to free Islam from Western control and purify it from Western corruption. Ironically, many of the Islamists who fought in this conflict received their military training from the United States: Viewing the war through Cold War lenses, American policymakers in the 1980s supported the Islamist struggle in Afghanistan as a way to weaken the Soviet Union. After Soviet troops withdrew from Afghanistan in defeat in 1989, the pro-Soviet Afghan government collapsed, and the Taliban, a revolutionary Islamist group, seized power.

Events in Afghanistan seemed a long way away from Europe and the United States—until September 11, 2001, when Islamists declared open war on the West in one of the most deadly episodes of terrorism yet seen. Islamist terrorists hijacked three passenger planes and smashed them into the World Trade Center in New York City and the Pentagon (the U.S. military headquarters in Washington, D.C.), while a fourth crashed in Pennsylvania. Almost 3,000 people died. American and European intelligence officers linked the suicide pilots to Al Qaeda, an Islamist terrorist organization run by Osama bin Laden, a wealthy Saudi exile based in Afghanistan. Evidence of ideological and financial links between bin Laden and the

Taliban led the United States to begin air attacks against Afghanistan in October 2001. The Taliban regime fell within weeks, but bin Laden remained at large and the "war against terror" continued.

In March 2003, this war took a new turn when U.S. and British forces attacked Iraq. No direct connection linked Osama bin Laden to Iraq's government. Iraq's secular dictator Saddam Hussein tortured and killed Islamists like bin Laden because he regarded their religious ideology as a threat to his personal power. But in the world after "9/11," Hussein's refusal to allow UN inspections of his weapons factories led the American and British governments to conclude—incorrectly—that Iraq possessed the ability to attack Western cities with biological, chemical, or nuclear weapons. Many Iraqis cheered the dictator's overthrow, but other Iraqis—and many Arabs in the surrounding states and many Muslims throughout the world—condemned the Anglo-American invasion as yet another episode in a long history of Western imperial intrusions on Arab territory and against Muslim people.

Subsequent terrorist attacks in Europe underscored this outrage. On March 11, 2004, approximately 200 people died after four bombs exploded on commuter trains during the rush hour in Madrid. Al Qaeda linked the bombing to Spain's support of the Iraq war. One year later, on July 7, 2005, a similar spate of bombings during the morning rush hour in London killed over 50 people and injured more than 700.

The men involved in "7/7" were not only linked to Al Qaeda, they were also British. The London bombings thus revealed the power of Islamism within the West itself. Some of the children and grandchildren of Muslim immigrants, young men in particular, felt betrayed by the cultures in which they lived. Their ongoing struggle against poverty, discrimination, and disempowerment turned them toward Islamism. In the wake of 9/11 and the attacks that followed, then, the question of Western identity was more troublesome than ever as a "Them" versus "Us" mentality that ignored the long, complex history of Islam in the West became more prevalent.

EURO-ISLAM   Yet the encounter between Islam and Europe was far from wholly negative. The majority of European Muslims rejected Islamism. Many, particularly those of the second and third generations of immigrant families, endeavored to create a new identity: **Euro-Islam.** Regarding themselves as fully Muslim and fully European, these individuals insisted that no contradiction existed between Islam and what many view as the core values of the West—democratic politics, respect for individual

AN IDENTITY STRUGGLE

In the wake of 9/11, European Muslims fought to assert their Western identity. Symbols became particularly important. This teacher won her battle in German courts to wear her Islamic head scarf in the classroom of a state school. In France, however, Islamic girls in head scarves were not permitted in schoolrooms.

differences, and civil liberties guaranteed by law to all, regardless of race and gender.

Euro-Islam produced significant theological and social innovations within the Islamic community. European Muslim women fought to eradicate such traditional practices as female circumcision and the forced marriage of young girls to men from their parents' or grandparents' homelands. More generally, they claimed an equal place for women within the context of both Europe and Islam. European Muslim theologians reinforced this claim. Traditional Islamic theology cut the world into two: the "house of Islam," and the "house of war." In the "house of Islam," Islamic law prevails. In the "house of war," or societies where Islamic law is not followed, Muslims live in a state of constant spiritual battle. Euro-Islamic proponents such as the Swiss scholar Tariq Ramadan (b. 1962) argued that Muslims should not view Europe and the United States as the "house of war." Instead, these regions form a third "house," the "house of testimony," where Muslims freely profess and live their faith in community with non-Muslims.

Into the Postmodern Era

The end of the Cold War, the formation of the European Union, and the growth of significant Muslim communities within western Europe all demanded a reevaluation and redefinition of West. So, too, did a number of intellectual, artistic, and technological developments that together helped created the postmodern era. Although the term **postmodernism** covers an array of styles and stances, at its core postmodernism rejects Western cultural supremacy. More specifically, postmodernism challenges the idea that Western science and rationality have constructed a single, universally applicable form of "modernity."

THE MAKING OF THE POSTMODERN Postmodernism first took form in architecture, perhaps because the failures of modernist architecture were so obvious by the early 1970s. Motivated by their faith in human rationality and modern technology, modernist architects had erected buildings that they believed would enable people to live better, more

beautiful lives. But the concrete high-rises they constructed failed to connect with the needs and emotions of their inhabitants, and many became derelict, crime-ridden, graffiti-scarred tenements.

Faced with this failure, a new generation—the postmodernists—insisted that modernist architecture was too elitist. The American architect Charles Jencks (b. 1939) argued that because people tend to rely on the familiar to make sense of their world, modernism was wrong to reject traditional forms. For example, most Europeans and Americans connect domestic housing with gabled roofs (ask a child to draw a picture of a house and see if he or she draws a flat roof). Was it surprising, Jencks asked, that the concrete rectangles so typical of modernist houses alienated so many people? Postmodernist *anti-elitism* thus led to *eclecticism,* to re-creating and combining forms and styles from past eras (such as gabled roofs), and to efforts to revive local and regional styles. Why should the streets of Tokyo look like the center of London or downtown Chicago? Instead, postmodernists embraced an architecture rooted in the specifics of time and place. In addition to being anti-elitist and eclectic, then, postmodernist architecture was also *anti-universalist:* It condemned modernism for its assumption that the same modern (and Western) ideals and forms fit all individuals and all societies.

The same sorts of criticism of modernism surfaced in the art world, as the politics of the late 1960s and early 1970s transformed the visual arts in three ways. First, in the wake of the protests of 1968, artists—many coming out of left-wing activist environments—rejected ideologies based on hierarchy and authority. This rejection led to an attack on the modernist idea of the "avant-garde," the concept of artistic geniuses fighting on the frontiers of aesthetic excellence. Second, the experience of political protest led many artists to try to communicate with a wider public—and, hence, to look to the past and to popular culture for forms and material that their audience would find familiar. As the art critic Edit DeAk explained, postmodernist art relied on "the shock of recognition instead of the shock of the new."[11] Finally, feminism influenced the new art. Feminists highlighted the systematic exclusion of women from gallery

POSTMODERNISM AT PLAY IN THE WEST:

Using the "shock of recognition," Marco Ventura blends six familiar images from the Western tradition in this playful painting that he entitled "Mona Lisa Contemplating the Bust of Nefertiti as God Creates Order Out of Chaos on a Starry Night on the Island of La Grande Jatte as the Infanta Margarita Looks On" (1993).

Source: Marco Ventura, "Mona Lisa Contemplating the Bust of Nefertiti as God Creates Order out of Chaos on a Starry Night on the Island of La Grande Jatte as the Infanta Margarita Looks On", 1993, oil on gessoed paper, 10"w × 8–1/2"h. Painting by Marco Ventura 1993.

and museum exhibitions. They also questioned the aesthetic hierarchy that fixed the patronizing label of "craft" to traditionally female art forms such as weaving.

By the end of the 1970s, postmodernist practices in art and architecture blended with a growing body of literary and cultural theory often called *poststructuralism*. The theory of poststructuralism centered on the work of an assorted group of French thinkers whose ideas were taken up in American universities and then filtered back into European intellectual circles. These thinkers

included Roland Barthes (1915–1980) and Jacques Derrida (1930–2004) in literary studies, Michel Foucault (1926–1984) in history, and Jacques Lacan (1901–1981) in psychoanalytic theory.

Like postmodernist theories in architecture and art, poststructuralism began as an exploration into the problems of communication. Barthes declared the "Death of the Author," by which he meant that the purpose of literary study is not to ask, "What does the author mean?" but instead to explore the way in which the reader creates his or her own meanings. Building on

Barthes, Derrida argued that the world we experience is structured by language—we cannot even understand or express our very selves apart from language. But because there is no inherent match between a word (what Derrida called a "signifier") and the thing or idea to which that word refers (the "signified"), communication is never straightforward. An endless variety of meanings and interpretations results, and thus, Derrida argued, we must abandon the idea of a fixed or single truth, of ultimate or universal meaning.

This effort to challenge any single "right answer" or any center of authority (sometimes called "decentering") linked the poststructuralist concern with communication to its analysis of power. Foucault and Lacan dissected hierarchies of authority (not only in the political sphere, but also in academic disciplines, for example, or in the medical world), and the way these authorities used seemingly objective bodies of knowledge to retain their hold on power.

The blending of these poststructuralist theories of communication and power with the critique of modernism already flourishing in architecture and the arts produced postmodernism. The postmodern view of culture as a global contest for power disturbed more traditional thinkers (with "modernist" now perceived as traditional), who insisted that criteria of aesthetic excellence ("Beauty") and objective standards of knowledge ("Truth") did exist, and who warned that cultural "decentering" would destroy the social cohesion and political stability of the West. (See *Different Voices* in this chapter.)

POSTMODERN CULTURES AND POSTINDUSTRIAL TECHNOLOGIES In many ways popular culture confirmed postmodern theories. In Britain, for example, the "Big Beat" songs that dominated the club scene in the late 1990s were produced by disc jockeys who lifted snatches from old records, played them at different speeds, and combined them with contrasting styles. Like

MAKING BUILDINGS DANCE

Designed by the American architect Frank Gehry and his Czech collaborator Vlado Mulunić, the "Dancing Building" fills a bomb site left vacant in central Prague since World War II. Also called "Fred and Ginger" (after the famous Hollywood dancing duo Fred Astaire and Ginger Rogers), this postmodernist piece delighted and enraged the people of Prague.

DIFFERENT VOICES HISTORY IN A POSTMODERN WORLD

In the late 1980s, postmodernist ideas penetrated the study of history. While many historians—such as Joan Wallach Scott, who wrote the first excerpt that follows—embraced postmodernist theories and methodologies, others—such as Gertrude Himmelfarb, the author of the second excerpt—condemned postmodernism as relativism run amok. This debate resonated beyond the rather small world of professional historians as the third excerpt shows. In an effort to establish uniform standards in elementary and secondary education, Margaret Thatcher sought a national curriculum for British state schools. As her account reveals, Thatcher's ideas about history clashed with those of professional historians.

I. Joan Wallach Scott: A "New" Historian's Defense

By "history," I mean not what happened, not what "truth" is "out there"...but what we *know* about the past, what the rules and conventions are that govern the production and acceptance of the knowledge we designate as history. My first premise is that history is...constructed by historians. Written history both reflects and creates relations of power. Its standards of inclusion and exclusion, measures of importance, and rules of evaluation are not objective criteria but politically produced conventions. What we know as history is, then, the fruit of past politics....

The pluralization of the subject of history challenges the notion...that "man" can be studied through a focus on elites. Instead, attention to women, blacks, and other Others demonstrates that history consists of many irreconcilable stories. Any master narrative—the single story of the rise of American democracy or Western civilization—is shown to be not only incomplete but impossible of completion in the terms it has been written. For those master narratives have been based on the forcible exclusion of Others' stories. They

are...stories which in their telling legitimize the actions of those who have shaped the laws, constitutions, and governments—"official stories."

The proliferation of Others' histories... has raised questions about difference and power:....How has the exclusion of some stories from the record of the past perpetuated inequalities based on attributions of difference? What is the connection between contemporary social hierarchy and measures of importance in historical writing? Answers to these questions...undermine claims by orthodox historians that...their history is but a transcription of how things really happened in the past....

...[H]istory is an interpretive practice, not an objective, neutral science. To maintain this does not signal the abandonment of all standards.... [Historians] share a commitment to accuracy and to procedures of verification and documentation.... [But we see] that the meanings attributed to events of the past always vary, that the knowledge we produce is contextual, relative, open to revision and debate, and never absolute.

II. Gertrude Himmelfarb: An "Old" Historian Rejects the New

Historians have always quarreled about the meaning and interpretation of facts and, indeed, about the facts themselves. But they...have traditionally assumed some correspondence between interpretation and fact, between language and reality. They are painfully aware of the imperfection of that correspondence—a past that always eludes them, a reality that is never fully revealed to them...But they have also been acutely aware of the need to try to close that gap as much as possible....Today, [however,] more and more historians...are making the past far more indeterminate, more elusive, less real than it has ever been—thus permitting themselves to be as

postmodernist paintings, Big Beat contained chunks of the past, recycled in new ways.

More generally, a series of technological developments meant that popular culture was

"decentered," that a multitude of popular cultures coexisted and that the individual consumer of culture, like Barthes's reader, was free to make meaning as he or she chose. The videocassette recorder

creative, innovative, and inventive as possible in interpreting the past. These have become the new "possibles" of history: the possibilities suggested by the historian's imagination and sensibility rather than by the contemporary experience*.... Contemporaries may have thought that their history was shaped by kings and statesmen, politics and diplomacy, constitutions and laws. New historians know better.... Race/gender/class—word-processors [early personal computers] all over the country must be programmed to print that formula with a single touch of a key.... The assumption that race, gender, and class are, and always have been, the basic determinants of history deconstructs the past not only as historians have known it but, in many cases, as contemporaries knew it.... Those benighted contemporaries, the argument goes, speak with no authority, because they were deluded by the "hegemonic culture" that was itself irredeemably sexist, racist, and elitist. Thus, all the past has to be deconstructed and constructed anew.

III. Margaret Thatcher: A Politician Weighs In

Perhaps the hardest battle I fought on the national curriculum was about history. Though not an historian myself, I had a very clear—and I had naively imagined uncontroversial—idea of what history was. History is an account of what happened in the past. Learning history, therefore, requires knowledge of events...[and] knowing dates. No amount of imaginative sympathy for historical characters or situations can be a substitute for the initially tedious but ultimately rewarding business of memorizing what actually happened....

In July 1989 the History Working Group produced its interim report. I was appalled. It put the emphasis on interpretation and enquiry as

*Here and throughout this essay, Himmelfarb uses the term *contemporary* to mean the period in the past that the historian is studying.

against content and knowledge. There was insufficient weight given to British history. There was not enough emphasis on history as chronological study....

[The *final report arrived in March 1990. Thatcher was not pleased.*] The attainment targets it set out did not specifically include knowledge of historical facts, which seemed to me extraordinary [and] the coverage of some subjects—for example, twentieth-century British history—was too skewed to social, religious, cultural and aesthetic matters rather than political events....By now I had become thoroughly exasperated....

Sources: Gertrude Himmelfarb, "Some Reflections on the New History," *American Historical Review*, 1989, 94:3, 665–666, 667, 668. Reprinted by permission of the author. Joan Wallach Scott, "History in Crisis? The Others' Side of the Story," *American Historical Review*, 1989, 94:3, 681, 682–683, 689–690. Reprinted by permission of the author. Margaret Thatcher, *The Downing Street Years*, 1993, 595–596. Copyright © 1993 by Margaret Thatcher. Reprinted by permission of HarperCollins Publishers.

For Discussion

1. What does Scott mean when she argues that "what we know as history" is actually "the fruit of past politics"? How would Thatcher have replied?

2. Himmelfarb argues that an overemphasis on race, gender, and class characterizes postmodernist interpretations of history. Why might postmodernists emphasize these three categories? Why does Himmelfarb object? Would Thatcher have sympathized with Himmelfarb's argument?

3. Imagine that you are present *in 1989* at a debate featuring Scott, Himmelfarb, and Thatcher. Each woman has been asked to define "the West." How do you think each might have responded?

(VCR), first marketed in 1975, and its technological successors, not only transported film viewing from the public to the private sphere, they also provided the film viewer with the possibility to

tailor the movie to his or her own preferences—to adjust the volume or choose another soundtrack entirely, to omit or fast-forward through certain scenes, to replay others endlessly. Similarly, the proliferation of cable and satellite television stations during the 1980s and 1990s fragmented the viewing audience and made it impossible to speak of popular culture in the singular.

Postmodernist concerns with communication, with the way in which interpretations can be endlessly modified, and with the abolition of a single center of authority certainly seemed appropriate for "the Information Age" or the **postindustrial society.** Emphasis on production characterized the industrial phase of economic development. But in the postindustrial phase, *making* things became less important than *marketing* them. If the factory symbolized industrial society, then the epitome of the postindustrial era was the home computer, with its capacity to disperse information, market products, and endlessly duplicate yet constantly alter visual and verbal images—all without any central regulating authority. Governments scrambled to impose control on the proliferating technologies of the postindustrial age, but in true postmodern fashion the centers of authority broke down. Existing laws that regulated pornography, for example, proved difficult to apply to the Internet, the vast global communications web.

Similarly, developments in medical technologies raised important questions about authority and ownership. In 1978, Louise Brown was born in Britain, the world's first "test-tube baby." Over the next 20 years, assisted fertility treatment resulted in more than one million births. As the technology grew more sophisticated, so did the ethical and political questions. Societies struggled to determine the legality of practices such as commercial surrogate motherhood, in which a woman rents her womb to a couple, and postmenopausal motherhood, in which a woman past childbearing age is implanted with a fertilized egg.

Genetic research provoked even more debate about which authorities or what principles should guide scientific research. In 1997, British scientists introduced the world to Dolly the sheep, the first mammal cloned from an adult. Many scientists assumed that the cloning of human beings, long part of science fiction and horror stories, was inevitable, even if religious leaders deemed it immoral and political authorities declared it illegal. The announcement in February 2001 that scientists had decoded the human genome—that they had mapped the set of instructions in every cell in the human body—raised such questions as, Who owns this information? Who has the authority to decide how it is to be used?

POSTMODERN PATTERNS IN RELIGIOUS LIFE Postmodern patterns—the fragmentation of cultures, the collapse of centers of authority, the supremacy of image—also characterized Western religious faith and practice after the 1970s. Christianity no longer served as a common cultural bond. In a time of increasing immigration and cultural diversity, Islam was the fastest-growing religious community in western Europe. In Britain, Muslims outnumbered Methodists by two to one. By the end of the twentieth century, regular churchgoers were a small minority of the

CHRONOLOGY: MEDICAL CHALLENGES AND ACHIEVEMENTS

1977	First diagnosed case of AIDS
1978	First test-tube baby
1980	Worldwide eradication of smallpox
1982	First use of genetic engineering (insulin manufactured from bacteria)
1983	First artificially created chromosome
1984	HIV identified
1985	First use of laser surgery to clear blocked arteries
1997	Successful cloning of sheep
2001	Human genome decoded

western European population—less than 5 percent in most countries. Religious faith became a private matter, the mark of subcultures (often defined by an "Us versus Them" mentality), rather than a bond tying together individuals and groups into a cohesive national culture.

At the same time, the long-reigning Pope John Paul II experienced unprecedented popularity. The most well-traveled and populist-oriented of twentieth-century popes, John Paul II became a media star, greeted with the same sort of cheering crowds and tee-shirt vendors that accompanied famous rock bands. Much of his popularity rested on his intimate connection with Poland's Solidarity and, therefore, with an image of liberation. But the pope's support for Solidarity did not mean he supported other forms of rebellion against authority. He adopted a firmly centralized approach to church government and opposed birth control, married clergy, and the ordination of women. Confronted with the postmodernist message that authority had fragmented and that no universal truth existed, many Christians found the pope's uncompromising stand a source of great comfort.

Yet throughout the West the pope's flock moved out of his control. In the United States, millions turned out to cheer John Paul II waving from an open car (the "popemobile"), yet the percentage of American Catholics using birth control—in direct violation of papal teachings—mirrored that of the population at large. Catholic Italy boasted the second-lowest birth rate in the world (after China), with the one-child family becoming the norm. It was hard to avoid the conclusion that in much of Western Roman Catholicism, as in much of postmodern society, image ruled while authority dissipated.

SEXUAL PRACTICE AND IDENTITY IN A POSTMODERN WORLD

The postmodern rejection of a single "right" answer or central authoritative voice was also apparent in sexual behaviors and the debates this behavior provoked. As many in the West abandoned traditional moral codes, rates of extramarital sex and divorce soared, the age at which individuals became sexually active tumbled, and sexual imagery in films, advertising, and publishing became more explicit.

Three developments contributed to this sexual revolution. First, the declining rates of religious belief and observance meant that religious-backed codes of sexual behavior carried less weight. At the same time, the rebellions of the 1960s and early 1970s glorified resistance to traditional conventions and rules. Second, breaking those rules seemed less risky for women as oral and barrier contraceptives and—particularly in eastern Europe—abortion became widely available. Third, feminism played an important role in encouraging women to see themselves as sexual beings.

The sexual revolution also meant greater visibity for sexual identities that did not conform to the dominant heterosexual pattern. Denmark became the first European state to legalize homosexual acts in 1933, but most European countries moved toward equalizing the legal treatment of homosexuality and heterosexuality during or after the 1960s. In England, for example, homosexual acts became legal in 1967, in Scotland in 1980. Denmark moved to the forefront once again in 1989 when it became the first state to legalize registered partnerships (also called civil unions) between couples of the same sex. By 2006, 20 European countries had done so. In the Netherlands, Belgium, Spain, Norway, Sweden, Iceland, Canada, and South Africa, gays and lesbians can legally marry on the same basis as heterosexuals.

The ongoing sexual revolution differentiated the West from much of the rest of the world, where more traditional sexual cultures remained strong. It also escalated the continuing debate within Western societies over what the "West" really means. Many, for example, saw the legalization of homosexual marriage as a logical and just extension of the concept of human rights—a central aspect of Western identity. Their opponents emphasized a different definition of the West when they argued that such a step violated the foundational Judeo-Christian values of Western culture. The growing numbers of Western citizens who were not Jewish or Christian but who adhered to religiously sanctioned sexual codes and roles—Muslim, Hindu, Sikh, and many others—intensified the debate still further.

The West in the Twenty-First Century

At the beginning of the twenty-first century, a worldwide environmental crisis raised significant questions about the ecological sustainability of Western habits of consumption. Environmental issues revealed the permeability of national borders and the limits of traditional political responses. As early as 1985, 257 multilateral treaties mandated some form of environmental protection—restrictions on trade in endangered species, wetlands preservation, forest conservation, regulation of industrial emissions. Yet the degradation of the planet proceeded apace. By 2000, half of the world's rivers were polluted or running dry, the number of people displaced by water crises stood at 25 million (versus 21 million war-related refugees), and the potential catastrophe of global warming loomed. Faced with this potential catastrophe, representatives of 192 countries from around the world gathered in Copenhagen for a United Nations-sponsored conference on climate change in December 2009.

Environmental issues such as climate change underlined the fact that global systems of production, distribution, and consumption linked the peoples of the world. Technological developments accelerated this **globalization.** Fiber-optic cables that transmitted signals 4,000 times faster than their copper predecessors made instant communication across national boundaries a reality. In this global economy, multinational corporations, with quick access to cheap Third World labor and raw materials, possessed significant economic—and political—power. So, too, did the World Bank and the IMF, the institutions that directed the flow of aid and loans throughout much of the world. The IMF, for example, insisted that governments receiving loans cut government spending on social and welfare programs and restrict the money supply to reduce inflation. Thus, economists or investors in offices far away, not elected leaders, called the shots in much of the world.

Multinational corporations, the World Bank, and the IMF embodied the characteristic Western confidence of the post-World War II era. Expert economists and agronomists taught that an infusion of Western capital and expertise would set the rest of the world on the path to economic growth. The growing gap between "North" and "South," however, called into question the reliability of Western economic models. Beginning in the 1990s, "antiglobalization" campaigners disrupted meetings of the World Bank, the IMF, and the "G8" (Japan, the United States, Britain, Canada, France, Germany, Italy, and Russia). These protesters sought to highlight the social costs of global capitalism.

In 2008, the globalized economy sharply declined when the explosion of a real estate-related stock bubble in the United States and western Europe sent shock waves across the industrialized world. Unemployment rates rose sharply, housing foreclosures escalated, and millions of people saw their retirement pensions dwindle. At the same time, Barack Obama (b. 1962), the first person of color to be elected president of the United States, took office and promised a new direction in economic and environmental policy. Many commentators began to talk about a turning point in the history of the West—but just where this turn was leading, no one was very clear.

CONCLUSION

Where Is the West Now?

In England, the most popular fast food is not fish and chips, long the quintessential English national supper, nor is it the Big Mac, as opponents of economic globalization might predict. Instead it is curry, the gift of the minority South Asian immigrant community. In the twenty-first century, "the West" may no longer serve as an important conceptual border marker. By many of the criteria explored in this textbook—economic, technological, political, and cultural—Tokyo would be defined as a Western city. So, too, would Melbourne—or Budapest or Shanghai. Nevertheless, the economic and social trauma that afflicted Russia and the poorer nations of the former Soviet bloc such as Romania and Bulgaria after 1989 demonstrates that the "West" retains its distinct identity, for the gap between it and the "East" remains wide. The admittedly hesitant, still incomplete spread of the Western ideal of democracy has thrown a fragile bridge across that gap. But perhaps the real divide for the twenty-first century stretches between "North" and "South"—the huge and growing difference between the global Haves and the Have-Nots. Whether any bridge can stretch across that span remains to be seen.

KEY TERMS

détente	perestroika
stagflation	lustration
new feminism	ethnic cleansing
Green politics	European Union (EU)
New Conservatism	Islamism
Helsinki Accords	Euro-Islam
Solidarity	postmodernism
civil society	postindustrial society
glasnost	globalization

CHAPTER QUESTIONS

1. How did economic and political developments in the 1970s and 1980s destabilize post-World War II national and international structures? (page 929)
2. What factors explain not only the outbreak but also the success of the revolutions of 1989–1991? (page 934)
3. What were the consequences of the revolutions of 1989 for the societies of eastern Europe? (page 943)
4. How and why was the West redefined at the end of the twentieth century and the beginning of the twenty-first? (page 949)

TAKING IT FURTHER

1. What do historians mean when they talk about the "postwar political consensus"? When did this consensus break apart and why?
2. How does the Hungarian uprising of 1956 and the Prague Spring (see Chapter 28) compare with Solidarity? Why did Solidarity succeed when the two earlier popular risings failed?
3. How can Western technological, religious, and sexual developments since 1980 be described as "postmodern"? How have these developments shaped the relationship between the West and the rest of the world?

✓• Practice on MyHistoryLab

GLOSSARY

absolutism (p. 492)   A form of government in the seventeenth and eighteenth centuries in which a ruler possessed unrivalled power.

acropolis (p. 79)   The defensible hilltop around which a polis grew. In classical Athens, the Acropolis was the site of the Parthenon (Temple of Athena).

Aeneid (p. 182)   Written by Virgil (70–19 B.C.E.), this magnificent epic poem celebrates the emperor Augustus by linking him to his mythical ancestor, Aeneas, the Trojan refugee who founded the Roman people. Considered by many to be the greatest work of Latin literature, the poem has had enormous influence in the West.

agora (p. 79)   An open area in the town center of a Greek polis that served as a market and a place for informal discussion.

agricultural revolution (p. 300)   Refers to technological innovations that began to appear during the eleventh century, making possible a dramatic growth in population. The agricultural revolution came about through harnessing new sources of power with water and wind mills, improving the pulling power of animals with better collars, using heavy plows to better exploit the soils of northern Europe, and employing a three-field crop rotation system that increased the amount and quality of food available.

agricultural societies (p. 65)   Settled communities in which people depend on farming and raising livestock as their sources of food.

alchemy (p. 534)   A form of learned magic that was intended to turn base metals into precious ones.

aldeias (p. 414)   Settlements for natives who had converted to Christianity in Brazil. In these settlements the Jesuit fathers protected the natives from enslavement.

Alexandrianism (p. 130)   A style of Hellenistic poetry that demonstrated a command of meter and language and appealed more to the intellect than the emotions.

Allies (p. 785)   During World War I, the states allied against the Central Powers of Germany and Austria-Hungary. During World War II, the states allied against the regimes of Nazi Germany, fascist Italy and imperial Japan.

Amarna Letters (p. 44)   A collection of over 370 cuneiform tablets discovered at Tell El-Amarna in 1887 that contains the diplomatic and imperial correspondence of the pharaohs from the mid-fourteenth century B.C.E.

Amarna Period (p. 39)   Time of religious ferment during the reign of Amenhotep IV (1351–1334 B.C.E.) in New Kingdom Egypt.

Anabaptism (p. 447)   Meaning "to rebaptize;" refers to those Protestant radicals of the sixteenth century who rejected infant baptism and adopted adult baptism. Anabaptists treated the Bible as a blueprint for reforming not just the church but all of society, a tendency that led them to reject the authority of the state, to live in self-governing "holy communities," and in some cases to practice a primitive form of communism.

anarchism (p. 737)   Ideology that views the state as unnecessary and repressive and rejects participation in parliamentary politics in favor of direct, usually violent, action.

anticlericalism (p. 765)   Opposition to the political influence of the Roman Catholic Church.

Antonine Decree (p. 180)   In 212 C.E. the emperor Aurelius Antoninus, called Caracalla, issued a decree that granted citizenship to all the free inhabitants of the Roman Empire. The decree enabled Roman law to embrace the entire population of the empire.

apartheid (p. 904)   System of racial segregation and discrimination put into place in South Africa in 1948.

appeasement (p. 860)   British diplomatic and financial efforts to stabilize Germany in the 1920s and 1930s and so avoid a second world war.

Arians (p. 213)   Christians who believe that God the Father is superior to Jesus Christ his Son. Most of the Germanic settlers in western Europe in the fifth century were Arians.

aristocracy (p. 587)   A term that originally applied to those who were considered the most fit to rule and later identified the wealthiest members of society, especially those who owned land.

asceticism (p. 215)   The Christian practice of severely suppressing physical needs and daily desires in an effort to achieve a spiritual union with God. Asceticism is the practice that underlies the monastic movement.

Auschwitz (p. 880)   Technically Auschwitz-Birkenau; death camp in Poland that has become the symbol of the Holocaust.

auto-da-fé (p. 466)   Meaning literally a "theater of faith," an *auto* was practiced by the Catholic Church in early modern Spain and Portugal as an extended public ritual of penance designed to cause physical pain among the sinful and promote fear of God's judgment among those who witnessed it.

Babylonian Captivity of the Church (p. 354) Between 1305 and 1378 seven consecutive popes voluntarily chose to reside in Avignon, France, in order to escape anarchy in the streets of Rome. During this period the popes became subservient to the kings of France.

Babylonian Exile (p. 67)   The period of Jewish history between the destruction of Solomon's temple in Jerusalem by Babylonian armies in 587 B.C.E., and 538 B.C.E, when Cyrus of Persia permitted Jews to return to Palestine and rebuild the temple.

balance of power (p. 501)   An arrangement in which various countries form alliances to prevent any one state from dominating the others.

Balfour Declaration (p. 817)   Declaration of 1917 that affirmed British support of a Jewish state in Palestine.

barbarians (p. 108)   A term used by Greeks to describe people who did not speak Greek and who were therefore considered uncivilized.

baroque (pp. 126, 498)   A dynamic style in art, architecture, and music that was intended to elicit an emotional response. Baroque buildings were massive, imposing structures with sweeping façades. The baroque style represented a development of Greek classicism in the Hellenistic period. In the seventeenth century the baroque style was closely associated with royal absolutism.

Berlin Wall (p. 908)   Constructed by the East German government, the wall physically cut the city of Berlin in two and prevented East German citizens from access to West Germany; stood from 1961 to 1989.

Big Three (p. 892)   Term applied to the British, Soviet, and U.S. leaders during World War II: until 1945, Winston Churchill, Joseph Stalin, and Franklin Roosevelt; by the summer of 1945, Clement Atlee, Joseph Stalin, and Harry Truman.

Black Death (p. 332)   An epidemic disease, possibly Bubonic plague, that struck Europe between 1348 and the 1350s killing at least one-third of the total population.

blitzkrieg (p. 861)   "Lightning war;" offensive military tactic making use of airplanes, tanks, and motorized infantry to punch through enemy defenses and secure key territory. First demonstrated by the German army in World War II.

Bolsheviks (p. 809)   Minority group of Russian socialists, headed by Vladimir Lenin, who espoused an immediate transition to a socialist state. It became the Communist Party in the Soviet Union.

boule (p. 83)   A council of 400 male citizens established by Solon in Greece in the sixth century B.C.E. It served as an advisory body for the general assembly of all male citizens.

Bourbon reforms (p. 560)   Measures introduced by the Bourbon Kings of Spain in the eighteenth century to make the Spanish empire more manageable and profitable.

bourgeoisie (p. 594)   A social group, technically consisting of those who were burghers in the towns, that included prosperous merchants and financiers, members of the professions, and some skilled craftsmen known as "petty bourgeoisie."

boyars (p. 488)   Upper-level nobles who dominated Russian society until the tsars began to supplant them in the fifteenth and sixteenth centuries.

Bretton Woods Agreement (p. 894)   Agreement signed in 1944 that established the post-World War II economic framework in which the U.S. dollar served as the world's reserve currency.

brinkmanship (p. 905)   Style of Cold War confrontation in which each superpower endeavored to convince the other that it was willing to wage nuclear war.

bronze (p. 36)   An alloy of tin and copper that produces a hard metal suitable for weapons, tools, ornaments, and household objects. Bronze production began about 3200 B.C.E.

Byzantine Empire (p. 225)   The eastern half of the Roman Empire, which lasted from the founding of Constantinople in 324 to its conquest by the Ottoman Turks in 1453.

caliphate (p. 250)   The Islamic imperial government that evolved under the leadership of Abu Bakr (r. 632–634), the successor of the prophet Muhammad. The sectarian division within Islam between the Shi'ites and Sunni derived from a disagreement over how to determine the hereditary succession from Muhammad to the caliphate, which combined governmental and some religious responsibilities.

calling (p. 442)   The Calvinist doctrine that God calls the Elect to perform his will on earth. God's calling gave Calvinists a powerful sense of personal direction.

canon law (p. 276)   The collected laws of the Roman Catholic Church. Canon law applied to cases involving the clergy, disputes about church property, and donations to the Church. It also applied to the laity for annulling marriages, legitimating bastards, prosecuting bigamy, protecting widows and orphans, and resolving inheritance disputes.

capital (p. 663)   All the physical assets used in production, including fixed capital, such as machinery, and circulating capital, such as raw materials; more generally the cost of these physical assets.

caravels (p. 397)   Hybrid three-masted ships developed about 1450 in the Iberian peninsula by combining the rigging of square with triangular lateen sails. These ships could be sailed in a variety of winds, carry large cargoes, be managed by a small crew, and be defended by guns mounted in the castle superstructure.

Carolingian Renaissance (p. 275)   The "rebirth" of interest in ancient Greek and Latin literature and language during the reign of the Frankish emperor Charlemagne (r. 768–814). Charlemagne promoted the intensive study of Latin to promote governmental efficiency and to propagate the Christian faith.

Catholic Reformation (p. 450)   A series of efforts during the sixteenth century to purify the Church that evolved out of late medieval spirituality and that included the creation of new religious orders, especially the Society of Jesus.

Central Powers (p. 785)   Germany and Austria-Hungary in World War I.

Chalcedonians (p. 213)   Christians who followed the doctrinal decisions and definitions of the Council of Chalcedon in 451 C.E. stating that Christ's human and divine natures were equal, but entirely distinct and united in one person "without confusion, division, separation, or change." Chalcedonian Christianity came to be associated with the Byzantine Empire and is called Greek Orthodoxy. In western Europe it is known as Roman Catholicism.

Chartists (p. 702)   A British group of workers and middle-class radicals who drafted a People's Charter in 1837 demanding universal male suffrage and other political reforms.

chinoiserie (p. 578)   A French word for an eighteenth-century decorative art that combined Chinese and European motifs.

Christian Democracy, Christian Democratic parties (p. 916)   Conservative and confessionally based (Roman Catholic) political parties that dominated much of western European politics after World War II.

Christian humanists (p. 430)   During the fifteenth and sixteenth centuries these experts in Greek, Latin, and Hebrew subjected the Bible to philological study in an attempt to understand the precise meaning of the founding text of Christianity.

Church Fathers (p. 220)   Writers in Late Antiquity from both the Greek and Latin-speaking worlds who sought to reconcile Christianity with classical learning.

circuit court (p. 321)   Established by King Henry II (r. 1154–1189) to make royal justice available to virtually anyone in England. Circuit court judges visited every shire in England four times a year.

civic humanism (p. 378)   A branch of humanism introduced by the Florentine chancellor Leonardo Bruni who defended the republican institutions and values of the city. Civic humanism promoted the ethic of responsible citizenship.

civilization (p. 12)   The term used by archaeologists to describe a society differentiated by levels of wealth and power, and in which religious, economic, and political control are based in cities.

civil society (p. 935)   Public organizations and activities separate from the state, commerce, or the family that help to create community life.

clans or kin groups (p. 267)   The basic social and political unit of Germanic society consisting of blood relatives obliged to defend one another and take vengeance for crimes against the group and its members.

class consciousness (p. 674)   The awareness of people from different occupations that they belonged to a class.

classicism (p. 591)   A style in art, architecture, music, and literature that emphasizes proportion, adherence to traditional forms, and a rejection of emotion and enthusiasm.

Cluny (p. 306)   A monastery founded in Burgundy in 910 that became the center of a far-reaching movement to reform the Church that was sustained in more than 1,500 Cluniac monasteries, modeled after the original in Cluny.

Cold War (p. 892)   Struggle for global supremacy between the United States and the Soviet Union, waged from the end of World War II until 1990.

collectivization (p. 840)   The replacement of private and village farms with large cooperative agricultural enterprises run by state-employed managers. Collectivization was a key part of Joseph Stalin's plans for modernizing the Soviet economy and destroying peasant opposition to communist rule.

colons (p. 581)   White planters in the French Caribbean colony of Saint Domingue (Haiti).

Columbian exchange (p. 418)   The trade of peoples, plants, animals, microbes, and ideas between the Old and New Worlds that began with Columbus.

Columbian question (p. 420)   The debate among historians and epidemiologists about whether syphilis or its ancestor disease originated in the Americas and was brought to the Old World after Columbus's voyages.

Common Market (p. 917)   Originally comprising West Germany, France, Italy, Belgium, Luxembourg, and the Netherlands, the Common Market was formed in 1957 to integrate its members' economic structures and so foster both economic prosperity and international peace. Also called the European Economic Community (EEC). Evolved into the European Union (EU).

communes (p. 303)   Sworn defensive associations of merchants and workers that appeared in north-central Italy after 1070 and that became the effective government of more than a hundred cities. The communes evolved into city-states by seizing control of the surrounding countryside.

communism (p. 690)   The revolutionary form of socialism developed by Karl Marx and Friedrich Engels that promoted the overthrow of bourgeois or capitalist institutions and the establishment of a dictatorship of the proletariat.

Companions (p. 110)   Elite regiments of cavalrymen armed with heavy lances formed by Philip of Macedon.

Concert of Europe (p. 696)   The joint efforts made by Austria, Prussia, Russia, Britain, and France during the years following the Congress of Vienna to suppress liberal and nationalist movements throughout Europe.

Conciliar Movement (p. 354)   A fifteenth-century movement that advocated ending the Great Schism and reforming church government by calling a general meeting or council of the bishops, who would exercise authority over the rival popes.

confessions (p. 456)   The formal sixteenth-century statements of religious doctrine: the Confession of Augsburg for Lutherans, the Helvetic Confessions for Calvinists, the Thirty-Nine Articles for Anglicans, and the decrees of the Council of Trent for Catholics.

Congress of Vienna (p. 649)   A conference of the major powers of Europe in 1814–1815 to establish a new balance of power at the end of the Napoleonic Wars.

conquistadores (p. 408)   Spanish adventurers in the Americas who explored and conquered the lands of indigenous peoples, sometimes without legal authority but usually with a legal privilege granted by the king of Spain who required that one-fifth of all things of value be turned over to the crown. The conquistadores extended Spanish sovereignty over new lands.

conservatism (p. 686)   A nineteenth-century ideology intended to prevent a recurrence of the revolutionary changes of the 1790s and the implementation of liberal policies.

containment (p. 896)   Cold War policy of blocking communist expansion; inaugurated by the Truman Doctrine in 1947.

corporatism (p. 834)   The practice by which committees (or "corporations") made up of representatives of workers, employers, and the state direct the economy.

Corpus Juris Civilis (pp. 143, 226)   The body of Roman law compiled by the emperor Justinian in Constantinople in 534. The Corpus became a pillar of Latin-speaking European civilization.

Cortes (p. 494)   Legislative assemblies in the Spanish kingdoms.

cosmology (p. 134)   A theory concerning the structure and nature of the universe such as those proposed by Aristotle in the fourth century B.C.E. and Copernicus in the sixteenth century.

counties (p. 275)   Territorial units devised by the Carolingian dynasty during the eighth and ninth centuries for the administration of the empire. Each county was administered by a count who was rewarded with lands and sent to areas where he had no family ties to serve as a combined provincial governor, judge, military commander, and representative of the king.

courtly love (p. 326)   An ethic first found in the poems of the late twelfth- and thirteenth-century troubadours that portrayed the ennobling possibilities of the love between a man and a woman. Courtly love formed the basis for the modern idea of romantic love.

creoles (p. 560)   People of Spanish descent who had been born in Spanish America.

Crusades (p. 288)   Between 1095 and 1291, Latin Christians heeding the call of the pope launched eight major expeditions and many smaller ones against Muslim armies in an attempt to gain control of and hold Jerusalem.

Cubism (p. 763)   Modernist artistic movement of the early twentieth century that emphasized the fragmentation of human perception through visual experiments with geometric forms.

cultural relativism (p. 422)   A mode of thought first explored during the sixteenth century to explain why the peoples of the New World did not appear in the Bible. Cultural relativism recognized that many (but not necessarily all) standards of judgment are specific to particular cultures rather than the fixed truths established by natural or divine law.

culture (p. 12)   The knowledge and adaptive behavior created by communities that helps them to mediate between themselves and the natural world through time.

cuneiform (p. 24)   A kind of writing in which wedge-shaped symbols are pressed into clay tablets to indicate words and ideas. Cuneiform writing originated in ancient Sumer.

curia (p. 309)   The administrative bureaucracy of the Roman Catholic Church.

Cynics (p. 132)   Followers of the teachings of Antisthenes (ca. 445–360 B.C.E.) who rejected pleasures, possessions, and social conventions to find peace of mind.

Darwinian theory of evolution (p. 753)   Scientific theory associated with nineteenth-century scientist Charles Darwin that highlights the role of variation and natural selection in the evolution of species.

Decembrists (p. 697)   Russian liberals who staged a revolt against Tsar Nicholas I on the first day of his reign in December 1825.

de-Christianization (p. 636)   A program inaugurated in France in 1793 by the radical Jacobin and former priest Joseph Fouché that closed churches, eliminated religious symbols, and attempted to establish a purely civic religion.

decolonization (p. 904)   The retreat of Western powers from their imperial territories.

deduction, deductive reasoning (pp. 24, 536)   The logical process by which ideas and laws are derived from basic truths or principles.

Defenders (p. 582)   Irish Catholic peasants who joined the United Irishmen in the rebellion against Britain in 1798.

deists (p. 545)   Seventeenth- and eighteenth-century thinkers who believed that God created the universe and established immutable laws of nature but did not subsequently intervene in the operation of nature or in human affairs.

Delian League (p. 92)   The alliance among many Greek cities organized by Athens in 478 B.C.E. in order to fight Persian forces in the eastern Aegean Sea. The Athenians gradually turned the Delian League into the Athenian Empire.

demand (p. 664)   The desire of consumers to acquire goods and the need of producers to acquire raw materials and machinery.

democracy (p. 82)   A form of government in which citizens devise their own governing institutions and choose their leaders; began in Athens, Greece, in the fifth century B.C.E.

de-Stalinization (p. 912)   Nikita Khrushchev's effort to decentralize political and economic control in the Soviet Union after 1956.

détente (p. 930)   During the 1970s, a period of lessened Cold War hostilities and greater reliance on negotiation and compromise.

dialectic (p. 688)   The theory that history advanced in stages as the result of the conflict between different ideas or social groups.

dialectical materialism (p. 689)   The socialist philosophy of Karl Marx according to which history advanced as the result of material or economic forces and would lead to the creation of a classless society.

Diaspora (p. 195)   Literally "dispersion of population;" usually used to refer to the dispersion of the Jewish population after the Roman destruction of the Temple in Jerusalem in 70 C.E.

diets (p. 494)   Legislative assemblies in German territories.

divination (p. 24)   The practice of discerning the future by looking for messages imprinted in nature.

divine right (p. 494)   The theory that rulers received their power directly from God.

division of labor (p. 660)   The assignment of one stage of production to a single worker or group of workers to increase efficiency and productive output.

domestication (p. 13) Manipulating the breeding of animals over many generations in order to make them more useful to humans as sources of food, wool, and other byproducts. Domestication of animals began about 10,000 years ago.

domestic system (p. 660) An economic arrangement developed in the sixteenth century in which capitalist entrepreneurs employed families in rural areas to spin and weave cloth and make nails and cutlery.

Dreyfus Affair (p. 730) The trials of Captain Alfred Dreyfus on treason charges dominated French political life in the decade after 1894 and revealed fundamental divisions in French society.

dualistic (pp. 88, 537) A term used to describe a philosophy or a religion in which a rigid distinction is made between body and mind, good and evil, or the material and the immaterial world.

Dutch Revolt (p. 479) The rebellion against Spanish rule of the seven northern provinces of the Netherlands between 1579 and 1648, which resulted in the independence of the Republic of the United Provinces.

Edict of Nantes (p. 477) Promulgated by King Henry IV in 1598, the edict allowed the Huguenots to build a quasi-independent state within the kingdom of France, giving them the right to have their own troops, church organization, and political autonomy within their walled towns, but banning them from the royal court and the city of Paris. King Louis XIV revoked the edict in 1685.

Einsatzgruppen (p. 879) Loosely translated as strike force or task force; SS units given the task of murdering Jews and Communist Party members in the areas of the Soviet Union occupied by Germany during World War II.

empires (pp. 20, 554) Large political formations consisting of different kingdoms or territories outside the boundaries of the states that control them.

empiricism (p. 535) The practice of testing scientific theories by observation and experiment.

enclosure (p. 663) The consolidation of scattered agricultural holdings into large, compact fields which were then closed off by hedges, bushes, or walls, giving farmers complete control over the uses of their land.

encomienda (p. 410) The basic form of economic and social organization in early Spanish America, based on a royal grant awarded to a Spaniard for military or other services that gave the grantee and

his successors the right to gather tribute from the Indians in a defined area.

English Parliament (p. 321) King Edward I (r. 1272–1307) began to call the English Parliament in order to raise sums of money for his foreign wars. The English Parliament differed from similar assemblies on the Continent. It usually included representatives of the "commons," which consisted of townsmen and prosperous farmers who lacked titles of nobility, but whom the king summoned because he needed their money. As a result, a broader spectrum of the population joined Parliament than in most other medieval kingdoms.

enlightened despots (p. 613) The term assigned to absolute monarchs who initiated a series of legal and political reforms in an effort to realize the goals of the Enlightenment.

Enlightenment (p. 596) An international intellectual movement of the eighteenth century that emphasized the use of reason and the application of the laws of nature to human society.

Epicureans (p. 131) Followers of the teachings of the philosopher Epicurus (341–271 B.C.E.). Epicureans tried to gain peace of mind by choosing pleasures rationally.

Estates General (p. 494) The legislative assembly of France in the Old Regime.

ethnic cleansing (p. 948) A term introduced during the wars in Yugoslavia in the 1990s; the systematic use of murder, rape, and violence by one ethnic group against members of other ethnic groups in order to establish control over a territory.

Etruscans (p. 139) A people of unknown origin who maintained a loose confederation of independent cities in central Italy and who strongly influenced the culture of ancient Rome.

Eucharist (p. 318) Also known as Holy Communion or the Lord's Supper, the Eucharistic rite of the Mass celebrates Jesus' last meal with his apostles when the priest-celebrant consecrates wafers of bread and a chalice of wine as the body and blood of Christ. In the Middle Ages the wafers of bread were distributed for the congregation to eat, but drinking from the chalice was a special privilege of the priesthood. Protestants in the sixteenth century and Catholics in the late twentieth century began to allow the laity to drink from the chalice.

eugenics (p. 832) The effort to improve the physical and intellectual capacities of the population by encouraging individuals with "desirable" traits to reproduce and/or by discouraging those individuals designated as "undesirable" from reproducing.

Euro-Islam (p. 956)   The identity and belief system being forged by European Muslims who argue that Islam does not contradict or reject European values.

European Economic Community (EEC) (p. 917) Originally comprising West Germany, France, Italy, Belgium, Luxembourg, and the Netherlands, the EEC was formed in 1957 to integrate its members' economic structures and so foster both economic prosperity and international peace. Also called the Common Market.

European Union (EU) (p. 949)   A successor organization to the EEC; the effort to integrate European political, economic, cultural, and military structures and policies.

excommunication (p. 309)   A decree by the pope or a bishop prohibiting a sinner from participating in the sacraments of the Church and forbidding any social contact whatsoever with the surrounding community.

existentialism (p. 822)   Twentieth-century philosophy that emerged in the interwar era and influenced many thinkers and artists after World War II. Existentialism emphasizes individual freedom in a world devoid of meaning or coherence.

Expressionism (p. 763)   Modernist artistic movement of the early twentieth century that used bold colors and experimental forms to express emotional realities.

factories (p. 416)   Trading posts established by European powers in foreign lands.

fanatic (p. 474)   Originally referring to someone possessed by a demon, during the sixteenth century a fanatic came to mean a person who expressed immoderate enthusiasm in religious matters or who pursued a supposedly divine mission, often to violent ends.

fascism (p. 833)   Twentieth-century political ideology that rejected the existing alternatives of conservatism, communism, socialism, and liberalism. Fascists stressed the authoritarian power of the state, the efficacy of violent action, the need to build a national community, and the use of new technologies of influence and control.

federalists (p. 628)   The name assigned by radical Jacobins to provincial rebels who opposed the centralization of the state during the French Revolution.

feminism, feminist movement (p. 741)   International movement that emerged in the second half of the nineteenth century and demanded broader political, legal, and economic rights for women.

Fertile Crescent (p. 13)   Also known as the Levantine Corridor, this twenty-five mile wide arc of land stretching from the Jordan River to the Euphrates River was the place where food production and settled communities first appeared in Southwest Asia (the Middle East).

feudalism (p. 281)   A term historians use to describe a social system common during the Middle Ages in which lords granted fiefs (tracts of land or some other form of income) to dependents, known as vassals, who owed their lords personal services in exchange. Feudalism refers to a society governed through personal ties of dependency rather than public political institutions.

fief (p. 281)   During the Middle Ages a fief was a grant of land or some other form of income that a lord gave to a vassal in exchange for loyalty and certain services (usually military assistance).

Final Solution (p. 879)   Nazi term for the effort to murder every Jew in Europe during World War II.

fin-de-siecle (p. 757)   French term for the "turn of the century;" used to refer to the cultural crisis of the late nineteenth century.

First Triumvirate (p. 163)   The informal political alliance made by Julius Caesar, Pompey, and Crassus in 60 B.C.E. to share power in the Roman Republic. It led directly to the collapse of the Republic.

Forms (p. 103)   In the philosophical teachings of Plato, these are eternal, unchanging absolutes such as Truth, Justice, and Beauty that represent true reality, as opposed to the approximations of reality that humans encounter in everyday life.

Forum (p. 138)   The political and religious center of the city of Rome throughout antiquity. All cities in the empire had a forum in imitation of the capital city.

Fourteen Points (p. 814)   The principles outlined by U.S. President Woodrow Wilson as the basis for a new world order after World War I.

franchise (p. 602)   The right to vote; also called suffrage.

freemasons (p. 611)   Members of secret societies of men and women that flourished during the Enlightenment, dedicated to the creation of a society based on reason and virtue and committed to the principles of liberty and equality.

French Wars of Religion (p. 475)   A series of political assassinations, massacres, and military engagements between French Catholics and Calvinists from 1560 to 1598.

friars (p. 315) "Brothers" who wandered from city to city and throughout the countryside begging for alms. Unlike monks who remained in a cloister, friars tried to help ordinary laypeople with their problems by preaching and administering to the sick and poor.

Gaullism (p. 923) The political ideology associated with twentieth-century French political leader Charles DeGaulle. Gaullism combined the advocacy of a strong, centralized state with social conservatism.

genocide (p. 807) The murder of an entire people.

German-Soviet Non-Aggression Pact (p. 859) Signed by Joseph Stalin and Adolf Hitler in 1939, the agreement publicly pledged Germany and the Soviet Union not to attack each other and secretly divided up Poland and the Baltic states between the two powers.

Girondins (p. 627) The more conservative members of the Jacobin party who favored greater economic freedom and opposed further centralization of state power during the French Revolution.

glasnost (p. 937) Loosely translated as openness or honesty; Gorbachev's effort after 1985 to break with the secrecy that had characterized Soviet political life.

globalization (p. 964) The process by which global systems of production, distribution, and communication link together the peoples of the world.

Gnostic, Gnosticism (p. 197) Religious doctrine that emphasizes the importance of *gnosis*, or hidden truth, as a way of releasing spiritual reality from the prison of the essentially unreal or evil material world.

Gothic (p. 327) A style in architecture in western Europe from the late twelfth and thirteenth centuries, characterized by ribbed vaults and pointed arches, which drew the eyes of worshipers upward toward God. Flying buttresses, which redistributed the weight of the roof, made possible thin walls pierced by large expanses of stained glass.

grand jury (p. 321) In medieval England after the judicial reforms of King Henry II (r. 1154–1189), grand juries were called when the circuit court judge arrived in a shire. The sheriff assembled a group of men familiar with local affairs who constituted the grand jury and who reported to the judge the major crimes that had been committed since the judge's last visit.

Great Depression (p. 834) Calamitous drop in prices, reduction in trade, and rise in unemployment that devastated the global economy in 1929.

Great Persecution (p. 207) An attack on Christians in the Roman empire begun by the emperor Galerius in 303 C.E. on the grounds that their worship was endangering the empire. Several thousand Christians were executed.

Great Purge (p. 842) Period of mass arrests and executions particularly aimed at Communist Party members. Lasting from 1934 to 1939, the Great Purge enabled Joseph Stalin to consolidate his one-man rule over the Soviet Union.

Great Schism (p. 354) The division of the Catholic Church (1378–1417) between rival Italian and French claimants to the papal throne.

Green movement, Green politics (p. 932) A new style of politics and set of political ideas resulting from the confluence of environmentalism, feminism, and anti-nuclear protests of the 1970s.

guilds (p. 345) Professional associations devoted to protecting the special interests of a particular trade or craft and to monopolizing production and trade in the goods the guild produced.

haciendas (p. 411) Large landed estates that began to be established in the seventeenth century replaced encomiendas throughout much of Spanish America.

habiru (p. 55) Peasants who existed outside the palace system of the Late Bronze Age; often seen as bandits.

Hallstatt (p. 122) The first Celtic civilization in central Europe is called Halstatt. From about 750 to about 450 B.C.E., Hallstatt Celts spread throughout Europe.

Hellenistic (p. 108) The word used to describe the civilization, based on that of Greece, that developed in the wake of the conquests of Alexander the Great.

helots (p. 82) The brutally oppressed subject peoples of the Spartans. Tied to the land they farmed for Spartan masters, they were treated little better than beasts of burden.

hetairai (p. 97) Elite courtesans in ancient Greece who provided intellectual as well as sexual companionship.

hieroglyphs (p. 32) Ancient Egyptian system of writing that represented both sounds and objects.

Holocaust (p. 877) Adolf Hitler's effort to murder all the Jews in Europe during World War II.

Homo sapiens sapiens (p. 13) Scientific term meaning "most intelligent people" applied to physically and intellectually modern human beings that first appeared between 200,000 and 100,000 years ago in Africa.

hoplites (p. 81)   Greek soldiers in the Archaic Age who could afford their own weapons. Hoplite tactics made soldiers fighting as a group dependent on one another. This contributed to the internal cohesion of the polis and eventually to the rise of democracy.

Huguenots (p. 474)   The term for French Calvinists, who constituted some 10 percent of the population by 1560.

humanists (p. 376)   During the Renaissance humanists were writers and orators who studied Latin and sometimes Greek texts on grammar, rhetoric, poetry, history, and ethics.

Hundred Years' War (p. 346)   Refers to a series of engagements (1337–1453) between England and France over England's attempts to assert its claims to territories in France.

hyperinflation (p. 827)   Catastrophic price increases and currency devaluation, such as that which occurred in Germany in 1923.

iconoclasm (p. 241)   The destruction of religious images in the Byzantine empire in the eighth century.

icons (p. 240)   The Christian images of God and saints found in Byzantine art.

ideologies (p. 684)   Theories of society and government that form the basis of political programs.

induction (p. 535)   The mental process by which theories are established only after the systematic accumulation of large amounts of data.

indulgences (p. 354)   Certificates that allowed penitents to atone for their sins and reduce their time in purgatory. Usually these were issued for going on a pilgrimage or performing a pious act, but during the Babylonian Captivity of the Church (1305–1378) popes began to sell them, a practice Martin Luther protested in 1517 in an act that brought on the Protestant Reformation.

industrial capitalism (p. 671)   A form of capitalism characterized by the ownership of factories by private individuals and the employment of wage labor.

intendants (p. 496)   French royal officials who became the main agents of French provincial administration in the seventeenth century.

interdict (p. 309)   A papal decree prohibiting the celebration of the sacraments in an entire city or kingdom.

Investiture Controversy (p. 308)   A dispute that began in 1076 between the popes and the German emperors over the right to invest bishops with their offices. The most famous episode was the conflict between Pope Gregory VII and Emperor Henry IV.

The controversy was resolved by the Concordat of Worms in 1122.

"Iron Curtain" (p. 892)   Metaphor for the Cold War division of Europe after World War II.

Islamism (p. 952)   Islamic radicalism or *jihadism*. The ideology that insists that Islam demands a rejection of Western values and that violence in this struggle against the West is justified.

Jacobins (p. 623)   A French political party supporting a democratic republic that found support in political clubs throughout the country and dominated the National Convention from 1792 until 1794.

Jim Crow (p. 777)   Series of laws mandating racial segregation throughout the American South.

Junkers (pp. 509, 705)   The traditional nobility of Prussia.

justification by faith (p. 432)   Refers to Martin Luther's insight that humanity is incapable of performing enough religious good works to earn eternal salvation. Salvation is an unmerited gift from God called grace. Those who receive grace are called the Elect.

Keynesian economics (p. 846)   Economic theories associated with the British economist John Maynard Keynes that advocate using the power of the democratic state to ensure economic prosperity.

knight (p. 281)   During the Middle Ages a knight was a soldier who fought on horseback. A knight was a vassal or dependent of a lord, who usually financed the knight's expenses of armor and weapons and of raising and feeding horses with a grant of land known as a fief.

Koine (p. 124)   The standard version of the Greek language spoken throughout the Hellenistic world.

La Tène (p. 122)   A phase of Celtic civilization that lasted from about 450 to 200 B.C.E. La Tène culture became strong especially in the regions of the Rhine and Danube Rivers.

laissez-faire (p. 686)   The principle that governments should not regulate or otherwise intervene in the economy unless it is necessary to protect property rights and public order.

late antiquity (p. 202)   The period between about 250 and 600, which bridged the classical world and the Middle Ages.

Latin Christendom (p. 214)   The parts of medieval Europe, including all of western Europe, united by Christianity and the use of Latin in worship and intellectual life. Latin served as an international language among the ruling elites in western Europe, even though they spoke different languages in their daily lives.

Latin War (p. 144)   A war that the Latin peoples of Italy waged against the Roman Republic between 340 and 338. B.C.E.

Law Code of Hammurabi (p. 25)   The world's oldest complete surviving compendium of laws, promulgated during the reign of Hammurabi (1792–1750 B.C.E.) of Babylon.

lay investiture (p. 307)   The practice of nobles, kings, or emperors installing churchmen and giving them the symbols of office.

League of Nations (p. 814)   Association of states set up after World War I to resolve international conflicts through open and peaceful negotiation.

Lend-Lease Act (p. 869)   Passed in March 1941, the act gave Britain access to U.S. industrial products during World War II, with payment postponed for the duration of the war.

Levantine Corridor (p. 13)   Also known as the Fertile Crescent, this arc of land stretching from the Jordan River to the Euphrates River was the place where food production and settled communities first appeared in Southwest Asia (the Middle East).

liberalism (p. 686)   An ideology based on the conviction that individual freedom is of supreme importance and the main responsibility of government is to protect that freedom.

"Linear B" (p. 47)   The earliest written form of Greek, used by the Mycenaeans.

linear perspective (p. 384)   In the arts the use of geometrical principles to depict a three-dimensional space on a flat, two-dimensional surface.

liturgy (p. 262)   The forms of Christian worship, including the prayers, chants, and rituals to be said, sung, or performed throughout the year.

lord (p. 276)   During the Middle Ages a lord was someone who offered protection to dependents, known as vassals, who took an oath of loyalty to him. Most lords demanded military services from their vassals and sometimes granted them tracts of land known as fiefs.

ma'at (p. 30)   Ancient Egyptian concept of the fundamental order established by the gods.

Macedonian Renaissance (p. 242)   During the Macedonian dynasty's rule of Byzantium (867–1056), aristocratic families, the Church, and monasteries devoted their immense riches to embellishing Constantinople with new buildings, mosaics, and icons.

The emperors sponsored historical, philosophical, and religious writing.

Mafia (p. 711)   Organizations of armed men who took control of local politics and the economy in late nineteenth-century Sicily.

magic (p. 469)   Learned opinion described two kinds of magic: natural magic, which involved the manipulation of occult forces believed to exist in nature, and demonic magic, which called upon evil spirits to gain access to power. Widely accepted as a reality until the middle of the seventeenth century.

Magisterial Reformation (p. 440)   Refers to Protestant churches that received official government sanction.

Magna Carta (p. 321)   In 1215 some English barons forced King John to sign the "great charter," in which the king pledged to respect the traditional feudal privileges of the nobility, towns, and clergy. Subsequent kings swore to uphold it, thereby accepting the fundamental principle that even the king was obliged to respect the law.

Malthusian population trap (p. 670)   The theory of Thomas Malthus (1766–1834) that the natural tendency of population to grow faster than the food supply would eventually drive the size of populations back to sustainable levels and end periods of economic expansion that usually accompany the growth of population.

Manhattan Project (p. 875)   Code name given to the secret Anglo-American project that resulted in the construction of the atom bomb during World War II.

manor (p. 301)   A medieval unit of agricultural management in which a lord managed and served as the presiding judge over peasants who worked the land.

marches (p. 275)   Territorial units of the Carolingian empire for the administration of frontier regions. Each march was ruled by a margrave who had special powers necessary to defend vulnerable borders.

Marshall Plan (p. 896)   The use of U.S. economic aid to restore stability to Europe after World War II and so undercut the appeal of communist ideology.

mass politics (p. 725)   A political culture characterized by the participation of non-elites.

matriarchy (p. 47)   A social or cultural system in which family lineage is traced through the mother and/or in which women hold significant power.

metropolis (p. 553).   The "mother state" that controlled an empire.

mechanical philosophy (p. 536)   The seventeenth-century philosophy of nature, championed by René

Descartes, holding that nature operated in a mechanical way, just like a machine made by a human being.

megalith (p. 000)   A very large stone used in prehistoric European monuments in the second millennium B.C.E.

mercantilism (p. 499)   The theory that the wealth of a state depended on its ability to import fewer commodities than it exported and thus acquire the largest possible share of the world's monetary supply. The theory encouraged state intervention in the economy and the regulation of trade.

meritocracy (p. 642)   The practice of appointing people to office solely on the basis of ability and performance rather than social or economic status.

mesmerism (p. 612)   A pseudoscience developed by Franz Anton Mesmer in the eighteenth century that treated sickness by massaging or hypnotizing the patient to produce a crisis that restored health.

mestizos (p. 574)   People of mixed white and Indian ancestry.

metropolis (p. 553)   The parent country of a colony or imperial possession.

Middle Passage (p. 571)   The journey taken by European ships bringing slaves from Africa to the Americas.

Modern Devotion (p. 355)   A fifteenth-century religious movement that stressed individual piety, ethical behavior, and intense religious education. The Modern Devotion was promoted by the Brothers of the Common Life, a religious order whose influence was broadly felt through its extensive network of schools.

modernism (p. 757)   Term applied to artistic and literary movements from the late nineteenth century through the 1950s. Modernists sought to create new aesthetic forms and values.

monastic movement (p. 215)   In Late Antiquity, Christian ascetics organized communities where men and women could pursue a life of spirituality through work, prayer, and asceticism. Called the monastic movement, this spiritual quest spread quickly throughout Christian lands.

Monophysites (p. 214)   Christians who do not accept the Council of Chalcedon (see Chalcedonians). Monophysites believe that Jesus Christ has only one nature, equally divine and human.

monotheism (p. 39)   The belief in only one god, first attributed to the ancient Hebrews. Monotheism is the foundation of Judaism, Christianity, Islam, and Zoroastrianism.

Montagnards (p. 627)   Members of the radical faction within the Jacobin party who advocated the centralization of state power during the French Revolution and instituted the Reign of Terror.

mosque (p. 247)   A place of Muslim worship.

Mountain, the (p. 627)   The radical faction of Jacobins in the National Convention during the French Revolution.

mulattos (p. 565)   People of mixed white and black race.

Munich Agreement (p. 859)   The agreement in 1939 between the governments of Nazi Germany, Britain, and France that granted Germany sovereignty over the Sudetenland; part of the effort to appease the Nazi government and avoid a second total war in Europe.

nabobs (p. 578)   Members of the British East India Company who made fortunes in India and returned to Britain, flaunting their wealth.

Napoleonic Code (p. 642)   The name given to the Civil Code of 1804, promulgated by Napoleon, which gave France a uniform and authoritative code of law.

nation (p. 690)   A large community of people who possess a sense of unity based on a belief that they have a common homeland and share a similar culture.

national consciousness (p. 691)   The awareness or belief of people that they belong to a nation.

nationalism (p. 690)   The belief that the people who form a nation should have their own political institutions and that the interests of the nation should be defended and promoted at all costs.

national self-determination (p. 690)   The doctrine advanced by nationalists that any group that considers itself a nation has the right to be ruled only by the members of their own nation and to have all members of the nation included in that state.

nation-state (p. 690)   A political structure sought by nationalists in which the boundaries of the state and the nation are identical, so that all the members of a nation are governed by the same political authorities.

natural law (p. 143)   A law that is believed to be inherent in nature rather than established by human beings.

nawabs (p. 575)   Native provincial governors in eighteenth-century India.

Nazism (p. 835)   Twentieth-century political ideology associated with Adolf Hitler that adopted many fascist ideas but with a central focus on racism and particularly anti-Semitism.

neoclassicism (p. 591)   The revival of the classical art and architecture of ancient Greece and Rome in the eighteenth century.

Neolithic Age (p. 10)   The New Stone Age, characterized by the development of agriculture and the use of stone tools.

Neoplatonism (pp. 221, 538)   A philosophy based on the teachings of Plato and his successors that flourished in Late Antiquity, especially in the teachings of Plotinus. Neoplatonism influenced Christianity in Late Antiquity. During the Renaissance Neoplatonism was linked to the belief that the natural world was charged with occult forces that could be used in the practice of magic.

New Conservatism (p. 932)   Political ideology that emerged at the end of the 1970s combining the free market approach of nineteenth-century liberalism with social conservatism.

New Economic Policy (NEP) (p. 824)   Vladimir Lenin's economic turnaround in 1921 that allowed and even encouraged small private businesses and farms in the Soviet Union.

new feminism (p. 931)   Reemergence of the feminist movement in the 1970s.

new imperialism (p. 766)   The third phase of modern European imperialism, that occurred in the late nineteenth and early twentieth centuries and extended Western control over almost all of Africa and much of Asia.

New Left (p. 926)   Leftwing political and cultural movement that emerged in the late 1950s and early 1960s; sought to develop a form of socialism that rejected the over-centralization, authoritarianism, and inhumanity of Stalinism.

New Testament (p. 197)   The collection of texts that together with the Hebrew Bible, or Old Testament, comprise the Christian Bible. New Testament texts include the Epistles (letters of Paul of Tarsus to early Christians), the Gospels (stories of Jesus Christ's life, death, and resurrection), and other early Christian documents.

95 theses (p. 434)   Propositions about indulgences Martin Luther announced he was willing to defend in debate. The publication of the 95 theses in 1517 started the Protestant Reformation.

nobility (p. 588)   Members of the aristocracy who received official recognition of their hereditary status, including their titles of honor and legal privileges.

nobility of the robe (p. 588)   French noblemen whose families acquired their status by appointment to office.

no-man's-land (p. 793)   The area between the combatants' trenches on the Western Front during World War I.

North Atlantic Treaty Organization (NATO) (p. 897)   Defensive anti-Soviet alliance of the United States, Canada, and the nations of western Europe established in 1949.

northern Renaissance (p. 430)   A movement in northern Europe that built on the foundations of the Italian Renaissance, especially to subject the Bible and the sources of Christianity to critical scrutiny.

Nuremberg trials (p. 874)   Post-World War II trials of members of the Nazi Party and German military; conducted by an international tribunal.

Old Regime (p. 613)   The political order of eighteenth-century France, dominated by an absolute monarch and a privileged nobility and clergy.

oligarchy (p. 82)   A government consisting of only a few people rather than the entire community.

Olympic Games (p. 79)   Greek athletic contests held in Olympia every four years between 776 B.C.E and 217. C.E.

Oppian Law (p. 147)   A law of the Roman Republic passed in 217 B.C.E. to help pay the cost of war. The law restricted the amount of gold or silver a single woman or widow could hold and restricted the articles of clothing they could wear.

Ottonian Renaissance (p. 285)   Under the patronage of the Saxon Emperor Otto I (936–973) and his brother Bruno, learned monks, Greek philosophers from Byzantium, and Italian scholars gathered at the imperial court, stimulating a cultural revival in literature and the arts. The writers and artists enhanced the reputation of Otto.

pagan (p. 211)   The Christian term for polytheist worship (worshiping more than one god). In the course of Late Antiquity, the Christian church suppressed paganism, the traditional religions of the Roman empire.

palace system (p. 52)   Late Bronze Age social system that concentrated religious, economic, political, and military power in the hands of an elite, who lived apart from most people in monumental fortified compounds.

pan-Arabism (p. 849)   Nationalist ideology that called for the political unification of all Arabs, regardless of religious affiliation.

panhellenic (p. 79)   This word means covering all Greek communities. It applies, for example, to the Olympic Games, in which competitors came from all over the Greek world.

papacy (p. 209)   The bishop of the city of Rome is called the Pope, or Father. The papacy refers to the administrative and political institutions controlled by the Pope. The papacy began to gain strength in the sixth century in the absence of Roman imperial government in Italy.

papal infallibility (p. 765)   The doctrine of the Roman Catholic Church proclaimed at the First Vatican Council in 1870 that the pope could not err when making solemn declarations regarding faith or morals.

paradigm (p. 538)   A conceptual model or intellectual framework within which scientists conduct their research and experimentation.

parlements (p. 496)   The highest provincial courts in France, the most important of which was the Parlement of Paris.

patriarchy (p. 28)   A social or cultural system in which men occupy the positions of power; in a family system, a father-centered household.

patricians (p. 140)   In ancient Rome, patricians were aristocratic clans with the highest status and the most political influence.

patrons and clients (p. 156)   In ancient Roman society, a powerful man (the patron) would exercise influence on behalf of a social subordinate (the client) in anticipation of future support or assistance.

Pax Romana (p. 168)   Latin for "Roman Peace," this term refers to the Roman Empire established by Augustus that lasted until the early third century C.E.

Pentateuch (p. 72)   The first five books of the Hebrew Bible.

perestroika (p. 939)   Loosely translated as "restructuring;" Gorbachev's effort to decentralize, reform, and thereby strengthen Soviet economic and political structures.

personal rule (p. 517)   The period from 1629 to 1640 in England when King Charles I ruled without Parliament.

phalanx (p. 81)   The military formation favored by hoplite soldiers. Standing shoulder to shoulder in ranks often eight men deep, hoplites moved in unison and depended on one another for protection.

pharaoh (p. 36)   Title for the Egyptian king, used during the New Kingdom period.

philology (p. 376)   A method reintroduced by the humanists during the Italian Renaissance devoted to the comparative study of language, especially to understanding the meaning of a word in a particular historical context.

philosophes (p. 596)   The writers and thinkers of the Enlightenment, especially in France.

pilgrimages (p. 219)   Religious journeys made to holy sites in order to encounter relics.

Pillars of Islam (p. 248)   The five basic principles of Islam as taught by Muhammad.

plantation colony (p. 399)   First appearing in the Cape Verde Islands and later in the tropical parts of the Americas, these colonies were established by Europeans who used African slave labor to cultivate cash crops such as sugar, indigo, cotton, coffee, and tobacco.

plebeians (p. 140)   The general body of Roman citizens.

plebiscite (p. 634)   A popular vote for or against a form of government or rule by a particular person.

pogroms (p. 740)   An organized and often officially encouraged riot or attack to persecute a particular ethnic or religious group, especially associated with eastern European attacks against Jews.

polis (p. 79)   A self-governing Greek city-state

polytheistic (p. 23)   Refers to polytheism, the belief in many gods.

pop art (p. 920)   Effort by artists in the 1950s and 1960s both to utilize and to critique the material plenty of post-World War II popular culture.

Popular Front (p. 846)   A political coalition of liberals, socialists, and communists to defeat fascist and racist-nationalist political rivals.

popular sovereignty (p. 636)   The claim that political power came from the people and that the people constituted the highest political power in the state.

positivism (p. 692)   The philosophy developed by August Comte in the nineteenth century according to which human society passed through a series of stages, leading to the final positive stage in which the accumulation of scientific data would enable thinkers to discover the laws of human behavior and bring about the improvement of society.

positivist (p. 756)   The emphasis on the use of the scientific method to reach truth; a stress on observable fact.

postindustrialism, postindustrial society (p. 962)   A service rather than manufacturing-based economy characterized by an emphasis on marketing and information and by a proliferation of communications technologies.

postmodernism (p. 957)   Umbrella term covering a variety of artistic styles and intellectual theories and practices; in general, a rejection of a single, universal, Western style of modernity.

Potsdam Conference (p. 895)   The meeting in July 1945 of the Allied leaders of Britain, the Soviet Union, and the United States in the German city of Potsdam.

Pragmatic Sanction of Bourges (p. 390)   An agreement in 1438 that guaranteed the virtual autonomy of the French Church from papal control, enabling the French king to interfere in religious affairs and exploit Church revenues for government purposes.

Prague Spring (p. 915)   Short-lived popular effort in 1968 to reform Czechoslovakia's political structures; associated with the phrase "socialism with a human face."

predestination (p. 442)   The doctrine promoted by John Calvin that since God, the all-knowing and all-powerful being, knew everything in advance and caused everything to happen, then the salvation of any individual was predetermined.

prerogative (p. 517)   The set of powers exercised by the English monarch alone, rather than in conjunction with Parliament.

Price Revolution (p. 462)   After a long period of falling or stable prices that stretched back to the fourteenth century, Europe experienced sustained price increases between about 1540 and 1640, causing widespread social and economic turmoil.

priesthood of all believers (p. 434)   Martin Luther's doctrine that all those of pure faith were themselves priests, a doctrine that undermined the authority of the Catholic clergy over the laity.

primogeniture (p. 514)   The legal arrangement by which the eldest son inherits the entire estate upon the death of the father.

proletariat (p. 690)   The word used by Karl Marx and Friedrich Engels to identify the class of workers who received their income from wages.

prophetic movement (p. 70)   An important phase in the development of what became Judaism. In the ninth century B.C.E., Hebrew religious reformers, or prophets, demanded the transformation of religious and economic practices to reflect ideals of social justice and religious purity.

protectionism (p. 562)   The policy of shielding domestic industries from foreign competition through a policy of levying tariffs on imported goods.

Protestant Reformation (p. 426)   Dominated European affairs between 1517 and 1560 when the movement for religious reform begun by Martin Luther led Germany, Britain, and most of northern Europe to break away from the Catholic Church.

Radical Reformation (p. 440)   Refers to Protestant movements that failed to gain official government recognition and were at best tolerated, at worst persecuted, during the sixteenth century.

rationalism (p. 536)   The theory that the mind contains rational categories independent of sensory observation; more generally that reason is the primary source of truth.

Realpolitik (p. 712)   The adoption of political tactics based solely on their realistic chances of success.

redistributive economies (p. 18)   Type of economic system characteristic of ancient Mesopotamian societies. The central political authority controls all agricultural resources and their redistribution.

regency (p. 496)   Rule by relative of a monarch during a period when the monarch was too young to rule or otherwise incapacitated.

Reign of Terror (p. 628)   A purging of alleged enemies of the French state between 1793 and 1794, superintended by the Committee of Public Safety, that resulted in the execution of 17,000 people.

Reinsurance Treaty (p. 787)   Treaty of 1887 in which the governments of Germany and Russia agreed to remain neutral if either was attacked.

relics (p. 219)   In Christian belief, relics are sacred objects that have miraculous powers. They are associated with saints, biblical figures, or some object associated with them. They served as contacts between Earth and Heaven and were verified by miracles.

Religious Peace of Augsburg (p. 439)   In 1555 this peace between Lutherans and Catholics within the Holy Roman Empire established the principle of *cuius regio, eius religio*, which means "he who rules determines the religion of the land." Protestant princes in the Empire were permitted to retain all church lands seized before 1552 and to enforce Protestant worship, but Catholic princes were also allowed to enforce Catholic worship in their territories.

Renaissance (p. 364)   A term meaning "rebirth" used by historians to describe a movement that sought to imitate and understand the culture of antiquity. The Renaissance generally refers to a movement that began in Italy and then spread throughout Europe from about 1350 to 1550.

reparations (p. 814)   Payments imposed upon Germany after World War I by the Versailles Treaty to cover the costs of the war.

republic (p. 139)   A state in which political power resides in the people or their representatives rather than in a monarch.

republicanism (p. 366)   A political theory first developed by the ancient Greeks, especially the philosopher Plato, but elaborated by the ancient Romans and rediscovered during the Italian Renaissance. The fundamental principle of republicanism as developed during the Italian Renaissance was that government officials should be elected by the people or a portion of the people.

Republic of Virtue (p. 628)   The ideal form of government proposed by Maximilien Robespierre and other Jacobins during the French Revolution. Its proponents wished to make the republic established in 1792 more egalitarian and secular and inspire civic pride and patriotism in the people.

requerimiento (p. 408)   A document read by conquistadores to the natives of the Americas before making war on them. The document briefly explained the principles of Christianity and commanded the natives to accept them immediately along with the authority of the pope and the sovereignty of the king of Spain. If the natives refused, they were warned they would be forced to accept Christian conversion and subjected to Spain anyway.

Resistance, the (p. 883)   Label given to the many different underground political and partisan movements directed against Nazi rule in German-occupied Europe during World War II.

revisionism, socialist revisionism (p. 736)   The belief that an equal society can be built through participation in parliamentary politics rather than through violent revolution.

rhetoric (p. 376)   The art of persuasive or emotive speaking and writing, which was especially valued by the Renaissance humanists.

Roman Forum (p. 136)   The central area in the city of Rome between the Palatine hill and the Capitoline hill.

Roman Republic (p. 137)   The name given to the Roman state from about 500 B.C.E., when the last king of Rome was expelled, to 31 B.C.E., when Augustus established the Roman Empire.

Romanesque (p. 327)   A style in architecture that spread throughout western Europe during the eleventh and the first half of the twelfth centuries and characterized by arched stone roofs supported by rounded arches, massive stone pillars, and thick walls.

Romanization (p. 177)   The process by which conquered peoples absorbed aspects of Roman culture, especially the Latin language, city life, and religion.

romanticism (p. 693)   An artistic and literary movement of the late eighteenth and nineteenth centuries that involved a protest against classicism, appealed to the passions rather than the intellect, and emphasized the beauty and power of nature.

Rome-Berlin Axis (p. 859)   Alliance between Benito Mussolini's Italy and Adolf Hitler's Germany formed in 1936.

salons (p. 611)   Private sitting rooms or parlors of aristocratic French women where discussions of philosophy, science, littérature, and politics took place in the eighteenth century.

sans-culottes (p. 623)   The militant citizens of Paris who refused to wear the pants worn by noblemen and provided support for the Jacobins during the French Revolution; literally, those without breeches.

satraps (p. 115)   Persian provincial governors who collected taxes and oversaw the bureaucracy.

Schlieffen Plan (p. 788)   German military plan devised in 1905 that called for a sweeping attack on France through Belgium and the Netherlands.

scholasticism (p. 324)   A term referring to a broad philosophical and theological movement that dominated medieval thought and university training. Scholasticism used logic learned from Aristotle to interpret the meaning of the Bible and the writings of the Church Fathers, who created Christian theology in its first centuries.

Scramble for Africa (p. 773)   The frenzied imposition of European control over most of Africa that occurred between 1870 and 1914.

scriptorium (p. 271)   The room in a monastery where monks copied books and manuscripts.

Sea Peoples (p. 54)   Name given by the Egyptians to the diverse groups of migrants whose attacks helped bring the International Bronze Age to an end.

Second Industrial Revolution (p. 723) A new phase in the industrialization of the processes of production and consumption, underway in Europe in the 1870s.

Second Triumvirate (p. 165) In 43 B.C.E. Octavian (later called Augustus), Mark Antony, and Lepidus made an informal alliance to share power in Rome while they jockeyed for control. Octavian emerged as the sole ruler of Rome in 31 B.C.E.

secularization (p. 545) The reduction of the importance of religion in society and culture.

seigneur (p. 593) The lord of a French estate who received payments from the peasants who lived on his land.

separate spheres (p. 609) The theory that men and women should conduct their lives in different social and political environments, confining women to the domestic sphere and excluding them from the public sphere of political involvement.

sepoys (p. 576) Indian troops serving in the armed forces of the British East India Company.

Septuagint (p. 125) The Greek translation of the Hebrew Bible (Old Testament).

serfs (p. 301) During the Middle Ages serfs were agricultural laborers who worked and lived on a plot of land granted them by a lord to whom they owed a certain portion of their crops. They could not leave the land, but they had certain legal rights that were denied to slaves.

settler colony (p. 399) A colony authorized when a private person obtained a license from a king to seize an island or parcel of land and occupied it with settlers from Europe who exported their own culture to the new lands. Settler colonies first appeared among the islands of the eastern Atlantic and portions of the Americas.

simony (p. 307) The practice of buying and selling church offices.

skepticism (p. 543) A tendency to doubt what one has been taught or is expected to believe.

Social Darwinism (p. 755) The later-nineteenth-century application of the theory of evolution to entire human societies.

social democracy (pp. 843, 887) Political system in which a democratically elected parliamentary government endeavors to ensure a decent standard of living for its citizens through both economic regulation and the maintenance of a welfare state.

socialism (p. 687) An ideology calling for the ownership of the means of production by the community with the purpose of reducing inequalities of income, wealth, opportunity and economic power.

socialist revisionism (p. 736) The belief that an equal society can be built through participation in parliamentary politics rather than through violent revolution.

Social War (p. 159) The revolt of Rome's allies against the Republic in 90 B.C.E. demanding full Roman citizenship

Solidarity (p. 935) Trade union and political party in Poland that led an unsuccessful effort to reform the Polish communist state in 1981; survived to lead Poland's first non-communist government since World War II in 1989.

Sophists (p. 102) Professional educators who traveled throughout the ancient Greek world, teaching many subjects. Their goal was to teach people the best ways to lead better lives.

soviets (p. 808) Workers' and soldiers' councils formed in Russia during the Revolution of 1917.

Spanish Armada (p. 478) A fleet of 132 ships, which sailed from Portugal to rendezvous with the Spanish army stationed in the Netherlands and launch an invasion of England in 1588. The English defeated the Armada as it passed through the English Channel. The defeat marked a shift in the power balance from Spain to England.

Spanish Reconquest (p. 260) Refers to the numerous military campaigns by the Christian kingdoms of northern Spain to capture the Muslim-controlled cities and kingdoms of southern Spain. This long, intermittent struggle began with the capture of Toledo in 1085 and lasted until Granada fell to Christian armies in 1492.

spiritualists (p. 448) A tendency within Protestantism, especially Lutheranism, to emphasize the power of personal spiritual illumination, called the "inner Word," a living form of the Scriptures written directly on the believer's soul by the hand of God.

stagflation (p. 930) Term coined in the 1970s to describe an economy troubled by both high inflation and high unemployment rates.

standing armies (p. 495) Trained and equipped military forces that were not disbanded after the conclusion of war. Standing armies often helped maintain order and enforce governmental policy at home.

states (p. 554) Consolidated territorial areas that have their own political institutions and recognize no higher political authority.

Stoics (p. 132) Followers of the philosophy developed by Zeno of Citium (ca. 335–ca. 263 B.C.E.) that urged acceptance of fate while participating fully in everyday life.

structuralism (p. 920) Influential post-World War II social theory that explored the common structures of language and thought.

Struggle of the Orders (p. 140) The political strife between patrician and plebeian Romans beginning in the fifth century B.C.E. The plebeians gradually won political rights and influence as a result of the struggle.

suffragettes (p. 746) Feminist movement that emerged in Britain in the early twentieth century. Unlike the suffragists, who sought to achieve the national vote for women through rational persuasion, the suffragettes adopted the tactics of violent protest.

suffragists (p. 745) Feminists who sought to achieve the national vote for women through rational persuasion and parliamentary politics.

supply (p. 664) The amounts of capital, labor, and food that are needed to produce goods for the market as well as the quantities of those goods themselves.

syncretism (p. 69) The practice of equating two gods and fusing their cults was common throughout the Roman Empire and helped to unify the diverse peoples and religions under Roman rule.

syndicalism (p. 737) Ideology of the late nineteenth and early twentieth century that sought to achieve a working-class revolution through economic action, particularly through mass labor strikes.

Talmud's (p. 217) Commentaries on Jewish law. Rabbis completed the Babylonian Talmud and the Jerusalem Talmud by the end of the fifth century C.E.

tetrarchy (p. 205) The government by four rulers established by the Roman emperor Diocletian in 293 C.E. that lasted until 312. During the tetrarchy many administrative and military reforms altered the fabric of Roman society.

Third Estate (p. 621) The component of the Estates General in Old Regime France that technically represented all the commoners in the kingdom.

Third Reich (p. 864) Term for Adolf Hitler's Germany; articulates the Nazi aim of extending German rule across Europe.

Third World (p. 909) Term coined in 1955 to describe nations that did not align with either the Soviet Union or the United States; commonly used to describe the industrially underdeveloped nations.

Thomism (p. 325) A branch of medieval philosophy associated with the work of the Dominican thinker,

Thomas Aquinas (1225–1274), who wrote encyclopedic summaries of human knowledge that confirmed Christian faith.

Time of Troubles (p. 489) The period from 1604 to 1613 when Russia fell into chaos, which ended when the national assembly elected Tsar Michael Romanov, whose descendants ruled Russia until they were deposed in 1917.

Torah (p. 72) Most commonly, the first five books of the Hebrew Bible; also used to refer to the whole body of Jewish sacred writings and tradition.

total war (p. 784) A war that demands extensive state regulation of economic production, distribution, and consumption; and that blurs (or erases entirely) the distinction between civilian and soldier.

trading posts (p. 401) Built by European traders along the coasts of Africa and Asia as a base for trade with the interior. Trading posts or factories were islands of European law and sovereignty, but European authority seldom extended very far beyond the fortified post.

transubstantiation (p. 318) A doctrine promulgated at the Fourth Lateran Council in 1215 that explained by distinguishing between the outward appearances and the inner substance how the Eucharistic bread and wine changed into the body and blood of Christ.

Treaty of Brest-Litovsk (p. 797) Treaty between Germany and Bolshevik-controlled Russia, signed in March, 1918, that ceded to Germany all of Russia's western territories.

trial by jury (p. 321) When disputes about the possession of land arose after the late twelfth century in England, sheriffs assembled a group of twelve local men who testified under oath about the claims of the plaintiffs, and the circuit court judge made his decision on the basis of their testimony. The system was later extended to criminal cases.

Triple Alliance (p. 787) Defensive alliance of Germany, Austria-Hungary, and Italy, signed in 1882.

Triple Entente (p. 787) Informal defensive agreement linking France, Great Britain, and Russia before World War I.

triremes (p. 90) Greek warships with three banks of oars. Triremes manned by the poorest people of Athenian society became the backbone of the Athenian empire.

troubadours (p. 326) Poets from the late twelfth and thirteenth centuries who wrote love poems, meant to be sung to music, which reflected a new sensibility, called courtly love, about the ennobling possibilities of the love between a man and a woman.

Truman Doctrine (p. 896)   Named after U.S. president Harry Truman, the doctrine that in 1947 inaugurated the Cold War policy of resisting the expansion of communist control.

Twelfth-Century Renaissance (p. 325)   An intellectual revival of interest in ancient Greek philosophy and science and in Roman law in western Europe during the twelfth and early thirteenth centuries. The term also refers to a flowering of vernacular literature and the Romanesque and Gothic styles in architecture.

tyrants (p. 81)   Rulers in Greek city-states, usually members of the aristocracy, who seized power illegitimately rather than acquiring it by heredity or election. Tyrants often gained political support from the hoplites and the poor.

Unitarians (p. 449)   A religious reform movement that began in the sixteenth century and rejected the Christian doctrine of the Trinity. Unitarians (also called Arians, Socinians, and Anti-Trinitarians) taught a rationalist interpretation of the Scriptures and argued that Jesus was a divinely inspired man, not God who became a man as did other Christians.

universal law of gravitation (p. 533)   A law of nature established by Isaac Newton in 1687 holding that any two bodies attract each other with a force that is directly proportional to the product of their masses and indirectly proportional to the square of the distance between them. The law was presented in mathematical terms.

universal male suffrage (p. 627)   The granting of the right to vote to all adult males.

vassals (p. 281)   During the Middle Ages men voluntarily submitted themselves to a lord by taking an oath of loyalty. Vassals owed the lord certain services—usually military assistance—and sometimes received in exchange a grant of land known as a fief.

Vatican II (p. 922)   Popular term for the Second Vatican Council that convened in 1963 and introduced a series of changes within the Roman Catholic Church.

vernacular languages (p. 480)   The native spoken languages of Europe, which became literary languages and began to replace Latin as the dominant

form of learned expression during the sixteenth century.

Versailles Treaty (p. 814)   Treaty between Germany and the victorious Allies after World War I.

Vichy, Vichy regime, Vichy government (p. 864) Authoritarian state established in France after defeat by the German army in 1940.

Vulgate (p. 214)   The Latin translation of the Bible produced about 410 by the monk Jerome. It was the standard Bible in western Christian churches until the sixteenth century.

Wahhabism (p. 850)   A religious reform and revival movement founded by Muhammad Abd al-Wahhab (1703–1787) in the eighteenth century to purify Islam by returning to a strict interpretation of the *Sharia*, or Islamic law. Revived during the 1920s in Saudi Arabia.

Warsaw Pact (p. 897)   Military alliance of the Soviet Union and its eastern European satellite states in the Cold War era.

Weimar Republic (p. 825)   The democratic German state constructed after defeat in World War I and destroyed by the Nazis in 1933.

wergild (p. 267)   In Germanic societies the term referred to what an individual was worth in case he or she suffered an injury. It was the amount of compensation in gold that the wrongdoer's family had to pay to the victim's family.

witch-hunt (p. 469)   Refers to the dramatic increase in the judicial prosecution of alleged witches in either church or secular courts from the middle of the sixteenth to the middle of the seventeenth centuries.

Yalta Conference (p. 894)   Meeting in 1945 of the leaders of the Allied states of Britain, the Soviet Union, and the United States to devise plans for postwar Europe.

ziggurat (p. 23)   Monumental tiered or terraced temple characteristic of ancient Mesopotamia.

Zionism (p. 741)   Nationalist movement that emerged in the late nineteenth century and sought to establish a Jewish political state in Palestine (the Biblical Zion).

Zoroastrianism (p. 88)   The monotheistic religion of Persia founded by Zoroaster that became the official religion of the Persian Empire.

CHAPTER 15. THE AGE OF CONFESSIONAL DIVISION

Anderson, M. S. *The Origins of the Modern European State System, 1494–1618.* 1998. The best short study for students new to the subject of the evolution of the confessional states in Europe. This book is very good at establishing common patterns among the various states.

Burke, Peter. *Popular Culture in Early Modern Europe.* 1994. This wide-ranging book includes considerable material from eastern Europe and Scandinavia, as well as the more extensively studied western European countries. Extraordinarily influential, it practically invented the subject of popular culture by showing how much could be learned from studying festivals and games.

Davies, Norman. *God's Playground: A History of Poland.* Rev. ed., 2 vols. 1982. By far the most comprehensive study of Polish history, this is particularly strong for the sixteenth and seventeenth centuries. Davies offers a Polish-centered view of European history that is marvelously stimulating even if he sometimes overstates his case for the importance of Poland.

Dukes, Paul. *A History of Russia: Medieval, Modern, Contemporary, ca. 882–1996,* 3rd ed. 1998. A comprehensive survey that synthesizes the most recent research.

Dunn, Richard S. *The Age of Religious Wars, 1559–1715,* 2nd ed. 1980. An excellent survey for students new to the subject.

Evans, R. J. W. *Rudolf II and His World: A Study in Intellectual History, 1576–1612.* 1973. A sympathetic examination of the intellectual world Rudolf created. Evans recognizes Rudolf's mental problems but lessens their significance for understanding the period.

Holt, Mack P. *The French Wars of Religion, 1562–1629.* 1996. A lucid short synthesis of the events and complex issues raised by these wars.

Hsia, R. Po-chia. *Social Discipline in the Reformation: Central Europe, 1550–1750.* 1989. An excellent, lucid, and short overview of the attempts to discipline the people in Germany.

Huppert, George. *After the Black Death: A Social History of Early Modern Europe.* 1986. Engaging, entertaining, and elegantly written, this is the best single study of European social life during the Early Modern period.

Levack, Brian P. *The Witch-Hunt in Early Modern Europe,* 2nd ed. 1995. The best and most up-to-date short examination of the complex problem of the witch-hunt. This is the place to begin for students new to the subject.

Ozment, Steven E. *Ancestors: The Loving Family in Old Europe.* 2001. This comprehensive study of family life demonstrates that families were actually far more loving than the theory of patriarchy would suggest.

Parker, Geoffrey. *The Dutch Revolt,* rev. ed. 1990. The classic study of the revolt by one of the most masterful historians of the period. This study is especially adept at pointing to the larger European context of the revolt.

Parker, Geoffrey. *The Grand Strategy of Philip II.* 1998. Rehabilitates Philip as a significant strategic thinker.

Wiesner, Merry E. *Women and Gender in Early Modern Europe.* 1993. The best short study of the subject. This is the best book for students new to the subject.

CHAPTER 16. ABSOLUTISM AND STATE BUILDING, 1618–1715.

Aylmer, G. E. *Rebellion or Revolution.* 1986. A study of the nature of the political disturbances of the 1640s and 1650s.

Beik, William. *Louis XIV and Absolutism: A Brief Study with Documents.* 2000. An excellent collection of documents.

Collins, James B. *The State in Early Modern France.* 1995. The best general study of the French state.

Elliott, J. H. *Richelieu and Olivares.* 1984. A comparison of the two contemporary absolutist ministers and state builders in France and Spain.

Goffman, Daniel. *The Ottoman Empire and Early Modern Europe.* 2002. A broad survey that challenges many of the Western stereotypes of Ottoman politics and culture, including the belief that Ottoman government was tyrannical.

Harris, Tim. *Politics Under the Later Stuarts*. 1993. The best study of Restoration politics, including the Glorious Revolution.

Hughes, Lindsey. *Russia in the Age of Peter the Great*. 1998. A comprehensive study of politics, diplomacy, society, and culture during the reign of the "Tsar Reformer."

Israel, Jonathan. *The Dutch Republic: Its Rise, Greatness and Fall, 1477–1806*. 1996. A massive and authoritative study of the Dutch Republic during the period of its greatest global influence.

Lincoln, W. Bruce. *Sunlight at Midnight: St. Petersburg and the Rise of Modern Russia*. 2000. The best study of the building of Peter the Great's new capital city.

Parker, David. *The Making of French Absolutism*. 1983. A particularly good treatment of the early seventeenth century.

Parker, Geoffrey. *The Military Revolution*. 1988. Deals with the impact of the military revolution on the world as well as European history.

Rabb, Theodore K. *The Struggle for Stability in Early Modern Europe*. 1975. Employs visual as well as political sources to illustrate the way in which Europeans responded to the general crisis of the seventeenth century.

Schama, Simon. *The Embarrassment of Riches: An Interpretation of Dutch Culture in the Golden Age*. 1987. Contains a wealth of commentary on Dutch art and culture during its most influential period.

Wilson, Peter H. *Absolutism in Central Europe*. 2000. Analyzes both the theory and the practice of absolutism in Prussia and Austria.

CHAPTER 17. THE SCIENTIFIC REVOLUTION

Biagioli, Mario. *Galileo, Courtier: The Practice of Science in the Culture of Absolutism*. 1993. Argues that Galileo's desire for patronage determined the type of research he engaged in and the scientific questions he asked.

Campbell, Mary Blaine. *Wonder and Science, Imagining Worlds in Early Modern Europe*. 1999. Explores the conceptual and celestial worlds opened by science as well as the geographical worlds found in voyages of discovery.

Cohen, H. Floris. *The Scientific Revolution: A Historiographical Inquiry*. 1995. A thorough account of all the different interpretations of the causes and significance of the Scientific Revolution.

Dear, Peter. *Discipline and Experience: The Mathematical Way in the Scientific Revolution*. 1995. Explains the importance of mathematics in the development of seventeenth-century science.

Debus, Allen G. *Man and Nature in the Renaissance*. 1978. Deals with the early history of the Scientific Revolution and develops many of its connections with the Renaissance.

Drake, Stillman, ed. *Discoveries and Opinions of Galileo*. 1957. Includes four of Galileo's most important writings, together with a detailed commentary.

Feingold, Mordechai. *The Newtonian Moment: Isaac Newton and the Making of Modern Culture*. 2004. A richly illustrated volume that contains valuable material on the reception of Newtonian ideas in the eighteenth century as well as a chapter on Newtonian women.

Grayling, A. C. Descartes: *The Life and Times of a Genius*. 2006. A biography that places Descartes in his proper historical context and suggests that he may have served as a spy.

Huff, Toby. *The Rise of Early Modern Science: Islam, China and the West*, 2003. Adresses the question why modern science arose only in the West despite the fact that non-Western science was more advanced in the Middle Ages.

Kuhn, Thomas S. *The Copernican Revolution*. 1957. The most comprehensive and authoritative study of the shift from an Earth-centered to a sun-centered model of the universe.

Needham, Joseph. *The Grand Titration: Science and Society in East and West*. 1979. Discusses the weaknesses and strengths of Chinese science.

Popkin, Richard. *The History of Scepticism from Erasmus to Spinoza*. 1979. Discusses skepticism as a cause as well as an effect of the Scientific Revolution.

Schiebinger, Londa. *The Mind Has No Sex? Women in the Origins of Modern Science*. 1989. Explores the role of women in all aspects of scientific endeavor.

Shapin, Steven. *The Scientific Revolution*. 1996. A study of the origins of the modern scientific worldview that emphasizes the social influences on the production of knowledge and the social purposes for which scientific knowledge was intended.

Shapin, Steven, and Simon Schaffer. *Leviathan and the Air Pump*. 1989. Discusses the difference between Robert Boyle and Thomas Hobbes regarding the value of experimentation.

Shea, William R., and Mariano Artigas. *Galileo in Rome: The Rise and Fall of a Troublesome Genius*. 2004. Attributes some of Galileo's troubles to his tactlessness and headstrong behavior.

Stewart, Matthew. *The Courtier and the Heretic: Leibniz, Spinoza, and the Fate of God in the Modern World*. 2006. Illuminates the conflicting philosophical ideas of Wilhelm Leibniz and Baruch Spinoza, arguing that Spinoza anticipated later philosophical and scientific developments by two and sometimes three centuries.

Thomas, Keith. *Man and the Natural World: A History of the Modern Sensibility*. 1983. A study of the shifting attitudes of human beings toward nature during the period from 1500 to 1800.

Webster, Charles. *The Great Instauration: Science, Medicine and Reform, 1626–1660*. 1975. Explores the relationship between Puritanism and the Scientific Revolution in England.

Westfall, Richard S. *Never at Rest: A Biography of Isaac Newton*. 1980. A superb biography of the most influential scientist in the history of the West.

CHAPTER 18. THE WEST AND THE WORLD: EMPIRE, TRADE, AND WAR, 1650–1815

Bailyn, Bernard. *Ideological Origins of the American Revolution*. 1967. A probing analysis of the different intellectual traditions upon which the American colonists based their arguments for independence.

Blackburn, Robin. *The Making of New World Slavery: From the Baroque to the Modern, 1492–1800*. 1997. Places European slavery in a broad world perspective.

Boxer, C. R. *The Dutch Seaborne Empire, 1600–1800*. 1965. A thorough account covering the entire period of Dutch expansion.

Brown, Christopher L. *Moral capital: Foundations of British Abolitionism*. 2006. Establishes the popular campaign as well as the work of parliamentary reformers like William Wilberforce.

Elliott, J. H. *Empires of the Atlantic World: Britain and Spain in America 1492–1830*. 2006. A superb comparative study of the two largest overseas empires in the early modern period.

Eltis, David. *The Rise of African Slavery in the Americas*. 2000. An analysis of the different dimensions of the slave trade based on a database of slave ships and passengers.

Goody, Jack. *The East in the West*. 1996. Challenges the idea that Western cultures are more rational than those of Asia.

Greene, Jack P. *Peripheries and Center: Constitutional Development in the Extended Polities of the British Empire and the United States, 1607–1788*. 1986. A study of the composition of the British Empire and its disintegration in North America.

Kamen, Henry. *Empire: How Spain Became a World Power*. 2003. Explains how Spain established the most extensive empire the world had ever known.

Langley, Lester D. *The Americas in the Age of Revolution, 1750–1850*. 1996. A broad comparative study of revolutions in the United States, Haiti, and Latin America.

Liss, Peggy K. *The Atlantic Empires: The Network of Trade and Revolutions, 1713–1826*. 1983. Places the American Revolution in a broader comparative setting and includes material on early Latin American independence movements.

Mungello, D. E. *The Great Encounter of China and the West, 1500–1800*. 1999. Studies China's acceptance and rejection of Western culture as well as the parallel Western reception of China.

Pagden, Anthony. *Lords of All the World: Ideologies of Empire in Spain, Britain and France, ca. 1500–ca. 1800*. 1996. Discusses the theoretical foundations of the Atlantic Empires.

Said, Edward. *Orientalism*. 1979. A study of the way in which Western views of the East have assumed its inferiority.

CHAPTER 19. EIGHTEENTH-CENTURY SOCIETY AND CULTURE

Alexander, John T. *Catherine the Great: Life and Legend*. 1989. A lively biography of the remarkable "enlightened despot."

Beckett, J. V. *The Aristocracy in England, 1660–1914*. 1986. A comprehensive study of this landholding and governing elite. Makes the important distinction between the aristocracy and the nobility.

Darnton, Robert. *The Forbidden Best-Sellers of Pre-Revolutionary France*. 1995. A study of the salacious, blasphemous, and subversive books that sold more copies than those of the philosophes in eighteenth-century France.

Dewald, Jonathan. *The European Nobility, 1500–1800.* 1996. A comprehensive study of this social class that emphasizes its adaptability.

Doyle, William. *The Old European Order, 1660–1800,* 2nd ed. 1999. The best general study of the period.

Houston, R. A. *Literacy in Early Modern Europe: Culture and Education.* 1991. The best survey of the subject for the entire period.

Israel, Jonathan. *Radical Enlightenment: Philosophy and the Making of Modernity 1650–1750.* 2001. Emphasizes the influence of the radical philosophical ideas of the followers of Benedict Spinoza on the Enlightenment.

Knott, Sarah, and Barbara Taylor, eds. *Women, Gender and the Enlightenment.* 2005. A valuable collection of 39 essays that reflect the influence of feminist scholarship on the study of the Enlightenment.

Lugee, Carolyn. *Le Paradis des Femmes: Women, Salons and Social Stratification in 17th-Century France.* 1976. A social study of the women of the salons.

Outram, Dorinda. *The Enlightenment.* 1995. A balanced assessment of the major historiographical debates regarding the Enlightenment.

Robertson, John. *The Case for Enlightenment: Scotland and Naples, 1680–1760.* 2005. Argues that the main unifying theme of the Enlightenment throughout Europe was not its philosophical ideas but the determination to achieve "human betterment" and material improvement.

Root, Hilton. *Peasants and King in Burgundy: Agrarian Foundations of French Absolutism.* 1979. A study of peasant communal institutions and their relationship with the crown as well as the nobility.

Smith, Adam. Introduction to *The Wealth of Nations.* 1776.

Williams, David, ed. *The Enlightenment.* 1999. An excellent collection of political writings with a long introduction.

CHAPTER 20. THE AGE OF THE FRENCH REVOLUTION, 1789–1815

Andress, David. *The French Revolution and the People.* 2004. Focuses on the role played by the common people of France—the peasants, craftsmen and those living on the margins of society—in the revolution.

Blanning, T. C. W. *The French Revolutionary Wars, 1787–1802.* 1996. An authoritative political and military narrative that assesses the impact of the wars on French politics.

Chartier, Roger. *The Cultural Origins of the French Revolution.* 1991. Explores the connections between the culture of the Enlightenment and the cultural transformations of the revolutionary period.

Cobban, Alfred. *The Social Interpretation of the French Revolution.* 1964. Challenges the Marxist interpretation of the causes and effects of the revolution.

Doyle, William. *The Oxford History of the French Revolution.* 1989. An excellent synthesis.

Ellis, Geoffrey. *Napoleon.* 1997. A study of the nature and mechanics of Napoleon's power and an analysis of his imperial policy.

Furet, François. *The French Revolution, 1770–1814.* 1992. A provocative narrative that sees Napoleon as the architect of a second, authoritarian revolution that reversed the gains of the first.

Hardman, John. *Louis XVI: The Silent King.* 2000. A reassessment of the king that mixes sympathy with criticism.

Higonnet, Patrice. *Goodness Beyond Virtue: Jacobins During the French Revolution.* 1998. Explores the contradictions of Jacobin ideology and its descent into the Terror.

Hunt, Lynn. *Politics, Culture and Class in the French Revolution.* 1984. Analyzes the formation of a revolutionary political culture.

Kennedy, Emmet. *The Culture of the French Revolution.* 1989. A comprehensive study of all cultural developments before and during the revolution.

Landes, Joan B. *Women and the Public Sphere in the Age of the French Revolution.* 1988. Explores how the new political culture of the revolution changed the position of women in society.

Lefebvre, Georges. *The Great Fear of 1789: Rural Panic in Revolutionary France.* 1973. Shows the importance of the rural unrest of July 1789 that provided the backdrop of the legislation of August 1789.

Schama, Simon. *Citizens: A Chronicle of the French Revolution.* 1989. Depicts the tragic unraveling of a vision of liberty and happiness into a scenario of hunger, anger, violence, and death.

CHAPTER 21. THE INDUSTRIAL REVOLUTION

Ashton, T. A. *The Industrial Revolution,* reprint edition with preface by P. Hudson. 1992. The classic statement of the optimist position, identifying the benefits of the revolution.

Berg, Maxine. *The Age of Manufactures, 1700–1820: Industry, Innovation and Work in Britain.* 1994. A study of the process and character of specific industries, especially those employing women.

Brinley, Thomas. *The Industrial Revolution and the Atlantic Economy: Selected Essays.* 1993. Essays challenging the view that Britain's Industrial Revolution was a gradual process.

Deane, Phyllis. *The First Industrial Revolution.* 1967. The best study of technological innovation in Britain.

Gutmann, Myron. *Toward the Modern Economy: Early Industry in Europe, 1500–1800.* 1988. A study of cottage industry, especially in France.

Hobsbawm, E. J. *Industry and Empire.* 1968. A general economic history of Britain from 1750 to 1970 that analyzes the position of Britain in the world economy.

Jacob, Margaret. *Scientific Culture and the Making of the Industrial West.* 1997. An exploration of the spread of scientific knowledge and its connection with industrialization.

Morris, R. J. *Class and Class Consciousness in the Industrial Revolution, 1780–1850.* 1979. A balanced treatment of the link between industrialization and class formation.

Pollard, Sidney. *Peaceful Conquest: The Industrialization of Europe, 1760–1970.* 1981. Links coal supplies to economic development.

Rule, John. *The Vital Century: England's Developing Economy, 1714–1815.* 1992. A general economic history establishing the importance of early eighteenth-century developments.

Stearns, Peter. *The Industrial Revolution in World History,* 2nd ed. 1998. The best study of industrialization in a global context.

Teich, Mikulas, and Roy Porter, eds. *The Industrial Revolution in National Context: Europe and the USA.* 1981. Essays illustrating similarities as well as national differences in the process of industrialization.

Wrigley, E. A. *Continuity, Chance and Change: The Character of the Industrial Revolution in Britain.* 1988. Includes the best discussion of the transition from an advanced organic economy to one based on minerals.

CHAPTER 22: IDEOLOGICAL CONFLICT AND NATIONAL UNIFICATION, 1815–1871

Anderson, Benedict. *Imagined Communities: Reflections on the Origin and Spread of Nationalism.* 1991. A discussion of the ways in which people conceptualize the nation.

Clark, Martin. *The Italian Risorgimento.* 1999. A comprehensive study of the social, economic, and religious context of Italian unification as well as its political and diplomatic dimensions.

Gellner, Ernest. *Nations and Nationalism.* 1983. An interpretive study that emphasizes the social roots of nationalism.

Holmes, Richard. *The Age of Wonder: How the Romantic Generation Discovered the Beauty and Terror of Nature.* 2009. Argues that science inspired the romantic imagination.

Hamerow, Theodore S. *Restoration, Revolution, Reaction: Economics and Politics in Germany, 1815–1871.* 1966. An investigation of the social basis of ideological encounters in Germany.

Honour, Hugh. *Romanticism.* 1979. A comprehensive study of romantic painting.

Hunczak, Tara, ed. *Russian Imperialism from Ivan the Great to the Revolution.* 1974. A collection of essays that illuminate Russian nationalism as well as imperialism over a long period of time.

Lichtheim, George. *A Short History of Socialism.* 1970. A good general treatment of the subject.

Nipperdey, Thomas. *Germany from Napoleon to Bismarck, 1800–1866.* 1996. An exploration of the creation of German nationalism as well as the failure of liberalism.

Onuf, Peter S. *Jefferson's Empire: The Language of American Nationhood.* 2000. A study of Jefferson's expansionary nationalism.

Pflanze, Otto. *Bismarck and the Development of Germany: The Period of Unification, 1815–1871.* 1963. The classic study of both Bismarck and the unification movement.

Pinckney, David. *The French Revolution of 1830.* 1972. The best treatment of this revolution.

Seton-Watson, Hugh. *Nations and States.* 1977. A clearly written study of the nation-state.

Sperber, Jonathan. *The European Revolutions, 1848–1851.* 1994. The best study of the revolutions of 1848.

Tombs, Robert. *The War Against Paris, 1871.* 1981. A narrative history of the Paris Commune.

CHAPTER 23. THE COMING OF MASS POLITICS: INDUSTRIALIZATION, EMANCIPATION, AND INSTABILITY, 1870–1914

Clyman, Toby W., and Judith Vowles, eds. *Russia through Women's Eyes: Autobiographies from Tsarist Russia*. 1999. Fascinating collection that allows us to see both women's history and Russian history in new ways.

Crossik, Geoffrey, and Serge Jaumin, eds. *Cathedrals of Consumption: The European Department Store, 1850–1939*. 1999. A set of essays exploring the impact of the retail revolution.

Hoerder, Dirk. *Cultures in Contact: World Migrations in the Second Millennium*. 2002. Wide-ranging study of the causes and consequences of human migration.

Kern, Stephen. *The Culture of Time and Space, 1880–1918*. 1983. An innovative work that explores the cultural impact of technological change.

Lidtke, Vernon. *The Alternative Culture: Socialist Labor in Imperial Germany*. 1985. Looks beyond the world of parliamentary politics to assess the meaning and impact of working-class socialism.

Lindemann, Albert. *Esau's Tears: Modern Anti-Semitism and the Rise of the Jews*. 1997. A comprehensive and detailed survey that challenges many assumptions about the roots and nature of modern anti-Semitism.

Mayer, Arno. *The Persistence of the Old Regime: Europe to the Great War*. 1981. Argues that landed elites maintained a considerable amount of economic and political power throughout the nineteenth century.

Maynes, Mary Jo. *Taking the Hard Road: Life Course in French and German Workers' Autobiographies in the Era of Industrialization*. 1995. Fascinating study of the "life course" of industrial workers.

Milward, A. S., and S. B. Saul. *The Development of the Economies of Continental Europe, 1850–1914*. 1977. A helpful survey.

Nord, Philip. *The Republican Moment: Struggles for Democracy in Nineteenth-Century France*. 1996. Illuminates the struggle to define and redefine France.

Pilbeam, Pamela. *The Middle Classes in Europe, 1789–1914: France, Germany, Italy, and Russia*. 1990. A comparative approach that helps clarify the patterns of social change.

Rendall, J. *The Origins of Modern Feminism: Women in Britain, France, and the United States*. 1985. A comprehensive comparative study.

Richards, Thomas. *The Commodity Culture of Victorian England: Advertising and Spectacle, 1851–1914*. 1990. Fascinating study of the manufacturing of desire.

Slezkine, Yuri. *The Jewish Century*. 2004. A good companion volume to Lindemann's *Esau's Tears*.

Steenson, Gary P. *After Marx, Before Lenin: Marxism and Socialist Working-Class Parties in Europe, 1884–1914*. 1991. Examines both ideology and political practice within Europe's socialist parties.

Weber, Eugen. *Peasants into Frenchmen: The Modernization of Rural France, 1870–1914*. 1976. A very important work that helped shape the way historians think about "nation making."

CHAPTER 24. THE WEST AND THE WORLD: CULTURAL CRISIS AND THE NEW IMPERIALISM, 1870–1914

Adas, Michael. *Machines as the Measure of Men: Science, Technology, and Ideologies of Western Dominance*. 1989. A superb study of the way in which the ideology of empire was inextricably connected with cultural and intellectual developments within the West.

Barnes, David S. *The Great Stink of Paris and the Nineteenth-Century Struggle against Filth and Germs*. 2005. Important study of developing attitudes toward public health.

Butler, Christopher. *Early Modernism: Literature, Music, and Painting in Europe, 1900–1916*. 1994. Wide-ranging and nicely illustrated

Crews, Robert. *For Prophet and Tsar: Islam and Empire in Russia and Central Asia*. 2006. Important study of an often-overlooked aspect of imperialism.

Dijkstra, Bram. *Idols of Perversity: Fantasies of Feminine Evil in* Fin-de-Siècle *Culture*. 1986. This richly illustrated work shows how anxiety over the changing role of women permeated artistic production at the end of the nineteenth century.

Dodge, Ernest. *Islands and Empires: The Western Impact on the Pacific and East Asia*. 1976. A useful study of Asian imperialism.

Ellis, John. *The Social History of the Machine Gun*. 1975. Lively, nicely illustrated, and informative.

Gould, Stephen Jay. *The Mismeasure of Man*. 1996. A compelling look at the manipulation of scientific data and statistics to provide "proof" for racist and elitist assumptions.

Headrick, Daniel R. *The Tools of Empire: Technology and European Imperialism in the Nineteenth Century*. 1981. Highlights the important role played by technology in determining both the timing and success of Western imperialism.

Hochschild, Adam. *King Leopold's Ghost*. 1998. Blistering account of Leopold's imperialist rule in the Congo.

Pick, Daniel. *Faces of Degeneration: A European Disorder, c. 1848–1918*. 1993. Argues that concern over degeneration formed a central theme in European culture in the second half of the nineteenth century.

Showalter, Elaine. *Sexual Anarchy: Gender and Culture at the* Fin de Siècle. 1990. An illuminating look at the turbulence that characterized gender relations in the *fin-de-siècle*.

Sperber, Jonathan. *Popular Catholicism in Nineteenth-Century Germany*. 1984. A look at the religious dimensions of popular culture.

Vandervort, Bruce. *Wars of Imperial Conquest in Africa, 1830–1914*. 1998. An up-to-date study by a military historian.

Weeks, Theodore. *Nation and State in Late Imperial Russia: Nationalism and Russification on the Western Frontier*. 1966. Important study of Russian imperialism and nation-making.

Weiner, Jonathan. *The Beak of the Finch: The Story of Evolution in Our Time*. 1994. Prize-winning study of Darwin's theory and its impact.

Wesseling, H. L. *Divide and Rule: The Partition of Africa, 1880–1914*. 1996. A solid survey of complex developments.

CHAPTER 25 THE FIRST WORLD WAR

Cooper, John Milton. *Breaking the Heart of the World: Woodrow Wilson and the Fight for the League of Nations*. 2001. Examines the failure of Wilson's new world order.

Ferguson, Niall. *The Pity of War*. 1999. A bold reconsideration of many accepted interpretations of the origins and experience of the war.

Cork, Richard. *A Bitter Truth: Avant-Garde Art and the Great War*. 1994. A beautifully illustrated work that looks at the cultural impact of the war.

Davis, Belinda. *Home Fires Burning: Food, Politics, and Everyday Life in World War I Berlin*. 2000. An important look at the German home front.

Figes, Orlando. *A People's Tragedy: A History of the Russian Revolution*. 1997. Award-winning, gripping account of the revolutionary years.

Fitzpatrick, Sheila. *The Russian Revolution, 1917–1932*. 1994. As the title indicates, Fitzpatrick sees the revolutions of 1917 as the opening battle in a more than ten-year struggle to shape the new Russia.

Gilbert, Martin. *The First World War: A Complete History*. 1994. A comprehensive account, packed with illuminating detail.

Higonnet, Margaret. *Lines of Fire: Women's Visions of World War I*. 1998. An important study of women's experiences.

Joll, James. *The Origins of the First World War*. 1984. One of the best and most carefully balanced studies of this complicated question.

Keegan, John. *The First World War*. 1999. Military history at its best.

Read, Christopher. *From Tsar to Soviets: The Russian People and Their Revolution, 1917–1921*. 1996. An up-to-date study of the popular revolution and its fate.

Steinberg, M. D. *Voices of Revolution, 1917*. 2001. The Russian Revolution in the words of the ordinary people who made and experienced it.

Winter, J. M. *The Experience of World War I*. 1989. Despite the title, this richly illustrated work not only covers the war itself but also explores the factors that led to its outbreak and outlines its chief consequences

Zuckerman, Larry. *The Rape of Belgium: The Untold Story of World War I*. 2004. Corrective account that takes a hard look at German atrocities.

CHAPTER 26. RECONSTRUCTION, REACTION, AND CONTINUING REVOLUTION—THE 1920s AND 1930s

Balderston, Theo, ed. *The World Economy and National Economics in the Interwar Slump*. 2003. Collections of essays exploring the impact of the Great Depression.

Berend, Ivan T. *Decades of Crisis: Central and Eastern Europe before World War II*. 2001. Surveys the complex history of these crucial regions.

Blinkhorn, Martin. *Fascism and the Right in Europe 1919–1945*. 2000. A clear and concise historical and historiographical survey, with a selection of key primary documents.

Bookbinder, Paul. *Weimar Germany: The Republic of the Reasonable*. 1996. An innovative interpretation.

Bosworth, R. J. B. *Mussolini's Italy: Life under the Fascist Dictatorship*. 2007. Crucial study of a crucial place and time.

Brendon, Piers. *The Dark Valley: A Panorama of the 1930s*. 2000. Fast-paced but carefully researched and comprehensive overview of the histories of the United States, Germany, Italy, France, Britain, Japan, Russia, and Spain.

Fischer, Conan. *The Rise of the Nazis*. 1995. Summarizes recent research and includes a section of primary documents.

Fitzpatrick, Sheila. *Everyday Stalinism. Ordinary Life in Extraordinary Times: Soviet Russia in the 1930s*. 1999. Explores the daily life of the ordinary urban worker in Stalinist Russia.

Fitzpatrick, Sheila. *Stalin's Peasants: Resistance and Survival in the Russian Village After Collectivization*. 1995. A superb history from the bottom up.

Getty, J. Arch, and Oleg V. Naumov. *The Road to Terror: Stalin and the Self-Destruction of the Bolsheviks, 1932–1939*. 1999. Interweaves recently discovered documents with an up-to-date interpretation of the Great Purge.

Gilbert, Bentley Brinkerhoff. *Britain 1914–1945: The Aftermath of Power*. 1996. Short, readable overview, designed for beginning students.

Jackson, Julian. *The Popular Front in France: Defending Democracy, 1934–1938*. 1988. A political and cultural history.

Kershaw, Ian. *Hitler*. 1991. A highly acclaimed biography.

Kitchen, Martin. *Nazi Germany: A Critical Introduction*. 2004. Short, clearly written, up to date. An excellent introduction and overview.

Lewis, Bernard. *The Shaping of the Modern Middle East*. 1994. Concise but comprehensive analysis.

Mack Smith, Denis. *Mussolini: A Biography*. 1983. An engaging read and a now-classic account.

Pedersen, Susan. *Family, Dependence, and the Origins of the Welfare State: Britain and France, 1914–1945*. 1993. Shows how welfare policy was inextricably linked to demographic and eugenic concerns.

Thomas, Hugh. *The Spanish Civil War*. 1977. An authoritative account.

Wolpert, Stanley. *Gandhi's Passion: The Life and Legacy of Mahatma Gandhi*. 2001. An intellectual and spiritual biography by one of the foremost historians of modern India.

CHAPTER 27. WORLD WAR II

Alperovitz, Gar. *Atomic Diplomacy: Hiroshima and Potsdam. The Use of the Atomic Bomb and the American Confrontation with Soviet Power*. 1994. The first edition of this book, published in 1965, sparked an ongoing scholarly debate over whether or not U.S. fears about Soviet power influenced the decision to use the atomic bombs against Japan..

Browning, Christopher. *Ordinary Men: Reserve Police Battalion 101 and the Final Solution in Poland*. 1992. A powerful account of the participation of a group of "ordinary men" in mass murder.

Calder, Angus. *The People's War: Britain, 1939–1945*. 1969. Lengthy—but worth the effort for students wishing to explore the war's impact on British society. (Those who want a shorter account can turn to Robert Mackay, *The Test of War: Inside Britain 1939–45* [1999].)

Frayn, Michael. *Copenhagen*. 1998. A remarkable play in which Frayn dramatizes a meeting (that actually did occur) between the German atomic physicist Werner Heisenberg and his Danish anti-Nazi colleague Niels Bohr. Contains both extremely clear explanations of the workings of atomic physics and a provocative exploration of the moral issues involved in the making of the atom bomb.

Friedlander, Saul. *Nazi Germany and the Jews, 1933–1939*. 1998. An important study of the evolution of Nazi anti-Semitic policy before the war.

Hilberg, Raul. *Perpetrators, Victims, Bystanders: The Jewish Catastrophe, 1933–1945*. 1992. As his title indicates, Hilberg looks at the three principal sets of participants in the Holocaust.

Iriye, Akira. *The Origins of the Second World War in Asia and the Pacific*. 1987. Part of Longman's "Origins of Modern Wars" series aimed at university students, this short and readable study highlights the major issues and events.

Keegan, John. *The Second World War*. 1989. Provides clear explanations of military technologies and techniques; packed with useful maps and vivid illustrations.

Kitchen, Martin. *Nazi Germany at War*. 1995. A short and nicely organized survey of the German home front.

Marrus, Michael R. *The Holocaust in History.* 1987. A clearly written, concise account of historians' efforts to understand the Holocaust. Highly recommended.

Maudsley, Evan. *Thunder in the East: The Nazi-Soviet War 1941–1945.* 2005. A wide-ranging account that looks at social and political contexts as well as military strategy and technology.

Merridale, Catherine. *Ivan's War: Life and Death in the Red Army, 1939–1945.* 2007. "From-the-bottom-up" military history, this account looks at the often harrowing experiences of ordinary soldiers.

Moore, Bob, ed. *Resistance in Western Europe.* 2000. A collection of essays that explores recent research on this controversial topic.

Overy, Richard. *Russia's War: A History of the Soviet War Effort, 1941–1945.* 1997. A compelling account, written to accompany the television documentary *Russia's War.*

Paxton, Robert. *Vichy France: Old Guard and New Order, 1940–1944.* 1972. A now-classic study of the aims and evolution of France's collaborationist government.

Rees, Laurence. *WWII Behind Closed Doors: Stalin, the Nazis and the West.* 2008. Winner of the British Book Award for History and companion volume to the BBC Television series, this account uses recently revealed archival documents and interviews to explore the morally complex issues involved in the strange alliance between Stalin and Western democracy.

Rhodes, Richard. *Masters of Death: The SS-Einsatzgruppen and the Invention of the Holocaust.* 2002. Compelling account of the Einsatzgruppen actions during the German invasion of the Soviet Union.

Rhodes, Richard. *The Making of the Atomic Bomb.* 1986. A lengthy but very readable account; very good at explaining the complicated science involved.

Rock, William R. *British Appeasement in the 1930s.* 1977. A balanced and concise appraisal.

Weinberg, Gerhard. *A World at Arms: A Global History of World War II.* 1994. Places the war within a global rather than simply a European context.

CHAPTER 28. REDEFINING THE WEST AFTER WORLD WAR II

Ansprenger, Franz. *The Dissolution of Colonial Empires.* 1989. A clear and comprehensive account (that unfortunately includes no maps).

Castles, Stephen, et al. *Here for Good: Western Europe's New Ethnic Minorities.* 1984. A useful exploration of the impact of postwar immigration, despite the rather rigid Marxist analysis.

Crampton, R. J. *Eastern Europe in the Twentieth Century—And After.* 1997. Detailed chapters on the 1950s and 1960s, including a substantial discussion of the Prague Spring.

De Grazia, Victoria. *Irresistible Empire: America's Advance through Twentieth-Century Europe.* 2005. A study of the Americanization of Europe.

Elkins, Caroline. *Imperial Reckoning: The Untold Story of Britain's Gulag in Kenya.* 2005. This controversial work won the Pulitzer Prize for Non-Fiction.

Fineberg, Jonathan. *Art Since 1940: Strategies of Being.* 1995. A big, bold, lavishly illustrated volume that makes the unfashionable argument that individuals matter.

Fink, Carole, et al. *1968: The World Transformed.* 1998. A collection of essays that explores both the international and the domestic political context for the turmoil of 1968.

Gaddis, John Lewis. *The Cold War: A New History.* 2005. A comprehensive overview by a prominent Cold War historian.

Gillingham, John. *European Integration, 1950–2003: Superstate or New Market Economy?* 2003. An important interpretive history of the European Union.

Gross, Jan T., ed. *The Politics of Retribution in Europe: World War II and Its Aftermath.* 2000. This series of essays makes clear that war did not end in Europe in May 1945.

Judge, Edward, and John Langdon. *A Hard and Bitter Peace: A Global History of the Cold War.* 1999. An extremely useful survey for students. Excellent maps.

Judt, Tony. *Postwar: A History of Europe since 1945.* 2005. An important interpretive survey.

Keep, John. *Last of the Empires: A History of the Soviet Union, 1945–1991.* 1995. Looks beyond the Kremlin to explore social, cultural, and economic developments.

Madara'z, Jeannette. *Working in East Germany: Normality in a Socialist Dictatorship, 1961–1979.* 2006. Examines ordinary life in an extraordinary society.

Poiger, Uta. *Jazz, Rock, and Rebels: Cold War Politics and American Culture in a Divided Germany.*

2000. Explores the interplay among youth culture, Americanization, and political protest.

Rees, Laurence. *WWII Behind Closed Doors: Stalin, the Nazis and the West*. 2008. Winner of the British Book Award for History and companion volume to the BBC Television series, this account uses recently revealed archival documents and interviews to explore the compromises that created Cold War Europe.

de Senarclens, P. *From Yalta to the Iron Curtain: The Great Powers and the Origins of the Cold War*. 1995. A look at the diplomatic, political and military concerns that created the Cold War.

Steege, Paul. *Black Market Cold War: Everyday Life in Berlin, 1946–1949*. 2007. History "from the bottom up" that explores the ways Berlin became the symbolic center of the Cold War and its impact on the people of Berlin.

Stromberg, Roland. *After Everything: Western Intellectual History Since 1945*. 1975. A swiftly moving tour through the major intellectual developments.

Taylor, Frederick. *The Berlin Wall: A World Divided, 1961–1989*. 2007. Uses the dramatic history of the Berlin Wall to explore the global impact of the Cold War.

Westad, Odd Arne. *The Global Cold War: Third World Interventions and the Making of Our Time*. 2007. Highly recommended study of the Cold War's globalization.

Wyman, Mark. *DPs: Europe's Displaced Persons, 1945–1951*. 1989. An important study of an often-neglected topic.

CHAPTER 29 THE WEST IN THE CONTEMPORARY ERA: NEW ENCOUNTERS AND TRANSFORMATIONS

NOTE: Many of the readings recommended for Chapter 28 supplement this chapter as well.

Ardagh, John. *Germany and the Germans: The United Germany in the Mid-1990s*. 1996. A snapshot of a society in the midst of social and economic change.

Kavanagh, Dennis. *Thatcherism and British Politics: The End of Consensus?* 1987. Kavanagh answers the question posed in his title with a convincing "yes."

Kenney, Padraic. *The Burdens of Freedom: Eastern Europe since 1989*. 2006. In only 160 pages, Kenney offers a lucid and very helpful account of postrevolutionary developments.

Lewis, Jane, ed. *Women and Social Policies in Europe: Work, Family and the State*. 1993. A series of essays exploring the position of women in western Europe. Packed with statistics and useful tables.

Lovell, Stephen. *Destination in Doubt: Russia Since 1989*. 2006. A clear and succinct account.

McNeill, John. *Something New Under the Sun: An Environmental History of the Twentieth Century*. 2000. Argues that twentieth-century human economic activity has transformed the ecology of the globe—an ongoing experiment with a potentially devastating outcome.

Ost, David. *Solidarity and the Politics of Anti-Politics: Opposition and Reform in Poland Since 1968*. 1990. Although the bulk of this account was written before the Revolution of 1989, it provides a compelling study of Solidarity's emergence, impact, and ideology.

Rogel, Carole. *The Breakup of Yugoslavia and the War in Bosnia*. 1998. Designed for undergraduates, this work includes a short but detailed historical narrative, biographies of the main personalities, and a set of primary documents.

Rosenberg, Tina. *The Haunted Land: Facing Europe's Ghosts After Communism*. 1995. Winner of the Pulitzer Prize, this disturbing account focuses on the fundamental moral issues facing postcommunist political cultures.

Sandler, Irving. *Art of the Postmodern Era: From the Late 1960s to the Early 1980s*. 1996. Much more broad-ranging than the title suggests, this well-written, blessedly jargon-free work sets both contemporary art and the theories of the postmodern within the wider historical context.

Stokes, Gale. *The Walls Came Tumbling Down: The Collapse of Communism in Eastern Europe*. 1993. A superb account, firmly embedded in history.

Young, John W. *Cold War Europe, 1945–1991: A Political History*. 1996. A solid survey.

NOTES

CHAPTER 15

1. Quoted in R. Po-Chia Hsia, *Social Discipline in the Reformation: Central Europe, 1550–1750* (1989), 147–148.
2. Quoted in Norbert Elias, *The Civilizing Process,* vol. 1: *The History of Manners.* Translated by Edmund Jephcott (1978), 119.
3. Quoted in R. J. Knecht, *The French Wars of Religion, 1559–1598,* 2nd ed. (1996), 13.
4. Michel de Montaigne, *Essays and Selected Writings.* Translated and edited by Donald M. Frame (1963), 219–221.

CHAPTER 16

1. Thomas Hobbes, *Leviathan,* C. B. Macpherson (ed.) (1968), 186.
2. Marshall Poe, "The Truth about Muscovy," *Kritika* 3 (2002), 483.
3. Quoted in Lindsey Hughes, *Russia in the Age of Peter the Great* (1998), 92.

CHAPTER 17

1. René Descartes, *Le Monde,* Book VI.
2. Thomas S. Kuhn, *The Structure of Scientific Revolutions* (1970).
3. René Descartes, *Discourse on the Method and Meditations on First Philosophy,* edited by David Weissmann (1996), 21.
4. Galileo, "Letter to the Grand Duchess Christina." In Stilman Drake (ed.), *Discoveries and Opinions of Galileo* (1957), 186.
5. Quoted in W. Hazard, *The European Mind, 1680–1715* (1964), 362.
6. François Poullain, *De l'égalite des deux sexes* (1673), 85.
7. Francis Bacon, *The Works of Francis Bacon,* vol. 3, J. Spedding (ed.) (1857–1874), 524–539.
8. Henry Oldenburg, "To the Reader." In Robert Boyle (ed.), *Experiments and Considerations in Touching Colours* (1664).

CHAPTER 18

1. Olaudah Equiano, *The Interesting Narrative of the Life of Olaudah Equiano, or Gustavus Vassa the African* (1789).

2. Thomas Rymer (ed.), *Foedera* vol. 18 (1704–1735), 72.
3. Quoted in Robin Blackburn, *The Making of New World Slavery* (1997), 325.

CHAPTER 19

1. Baron d'Holbach, *Good Sense* (1753).
2. David Hume, *Essays Moral, Political, and Literary* (1742), Essay 10: "Of Superstition and Enthusiasm."
3. Cesare Beccaria, *An Essay on Crimes and Punishments* (1788), Chapter 47.
4. Voltaire, "Religion," *The Philosophical Dictionary* (1802).

CHAPTER 20

1. H. Wallon, *Histoire du tribunal révolutionnaire de Paris* vol. 4 (1880–1882), 511.

CHAPTER 21

1. Lord Ashley's Commission on Mines, *Parliamentary Papers,* Vols. 15–17 (1842), Appendix 1, Note 26.
2. Sir James Kay-Shuttleworth (1832), quoted in John Rule, *The Labouring Classes in Early Industrial England* (1986).
3. John Richardson, *The Friend: A Religious and Literary Journal,* 30 (1856), 97.
4. "Report of the Select Committee on the Factories Bill," *Parliamentary Papers,* Vol. 20 (1833).
5. John O'Rourke, *The History of the Great Irish Famine of 1847* (1902).
6. David Gillard, ed., *British Documents on Foreign Affairs,* Vol. 1: *The Ottoman Empire in the Balkans, 1856–1875* (1984–1985), 20.

CHAPTER 23

1. Leslie Moch, *Moving Europeans: Migration in Western Europe Since 1650* (1992), 147.
2. Quoted in Eugen Weber, *Peasants into Frenchmen: The Modernization of Rural France, 1870–1914* (1976), 332–333.

3. Norman Kleeblatt, *The Dreyfus Affair: Art, Truth, and Justice* (1987), 96.
4. Quoted in Eric Cahm, *The Dreyfus Affair in French Society and Politics* (1994), 167.
5. Quoted in Robert Gildea, *Barricades and Borders: Europe, 1800–1914* (1987), 317.
6. Eugen Weber, *France, Fin-de-Siècle* (1986), 126.
7. Albert Lindemann, *Esau's Tears: Modern Anti-Semitism and the Rise of the Jews* (1997).
8. Maria Desraismes, "La Femme et Le Droit," *Eve dans l'humanite* (1891), 16–17.

CHAPTER 24

1. Winston Churchill, *The River War: An Account of the Re-Conquest of the Sudan* (1933); quoted in Daniel Headrick, *The Tools of Empire: Technology and European Imperialism in the Nineteenth Century* (1981), 118.
2. Quoted in Anne McClintock, *Imperial Leather: Race, Gender, and Sexuality in the Colonial Contest* (1995), 50.
3. From Rider Haggard, *She* (1887).
4. Quoted in H. Stuart Hughes, *Consciousness and Society* (1958), 296.
5. Quoted in Shearer West, *Fin de Siècle* (1993), 24.
6. Stephen Kern, *The Culture of Time and Space, 1880–1918* (1983), 195.
7. From *Elementary Forms*. Quoted in Hughes, *Consciousness and Society*, 284–285.
8. Quoted in William Schneider, *An Empire for the Masses: The French Popular Image of Africa, 1870–1900* (1982), 72.
9. Heinrich von Treitschke, *Politics* (1897).
10. Yves-Alain Bois, "Painting as Trauma," in Christopher Green, *Picasso's Les Demoiselles d'Avignon* (2001), 49.
11. Brassaï, *Conversations with Picasso*, trans. Jane Marie Todd (1999), 32.
12. John Golding, "*Les Demoiselles D'Avignon* and the Exhibition of 1988," in Green, *Picasso's Les Demoiselles*, 29.
13. Mary Kingsley, in *West African Studies* (1901), 329–330.
14. Rudyard Kipling, *Verse* (1920).
15. Headrick, *The Tools of Empire*, 101. Headrick is the historian who identified the crucial role of the steamship, the quinine prophylaxis, and the breech-loading, repeating rifle in the conquest of Africa.
16. Quoted in Thomas Pakenham, *The Scramble for Africa, 1876–1912* (1991), 22.

17. Quoted in F. K. Crowley (ed.), *A New History of Australia* (1974), 6.
18. Ibid., 207.
19. Quoted in W. G. Beasley, *Japanese Imperialism, 1894–1945* (1987), 31–33.

CHAPTER 25

1. Quoted in Niall Ferguson, *The Pity of War* (1999), 152.
2. Quoted in Eric Leeds, *No Man's Land: Combat and Identity in World War I* (1979), 17.
3. Allister Horne, *The Price of Glory: Verdun, 1916* (1967), 27.
4. Siegfried Sassoon, *Memoirs of an Infantry Officer* (1937), 228.
5. Ernst Lessauer, "Hymn of Hate" (1914), in *Jugend* (1914). Translated by Barbara Henderson, *New York Times*, October 15, 1914.
6. Quoted in W. Bruce Lincoln, *Red Victory: A History of the Russian Civil War* (1989), 32.
7. Quoted in Edvard Radzinsky, *The Last Tsar*, trans. Marian Schwartz (1993), 336.
8. From the written account of Yakov Yurovsky, quoted in Radzinsky, *The Last Tsar*, 355.
9. Quoted in William Henry Chamberlin, *The Russian Revolution, 1917–1921, Vol. 2: From the Civil War to the Consolidation of Power* (1987), 91.
10. Quoted in Lincoln, *Red Victory*, 151.
11. Ibid., 155.
12. Quoted in Radzinsky, *The Last Tsar*, 326.
13. Richard Pipes et al. (eds.), *The Unknown Lenin* (1999), 6.
14. Ibid., Document 59.
15. Quoted in Richard Cork, *A Bitter Truth* (1994), 198.

CHAPTER 26

1. Quoted in Peter Gay, *Weimar Culture* (1970), 99.
2. Martin J. Sherwin, *A World Destroyed: Hiroshima and the Origins of the Arms Race* (1987), 17.
3. Quoted in Michael Burleigh, *The Third Reich: A New History* (2000), 36.
4. Quoted in Ibid., 52.
5. Quoted in Joachim Fest, *Hitler* (1973), 190–193.
6. Ibid., 192, 218.
7. Quoted in Wendy Goldman, *Women, the State, and Revolution: Soviet Family Policy and Social Life, 1917–1936* (1993), 5.
8. Quoted in Claudia Koonz, *Mothers in the Fatherland* (1987), 130.

9. Quoted in Fest, *Hitler*, 445.
10. Quoted in Koonz, *Mothers in the Fatherland*, 194.
11. Ibid., 178.
12. Ibid., 56; Victoria DeGrazia, *How Fascism Ruled Women: Italy, 1922–1945* (1992), 234.
13. Quoted in Mark Mazower, *Dark Continent: Europe's Twentieth Century* (1998), 123.
14. Quoted in Sheila Fitzpatrick, *Everyday Stalinism* (1999), 68.
15. See Stephen G. Wheatcroft, "More Light on the Scale of Repression and Excess Mortality in the Soviet Union in the 1930s," in J. Arch Getty and Roberta Manning, *Stalinist Terror: New Perspectives* (1993), 275–290.
16. "Appendix 1: Numbers of Victims of the Terror," in J. Arch Getty and Oleg V. Naumov, *The Road to Terror: Stalin and the Self-Destruction of the Bolsheviks, 1932–1939* (1999), 587–594.
17. Quoted in Felix Gilbert, *The End of the European Era* (1991), 162.
18. Mohandas K. Gandhi, *An Autobiography: The Story of My Experiments with Truth* (1957), 120.
19. Quoted in Tyler Stovall, *Paris Noir: African Americans in the City of Light* (1996), 32.

CHAPTER 27

1. Quoted in Robert H. Abzug, *Inside the Vicious Heart: Americans and the Liberation of Nazi Concentration Camps* (1985), 19.
2. Quoted in Gordon Horwitz, *In the Shadow of Death: Living Outside the Gates of Mauthausen* (1991), 167.
3. Quoted in Piers Brendon, *The Dark Valley: A Panorama of the 1930s* (2000), 282.
4. Quoted in Richard Overy, *Russia's War* (1998), 95.
5. Quoted in Mark Mazower, *Dark Continent: Europe's Twentieth Century* (1999), 157.
6. Quoted in Peter Clarke, *Hope and Glory: Britain, 1900–1990* (1996), 204.
7. Quoted in Joachim Fest, *Hitler* (1973), 665.
8. Quoted in Richard Rhodes, *The Making of the Atomic Bomb* (1988), 474.
9. Elie Wiesel, *Night* (1960), 39.
10. Gideon Hausner, *Justice in Jerusalem* (1966), 291.
11. Ibid., 323–324.
12. From Hausner's opening statement; quoted in Moshe Pearlman, *The Capture and Trial of Adolf Eichmann* (1963), 149.
13. Ibid., 463–465.
14. Ibid., 603; Hausner, *Justice in Jerusalem*, 422.
15. Quoted in Ulrich Herbert, *Hitler's Foreign Workers* (1997), 306.

CHAPTER 28

1. Stalin to Maxim Litvinov, cited in Vladislav Zubok and Constantine Pleshakov, *Inside the Kremlin's Cold War: From Stalin to Khrushchev* (Cambridge, 1996), 37–38.
2. Leo Crowley, director of the Foreign Economic Administration under Roosevelt and Truman; quoted in William Appleman Williams, *The Tragedy of American Diplomacy* (New York, 1972), 241.
3. Lawrence Rees, *World War II Behind Closed Doors: Stalin, the Nazis, and the West* (2008), 221, 236.
4. Quoted in William Hardy McNeill, *America, Britain, and Russia: Their Cooperation and Conflict 1941–1946* (New York, 1970), 700, note 2.
5. Quoted in Karel Kaplan, *Report on the Murder of the General Secretary* (1990), 159.
6. Ibid., 242.
7. Ibid., 231.
8. Quoted in John Hargreaves, *Decolonization in Africa* (1996), 113.
9. Quotation from *Time* magazine, 1950; quoted in Martin Walker, *The Cold War and the Making of the Modern World* (1993), 66–67.
10. Quoted in Walker, *The Cold War*, 83.
11. Quoted in Stephen Ambrose, *Rise to Globalism* (1971), 225.
12. Quoted in Donald White, *The American Century* (1999), 286.
13. Quoted in John L. H. Keep, *Last of the Empires: A History of the Soviet Union, 1945–1991* (1995), 79.
14. Quoted in Michael Scammell, *From Gulag to Glasnost: Nonconformist Art in the Soviet Union*, eds. Alla Rosenfeld and Norton T. Dodge (1995), 61.
15. Quoted in Walker, *The Cold War*, 105.
16. Quoted in Robert Paxton, *Europe in the Twentieth Century* (1997), 578.
17. Quoted in Jonathan Fineberg, *Art Since 1940: Strategies of Being* (1995), 144.
18. Ibid., 89.
19. Quoted in Adrian Hastings, *Modern Catholicism: Vatican II and After* (1991), 29.
20. Reinhold Wagnleitner, *Coca-Colonization and the Cold War: The Cultural Mission of the United States in Austria After the Second World War* (1994).

21. Quoted in Felix Gilbert, *The End of the European Era, 1890 to the Present* (1991), 429.

22. Quoted in Richard Kuisel, *Seducing the French: The Dilemma of Americanization* (1993), 147.

CHAPTER 29

1. Quoted in Robert Paxton, *Europe in the Twentieth Century* (1997), 613.

2. Kenneth Boulding, "The Economics of the Coming Spaceship Earth," first published in 1966, reprinted in *Toward a Steady-State Economy*, ed. Herman Daly (1973).

3. Quoted in D. J. Peterson, *Troubled Lands: The Legacy of Soviet Environmental Destruction* (1993), 12.

4. Quoted in Archie Brown, *The Gorbachev Factor* (1996), 125.

5. Stephen Lovell, *Destination in Doubt: Russia Since 1989* (2006), 99.

6. Salman Rushdie, "Please, Read *Satanic Verses* Before Condemning It," *Illustrated Weekly of India* (October 1988). Reprinted in M. M. Ahsan and A. R. Kidwai, *Sacrilege Versus Civility: Muslim Perspectives on The Satanic Verses Affair* (1991), 63.

7. Quoted in Malise Ruthven, *A Satanic Affair: Salman Rushdie and the Wrath of Islam* (1991), 562.

8. Quoted in Ruthven, *A Satanic Affair,* 100.

9. *Bookseller,* London (February 24, 1989). Quoted in Lisa Appignanesi and Sara Maitland, *The Rushdie File* (1990), 103–104.

10. *The Sunday Telegraph* (June 24, 1990). Quoted in Ahsan and Kidwai, *Sacrilege Versus Civility,* 80.

11. Quoted in Irving Sandler, *Art of the Postmodern Era* (1996), 4.

PHOTO CREDITS

Jerusalem, Israel/Vera & Arturo Schwarz Collection of Dada and Surrealist Art/The Bridgeman Art Library; **page 604:** William Hogarth, Sarah Malcolm in Prison. 1733. Oil on canvas. 48.80 × 38.70 cm (framed: 56.20 × 46.40 × 9.00 cm). National Galleries of Scotland, Scottish National Gallery of Modern Art; **page 606:** Private Collection/The Bridgeman Art Library; **page 608:** Bibliotheque Nationale de France; **page 614:** Vigilius Erichsen (1722–82), "Equestrian Portrait of Catherine II (1729–96), the Great of Russia", oil on canvas. Musee des Beaux-Arts, Chartres, France/The Bridgeman Art Library; **page 619:** Chateau de Versailles, France/Giraudon/The Bridgeman Art Lirary Nationality; **page 621:** Musee Carnavalet, Paris, France/ The Bridgeman Art Library, London/New York; **page 623:** Snark/Art Resource, NY/Art Resource, NY; **page 626 (from left to right):** The Art Archive/Musee Carnavalet Paris/Dagli Orti; The Art Archive/Private Collection/ Marc Charmet; **page 631:** Bibliotheque Nationale, Paris, France/The Bridgeman Art Library; **page 637:** Musee de la Ville de Paris, Musee Carnavalet, Paris, France/The Bridgeman Art Library; **page 638:** Giraudon/Musees Royaux des Beaux-Arts de Belgique, Brussels/Art Resource, NY; **page 639:** Jacques Louis David (1748–1825), "Consecration of the Emperor Napoleon I and Coronation of Empress Josephine," 1806–07. Louvre, Paris. Bridgeman-Giraudon/Art Resource, NY; **page 646:** Jean-Charles Tardieu (1765–1830), "Troops Halted on the Banks of the Nile, 2nd February 1812", oil on canvas. Chateau de Versailles, France/Lauros/Giraudon/The Bridgeman Art Library; **page 648:** Francisco de Goya, (Spanish, 1746–1828). "The Third of May, 1808". 1814–1815. Oil on canvas, approx. 8'8" × 11'3". Derechos reservados © Museo Nacional Del Prado-Madrid. Photo Oronoz; **page 655:** Library of Congress; **page 656:** Guildhall Library, City of London/The Bridgeman Art Library; **page 657:** © RCAHMS. Reproduced courtesy of J R Hume. Licensor www.rcahms.go.uk; **page 659:** Science Museum London/Bridgeman Art Library; **page 661:** Private Collection/The Bridgeman Art Library; **page 668:** Archiv/Photo Researchers, Inc; **page 673:** Getty Images Inc. Hulton Archive Photos; **page 676:** The Image Works; **page 678:** The Bridgeman Art Library International; **page 679:** Joseph Mallord William Turner, 1775–1851, "Rain, Steam, and Speed—The Great Western Railway." Oil on canvas, 90.8 × 121.9. © The National Gallery, London; **page 685:** Eugene Delacroix (1798–1860) "July 28th, 1830; Liberty Guides the People", oil on canvas, 260 × 325 cm. Louvre, Dept. des Peintures, Paris, France. © Photograph by Erich Lessing/Art Resource, NY; **page 690:** The Granger Collection, New York; **page 693:** Hamburger Kunsthalle, Hamburg, Germany/The Bridgeman Art Library; **page 697:** Getty Images/De Agostini Editore Picture Library; **page 701:** The Illustrated London News Picture Library, London, UK/The Bridgeman Art Library; **page 705:** Ullstein Bild/The Granger Collection, New York; **page 707:** Image Works/Mary Evans Picture Library Ltd; **page 711:** © Hulton-Deutsch Collection/CORBIS; **page 714:** Art Resource/Bildarchiv Preussischer Kulturbesitz; **page 718:** Bildarchiv Preussischer Kulturbesitz/Art Resource, NY; **page 721:** Pierre Auguste Renoir. Le Moulin de la Galette, 1876. Oil on canvas. © 2004 Artists Rights Society (ARS), New York. Louvre Museum/Art Resource, NY; **page 722:** Getty Images; **page 725:** Private Collection/Roger Perrin/The Bridgeman Art Library Nationality; **page 727:** The Children's Class, 1889 (oil on canvas) by Henry Jules Jean Geoffroy (1853–1924). Ministere de L'Education Nationale, Paris, France/Archives Charmet/The Bridgeman Art Library Nationality; **page 728:** Getty Images Inc.—Hulton Archive Photos; **page 732:** Getty Images Inc.—Hulton Archive Photos; **page 734:** Sovfoto/Eastfoto; **page 737:** Getty Images/De Agostini Editore Picture Library; **page 740:** The Black Banner (Czarny Sztandar), 1905. Oil on canvas, 30 × 81". Gift of the Estate of Rose Mintz, JM 63–67a. Photo by Richard Goodbody, The Jewish Museum, New York, NY, U.S.A; **page 743:** Réunion des Musées Nationaux/Art Resource, NY; **page 751:** Giraudon/Art Resource, NY; **page 752:** Adalbert Franz Seligmann "Allgemeines Krankenhaus" (General Hospital) 19th Century Painting, canvas. "Professor Theodor Billroth lectures at the General Hospital, Vienna. 1880". Erich Lessing/Art Resource, NY; **page 754:** National History Museum, London, UK/Bridgeman Art Library; **page 758:** Edgar Degas, "The Glass of Absinthe," 1876. Oil on canvas, 36 × 27 in. Musee d'Orsay, Paris. Scala/Art Resource, NY; **page 759:** Erich Lessing/Art Resource, NY; **page 761:** The Granger Collection, New York; **page 763:** Egon Schiele (1890–1918), "Standing Nude, Facing Front (Self Portrait)," 1910. Graphische Sammlung Albertina, Vienna, Austria/The Bridgeman Art Library; **page 764:** William Holman Hunt (1827–1910), "The Light of the World", c. 1852, oil on canvas. © Manchester Art Gallery, UK/The Bridgeman Art Library; **page 767:** Bodleian Library, University of Oxford, Shelfmark 2523; **page 768:** Pablo Picasso, "Les Demoiselles d'Avignon". 1907. Oil on Canvas. 8' × 7'8" (2.44 × 2.34 m). Acquired through the Lillie P. Bliss Bequest. Digital Image © The Museum of Modern Art/Licensed by Scala-Art Resource, NY. © 2008 ARS Artists Rights Society, NY; **page 780:** Hulton Archive/Getty Images; **page 785:**

INDEX

Abd al-Wahhab, Muhammad, 850
Abolition and abolitionism, 572
Aboriginal peoples, 777–778, 779
Abortion, 931, 963
Absinthe (Degas), 758 (illus)
Absolutism, 492
   in central and Eastern Europe,
     506–514
   Dutch Republic and, 516–525
   England and, 516–525
   enlightened, 613–615
   in France, 494–496, 497
   of Louis XIV (France), 497–498
   in Prussia, 509
   in Spain, 495–496, 501–502
   theory of, 493–494
   warfare and, 494–495
Abstract art, 918–919
Abstract Expressionism, 918–919, 920
   (illus)
Académie des Sciences (France), 500
Academies. *See also* specific academies
   in France, 480, 634–635
Academy of Experiment (Florence),
   540–541
Academy of Fine Arts (France), 500
Academy of Music (France), 500
Academy of Sciences, 540. *See* French
   Academy of Sciences
Academy of the Lynxes (Rome),
   540–541
Administration. *See also* Government(s)
   of France, 642
Adowa, Battle of, 775
Adriatic Sea, 797–798
Afghanistan, 956
   Soviets and, 933
Africa. *See also* North Africa;
   Sub-Saharan Africa
   anti-Western sentiment in, 849
   Belgium and, 774–775
   Boer War and, 781–782
   British Empire and, 781–782
   conquests of, 774–775
   decolonization and, 903 (map)
   in First World War, 800 (map)
   after First World War, 818
   Germany and, 781–782, 782
   immigrants from, 924
   imperialism and, 773 (map), 781
   (illus), 781–782
   Islam in, 849
   national self-determination and,
   849, 853

   new imperialism in, 750, 766, 769,
   772 (map), 773 (map), 773–775
   resistance in, 775
   scramble for (1876, 1914), 772
   (map), 773 (map), 773–775
   in Second World War, 865
   slave trade and, 774
   slavery and, 571
   South Africa, 781 (illus)
African Americans, 777
Africans. *See* Slaves and slavery
Afrikaners, Boers as, 781–782
Age of Affluence, 917, 923, 923–926
Aggression. *See* specific countries
Agriculture
   in Europe, 460
   productivity of, 663
   Soviet, 840–841, 912–913
AIDS, 962
Air pump (Boyle), 534 (illus)
Air Raid Protection services, 886
Air raid shelters, 887
Airplanes, 823, 861
Akhenaten (Egypt). *See also* Amenhotep
   IV (Egypt)
Al Qaeda, 955–956
Alaska, Russia and, 561
Alba, Duke of, 479
Albania, 915
   in 1920s and 1930s, 827
   authoritarianism in, 827
   after the fall of communism, 945
   in First World War, 797–798
   after First World War, 858
Albanians, 946
Alchemy, 534
Alembert, Jean le Rond d’. *See*
   D’Alembert, Jean le Rond
Aleuts, 561
Alexander I, 827
Alexander I (Russia), 697
Alexander III (Russia), 809
Alexander Ypsilantis (Greece), 696
Alexandra (Russia), 807, 810 (illus),
   810–812
Alexei (Russia), 807, 810, 810 (illus)
Algeria
   in First World War, 798
   Franco-Algerian War and, 906
   independence of, 901
   in Second World War, 871
Alien Land Law (1913), 777
Alliances. *See also* specific alliances
   in First World War, 787–788

   against Napoleon, 626
Allies (First World War), 785–791, 789
   (map), 792–802, 797 (map),
   821–822, 825, 826 (map), 862–863
   in First World War, 800 (map)
   after First World War, 813–816
   German reparations and, 827–828
Allies (Second World War), 856–890,
   871–874, 892
   Holocaust and, 880, 883
   victory of, 872 (map)
Alsace
   in First World War, 789
   after First World War, 815 (map)
Amenhotep III (Egypt). *See also*
   Akhenaten (Egypt)
Amenhotep IV (Egypt). *See also*
   Akhenaten (Egypt)
America. *See also* England (Britain);
   specific countries and regions;
   United States as
   plantation colonies in, 560
American Indians, 568
American Revolution, 563, 565,
   579–581
   Paine and, 609
Americanization, 923–924
Amsterdam: stock exchange in, 523,
   524 (illus)
Anarchism, 737
Anastasia (Russia), 810, 810 (illus)
Anatolia (Turkey). *See also* Turkey
Anatomy
   dissection and, 535
Andropov, Yuri, 937
Anesthetics, 753
Anglo-French rivalry, 563–565
Anglo-Irish War, 847, 848 (map)
Angola
   Portuguese trading post in, 560
Annam (Vietnam), 776, 781
Anne of Austria, 497
Anschluss, 859
Anti-Corn Law League (England), 701
Anti-elitism, postmodernist, 957
Anti-Semitism, 817, 835–836, 883,
   898. *See also* Jews and Judaism
   Dreyfus Affair and, 730–733
   Herzl and, 741
   in mass politics, 739–740
   in Nazi Germany, 835–838
   in Second World War, 877–883
Anti-universalism, of postmodernist
   architecture, 957

Antwerp, 460, 479
Anxiety
  Price Revolution and, 462–463
  scientific developments and, 750–757
Apartheid, 852
Appeasement, at Munich, 859,
  860–861, 862–863, 864
Aquinas. *See* Thomas Aquinas
Arab nationalists, *816* (map), 817
  in First World War, *797* (map), 799
Arabia, 850
Arabian Peninsula
  First World War and, 799
Arabs, 816–817, *826* (map)
  Israel and, 902
  Pan-Arabism and, 849
Aragon, 502
Archbishop of Paris, 764
Architecture
  after First World War, 822–823
  modern, 822, 957
  postmodern, 957, *959* (illus)
  of St. Petersburg, 515–516
Arcimboldo, Giuseppe, *484* (illus)
Arendt, Hannah, 882
Argentina, 812, 881
Aristarchus of Samos, 538
Aristocracy, 587–592. *See also* Nobility
  bourgeoisie and, 595–596
  challenges to, 592–596
  cultural world of, 591–592
  decline of, 586
  in post-World War I Germany, 827,
    829, 837 political power of,
    590–591
  salons and, 611
  use of term, 587
  wealth of, 588–589
  women and, 588–589
Aristotelianism, education and, 543
Aristotle
  geocentric theories of, 530
  impetus theory and, 537
  on physics, 532, 537
Arizona, 777
Arkwright, Richard, 656, 658
Armada, Spanish, 480
Armed forces
  standing armies and, 494–495
Armenia, 944
  in 1920s and 1930s, *826* (map)
  after First World War, 824
Armenian massacre, *806* (illus)
Arms race, 939–940
Armstrong, Neil, 921–922
Arouet, François Marie. *See* Voltaire
"Art for art's sake," 762
Art(s)
  in 1950s and 1960s, 918–919

African influences on, 768–769,
  772, 850
Cubism (painting), 763, 768–769
of the *fin-de-siècle, 758* (illus)
at the *fin-de-siècle,* 759
after First World War, 821–823
modernism in, 762–764, 783, 957–958
postmodernism in, 957–958
representing First World War, 796
  (illus)
romanticism and, 693–694
in Soviet Union, *841* (illus), 913, 914
Asia. *See also* Middle East; Southwest
  Asia; specific countries
  in 1920s and 1930s, 847
  decolonization and, *901* (illus)
  emerging nations in, 926
  European attitudes toward, 576–579
  in First World War, *800* (map)
  France and, 781
  immigrants from, 924
  imperialism and, 750, 766, 775–776,
    776 (illus), 777–781, 782
  industrialization and, 930–931
  Opium War in, 680–681
  Russia and, 779
  scramble for, 776
  after Second World War, *901* (illus)
Assassinations. *See* specific individuals
Assayer, The (Galileo), 546
Assemblies. *See* Diet (assembly);
  Legislatures; Parliament; specific
  assemblies
Assembly line, 669
Assignats (paper money, France), 633
Assyria and Assyrians, 817. *See also*
  Neo-Assyrian Empire
Aswan Dam, 909
Ataturk, Kemal. *See* Kemal Pasha,
  Mustafa ("Ataturl")
Athletics, Greek. *See also* sports
Atlantic Ocean region
  slave trade in, 567, 570–573
Atomic bomb, 874, 875–876, 877, 895,
  897, 918–919
Atoms, 823–824
  Boyle on, 538
Attlee, Clement, 895, 900, 905
Auerstädt, battle at, 644
Auschwitz-Birkenau, 880
Australia, 781, 782
  in 1920s and 1930s, 847
  Aboriginal peoples in, 777–778, 779
  Chinese immigrants to, 778
  in First World War, 798, 799
  after First World War, 818
  imperialism and, 777–778
  in Second World War, 874–875
  territorial expansion of, 777

Austria, 812, 929
  in Concert of Europe, 696
  enlightened despots in, 613
  expansion of Nazi Germany
    and, 859
  in First World War, 784–786, 787
  after First World War, 858, 862
  France and, 627
  Napoleon and, 627
  nationalities in, *715* (map)
  revolution of 1848 in, 702–704
  in Second Coalition, 633
  after Second World War, *893* (map)
  in Third Coalition, 644
Austria-Hungary, 784–786
  China and, 780
  in First World War, 787–790,
    795–802, 806
  after First World War, 814
  nationalism in, 738
Austrian Habsburg Monarchy,
  506–507, 614
Authoritarianism, 888
  in 1920s and 1930s, 833–835
  in Eastern and Central Europe,
    825–828
  after First World War, 824–828,
    827–828
  First World War and, 803
  in Germany, 827
  in Russia, 824–825, 944
Auto-da-fé, 466–467
  in Lisbon, *467* (illus)
Automobiles, 823
Auxiliary Service Law (Germany), 803
Avant-garde, 918–919
Azerbaijan, 942, 944
  after First World War, 824
Aztecs
  chocolate and, 568

Babeuf, François-Noël, 690
Baby boom, 925
Bacon, Francis (painter), 918, 920,
  920 (illus)
Bacon, Francis (philosopher), 535,
  542–543, 548
Bacteria, Pasteur and, 753
Baghdad, 817
Baker, Josephine (illus), *854* (illus)
Balance of power, 501, 726, 787
Baldwin, Stanley, 860
Balfour Declaration, 817
Balkan region, 835
  after the fall of communism, 945
  in First World War, 797–798
  after First World War, 816
  in Second World War, 865
  after Second World War, 897

Baltic region, 809, 813, 944
  after the fall of communism, 945
  after First World War, *815* (map)
  German-Soviet Non-Aggression Pact
    and, 860
Bandung Conference, 901, 909
Banks and banking
  continental industrialization and,
    664, 668
  Great Depression and, 834
  industrial funding by, 664
Baroque style, in Spanish painting, 505
Barth, Karl, 822
Barthes, Roland, 958, 960
Barton, Edmund, 777
Bartonnet, Marie-Jeanne, 604
Basque separatists: terrorism by, 951
Basra, 817
Bastille: storming of, 618, *618*
    (illus), 620
Batavia (Jakarta), 557
Batouala (Maran), 853–854
Battery Shelled, A, *793* (illus)
Battle of Britain, 864
Battle of the Nations at Leipzig,
    647, 649
Battle of the Somme, The (movie)
    (illus), *785* (illus)
Battles. *See* specific battles and wars
Bauhaus, 822
Bavarian separatism, 829
Beatles, 924
Beccaria, Cesare, 601, 605, 607
Beckett, Samuel, 918
Beer Hall Putsch, 827, 829, 836
Beethoven, Ludwig van, 640, 694
Beijing, 780
Belarus, 813, 937
  after First World War, *815* (map)
Belgium
  in 1920s and 1930s, 832
  in 1950s and 1960s, 916, 917
  Africa and, 774–775
  in First World War, 789–792
  nationalist revolution in (1830),
    697–698
  in Second World War, 873
Benelux states, 917
Bengal, 565
Ben-Gurion, David, 881
Bergen-Belsen concentration camp, 856,
    857 (illus)
Berlin, 813, 897, 928–929, *929* (illus)
Berlin Airlift, 897
Berlin Conference (1884), 774–775
Berlin Wall, 905, 908
  construction of, 890, *891* (illus)
  fall of, 928–929, *929* (illus), 941
Bethmann-Hollweg, Theobold
    von, 788

Beveridge Report (Britain), 888
Bevin, Ernest, 895, 896, 900
Bible (Christian), 753, 822. *See also*
    Bible (Hebrew)
  on motion of sun, 540
  science and, 540
Bible (Hebrew), 753. *See also* Bible
    (Christian)
Bicycles, 725
Bidault, Georges, 896
"Big Beat" songs (England),
    959–960
Big Three
  at Potsdam, 895
  at Tehran, 892, 894
  at Yalta, 894, *894* (illus), 895
Bill of Rights (England), 522
bin Laden, Osama, 955–956
Biology, 753–754
Birth control, 923, 963
  in 1920s and 1930s, 832
  in Nazi Germany, 839
Birth rate
  in 1930s, 839, 842
Bismarck, Otto von, 787
Black Banner, The (Hirszenberg),
    740 (illus)
Black Hand (Bosnian Serbs), 786
Black Sea region, *778* (illus), 779
Black-Haired Girl (Schiele), 759
Blake, William, 672
Blanc, Louis, 687
Bligh, William, 558
Blitzkrieg, by Nazis, 861, 864, 865,
    868, 872
Blood circulation, 534–535
Blood transfusions, 922
"Bloody Sunday" (Russia), 733
Blue Prussians (Giants of Potsdam), 510
Blum, Léon, 846
Bodin, Jean, 473, 493
Boer War, 781–782
Boers, 781–782
Bohemia. *See also* Czech Republic
  Diet in, 506
  under Habsburgs, 505
  industry in, 669
  religious toleration in, 483
Bolívar, Símon, 583–584, 615
Bolshevik Revolution, 802, 809–812,
    813, 840, 842
  women in, 832–833
Bolshevik Ural Regional Soviet,
    810–811
Bolsheviks and Bolshevism (Russia),
    809–812, 818, 824–825, 836,
    840, 864
  in First World War, 796–797
Bombs and bombings, 726, 787, 875,
    886. *See also* Atomic bomb

Bonaparte family. *See also* Napoleon I
    Bonaparte (France); Napoleon III
    Bonaparte (Louis-Napoleon,
    France)
  Joseph, 644, 695
Boniface VIII (Pope). *See also* Napoleon
    III Bonaparte (Louis-Napoleon,
    France)
Bonn, West Germany, *933* (illus)
Books
  burning of Cathar heretical books.
    See also Libraries
  in Enlightenment, 612
  salons and, 611
Books of the Polish Nation, The
    (Mickiewicz), 695
Boris III, 827
Borodino, battle at, 649
Bosnia, 948, *948* (map), 952
  in First World War, 786, 790
Bosnia-Herzegovina, 948
Bosnian Croats, 948
Bosnian Serbs, 786, 948
  in First World War, 806
Boston Tea Party, 580, *580* (illus)
*Bostonian's Paying the Excise Man or
    Tarring and Feathering, The* (illus),
    580 (illus)
Boundaries. *See also* Borders
  of Russian Empire, 513–514
Bounty (ship), mutiny on, 558–559
Bourbon, Henry. *See* Henry IV (France)
Bourbon family
  in France, 648
  in Kingdom of the Two Sicilies, 705
Bourgeoisie, 594–595. *See also* Middle
    class
  critique of aristocracy by, 595–596
  Marx and Engels on, 688–689
Boxer Rebellion, 780, *780* (illus), 781
Boyars (Russia), 488
Boyle, Robert, 533–534, *534* (illus)
Brabenec, Vratislaw, 938
Bradshawe, John, 519, 521
Brahe, Tycho, 531
Brahms, Johannes, 694
Brandenburg, 507
Brandenburg-Prussia, *509* (map)
    1618-1786, *509* (map)
Brandt, Willy, 930
Braque, Georges, 768
Brazil
  Dutch in, 696
  in First World War, 801
  Portugal and, 561
  slavery in, 553
  social structure in, 574
Brenz, Johann, 472–473
Brest-Litovsk, Treaty of, 797, 802
Bretton Woods Agreement, 894–895, 930

Brezhnev, Leonid, 905, 912, 913–914, 915, 937
Brezhnev Doctrine, 915
Brighton, pavilion in, 578, 578 (illus)
Brindley, James, 666
Brinkmanship, 905, 908
Brissot, Jacques-Pierre, 626, 629
Britain. See England (Britain)
Britain, Battle of, 864, 875
British East India Company, 576
British Empire, 766
  Africa and, 781–782
  Asia and, 775
  Australia and, 777–778, 779
  Boer War and, 781–782
  decolonization and, 902
  expansion of, 554–555
  in First World War, 798–799
  imperialism and, 775, 775–776
  India and, 779, 852–853
  India in, 577 (map)
  industry, trade, and, 680
  Irish Revolution and, 847, 848 (map)
  Kenya and, 902
  nationalism and, 902
  Samoa and, 775–776
  after Second World War, 900–901
British parliament, 864
British Restoration of Pre-War Practices
    Act (1919), 805
Broadlie Mill, 657 (illus)
Bronze Age. See International
    Bronze Age
Brooke, Rupert, 794, 795
Brown, Louise, 962
Broz, Josip, 884. See also Tito
Bruning, Heinrich, 837
Bruno, Giordano, 484
Bubonic plague, as Black Death.
    See also Black Death
Budapest, Hungary, 927
Buenos Aires, 812
Bukharin, Nikolai, 840
Bulgaria, 941
  in 1920s and 1930s, 827
  after the fall of communism, 945
  in First World War, 797–798, 802
  after Second World War, 894
Bultmann, Rudolf, 822
Bureaucracy, 756–757
Burke, Edmund, 686
Burma (Myanmar), 871, 874, 902
  in British Empire, 766
  independence of, 901
  nationalism in, 849
  in Second World War, 869
Business. See also Commerce; Trade
Byelorussia, 824
Byrnes, James, 896
Byron, George (Lord), 696

Byzantine Empire (Byzantium). See also
    specific emperors
Byzantium (city). See Byzantine Empire
    (Byzantium)

Cacao. See Chocolate
Calas, Jean, 606
California, 777
  Russia and, 561
  United States and, 714
Calvin, John, and Calvinism
  in France, 474
  French Huguenots and, 474–475, 497
  spread of, 474
Cambodia, 776, 781, 901 (illus)
Camões, Luis Vaz de, 481
Canada, 933
  English and, 565
  in First World War, 798
  French and, 565
  in Second World War, 873
Candide (Voltaire), 606–607
Cape Colony, 781 (illus), 781–782, 782
Capital
  for continental industrialization, 664
  formation and accumulation of,
    663–664
Capital (Marx), 690
Capitalism, 759, 891, 946, 949
  critics of, 772–773
  imperialism and, 772–773
  science and, 542
Capitalist Realism (West Germany), 920
Captive Wife, The (Gavron), 926
Caribbean region
  British colonies in, 566 (map)
  immigrants from, 924
Carlsbad Decrees (1819), 703
Carol, 827
Carol II (Romania), 835
Carson, Edward, 760
Carthage. See also Punic Wars
Cartwright, Edmund, 657–658
Casanova, Giacomo, 610
Castile, Aragon united with, 502
Castro, Fidel, 908
CAT scan, 922
Catherine de Médicis, 475
Catherine II (the Great, Russia)
  as enlightened despot, 614–615
  French revolution and, 615
  Pugachev and, 594, 615
Catherine of Braganza, 561
Catholic League, procession of, 457 (illus)
Catholicism. See Christianity; Roman
    Catholicism
Catholics
  in Ireland, 847
  in Nazi Germany, 838

  in Second World War, 884
Caucasus region, 778 (illus), 779, 826
    (map), 871
Cavaliers. See Royalists, in England
Cavendish, Margaret, 549
Ceausescu, Nicolai, 914–915, 941
Cellarius, Andreas, 531 (illus)
Censorship
  in Soviet Union, 914
  in wartime, 806
Central America. See also Latin America
Central Europe
  authoritarianism in, 825–828
  democracy in, 820, 945–946
  enlightened despots in, 613
  after the fall of communism, 944–945
  after First World War, 815 (map),
    825–828
  reconstruction of national politics in,
    825–828
Central Powers (First World War),
    785–791, 789 (map), 792–802,
    797 (map), 797–798
Cervantes, Miguel de, 481, 505
Cesi, Federico, 540
Cézanne, Paul, 763
Chadwick, James, 823
Chaldean Empire. See Neo-Babylonian
    Empire
Chamber of Deputies, 698
Chamberlain, Neville, 859, 860, 862, 864
Charles Albert (Piedmont-Sardinia), 708
Charles I (England), 517, 518
  Parliament and, 518
  trial of, 518, 519–521, 520 (illus)
Charles III (Spain), 501
Charles V (Holy Roman Empire), 484
  inflation and, 462
Charles X (France), 698
Charleston (dance), 823, 823 (illus)
Charter 77 (Czechoslovakia), 938
Chartists (England), 701 (illus), 702
Chechnya, nationalism in, 944–945, 952
Cheops. See Khufu (Cheops, Egypt)
Chernenko, Konstantin, 937
Chernobyl nuclear disaster, 937
Chetniks, 884, 885, 948
Child labor
  in mining, 655 (illus)
  Sadler Committee on (Britain), 676–677
Childbearing
  in Protestant and Catholic families, 673
Children. See also Families
China, 779. See also Manchuria
  Austria-Hungary and, 780
  Boxer Rebellion in, 780, 780 (illus), 781
  détente and, 930
  England (Britain) and, 780
  Europeans and, 575–579
  in First World War, 798

China (*Continued*)
France and, 780
Germany and, 780
imperialism and, 766, 776, 776
(illus), 777, 780
Japan and, 779, 780, 781, 798, *858*
(illus), 860
Korean War and, 904–905
nationalism in, 849
Rape of Nanking and, 858
revolution in, 781
Russia and, 779, 780
scramble in, 780
United States and, 780, 781
Vietnam War and, 909
Chinese Exclusion Act (1882), 777
Chinese immigrants, 777, 778
Chinoiserie, 578
Chiswick House (England), 592
Chocolate
as a beverage, 568
Chocolate, in Old World and New
World, 568–569
Chocolate House, The, 569 (illus)
Cholera, 752
Chopin, Frédéric, 695
Christ. *See* Jesus Christ (Jesus of
Nazareth)
Christian, Fletcher, 558
Christian Church. *See also* Christianity;
Roman Catholicism
Christian Democrats, 916–917, 922,
932, 945
Christianity, 890, 922, 962. *See also* Bible
(Christian); Jesus Christ (Jesus of
Nazareth); Latin Christianity; Ortho-
dox Christianity; Roman Catholicism
evolutionary theory and, 753, 754, 765
at the *fin-de-siècle*, 764–765
after First World War, 822
imperialism and, 769
after Second World War, 922
Voltaire on, 606
Christians, 817, 962–963
Church(es), 922. *See* Roman Catholicism
Churchill, Winston, 791, 864, 875, 887,
892, 894, *894* (illus), 895, 897
on appeasement, 862–863
Battle of Omduran and, 750
Iron Curtain and, 892, 897
Second World War and, 871
at Tehran, 892, 894
at Yalta, 894, *894* (illus), 895, 897
Cities and towns. *See also* City-states;
specific locations; Villages
growth of, 460–461
industrial, 679–680, 724
wealthy and poor in, 457
workers' lifestyles in, 735–736
Civil Code (France), 641–642, 644

Civil Constitution of the Clergy
(France, 1790), 620, 622, 641
Civil society, 935, 936, 946
Civil war(s)
in England, 474, 517–521
French Wars of Religion as, 474–477
Civilization(s). *See also* specific civiliza-
tions; Western world (the West)
Western, 755, 766, 768, 777, 818,
851, 856, 860, 904, 929, 951,
954–955
Class consciousness, 673
Classes. *See also* Elites; Society; specific
groups
in industrial Europe, 673–674
Classical Age: in Greece. *See also*
Classical learning; Greece
(ancient); Hellenistic Age
Classicism: in arts, 693
Cleland, John, 610
Clemenceau, George, 803, 814
Clergy
celebacy of, 923
in France, 620, 622
Voltaire on, 606
Clermont (ship), 774
Clients. *See* Patron-client system
Climate change, 964
Clinton, Bill, on terrorism, 951
Clive, Robert, 576
Cloning, 962
Cloth and clothing. *See* Textiles and
textile industry
Coal and coal mining
in Britain, 659
child labor in, *655* (illus)
Coalbrookdale by Night (Louther-
bourg), *659* (illus)
Coca-Cola, 923
Coca-Colonization, 923–924
Code breakers, 883
Coffee, 569
Coffeehouses, 568–570, 611
Colbert, Jean-Baptiste, 499, 505
Cold War, 888, 890–891, 891–900,
892–900, *893* (map), 921, 927,
930, 933, 949
in 1950s and 1960s, 911–915
decolonization and, 900–910
détente during, 930, 932–933, 934
end of, 928–929, 934, 939–940,
942, 957
Europe and, *911* (map)
globalization of, 904–905, 908
Middle East and, 909, *910* (map)
protests and, 926
Vietnam War and, 909
women and, 925
Coleridge, Samuel Taylor, 578, 693
Collectivization, 840–841, 912, 914

Colleges. *See* Universities and colleges
Collingwood, Luke, 571
Cologne, Germany, 875
Colonies and colonization. *See also*
Empire(s); Imperialism; New
imperialism; Revolution
Portuguese, 560–561
Colorado, 777
Comédie Française, 500
Commerce. *See also* Trade
Dutch Empire and, 557–558
Commercial agriculture, 459–460
Commission of Science and Arts
(France), 646
Committee of Public Safety (France),
628–629, 632–633
Common Life. *See* Brothers of the
Common Life
Common Market, 917. *See also*
European Economic Community
Common Sense (Paine), 609
Communards (Paris), 684, 718
(illus)
Communes. *See also* Paris Commune
Communication(s). *See* Transportation;
Writing
Communion. *See also* Eucharist
Communism and communists, 840,
849, 854, 864, 890–891, 912, 929,
945–946
British fears of, 861
in China, 849
collapse of, 928–929, 934–937
in concentration camps, 880
in Czechoslovakia, 898–900, 915
in Eastern Europe, 895–896
fears of, 837
in Germany, 813, 827
in Greece, 895
Marx and, 690
in Nazi Germany, 838
in Poland, 914
in Romania, 914–915
in Russia, 824
in Second World War, 879, 884
in Soviet Union, 840–842
women and, 832–833
Communist Manifesto, The (Marx and
Engels), 674, 688–690
Communist Party, 824, 912
in China, 849
in Germany, 837
in Soviet Union, 840, 842, 939
in Western Europe, 916
Communist Party of Czechoslovakia
(CPC), 898–900
Comte, August, 693
Concentration camps, *878* (illus)
in Boer War, 782
death camps as, 880

in Second World War, 856, *857*
(illus), 881–882
Concert of Europe, 696
Concord (city), 580
Concordat (France), 641, 644
*Condition of the Working Class in
England in 1884, The* (Engels), 672
Condorcet, Marquis de, 607, 630
Confession of Augsburg, 463
Confessions, 456
confessional states and, 472–483
Congo, 774–775, 901
Congress of Victors, 840, 842
Congress of Vienna (1815), 649, 695
Conservative Party (Britain), 862, 932.
See also Tories (England)
Conservatives and conservatism,
686–687, 916
Constantinople (Istanbul). *See also*
Byzantine Empire
Consulate (France), 633, 644
Consumers
demand by, 664
Consumption, 917, 917–923
chocolate and patterns of, 568
imperialism and, 766
secularism and, 765
Contraceptives, 923, 963
Convents. *See* Nunneries; Nuns
Cook, James, 555, 777
Copernicus, Nicolaus, 532, 538
heliocentric theory of, 531, 540
papacy and, 540–541
Corday, Charlotte, 638
Corn Law (England, 1815), 701
Corporal punishment, in Germany,
706–707
Corporate capitalism, 759
Corporatism, 834
Cortes (Spanish assembly), 494, 695
Cosimo II de' Medici, 540
Costa Rica, 801
Cottage industry
in United States, 669
Cotton and cotton industry, 657
production of, 657
Cotton mills, 657
Council of Trent, 463
Counter Reformation. *See* Catholic
Reformation
Court (royal):
of Rudolf II (Holy Roman Empire), 484
at Versailles, 498
Court Chamber (Austria), 510
Court-martial, of Bounty mutineers,
558–559
Covenant of the League of
Nations, 816
Credulity, Superstition, and Fanaticism
(Hogarth), *602* (illus)

Creoles
in Spanish America, 583
Crick, Francis, 920–921
Crime
auto-da-fé and, 466–467
in cities, 735–736
infanticide in Enlightenment, 604
Crimean War, 716–717
Russia, Ottoman Empire, and, 716–717
Critique of Pure Reason (Kant), 607
Croatia, 946, 947, 948, *948* (map)
Croats, 825, 885, 948
Crompton, Samuel, 656–658
Cromwell, Oliver, 518, 521
Crops. *See also* Agriculture
Crystal Palace Exhibition (London,
1851), *656* (illus)
Cuba, 801, 891, 905
U.S. acquisition of, 777, 781
Cuban Missile Crisis, 905, 908
Cubism, 763
Cugoano, Quobna Ottobah, 572–573
"Cult of the Duce" (Italy), 834
Cult of the leader, 834, 844–845
Cult of the Supreme Being, 637
Cultural theory, 958–959
Culture(s). *See also* Art(s);
Enlightenment; Popular culture;
Renaissance; Society
in 1950s and 1960s, 917–923
Atlantic world, 573–574
European attitudes toward Asian,
576–579
ideology and, 692–695
non-European, 599
scientific rationalism and, 692–693
Curie, Marie, 756
Customs unions
in continental Europe, *667* (map)
Zollverein as, 666, 703
Czech people
revolutions of 1848 and, 702–704
Czech Republic, 941, 942, *950* (map).
See also Bohemia; Poland-Lithuania
after the fall of communism, 945
Czechoslovakia, 899, 909, 936–937,
938, *950* (map)
collectivization in, 914
communism in, 897, 898–900
democracy in, 825
de-Stalinization of, 915
expansion of Nazi Germany and, 859
fall of communism in, 941, 942
in First World War, 786
after First World War, 814, *815*
(map), 816, 825, 858, 862
Marshall Plan and, 896
Prague Spring and, 915
Resistance movement in, 884
in Second World War, 860

after Second World War, 892, *893*
(map), 894
Slánský trial in, 898–900
Czechoslovakian Communist Party, 915
Czechs, 816

Daladier, Edouard, 859
Dalhousie, Lord, 576
Damascus, Syria, *826* (map)
Dance, *854* (illus)
after First World War, 823, *823* (illus)
"Dancing Building," *959* (illus)
Dandyism, 761
Danton, George-Jacques, 627
Danube River, 936
Darwin, Charles, 753, 754, *754* (illus),
755, 765, 782
Das Kapital (Marx). *See Capital* (Marx)
David, Jacques-Louis, 635
Dawes Plan, 828
Daylight Saving Time, 803
Dayton Accords, 946, 948
D-Day, 873
De Beauvoir, Simone, 925
De Bonald, Louis, 687
De Gaulle, Charles, 884, 904, 923
De Gouges, Marie Olympe Aubrey,
624–625, 632
De Maistre, Joseph, 687
De Sade, Donatien François (Marquis
de), 610
DeAk, Edit, 957
Death camps, in Second World War,
856, 880
Death of Marat, The (David), *638* (illus)
Debret, Jean-Baptiste, 553
Decembrist Revolt (Russia), 697–698
De-Christianization: in France, 636
Declaration of Independence, 580
Enlightenment and, 615–616
Locke's Two Treatises and, 522
Paine and, 609
*Declaration of the Basic Rights of the
German People* (1848), 702, 704
*Declaration of the Rights of Man and
Citizen* (France, 1789), 620,
624–625, 691
Decolonization, *903* (map)
protests and, 926
after Second World War, 900–910
Decorative art, chinoiserie as, 578
Deductive reasoning, 536
Dee, John, 484
Defenestration of Prague, 506, *507*
(illus)
Deffand, Madame du, 611
Degas, Edgar, *758* (illus)
Degeneration, 757, 758
Deities. *See* Gods and goddesses;
Religion(s); specific deities

Delacroix, Eugène, *685* (illus), 696
Demand, 462
    inelastic, 462
Democracy, 891
    in 1930s, 839–840
    in Eastern Europe, 825
    after First World War, 820
    First World War and, 803
    in Germany, 814
    in West, 916–917
Democritus of Abdera (Greece), 538
Demoiselles d'Avignon, Les (Picasso),
    768 (illus), 768–769
Demonic magic, 470
Demonstrations. *See also* Protest(s)
Denmark, 885, 949–950, 963
    in the 1970s, 931
    in Second World War, 861, 868
Depression (economic). *See* Great
    Depression
Derrida, Jacques, 958–959
Descartes, René, 536, 543, 549
    dualism of, 537
Descent of Man, The (Darwin), 754
Desmoulins, Camille, 618
Despots, enlightened, 613
De-Stalinization, 912–913, *913* (illus)
    of Hungary, 914
Détente, 930, 934
    end of, 932–933
    Helsinki Accords and, 933
Developing world. *See also* South
    (global); Third World
Devil
    witchcraft and, 470
DeVries, Hugo, 754
Diabolism, 470
Dialectic, 689
Dialectic materialism, 689
*Dialogue Concerning the Two Chief
    World Systems* (Galileo), 533,
    546–547
Dictatorships, 827–828
Diderot, Denis, *598* (illus)
    Catherine II (Russia) and, 614
Dien Bien Phu, Battle of, 902, *904*
    (illus), 909
Diet (assembly)
    of Brandenburg, 510
Diet (food), chocolate in, 568
Directory (France), 632–633
Discipline
    of children, 465
    confessional identities and,
    463–464
Discourse on the Method (Descartes),
    543, 546
*Discourse on the Origin on Inequality
    Among Men* (Rousseau),
    603, 608

*Discourses on the Two New Sciences
    of Motion and Mechanics*
    (Galileo), 533
Disease. *See also* Black Death
    in cities, 735–736
Displaced persons (DPs), after Second
    World War, 892. *See also* Refugees
*Disquisition on the Spiritual Condition
    of Infants*, 465
Dissection, 535, *535* (illus)
Dissenters, in American colonies. *See
    also* Puritans
Dissidents, 933. *See also* Revolts and
    rebellions
Divine right, 687
    Charles I (England) and, 521
    theory of, 494, 521–522, 607
Dix, Otto, *821* (illus), 822
DNA, 920–921, 922
Doctors. *See* Medicine
Dodd, Robert, 558
Does Germany Need Colonies?, 771
Dolly the sheep, 962
Domesticity
    separate spheres theory, 609
    women and, 609
Don Quixote (Cervantes), 481, 505
Doré, Gustave, 673
Double standard: sexual, 744–745
Douglas, Alfred (Lord), 760–761,
    761 (illus)
Dr. Jekyll and Mr. Hyde (Stevenson), 757
Dracula (Stoker), 757
Draft (military).. *See* Conscription
Drama
    Comédie Française as, 500
Dreyfus, Alfred, 730–733, *732* (illus)
Dreyfus Affair (France), 730–733
    anti-Semitism and, 730–733
    French national identity and, 730–733
Drinking. *See* alcohol
Dual Alliance, 787
Dualism: of Descartes, 537
Dubcek, Alexander, 915
Duce (Leader), Mussolini as, 834
Dulles, John Foster, 905
Duma (Russia), 733, 808
Duncan, Isadora, 820
Dunkirk, 861
Durkheim, Emile, 765
Dutch, 779. *See also* Dutch Republic;
    Holland; Netherlands
    Boer War and, 781–782
    revolt against Spain by, 478, 479
    (map)
    slave trade and, 570
    trading companies of, 523
Dutch East India Company, 557
Dutch Factory of Batavia in Indonesia,
    557 (illus)

Dutch Reformed Church, 524
Dutch Republic (United Provinces of
    the Netherlands), 479 (map), 480,
    523–525. *See also* Dutch; Holland;
    Netherlands
    industry in, 669
Dynasties. *See also* specific dynasties

Early Modern Europe, peoples of,
    458–463
Earth
    Aristotle on, 530
East, the, 576
East Asia, Opium War in, 680–681
East Berlin, 890, *891* (illus), 897, 905,
    908, 928–929, *929* (illus)
East Germany, 890, *891* (illus), 897,
    905, 908, 928–929, *929* (illus),
    936, 945. *See also* Germany and;
    West Germany
    fall of Berlin Wall and, 941
    fall of communism in, 941, 942
East Jerusalem, 952
East Prussia
    in First World War, 796–798
    after Second World War, *893* (map)
Easter Rising (Ireland), 847
Eastern Christianity. *See* Orthodox
    Christianity
Eastern Europe, 933, 949. *See also*
    specific countries
    in 1950s and 1960s, 911–915, 927
    anti-Semitism in, 898
    authoritarianism in, 825–828
    Cold War and, 911–915
    collectivization in, 914
    communism in, 895–896
    crises in 1970s, 934–937
    democracy in, 820, 825, 945–946
    de-Stalinization of, 912, 914
    dissent in, 914–915
    diversity of, 914–915
    economies in, 934–935
    environmentalism in, 936–937
    after the fall of communism, 944–945
    fall of communism in, 940–941, *943*
    (map)
    in First World War, 784–786, *785*,
    795–798, *797* (map), 805
    after First World War, *815* (map),
    818, 825–828
    national self-determination and,
    814–815
    nationalism in, 714–716, 785–786, 942
    peasant rebellions in, 594
    reconstruction of national politics in,
    825–828
    revolutions of 1989 in, 940–941
    after Second World War, 888
    states and confessions in, 483–490

Eastern Front, 885, 886, 887
  in Second World War, 872, 873
Eastern Front (First World War),
  795–798, 797 (map)
Eastern Roman Empire. *See also*
  Byzantine Empire; Western Roman
  Empire
Eating habits, table fork and, 468,
  468 (illus)
Ebert, Friedrich, 813
Eclecticism, postmodernist, 957
Ecology. *See* Environment and
  environmentalism
economic crisis of 1970s, 930–931
Economy and economics. *See also*
  Great Depression; Industrial
  Revolution; Industrialization
  in 1920s and 1930s, 848–849
  in Atlantic region, 565–574, 567,
    567 (map)
  ideology and, 848–849
  imperialism and, 766–767
  laissez-faire and, 686, 755
ECSC. *See* European Coal and Steel
  Community (ECSC)
Eden, Anthony, 909
Edict of Nantes, 477, 497, 499
Edison, Thomas, 723
Education. *See also* Schools
  humanism and, 543
  Scientific Revolution and, 543
Egypt, 909
  in 1920s and 1930s, 850
  after First World War, 817
  France and, 646
  Napoleon and, 633
  nationalism in, 849
  in Second World War, 870
  Suez Crisis and, 909
Egypt (ancient). *See also* Gods and
  goddesses
  Muslim Brotherhood in, 850
Eichmann, Adolf, 879
  trial of, 881 (illus), 881–883
*Eichmann in Jerusalem: A Report on
  the Banality of Evil* (Arendt), 882
Eiffel, Gustave, 723
Eiffel Tower, 723
Einsatzgruppen, 879, 879 (illus), 883
Einstein, Albert, 756, 823
Eire, 826 (map)
Eisenhower, Dwight, 876, 905,
  908, 909
Ekaterinburg, 810
El Alamein, Battle of, 869, 870–871, 871
Élan, 792
Elba: Napoleon on, 649
Elbe River, 877
Electors, of Brandenburg, 508
Eliot, T. S., 822

Elisabeth of Bohemia, 549
Elites. *See also* Aristocracy; Nobility
Elitism, 957
Elizabeth I (England), 482, 482 (illus).
  See also Elizabethan Renaissance
  inflation and, 462
Elizabethan Renaissance (England), 482
Emigration. *See also* Slave trade
  after 1870, 724
Emile, or an Education (Rousseau), 607
*Emperor Napoleon Crowning his Wife,
  Josephine, Empress of the French
  in the Cathedral of Notre Dame*
  (David), 639 (illus)
Emperors. *See also* specific empires and
  emperors
  Napoleon as, 633
Empire(s). *See also* Byzantine Empire;
  Colonies and colonization; Roman
  Empire; specific empires
  in Americas, 554
  Dutch, 557
  European overseas, 554 (map)
  French, 556–557
  Portuguese, 560–561
  Spanish, 560
Empirical data, 535
Empirical observation, 535
Employment. *See also* Labor; Workers
  of children, 672–673
Enabling Act (Germany), 836, 837
Encyclopedia (Diderot and Alembert),
  598, 607, 611–612
Energy. *See* Power (energy)
Engels, Friedrich, 675, 688
  Communist Manifesto, The (Marx
    and Engels), 674, 688–690
England (Britain), 847, 848 (map), 868,
  934 (illus), 949–950
  in 1920s and 1930s, 826 (map), 832
  in 1930s, 846
  in 1950s and 1960s, 916, 920
  in the 1970s, 931
  absolutism and, 521–526
  anti-Semitism in, 883
  Asia and, 775
  British East India Company and, 576
  Chartist movement in, 701 (illus)
  China and, 780
  coal industry in, 659
  in Concert of Europe, 696
  continental industrialization and, 664
  Corn Laws in, 701
  decolonization and, 900–901
  Elizabethan Renaissance in, 482
  expansion of Nazi Germany and, 859
  in First World War, 784–785, 787,
    790–791, 797 (map), 798–805,
    805 (illus), 806
  after First World War, 821–822

  franchise extended in, 726
  game laws in, 586
  German rearmament and, 905
  Glorious Revolution in, 518,
    521–526, 590
  Great Depression in, 835
  Haitian Revolution and, 581
  Hong Kong ceded to, 681
  immigration to, 924 (illus), 931
  imperialism and, 750, 767, 775–776
  India and, 851, 900–901
  Ireland and, 582
  Israel and, 902
  liberal reforms in, 699–702
  Middle East and, 817, 826 (map), 902
  monarchy in, 517
  mutiny on *Bounty* and, 558–559
  North America and, 566 (map)
  Price Revolution in, 462–463
  religion and, 922
  religion in, 764
  Samoa and, 775–776
  in Second Coalition, 633
  in Second World War, 856, 860–865,
    868–875, 883–884, 887–888
  after Second World War, 892,
    894–897, 900
  slave trade and, 570–571
  social welfare in, 887–888
  Spanish Civil War and, 846
  Sudan and, 750
  Suez Crisis and, 909
  textile industry in, 669
  in Third World, 644
  in United Kingdom, 518
  Voltaire on, 606
  women in, 886
  at Yorktown, 580
Enigma, 883
Enlightened absolutism, 613–615
Enlightened despots, 613
Enlightenment, 596–610
  Americas and, 615
  Asian cultures and, 598–599
  in Europe, 597 (map)
  impact of, 610–612
  limits of, 612–613
  literacy and, 610
  political theory in, 606–610
  revolution and, 615–616
  scientific rationalism and, 692–693
  sexuality and, 610
  themes of, 596–602
  Voltaire and, 606
  women in, 609
Enola Gay (airplane), 876
*Enquiry Concerning Human
  Understanding* (Hume), 607
Entertainment. *See also* specific types
Environment and environmentalism, 964

environmentalism, 931, 932, 936–937
Epic literature. *See also* specific works
Epidemics. *See also* Black Death;
    Disease
    in cities, 735–736
Episcopalian Church. *See* Church of
    England
Equiano, Olaudah, 552
Essay Concerning Human Understanding (Locke), 607
Essay on Crimes and Punishments
    (Beccaria), 601, 607
Essay on the Principle of Population
    (Malthus), 670
Essen, German, Krupp steel in, 668
    (illus)
Estates General (France), 494, 620
Estonia, 809, 826 (map)
    in 1920s and 1930s, 827
    authoritarianism in, 827
    after First World War, 815 (map)
Eta (Basque separatists), 951
Ethiopia, 772 (map), 775, 858
    Italy and, 858, 860
Ethnic cleansing, in former Yugoslavia,
    948, 949
Ethnic groups and ethnicity, 924–925
Ethnographic Museum, 768
EU. *See* European Union (EU)
Eucharist. *See also* Communion
Eugenics, 832
Euro (currency), 949
Euro-Islam, 956 (illus), 956–957
Europe. *See* Europe and Europeans
    contemporary, 950 (map)
    Islam and, 951–957
    Muslims in, 956, 956 (illus)
Europe and Europeans, 923
    in 1920s and 1930s, 821–828, 826
        (map)
    in 1950s and 1960s, 915–926, 927
    age of affluence in, 917
    Americanization and, 923–924
    Asia and, 575–579
    Cold War and, 892–900, 911 (map)
    after Congress of Vienna (1815), 650
        (map)
    democracy and, 916–917
    economic integration of, 917
    expansion by, 556 (map)
    before First World War, 789 (map)
    after First World War, 815 (map)
    ideological encounters in, 695–708
    immigration to, 924–925
    imperialism and, 766–769, 773–781,
        776 (illus)
    industrialization on Continent, 666
    in late nineteenth century, 729 (map)
    McDonald's in, 924
    under occupation, 885–886

    overseas empires of, 556 (map)
    religion and, 764
    after Second World War, 890–891,
        892–900, 893 (map)
European Community (EC), 949
European Court of Justice, 949
European Economic Community
    (EEC), 917, 949. *See also* Common
    Market
European Parliament, 949
European Union (EU), 949–951, 950
    (map), 957
"Evil Empire," Soviet Union as, 933
Evolution of humans, 753–754, 754
    (illus)
Evolutionary science, 753–754, 754
    (illus), 765, 782
Exchange Bank (Amsterdam), 523
Executions
    by guillotine, 628
    of Louis XVI (France), 629,
        631 (illus)
Existentialism, 822, 918, 920
Expansion. *See also* Empire(s)
    European, 556 (map)
Experimentation, scientific, 535
Expressionism, in painting, 763

Fabri, Friedrich, 771
Factories
    child labor in, 676–677
    industrial, 659–660
    working conditions in, 672
Factory Act (Britain, 1833), 673
Faisal (Syria and Iraq), 817
Faith. *See also* Confessions;
    Justification by faith;
    Theology
Falkenhayn, Erich von, 795
Families
    in 1950s and 1960s, 925
    children in, 672–673
    Lenin on, 832–833
    in Nazi Germany, 838–839
    in Soviet Union, 832–833, 842
Famine. *See also* Starvation
    Ireland and, 682
Fanatic and fanaticism, 487
    assassination of Henry IV (France)
        and, 477, 496, 497
    use of term, 474
Far East. *See also* East, the; specific
    countries
Farms and farming. *See also*
    Agriculture; Peasants
Fascism, 840, 843–847, 888, 916
    in Italy, 833–834, 844–845
    spread of, 834–835
    women and, 838–839, 839 (illus)
Fascist Party, 833–835

Fathers. *See* Families
Fauves (artists), 772
Feast of the Federation (France), 637,
    637 (illus)
February Revolution, 807–808, 808
    (illus)
federalism, 945–946
Feminine Mystique, The (Friedan), 926
Feminism, 741, 931–932, 934, 957–958,
    963. *See also* specific rights; Women
    in 1950s and 1960s, 925–926
    at the *fin-de-siècle*, 758–759
Ferdinand II (Aragon), 502
Ferdinand II (Bohemia, Hungary, Holy
    Roman Empire), 510
Ferdinand II (Kingdom of the Two
    Sicilies), 705, 708
Ferdinand VII (Spain), 695
Ferry, Jules, 770–771
Fertile Crescent. *See* Levantine Corridor
Fertility, 925
Fertility treatments, 962
Figure with Meat (Bacon), 920 (illus)
Film. *See* Movies
Final Solution, 879, 880
Finances. *See also* Taxation
Fin-de-siècle (end of the century)
    culture, 757–765
Finland, 809
    in 1920s and 1930s, 826 (map)
    after First World War, 815 (map)
First Balkan War, 797
First Consul, Napoleon as, 634
First Opium War, 681
First World War, 783–819, 785 (illus),
    793 (illus), 798 (illus), 848,
    857, 886
    aftermath of, 818, 820–824
    Eastern Front, 795–798, 797 (map)
    end of, 802
    Europe before (map), 789 (map)
    events leading to Second World War
        after, 858
    genocide and, 806–807
    globalization of, 800 (map)
    home fronts in, 802
    impact of, 804–805
    naval warfare in, 799–801
    origins of, 784–791
    propaganda in, 805–807
    revolution and, 807–817
    social impact of, 804–805
    trench warfare in, 792 (illus),
        792–795, 818
    war effort in, 805–807
    Western Front, 792–795, 801–802
Fission. *See* Nuclear fission
Five Orchestral Pieces (Schoenberg), 763
Flanders, 885
Flanders (Dix), 821 (illus), 822

Florida, 714
  colonization of, 563
Foch, Ferdinand, 795
Fontenelle, Bernard de, 543
Forced labor
  in Africa, 775
  from concentration camps, 880
  in Nazi-occupied Europe, 878 (map),
    880, 883, 885
  in Soviet Union, 842
Fort William, India, 575
Forts. See Trading posts
Forum. See Roman Forum
Foucault, Michel, 958, 959
Fouché, Joseph, 636
Fournier, Jacques. See Benedict XII (Pope)
Fourteen Points, 814
Fox, George, 555
France, 765
  in 1920s and 1930s, 828, 832
  in 1930s, 846
  in 1950s and 1960s, 916, 917,
    919, 920
  in the 1970s, 931
  absolutism in, 494–497
  academies in, 480, 634–635
  administration of, 642
  Algeria and, 902, 904
  anti-German policies of, 814, 828, 861
  Asia and, 775, 781
  boundaries of, 500 (map)
  China and, 780
  Concert of Europe and, 696
  decolonization and, 900–901, 902,
    904, 904 (illus)
  Dreyfus Affair and, 730–733
  expansion of Nazi Germany and, 859
  feudalism in, 620
  in First World War, 784–785,
    789–795, 801–805
  after First World War, 814, 816, 818,
    821–822
  Franco-Algerian War and, 906
  Gaullism and, 923–924
  German occupation of, 864, 868,
    871, 873, 884
  Goncourt Prize in, 853
  Great Depression in, 835
  Haitian Revolution and, 581
  Huguenots in, 474–475
  immigration to, 931
  imperialism and, 766, 775, 781
  Indochina and, 776, 900–902, 904
    (illus), 904–905, 909
  liberation of, 873
  Middle East and, 826 (map)
  under Napoleon, 640–642
  Paris Commune in, 627, 633
  political culture in, 635–638
  protests in, 926

  republic in (1792-1799), 623–634
  Resistance movement in, 884
  Revolution of 1848 in, 702–703
  revolutionary calendar in, 637
  Second Empire in, 717
  in Second World War, 860–864, 868,
    871, 873, 884
  after Second World War, 894, 895,
    897, 900
  slave trade and, 570
  Soviet Union and, 923
  Spanish Civil War and, 846
  Suez Crisis and, 909
  textile industry in, 669
  Third Republic in, 717, 729–730
  Voltaire on, 606
Franchise, 745
  expansion of, 726
Francis I (France), 475
Francis II (Kingdom of the two
  Sicilies), 705
Francis Joseph (Austria-Hungary), 715
Franco, Francisco, 846
Franco-Algerian War, 901, 902, 904,
  906–907
Franco-Prussian War, 712, 717–718,
  757, 787
Franco-Russian Alliance, 787,
  788–789
Frankenstein (Shelley), 695
Frankfurt Parliament, 702
Franks. See also Carolingian empire
Franz Ferdinand (Austria), assassina-
  tion of, 784, 786, 786 (illus), 787,
  790, 791
Frederick II (the Great, Prussia), 613
Frederick William (Great Elector), 508
Frederick WIlliam IV (Prussia), 702
  Frankfurt Parliament and, 702
Free coloreds, in Haiti, 581
Free Corps (Germany), 827
Free French, 884
Free trade
  in Britain, 701
Freedom of the Sea, The (Grotius), 523
Freemasons, 611
Freethinking, of Spinoza, 544
Free-trade zones
  United Kingdom as, 666
French, John, 795
French Academy of Sciences, 500,
  540, 612
French and Indian War. See Seven
  Years' War
*French Army Halts at Syene, Upper
  Egypt. . ., The* (Tardieu),
  646 (illus)
French Assembly, 864
French Departments during the
  Revolution, 643 (map)

French East India Company, 556
French Empire, 556–557
  in First World War, 798
  under Napoleon, 645 (map)
French Indochina, 781
French language, 480, 500
French National Assembly, 770–771
French Revolution (1789 and 1792),
  492, 565. See also Napoleon I
  Bonaparte (France)
  beginning of, 620–622
  culture change during, 634–638
  Enlightenment and, 615
  First (1789-1791), 620–622
  Jacobins and, 623, 627–629
  legacy of, 651–652
  Reign of Terror in, 628–632
French Revolution (1830), 697, 698
French Revolution (1848), 702–703
French Wars of Religion, 474–477
French West Africa, First World War
  and, 798
Freud, Sigmund, 755, 757, 851
Friars Minor (Lesser Brothers). See
  Franciscans
Friedan, Betty, 926
Fronde (France), 497
Front National, 931
Fustat, Egypt. See Cairo
Futurists (painters), 762

G8, 964
Gaelic people, in Ireland, 582
Galicia, 796–798
  after First World War, 815 (map)
  in Second World War, 866
Galilei, Galileo, 528, 539
  mathematics and, 536
  physics and, 532
  on separation of religion and
    science, 545
Gandhi, Mohandas (Mahatma), 851,
  852 (illus), 852–853, 902
Garibaldi, Giuseppe, 709, 711 (illus)
Gas, Boyle on, 533
Gas chambers, 880
Gauguin, Paul, 751 (illus), 772, 783
Gaullism, politics of, 923–924
Gavron, Hannah, 926
Gay rights, 963
Gehry, Frank, 959 (illus)
Gender and gender issues, 755,
  832–833, 923, 925–926. See also
  Men; Women
  in 1920s and 1930s, 828, 831–833
  at the *fin-de-siècle*, 758–759
  in First World War, 804–805
  after First World War, 805, 824
  Social Darwinism and, 755
  in Soviet Union, 832 (illus)

General Will
  de Gouges and, 625
  Robespierre and, 629
  Rousseau on, 608, 615, 629
Genetics, 754, 757, 832, 920–921, 962
Geneva summit, 905, 908
Genocide, 878–879, 946
  Armenian massacre, 806 (illus)
  Eichmann trial, 881–883
  evolution in Second World War,
    877–880
  in First World War, 806–807
  in former Yugoslavia, 948
Geoffrin, Madame, 587, 611
Geoffroy, Jean Jules Henri, 727 (illus)
Geology, 753–754
George III (England), 777
Georgia (republic), 812, 942, 944
  after First World War, 824
German Empire. See also Germany
  proclamation of, 712
German National Assembly, 702
German Social Democratic Party, 916
German Surgeon Theodor Billroth at
    Work in Vienna (Seligmann), 752
    (illus)
Germanic tribes. See also specific tribes
German-Soviet Non-Aggression Pact,
    859 (map), 859–860, 861, 865,
    868, 878, 892, 894
Germany, 825, 890, 891 (illus), 897,
    932. See also German Empire; Holy
    Roman Empire; Nazi Germany
  in 1920s and 1930s, 825, 825–828,
    835–838, 847
  Africa and, 781–782, 782, 847
  annexation of Southwest Africa,
    781, 782
  Asia and, 847
  Battle of Britain and, 864
  Carlsbad Decrees in, 703
  China and, 780
  communists in, 813
  democracy in, 814
  expansion of Nazi Germany,
    858–860, 859 (map)
  in First World War, 784, 787–790,
    790 (illus), 791–800, 800 (map),
    801–806
  after First World War, 814, 815
    (map), 816, 825–828, 862
  German-Soviet Non-Aggression Pact,
    859–860
  Great Depression in, 835, 837
  imperialism and, 766, 767, 775–776
  industrialization of, 666
  invasion of Soviet Union, 864–868
  Junkers in, 667
  League of Nations and, 858
  Nazi Empire, 866 (map)

prostitution in, 706–707
  rearmament of, 837–838
  reparations after First World War,
    814, 827–828
  reunification of, 941, 945
  revolution in, 812–813
  revolution of 1848 in, 702–704
  Samoa and, 775–776
  in Second World War, 856–857,
    860–871, 873–875, 877–883, 885
  after Second World War, 892, 893
    (map), 894–896
  Soviet Union and, 861
  Spanish Civil War and, 846
  steel industry in, 669
  Thirty Years' War and, 474, 506
  unification of, 711–712, 787
  Versailles Treaty and, 814
  Weimar Republic (Germany), 825–829
  women in, 886
  Zollverein in, 666, 703
Gestapo, 881
Ghana
  independence of, 901, 903 (map)
Gheorghiu-Dej, Gheorghe, 914–915
Ghettoization, 877–878
Giacometti, Alberto, 918, 918
    (illus), 920
Girondins, in French Revolution,
    627–629, 630
Glasnost, 937, 940 (illus)
Global economy, chocolate and, 568
Global North. See North (global)
Global South. See South (global)
Globalization, 964
Glorious Revolution (England), 518,
    521–526
Goa, Portugal and, 560
Gods and goddesses. See also
    Religion(s); specific dieties
"God's Wife" (Egypt). See also
    Hatshepsut
Goebbels, Joseph, 886
Golan Heights, 909, 952
Gold coins: in Rome. See also Coins
Golden Age, in Spanish literature,
    481–482
Golding, John, 768
Golding, William, 919
Goldsmith Girls in a Peugeot. . .(Julius
    LeBlanc Stewart), 743 (illus)
Gömbös, Gyula, 827
Gomulka, Wladislaw, 912, 914
Goncourt Prize, 853
Gorbachev, Mikhail, 934, 937, 939,
    941, 942
Gottwald, Klement, 898
Gouges, Marie Olympe Aubrey de. See
    De Gouges, Marie Olympe
    Aubrey

Government(s). See also specific
    countries
  in continental industrialization, 664
  in First World War, 803, 805–807
  Hobbes on, 494
  Locke on, 522
  Price Revolution and, 462–463
  standing armies of, 494–495
  Voltaire on, 606
Goya, Francisco, 648
Grand Alliance, 501
Grand Army, of Napoleon, 647
Gravitation, 532–533
  Newton on, 533
Great Britain. See England (Britain)
Great Depression, 834–835, 839–840,
    844–846, 848–849, 858, 860, 888
  of 1873, 721–722
  in Germany, 836–837
"Great Fear" (France), 620, 622
Great Northern War, 505, 514
Great Purge, 840, 842–843
Greece, 850, 865, 895, 911 (map)
  in the 1970s, 932
  in First World War, 797
  after First World War, 814, 816
  immigrants from, 924
  independence of, 698
  nationalist revolt (1821) in, 696–698
  Resistance movement in, 884
  in Second World War, 865, 868, 884
Greece (ancient). See also Hellenistic Age
  Africa and, 773
  communism in, 896
Green politics, 932
Greenham Common Protests, 934
    (illus)
Gropius, Walter, 822
Gross National Product, 925 (table)
Grosz, George, 828 (illus)
Grotius, Hugo, 523
Guadalcanal, 871
Guam, 777, 869
Guatemala, 801
Guestworkers, 924. See also Immi-
    grants and immigration
Guillotine (France), 628
Guise family, 476–477
Gulag Archipelago, 912
Gulf War (1991), 952
Gunpowder, 495
Gypsies. See Roma (Gypsies)

Habsburg Empire. See also Austria;
    Austrian Habsburg Monarchy;
    Habsburg Monarch; Holy Roman
    Empire; specific rules
  after First World War, 815
  industry in, 669
  Treaty of Utrecht and, 501

Habsburg Monarchy, 510–511. *See also* Austria; Austrian Habsburg Monarchy
Philip II (Spain) and, 477
the Hague, 946
Hahn, Otto, 824
Haig, Douglas, 795
Haile Selassie (Ethiopia), 858
Haiti, 581. *See also* Saint Domingue
in First World War, 801
revolution in, 581–582
Hall of Mirrors, Versailles, 497–498
German Empire proclaimed at, *714* (illus)
Hals, Franz, 524
Hamburg, Germany, 875
Hamilton, Richard, 920, *921* (illus)
Hammer of Witches, The, 470
Hansen's disease. *See* Lepers
Hapiru people. *See also* Hebrews
Hargreaves, James, 656, 658
Harvey, William, 533, 534–535, 538
Hashemites, 817
Hastings, Warren, *576* (illus)
Hausner, Gideon, 881
Havana, 562
Havel, Václav, 934, 938, 939, 942
Hawaii
Japanese attack on, 869
U.S. acquisition of, 777, 781
Haydn, Franz Joseph, 592
Head scarves, *956* (illus)
Hebrews. *See also* Bible (Hebrew); Jews and Judaism
Hegel, Georg Wilhelm Friedrich, 688, 693
Heliocentric theory. *See* Sun-centered theory
Helsinki Accords, 933
Helvetic Confessions, 463
Henry II (France), 474
Henry IV (France), 475, 496
Henry V (Shakespeare), 887
Henry VIII (England)
Anne Boleyn and, 482
Henty, G. A., 755
Hera (goddess)
temple of (illus), 3
Herder, Johann Gottfried von, 695
Hereditary social status. *See also* Aristocracy
abolition of privileges in France, 620
Herero people, 772 (map), 775
Heresy. *See also* Crusades; Inquisition
auto-da-fé and, 466–467
Galileo and, 543
Roman Inquisition and, 546
Herzl, Theodor, 741
Hesse, Herman, 853

Hevelius, Elisabetha and Johannes, *550* (illus)
Heydrich, Reinhard, 884
Hidalgos (Spain), 588
Higher education, 926
Hildebrand. *See* Gregory VII (Pope)
Himmelfarb, Gertrude, 960–961
Hindenburg, Paul von, 796, 804, 837
Hindu caste system, 851, 852
Hinduism, 851, 852
Hindus, 851, 902, 963
Hirohito (Japan), 877
Hiroshima, Japan, bombing of, *876* (illus), 876–877, 889, 897
Hirszenberg, Samuel, *740* (illus)
Hispaniola. *See also* Haiti; Saint Domingue
History and historians. *See also* specific individuals
postmodern, 959–960
Hitler, Adolf, 827, 838, 856, 857–863, 865, 868–869, 871, 873, *874* (illus), 883, 888, 892, 902. *See also* Holocaust; Nazi Germany
anti-Semitism of, 835–836, 856, 878–879
assassination attempt against, 884
cult of the leader and, 844–845
rise to power, 835–838
suicide by, 873–874, 877
total war by, 856
trial of, 829–831, *830* (illus), 836
on women's roles, 886
Hlavsa, Milan, 938
Ho Chi Minh, 902, 909
Hobbes, Thomas, 492
Leviathan by, 492
Hobson, J. A., 772–773
Hoffmansthal, Hugo von, 782
Hogarth, William, 589, 602
Holland. *See also* Dutch; Dutch Republic; Netherlands
Hollywood. *See* Movies
Holocaust, 877–883, 889, 918
Allies' knowledge about, 880, 883
Eichmann and, 879, 881–883
Holy Office of the Inquisition, 543
Galileo and, 543
Holy Roman Empire, 483, 510. *See also* Crusades; Inquisition
Charles V and, 484
dissolution of, 644
imperial diet in, 483
Homosexuals and homosexuality, 923, 963
deaths in Holocaust, 878
at the *fin-de-siècle*, 758–759, 760–762
Wilde, Oscar and, 760
Honduras, 801

Hong Kong
Chinese cession to British, 681
in Second World War, 869
Hongerwinter, 885 (illus)
Hooch, Pieter de, *465* (illus)
Hosius, Stanislas, 486
"House of Islam," 957
House of Trade (Spanish council), 560
"House of War," 957
Howe, Elias, 658–669
Hugo, Victor, 694
Huguenots
Edict of Nantes and, 477, 497, 499
in France, 474–475
Human body. *See also* Medicine
Harvey on, 533, 534–535
Human genome, mapping of, 962
Human rights, 951
Hume, David, 607
Humors (bodily fluids)
Galen and, 534
Hunchback of Notre Dame (Hugo), 694
Hundred Years' War, 563
Hungarian Revolution, 912, *913* (illus), 927
Hungary, 516, 812, 927, 928, 929, 936–937, 941
in 1920s and 1930s, 827
de-Stalinization and, 912, *913* (illus)
de-Stalinization of, 914
after the fall of communism, 945
fall of communism in, 940–941, *941*, *942* (illus)
after First World War, 815, 816, 825, 858, 862
in Hapsburg Empire, 510
Magyars and, 702
revolution of 1848 in, 702–704
revolutionary efforts in, 702
in Second World War, 872
after Second World War, 892, 894
Soviets and, 914
uprising in, 905
Warsaw Pact and, 914
Hunt, William Holman, 763–764, *764* (illus). *See* Holman Hunt, William
Husayn (Hussein) ibn Ali (Hashemite dynasty), 817
Hussein, Saddam, 956
Hydrogen bomb, 897, 905
Hyperinflation, in Germany, 827–828, 829, 838
Hypnosis, 612

Iberian peninsula. *See* Portugal; Spain
Ibn Saud, Abd al-Aziz, 850
ICBMs. *See* Intercontinental ballistic missiles (ICBMs)
Ice Man. *See* Otzi (Ice Man)

Ideologies, 684. *See also* communism; conservatism; fascism; liberalism; nationalism; socialism
  in 1920s and 1930s, 848–849, 854
  economics and, 848–849
Iliescu, Ion, 941–942
Images (religious). *See* Iconoclasm
Immigrants and immigration, *924* (illus), 924–925, *925* (table). *See also* Slave trade
  Asian in U.S., 777
  Chinese immigrants to Australia, 778
  Irish, 682
  Jews and, 740
Imperial Diet
  in Holy Roman Empire, 483
Imperialism, 750, 798, 889. *See also* Empire(s)
  in 1920s and 1930s, 847–851, 853
  advocates of, 770–771
  in Africa, *772* (map), *773* (map), 773–775, *781* (illus), 781–782
  in Asia, 775–776, *776* (illus), 777–781
  Asia and, 782
  capitalism and, 772–773
  China and, 776, 777, 780
  Christianity and, 769
  critics of, 772–773
  economics and, 766–767
  idea of, 767, *767* (illus), 769
  Japan and, 779
  new, 765–782
  politics and, 766–767
  Russia and, 781
  science and, 774
  Social Darwinism and, 755, 766
  technology and, 766–767, 769, 774
Imports. *See* trade
In vitro fertilization, 962
Independent Group, 920
India, 902. *See also* Mughal empire
  in 1920s and 1930s, 851
  annexation, trade, and, 575, 681
  Britain and, 681, 900–901
  British Empire and, 779
  in First World War, 798, 799, *799* (illus)
  after First World War, 818
  imperialism and, 766
  independence of, 900, 901
  modernization of, 851
  nationalism in, 851
  Portugal and, 560
  in Second World War, 874
  Second World War and, 900
Indian National Congress, 851
"Indian wars," 777
Indians. *See* American Indians; Native Americans
Indigo, 6, 7

Indochina, 781, 900, 901, *901* (illus), 902, *904* (illus), 904–905, 909. *See also* Cambodia; Laos; Vietnam
  in First World War, 798
  France and, 776
  independence of, 901
  nationalism in, 849
  in Second World War, 869
Indonesia, 900
  nationalism in, 849
  in Second World War, 869
Induction, 535
"Indulgents" (France), 632
Industrial capitalism, 687
Industrial regionalism, 669–670
Industrial Revolution, 654–683, 784. *See also* Industrialization
  conditions favoring, 662–665
  depression of 1873 and, 722
  factories and, 659–660
  mechanization and, 660
  mineral sources of energy for, 658–659
  nature of, 655–662
  population growth and, 662, 670–671
  Second, 766
  steam engine and, 658
  technology in, 655–658
  transportation and, 660–662
Industrialism, 889
Industrialization, 766. *See also* Industrial Revolution
  cities and, 679–680
  consumer and producer demand, 664–665
  on Continent, 666–667, 667–668
  economic growth and, 670–671
  effects of, 670–680
  new imperialism and, 680–681, 766
  population and, 662, 670–671
  Sadler Committee on child labor and, 676–677
  social unrest from, 724–725
  in Soviet Union, 840–841
  standard of living and, 671–672
  in United States, 669
  warfare and, 802–804, 818
  women and children as labor for, 672–673
Industry. *See also* Industrial Revolution
  Britain and, *665* (map)
  railroad, 661
INF (Intermediate Nuclear Forces) Treaty, 939–940
Infantry. *See* Armed forces; Military; Soldiers; War and warfare
Infectious diseases, 751–753
Information Age, 962
Innocent III (Pope)
  monarchy of, 501

Inquiry into the Nature and Causes of the Wealth of Nations (Smith), 599, 607
Inquisition(s)
  in Portugal, 696
  in Spain, 502
Institutions de physique (Madame du Châtelet), *606* (illus)
Intellectual thought. *See also* Enlightenment; Italian Renaissance; Jews and Judaism; philosophy
  scientific rationalism and, 692–693
Intercontinental ballistic missiles (ICBMs), 908
International competition
  in First World War, 787–788
International Monetary Fund (IMF), 664, 895, 909, 964
  Eastern Europe and, 940, 945
International organizations. *See* League of Nations; specific organizations; United Nations
International War Crimes Tribunal: Milosevic trial by, 949
Interpretation of Dreams, The (Freud), 757
Intolerable Acts (1774), 580
Inventions. *See* specific inventors and inventions
Invincible Armada: Spanish, 480
IRA. *See* Irish Republican Army (IRA)
Iran, 817, 952, 953–955, *954* (illus). *See also* Persia
Iranian hostage crisis (1979–1980), 952
Iraq, 817, 909, 952. *See also* Mesopotamia
Ireland, 847, *848* (map)
  in 1920s and 1930s, *826* (map)
  discrimination against Irish in, 735
  England and, 582
  in First World War, 798
  immigrants from, 682
  potato famine in, 682
  rebellion in (1798-1799), 582–583
  revolution in, 579
  in United Kingdom, 682
  Whiteboys in, 594
Ireton, Henry, 521
Irish Republican Army (IRA), 847, 951
Irish Revolution, 847, *848* (map)
Iron and iron industry, 669
Iron Curtain, 892, 897
Iron Guard (Balkans), 835
"Iron Lady," 933
Isabella (Castile)
  Ferdinand II of Aragon and, 502
Isabella II (Spain), 696

Islam, 962. *See also* Crusades; Muslims in; Ottomans
  African slavery and, 571
  Europe and, 951–957
  after First World War, 849–851
  in Spain, 478
Islamic Brotherhood, 850
Islamic law, 850, 953–955, 957
Islamism, *952, 953–955, 954* (illus)
Israel, 898, 951–952. *See also* Zionism
  creation of, 901, 902
  Eichmann trial by, 881–883
  Six-Day War and, 909
Istanbul. *See* Constantinople (Istanbul)
Italy, 850, 873, 916. *See also* Roman Empire; Rome (ancient)
  in 1920s and 1930s, 832, 833–834, 833–835
  in 1950s and 1960s, 917, 927
  in the 1970s, 931
  Ethiopia and, 858, 860
  fascism in, 833–834, 835
  in First World War, 787, 795–796
  after First World War, 814, 833–834, 858
  Futurism in, 762
  Great Depression in, 835
  immigrants from, 924
  imperialism and, 766, 767
  invasion of Greece, 865
  invasion of North Africa, 865
  Napoleon and, 633
  nationalism in, 708
  revolutions of 1848 in, 705, 708
  in Second World War, 865, 869, 870, 871, 872, 873
  Spanish Civil War and, 846
Ivan III ("the Great," Russia), 489
Ivan IV ("the Terrible," Russia), 488–490
Iwo Jima, Battle of, 875, 877

Jacobins (France), 623, 627–629
Jakarta. *See* Batavia (Jakarta)
Jamaica, 562
  Anglo-Spanish war over, 562
James I (England), 517–518, 519–520
James II (England), 518, 521
James VI (Scotland). *See* James I (England)
Japan, 788, 889, 895
  in 1920s and 1930s, 847
  China and, 779, 780, 781, 798, 858, *858* (illus), 860
  in First World War, 798, *800* (map)
  after First World War, 858
  imperialism and, 766, *776* (illus), 779
  industrialization and, 779
  invasion of Manchuria, 858, 860
  Korean War and, 904–905

Manchuria and, 779
Russia and, 779
Russo-Japanese War and, 734
in Second World War, 856, 869, 870, *870* (illus), 871, 874–877, *877,* 889
after Second World War, 892
surrender of, 877
Western world (the West) and, 779
Japanese immigrants, 777
Jaruzelski, Wojciech, 935, 940
Java: in mercantilist empire, 775
Jazz, 762
Jefferson, Thomas, 609, 615
Jehovah's Witnesses, 880
  in Nazi Germany, 838
Jena, battle at, 644
Jencks, Charles, 957
Jenkins, Robert, 562
Jenny. *See* Spinning jenny
Jerusalem, 952
  First World War and, 799, 802
Jesuits
  in Poland, 487
Jesus Christ (Jesus of Nazareth), 822. *See also* Christianity
Jewish nationalists, *816* (map)
Jewish State, The (Herzl), 741
Jews and Judaism, 740–741, 898–900, 963. *See also* Anti-Semitism; Bible (Hebrew)
  Balfour Declaration and, 817
  in concentration camps, *878* (illus). *See also* Holocaust
  deaths in Holocaust, 877
  Dreyfus Affair and, 730–733
  in France, 613
  French Revolution and, 623, 641
  ghettoization of, 877–878
  Nazi Germany and, 838, 877–883
  Nazism and, 836
  in Poland, 825
  Resistance movement (Second World War), 884
  in Second World War, 864, 877–883, *878* (illus), *879* (illus), 884
  Soviets and, 912
  Spinoza and, 544
  Zionism and, 817
Jihadism, 952
Jim Crow: in southern U.S., 777
Jinnah, Muhammad Ali, 902
Jirous, Ivan, 938
Joanna ("The Mad," Spain), 484
Jobs: for women. *See also* Careers; Employment
Jodl, Alfred, 874
Joffre, Joseph, 795
John Paul II, 540, 935, *936* (illus), 963
John XXIII (Pope), 922

Johnson, Lyndon B., 909
Jordan, 817, 909
Joseph II (Austria), 614
Josephine (France), *639* (illus)
Journal des savants, 500
Judaism. *See* Jews and Judaism
Judea. *See* Jews and Judaism
Judiciary. *See also* Court (judicial)
  Montesquieu on, 607
July Ordinances (France), 698
Jung, Carl, 851
Junkers (Prussia), 509
Just a Kiss (musical), *823* (illus)
Just What Is It That Makes Today's Homes So Different, So Appealing? (Hamilton), 920, *921* (illus)
Justine (de Sade), 610

Kádár, János, 914
Kandinsky, Wassily, 763
Kant, Immanuel, 607
Kashmir: in British Empire, 766
Katyn forest massacre, 874
Kazakhstan, 841
Kemal Pasha, Mustafa ("Ataturk"), 850
Kennedy, John F., 908–909
Kenya, 901–902
Kenyatta, Jomo, 901, 902
Kepler, Johannes, 484, 533, 548
Kerch, Massacre at, *867* (illus)
Kerensky, Alexander, 809
Kershaw, Patience, 654
Keynes, John Maynard, 846
Keynesian economics, 846
Khomeini, Ayatollah, 952, 953–955, *954* (illus)
Khrushchev, Nikita, 905, 908, 912, 914, 935
  de-Stalinization and, 912–913, *913* (illus)
Kiev
  in Second World War, 865
King George's War. *See* War of the Austrian Succession
Kingdom of the Two Sicilies, 705, 710
Kings and kingdoms. *See also* Absolutism; Monarchs and monarchies; specific rulers
Kingsley, Mary, 769
Kipling, Rudyard, 2, 769, 772
Klement, Ricardo, 881
Klimt, Gustav, 759, *759* (illus)
Kneller, Godfrey, *533* (illus)
Knolles, Richard, 512–513
Koch, Robert, 753
Kohl, Helmut, 932, *933* (illus), 945
Korea, 891. *See also* Korean War; North Korea; South Korea
  imperialism and, 766
  Japanese seizure of, 779

Korean War, 904–905
Kosovo, 946, *948* (map), 949
Kremlin (Moscow), *488* (illus)
Krupp, Alfred, 669
"Kubla Khan" (Coleridge), 578
Kuhn, Thomas, 538
Kun, Bela, 812
Kurdistan, *826* (map), 850
Kurds: in Iraq, 817
Kuwait, 952

Labor. *See also* Industrial Revolution;
    Slaves and slavery; Workers;
    Working women
  in First World War, 803
  syndicalism and anarchism in, 737
  women and, 926
Labour Party (Britain), 895
Lacan, Jacques, 958, 959
Laissez-faire, 755
  manufacturing and, 686
Lamarck, Jean-Baptiste, 755, 757
Landsberg Prison, *830* (illus)
Landscape: industrial, 679–680
Language(s), 958–959. *See also* Alphabet;
    specific languages; Writing
  Americanization of, 923
  French, 480, 500
  vernacular, 480
Laos, 776, 781, *901* (illus)
Latin America. *See also* America(s);
    Spanish America; specific regions
    and countries
  emerging nations in, 926
  in First World War, *800* (map), 801
  industrialization and, 930–931
  trade with, 681–682
Latin Christianity. *See also* Roman
    Catholicism; Western Christianity
Latvia, 809, 937
  in 1920s and 1930s, *826* (map), 827
  authoritarianism in, 827
  after First World War, *815* (map)
Laud, William, 556
Lavoisier, Antoine, 632
Law codes
  Napoleonic, 743
  women in, 743
Law of War and Peace, The
    (Grotius), 523
Lawrence, T.E. ("Lawrence of
    Arabia"), 799
Law(s). *See also* Law codes; Legal reform
  Montesquieu on, 607
Lay investiture. *See also* Investiture
    Controversy
Le Corbusier, 822
Le Pen, Jean-Marie, 931
League of Nations, 814, 816, 858, 894
Leahy, William, 876

Learning. *See also* Classical learning;
    Intellectual thought
LeBon, Gustave, 755, 756
Legislative Assembly (France), 620,
    622–623
Lend-Lease Act (1941), 868, 869, 873
Lenin, Vladimir, 809, 813, 824, 840,
    842, 849
  death of, 840
  on women's roles, 832–833
Leningrad. *See* St. Petersburg
  in Second World War, 865
Leopold II (Austria), 626
Leopold II (Belgium): in Congo, 774–775
Les Misérables (Hugo), 694
Leuillette, Pierre, 906–907
Levellers (England), 518
Leviathan (Hobbes), 493
Lévi-Strauss, Claude, 920
Lewis, Percy Wyndham, *793* (illus)
Lexington, 580
Libel trial: of Oscar Wilde, 760–762
Liberalism, 685–686, 759, 891
  German prostitution and corporal
    punishment, 706–707
  Polish revolt of 1830 and, 697–699
Liberia, *772* (map)
Liberty
  Rousseau on, 608
"Liberty, Equality, Fraternity," 643
Liberty Leading the People (Delacroix),
    685 (illus)
Libraries
  in France, 635
Libya, 909
  in Second World War, 865, 870
Lidice, 884
Liebknecht, Karl, 813, 827
Light: Newton's theory of, 533
Light of the World, The (Holman
    Hunt), 763–764, *764* (illus)
Lightbulb, 723
Lincoln, Abraham, 7
Lindbergh, Charles, 823
Lissauer, Ernst, 806
Literary theory, 958–959
Literature. *See also* Bible (Christian);
    Bible (Hebrew); specific works
  in 1930s, 853
  about First World War, 794, 795
  in Elizabethan England, 482
  of the *fin-de-siècle*, 757
  after First World War, 822
  in France, 480
  Goncourt Prize, 853
  romantic, 693–694
Lithuania, 827. *See also* Poland-Lithuania
  in 1920s and 1930s, *826* (map)
  authoritarianism in, 827
  after First World War, *815* (map)

Living with Pop (Richter), 920
Livingstone, David, 769
Livy (historian), 3
Lloyd George, David, 803, 814
Locke, John, 580, 596
  on Glorious Revolution, 522, 580
  reason, religion and, 545
Locomotives, 658
London, 460
  Crystal Palace Exhibition, *656* (illus)
  Islamist terrorist bombings in, 956
Lone Ranger (TV series), 923
Long Parliament (England), 517–518
Loom: power, 648
Lord of the Flies (Golding), 919
Lorenzo the Magnificent.. *See* Medici
    family
Lorraine, 789, *815* (map)
Louis XIII (France), 496–497
Louis XIV (France), 497
  absolutism and, 499–500
  Mazarin and, 497, 499
  mercantilism and, 499
  portrait of, *502* (illus)
  revocation of Edict of Nantes by,
    497, 499
  standing army of, 494–495
  warfare by, 500–501, 505
Louis XVI (France), *623* (illus)
  French Revolution and, 620
  trial and execution of, 628, 629,
    630–631
Louis XVIII (France), 648
Louisbourg, Canada, 565
Louis-Napoleon (France). *See* Napoleon
    III Bonaparte (Louis-Napoleon)
Louis-Philippe I (France), 698, 703
Lourdes: shrine at, 764
Louvre palace: museum in, 635
Luddites, 678
Ludendorff, Erich von, 796, 804, 829
Luftwaffe, 861
Lum, Wing Tek, 2
Lutherans and Lutheranism
  confessional identity of, 463
Luxembourg, 813, 917
  in Second World War, 873
Luxury goods
  chocolate as, 568
Lyell, Charles, 753

Macao, Portugal and, 560
MacArthur, Douglas, 876
Macedonia, *948* (map)
  after First World War, 815–816
Machine age. *See* Industrialization
Machine guns, 802
Machinery, 822–823. *See also*
    Industrialization
  industrial, 655–658

in Industrial Revolution, 655–658
technology and, 655–658
Madrid, Spain
Islamist terrorist bombings in, 956
Mafia
in Sicily, 711
Magic, 469
Magyars
in Hungary, 702
Malaria: in Africa, 774
Malaya, 869
Malcolm, Sarah, 604
Maleficia, 470
Malthus, Thomas, 670, 753
Man Pointing (Giacometti), *918* (illus)
Manchester, 679
Peterloo Massacre in, 678
Manchu dynasty (China), 781
Manchuria, 779, 858, 860
Manhattan Project, 875–876
Maran, René, 853–854
Marat, Jean-Paul, 627, 630, 638
Marcuse, Herbert, 926
Marguerite of Angoulême, 475
Marguerite of Navarre, 475
Marguerite of Valois (France), 476
Maria (Russia), 810, *810* (illus)
Maria Theresa (Austria), 563–565, 613
torture abolished by, 614
Marie Antoinette (France), 626, 629
Marie de' Medici, 496
Marie-Louise (Habsburg): Napoleon
and, 644, 649
Mariner's Compass, *5* (illus)
Marketing, 962
Marne, Battle of the, 802
Marne River, 792
first Battle of, 802
Marriage, 925
in Early Modern Europe, 464
Lenin on, 832–833
in nobility, 589
women's rights and, 743
Marriage à a Mode (Hogarth), *589*
(illus)
Marshall, George, 896, 897
Marshall Plan, 896
Marx, Karl, 687, 688, *690* (illus), 693,
736, 824, 927
Communist Manifesto, The, 674,
688–690
Marxism, 807, 818, 824
Mary (mother of Jesus), 925
Mary, Duchess of Richmond
(Reynolds), *595* (illus)
Mary I (England), Phillip II (Spain) and,
478
Mary II (England). *See also* William and
Mary (England)
Mary of Modena, 522

Masons. *See* Freemasons
Mass materialism, 920
Mass politics, 738
Anti-Semitism in, 739–740
Massacres
at Kerch, *867* (illus)
Russia's "Bloody Sunday" and, 733
St. Bartholomew's Day, 476–477
at Vassy, France, 476
Matamoe (Gaugin), *751* (illus)
Materialism, 920
*Mathematical Principles of Natural Phi-
losophy* (Newton), 533, 607
Mathematics
deductive reasoning and, 536
nature and, 536
Newton and, 536
Matisse, Henri, 768, 772
Mau Mau rebellion, 901, 902
Mauthausen, Austria, concentration
camp in, 856
May Laws (Russia, 1882), 734
Mayans
chocolate and, 568
Mazarin, Jules, 497, 499
Mazzini, Giuseppe, 692, 708
McDonald's, 924
Mechanics
Archimedes on, 538
Aristotle on, 537
Medici family
Catherine de Médicis, 475
Cosimo II de', 540
Medicine, 751–753, *752* (illus),
920–922, 962
dissection and, 535
religion and, 765
urbanization and, 752–753
Medvedev, Pavel, 810–811
Meiji Restoration, 779, 781
Mein Kampf ("My Struggle") (Hitler),
836
Memoirs of a Woman of Pleasure (Cle-
land), 610
Mendel, Gregor, 754
Mercantilism. *See also* Colonies and
colonization; Empire(s); specific
empires
Dutch, 523, 525
in France, 499
Meritocracy: in France, 642
Merkel, Angela, 945
Mesmer, Franz Anton, 612
Mesmerism, 612
Mestizos, 574
Metals: Phoenician commerce and. *See
also* specific metals
Metternich, Clemens von
conservatism of, 704
Mexico, 801

United States and, 777
Mickiewicz, Adam, 695
Microbes, 751–753
Middle Ages
science in, 537
Middle class, 688–689. *See also*
Bourgeoisie
liberalism among, 686, 688
Middle East, *826* (map), 898
in 1920s and 1930s, 847, 849–850
in First World War, 797 (map),
798–799
after First World War, *816* (map),
816–817, 818
Pan-Arabism and, 849
in Second World War, 869
after Second World War, 909, *910*
(map), 911
Middle Passage, 571
Midway, Battle of, 869, 870, 871
Midway Island, 870
Military. *See also* Armed forces;
Conscription; Soldiers; Wars and
warfare
Anglo-French rivalry and, 563–565
Scientific Revolution and,
542–543
Mill, James, 688
Millennium: Protestant belief in, 539
Millones (Spanish tax), 502
Milner, Lord, 769
Milosevic, Slobodan, 946, 948–949
Minarets, 951
Mind-body dualism
Descartes on, 537
Spinoza on, 543
Ministry of Information (MOI), 887
Missions and missionaries, 769, 774
Mobilization, 788–790
for First World War, 791
*Modern Warfare: A French View of
Counterinsurgency* (Trinquier),
906
Modernism, 757, 762–765, 822–823,
957–958. *See also* Postmodernism
Modernity, 957
Molière, Jean Baptiste, 500
Moltke, Helmut von, *790* (illus), 795
*Mona Lisa Contemplating the Bust of
Nefertiti...* (Ventura), *958* (illus)
Monarchs and monarchies, 494. *See
also* Carolingians; Empire(s); Ger-
man Empire; Holy Roman Empire;
Kings and kingdoms; Ottomans;
specific rulers and empires
absolutism and, 494
in England, 494
in France, 494
French Revolution and, 623, 629
Montesquieu on, 607

Monasticism. *See also* Monasteries; Monks

Mongols. *See* Tartars

Monks. *See also* Monasteries; Monasticism; specific monks

Montagnards (the Mountain). *See* Mountain

Montaigne, Michel de, 480–481

Montenegro, *948* (map)

Montesquieu, Baron de (Charles-Louis de Secondat), 607–608

Moon landing, 921–922

Moore, Henry, 887

Morale: in Second World War, 887

Morality
  in Enlightenment, 600–601

Moriscos, 480

Morocco, 871

Moscow, 824, 868
  Kremlin in, *488* (illus)
  Napoleon's invasion of, 647, 649
  in Second World War, 865

Mosul: in Iraq, 817

Motherhood, 832, 925

Motion, 532–533
  Galileo's theory of, 537

Moulin de la Galette, Le (Renoir), 721 (illus)

"Mountain, the," in French Revolution, 627, 628, 630

Movement. *See* Immigrants and immigration; Migration

Movies, *785* (illus), 887, 923
  after First World War, 823
  Russian Revolution of 1905 in, *734* (illus)

Mozambique: Portugal and, 560

Mozart, Wolfgang Amadeus, 592

Mughal empire (India), 554

Muhammad, 850, 952, 953–955, *954* (illus)

Mulattos, 565

Mule spinning, *661* (illus)

Multiculturalism, 924–925, 931, 964–965

Multinational corporations, 964

Multinational empires: in eastern Europe, 714–716

Mulunic, Vlado, *959* (illus)

Munich, 827, 829, 836

Munich Agreement, 859, 860, 862–863

Munich Conference, 859, 860

Museum of Modern Art, 768

Museums
  in France, 635

Music, 924
  classical, 592
  modernism in, 762–763
  postmodern, 959–961
  romantic, 694

Muskets, 774

Muslim Brotherhood, 850

Muslims, 817, 888, 948, 962–963. *See also* Islam; Islamic Empire
  in Europe, 951–952, *956* (illus), 956–957
  expulsion from Spain, 480
  after First World War, 849–851
  in Pakistan, 902
  in Russia, *778* (illus), 779
  in Second World War, 884
  slavery and, 571
  terrorism and, 951–952

Muspratt, William, 559

Mussolini, Benito, 833–834, 835, 838, 839, 859, 860, 865, 869, 872
  cult of the leader and, 844

Mutineers Casting Bligh Adrift in the Launch (Dodd), *558* (illus)

Mutiny: on *Bounty*, 558–559

Mutsuhito (Japan), 779

NAACP. *See* National Association for the Advancement of Colored People (NAACP)

Nagasaki, Japan, 779
  bombing of, 877, 889, 897

Nagy, Imre, 914

Naples (Neapolis)
  in Second Coalition, 633

Napoleon I Bonaparte (France), 619
  abdication of, 648–649
  downfall of, 644–650
  as emperor, 642–644
  as First Consul, 634
  French adminstration under, 640–642
  French Empire under, 642–644, *645* (map)
  French Revolution and, 633, 638–650, 640
  rise to power, 638–640
  Russia invaded by, 645, 649

Napoleon III Bonaparte (Louis-Napoleon, France), 702–703, 717

Napoleonic Code (France), 648, 743

Nash, Paul, *796* (illus)

Nasser, Gamel Abdel, 909

nation, 690

National Assembly (France), 620–621, 717
  move to Paris, 620

National Assembly (Germany), 705

National consciousness, 691

National Convention (France), 628–629, 633

National Covenant (Scotland), 517

National Guards (France)
  Paris Commune and, 627

National identity, 726–728. *See also* Identity
  in France, 728–729
  in Ireland, 728–729
  schools and, 727

National Liberation Front, 884

National self-determination, 690, 825–828, 847
  failure of, 814–815

National Society for Women's Suffrage (England), 745

Nationalism, 685, 690–692, 849. *See also* Unification
  in Eastern Europe, 715, 785–786, 944, 946–949
  in First World War, 786, 788, 791
  after First World War, 849–851
  after French Revolution, 691
  German unification and, 711–712
  in India, 851
  inventing traditions and, 728
  in Italy, 708
  romanticism and, 696
  after Second World War, 902
  in Soviet Union, 842, 942
  terrorism and, 945, 951

Nation(s). *See* Nationalism; Nation-states; State (nation)

Nation-states, 690
  in Italy, 709–710

Native Americans, 777. *See also* American Indians

Native peoples. *See* Indigenous peoples; specific groups

NATO. *See* North Atlantic Treaty Organization (NATO)

Natural law(s)
  in Enlightenment, 599

Natural magic, 469

Natural resources. *See* Resources

Natural rights, 687
  in France, 623

Natural selection, 753

Nature
  control of, 548–549
  Frankenstein and, 698
  mechanical philosophy of, 536–537
  Neoplatonists and, 538
  universal laws of, 533
  women, men, and, 549–550

Nausea (Sartre), 822

Navarre
  Bourbon family in, 475
  Huguenots in, 475
  kingdom of, 475

Navies
  mutiny on *Bounty* and, 558–559
  trading post empires and, 562

Navigation Acts (England), 562

Nawabs (India), 575

Nazi Germany, 854, 856–858, 862–863, *866* (map), 892, 894. *See also* Hitler, Adolf
  Battle of Britain and, 864
  Birth control in, 839
  expansion of, 858–860, *859* (map)
  fall of, 873–874
  families in, 838–839
  Final Solution and, 879, *879* (illus)
  invasion of Soviet Union, 864–868
  Jews in, 877–883
  occupation of Europe by, *885* (illus), 885–886
  in Second World War, 860–868, 869, 870–871, 875, 877–883, 888
  Spanish Civil War and, 846
  surrender of, 873, 874, 877
  women in, 886
Nazi Party, 829, 836–838
Nazism, 833, 835–838, 840, 843–847, 844–845, 888, 916
  women and, 838–839, *839* (illus)
Négritude movement, 853
Negro Americans. *See* African Americans
Nelson, Horatio, 633
Nemesis (gunboat), 681
Neoclassicism, 591
Neoplatonism, 538
Neo-Realist filmmakers, 887
Netherlands, 885, *885* (illus), 949. *See also* Durtch Republic; Dutch; Holland
  in 1950s and 1960s, 917
  in the 1970s, 931
  Asia and, 775
  decolonization and, 900–901
  immigration to, 931
  imperialism and, 775
  Indonesia and, 900, 901
  painting in, 524
  in Second World War, 869, 873
Nevada, 777
New Amsterdam, 562
New Astronomy (Kepler), 532–533
New Conservatism, 931, 932
New Conservatives, *933* (illus)
New Deal (U.S.), 845
New Economic Mechanism, 914
New Economic Policy (NEP), in Russia, 824–825, 833, 840
new feminism, 931–932
New Guinea, 875
New Harmony, Indiana, 687
New Lanark, 687
New Left, 926, 932
New Mexico, 714, 777, 801, 895
New Model Army (England), 518
New Organon (Bacon), 535

New Realism (France), 920
New Stone Age. *See* Neolithic (New Stone) Age
New Testament. *See* Bible (Christian)
"New Woman": after First World War, 828, 831, *831* (illus)
New World. *See also* America(s); specific regions
  imperialism and, 766
New York City
  Islamic terrorist attacks on, 954, 955–956
New Zealand
  in 1920s and 1930s, 847
  in First World War, 798, 799
Newton, Isaac, 533, *533* (illus), 596, 755–756
  mathematics and, 536
Nicaragua, 801
Nicholas I (Russia), 697, 698
Nicholas II (Russia), 801, 807, 808, 809, *810* (illus), 810–812
Nietzsche, Friedrich, 758
Nigeria, 901
Nile, Battle of the, 633
Nile River region, 1, 909
Nixon, Richard, 930
Nobility, 588. *See also* Aristocracy
"Noble savage": Rousseau on, 608
No-man's-land, 793
Nonconformists: in England, 700
Nonviolence, 851
Norseman (Northmen). *See* Vikings in
North Africa, 873. *See also* Carthage
  Italian invasion of, 865
  in Second World War, 868, 869, 870–871, 871
North America
  England and, *566* (map)
  imperialism and, 777
North Atlantic Treaty Organization (NATO), 897, 908, *911* (map), *934* (illus), 948, 951
  bombing of Serbs by, 946, 949
  France and, 923
  German rearmament and, 905
North Korea, 904–905
North Vietnam, 909
Northern Ireland, 951
  in 1920s and 1930s, *826* (map)
Norway, 885
  in Second World War, 861, 868
Notables (France), 642
Novels. *See also* Literature; specific works
Novgorod, 488
Nuclear power. *See* Atomic bomb
Nuclear Test Ban Treaty (1963), 905, 908
Nuclear testing: suspension of, 905, 908

Nuclear weapons, 905, 908, 918–919, 933
Nude Self-Portrait with Open Mouth (Schiele), *763* (illus)
Nunneries. *See* Convents
Nuremberg Laws (Germany, 1935), 838
Nuremberg trials, 874
Oath of the Tennis Court (David), *621* (illus)

Oaths
  in France, 637
Obama, Barack, 964
Observation: empirical, 535
Octavian (Rome). *See* Augustus (Octavian, Rome)
October Revolution, 809–812
"Ode to Joy" (Beethoven), 694
OEEC. *See* Organization for European Economic Cooperation (OEEC)
Okinawa, Battle of, 875, 876, 877
Old Regime (France), 613, 618. *See also* French Revolution
  destruction of, 619, 623
  Enlightenment and, 613
Old Stone Age. *See* Paleolithic (Old Stone) Age
Old Testament. *See* Bible (Hebrew)
Olga (Russia), 810, *810* (illus)
Olivares, Count-Duke of, 503–504
Olivier, Fernande, 768
Olivier, Laurence, 887
Omdurman, Battle of, 750
On the Admission of Women to the Rights of Citizenship (Condorcet), 609
On the Revolution of the Heavenly Spheres (Copernicus), 531, 533, 540
OPEC (Organization of Petroleum Exporting Countries), 930
Open City (movie), 887
Operation Bagration, 873
Opium Wars, 680–681
Optics, 532
Orange Free State, *772* (map), *781* (illus), 782
Organic Articles of Confederation, 641
Organic energy sources, 658
Organization for European Economic Cooperation (OEEC), 896
Origin of Species, The (Darwin), 754, 755
Orphan of China (Voltaire), 587
Orthodox Christianity, 912
  in Russia, 488, 514
Ossies, 945
Ostpolitik (Eastern policy): by West Germany, 930
Otto I (Greece), 698

Ottoman Empire, 511–513, 554,
    849–850, 951
    Armenian massacre and, 806–807
    disintegration of, 739 (map)
    in First World War, 797 (map),
        798–799, 802
    after First World War, 815, 815
        (map), 816, 817, 826 (map)
    Greece in, 698
    Hungary and, 511
    nationalist politics in, 738
    Russia, Crimean War, and, 716–717
Overseas empire. See Empire(s)
Owen, Robert, 687
Owen, Wilfred, 794, 795

Pacific islands, 775
Paine, Thomas, 609
Painting
    Cubism, 763, 768–769
    Expressionism, 763
    of the fin-de-siècle, 758 (illus)
    at the fin-de-siècle, 759
    after First World War, 822
    modernism in, 762–764
    representing First World War, 793
        (illus)
    romantic, 693
Pakistan
    creation of, 901, 902
Palaces
    at Versailles, 498 (illus)
Palestine, 817, 902, 909
    after First World War, 817
Palestine Liberation Organization
    (PLO), 952
Palestinian-Israeli conflict, 909,
    951–952
Palladio, Andrea, 592
Panama
    in First World War, 801
Pan-Arabism, 849
Pan-Slav Congress (Prague, 1848),
    702, 708
Papacy. See also Pope(s); specific
    popes
    Napoleon and, 641
    science and, 540–541
Papal decree against heliocentrism, 541
Papal infallibility, 765
Papal States, 645
Papen, Franz von, 837
Paradigms: collapse of scientific,
    538–539
Paris, 813. See also French Revolution
    in First World War, 789, 792
    French Revolution and, 633
    liberation of, 873
    Parlement of, 604–605
    salons in, 611

Paris, Treaty of
    of 1763, 566
    in 1814, 649
Paris, 68, 926
Paris Commune
    of 1792, 627
    of 1871, 717
Parlement of Paris (court)
    Fronde of, 497
Parlements (French courts), 591
Parliament (England). See also House of
        Commons (England); House of
        Lords (England)
    Charles I and, 518
    Charles II and, 521
Partisans, 884, 885
Pascal, Blaise, 545
Pasteur, Louis, 753
Patriarchy, 464
Patriotism. See Nationalism
Patronage
    science and, 539–542
Paul VI (Pope), 922
Paulus, Friedrich von, 871
Peace (Roman). See Pax Romana
Peace of Augsburg, 485
Peace of Riga, 813
Pearl Harbor: Japanese attack on, 869,
    871, 875
Peasants. See also Serfs
    aristocracy and, 593–594
Penance
    pain and suffering as, 467
Penicillin, 922
Pennsylvania, 955
Peoples Republic of China. See China
Perestroika, 937, 939, 942
Perry, Matthew, 777, 779, 781
Persecution. See also Anti-Semitism;
        Holocaust
Persia, 817. See also Iran; Persian
        Empire; Safavid Empire
    in First World War, 799
Persian Letters, The (Montesquieu),
    607
Persons with disabilities, 838
Pétain, Philippe, 864, 884
Peter I ("the Great," Russia), 514
Peter the Great, 842
Peterloo Massacre (1819), 678 (illus)
Petrograd: Russian Revolution in,
        807–809, 812, 824. See also
        St. Petersburg
Petrograd Soviet, 808–809
Philip II (France), 477
Philip II (Spain)
    inflation and, 462
Philip of Anjou. See Philip V (Spain)
Philip V (Spain), 501, 563
Philippines, 772, 777

in Second World War, 869, 871, 873
    U.S. acquisition of, 777, 781
Philosophical Dictionary (Voltaire),
    606–607
Philosophy. See also Enlightenment;
        Science
    of the fin-de-siècle, 758
    after First World War, 822
    Neoplatonism, 538
    after Second World War, 918, 920
Phoenicians. See also Carthage
Physicians. See also Medicine
    women as. See also Disease
Physics
    after First World War, 823–824
    revolution in, 755–756
Picasso, Pablo, 763, 768 (illus),
    768–769, 772, 783
Pictor. See Fabius family
Pictureque and Historic Voyage to
        Brazil (Debret), 553
Pillars of Society, The, 828 (illus)
Pilsudski, Joseph, 813, 827
Pius IX (Pope), 765
Pius XII (Pope), 925
Plague. See also Black Death
Planck, Max, 756
Planets. See also Astronomy;
        Universe
Plantation colonies, 560
    Brazil as, 560
Plassey, Battle of, 576
"Plastic People of the Universe, The"
    (PPU), 938–939, 939 (illus)
Platonic thought
    Copernicus and, 538
Plays. See Drama
PLO. See Palestine Liberation
        Organization (PLO)
Plotinus (philosopher), 538
Pogroms: against Jews, 740
Poison gas, 794, 802
Poland, 809, 813, 912, 928, 936 (illus),
        941, 963
    in 1920s and 1930s, 826 (map), 827
    authoritarianism in, 827
    collectivization in, 914
    communism in, 914
    expansion of Nazi Germany and,
        859 (map)
    after the fall of communism, 945
    fall of communism in, 940–941, 941
    in First World War, 786
    after First World War, 814, 825
    German occupation of, 860, 861,
        864, 868, 872, 874, 878, 878 (illus)
    German-Soviet Non-Aggression Pact
        and, 860
    Jews in, 487, 878 (illus), 878–879
    national minorities and, 825

nationalist rebellion in (1830), 697–699
pogroms in, 740
Resistance movement in, 883–884
Roman Catholicism in, 914
in Second World War, 860–861, 864, 868, 872, 874, 878, *878* (illus), 878–879, 880
after Second World War, 892, 894, 895, 897
Solidarity movement in, 935–936
Soviets and, 914
Poland-Lithuania, 516, 813
Commonwealth of, 489
Russia and, *483* (map)
Polio vaccine, 922
Politburo (Soviet Union), 937
Political Discourses (Hume), 599
Political parties. *See also* specific parties
Political theory, in Enlightenment, 606–610
Politics
in 1920s, 824–839
in 1930s, 839–847
after First World War, 824–847
imperialism and, 766–767
race and nationalism in, 738–741
romanticism and, 694
Pollock, Jackson, 919, *920* (illus)
Pomerania
after Second World War, *893* (map)
Poor. *See* Poverty
Pop art, 920
Pope(s). *See also* Papacy; Roman Catholicism; specific popes
Popular culture
Americanization of, 923–924
after First World War, 823, *823* (illus)
French political culture as, 635–638
postmodern, 959–962
Popular Front, 846
Popular sovereignty
after French Revolution, 636
Population
of fourteenth-century Europe, 458
of Early Modern Europe, 458
Porajmos, 877
Portrait of Pope Innocent X (Velazquez), *920* (illus)
Portrait of the Prince Baltasar Carlos . . . . (Velázquez), *504* (illus)
Portugal
in 1920s and 1930s, 847
in the 1970s, 932
Africa and, 847
Asia and, 775
Brazil and, 696
in First World War, 798, *800* (map)
immigrants from, 924

imperialism and, 775
India and, 560
liberal revolt in, 698
Spain and, 504
Portuguese Empire, 480, 560–561
Portuguese Inquisition, 696
Positivism, 692, 756–757
Postindustrial society, 961
Postindustrial technologies, 959–962
Postmodernism, 957–964, *958* (illus)
culture of, 959–962
historical writing and, 959–960
religion and, 962–963
Poststructuralism, 958–959
Potatoes
in Ireland, 582–583
Potsdam Conference (1945), 895, 897
Power loom, 655, 658
POWs (prisoners of war): Nazi treatment of, 885
Prague
Defenestration of, 506, *507* (illus)
Prague, Czechoslovakia, 912, 915, 927, 938, *959* (illus)
Prague Spring, 912, 915, 927, 938
Prerogative, 517
Price Revolution, 461–463
inflation and, 462–463
Primitive, the, 851, 853, *854* (illus)
Primogeniture
abolition in France, 623
Princes
Fronde of (France), 497
Princip, Gavrilo, *786* (illus)
Principles of Geology (Lyell), 753
Principles of Political Economy and Taxation (Ricardo), 686
Printing press
Scientific Revolution and, 542
Procession of the Catholic League, 457 (illus)
Production. *See also* Factories; Industrialization; Productivity
Progress
Enlightenment and, 601–606
Proletariat: Marx and Engels on, 690
Proselytizing: by Christians. *See also* Conversion (to Christianity)
Prostitution
feminism and, 745
in Germany, 706–707
Protectionism
continental industrialization and, 664
mercantilism and, 499
Protectorate (England), 518
Protestant Reformation. *See also* Protestants and Protestantism

Protestants and Protestantism, 765, 769, 922. *See also* Huguenots; Puritans; specific countries; St. Bartholomew's Day Massacre and
in Austrian Habsburg lands, 510
English nonconformists as, 700
French Revolution and, 623
in Ireland, 847
in Prussia, 510
science and, 539
St. Bartholomew's Day Massacre and, 476–477
Protest(s)
in 1960s, 926
Provisional Government (Russia), 808–809, 812
Prussia, 507–508, 813
absolutism in, 508
in Concert of Europe, 696
after Congress of Vienna, 650
enlightened despots in, 613
Hohenzollerns in, 508
Junkers in, 509
Psychoanalytic theory, 958
Psychology, 757, 851
Ptolemaic universe, *530* (illus)
Ptolemy, Claudius (astronomer), 530, 538
Puerto Rico
U.S. acquisition of, 777, 781
Pugachev, Emelian, 594
Punishment of a Slave (Debret), *553* (illus)
Purges. *See also* Great Purge (Soviet Union)
Puritans
in Americas, 555
Putin, Vladimir, 944–945
Pyramids, Battle of the, 633

Quakers, 555
Queen Anne's War. *See* War of the Spanish Succession
Queensberry, Marquis of, 760–762
Quinine: malaria and, 774
Qur'an, 951

Rabelais, François, 480
Race and racism. *See also* Discrimination; Immigrants and immigration
African slavery and, 571
politics of, 738–741
racial conflict in the 1970s, 931
Social Darwinism and, 755
theories of, 579
Radical Left, 844
Radical Right, 829
after First World War, 833–839
women and, 838–839

Radicalism
of Paine, 609
of Rousseau, 608
in trade unions, 737
Radio Free Europe, 915
Railroads, 661, 777
continental industrialization and, 668
new imperialism and, 767
trans-Siberian, 779
in United States, 777
Rain, Steam and Speed: THe Great Western Railway (Turner), 679 (illus), 680
Ramadan, Tariq, 957
Rape
First World War and, 807
in former Yugoslavia, 949
Rape of Nanking (Nanjing), 858, 860
Rasputin, Grigorii, 807
Rationing, 886
Raw materials: in Britain vs. Continent, 667
Raynal, Guillaume Thomas, 577
Reagan, Ronald, 932, 933, 933 (illus), 939–940
Realism, in Dutch Painting, 525
Realpolitik, 712
Reason and reasoning
deductive, 536
in Enlightenment, 596–597
independent, 543–544
Reasonableness of Christianity (Locke), 545
Rebaptism. *See* Anabaptists
Red Army, 928
in Second World War, 860, 864–868, 868 (map), 869, 871, 873, 877
Red Sea, 799
Reflections on the Revolution in France (Burke), 686
Reformation(s). *See also* Catholic Reformation; Protestant Reformation
Reform(s). *See also* Reformation(s)
Enlightenment and, 601–606
Refugees
in First World War, 798 (illus)
from former Yugoslavia, 949
Jewish, 902
Palestinian, 902, 909
Regency, 496
Regionalism: industrial, 669–670
Regression, 755
Reichstag (Germany), 506, 813, 836, 837
Reign of terror
in France, 628–632
Reinsurance Treaty, 787
Relajados (sinners), 466
Relativity theory, 756

Religion(s). *See also* Bible (Christian); Bible (Hebrew); Catholic Reformation; Gods and goddesses; Protestant Reformation; *Qur'an*; Secular culture; specific religions; Toleration
in 1950s and 1960s, 920–923
confessional identities and, 463–464
in Enlightenment, 600
at the *fin-de-siècle*, 764–765
Hume on, 600
in Ireland, 582–583
medicine and, 765
postmodernism and, 962–963
science and, 765
Voltaire on, 606
Religious orders. *See also* specific orders
Religious Peace of Ausburg (1555), 472
Rembrandt (van Rijn), 524, 525
Renaissance
of Poland-Lithuania, 485–487
Reparations, 895–896
after First World War, 814, 827–828, 835, 861
after Second World War, 896
Republic of Letters, 596–597
Republic of the United Provinces, 479
Republic of Virtue, 628
Republicans, 932
Republic(s)
in France, 702
Montesquieu on, 607
Research. *See also* Scientific Revolution
Resistance. *See* Revolts and rebellions
Resistance Charter of 1944, 884
Resistance movement (Second World War), 883–884, 887–888, 917, 918
Re-Stalinization, 913–914
Revolts and rebellions
in 1820–1848, 700 (map)
Dutch Revolt against Spain, 478–479
in Ireland, 582–583
liberalism in, 695–696
in Poland (1830), 697–698
in Portugal, 695–696
Sepoy Mutiny as, 681
in Spain, 695–696
Revolution(s). *See also* American Revolution; French Revolution; Russian Revolutions
of 1820-1848, 700 (map)
in Belgium (1830), 697–698
after First World War, 807–817
in Italy (1848), 702, 708
in Russia (1905), 734
Revolutions of the Heavenly Spheres, The (Copernicus), 533, 540
Reynolds, Joshua, 595 (illus)
Rhineland, 859, 859 (map), 860

Ricardo, David, 686
Rich. *See* Wealth
Richelieu, Cardinal (Armand Jean du Plessis de Richelieu), 496 (illus), 496–497, 499
Richter, Gerhard, 920
Rifles: repeating, 774
Riga, Peace of, 813
Right (political). *See* Conservatives and conservatism; Reaction; Right wing
Right wing. *See also* Radical Right
Rights
of married women, 743
U.S. Constitution, 714
Rights of Man, The (Paine), 607, 609, 612
Rights of Women, The (De Gouges), 624–635
"Rime of the Ancient Mariner" (Coleridge), 693
Rite of Spring, The (Stravinsky), 762–763
Rivers and river regions. *See* specific rivers and river regions
Robespierre, Maximilien, 627, 629–630
Cult of the Supreme Being and, 637
Rousseau and, 608
Robinson, John, 922
Rock and roll, 938
Roma (Gypsies), 838, 880, 945
deaths in Holocaust, 877
Roman Catholic Church, 764, 765, 834, 922, 925, 935
Roman Catholicism, 916–917, 922, 963. *See also* Catholic Reformation; Missions and missionaries; Protestant Reformation
auto-da-fé in, 466–467
conversions to, 499
at the *fin-de-siècle*, 764, 765
James II (England) and, 521
Philip II and, 477
in Poland, 914, 935
St. Bartholomew's Day Massacre and, 476–477
Voltaire on, 606
women's suffrage and, 745
Roman Empire. *See also* Eastern Roman Empire; Roman Republic; Western Roman Empire
Roman Inquisition. *See* Holy Office of the Inquisition
Roman Republic. *See also* Roman Empire; Rome (ancient)
Romania
in 1920s and 1930s, 827
authoritarianism in, 827
collectivization in, 914
communism in, 914–915
after the fall of communism, 945

fall of communism in, 941–942
in First World War, 797, 797 (map)
after First World War, 814, *815*
  (map), 825
in Second World War, 872
after Second World War, 892, 894
Romanov family (Russia). *See also* specific tsars; Tsars
  Michael Romanov and, 489
Romanticism, 693–695
Rome (ancient). *See also* Gods and
  goddesses; Punic Wars
Rome (city)
  liberation of (Second World War), 873
Rome-Berlin Axis, 859, 860
Roosevelt, Franklin D., 844–845, 875,
  892, 894, *894* (illus), 895
  at Tehran, 892, 894
  at Yalta, 894, *894* (illus), 895, 897
Rossellini, Roberto, 887
Roundheads (England), 518
Rousseau, Jean-Jacques, 607, 608
  on civil liberty, 608
  French Revolution and, 608
Royal Air Force (RAF, Britain),
  861, 864
Royal Navy. *See* British Empire;
  England (Britain); Navies
Royal Society (England), 540, 542
Royalists
  in England, 518
Rudolf II (Holy Roman Empire), 484
  portait of, 484 (illus)
Rudolph, Gesche, 706–707
Ruhr Valley, 828
Rural areas. *See also* Peasants
Rushdie, Salman, 952, 953–955, *954*
  (illus)
Russia, 802, 807, *943* (map). *See also*
  Russian Revolutions; Soviet Union
  in 1920s and 1930s, *826* (map)
  Asia and, 779, 781
  Black Sea region and, *778* (illus), 779
  Caucasus region and, *778* (illus), 779
  Chechens and, 952
  China and, 779, 780
  civil war in, 812, 824, 840
  in Concert of Europe, 696
  crises in 1990s, 944
  Decembrist Revolt (1825) in, 697–698
  economy in, 942, 944
  expansion of, *778* (illus), 778–779, 781
  after the fall of communism, 943–944
  in First World War, 785, 787–789,
    791, 796–798, 797 (map), *798*
    (illus)
  after First World War, 814, *815*
    (map), 816, 818, 824–825
  imperialism and, *778* (illus),
    778–779, 781

industry in, 669
Ivan the Terrible in, 488–490
Japan and, 779
Middle East and, 817
Muslims in, *778* (illus), 779
Napoleon and, 645
nationalism in, 944–945
under Putin, 944–945
reconstruction of, 824–825
revolution of 1905 in, 734
Russian Revolutions, 807–812
  in Second Coalition, 633
  in Third Coalition, 644
West and, 513–514
westernization in, 514
Yeltsin in, 942, 944–945
Russian Empire, 824–825
  expansion of, 513–514
Russian Revolutions, 779, 807
  of 1905, 733–734
  of 1917, 801, 802, 807–812, *808*
    (illus), 818
Russian-American Company, 561
Russo-Japanese War (1905), 734, 779,
  781, 788
Rutherford, Ernest, 823
Ryswick, Treaty of, 501, 505

SA (Nazi Germany), 836, 838
Sadler, Michael, 676
Sadler Committee: on child labor
  (Britain), 676–677
Safavid Empire, 554
Sailing and sailors. *See also* Navigation;
  Ships and shipping
Saint Cyr, 792–795
Saint Domingue
  independence of, 557
  revolution in, 579, 580–581
  slaves in, 579
Salk, Jonas, 922
Salons, 611–612
SALT Talks. *See* Strategic Arms
  Limitation Talks
Samizdat (self-publishing), 914
Samoa, 775
"Sans Souci" (palace), 613
Sans-culottes, in French Revolution,
  623, 627, 636
Sartre, Jean-Paul, 822, 918
Sasson, Siegfried, 792
Satan. *See* Devil
Satanic Verses (Rushdie), 953–955,
  954 (illus)
Satellite states (Soviet). *See also*
  Eastern Europe; specific
  countries
Satyagraha (India), 853
Saudi Arabia, 850
Savior. *See* Messiah

Scandinavia
  religion and, 922
Schabowski, Gunter, 928
Schiele, Egon, 759, 762, 763, *763* (illus)
Schlieffen, Alfred von, 788, *790* (map)
Schlieffen Plan, 788–789, *790*
  (map), 792
Schoenberg, Arnold, 762–763
Scholarship. *See also* Intellectual
  thought
Schools, 727. *See also* Education
Schubert, Franz, 694
Science, 782. *See also* Scientific
  Revolution; Technology
  after 1870, 750–757
  in 1950s and 1960s, 919, 920–923
  collapse of paradigms in, 538–539
  coming of millennium and, 539
  cultural superiority and, 889
  after First World War, 823–824
  imperialism and, 774
  intellectual developments outside,
    539–542
  in later medieval period, 537–538
  patronage and, 539–542
  printing press and, 542
  Protestantism and, 539
  religion and, 540–541, 765
  in Renaissance, 538
  theology and, 765
  Voltaire and, 606
Scientific method, 765
Scientific rationalism, 692–693
Scientific Revolution, 528–551, 692
  in astronomy, 530–532
  in biology, 534–535
  causes of, 537–542
  chemistry and, 534
  intellectual effects of, 543–548
  natural law and, 548–550
  in physics, 532–533
  search for scientific knowledge in,
    535–537
"Scorched earth" policy, 798 (illus)
Scotland
  Charles I and, 518
  England and, 518
  in United Kingdom, 518
Scots Irish, 582
Scott, Joan Wallach, 960
Scott, Samuel, *A Thames Wharf,*
  555 (illus)
Scott, Walter, 680, 693
Scriptures, 540
Sea of Japan, 778
Second Balkan War, 797
Second Coalition, 633
"Second Culture" (Czechoslovakia), 938
Second Empire (France), 717
Second Industrial Revolution, 766

Second Republic (France), 717
Second Sex, The (de Beauvoir), 925
Second Vatican Council, 922. *See* Vatican II
Second World War, 856–890, 917
  air war in, 874, 875
  Allied victory in (1942-1945), 871–874, *872* (map)
  India and, 900
  myth making and morale in, 887
  reconstruction plans, 887–888
  Resistance movement in, 883–884
  war effort, 887–888
  wartime gains from, *887* (illus)
Secret police, 938
secret societies
  of freemasons, 611
"Secret Speech" (Krushchev), 912, 914
Secularization, 764–765
Segregation, 777
Seigneurs: rights of, 593
Self-determination: national, 690
Self-flagellation, 466
Seligmann, Adelbert, *752* (illus)
Senghor, Leopold, 853
Separate spheres ideology. *See also* Domesticity
Separation of powers: Montesquieu on, 607–608
Separatist revolts: in Spanish territories, 504
Sepoy Mutiny, 681
Serbia, 785–786, 946, *948* (map), 948–949
  in First World War, 784–788, 790–791, 797, *797* (map), 806
  after First World War, 814, *815* (map)
Serbs, 816, 825, 884, 946, 947, 948
Servatius, Robert, 882
Seven Years' War, 556, 563–565
Sewing machine, 658–669
Sex and sexuality, 922, 923
  in 1960s, 926
  double standard in, 744–745
  in Enlightenment, 610
  at the *fin-de-siècle*, 759
  Oscar Wilde trial and, 760–762
Sex-change operations, 922
Sexual revolution, 926, 963–964
Sexuality, 963–964
Shaftesbury, Earl of, 521
Shakespeare, William, 482, 887
Sheba, Queen of. *See* Sabaea (Sheba)
Shelley, Mary, 695
Shelley, Percy, 696
Shimmering Substance (Pollock), *920* (illus)
Ships and shipping
  slave ships and, 567

Siberia, 779
  slave trade and, 779
Sicily, 871–872
  Mafia in, 711
Siddiqui, Kalim, 954
Sieyès, Emmanuel-Joseph, 634
Sikhs, 902, 963
  in First World War, *799* (illus)
Silesia
  after Second World War, *893* (map)
Sinai Peninsula, 909
Singapore, 871
Singer, Isaac, 669
Sinn Fein (Ireland), 735
Sino-Japanese War, 779, 780, 781
Siraj-ud-Daulah (nawab of Bengal), 575–576
Six Books of a Commonweal (Bodin), 493–494
Six-Day War (1967), 909, 952
Skepticism, 543
  of Spinoza, 544
Sketch for a Historical Picture of the Progress of the Human Mind (Condorcet), 602, 607
Slánský, Rudolf, 898–900, *899*
Slave labor, 912
  in death camps, 880
Slave Ship, The (Turner), *574* (illus)
Slave trade, 774
  in Atlantic region, 570–573
  Equiano on, 552
  Portugal and, 570
  in Siberia, 779
  Spain and, 570
Slaves and slavery, 774, 775, 779
  abolition of, 572
  Haitian Revolution and, 581
  plantation labor and, 570
Slavs, 878, 885–886
  in First World War, 787
Slovakia, 941, 942
  after the fall of communism, 945
Slovaks, 816
Slovenes, 825
Slovenia, *948* (map)
  in First World War, 786
Slums, 672
Smallpox
  eradication of, 962
  in Seven Years' War, 565
Smetona, 827
Smith, Thomas, 512–513
Smoking. *See also* Tobacco
Social Contract, The (Rousseau), 607, 609, 622
Social Darwinism, 755, 769
  imperialism and, 766
Social Darwinism and, 834

Social democracy, 843–847, 916–917, 931
Social Democratic Party (SPD, Germany), 813, 825, 827, 829
Social Democratic Party (Sweden), 846
Social Democrats, 916
Social Security Act, 845
Social thought: positivism and, 756–757
Social welfare, 832
  in England, *887* (illus), 887–888
  after Second World War, *887* (illus), 887–888
  social welfare in, *887* (illus)
Socialist parties. *See also* Socialists and socialism; specific parties
Socialist Realism, *841* (illus), 912
Socialists and socialism, 687–688, 765, 912, 916. *See also* specific parties
  in Germany, 825–826, 827
  in Italy, 833–834
  revolutionary, 736
  in Second World War, 884
  working-class, 736
Society. *See also* Classes
  in the Age of Affluence, 923–926
  First World War and, 804–805
  under French Directorate, 633
  natural law and, 599
  Rousseau on, 602
  Voltaire on, 606
Society of Friends. *See* Quakers
Society of Jesus. *See also* Jesuits
Society of United Irishmen, 582
Sociology, 765
Sokoto caliphate, West Africa, *772* (map)
Solidarity movement, 935–936, *936* (illus), 941, 963
Solmitz, Louise, 844
Solzhenitsyn, Alexander, 912
Somme, Battle of the, 784, *785* (illus), 795, 818
Somnium (Lunar Astronomy) (Kepler), 548
Sorel, Georges, 737
South (global), 889, 891
South Africa, 769, *772* (map), *781* (illus), 781–782, 852–853. *See also* Africa
  in First World War, 798, *800* (map)
South America
  imperialism and, 766
  industrialization and, 930–931
South Korea, 904–905. *See also* Korean War
South Pacific region. *See also* Pacific Ocean region
Southwest Asia. *See also* Middle East
Soviet bloc, 933
Soviet Union, 933, 936, *950* (map). *See also* Russia

in 1920s and 1930s, *826* (map), 854
in 1930s, 840–843
in 1950s and 1960s, 911–915, 927
in the 1980s, 928–929, 934,
    936–937, 939, *940* (illus)
Afghanistan invasion by, 955
anti-Semitism in, 898
arts in, 913, 914
Berlin Wall and, 890, 928–929
Chernobyl nuclear disaster and, 937
Christianity in, 912
Cold War and, 892–900, 900–910,
    911–915
collectivization in, 840–842, 912
crises in 1970s, 934–937
détente and, 930
disintegration of, 928–929, 942,
    943 (map)
dissent in, 914
Eastern Europe and, 892–900
economy in, 942
economy of, 934–935
end of Communist monopoly in, 939
establishment of, 812
expansion of Nazi Germany and,
    859, *859* (map), 859–860
Families in, 832–833
families in, 842
after First World War, 818, 824–825
forced labor in, 842
France and, 923
German-Soviet Non-Aggression Pact,
    859–860
Germany and, 861
Gorbachev in, 937
Hungary and, 912, *913* (illus),
    914, 927
ideology and, 849
industrialization and, 840–842
Jews in, 912
League of Nations and, 858
nationalism in, 842
non-Russians in, 937
Palestinian-Israeli conflict and, 909
Poland and, 813, 914
post-war Europe and, 892–900
Prague Spring and, 915, 927
Resistance movement in, 884
Re-Stalinization in, 913–914
in Second World War, 860, 864–868,
    868 (illus), 869, 871, 872, 872–874,
    877, *878* (illus), 883–885
after Second World War, 888, 890
society in, 842–843
Stalinism in, 840–843, 845
Velvet Revolution and, 938
Vietnam and, 909
Warsaw Pact and, 897
women in, *832* (illus), 832–833,
    842, 886

Soviet-Afghan War, 955
Spaak, Paul-Henri, 917
Space exploration, 905, 921–922
Spain, 860. *See also* Spanish Civil War
    in 1920s and 1930s, 832, 854
    in 1930s, 846
    in the 1970s, 932
    Basque terrorism in, 951
    chocolate and, 568
    civil war in, 858
    decline of, *503* (map)
    Haitian Revolution and, 581
    immigrants from, 924
    Inquisition in, 502
    liberal revolt of 1820 in, 698
    overseas empire of, 502
    unification of, 708–709
Spanish America. *See also* Spain;
    specific locations
    national revolutions in, 583–584
Spanish Civil War, 846, *847* (illus),
    858, 860
Spanish Empire, 560
Spanish Inquisition, 479
    restoration of, 695
Spanish-American War, 777, 781
Spartacists: in Germany, 813
SPD. *See* Social Democratic Party (SPD,
    Germany)
Spencer, Herbert, 755
Spending. *See* Defense spending
Spice Islands
    Portugal and, 478
Spices and spice trade
    chocolate and, 568
Spinning jenny, 656, 658
Spinning: mule, 657–658, *661* (illus)
Spinoza, Baruch, 524, *544* (illus)
Spirit of the Laws (Montesquieu), 607
Spiritualists and spiritualism
    in Enlightenment, 612
Sputnik, 905, 908
SS (Nazi Germany), 838, 879, 880. *See
    also* Einsatzgruppen (SS unit)
St. Bartholomew's Day Massacre,
    476–477, *477* (illus)
*St. Michael and the Dragon: Memoirs
    of a Paratrooper* (Pierre Leuillette),
    906–907
St. Petersburg, Russia, *514*, *516* (illus),
    807–808, 824
    March Revolution in, 807–809, 812
    in Second World War, 873
    West and, 515
Stadholder (United Provinces), 479
Stagflatin, 930–931
Stalin, Joseph, 840–843, 845, 888
    consolidation of power by, 842–843
    death of, 905, 911, 912
    on the family, 842

at Potsdam, 895, 897
    rise to power, 840
    after Second World War, 892, 894,
        894 (illus), 895–900
    Second World War and, 865, 867,
        871, 888
    Slánsk‡ trial and, 898–900
    Soviet Union under, 840–843, 865,
        867, 871, 888, 892, *894* (illus),
        894–900
    at Tehran, 892, 894
    at Yalta, 894, *894* (illus), 895, 897
Stalingrad, Battle of, 869, 871, 873, 886
Stalinism, 840–843, 846, 926
Stamp Act (1765), 580
Standard of living. *See also* Economy;
    Lifestyle
    industrialization and, 671–672
Standing armies
    after Thirty Years' War, 494–495
START treatie. *See* Strategic Arms
    Reduction Treaty (START I)
Starvation. *See also* Famine
State (nation)
    confessional, 472–483
    expansion of, 803
    in Prussia, 507–508
State of nature
    Rousseau on, 608
Steam engine, 658
Steam locomotive, 658
Steamship, 774
Steen, Jan, 524
Stephenson, George, 658
Sterilization: in Nazi Germany, 838
Stevenson, Robert Louis, 757
Stock exchange: in Amsterdam, *524*
    (illus)
Stoker, Bram, 757
Strassman, Fritz, 824
Strategic Arms Limitation Talks: SALT I
    (1972), 930
Strategic Arms Reduction Treaty
    (START I), 940
Stravinsky, Igor, 762–763
Structuralism, 920
Stuart dynasty (England)
    Glorious Revolution and, 521–526
    later absolutism of, 521–526
student protests, 931
Submarines: in First World War,
    799–801
Sub-Saharan Africa. *See also* Africa
Sudan, 774, 909
    Britain and, 750
Sudetenland
    expansion of Nazi Germany and, 859
    after First World War, 862
    in Second World War, 860
    after Second World War, *893* (map)

Suez Canal, 799, 909
Suez Crisis, 909
Suffrage, 687, 701–704, 717, 726, 730
  for women, 741, 745–747
Suffragettes, 746–747
Sugar industry, 568–569
  in Brazil, 561
  in plantation colonies, 560
Sukarno, Ahmed, 900
Sultan (Ottoman Empire). *See also*
    specific rulers; Turks
Sun-centered theory, 531
Supernatural: magic and, 470. *See also*
    Magic; Religion(s)
Superpowers: in Cold War. *See also*
    Soviet Union; United States
*Supplement to the Voyages of
    Bougainville* (Diderot), 598
Supply and demand: inflation and, 462
Surgery: improvements in, 752
    (illus), 753
Surrender of Breda, The (Velázquez), 505
Survival of the fittest, 755
Sweden, 846, 949–950
  in 1930s, 846
  in the 1970s, 931
  immigration to, 931
Switzerland
  in 1950s and 1960s, 917
  in the 1970s, 931
  immigration to, 931
Syllabus of Errors (Pius IX), 765
Symphonic music, 762
*Syndics of the Clothmakers of
    Amsterdam* (Rembrandt),
    525 (illus)
Syria, 807, 909
  after First World War, 817
Szlachta (Polish nobility), 485–486, 588

Tahiti, 558, 598
Taiwan: Japanese seizure of, 779
Taliban, 956
Tannenberg, Battle of, 796, 804
Tardieu, Jean Charles, 646
Tariffs. *See also* Protective tariffs
Tatiana (Russia), 810, 810 (illus)
Taxation. *See also* Revenue
  for maintaining armies, 495
"Taxation without representation," 580
Tchaikovky, Peter, 694
Technology. *See also* Science
  in 1950s and 1960s, 919
  cultural superiority and, 889
  fascism and, 834
  after First World War, 822–823
  genocide and, 879–880
  imperialism and, 766–767, 769, 774
  industrial landscape and, 679–680
  in Industrial Revolution, 658

Luddites and, 678
  warfare and, 802–804
Tehran Conference (1943), 892, 894
Telescope, 528–529, 529 (illus)
Television, 923, 960–961
Temple(s). *See also* Pyramids
Tennis court oath (France), 620
Tennyson, Alfred Lord, 754
Terror, the. *See* Reign of terror, in France
Terrorism, 779
  in Franco-Algerian War, 906
  Islam and, 951–952
  in London, 956
  on September 11, 2001, 952, 955–956
Test Act of 1673, 522
Test-tube babies, 962
Texas, 714
Textiles and textile industry
  child labor in, 676 (illus)
  industrial regionalism and, 669
  in Industrial Revolution, 656–658
  in Ulster, 682
Thatcher, Margaret, 932, 933, 933
    (illus), 961
"The Ballad of East and West"
    (Kipling), 2
The First Authors of the Revolution, 615
The Junior Class (Geoffroy), 727 (illus)
The Massacre at Chiox (Delacroix),
    697 (illus)
Theater. *See* Drama
Theology
  evolutionary theory and, 753, 754
  after First World War, 822
  science and, 538, 765
Theory of motion: of Galileo, 537
Thiers, Adophe, 684
Third Balkan War: First World War as,
    797–798
Third Estate (France), 620–621, 634
Third of May, The (Goya), 648 (illus)
Third Reich: Nazi Germany as, 864
Third Republic (France), 717
  Dreyfus Affair and, 730–733
Third Symphony (Beethoven), 640
Third World, 901, 909
Thirty Years' War, 492, 505
  Germany and, 474, 485, 506–507
  standing armies after, 492, 494–495
Thirty-Nine Articles, 463
*Thoughts and Sentiments on the Evil
    and Wicked Traffic of the Slavery
    and Commerce of the Human
    Species* (Cugoano), 572–573
Three Romes: Russian theory of, 488
Time of Troubles (Russia), 489
Tito (Yugoslavia), 885, 896, 897,
    945–946
Titulos (Spain), 588
Tobacco, 568–569

Tokutomi Soho, 779
Toleration. *See also* Religion(s)
Tonkin (Vietnam), 776, 781
Torah. *See also* Bible (Hebrew)
Tories (England), 726
Torschlusspanik (fear of the closing
    door), 766
Torture
  in *auto-da-fé*, 466–467
  in Franco-Algerian War, 906–907
Total war, 784, 792–793, 795–802,
    805–807, 818
  politics of, 803–804
Townshend, Charles ("Turnip,"
    590, 666
Trade. *See also* Commerce; Market(s);
    Slave trade
  with Asia, 578
  with China, 578
  chocolate and, 560
  Portuguese, 561
Trading companies
  Dutch, 523
Trading posts. *See also* Factors and
    factories (trading posts)
Traditions, 728
Transexuality, 922
Transjordan: England and, 817
Transplants, 922
Transportation. *See also* specific types
  Industrial Revolution and,
    660–662
trans-Siberian railway, 779
Transvaal, 772 (map), 781, 781
    (illus), 782
Transylvania
  peasant rebellion in, 594
Travels in Upper and Lower Egypt
    (Vivant-Denon), 647
Treason: Dreyfus Affair and, 730–733
Treaties. *See also* specific treaties
Treatise of Human Nature (Hume), 599
*Treatise on Religion and Political Phi-
    losophy, A* (Spinoza), 543
Treatise on Toleration (Voltaire), 607
Treatises on the Plurality of Worlds
    (Fontenelle), 543, 548
Treaty of Lausanne, 850
Treaty of Sèvres, 849–850
Treitschke, Heinrich von, 767
Trench warfare, 792 (illus),
    792–795, 818
Trials
  of *Bounty* mutineers, 558–559
  of Charles I (England), 518–521, 520
    (illus)
  of Galileo, 546–547, 547 (illus)
  for infanticide in Enlightenment, 604
  of Oscar Wilde, 760–762
  for witchcraft, 469–471, 471

Tricolor: in France, 636
Trieste, 844
Trinity test: of atomic bomb, 875
Trinquier, Roger, 906
Triple Alliance, 787, 788
Triple Entente, 787
Trojan War. *See also Iliad, The* (by Homer)
Trotsky, Leon, 840
Truman, Harry, 876, 895, 896, 904–905, 905
Truman Doctrine, 896, 897
Tsars (Russia). *See also* Russia; specific rulers
Tuberculosis, 753
Tudor dynasty (England). *See also* specific rulers
Tuileries Palace
    in French Revolution, 629
    Paris Commune burning of, 684
Tunisia, 818
Turkey, *911* (map), 951. *See also* Anatolia; Ottoman Empire
    in 1920s and 1930s, 849–850
    Armenian massacre and, *806* (illus)
    Cuban Missile Crisis and, 905
    after First World War, 815, *815* (map)
    immigrants from, 924
    nationalism in, 849–850
    Second Coalition, 633
    Westernization of, 849–850
Turks. *See also* Ottoman Empire; Ottoman Turks
    absolutism and, 511
Turner, J. M. W., 574, 679, 680
Two Treatises of Government (Locke), 522

Ukraine, 807, 812, 813, 841, 937, 944
    in 1920s and 1930s, *826* (map)
    in First World War, 786
    after First World War, *815* (map), 824
    Resistance movement in, 884
    in Second World War, 865, 866, 884
Ukrainians
    in Poland, 825
Ulbricht, Walter, 908
Unconscious: Freud and, 757
Unification. *See also* Reunification
    of Germany, 708–709, 711–712, 713 (map)
    of Italy, 709, *710* (map)
    of Spain, 708–709
    in United States, 708–709, 712–714
Union of French Indochina, 776, 781
Union Pacific railroad, 777
Unionists (Ulstermen), 735
Union(s). *See* Labor unions; Trade unions
unions, 931

United Irishmen, 582
United Kingdom, 666. *See also* England (Britain)
    formation of, 518, 691
    Ireland in, 691
    Scotland in, 518, 691
United Nations (UN), 894, 930, 948, 956, 964
    Israel and, 902
    Middle East and, 817
    Palestinian-Israeli conflict and, 951–952
United Provinces of the Netherlands. *See* Dutch Republic (United Provinces of the Netherlands)
United States, 782, 933. *See also* Cold War
    in 1930s, 840, 844–846
    in the 1970s, 932
    in the 1980s, 939–940
    anti-Asian sentiment in, 777
    anti-Semitism in, 883
    China and, 780, 781
    Cold War and, 892–900, 900–910
    détente and, 930
    in First World War, 784, 799–801, *800* (map), 801–802, 805, 807
    after First World War, 813–816, 818, 823
    GNP in 1930s, 845
    Great Depression in, 835
    immigration to, 777
    imperialism and, 766, 775–776, 776 (illus), 777–778
    Iran and, 952
    Korean War and, 904–905
    League of Nations and, 858
    Mexico and, 777
    Middle East and, 817
    Palestinian-Israeli conflict and, 909
    religion and, 922
    Samoa and, 775–776
    in Second World War, 856, 860, 868–877
    Spanish Civil War and, 846
    unification in, 708–709
    Vietnam War and, 905, 909, 926
    women in, 886
Universal Law of Gravitation, 533
Universal male suffrage
    in England, 702
    in France, 627, 703
Universe. *See also* Solar system
    Aristotle on, 530–531
    Democritus on, 538
    geocentric theory of, 548
    heliocentric theory of, *531* (illus), 548
    humans in, 548
    Neoplatonists on, 538
    pre-Copernican, *530* (illus)

Universities and colleges
    protests in, 926
    women in, 744
Urban areas
    industrial landscape of, 679–680
Urban VIII (Pope), 533
Urbanization, 724, 757, 759
    medicine and, 752–753
    Social Darwinism and, 755
U.S. Strategic Bombing Strategy, 876
Utah, 777
Utopian socialism, 687
Utrecht, Treaty of, 501, 505, 563

Valmy, Battle of, 629
Valois family
    Marguerite, 476
Variation, 753
Vassy, France, massacre at, 476
Vatican II (1963), 922, 923
VE Day, 877
Velazquez, Diego, *920* (illus)
Velázquez, Diego de, 505
Velvet Revolution, 938
Ventura, Marco, *958* (illus)
Venus di Milo. *See* Aphrodite of Melos (statue)
Vernacular languages, 480, 922
Versailles, 620
    Louis XVI and, 497–498, 620
Versailles Treaty, 814, *815* (map), 816, 827, 827–828, 858, 859, 860, 861
Vichy France, 864, 884
Victor Emmanuel III (Italy), 834
Victoria (England), 753
Videocassette recorder (VCR), 960–961
Vienna, 812
Vietnam, *901* (illus), 902, 905, 909, 926
Vietnam and, 891
Vietnam War, 905, 909, 926
Villages. *See also* Cities and towns; specific communities
Vindication of the Rights of Woman, A (Wollstonecraft), 607, 609
Violence
    by suffragettes, 747
Virgin Mary. *See* Mary (mother of Jesus)
Visual arts
    romanticism in, 694
V-J Day, 877
Vladivostok, 778
Volga River, 871
Voltaire, 606, 608
    Asian cultures and, 577
    Catherine II (Russia) and, 614
    Frederick the Great and, 613
    French Revolution and, 615
    sexuality and, 610

Wafd party (Egypt), 849
Wagner, Richard, 694
Wahhabi religious revival, 850
Waiting for Godot (Beckett), 918
Wake Island, 869
Wales
    England and, 691
    language in, 691
    in United Kingdom, 691
Walesa, Lech, 935, 936 (illus), 941
Wanderer Above the Sea of Fog
    (Friedrich), 693 (illus)
WannSee Conference, 879
"War Communism" (Russia), 824
War effort, 805–807, 887–888
War of Independence. *See* American
    Revolution
War of Jenkins' Ear, 562
War of the Austrian Succession,
    563–564, 564 (map)
War of the Spanish Succession, 501,
    505, 563–564
Ward, Mrs. Humphry, 746
Wars and warfare, 561–565. *See also*
    specific wars; Weapons
    British in India and, 563
    by Europeans, 561–565
    against French
        Revolutionaries, 563
    gunpowder and, 495
    industrialization and, 784, 788–790,
        802–804, 818
    mercantilist, 562–563
    myth making and morale in, 887
    in Second World War, 861, 864
    technology and, 802–804
    total war, 784, 792–793, 795–802,
        803–804, 805–807
    trench warfare, 792 (illus),
        792–795, 818
Warsaw, 778
Warsaw, Battle of, 813
Warsaw ghetto: uprising in, 884
Warsaw Pact, 897
    Czechoslovakia and, 915
    Hungary and, 914
"Waste Land, The" (Eliot), 822
Water frame, 658
Water Serpents, 759 (illus)
Waterloo, Battle of, 649, 697
Watson, James, 920–921
Watt, James, 658
We Are Making a New World (Nash),
    796 (illus)
Wealth. *See also* Aristocracy; Elites
Wealth of Nations, See *Inquiry into the*
    Nature and Causes of the Wealth
    of Nations (Smith)
Weapons. *See also* Bombs and
    bombings; specific weapons

gunpowder and, 495
    repeating rifles, 774
Weapons of mass destruction, 956
Weber, Max, 756–757
Wedgwood, Josiah, 665
Weimar Republic (Germany), 825–826,
    828 (illus), 829, 836, 837
    collapse of, 827–828
Welfare benefits. *See also* Social welfare
Wellesley, Arthur. *See* Wellington,
    Duke of
Wellington, Duke of, 644
Weltpolitik (world policy), 787
Wessies, 945
West Africa
    Portugal and, 560
West Bank, 909, 952
West Berlin, 890, 891 (illus), 897
West Francia: kingdom of. *See also*
    France
West Germany, 890, 891 (illus), 897,
    916, 927–930, 933 (illus), 942, 945.
    See also East Germany; Germany
    in 1950s and 1960s, 920
    in the 1970s, 931, 932
    immigration to, 931
    rearmament of, 905
    religion and, 922
Western Christianity. *See also* Roman
    Catholicism
Western Europe
    monarchies of, 494
    after the Second World War, 915–926
    table fork in, 468
Western Front (First World War),
    792–795, 801–802
Western Roman Empire. *See also*
    Eastern Roman Empire
Western world (the West), 799 (illus),
    930–931. *See also* America(s);
    Europe and Europeans; specific
    countries
    in 1950s and 1960s, 915–926, 927
    in the 1970s, 929, 930–931
    in the 1980s, 929, 930, 931–934
    in the 1990s, 929
    age of consumption in, 917–923
    core lands of, 7 (map)
    cultural superiority and, 769, 772,
        853, 889
    economic crisis of 1970s, 932
    expansion of, 782–783
    fragmentation of, 782–783
    imperialism and, 769, 773–781
    Islamism and, 952
    Japan and, 779
    redefinition of, 949–964
    responses to fascism, Nazism, and
        Stalinism, 843–847
    satellite photo, 2 (illus)

after Second World War, 888
    Social Darwinism and, 755
    St. Petersburg and, 514–515
    in the twenty-first century,
        964–965
Westernization, 849–851
Westernization: of Russia, 514
Westphalia, Treaty of, 505, 507
    Europe after, 508 (map)
Weyer, Johann, 472–473
Whigs (England), 521
"White Australia," 777
White Mountain, Battle of, 505, 510
White Terror (France), 632
Whiteboys (Ireland), 594
Wiesel, Elie, 880
Wilberforce, William, 572
Wilde, Oscar, 760–762, 761 (illus)
"Will to war," 790–791
William and Mary (England), 522
William II (Germany), 728 (illus), 787
    abdication of, 802
William III (Orange). *See* William and
    Mary (England)
William the Silent (House of Orange),
    456, 479–480
Wills, Alfred, 761
Wilson, Woodrow, 801, 807, 815, 820,
    825, 833
    Fourteen Points of, 814
    League of Nations, 816
    League of Nations and, 814
Wilusa (site of Troy). *See also* Troy
Witchcraft, 472
    Dutch Republic and, 471
    ordeals in witch trials, 471
Witte, Sergei, 734
Wives
    in Napoleonic Code, 743
Wojtyla, Karol. *See* John Paul II (Pope)
Wollstonecraft, Mary, 607, 609
Woman suffrage, 741
Women, 925–926, 926. *See also*
    Feminism; Wives
    in 1920s and 1930s, 828, 831–833
    birth control and, 742, 923, 963
    Bolshevik Revolution and, 832–833
    education for, 744
    education of, 805
    employment of, 744
    Enlightenment and, 609, 611
    fascism and, 838–839, 839 (illus)
    in First World War, 804–805, 805
        (illus)
    French Revolution and, 624–625,
        642, 651
    gender boundaries and, 925–926
    law and, 742–743
    Lenin on, 832–833
    marriage, and, 743, 925–926

in middle class, 742, 926
as mothers, 832, 925
nature and, 549–550
Nazism and, 838–839, 839 (illus)
ordination of, 923
as priests, 923
Radical Right and, 838–839, 839
   (illus)
in Roman Catholicism, 925
as "second sex," 925
in Second World War, 886
sexuality and, 744–745, 925, 963
Social Darwinism and, 755
in Soviet Union, 832 (illus),
   832–833, 842
in Spanish Civil War, 847 (illus)
Virgin Mary and, 925
Voltaire and, 610
witchcraft and, 471, 473
in workforce, 804–805, 805 (illus),
   832, 832 (illus), 839, 842, 886, 926
Women's Bureau, 833
Women's movement: international,
   742–747, 931–932 See also
   Feminism
Women's rights. See also Feminism
Women's suffrage, 745–747, 805, 916
Workers. See also Labor; Workforce
   laissez-faire and, 686

Marx and Engels on, 674
Peterloo Massacre and, 678
Workforce
   assembly line and, 669
   children in, 672–673
Working class
   politics of, 735–741
World Bank, 895, 964
   Eastern Europe and, 940
World Trade Center: Islamist terrorist
   destruction of, 954, 955–956
World War I. See First World War
World War II, 891–892, 895. See
   Second World War

X-ray, 756

Yalta Conference (1945), 894, 894
   (illus), 895, 897
Year of Mary (1954), 925
Yeltsin, Boris, 942, 944–945
Yom Kippur War, 930
Yorktown: British surrender at, 580
Yugoslav army, 948
Yugoslavia, 896, 897, 948, 950 (map)
   in 1920s and 1930s, 827
   authoritarianism in, 827
   breakup of, 945–946, 947–949,
   948 (map)

civil war in, 884–885, 928–929,
   945–948
after First World War, 814, 815
   (map), 858
immigrants from, 924
national minorities and, 825
nationalism in, 946,
   947–949
in Second World War, 865, 868,
   884–885
after Second World War, 892

Zamosc, 487
Zamoyski, Jan (Count), 487
Zappa, Frank, 938, 939
Zarathustra. See Zoroaster and
   Zoroastrianism
Zhivkov, Todor, 941
Zimbabwe, 773
Zimmermann, Arthur, 801
Zimmermann telegram, 801
Zionism, 741, 817, 898. See also
   Jews and Judaism
   Palestine and, 741
Zog, 827
Zola, Émile, 731, 757
Zollverein (customs union), 666
Zong (slave ship), 571, 574
Zuckmayer, Carl, 791